MW01241378
Special Edition
USING
Lotus®
Approach® 96
QUE®

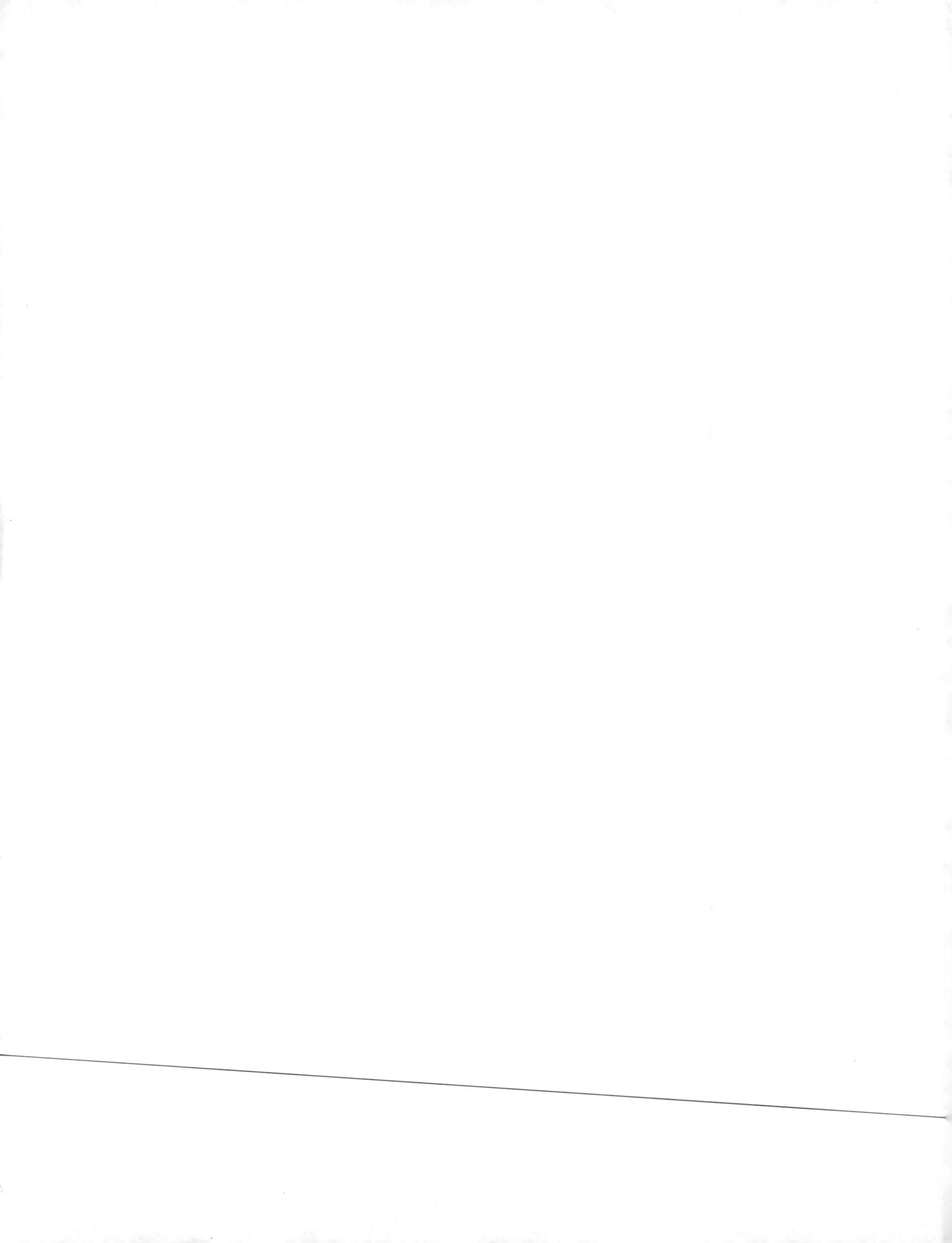

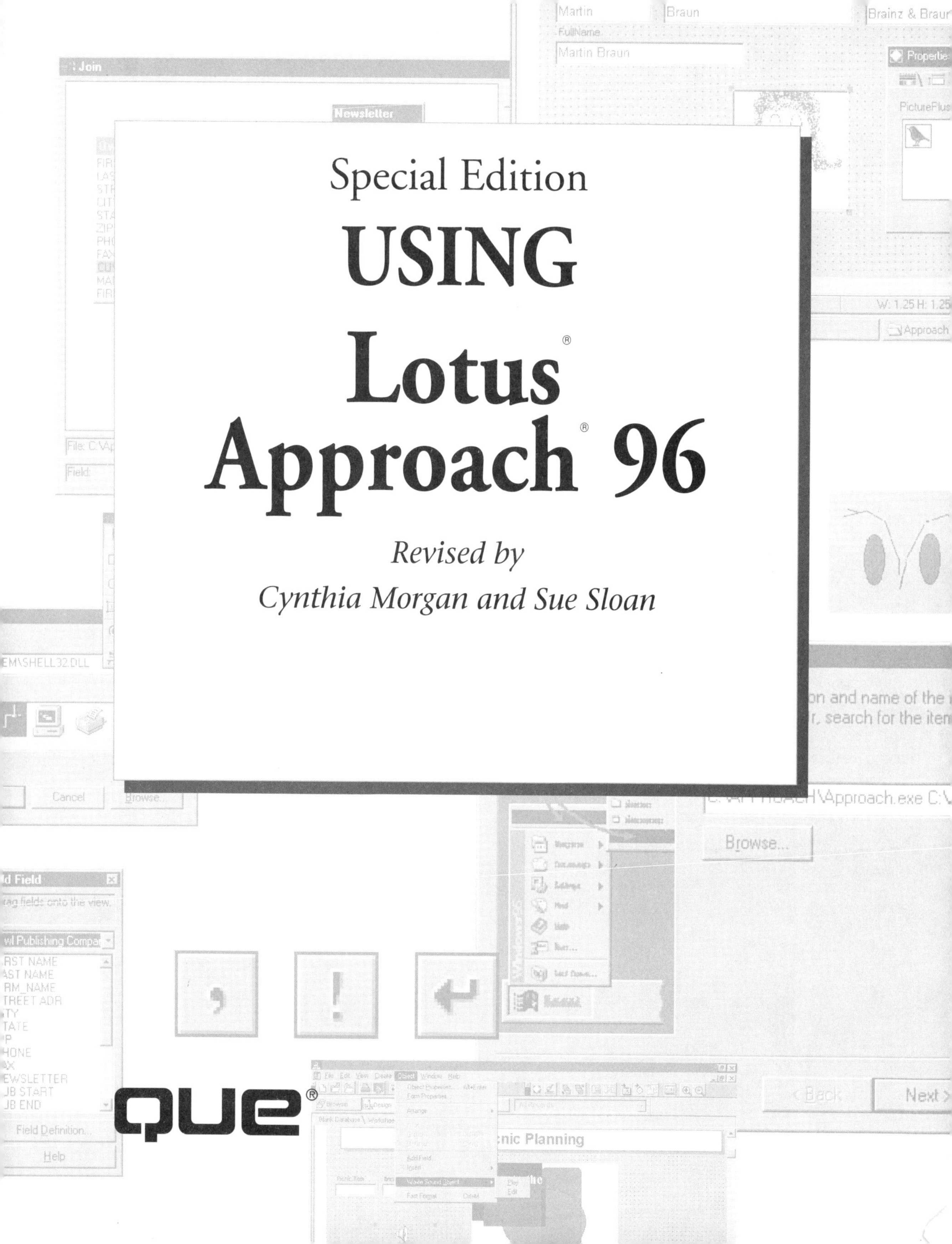

Special Edition

USING Lotus® Approach® 96

Revised by

Cynthia Morgan and Sue Sloan

QUE®

Special Edition Using Lotus Approach 96

Library of Congress Catalog No.: 95-71749

ISBN: 0-7897-0208-8

98 97 96 4 3 2 1

Interpretation of the printing code: the rightmost double-digit number is the year of the book's printing; the rightmost single-digit number, the number of the book's printing. For example, a printing code of 96-1 shows that the first printing of the book occurred in 1996.

Screen reproductions in this book were created using Collage Plus from Inner Media, Inc., Hollis, NH.

Composed in *Stone Serif* and *MCPdigital* by Que Corporation

Credits

President and Publisher
Roland Elgey

Associate Publisher
Joseph B. Wikert

Editorial Services Director
Elizabeth Keaffaber

Managing Editor
Sandy Doell

Director of Marketing
Lynn E. Zingraf

Senior Series Editor
Chris Nelson

Title Manager
Bryan Gambrel

Acquisitions Editor and Coordinator
Angela C. Kozlowski

Product Director
Stephen L. Miller

Production Editor
Susan Shaw Dunn

Editors
David Bradford
Thomas Cirtin
Don Eamon
Kelly Oliver

Assistant Product Marketing Manager
Kim Margolius

Technical Editor
Jeff Hester

Operations Coordinator
Patricia J. Brooks

Editorial Assistant
Andrea Duvall

Technical Support Specialist
Nadeem Muhammed

Book Designer
Ruth Harvey

Cover Designer
Dan Armstrong

Production Team
Bryan Flores
DiMonique Ford
Trey Frank
Jason Hand
Sonja Hart
Clint Lahnen
Glenn Larsen
Bob LaRoche
Michelle Lee
Julie Quinn
Laura Robbins
Bobbi Satterfield
Michael Thomas
Paul Wilson
Jody York

Indexer
Gina Brown

To Salman, Abou, Rani, Chinni, Rajah, and Presley, whose patience, purrs, and perseverance helped me survive to see this book in print!

—Cynthia Morgan

This book would not have been possible without the support and encouragement of my life partner, Rodger Kellermann. He kept everything else under control so I could focus on the job at hand, including the care and feeding of me and our cats.

—Sue Sloan

About the Authors

Cynthia Morgan, the Software Reviews Editor at *Windows Magazine*, has worked with PC databases for more than 10 years. A computer consultant as well as a writer, she frequently serves as a software expert on East Coast radio shows. She's currently engaged in several consulting projects involving databases and the Internet.

Susan Sloan is the owner of Cross-W Systems, a consulting firm for small-business automation in Pound Ridge, New York. Susan has more than 30 years' experience in the computer industry, both in technical development of database systems and in management, ranging from field sales to corporate training. Susan recently retired from corporate life and is applying her skills to small retail and blue-collar businesses that the larger consulting firms often overlook. This is her first project for Que Corporation.

Acknowledgments

The authors wish to acknowledge the valuable and understanding assistance of Terry Ridgeway and the Lotus Approach beta team.

Also, to Susan Dunn, Stephen Miller, and Angela Kozlowski, who kept us on our toes while working on this book for Que.

Also, from Sue Sloan: To my many friends and fellow Approach users on the LOTUSB forum on CompuServe, your constant stream of "Why does it...?" and "How do I...?" messages were an inspiration to do the best possible job on this book and make
Approach 96 even easier to use than the prior releases.

We'd Like To Hear From You!

As part of our continuing effort to produce books of the highest possible quality, Que would like to hear your comments. To stay competitive, we *really* want you, as a computer book reader and user, to let us know what you like or dislike most about *Special Edition Using Lotus Approach 96* or other Que products.

You can mail comments, ideas, or suggestions to the address below, or send us a fax at (317) 581-4663. For the on-line inclined, Macmillan Computer Publishing has a forum on CompuServe (type **GO QUEBOOKS** at any prompt) through which our staff and authors are available for questions and comments. The address of our Internet site is **http://www.mcp.com** (World Wide Web).

In addition to exploring our forum, please feel free to contact me personally on CompuServe at **76103,1334** to discuss your opinions of this book. You can also reach me on the Internet at **smiller@que.mcp.com**.

Thanks in advance—your comments will help us to continue publishing the best books available on computer topics in today's market.

Stephen L. Miller
Product Development Specialist
Que Corporation
201 W. 103rd Street
Indianapolis, Indiana 46290
USA

Contents at a Glance

Contents

Introduction

As computers become more common in today's offices and homes, it's only appropriate that databases also become easier to develop and use without extensive computer programming skills. Approach 96 for Windows 95 maintains a very high level of usability by non-technical computer users by retaining and extending the ease-of-use features of Approach 3 for Windows, such as the Form and Report SmartAssistants, which guide you step by step in developing professional-looking database programs.

By following the examples and using the tips in this book, even novice database designers will be able to create fully functional databases with easy-to-use data-entry screens and comprehensive reports. Professional database designers and consultants will find that Approach 96 is up to their most demanding tasks, while improving their productivity substantially compared to using the more traditional programming and database tools.

What's New in Approach 96?

Approach 96 builds on the successful base established with Approach 3.0, not just by adding 32-bit and Windows 95 support but by extending the base to include many new and desirable features. Many common PC applications are now available as built-in SmartMasters—either as templates containing only the outline of the databases needed, or as fully developed applications needing only your data to be entered. New "assistants" have been added to help you create and save sophisticated database queries, generate envelopes, and define and store SQL queries.

For the analysts among you, Approach 96 has enhanced the crosstabs with improved filtering and groupings, and added a new drill-down capability to pinpoint the underlying data in a crosstab cell or chart section. Reports can now be organized using smart dates (for example, months and quarters) or alphabetic groupings.

Form letters and forms can now be multi-page with text flowing smoothly from one page to another as your fields change in size. And when changes occur, you can use the new Find & Replace text functions to search your database and replace text anywhere it appears.

Also, you can improve database usability without compromising security using the new TeamSecurity function to specify users and groups who have access to your data at various levels. Rather than have to provide passwords for each file or database, you can use one password to cover an entire spectrum of database access.

Finally, the ability to use LotusScript in Approach by the more technical database developers will enable the building of applications using object-oriented programming tools. LotusScript is a cross-product scripting language, much like the industry standard BASIC, that's common to multiple Lotus products.

Who Should be Using This Book?

Special Edition Using Lotus Approach 96 is designed for anyone who has information accumulating on paper (or in their brain) and needs a computer to make that information easier to maintain and use. This book can also unlock the secrets of databases built for your use by others by showing you how to import and use these information sources without contracting for programming assistance.

This book does assume that you know how to perform the more common tasks that the Windows 95 operating environment requires, such as selecting an item by clicking it, pulling down a menu, opening and closing files and windows, and using drag-and-drop to move objects on-screen.

We, the authors, highly recommend that you read (perhaps *experience* is a better term) this book by sitting down at your computer with Approach 96 at your fingertips. Try out the examples as you go through the book rather than just read them. Add your own ruffles and flourishes as you go; just because a particular type style or field object type was used on the example forms is no reason for you not to try out others. Be creative! Have fun!

What's Covered in This Book?

Special Edition Using Lotus Approach 96 covers all of the features of Approach with the exception of LotusScript, which is beyond the scope of this book. In addition to explaining these features, examples are included to illustrate how they would be used in creating a database for a fictitious company, Owl Publishing. Tips and techniques for using Approach more effectively or avoiding common errors are included throughout the book.

This book is divided into four major parts:

- Part I, "Getting Started with Approach," covers the basics of using Approach and creating simple forms and databases. Queries and sorts, as well as basic reports and mailing labels, are included.
- Part II, "Using Forms, Queries, and Reports," covers more advanced features, such as using multiple related databases, TeamSecurity, calculated fields, and

more complex queries, forms, and reports. Approach's macro functions are also covered here.

- Part III, "Getting the Most from Approach," describes Approach's worksheet, crosstab report, and charting features. It also covers the infamous "many-to-many" relational database problem and ends with a discussion of ways to customize Approach's look and feel.
- Part IV, "Integrating Approach with Other Applications," covers importing and exporting database, text, and spreadsheet files. Interaction of Approach with other software programs in the Lotus SmartSuite is also described.

Part I: Getting Started with Approach

Chapter 1, "Learning Approach Basics," explains how Approach can help you organize your information into databases. It also familiarizes you with Approach's on-screen tools, action and status bars, and SmartIcons. Various computer files that Approach creates for you are explained, and you learn how to save your work.

Chapter 2, "Creating Database Tables," shows you how to create and modify database tables using Approach. In addition to direct data entry, existing text and spreadsheet files can be converted to Approach databases by using Approach's import facilities. Data-entry options and field content validation are discussed. TeamSecurity is introduced, as are the simpler forms of password protection for your data and programs.

Chapter 3, "Building Data Input Forms," shows you how to create forms on-screen in which to enter or display your database information. The Form Assistant is explored, as are the various layout tools available for building forms.

Chapter 4, "Enhancing Data Input Forms," builds on the skills you acquired in Chapter 3. It explains the various formats for field objects that display your database field content, and shows you how to add color and shadows as well as change fonts, sizes, and effects for text.

Chapter 5, "Working with Your Data," explores data entry on your forms and how to sort, edit, and delete the information. You can establish a default sort order so that your information is always displayed in an order useful to you.

Chapter 6, "Finding Records," discusses the basics of using input forms to build queries for finding records that meet your criteria. The new Find Assistant is highlighted as it makes finding data in your database a "point-and-click" operation using plain English to confirm to you the criteria you've specified. Simple matches to exact values, ranges of values, and combinations of criteria across multiple fields are discussed.

Chapter 7, "Creating Reports and Mailing Labels," expands the usability of your database by showing how to create reports and labels using many of the skills you acquired in building forms earlier. The Report Assistant is highlighted as well as various customization features and summarization capabilities. Labels are easy to create using predefined standard templates for common label sizes and shapes.

Part II: Using Forms, Queries, and Reports

Chapter 8, "Understanding Relational Databases," describes how to create and link multiple databases that have related information in them. Relational links can virtually eliminate maintaining duplicate information in several computer databases while enhancing the analysis and reporting aspects of your system.

Chapter 9, "Designing Advanced Forms," covers how to design forms using relational databases. In addition to database field selection and placement, repeating panels are described, showing you how to display multiple joined database records on one form. Techniques for using related databases to provide the values displayed in drop-down lists are also described.

Chapter 10, "Using Advanced Field Types," covers how to define fields to import pictures and to perform calculations. You can set up constants using variable-type fields. Approach's extensive formula-creating capabilities are discussed, including text and numeric data-manipulation functions.

Chapter 11, "Performing Advanced Finds," discusses advanced query techniques such as performing a query using the result of a calculation and using the `If()` function to test logically for various criteria being met.

Chapter 12, "Creating Advanced Reports," shows how to set up reports using the Report Assistant, and then how to modify reports so you can create complex summaries and totals. Form letters are also discussed, as is the new Envelope Assistant.

Chapter 13, "Automating Your Work," explains how to use Approach's macro capabilities to perform a series of actions automatically whenever needed. You can attach macros to buttons, fields, pictures, and forms. These macros can do simple things, such as switch to a different form, perform complex logic to determine whether the data entered is acceptable, display error messages, or branch to various other macros to handle conditions encountered.

Part III: Getting the Most from Approach

Chapter 14, "Using Worksheets and Crosstabs," details how to customize and use a spreadsheet-like worksheet to enter and edit data in your Approach database. A crosstab allows you to analyze and summarize your data easily by grouping data into rows and columns based on criteria you specify, such as totaling sales in columns by product and rows by month.

Chapter 15, "Creating Charts," shows you how to view your database's content in meaningful charts or diagrams to highlight trends or spot changes that may be difficult to see in the raw numbers. The Chart Assistant leads you through creating charts easily in two- and three-dimensional layouts.

Chapter 16, "Exploring Advanced Database Relationships," gives you guidance on resolving complex relational database situations.

Chapter 17, "Customizing Approach," shows you how to set up user preferences for your database systems, including default styles (such as color, font, and borders), the optional display of on-screen features such as the action bar and SmartIcon bar, and developing custom SmartIcon bars and menus.

Part IV: Integrating Approach with Other Applications

Chapter 18, "Importing and Exporting Files," discusses the exchange of data with other common computer applications in various common file formats. These formats include dBASE III+ and IV, Paradox, Excel, and Lotus 1-2-3.

Chapter 19, "Using Approach with Lotus SmartSuite 96," discusses data sharing and functional integration with other members of the Lotus SmartSuite application set. By using object linking and embedding (OLE), Approach lets you access current database information in WordPro tables and Lotus 1-2-3 spreadsheet cells. You can paste drawings and even complete presentations into Approach forms and reports from Freelance.

Conventions Used in This Book

Names of all dialog boxes and dialog box options are written with initial capital letters. Messages that appear on-screen and all program code and Access commands appear in a special monospace font, as in the following example: `Variable undefined`. New terms are introduced in *italic* type. Text that you are to type appears in **`monospace boldface`**.

Uppercase letters are used to distinguish field names and file and directory names.

Tip

This paragraph format suggests easier or alternative methods of executing a procedure.

Note

This paragraph format indicates additional information that may help you avoid problems or that should be considered in using the described features.

Caution

This paragraph format warns you of hazardous procedures (for example, activities that delete tables).

Part I

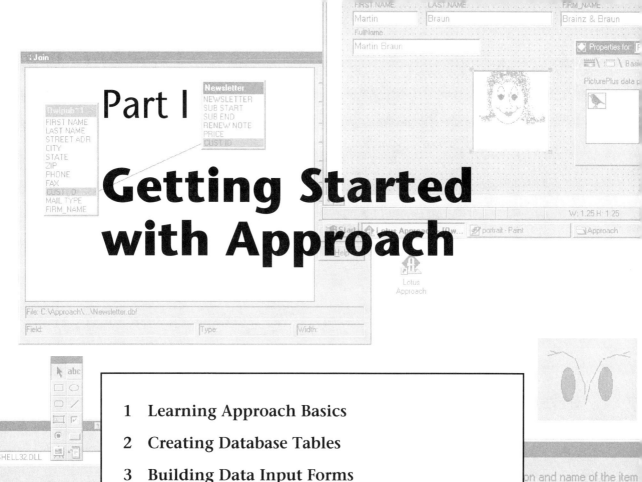

Getting Started with Approach

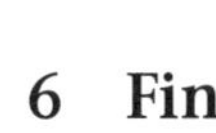

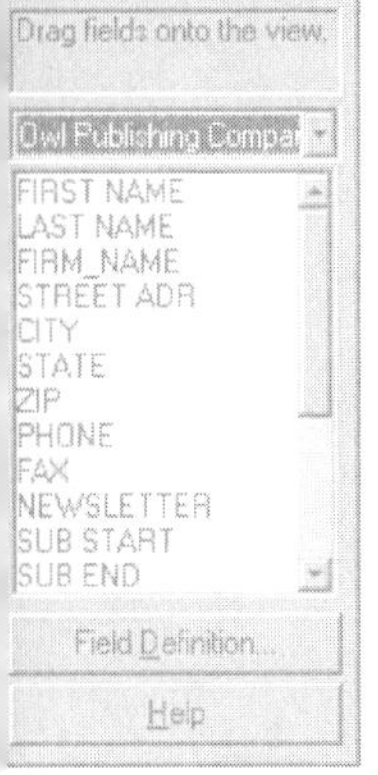

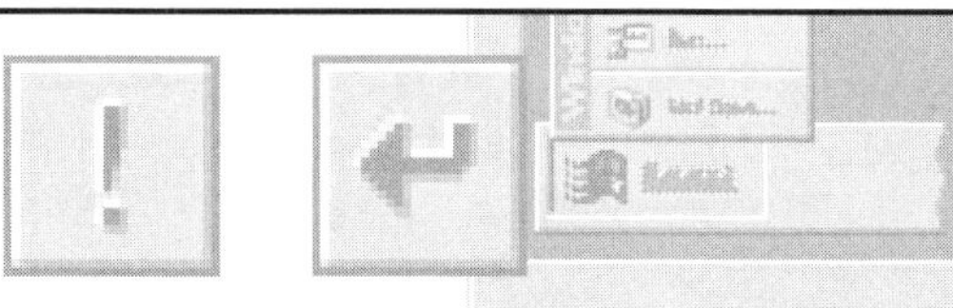

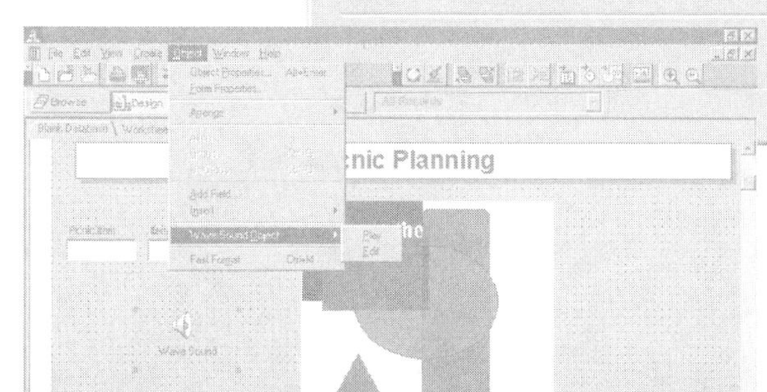

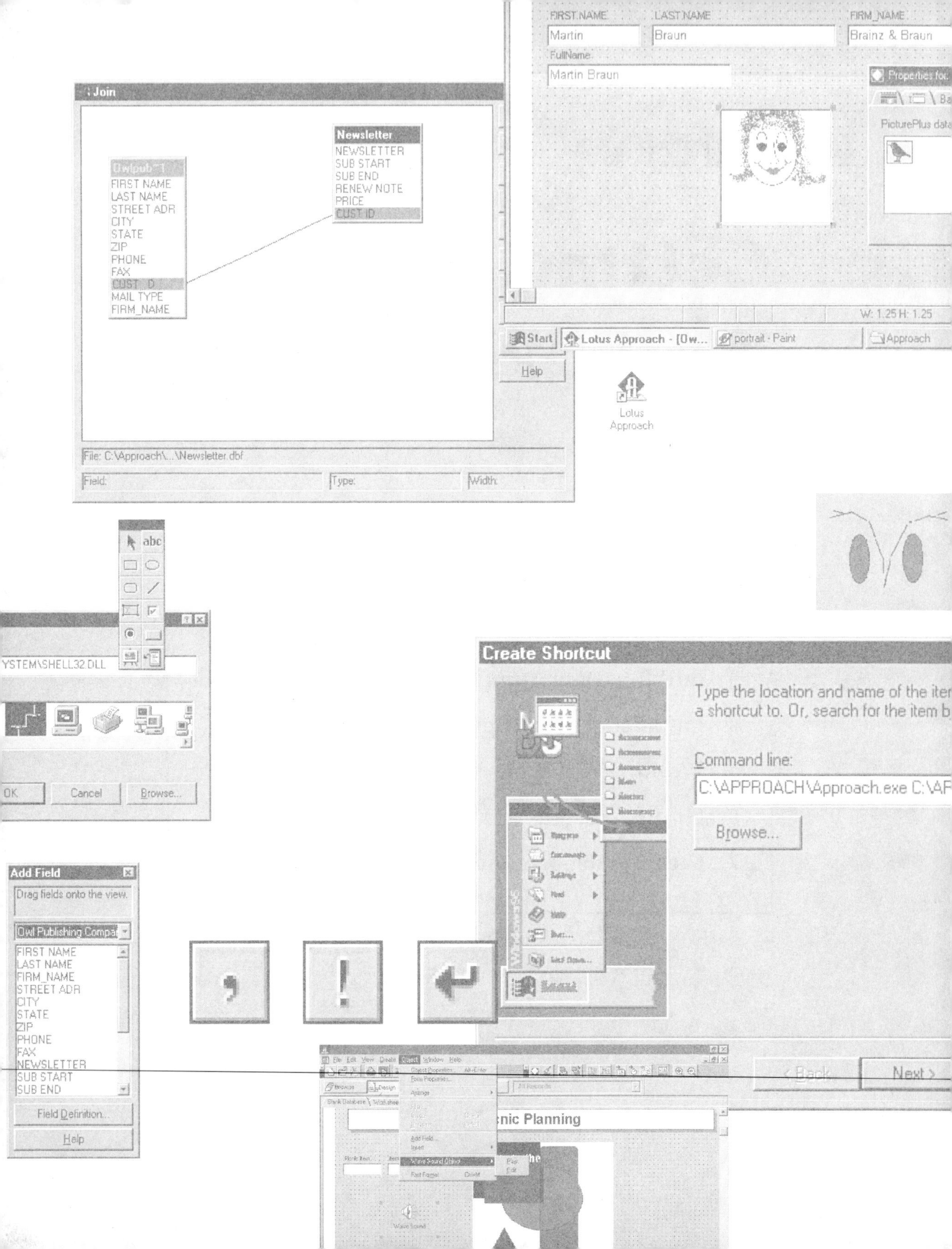

FIRST NAME
LAST NAME
FIRM_NAME
Martin
Braun
Brainz & Braun
FullName
Martin Braun
PicturePlus data
W: 1.25 H: 1.25
Start
Lotus Approach - [Ow...
portrait - Paint
Approach
Help
Lotus Approach
Join
Newsletter
NEWSLETTER
SUB START
SUB END
RENEW NOTE
PRICE
CUST ID
FIRST NAME
LAST NAME
STREET ADR
CITY
STATE
ZIP
PHONE
FAX
MAIL TYPE
FIRM_NAME
File: C:\Approach\...\Newsletter.dbf
Field:
Type:
Width:
abc
YSTEM\SHELL32.DLL
OK
Cancel
Browse...
Create Shortcut
Type the location and name of the iter
a shortcut to. Or, search for the item b
Command line:
C:\APPROACH\Approach.exe C:\AF
Browse...
Add Field
Drag fields onto the view.
Owl Publishing Compa
FIRST NAME
LAST NAME
FIRM_NAME
STREET ADR
CITY
STATE
ZIP
PHONE
FAX
NEWSLETTER
SUB START
SUB END
Field Definition...
Help
< Back
Next >
nic Planning

CHAPTER 1

Learning Approach Basics

Approach 96 for Windows 95 combines a powerful set of tools with Windows 95's intuitive interface to provide an easy-to-learn and easy-to-use database program. People with little or no programming experience can now build databases and design data-entry forms and reports to track and manage home and business information.

The following Approach basics are covered in this chapter:

- Understanding computerized database concepts and benefits
- Using Approach on-screen elements (menus, icons, and tools)
- Working with Approach files
- Establishing security over your databases and Approach files
- Creating a Windows 95 Start or Programs menu entry to quickly access your database
- Adding descriptive information to an Approach file
- Using keyboard shortcuts

Understanding Computerized Databases

A *database* is an organized collection of related information. You can store database information on paper or in a computer.

An example of a database stored on paper is an address book—certainly one of the most common databases people have. Of course, you can also keep an address book in a database on a computer.

The information in a computerized database is usually stored in the form of a table with rows and columns. Each table is given a unique name, such as *My Address Book*. Table 1.1 shows the rows and columns in an address book database. Each row in table 1.1 contains a set of information, labeled Name, Address, City, State, ZIP, and Phone. Rows in such a table are called *records*. The second row in table 1.1, for example, containing the name Mary Smith and her address and phone number, is a record.

The columns represent categories of related information in each record (row). Each category (column) is called a *field*. City, for example, is the name of one field in table 1.1.

Table 1.1 Records and Fields in the My Address Book Database

Name	Address	City	State	ZIP	Phone
Joe Change	23 West 14th	New York	NY	10034	(212) 555-1234
Mary Smith	44 Gulf Ct.	Concord	NH	02457	(304) 555-5908
Mike Carter	98 Tone Ave.	Myers	AZ	88907	(206) 555-4689

Your address book is probably similar to table 1.1. The information that pertains to one person is a single record. (However, you may have additional fields for other information you want to track, such as birthdays and anniversaries.) An address book database thus contains many records—one for each person you've listed. Each record contains many fields, such as the person's name, address, phone number, and so on.

The address book example represents a simple type of database called a *flat-file database*. In a flat-file database, all the information about a particular subject is stored in a single table. A more sophisticated type of database is a *relational database*, which allows you to store related information in multiple tables and link the information in those tables in a logical manner. A relational database gives you more flexibility in working with your data and creating reports than a flat-file database. For example, your address book database could be linked to another database containing the City, State, and ZIP so that your address book database would contain only the ZIP field. The link would be the ZIP field. This would save computer storage space and perhaps speed up access to your data when searching for people in particular cities or states.

Approach lets you create flat-file and relational databases. Although this book initially discusses using Approach with a flat-file database, you'll learn about its relational capabilities in Chapter 8, "Understanding Relational Databases."

Why Use a Computerized Database?

Chances are, you frequently need to revise your address book database—add new names, change addresses and phone numbers when people move, and so on. Although keeping a simple database (such as an address book) in printed form makes sense, large databases quickly become unmanageable when you try to maintain them on paper.

Keeping your database on a computer has some significant advantages over the paper method:

- You can store a large amount of information in a relatively small amount of space.
- The computer can find particular information quickly.

- You can tell the computer to print reports, mailing labels, and form letters from all, or a part, of your database.
- You can sort your database based on any piece of information (field contents).
- You can easily add fields or change the type of information you want to store in your database.
- You can tell the computer to perform complex calculations and summarize the data contained in your database.

If you want to rearrange your database based on a different piece of information, you can sort your address book database by any field—by phone number instead of by last name, for example. This way, you can group all the people with the same area codes. At any time, you can also add another category of information to the database—such as a fax number field or a check box field for whether someone sent you a Christmas card last year. Although all these things are possible with a paper-based database, managing that database would require much more manual labor. A computerized database allows you to manage your information more efficiently and frees you to pursue more enjoyable interests.

Why Design Your Own Database?

Databases in one form or another are critical sources of information for individuals and businesses. Databases can improve your life and influence how your business operates. You can keep your financial data in a database, for example, and make decisions about how to manage your money based on that data. A business may keep virtually all the information it needs to operate in databases. This information can include data about employees, salaries, the products the business sells, and customers. But how do you create and manage the databases containing the information you need?

A variety of programs for building databases and programs to manage them—called *applications*—have been available for years. Paradox, dBASE, FoxPro, Access, and other database programs enable people to design databases and create their own applications. Unfortunately, despite advances in user-friendliness, creating applications with these programs is still beyond the reach of most people because it's necessary to learn a computer programming language to use the programs effectively.

The tendency, therefore, is to hire a consultant to build a database application for you with one of these tools. Hiring a consultant has several disadvantages:

- *Cost.* Hiring a consultant can be expensive. The price varies widely, depending on the person's experience and the location of your business, but it can range from as little as $35 per hour to as much as $125 per hour.
- *Inaccuracy.* The finished application often doesn't quite reflect what you had in mind. Because describing your requirements to a consultant can be difficult, the finished application may not do everything you need.
- *Inappropriateness.* You're bound to find many annoying little things that you don't like—perhaps the labeling on a menu screen is confusing, or the color

scheme is annoying. Unfortunately, getting such problems fixed means having the consultant return—and paying for that time. As a result, all too often these unsatisfactory aspects of the application never get fixed.

- *Availability*. The original consultant may be unavailable, meaning that a new consultant would have to become familiar enough with the application to make the changes for you. Not only might it be difficult to find another consultant, but the new person would charge you for the time spent learning your application!

With Approach, you can create your own databases without becoming a computer expert. You can design attractive forms for data input, print reports and mailing labels, and make corrections to fine-tune your creation as you see fit. As your needs or your company's needs change, you can change the database to match—all without incurring huge consulting bills. Also, because Approach is a Windows 95 program, training someone to enter the data takes much less time than if the application were built using older technologies. Training someone to enter data is even easier if the person has used other Windows 3.x or Windows 95 programs.

Starting Approach

Approach can be launched just like any other Windows 95 application. Follow these steps:

1. Click the Start button on the Windows 95 task bar and then choose Programs.
2. On the Programs menu, point to the folder that contains the Approach program.
3. Click the Approach program icon in the folder to run Approach.

Note

If the program you want to start doesn't appear on the Programs menu or one of its submenus, choose Find on the Start menu, and then choose Files or Folders. Use the Find: All Files dialog box to locate the program file, Approach.exe, which is probably on your C drive. Make sure that the Include Subfolders check box is selected.

Introducing Approach

Approach is a very flexible product. As you perform tasks in Approach, you'll use several different modes: Browse, Design, Print Preview, and Find. Browse mode allows you to enter database information on a form, worksheet, or report. Design mode lets you create views (your own forms, worksheets, crosstabs, charts, reports, form letters, and mailing labels). Print Preview mode shows you what your information on-screen will look like when you print it. Finally, you can locate records that meet special criteria by using Find mode. You can switch between the modes by using the action bar near the top of the screen, the status line at the bottom of the screen, or the SmartIcon bar at the top of the screen.

Approach uses two special kinds of files: database files and Approach files (called *View files* in some earlier Approach versions). Your information (records and fields) is stored in a database file, whereas the details of your application (forms, reports, queries, and temporary calculated and variable fields) are stored in an Approach file. These details include how your forms and reports look, and special features of your application.

Although Approach is designed to be used primarily with a mouse, you can use the keyboard to perform some operations, such as selecting items from menus and making selections from dialog boxes. However, the mouse is more efficient for some actions, such as placing and sizing objects on a form.

Using Approach Screen Elements

The first step in beginning to use Approach is to learn the various screen elements. Figure 1.1 shows the data input form of the example scenario, a legal publishing company called Owl Publishing. The form is displayed in Design mode. Study this figure carefully as the various items on-screen are discussed.

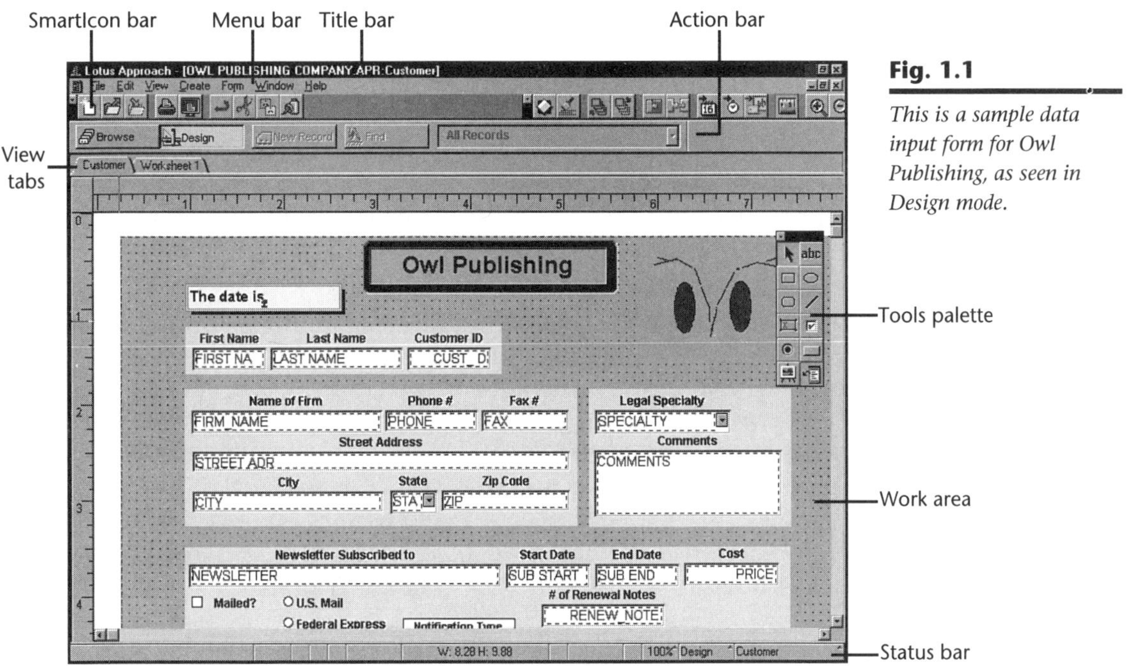

Fig. 1.1

This is a sample data input form for Owl Publishing, as seen in Design mode.

Tip

You can use the View menu commands to display or hide many of the on-screen items discussed in the following sections. For example, you can hide the SmartIcons, action bar, status bar, and view tabs.

The Title Bar

Across the top of the Approach window is the title bar. The text in the title bar normally includes the words `Lotus SmartSuite 96 - Approach -`, specifies in brackets the name of the Approach file that's now in use, and shows the name of the current view (form or report) that's being displayed in the middle of the screen. The title bar also will show you a quick explanation of the function of any menu bar item that you move your mouse pointer over or select.

The control icon at the left of the title bar and the Minimize, Maximize, and Close boxes at the right side are standard Windows 95 controls for an on-screen window.

The Menu Bar

Below the title bar is the menu bar, which contains the standard File, Edit, and Help drop-down menus present in virtually all Windows 95 applications. The other menu names will vary depending on your mode and the type of view you're now displaying.

To use the mouse to make a selection from a menu, move the pointer to a menu name and then click. The menu opens, showing the commands available. You can choose one of these commands by clicking it. For example, to quit Approach, open the File menu and choose Exit.

Menu commands that are available for you to choose are shown in black letters; commands that are "grayed out" can't be chosen, as they aren't useful to you in the current mode.

You can also access the menus from the keyboard. For example, press and hold down the Alt key and then press the F key to display the File menu. (Notice on the File menu that you can use the Ctrl+O keystroke combination to open a file. For more information, see "Using Keyboard Shortcuts" later in this chapter.)

The SmartIcon Bar

Below the menu bar is the SmartIcon bar. The SmartIcon bar contains one or more sets of icons that act like little buttons to make the most common Approach tools and commands easy to use. SmartIcons duplicate commands available from the pull-down menus on the menu bar. To use a SmartIcon, click it with the mouse.

Approach offers help with the function of a SmartIcon in two ways:

- The icon shows a little picture indicating the tool or command that's available. For example, the icon with the little printer on it lets you print the current view immediately.

- You can right-click and hold down the mouse button on a SmartIcon to display a balloon that describes the icon's function. Or, if you've selected the Show Icon Descriptions check box in the SmartIcons Setup dialog box, you can simply position the mouse pointer over a SmartIcon and the description balloon will appear immediately. The balloon disappears when you move the mouse pointer away from the SmartIcon bar.

Tip

To open the SmartIcons Setup dialog box, open the File menu, choose User Setup, and then choose SmartIcons Setup.

The SmartIcon bar content varies with the mode (Browse, Design, Find, or Print Preview) and the context (form, worksheet, crosstab, report, form letter, labels, or envelope) that you're now using. You can also customize the SmartIcon bar, hide all or part of the SmartIcon bar, or create an entirely new SmartIcon bar, as detailed in Chapter 17, "Customizing Approach."

You can display or hide the entire SmartIcon bar by opening the View menu and choosing Show SmartIcons. Individual sets of SmartIcons have an arrow at the left of the leftmost SmartIcon in the set. Clicking this arrow displays a menu of items related to the entire SmartIcon bar's visibility and content, and access to the SmartIcons Setup dialog box.

Tip

To display the SmartIcon bar by default in the current session, click the SmartIcons check box in the Show section of the Display page in the Approach Preferences dialog box. To make the change permanent, click the Save Default button in the same dialog box. You can access this dialog box from the File menu by choosing User Setup and then Approach Preferences.

Each SmartIcon set can be moved anywhere on-screen and "float" in its own little window (see fig. 1.2). To move a set, place the mouse pointer on the blue space below the arrow at the left end of the set. When the little hand appears, click and drag the set to where you want it to appear.

You can change the shape of a SmartIcon set's window into a little box or palette by resizing the set's window. To resize the window, move the mouse pointer over one of the window borders until it changes into a two-headed arrow, and then click and drag the border in any direction you desire.

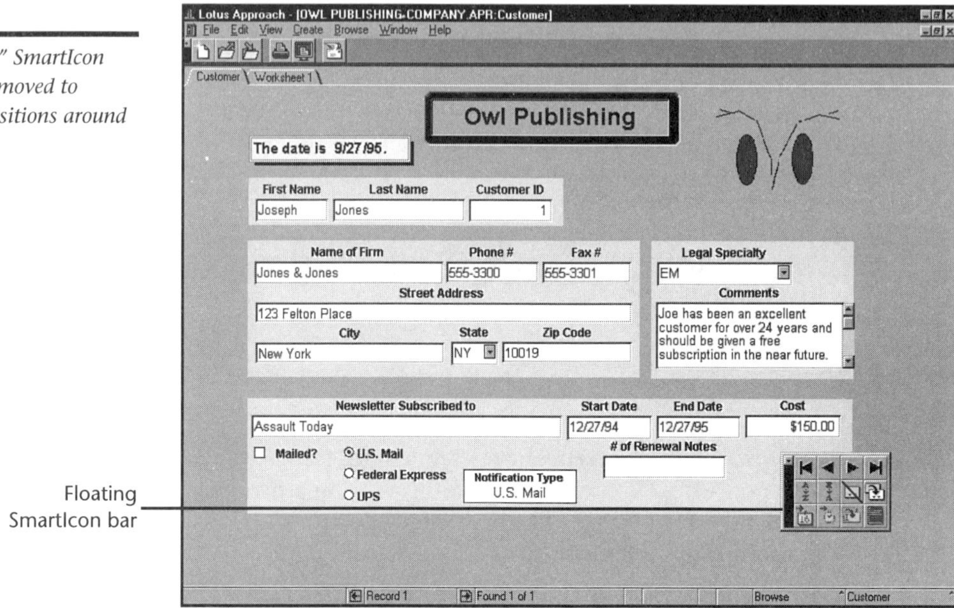

Fig. 1.2

A "floating" SmartIcon bar can be moved to different positions around the screen.

> **Note**
>
> If you move all the SmartIcons sets off the SmartIcon bar, the bar will disappear from view. You can cause the bar to reappear by moving a SmartIcon set back to its original position under the menu bar.

Chapter 5, "Working with Your Data," discusses using the Browse mode SmartIcon bar. Using the Design mode SmartIcon bar is discussed in chapters 4, 7, and 9. Using the Find mode SmartIcon bar is discussed in chapters 6 and 11. Chapter 7, "Creating Reports and Mailing Labels," discusses using the Print Preview mode SmartIcon bar.

Context-related SmartIcon sets are discussed in the chapters where the associated view is explained. Chapter 5, "Working with Your Data," covers forms; Chapter 7, "Creating Reports and Mailing Labels," covers reports and mailing labels; and Chapter 12, "Creating Advanced Reports," covers advanced reports and form letters. Chapter 14, "Using Worksheets and Crosstabs," explores worksheets and crosstabs, and Chapter 15, "Creating Charts," covers charts.

The Action Bar

The action bar is a set of buttons located at the top of the Approach work area, below the SmartIcons. The set of buttons you see most often lets you

- Switch to Browse or Design mode
- Create a new database record

- Switch to the Find mode (see Chapter 6, "Finding Records")
- Execute a named sort or find (see Chapter 5, "Working with Your Data," and Chapter 6, "Finding Records")

The action bar changes its appearance or content to support various modes. In Design mode, the buttons for creating a new record, doing a find, or executing a named find are visible but not available. In Find mode, the entire content of the action bar is replaced, as shown in Chapter 6, "Finding Records." The action bar also changes to assist in some design operations, such as setting the tab order of your fields in a form.

To display or hide the action bar, open the View menu and choose Show Action Bar. You can also hide or move the bar—right-click the bar in a space between buttons, and then choose an option or location from the menu. If you select Float, the action bar is put into its own little window. To move the action bar window, position your mouse pointer anywhere but on a button in the little window. Click and hold down the left mouse button and move (drag) the action bar wherever you want. Release the mouse button (drop) to leave the action bar where you want it.

The Tools Palette

The tools palette provides a set of tools for designing screens (views) interactively. You see what you've designed as you do it! The palette is in a floating window of its own in the work area of the screen when you're in Design mode. The tools palette includes the following:

- Graphic shapes you can use to draw on-screen (rectangles, ovals, lines, and so on)
- Various field types that you can place on-screen (data-entry fields, database fields, buttons, check boxes, and radio buttons)
- A text block tool to add text headings, instructions, and labels for areas of the screen or for fields
- A button tool to add a button to your screen to indicate special functions that can be performed—usually a set of commands you've placed in a macro to do several Approach operations with only one click (macros are discussed in Chapter 13, "Automating Your Work")
- A PicturePlus tool to place photographs or graphics fields from your database on-screen

The tools palette is visible only in Design mode. You can toggle the display of the tools palette by opening the View menu and choosing Show Tools Palette (or pressing Ctrl+L). You can also move the palette anywhere you want by using the drag-and-drop Windows feature.

Tip

To display the tools palette by default in the current session, click the Tools Palette check box in the Show in Design section of the Approach Preferences dialog box's Display page. To make the change permanent, click the Save Default button in the same dialog box. You can access this dialog box from the File menu by choosing User Setup and then Approach Preferences.

The Approach Work Area

The Approach work area—the largest portion of the screen—displays a "view" that shows the data from your database. A view can be a form, report, worksheet, crosstab, chart, form letter, mailing label, or envelope. The Approach work area is where you enter or modify your data or design your views.

Besides your database fields, you can place other objects in the work area. These objects can be text labels (perhaps to indicate what information is expected in a particular field), pictures, and graphics. You can also place buttons in this area and then click those buttons to execute certain tasks. (See Chapter 13, "Automating Your Work," for more information on how you can add buttons to a view.)

The View Tabs

Just under the action bar are the view tabs. Approach displays a tab for each view that you create. The name of the view is displayed on the tab. Approach creates default names such as Form 1 during design, but you can rename your views to make more sense to you.

You can switch to a particular view by clicking the tab for that view. If there are more tabs than Approach can fit on-screen, a pair of triangular arrow buttons appear to the far right of the view tabs. You can scroll the list of tabs left or right by clicking the left- or right-arrow button, respectively.

The view tabs can be very useful in that you can design your application to resemble a file cabinet with folders containing various information. For example, displaying a particular report on-screen could be as simple as clicking on your report view tab. Viewing the details of one of the items on the report would be easy—just select a database record on the report and use a view tab to switch to the data-entry form for that record.

To display or hide the view tabs, open the View menu and choose Show View Tabs. To rearrange the view tabs from within Design mode, simply click and drag a tab to a new location in relation to the other tabs. Finally, you can hide individual view tabs if you don't want to have them shown by changing the view's InfoBox setting, which is discussed later in this chapter.

Tip

To display the view tabs by default in the current session, select the View Tabs check box in the Show section of the Display page in the Approach Preferences dialog box. To make the change permanent, click the Save Default button in the same dialog box. You can access this dialog box from the File menu by choosing User Setup and then Approach Preferences.

The Status Bar

At the bottom of the work area is the status bar. This line contains additional information about the current Approach environment and provides a place to make selections. You can display or hide the status bar by opening the View menu and choosing Show Status Bar.

Tip

To display the status bar by default in the current session, click the Status Bar check box in the Show section of the Display page in the Approach Preferences dialog box. To make the change permanent, click the Save Default button in the same dialog box. You can access this dialog box from the File menu by choosing User Setup and then Approach Preferences.

Many areas of the status bar are "live"—that is, when you click an area, Approach presents you with a list of choices. The contents of the status bar vary depending on whether you're in Design mode, Browse mode, Find mode, or Print Preview mode.

In Browse and Print Preview modes, the status bar contains the following items, from left to right:

- *The previous record button.* Click this button to move to the preceding record in your database.

  Note

  This button moves to the previous page if Approach is in Print Preview mode and you're viewing a report or mailing labels.

- *The current database record number.* Click this indicator to open the Go to Record dialog box, in which you can type the record number that you want to view. When you click OK, Approach displays that record.

> **Note**
>
> This button displays the current page number if Approach is in Print Preview mode. Clicking this indicator under these circumstances opens the Go to Page dialog box, in which you can type the page number you want to look at. When you click OK, Approach displays that page.

- *The next record button.* Click this button to move to the next record in your database.

> **Note**
>
> This button moves to the next page if Approach is in Print Preview mode and you're viewing a report or mailing labels.

- *The active records indicator.* This part of the status bar displays the total number of records in your database and how many of those records are now available for viewing or editing. Normally, all records are available. If you execute a find, however, only those records that match the criteria of the find are available for editing.

> **Tip**
>
> To return to working with all the records in the database, open the Browse menu and choose Find and then Find All (or press Ctrl+A).

- *The magnification indicator.* If you click this indicator (which is available only in Print Preview mode), a range of zoom percentages from 200% to 25% is displayed. If you select from this list, the view will zoom in or out based on whether you select a higher or lower percentage than you're currently using.
- *The current mode.* If you click this indicator, Approach presents a list of modes: Browse, Design, Print Preview, and Find. You can switch to another mode by choosing the mode from this list. If you select Print Preview while Approach is already in a Print Preview mode, the Print Preview mode is turned off and the mode returns to the last-used mode—Browse or Design.
- *The name of the view now on-screen.* If you click this name, Approach displays a list of view names included in the Approach file you're using. You can switch to another view by selecting it from this list.

In Design mode, the status bar contains the following items, from left to right:

- *The text size.* This indicator displays the size of the text in the selected object. To change the size, click the size indicator and select a new size from the popup list. If the object doesn't have a size, this indicator is blank.

Note

Text sizes are measured in a unit of measurement called *points*. There are 72 points in an inch. The larger the number selected, the larger the text will appear on-screen.

- *The effects buttons.* The next three indicators on the status bar display the text effects for the selected object. The three indicators show whether the selected object's text is currently bold (**B**), italic (*I*), or underlined (U). If the object doesn't have text, these indicators are blank.
- *The style name indicator.* Approach lets you define a set of properties that you can attach to an object. These properties include font, size, effects, colors, borders, drop shadows, and many others. When you attach a style to an object, that object takes on the properties defined by the style. The style name indicator on the status bar displays the style attached to the selected object. If the object doesn't have a style, this indicator is blank.
- *X- and y-coordinates/dimensions.* This section of the status bar displays the x- and y-coordinates of the mouse pointer if no object is selected. If an object is selected, this section of the status bar displays either the left and top coordinates of the selected object (the status bar shows `L:` and `T:`) or the width and height of the selected object (the status bar shows `W:` and `H:`). You can toggle between the coordinates and dimensions by clicking this section of the status bar.
- *The magnification indicator.* This indicator is available in Design and Print Preview modes. Click this indicator for a list of available magnifications (from 25 to 200 percent) from which you can choose. Selecting a magnification smaller than 100 percent allows you to see more of your data or design on-screen. Selecting a magnification greater than 100 percent allows you to enlarge a portion of the screen, making it easier to do detailed design work.

Tip

In Print Preview mode, the mouse pointer turns into an outline of a mouse and magnifying glass. Click the left mouse button to increase the magnification one step (for example, from 50 to 75 percent); click the right mouse button to decrease the magnification one step.

- *The current mode.* Click this indicator to see a list of modes. You can switch to another mode by selecting the mode from this list.
- *The name of the view now on-screen.* If you click this name, Approach displays a list of view names included in the Approach file you're using. You can switch to another view by selecting it from this list.

In Find mode, the status bar contains the following items, from left to right:

- *The previous record button.* This button is visible but not operative in this mode.
- *The current database record number.* Like the previous record button, this button is visible but not operative in this mode.
- *The next record button.* Like the preceding two buttons, the next record button is visible but not operative in this mode.
- *The active records indicator.* This will not change from the previous mode you left when you switched to Find mode.
- *The current mode.* If you click this indicator, Approach presents a list of modes: Find, Browse, and Design. (You also get Print Preview mode if you're not already in Find mode.) You can switch to another mode by choosing the mode from this list.
- *The name of the view now on-screen.* If you click this name, Approach displays a list of view names included in the Approach file you're using. You can switch to another view by selecting it from this list.

The InfoBox

The InfoBox is a special window that's available in Design mode (see fig. 1.3). To display the InfoBox for an object such as a field or text block, double-click the object, press Alt+Enter while an object is selected, or choose Object Properties from the Object menu or from the popup menu that appears when you right-click a screen object. The view you're designing also has an InfoBox to set overall properties for your form or report, such as the name for the view, the main database used, page margins, and style. To display the view's InfoBox, double-click anywhere an object isn't displayed, or press Alt+Enter after selecting a spot where no object is displayed.

> **Note**
>
> The Change the Properties of a Selected Object SmartIcon will display the InfoBox for any object selected with the mouse. A selected object has handles around it, which make it look different from when it's not selected.

The InfoBox provides a set of pages for customizing the look of a screen object. For example, you can set the font, size, and effects of text in a text box or field. You can also set the background color, borders, frame style, and shadow color for most types of objects. You can even change the size and position of a screen object using the InfoBox. These pages are accessed by clicking the tabs near the top of the InfoBox.

You can leave the InfoBox visible on-screen while doing your design work, and the InfoBox will change as you click different objects. To get help with an InfoBox, click the question mark in the upper right corner. To close the InfoBox, click the Close button in the upper right corner.

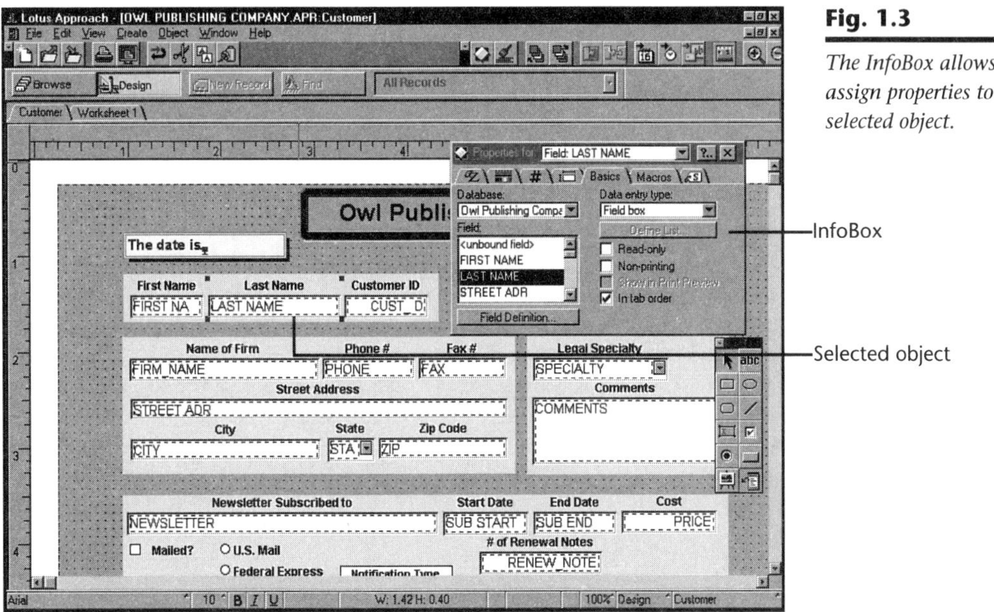

Fig. 1.3

The InfoBox allows you to assign properties to a selected object.

You also can shrink the InfoBox to a smaller size so that it'll still be handy on-screen but won't hide as much of the view. To shrink the InfoBox, double-click its title bar and the page portion of the InfoBox disappears, leaving only the title bar and tabs; to return the InfoBox to its full size, double-click the title bar again.

The various view and object properties that you can set from the InfoBox are discussed throughout this book.

Working with Files

A set of related databases and views to create them and manage them is stored on your computer's hard disk in files. Computer experts tend to call this set of information and screens an *application*. An application that you build with Approach has two major kinds of files:

- *Database files* contain the data that you enter on a form or report and include field indexes to make sorting and finding information more efficient.
- An *Approach file* contains the details of your application. These details include the layout of all your views, any calculations or special functions you've defined, and the names of all databases that your application must access.

> **Note**
>
> It's important to understand that you can have several applications in Approach that work with the same databases or different ones. This means you may have several Approach files doing different things with the same copy of your database(s), or your Approach files may be doing totally unrelated applications that have no databases in common.

You never need to worry about saving a database file, because the data is saved automatically as you enter it. An Approach file, on the other hand, needs to be saved any time you make changes to any items on-screen (for example, when you move fields around on a form, add a new report, use a new database in your application, or build a new form). If you make changes that affect the Approach file and try to exit Approach or close the Approach file without saving the changes, Approach reminds you to save your Approach file changes.

The Approach file defines everything you've designed in your Approach application, including the relationships between databases (see Chapter 8, "Understanding Relational Databases"), and the details of input forms (see Chapter 4, "Enhancing Data Input Forms") and reports (see Chapter 7, "Creating Reports and Mailing Labels"). Thus, your application's Approach file is a very important file. In fact, after you define the database tables to hold your data (see Chapter 2, "Creating Database Tables"), you'll likely never work with any file except the Approach file. The next sections discuss how to work with Approach files in more detail.

Creating an Approach File

When you want to use an existing database but don't yet have an Approach file for it, you can create one quickly by simply opening your database file with Approach. Approach will create a basic application consisting of one form and one worksheet view. (The types of databases that will open directly in Approach and other details about this process are described later in this chapter.)

Common types of database templates (such as address books and video libraries) and some generic applications (such as contact management) are provided with Approach as *SmartMasters*. They contain either database definition "templates" or working applications with forms and reports. You can use SmartMasters to create databases and Approach files for your own use rather than start with a blank screen. From the File menu, choose New Database. The New dialog box lists the available SmartMasters in the categories *templates* and *applications*.

Several types of SmartMasters are available:

- *Blank Database*. This takes you directly to a window to define your database fields yourself and name your Approach file. An empty database named Blank.dbf is created, as well as a form and a worksheet with your fields placed on them.

- *Templates*. These SmartMasters create an empty database, a form, and a worksheet, but unlike the blank one, a database is already defined with fields appropriate to the SmartMaster title. For example, Friends and Family creates an address book database. Some others are Art Collection, Inventory, Stocks and Bonds, and Video Library.
- *Applications*. These SmartMasters do all the things that the templates do, but also include reports and other views, as well as logic, to make the entire application work immediately.

Although you may find the resulting Approach files from using the SmartMasters aren't entirely satisfactory for your needs, they're an excellent way to get started for many common computer applications. This is because Approach lets you add, change, and delete views and database fields to improve or extend these "starter-uppers."

Opening an Approach File

When you need to use your application, simply open the Approach file you created (as described in the preceding section). Approach then has access to everything you've built as part of that application.

> **Note**
>
> To open your Approach file, you must have previously "saved" it. Saving your Approach file is covered under "Saving an Approach File" later in this chapter.

If you've configured Approach to display the Welcome to Lotus Approach dialog box, you can open an existing file by using the Open an Existing Approach File page (see fig. 1.4). The displayed file list contains the most recent Approach files you've used. Select the file you want to open and click OK. If you don't see the file you want, use the Browse for More Files button to look for the file anywhere on your computer using the Open dialog box.

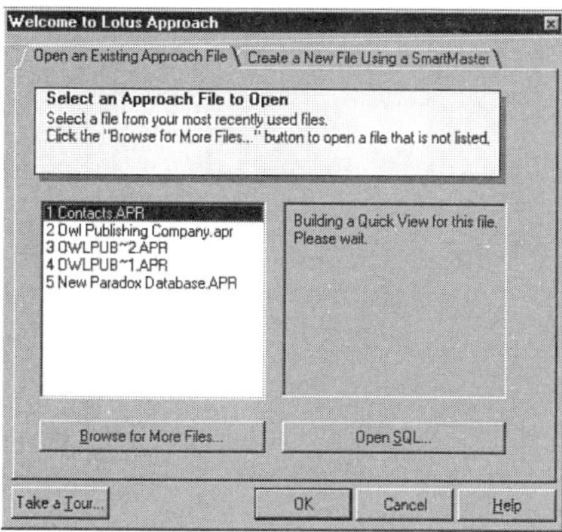

Fig. 1.4

This dialog box lets you select from Approach files that you've used recently.

You can also open an Approach file by opening the File menu and choosing Open to display the Open dialog box (see fig. 1.5). The Open dialog box is similar to other Open dialog boxes in Windows 95. In this dialog box, you can open files, change folders, and specify the file type you want to see.

Fig. 1.5

Use the Open dialog box to open your files.

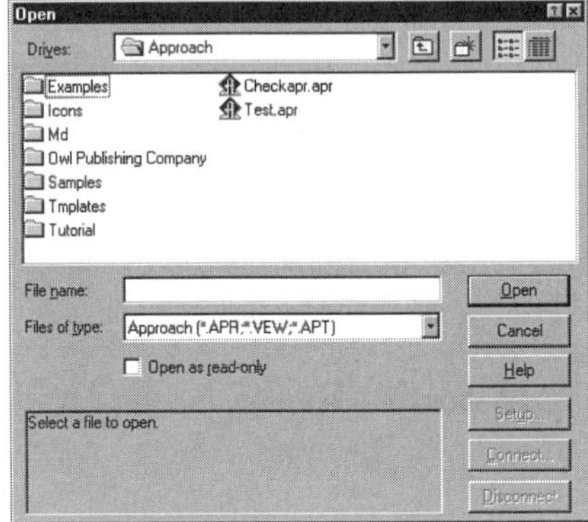

The area in the center of the Open dialog box displays folders in the current drive and any files that match the current file type selected. To select one of these files, click the file name. The name appears in the File Name text box. To open one of the folders, double-click the folder name and the area will display the contents of that folder.

At the top of the Open dialog box is an area from which you can set the drive and folder that contain the file you want to open. To change drives, use the Drives drop-down list and select the appropriate entry from the hierarchy shown. To open the folder one level higher, click the icon to the right of the list box. The next icon to the right creates a new folder in the current drive. The other two icons control the level of detail displayed (icons and names only, or icons, names, size, and modification date and time detail) in the center of the dialog box.

Below the file name is a drop-down list box of file types that Approach can open. By default, this list has Approach (*.APR, *.VEW, *.APT) selected; if they aren't selected, click the down arrow to the right of this line to access a list of file types. Click the Approach (*.APR, *.VEW, *.APT) line, and all available Approach files appear in the center of the dialog box.

Below the file types is the Open as Read-Only check box. Selecting this mode allows you to view the contents of the file but not to modify those contents.

Tip

The Open as Read-Only check box must be selected any time you want to open the file in read-only mode; however, Approach doesn't remember the mode from the last time you opened the Approach file unless you've set up TeamSecurity to control this aspect of your application (see Chapter 8, "Understanding Relational Databases").

At the bottom of the Open dialog box, information about the currently selected folder or file is displayed. For folders, the date, time, and size of any files in it are shown. For a file, the author, date, time, and size are shown. You can see more details about files and folders by clicking the Details button at the top right of the dialog box.

After you select the desired file, click Open to open the file. Or you can double-click the file to open it.

Caution

The Approach file and the databases can get out of synch if you change the database structure (for example, if you change a field name or delete a field from the database) and don't save the Approach file after the change. The next time you open the Approach file, Approach will automatically display the Field Mapping dialog box. You must use this dialog box to map the fields in the Approach file to the fields in the database. To avoid this problem, always save the Approach file after making changes to the database structure.

Saving an Approach File

The first time you need to save an Approach file, open the File menu and choose Save Approach File. The Save Apr dialog box appears (see fig. 1.6).

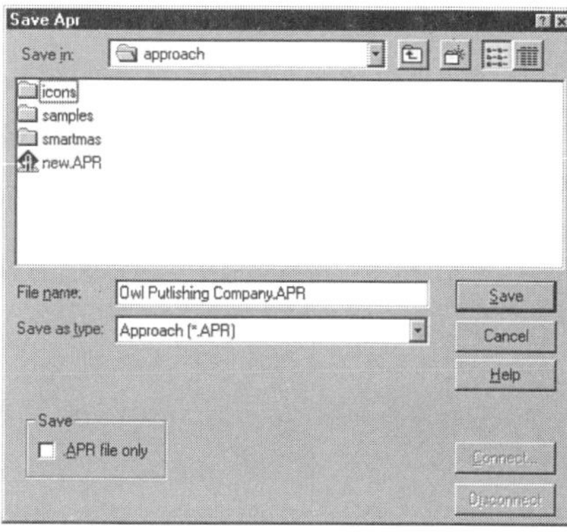

Fig. 1.6

The Save Apr dialog box is nearly identical to the Open dialog box, except that it has a Save button instead of an Open button.

In the File Name text box, type a name for the file. A file name can contain up to 255 characters, including spaces. But it can't contain any of the following characters: \ / : * ? " < > and ¦. You can also accept the default name, which is the same as the database name. You don't need to include a file extension; Approach appends an .APR extension by default. The first time you save an Approach file, the file automatically saves the information on the name of the open database and the default form created from that database.

Note

After you create and save an Approach file for the first time, Approach saves the Approach file to the same file name each time you open the File menu and choose Save Approach File.

By default, Approach saves the Approach file to the folder selected in the drive list box. If you need to save the file to a different drive or folder, change the drive with the Save In drop-down list box and select the appropriate folder.

Setting Your Approach File Passwords. If you need to protect an Approach file, you can use one or more passwords. Although users can still enter data using a password-protected Approach file, they can't modify the Approach file in Design mode. If someone tries to enter Design mode, that person is prompted for the password before proceeding.

Caution

Consider very carefully whether you want to assign passwords to an Approach file. If you forget the passwords, you can't access the file in Design mode and must rebuild the Approach file to modify it.

To set an Approach file password, follow these steps:

1. Open the File menu and choose TeamSecurity. The Team Security dialog box appears. Approach defaults to Manager, Editor, Designer, and Reader as the types of people who may use your Approach file.
2. Select from the classes of user displayed or enter a new one; the Edit Team Security dialog box appears. You may edit the Group or User Name text box, or add a new name if it's blank.
3. Enter the password you want to use in the Approach File Password text box. The typed text appears as asterisks so that someone watching you enter the password won't be able to read your password.

Tip

Pick a password that's easy to remember but difficult for someone else to guess. Adding a non-alphanumeric character to the password, such as an asterisk (*) or comma, can foil an intruder.

4. Click the Advanced tab and set the check boxes to allow or prevent design changes (Designer Privileges) or Approach file password changes (Change Passwords). Selecting the check boxes allows the options; deselecting denies these options.
5. Click OK. The Confirm Approach File Password dialog box appears, asking you to retype your password to ensure that you typed it correctly the first time.
6. Retype the password in the Retype Approach File Password text box and click OK.

Tip

An overall password for the Approach file can be established by opening the File menu and choosing User Setup and then Approach Preferences. In the Approach Preferences dialog box, click the Password tab. Select the appropriate check box and enter your Approach file password in the appropriate text box.

Changing or Deleting Approach File Passwords. To change or delete Approach file passwords, follow these steps:

1. Open the password-protected Approach file.
2. Open the File menu and choose TeamSecurity. You can do this only if your user class allows password changes. The user class and TeamSecurity are set up by the application author as a part of group or individual user security, so be sure to remember how you set them up.
3. Type in new passwords in the same way you entered the original passwords for each group or user. Press Delete to delete a password. Save your changes by clicking OK. Repeat for each group or user as needed.
4. Open the File menu and choose Save Approach File to save your security settings.

Tip

The overall password for the Approach file can be changed by opening the File menu and then choosing User Setup and Approach Preferences. In the Approach Preferences dialog box, click the Password tab. Deselect the appropriate check box to delete the password, or enter your new Approach file password in the appropriate text box.

Copying an Approach File

An Approach file contains the information about your entire application. Because you can spend a considerable amount of effort building an Approach file and getting it just right, Approach lets you copy an Approach file so that you can create a similar application without building it from scratch. For example, you may want to build an address book database for yourself and another similar address book just for business associates. Remember, however, that an Approach file can't be created unless it's associated with at least one database. Thus, when you copy an Approach file, you must also link the new Approach file to existing databases or have Approach create new databases to link to the new Approach file.

To create a new Approach file from an existing one, follow these steps:

1. Open the existing Approach file.
2. Open the File menu and choose Save As. The Save Apr dialog box appears (refer to fig. 1.6).
3. In the File Name text box, type the name of the new Approach file.
4. Set the folder and drive where you want the Approach file saved.
5. In the bottom right corner of the dialog box, you can select the APR File Only check box. (The implications of this are explained after these steps.)
6. Click Save to save the new Approach file.

If you select the APR File Only check box, Approach doesn't copy the databases at all. Instead, it links the new Approach file to the same databases as the original Approach file. You can then modify the new Approach file to change your application or to create an entirely new application (with new forms, reports, validation criteria, and so on) linked to the same databases as your original application. Creating a new .APR file is useful if you want two different sets of people—perhaps with access to different subsets of the database information—to use the same database.

If you don't select the APR File Only check box, the Save Table dialog box will appear for each database you have access to (see fig. 1.7). You'll need to select one of three options for each database. These options allow you to create a blank copy of your database, copy the database with its data, or use the existing database associated with your original Approach file. You can choose only one option per database. (These options are discussed in the following sections.)

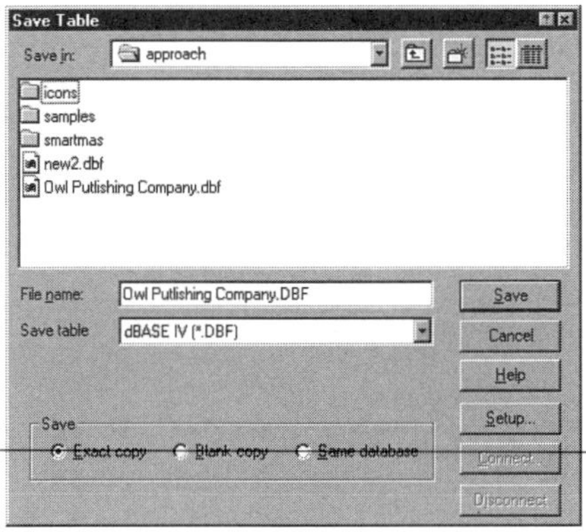

Fig. 1.7

The Save Table dialog box lets you save a database under a new name, among other options.

Using the Exact Copy Option. The Exact Copy option duplicates a database. The newly created Approach file is linked to the copied database rather than the original database. Thus, you can create a complete copy of your application, including the Approach file and databases. You can then make any changes to this copy without affecting the original application.

If you choose this option, rename the database before you click Save in the Save Table dialog box. You can type over the name of the current database that appears in the File Name text box. You must specify either a new name for the database or a new folder for the database.

To save the new database under a different name or as a different type, follow these steps:

1. In the File Name text box, type the new name for the file.
2. If you want to change the type of database—for example, from dBASE III+ to FoxPro—drop down the Save as Type list box and choose the type of database you want for the copy.
3. Specify where you want the database to be stored by using the folders and Save In options.
4. Click Save to create the copy of the database.

Note

Clicking Cancel in any of the Save Table dialog boxes cancels the entire operation and returns you to the original Approach file without saving the Approach file or making any database copies.

Using the Blank Copy Option. The Blank Copy option duplicates just the database structure (see Chapter 2, "Creating Database Tables," for information on how to create a database structure). The new database has the same fields as the old database, but no actual records are in it. This way, you can fill the new database with new data. When you click Save in the Save Table dialog box, the Save Table dialog box appears again (once for each database in the application) so that you can specify options for the other databases. Selecting Cancel in any Save Table dialog box cancels the entire operation and returns you to the original Approach file.

Using the Same Database Option. The Same Database option links the new Approach file to the same database as the original Approach file. This is useful if you're creating a new application with one or more of the same databases as the original Approach file, and you also need new or blank copies of some of the databases.

Deleting an Approach File or Database File

You can delete an Approach file or database file from within Approach. If you delete a database file, Approach will delete all related files, such as the accompanying indexes for the database. If you delete an Approach file, Approach will give you the option to delete each associated database file and all related files (see fig. 1.8).

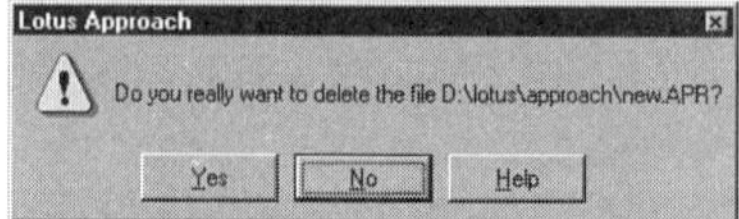

Fig. 1.8

You'll be asked if you want to delete each associated database.

> **Note**
>
> Approach files and database files must be closed before you can delete them.

To delete a database or Approach file, follow these steps:

1. Open the File menu and choose Delete Approach File. The Delete File dialog box appears.
2. To delete a database file, select the database file type in the Delete Type drop-down list. The file type is preset to show Approach's .APR, .VEW, or .APT files, so if you want to delete an Approach file, you don't need to change the file type in this drop-down list.
3. Adjust the Delete In and folder selections until the file name appears in the list box. Select the file you want to delete and click OK. Approach asks if you're sure that you want to delete the file. A password may also be requested, if the file is password protected.
4. Click Delete to delete the file. If deleting an Approach file, Approach asks if you're sure that you want to delete each associated database file. You can click No in any of these alert boxes to keep a particular database file. If you click Yes, the database file is deleted.

> **Caution**
>
> Be careful when deleting database files! Once a database file is deleted, it's no longer available for any use—including use by another Approach file. You can't recover the database files from Windows 95's Recycle bin because Approach does not save them there on delete operations.

Creating a Windows 95 Menu Entry to Open an Approach File

You can create an entry in the Windows 95 Start or Programs menu that serves as a shortcut for running Approach and for opening a specific Approach file. When you double-click the entry, Approach runs and the Approach file opens automatically. Follow these steps:

1. Click the Start button on the Windows 95 taskbar and choose Settings and then Taskbar. The Taskbar Properties sheet appears.

2. Select the Start Menu Programs tab. Click the Add button to open the Create Shortcut dialog box (see fig. 1.9).

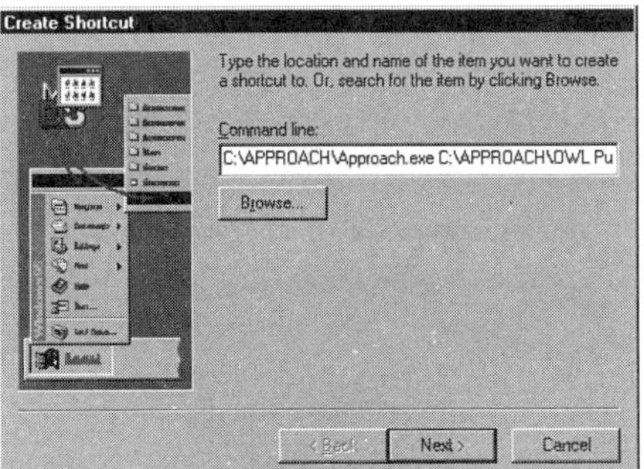

Fig. 1.9

You can create a shortcut to a specific Approach file by using the Create Shortcut dialog box.

3. In the Command Line text box, type the full path name of the Approach file (for example, **`c:\approach\owl.apr`**). If you don't know the full path, click the Browse button to locate the program you want to add. When you find it, double-click the name.
4. Click Next to move to the Select Program Folder dialog box. Double-click the menu (Start or Programs) on which you want the shortcut to appear.
5. Click Next. The Select a Title for the Program dialog box appears.
6. In the Select a Name for the Shortcut text box, type the text that you want to appear with your icon (for example, **`Owl Publishing`**). Then click Finish.

The Start or Programs menu now contains your application with an icon that looks just like the Approach icon and the shortcut name you provided.

To change the icon (or other properties of your program, such as the folder to use and the window size at startup), follow these steps:

1. Repeat step 1 from the preceding steps and select the Start Menu Programs tab.
2. Click the Advanced button. The Windows Explorer is launched, with your Start Menu folder and its contents displayed.
3. Click the folder that contains your program and then select the program name. Open the File menu and choose Properties; the Properties sheet for your program appears. Notice the various properties that you can change.
4. Click the Shortcut tab. Notice the additional program properties in this dialog box. Click the Change Icon button to open the Change Icon dialog box (see fig. 1.10).
5. Choose an icon from the Current Icon list.

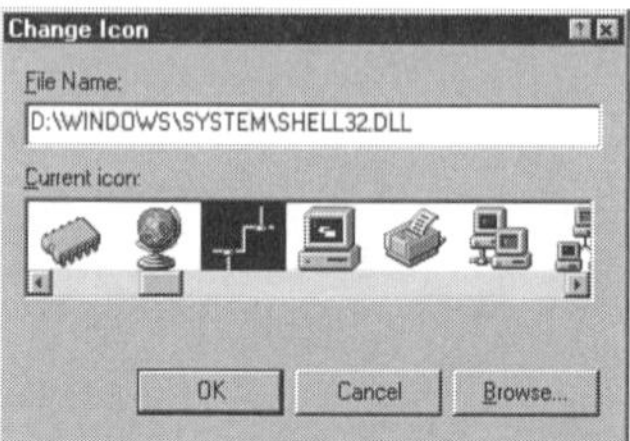

Fig. 1.10

Change the icon for the new Start menu item by using the Change Icon dialog box.

> **Note**
>
> If you want a different set of icons to choose from, type another file name in the File Name text box. Good files to use are the Shell32.dll in the \Windows\System directory (folder), or the Progman.exe and Moricons.dll files in the \Windows directory, which contain a large assortment of icons. To see all the icon files on your computer that you can pick from, choose Browse. You can literally use any icon for your program just by clicking the icon file in the middle of this new Change Icon dialog box and clicking the Open button. After you choose the file you want, you'll see all the icons in it in the middle of the first Change Icon dialog box. Choose the icon you like from the Current Icon list.

6. Click OK in the Change Icon dialog box and Properties sheet. Close the Windows Explorer. Then click OK on the Taskbar Properties sheet. Your Start button's menu now shows the new icon for your application (see fig. 1.11).

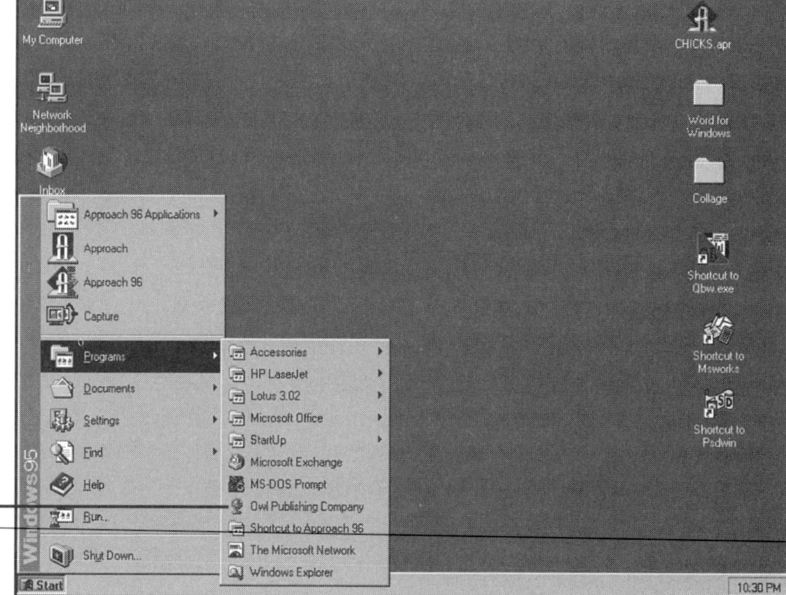

Fig. 1.11

The new entry for your Approach file appears on the Start menu.

Opening Database Files

Besides opening Approach files, as described earlier, Approach can open different types of external database files directly. These file types include dBASE III+ and IV, FoxPro, and Paradox.

Always open the Approach file (the .APR, .VEW, or .APT file) to open a database created in Approach. (Opening the Approach file automatically opens the database file.) If the database was created in an application other than Approach, however, you must open the database file directly because that file doesn't yet have an Approach file attached to it. When you open a database file directly, Approach creates a new Approach file of the same name. You can save the newly created Approach file to avoid having to open the database directly again.

To open a database file, follow these steps:

1. Open the File menu and choose Open. The Open dialog box appears (see fig. 1.12).

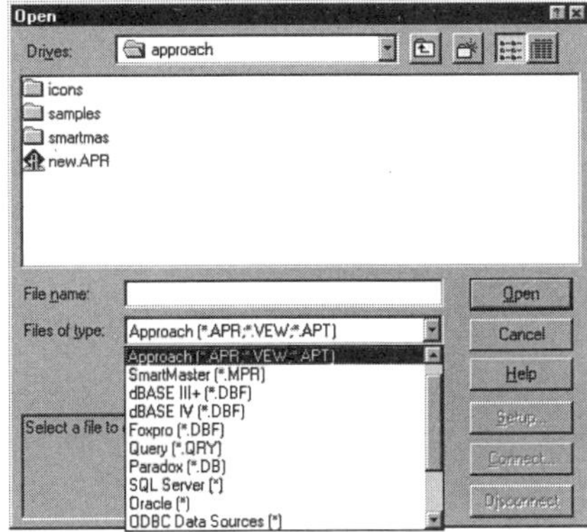

Fig. 1.12

You can open other database files by using the Open dialog box.

2. From the Files of Type drop-down list, choose the type of database file you want to open.
3. From the Drives drop-down list, specify where the database is located.
4. In the area below the Drives drop-down list box, select one of the file names. The file name appears in the File Name text box.
5. After you select the file you want, click Open to start opening the file. An Approach file is automatically created with minimal help from you, but don't forget to save your newly created files before quitting Approach.

Adding Approach File Information

Approach can store general information about an Approach file. This information includes the name of the author, title and description of the Approach file, and descriptive keywords.

To add information to an Approach file, first open the proper Approach file, and then open the File menu and choose Approach File Properties. The Approach File Properties dialog box opens (see fig. 1.13). You can enter the following information:

- *The name of the author of the file.* Type the name into the Author text box. The default entry is the name of the person to whom the copy of Approach is registered.
- *A title for the file.* Type the title into the Title text box. This title is for documentation purposes and need not be the same as the Approach file name.
- *A description of the file.* Type the description into the Description text box.

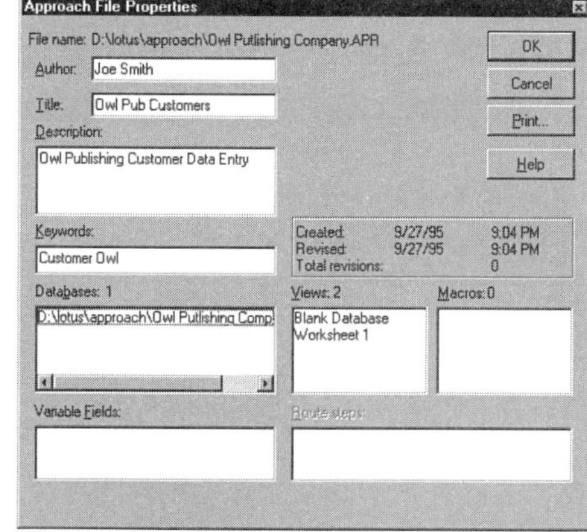

Fig. 1.13

The Approach File Properties dialog box provides basic information about your database application.

- *Descriptive keywords for the file.* Type the keywords into the Keywords text box.
- *Variable fields for the file.* To enable a variable field for sharing with Notes/FX in the Approach File Properties dialog box, select the check box to the left of the variable field name in the FX Enable column.
- *Route steps for the file.* Enter the names of those people who you want to receive your e-mail of Approach views and data. This will create a routing list. You must be connected to a network and have access to an e-mail package to use this feature.

Approach also displays certain information about the file, including the associated databases, views, macros, variable fields, Route Steps, and the date and time that the file was originally created and last modified.

Using Keyboard Shortcuts

The menu bar at the top of the screen is one way to choose commands in Approach. Sometimes, however, taking your hands off the keyboard to use the mouse is inconvenient. Approach offers some keyboard shortcuts so that you can give commands without having to use the mouse.

As with any Windows application, you can press Alt and another key to access a menu, and then press a third key to activate a command on that menu. Pressing Alt+F, for example, accesses the File menu. You can then press the letter O to access the Open command and open a new file.

The letters that you use to activate commands are underlined. These underlined letters, called *hot keys*, are underlined throughout this book. On the File menu, for example, the F is underlined. After you pull down the menu, notice that the O in Open is also underlined (see fig. 1.14).

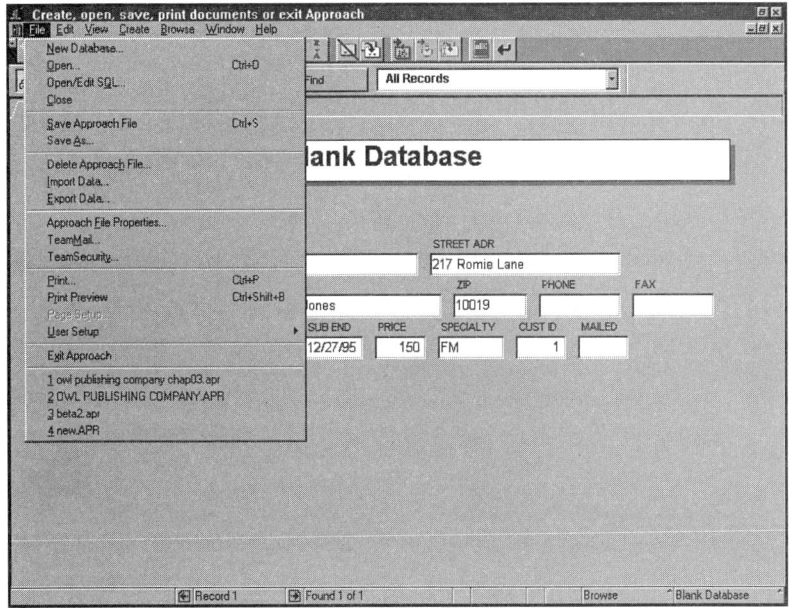

Fig. 1.14

Shortcut keyboard commands are shown to the right of menu choices.

Approach also lets you use even more efficient keyboard shortcuts to access some common commands. Shortcut keystrokes consist of the Alt or Ctrl key and a single letter. (You press these two keys at the same time.) Pressing Ctrl+N, for example, brings up a new record.

The keyboard shortcuts, listed in online help, are shown on the menus. As you use the menus, note these keyboard shortcuts—they make navigating through Approach much quicker and easier.

From Here...

In this chapter, you learned what a database is and the advantages of using a computerized database. You also learned about Approach's screen layout and the Browse, Design, Print Preview, and Find modes, as well as the different types of files that Approach uses to allow you to create and use your applications.

Giving commands to Approach is another important concept covered in this chapter. Using the mouse and menus, keyboard shortcuts, the status bar, the action bar, and the SmartIcon bar were also discussed. You also discovered how to save, copy, and delete Approach files, how to protect them with file passwords, and how to add descriptive information to an Approach file.

For more information about working with database files and Approach files, refer to the following chapters in this book:

- Chapter 2, "Creating Database Tables," leads you through the process of creating databases.
- Chapter 3, "Building Data Input Forms," shows you how to build a form for data input and then save the form.

CHAPTER 2

Creating Database Tables

This chapter covers some of the theory of designing a database. It also discusses how to select a file type, how to specify fields to hold your data, and how to choose special options to ensure that the fields behave the way you want. You'll learn how to modify your database structure if you need to. At the end of this chapter, you'll also learn how to build an example database file to illustrate these concepts.

In this chapter, you learn how to

- Create a database from scratch
- Create a database by converting spreadsheet and text files
- Select the best file type for your database format
- Define new fields and their types
- Rearrange fields in your table structure
- Simplify data entry with default and calculated values
- Add formulas to your database fields
- Add passwords to your files
- Modify the table structure and fields
- View your data in an Approach worksheet

Designing a Database

As mentioned in Chapter 1, "Learning Approach Basics," you can think of a database as an organized collection of information (data). The data is arranged in tables; each column in the table is a field in the database.

The first task in setting up a new database is to plan what the table will look like. Although leaping in and creating your new table immediately may tempt you greatly, this method isn't the best way to proceed. You should carefully plan the table's content. All too often, a new Approach owner creates a database and starts entering data, only to find that the database doesn't provide all the necessary reports required or the information isn't stored in the format needed.

Although Approach is powerful enough to allow you to correct these kinds of errors, the process of repairing your mistakes can be tedious and time-consuming, and may require you to re-enter some of the data. By spending a little time planning the database early on, you can save time later.

You can divide the process of designing a database roughly into two steps. The first step is *data definition*, in which you list the fields of the database. The second is *data refinement*, in which you use several techniques to answer these questions:

- Has all necessary data been included in the database?
- Is any unnecessary data being stored in the database?
- Is the data in the database being stored in the correct format?
- Can you use the database for all the purposes you want?

In the following sections, read through the two steps involved in designing a database using Owl Publishing, a fictional company that publishes law-related newsletters and magazines, as an example.

Step 1: Defining Data

The first step is to list on a sheet of paper as many pieces of data as you can think of that you need to store in the database.

Keep in mind how you plan to use the data. The usage directly affects how the data is stored. If you want to create mailings to people in specific ZIP codes, for example, ZIP CODE must be a separate field in the database—as opposed to being combined with the rest of the address information.

Note

You should list all the possible fields of the database. You can eliminate unwanted fields in the second step.

In this example, the Owl Publishing Company has decided to create a database to keep track of its newsletter customers. The necessary information includes

Customer name	Newsletter name
Address	Date when subscription started
Phone number	Length of subscription
Birth date	

Step 2: Refining Data

Next comes the all-important step of refining the data. You should carry out this step with as many of the people who'll use the database as possible—the more people involved in this process, the closer your final product is to being right.

During the data refinement process, you need to ask yourself what each piece of data will be used for and what kinds of questions you expect the database to answer. By considering these things, you can decide whether the data in the database can provide the information you need.

Ask yourself these questions:

- Why will I use each piece of data? Can I efficiently use the data for that purpose?
- Can I get the type of information I need from the database? If not, what missing data will allow me to fulfill my needs?

Keep in mind that even after you design the database, your design isn't permanent. You can always make changes later, if necessary. However, even something as simple as adding a new field involves a great deal of extra work that would have been unnecessary if you had included the field in the first place. At a minimum, you must go through and type the information in the new field of every record in the database. Adding the information in this field as you enter each new record is, of course, much more efficient.

Careful planning and time spent designing the database can help you avoid such problems. If you follow the systematic approach to database design outlined in this chapter, the chances are much better that you won't create a database that you later must redesign extensively.

Owl Publishing needs to target its customers by state or ZIP code for mailings regarding new newsletters. You could create a field called ADDRESS for this information, but then you couldn't sort the information by just state or ZIP code. Breaking the address line into STREET ADDRESS, CITY, STATE, and ZIP CODE fields would be more helpful. Also, because many prospective customers belong to firms, you need to record the firm name. Because Owl Publishing doesn't plan to send out birthday cards, the birth date of the customer isn't important.

Next you need to ask, "What's the purpose of the Length of Subscription field?" Because Owl Publishing sends out renewal notices just before a subscription expires, a report of all customers whose newsletter subscriptions expire in the next three months would be helpful. Given this usage, the expiration date of the subscription should replace the LENGTH OF SUBSCRIPTION field. An expiration date field lends itself much more effectively to determining who needs to get a renewal notice. Also, if Owl Publishing is sending out renewal notices, you may want to record how many notices have been sent to a particular customer so that you can use different form letters for the second and subsequent notices. You'll also want to record whether a flyer has been mailed and how it was sent.

The customer database should also contain all the information necessary to create and send out an invoice—except the newsletter price. Therefore, you need to add pricing information as well.

Finally, because lawyers specialize in various kinds of law, recording their specialties is important so that you can target the correct potential customers for subscription drives.

Given all these considerations, Owl Publishing came up with this list of fields for its customer database:

FIRST NAME	STATE	SUBSCRIPTION END DATE
LAST NAME	ZIP	NUMBER OF RENEWAL NOTICES SENT
FIRM NAME	SPECIALTY OF LAW	PRICE OF NEWSLETTER
STREET ADDRESS	NEWSLETTER NAME	FLYER MAILED?
CITY	SUBSCRIPTION START DATE	MAIL METHOD

Creating a Database File

After you figure out the fields you're going to need in your database, you're ready to create the new database file. You can create an entirely new database file, or convert an existing spreadsheet or text file to a database file.

Creating an Entirely New File

You may create a new database file by using the Welcome to Lotus Approach dialog box or the File menu.

> **Note**
>
> The Welcome to Lotus Approach dialog box appears when you first start Approach and when you close all Approach files. If the Welcome to Lotus Approach dialog box doesn't appear under these circumstances, open the File menu and choose User Setup and Approach Preferences. On the Display page, select Welcome Dialog.

From the Welcome to Lotus Approach dialog box, select Create a New File Using a SmartMaster and select an option from the list. You can create a Blank Database or choose one of the commonly used SmartMaster templates provided, such as Accounts, Contact Database, Customer, Employee, and so on. If you select a SmartMaster, Approach automatically includes the appropriate database fields in the new file. Refer to the "Working with Files" section of Chapter 1, "Learning Approach Basics," for additional information about Approach files.

Approach opens the New dialog box (see fig. 2.1). Follow these steps to create a new file:

1. In the File Name text box, type a name for the file. You don't need to type a file extension—Approach automatically assigns the proper extension after you choose a file type.

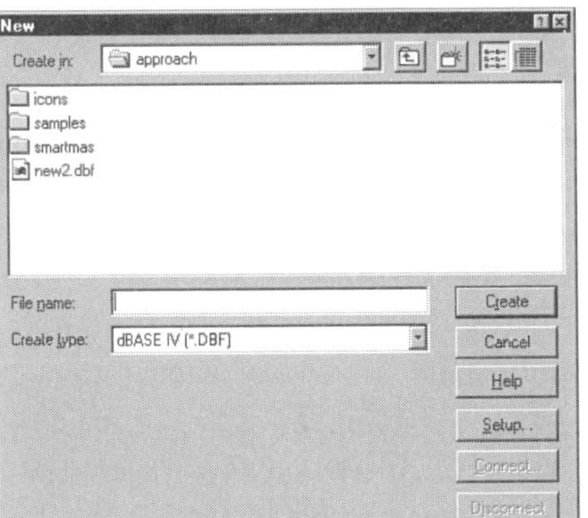

Fig. 2.1

The New dialog box indicates the types of files Approach can create.

2. Choose the file type you want from the Create Type drop-down list. (The available file types are explained later in the section "Understanding the File Types.")
3. Click Create.

To create a new file by using the menu bar, open the File menu and choose New Database. The New dialog box appears. Follow the preceding steps.

Converting a Database from a Spreadsheet

You can open a spreadsheet file in Lotus 1-2-3 or Excel format, and Approach creates a new database and Approach file by using the information in the spreadsheet. When you use a spreadsheet to create a new database, the columns in the spreadsheet become fields in the database, and the rows become records.

If the first row in the spreadsheet contains information (headings, for example) that identifies the rest of the contents, you can use the first row to provide the field names. Otherwise, the fields are initially named A, B, C, and so on. You can use the Field Definition dialog box to change the field names (see "Modifying the Table Structure" later in this chapter).

To create a new database from a spreadsheet, follow these steps:

1. Click the Open File SmartIcon, or open the File menu and choose Open. If the Welcome to Lotus Approach dialog box appears, select the Open an Existing Approach File tab and click the Browse for More Files button. The Open dialog box appears.
2. Select Lotus 1-2-3 (*.WK*) or Excel (*.XL*) in the Files of Type drop-down list. Choose the file you want to open in the center of the dialog box. You can change the folder and drive to locate your spreadsheet file.

3. Click Open. To create a database from a Lotus 1-2-3 spreadsheet, select the sheet or named range with the data you want in the Select Range dialog box.
4. To use the first row in the spreadsheet for the field names, make sure that the First Row Contains Field Names check box is selected in the Select Range dialog box (for Lotus 1-2-3) or the Field Names dialog box (for Excel). Otherwise, deselect this box. Then click OK.
5. The New dialog box appears. Type a name for your new database file into the File Name text box. You don't need to specify a file extension because Approach will provide the extension for you. You can change the folder and drive if you want to specify a different location for the new file.
6. Choose a file type from the Create Type drop-down list. (For more information on file types, see "Understanding the File Types" later in this chapter.)
7. Click Create. Approach creates the new file for you and displays the contents of the database on a standard form. Be sure to save the new Approach file by opening the File menu and choosing Save Approach File.

Converting a Database from a Delimited Text File

You can open an ASCII text file with delimited text, and Approach will create a new database and Approach file by using the information in the text file.

A *delimited text file* contains text separated into distinct units using delimiters such as commas, spaces, or tabs. The delimiters mark where one field, such as the city name, ends and another field, such as the state name, begins. You can specify the delimiter when you convert the text file into a database. Each line from the text file becomes a record in the database.

If the first row in the text file contains information that identifies the rest of the contents (for example, headings), you can use the first row to provide the field names. Otherwise, the fields are initially named Field1, Field2, Field3, and so on. You can use the Field Definition dialog box to change the field names, as discussed later in the section "Modifying the Table Structure."

To create a new database from a delimited text file, follow these steps:

1. Click the Open File SmartIcon, or open the File menu and choose Open. If the Welcome to Lotus Approach dialog box appears, select the Open an Existing Approach File tab, and then click the Browse for More Files button.
2. Select Text – Delimited (*.TXT) in the Files of Type drop-down list. Choose the file you want to open in the center of the dialog box. You can change the folder and drive to locate the text file.
3. Click OK. The Text File Options dialog box appears. Select the delimiter from the Separate Fields With section: Commas, Semicolons, Spaces, or Tabs. If the text in the file is separated with a different delimiter, select Other and then type the delimiter into the adjacent text box.

To use the first row in the text file for the field names, make sure that the First Row Contains Field Names check box is selected. Otherwise, deselect this option.

4. Click OK. The New dialog box appears. Type a name for your new database file into the File Name text box. You don't need to specify a file extension because Approach will provide the extension for you. You can change the folder and drive if you want to specify a different location for the new file.
5. Choose a file type in the Create Type drop-down list. (For more information on file types, see "Understanding the File Types" later in this chapter.)
6. Click Create. Approach creates the new file and displays the contents of the database on a standard form. Be sure to save the new Approach file by opening the File menu and choosing Save Approach File.

Converting a Database from a Fixed-Length Text File

You can open an ASCII text file with fixed-length text, and Approach will create a new database and Approach file using the information in the text file.

A *fixed-length text file* contains text separated into one or more distinct blocks of a fixed length. If the text in a block doesn't fill the entire length, the text has spaces after it until the next block begins.

When you create a database from a fixed-length text file, you must tell Approach how long each text block is. Each fixed-length block becomes a field (column) in the database, and each row (set of text blocks) becomes a record. If the first row in the text file contains information that identifies the rest of the contents, you can use the first row to provide the field names. These field names must start at the far left position of the corresponding text block in the following rows and must contain no blanks. Otherwise, you must name the fields when you create the database. You can use the Field Definition dialog box to change the field names, as discussed later in the section "Modifying the Table Structure."

To create a new database from a fixed-length text file, follow these steps:

1. Click the Open File SmartIcon, or open the File menu and choose Open. If the Welcome to Lotus Approach dialog box appears, select the Open an Existing Approach File tab, and then click the Browse for More Files button.
2. Select Text – Fixed-Length (*.TXT) from the Files of Type drop-down list. Choose the file you want to open in the center of the dialog box. You can change the folder and drive to locate the text file.
3. Click Open. The Fixed Length Text File Setup dialog box appears (see fig. 2.2). If the first row of the text file contains the field names, check the First Row Contains Field Names check box. Otherwise, type the name of the first field name in the first row of the Field Name column, and then tab to the next column.

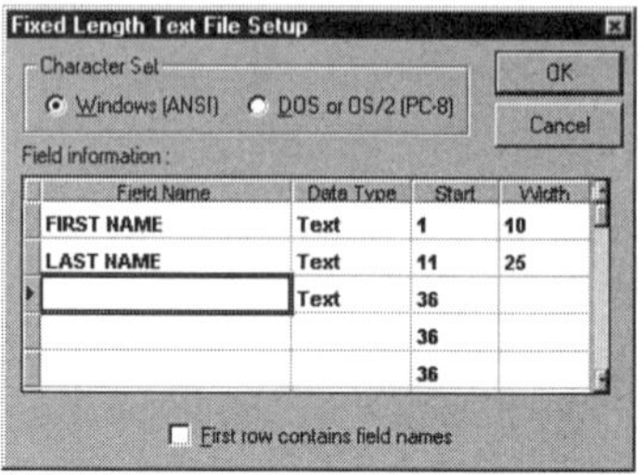

Fig. 2.2

Import fixed-length text files from the Fixed Length Text File Setup dialog box.

4. Choose the Data Type of the field from the drop-down list and then tab to the next column. For more information on data types, see "Defining New Fields" later in this chapter.

> **Note**
>
> You may tend to set the data type for all your fields to Text when importing a text file. However, Approach is smart enough to convert data from text to other types, if the resulting database fields are really dates, numbers with decimals, or other types.
> For example, 105.50 will convert correctly from text into a numeric field type, but ---105.50-- won't. If your data doesn't match the type selected, the resulting field in your database will be blank or empty.

5. Type the starting position for the first text block in the Start column. For example, if your first text block starts in column 1 in the row of text, type **1** in the Start column for that field.
6. Type the width, in characters, of the text block in the Width column.
7. Click the next line in the Fixed Length Text File Setup dialog box. Approach automatically inserts the starting position for the next field in the Start column. Enter the field name and width of the next text block. Repeat this step for all blocks in the text file.
8. Click OK. The New dialog box appears. Type a name for your new database file into the File Name text box. (You don't need to specify a file extension because Approach will provide the extension for you.) You can change the folder and drive if you want to specify a different location for the new file.
9. Choose a file type in the Create Type drop-down list. (For more information on file types, see the following section.)
10. Click Create in the New dialog box. Approach creates the new file for you and displays the contents of the database on a standard form. Be sure to save the new Approach file by opening the File menu and choosing Save Approach File.

Understanding the File Types

As stated earlier, Approach doesn't have its own database file format. But Approach can create, open, and use the most common of the existing commercially available database file formats. These include dBASE III+, dBASE IV, FoxPro, and Paradox. The one you choose depends on the file format that's most appropriate for your working environment. You don't need to have access to the original database programs to use these file formats in Approach.

The following sections discuss some things you need to remember when choosing a file type.

Choosing dBASE Files

Two "flavors" of dBASE files exist: dBASE III+ and dBASE IV. The two file types are very similar, but some differences exist, such as the way indexes are handled. You may want to choose the older dBASE III+ format for compatibility with older applications built with that popular program.

If you choose dBASE III+ or dBASE IV as the file type, you can use Boolean (yes/no or true/false), date, time, text, numeric, and memo (free-form text) fields. (For a description of these field types, see the later section "Defining New Fields.") Field names can contain up to 32 characters in Approach; if you open the dBASE file in another dBASE application, however, you'll see modified field names (dBASE normally allows only 10 characters). A dBASE text field length must be between 1 and 254 characters. If you need more characters for text, you must use a memo field (which has unlimited length). Numeric fields in dBASE can contain a maximum of 19 digits and display up to 15 decimal places.

You can use any character to name a field, but it must begin with a letter. However, because dBASE normally allows only letters A to Z, whole numbers, and the underscore character, the field names will appear differently if you open the dBASE file in another application.

Note

Although you can create memo fields of unlimited length in Approach, you can't open a memo field longer than 4,000 characters in dBASE III+ or longer than 64,000 characters in dBASE IV.

If you choose a dBASE file, you can use Approach PicturePlus fields (which hold graphics and linked or embedded objects), but you can't view the PicturePlus fields in dBASE. PicturePlus fields are very handy for storing non-textual data (such as pictures) in each record of the database. (See Chapter 10, "Using Advanced Field Types," for more information on PicturePlus fields.)

One special feature of dBASE files is when you "delete" a record, the record isn't actually removed from the database. Instead, the record is marked as deleted and doesn't appear on forms or in reports. However, the deleted record continues to take up space in the database. Approach provides a way to remove these deleted records permanently, decreasing the size of the file. To remove deleted records (a process that dBASE calls *packing*), follow these steps:

1. Open the File menu and choose User Setup and Approach Preferences. The Approach Preferences dialog box opens.
2. Click the Database tab, the Compress button, and then OK. Approach removes all deleted records from the database file.

Choosing FoxPro Files

FoxPro (DOS) files work exactly the same way dBASE files do. FoxPro files are identical to dBASE files except for the format of the memo field. Approach can open and read FoxPro memo fields as well as dBASE memo fields, but can't share FoxPro files across a network.

Choosing Paradox 3.5 Files

If you choose a Paradox 3.5 file type, you can select from date, numeric, text, Boolean, and time fields. The date, numeric, and text field names can contain up to 25 characters each, and the Boolean and time fields can contain up to 18 characters each. A Paradox text field can be between 1 and 255 characters long. Approach—and Paradox, for that matter—automatically sets the field length of all other field types.

To name a field, you can use letters A to Z, whole numbers, symbols, and spaces. The field name can't begin with a space or contain square brackets ([]), braces ({}), or parentheses. The field name also can't contain the number (pound) sign (#) by itself, although the # can be combined with other symbols (for example, CUSTOMER #).

If you choose a Paradox 3.5 file, you also can use memo fields and Approach PicturePlus fields, but you can't view these fields in Paradox. The field names for memo and PicturePlus fields can contain up to 18 characters. These field types are discussed in Chapter 10, "Using Advanced Field Types."

As discussed later in "Saving the Database Files," when you use a Paradox file, you also must identify a field (or combination of fields) that uniquely identifies each record in the database. This field is called a *key field*. If for some reason your database doesn't have a key field, Approach can create one for you.

Choosing a Paradox 4 or Paradox for Windows File

All the limitations mentioned for Paradox 3.5 also apply to Paradox 4 and Paradox for Windows, except that you can open memo fields and PicturePlus fields in Paradox 4 and Paradox for Windows.

Defining the Database Structure

What happens after you enter the file name and file type in the New dialog box depends on how you chose the new database. If you used the Welcome to Lotus Approach dialog box or chose New Database from the File menu and picked a SmartMaster other than Blank Database, Approach creates the new database automatically and displays the default data-entry form and a worksheet.

However, if you selected a Blank Database from the SmartMaster list, the Creating New Database dialog box appears (see fig. 2.3). In this dialog box you can assign names, types, number of decimal places, and lengths to your fields.

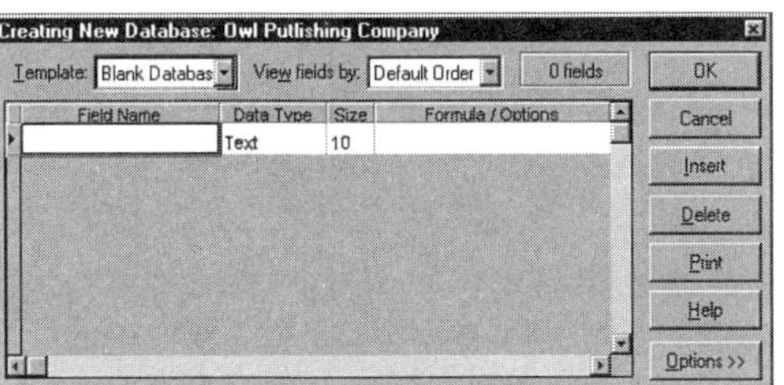

Fig. 2.3

Select the Blank Database SmartMaster to display the Creating New Database dialog box.

You can select a SmartMaster template from the Template drop-down list. Approach populates the field information portion of the dialog box with the appropriate fields from the template. You can change field characteristics, add additional fields, or remove any of the existing fields.

You don't need to specify a value for every field you create. Approach makes available only the boxes needed for a given field type. The Size column, for example, is available for text fields because you must set the length of a text field. For a date field, however, the length is set automatically, so the Size column shows the word `fixed`. For numeric fields, the size is displayed as a decimal number (for example, 10.2). The digits indicate the number of places to the left of the decimal point (10) and to the right of the decimal point (2). The maximum digits allowed for numeric fields is 19, ranging from 19.0 to 4.15 in your definition. For text fields, you enter a whole number such as 8 or 55 in the Size column—no decimal places are allowed.

Defining New Fields

The first step in defining new fields (the columns in the database table) is to type a field name in the Field Name column at the left side of the Creating New Database dialog box. Remember to follow the rules as noted in the preceding section for length of field names and allowable characters; otherwise, Approach won't create the new field in the database.

The second step is to specify the type of field you want by using the drop-down list box in the Data Type column.

> **Note**
>
> Not all field types that appear in the Data Type drop-down list are explained here. Refer to Chapter 10, "Using Advanced Field Types," for an explanation of Calculated, PicturePlus, and Variable fields.

Boolean Field Types. Boolean fields can contain only one of two possible values. These values may be entered in the fields as yes (or y or 1) for true and no (or n or 0) for false. A Boolean field is often represented on a form as a check box, which also can have only two possible states: checked and unchecked.

Date Field Types. Date fields contain only dates. The date must be entered in the Windows short format specified in the Control Panel under Regional Settings—that is, m/d/yy for English (United States). Although the date can be entered only this way, Approach can display the date in a wide variety of on-screen formats.

Memo Field Types. Memo fields can contain an unlimited amount of text. Such fields are ideal for recording comments, giving the ongoing status of a project or situation, and so on. Since they don't reserve a specific minimum text area in your database like a text-type field does, memo fields can save you a lot of disk space.

Numeric Field Types. Numeric fields contain numbers such as dollar amounts, percentages, phone numbers, ZIP codes, and other quantities.

Text Field Types. Text fields hold text strings up to 255 characters long (254 in dBASE III+, dBASE IV, and FoxPro). You can enter any kind of text or symbol in text fields, even numbers (such as ZIP codes). The text field is the most useful field because you can type virtually anything into it.

Time Field Types. Time fields are used to hold times. Approach lets you record time to the nearest 1/100 of a second. You can enter any portion of the time (such as hours, or hours and minutes) or separate the numbers with colons or other nonnumeric symbols. Times can be entered using a 24-hour clock or an AM/PM designation.

Completing the Field Definition

The third step in defining new fields is to type the length of each field in the Size column. A size is required for text-type fields in all types of databases, and for numeric fields in dBASE and FoxPro files. For numeric fields that contain a decimal point, specify the number of places to the left of the decimal point, a decimal point, and the number of places to the right of the decimal point. For numeric fields in dBASE and FoxPro files, you can specify up to 15 decimal places.

You don't need to fill in the last column, Formula/Options, at this point. This column provides you with methods for providing default values for your fields and for validating data entered into fields. These methods are discussed in detail later in the section "Setting Up Field Options."

If you're ready to define all your fields, type the required information (name, type, and size) in the rows of the Creating New Database dialog box. When you're finished defining the fields, click OK to create the database.

Rearranging Fields in the Creating New Database Dialog Box

You can insert, delete, and rearrange the order of the field definitions (rows) in the Creating New Database dialog box. You can also print out a list of rows by clicking the Print button.

To insert a new field row, click anywhere on the row above which you want to insert a blank row and click the Insert button. To delete a row, click anywhere on the row that you want to delete and click the Delete button. Confirm that you want to delete the row in the alert box that appears.

The Creating New Database dialog box normally displays the fields in the order you enter them. This is the default order, and also the order in which Approach creates the fields in the database.

> **Note**
>
> Approach creates the fields in the database in the default order, regardless of the order in which you view the fields in the Creating New Database dialog box. Approach also uses the default order when it creates the default Blank Database form and Worksheet 1 worksheet.

You can change the order in which the Creating New Database dialog box displays the fields by using the View Fields By drop-down list. The fields can be sorted by Field Name, Data Type, or Custom Order. If you select Custom Order, you can drag rows in the Creating New Database dialog box to rearrange the order in which the fields are displayed. To rearrange the viewed field order, follow these steps:

1. Move the mouse pointer over the row-select button at the left end of the row that you want to drag to a new location. For the row you're now editing, this button contains a small triangle pointing to the right.
2. Click the button to highlight the row. If you want to highlight multiple rows, click the first row and then hold down the Shift key and click the last row. All rows between these two rows are selected to be moved.

> **Tip**
>
> To deselect a row or a collection of rows, click anywhere except on the row-select button in a selected row.

3. Drag the mouse to reposition the selected row(s). The mouse pointer becomes an open hand to indicate that the move operation is taking place. A dark bar appears between field rows in the Creating New Database dialog box to indicate where the row(s) will be located when you release the mouse button (see fig. 2.4).

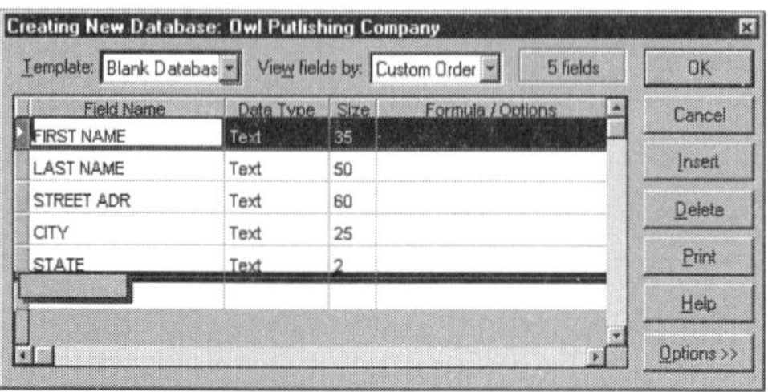

Fig. 2.4

Change the order of fields by dragging rows to a new location.

Modifying a Field Specification

As you're working, you can modify or delete the fields you've entered.

To modify a field, click its row-select button in the Creating New Database dialog box. Make any necessary changes to the field name, data type, or size.

> **Note**
>
> If you click and drag a field row-select button without switching the View Fields By list to Custom Order, Approach switches to Custom Order automatically.

Setting Up Field Options

Approach lets you customize the fields you define for a database in two ways:

- You can set up a field so that Approach automatically enters default data into it.
- You can have Approach ensure that the data entered into a field is valid by meeting certain criteria.

To customize a field either of these ways, the bottom portion of the Creating New Database dialog box, which displays the Default Value and Validation information, must be visible (see fig. 2.5). If the lower portion of the Creating New Database dialog box isn't visible, click the Options button. Select the field that you want to set the Default Value or Validation information for in the rows that display the database fields. You can switch fields and set the Default Value or Validation values for any field. To set the Default Value or Validation options for a field, click the tab for the page you want.

> **Note**
>
> The best approach for saving your table is to set the Default Value and Validation options before choosing OK in the Creating New Database dialog box. If you need to add these options to an existing table, see "Modifying the Table Structure" later in this chapter.

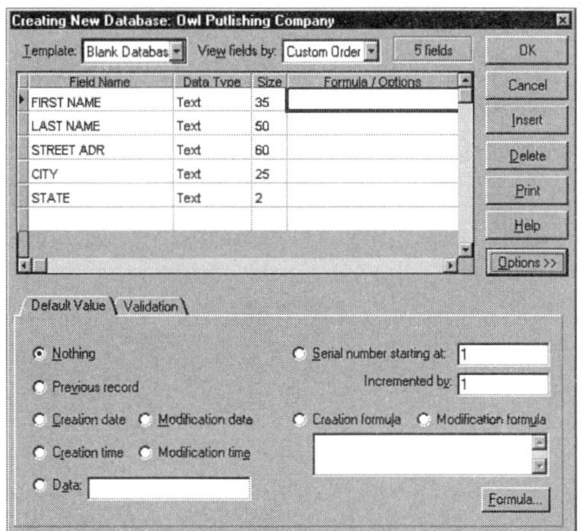

Fig. 2.5

Click the Options button to have Approach set default values or validate your data entry.

Using Automatic Data Entry

The first page allows you to set the default values, which tell Approach that you want specific information entered into a field every time a new record is created or modified, in some instances. The Default Value options are described in the following sections.

> **Note**
>
> Although Approach automatically enters information in fields that you've set the Default Value options for, you still can modify the information in the field.

The Nothing Option. The Nothing option is the default. If this button is highlighted, Approach enters nothing in the field when you create a new record. This option is also helpful when you're modifying the Default Value options, because choosing the Nothing option clears any previous choice.

The Previous Record Option. Choosing the Previous Record option enters the data from the same field that was entered into the previous new record. This option is helpful if you're creating many new records with the same data in a field.

The Creation Date and Modification Date Options. The next two options, Creation Date and Modification Date, are available only if the selected field is a date field or a text field long enough to hold the date. The creation date is the date on which the record was created. The modification date is the date on which the record was last modified. You can attach these options to fields for databases in which keeping track of these dates is important.

The Creation Time and Modification Time Options. The next two options, Creation Time and Modification Time, are available only if the field is a time field or a text field that's long enough to hold the time. The creation time is the time at which the record was created. The modification time is the time at which the record was last modified. You can attach these options to fields for databases in which keeping track of these times is important. These time fields are often used with the Creation Date and Modification Date options assigned to other fields in the database.

The Data Option. If you want the same data entered in a field each time a record is created, enter this data in the text box next to the Data option. Suppose that you're specifying options for a state field and know that most of your customers live in a certain state. You can enter that state name in the Data text box as you customize the STATE field. When you enter records later, you can edit those fields in which the value entered by Data isn't accurate.

The Serial Number Option. Approach enters a sequential number into a serial number field whenever you create a new record. This type of field works well for arbitrary numbers, such as customer ID. You can specify the starting number by typing the number in the Serial Number Starting At text box. You can also specify the increment to the next number by typing the number in the Incremented By text box. If you specify that the number starts at 10 and is incremented by 5, for example, the numbers Approach uses are 10, 15, 20, 25, and so on.

The Creation Formula Option. The Creation Formula option tells Approach to enter the result of a formula into the field when you first create a record. For example, you could have a formula generate a date seven days from when the record was created so that you can contact a person listed in that record. The formula is evaluated only when the record is first created, not when the record is later changed. To enter a formula, click the Creation Formula radio button. You can enter a formula in two ways:

- Type the formula into the text box below the Creation Formula radio button.
- Click the Formula button to open the Formula dialog box. When you're finished entering the formula in the Formula dialog box, click OK. The new formula appears in the text box below the Creation Formula radio button. To modify the formula, click the Formula button to reopen the Formula dialog box. (For more information on using formulas, see "Using Formulas" later in this chapter.)

The Modification Formula Option. The Modification Formula option tells Approach to enter the result of a formula when you first create a record and whenever you modify the value of any field in that record. The value of the field will change if any of the values that the formula depends on are changed. For example, you might want to keep a running record of when you next need to contact a client. If you have a field that records the last time you contacted that client, the Modification Formula field could calculate a date one month later. When you call the client again (and record the new contact date), the Modification Formula field automatically updates to show the next contact date. You can override the value Approach places in the field, but the next time you change the value of any field in that record, Approach will replace the value in the field with the results of the formula.

To enter a formula, click the Modification Formula radio button. Enter the formula exactly the same way you would for creation formulas by clicking the Formula button to open the Formula dialog box. When you're finished entering the formula in the Formula dialog box, click OK.

Validating Entered Data

You use the second page in the lower portion of the Creating New Database dialog box for setting up data validation criteria (see fig. 2.6). Use the Validation page to tell Approach that the data entered into a field must meet certain tests, or it can't be accepted. If, when entering a record, you enter data that doesn't meet the criteria, Approach displays an error message telling you that the data can't be accepted because it doesn't meet the data validation.

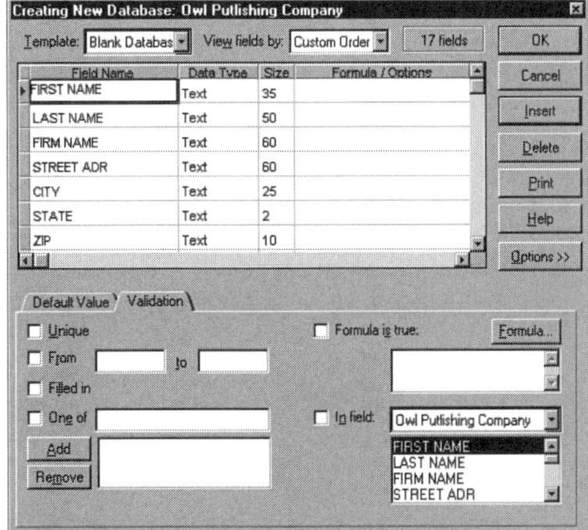

Fig. 2.6

Validate entered values by using the Validation page of the Creating New Database dialog box.

> **Note**
>
> Since you can't override the validation criteria, you must carefully define your criteria.

The Unique Option. The value entered into a field with the Unique option can't be duplicated in this field when it appears in any other record. This option is handy for fields such as CUSTOMER ID, in which each number should be different.

The From Option. When you choose the From option, Approach ensures that the value entered into the field falls between the values specified. Next to this option is a pair of text boxes with the word To between them. The left text box is for the lowest acceptable value in the range; the right text box is for the highest acceptable value in the range. If the value falls between 1 and 100, for example, enter the value **1** in the left box, and **100** in the right box. You can also use alphabetic characters (such as a range from ab to xz). An alphabetic range is useful to ensure that the entered data is letters rather than numbers.

When entering records, if you try to enter a value outside the acceptable range, an error message appears. The error message reminds you of the acceptable range.

The Filled In Option. When you choose the Filled In option, Approach requires you to enter a value into the field. If you leave the field blank when entering records, Approach doesn't proceed until a value is filled in (see fig. 2.7). This option is handy if you must be certain that a field isn't left blank.

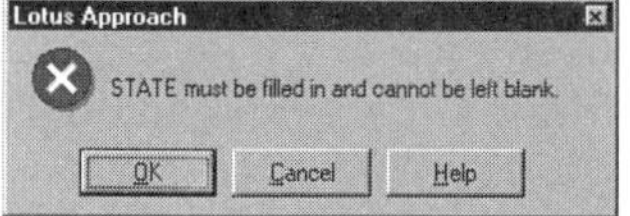

Fig. 2.7

An error message appears if your data entry falls outside the validation criteria.

The One Of Option. When you choose the One Of option, Approach ensures that the value entered into a field is one of those in the list available to the right of this option. This option is handy to limit the values entered to a predetermined list.

To add values to the list, type a value into the text box next to the One Of option and click Add. The value is added to the list below the text box.

You can't edit an item on the list. Instead, you must remove the item and add a new one. To remove an item from the list, click the item you want to remove and then click Remove.

When you use the One Of data validation option, Approach automatically generates a drop-down list that provides the valid values for you to choose (see fig. 2.8).

Fig. 2.8

The One Of option automatically generates a drop-down list of acceptable values.

Tip

Another way to limit values to a valid list is to use the drop-down list format for a field and provide the valid values for the list. See Chapter 4, "Enhancing Data Input Forms," for more information on data input forms.

The Formula Is True Option. When you choose the Formula Is True option, Approach accepts a value typed into the field only if that value causes the formula you enter in the text box to evaluate true. You can design highly complex validations by building a formula. An example of a valid formula is

```
NAME>'A'
```

This formula ensures that the NAME field starts with a letter greater than A.

You can enter a formula in two ways:

- Select the Formula Is True check box, and then type the formula into the text box below the Formula Is True check box.
- Select the Formula Is True check box, and then click the Formula button to open the Formula dialog box. When you're finished entering the formula in the Formula dialog box, click OK. The new formula appears in the text box below the Formula Is True check box. To modify the formula, click the Formula button to reopen the Formula dialog box.

For more information on using formulas, see "Using Formulas" later in this chapter.

The In Field Option. The In Field option ensures that the value you enter into a field is a value that's already entered into another field (called a *validation field*) in the same or in a different database. If the value you type into the field is *not* contained in the validation field, Approach doesn't accept the value. Choose In Field and then select the validation field from the list of fields that appears beside this option.

When you use the In Field validation option, Approach automatically provides a drop-down list of values in the validation field. You can also create your own drop-down field on the form and attach the list to the validation field. See Chapter 4, "Enhancing Data Input Forms," for information on how to set up such a drop-down list.

Note

The normal use of the In Field option is to make sure that the value entered into a field in one database is a value that already has been entered into a field in another database. Before you can access other databases, however, you must link them to the current database. These relational links are covered in Chapter 8, "Understanding Relational Databases," which also tells you how to use the In Field option with relational linked databases.

Using Formulas

Three of the options available for setting the Default Values and Validations pages in the Create New Database dialog box involve using formulas. As you'll see later in this book, formulas play an important part in tapping the power of Approach. For example, in Chapter 10, "Using Advanced Field Types," you'll use fields that get their values from the evaluation of a formula (*calculated fields*). To use the Default Value and Validation options, and to use calculated fields later, you must understand how to build formulas.

Examining the Parts of a Validation Formula

Validation formulas are constructed from four kinds of building blocks:

- References to field values
- References to constant values
- Operators (arithmetic, comparison, and Boolean)
- Functions

References to Field Values. To include a field value in a formula, type the name of the field. If the field name contains spaces, you must enclose the field name in double quotation marks (""). To refer to the value in the field NAME, for example, type **NAME** in the formula.

In the formula, you must refer to the value of the field that you're trying to validate. You can also refer to the values in other fields.

References to Constant Values. *Constant values* are values you type into the formula that don't change from record to record. You must follow certain rules when typing constant values into a formula:

- Enclose text string constants in single quotation marks (for example, **'Approach'**).
- Type date constants in the order of month, date, and year, separated by slashes and enclosed in single quotation marks (for example, **'03/12/56'**).
- Type time constants in the order of hours, minutes, seconds, and hundredths of seconds. Separate hours, minutes, and seconds with a colon (:). Separate seconds and hundredths of seconds with a decimal point. Enclose time constants in single quotation marks (for example, **'12:25:00.45'**).
- Type Boolean constants as **'Yes'** or **'No'** and enclose them in single quotation marks. You can also use **Y** or **1** for yes and **N** or **0** for no (without quotation marks).
- Don't type numeric constants in scientific notation (for example, 4.5E4).

To refer to the value A in a formula, for example, type the value in the formula as **'A'**.

Arithmetic Operators. You can use arithmetic operators to build arithmetic equations in the formula:

+	addition
–	subtraction
/	division
*	multiplication
%	percentage
`NOT`	negation operator

Approach evaluates arithmetic operations in a specific order:

- Multiplication (*) and division (/) operations are evaluated first.
- Addition (+) and subtraction (–) operations are evaluated second.
- The % operation is third, followed by the `NOT` operation.
- If any operations are on the same evaluation level (such as multiplication and division), they're evaluated from left to right in the formula.

The following examples show how arithmetic operations work:

`5*6/2 = 15`, because `5*6 = 30` and `30/2 = 15`

`4+3*2 = 10`, because `3*2 = 6` and `6+4 = 10`

You can use parentheses to modify the evaluation order of arithmetic operators. Approach always evaluates the contents of parentheses before evaluating other parts of the formula. Within a set of parentheses, the evaluation order is the same as outside the parentheses. The following example shows how parentheses are used:

`(2+4)*3 = 18`, because `2+4 = 6`, and `6*3 = 18`

Comparison Operators. You use comparison operators to compare two values or fields. The comparison operators consist of the following:

=	equal
>	greater than
<	less than
<>	not equal to
>=	greater than or equal to
<=	less than or equal to

To ensure that the value in the NAME field starts with a letter greater than or equal to A, for example, use

```
NAME>='A'
```

Alternatively, to ensure that the number in the NEWNUM field is greater than twice the value in the OLDNUM field, use

```
NEWNUM>OLDNUM*2
```

To make sure that the date in the field SUB DATE is at least five days later than the date in the MOD DATE field, use

```
"SUB DATE">="MOD DATE"+5
```

Boolean Operators. You can use the Boolean operators `AND` and `OR` to connect parts or clauses of the formula.

A clause containing the `AND` operator evaluates true only if both parts connected by the `AND` operator are true. The formula `5>6 AND 'A'<'B'` is false, for example, even though `'A'` is less than `'B'`, because 5 isn't greater than 6. The formula `5<6 AND 'A'<'B'` is true, however, because both parts of the equation are true.

A clause containing the `OR` operator evaluates true if either part connected by the `OR` is true. The formula `5>6 OR 'A'<'B'` is true, for example, because `'A'` is less than `'B'`. The formula `5>6 OR 'A'>'B'` is false, however, because both sides are false.

You can connect multiple clauses with combinations of `AND`s and `OR`s. Approach normally evaluates clauses from left to right (`AND` and `OR` have the same evaluation level). You can use parentheses to modify this order. Approach then uses the result of each clause (true or false) to evaluate the next clause. The formula `5>6 AND 'A'<'B' OR 10<12`, for example, evaluates true. The first clause is `5>6 AND 'A'<'B'`. Because 5 isn't greater than 6, the entire clause evaluates as false. Approach then uses the result (false) with `OR 10<12`. The entire clause evaluates as false *or* true, which results in a true value.

To ensure that the value in the NAME field begins with an alphabetic character, for example, use

```
NAME>='A' AND NAME<='Z'
```

Functions. Approach supports 85 functions that can perform various operations on text and numeric values.

The value by which a function operates (called an *argument*) can be a field value or a constant value. If a function uses multiple arguments, you must separate the arguments with commas.

> **Note**
>
> The delimiter is determined by the Regional Settings in the Windows Control Panel. In the United States, the comma serves as the delimiter. Most European countries use the semicolon (;).

The `Middle()` and `Length()` functions are especially useful when writing validation formulas, as illustrated by the following examples.

The `Middle()` function returns a text string of a certain size from a specified position in a text field. It has the following syntax:

```
Middle(Fieldname, Position, Size)
```

The `Length()` function returns the length of a field. It has the following syntax:

```
Length(Fieldname)
```

To make sure that the length of the value typed into the ZIP field is 5, use

```
Length(ZIP)=5
```

To make sure that the length of the value typed into the ZIP field is 5 or 10, use

```
Length(ZIP)=5 OR Length(ZIP)=10
```

To make sure that the length of the value typed into the ZIP field is 5 or 10, and that the sixth character is a hyphen (using the ZIP+4 formatting), use

```
Length(ZIP)=5 OR (Length(ZIP)=10 AND Middle(ZIP,6,1)='-')
```

Approach evaluates the preceding formula as follows:

- If the length of ZIP is 5, the entire formula is true because a true statement (`Length(ZIP)=5`) OR a false statement (`Length(ZIP) = 10 AND Middle(ZIP,6,1)='-'`) evaluates as true. If both were false, the entire formula would evaluate as false.
- If the length of ZIP is 10 and the sixth character is a hyphen (-), this entire formula is true because the `AND` clause is true (a false statement OR a true statement evaluates as true).
- If the length of ZIP is 10 but the sixth character isn't a hyphen, the entire formula evaluates false. The reason is that the `AND` clause is false, and both sides of the `OR` clause are also false (a false statement OR a false statement evaluates as false).

Entering Invalid Values

If you attach a validation formula to a field using the Validation page in the Creating New Database dialog box, Approach doesn't accept any values that don't make the formula evaluate true. If you enter an invalid value, Approach displays an error message and doesn't let you exit the field until you enter a valid value.

If a formula refers to values in more than one field, Approach checks that the formula is true after you enter a value in any field referenced in the formula. If the value you enter is invalid, Approach lets you modify it in any of the referenced fields. However, Approach doesn't give you access to any other fields. To ensure that a field called SUB DATE is at least five days after a field called MOD DATE, for example, you can use the following formula:

```
"SUB DATE">="MOD DATE"+5
```

On a form, the `Invalid value` error message appears if you modify the value in either field (SUB DATE or MOD DATE) so that the formula is no longer true. At that point, Approach lets you access either field to modify the values so that the formula is true. But you can't access any other fields until you fix this problem.

Entering References to Different Fields

For a validation formula, you can't separate references to values in different fields with Boolean operators (AND and OR). If you do, any portion (clause) of the formula that doesn't include the field being validated is ignored. If you try to write a formula for the NAME field such as

```
NAME>'A' AND "SUB DATE">12/21/92
```

the reference to SUB DATE is ignored.

Entering the Formula into Approach

To enter formulas into Approach, choose the Formula button in the Creating New Database dialog box to call up the Formula dialog box (see fig. 2.9).

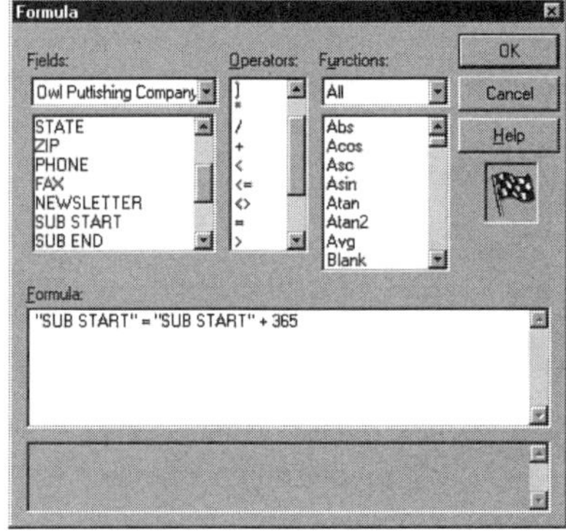

Fig. 2.9

The Formula dialog box ensures that the syntax for the formula is correct before it makes the OK button available.

The Formula dialog box has five major sections you can use when setting up a validation formula:

- The Fields list box lists all the fields available in your database.
- The Operators list box lists all the available operators—arithmetic, comparison, and Boolean.
- The Functions list box lists all the available functions, including summary, trigonometric, logarithmic, and statistical functions.
- The function help box at the bottom of the dialog box shows you the purpose and syntax of a selected function.
- The Formula text box is where you build your formula.

To build a formula in the Formula dialog box, follow these steps:

1. Select an entry in the Fields, Operators, or Functions list box. Approach transfers your selection into the Formula text box.
2. Type any constant values (such as `'A'` or `'01/01/93'`) in the Formula text box.
3. Continue entering the other parts of the formula by choosing from the text boxes or by typing information.

4. After you finish building the formula, click OK to return to the Creating New Database dialog box.

If the OK button isn't available in the Formula dialog box, the formula wasn't entered correctly or completely. Correct this syntax error and click OK. The formula you built appears in the box next to the formula option (Creation Formula, Modification Formula, or Formula Is True) in the Creating New Database dialog box.

Saving the Database Files

After you finish defining the fields in your newly defined database, click OK in the Creating New Database dialog box. Approach creates and saves your database in the file format you chose (dBASE, Paradox, or FoxPro).

Tip

After you create and save the database, Approach creates and displays a default form named Blank Database for data entry. You can use this form to begin entering your database's data.

If you chose a Paradox file format, Approach displays the Select Key Field dialog box so that you can select the key field(s) that make each record in the Paradox database unique (see fig. 2.10). Using the Select Key Field dialog box, you must select the field or combination of fields that uniquely identifies each record in the database. For example, you might choose a CUSTOMER ID field that must be unique, or perhaps the combination of PHONE NUMBER and LAST NAME.

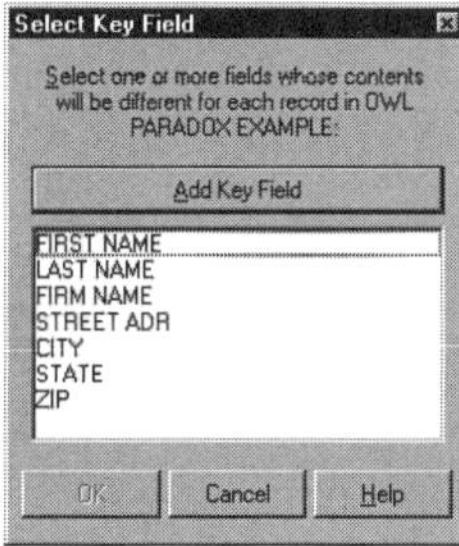

Fig. 2.10

Use the Select Key Field dialog box to choose key field(s) for a Paradox database or to create a new field to use as a key.

The list of fields in the Paradox database appears in a list box at the bottom of the Select Key Field dialog box. To select a key field, click any fields in this list. If the key field is a combination of fields (such as LAST NAME and FIRST NAME), click the first field, press Ctrl, and then click any additional fields.

If no fields are unique in your Paradox database, choose Add Key Field to tell Approach to create a key field for you. The key field created in this manner is numeric, and Approach automatically fills in a sequential number in this key field each time you create a new record.

Adding a Password to the Database

In Chapter 1, "Leaning Approach Basics," you saw how you can add a password to an Approach file to keep others from modifying the design of the database application or changing the structure of the underlying database. Chapter 1 also looked briefly at the TeamSecurity security options. You can also attach passwords to the database itself to limit access to the data.

You can attach two kinds of passwords to a database:

- With a *read/write password*, the user must enter the correct password before gaining *any* access to the database or the Approach file. If the user enters an incorrect password, the user won't be able to see (read) the values in the database or enter (write) new values. The user also won't be able to change the database structure (change or add fields).
- With a *read-only password*, the user can view the data in the database but can't modify the data or the structure.

You can attach both password types to a database. In this case, if the user enters the read-only password, the user can view the database. If the user enters the read/write password, full access to the database is available. If neither password is entered correctly, the user is denied access to the database.

To set the passwords, follow these steps:

1. From the File menu, choose Open to open the database for which you want to set the password(s).
2. Open the File menu again and choose User Setup and then Approach Preferences.
3. Select the Password tab to open the Password page of the Approach Preferences dialog box (see fig. 2.11).

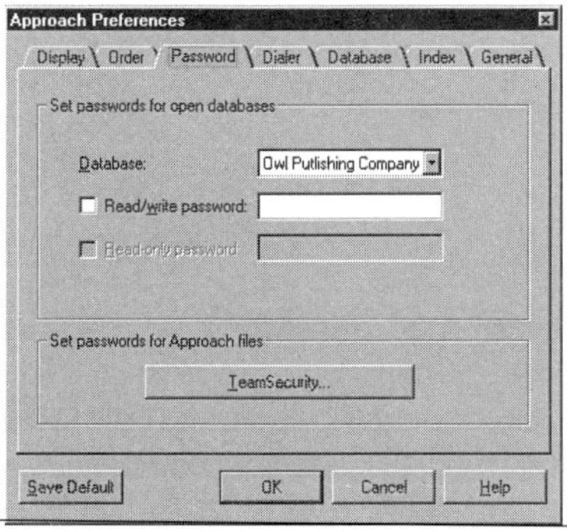

Fig. 2.11

You can limit access to your data with passwords from the Password page of the Approach Preferences dialog box.

4. To set a read/write password, select Read/Write Password and type the password in the text box. The password appears as asterisks in the box to prevent anyone from reading the password as you type it.
5. Press Tab, Enter, or click OK. Approach displays the Confirm Password dialog box. Retype your password and click OK to close the dialog box and set the read/write password.

When you've set a read/write password, you can set the read-only password. (Note that you can set a read-only password only if you have first set a read/write password.) To set the read-only password, follow these steps:

1. Select the Read-Only Password check box.
2. Type the read-only password. This password also appears as asterisks in the box.
3. Press Tab, Enter, or click OK. Approach displays the Confirm Password dialog box. Retype the password and click OK to close the dialog box and set the read-only password.

The next time someone tries to open this database, that user must enter either password before access to the database is granted.

Restricting Access Without a Password

You can make a database's fields read-only without using a password. To do so, open the File menu and choose User Setup and Approach Preferences to open the Approach Preferences dialog box. Select the Database tab. Select the Make All Fields in Database Read-Only check box and click OK.

Caution

Selecting the Make All Fields in Database Read-Only check box doesn't prevent someone from changing the database. If a database has no password protection, any user can open the Approach Preferences dialog box and disable this option.

Enabling Approach to Update dBASE and FoxPro Indexes

Indexes give a database speed when searching for specific records. Although Approach doesn't use dBASE- or FoxPro-type indexes, the program can update existing indexes as you add new records. If you update existing indexes when using Approach, you can open the database by using dBASE (III+ or IV) or FoxPro, and the indexes will be current and usable.

> **Note**
>
> Approach can't create dBASE and FoxPro indexes; it can only update them.

To have Approach update these indexes, follow these steps:

1. From the File menu, choose Open to open the dBASE or FoxPro database you want to work with.
2. Open the File menu and choose User Setup and then Approach Preferences to open the Approach Preferences dialog box.
3. Select the Index tab (see fig. 2.12). The dBASE and FoxPro Indexes list contains the indexes that Approach will update (the box is empty if you haven't identified any indexes yet).
4. To add an index to this list, choose Add Index; the Add Index dialog box appears (see fig. 2.13).

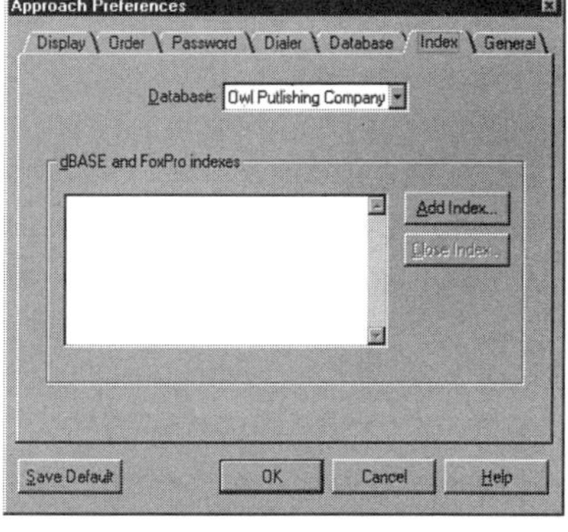

Fig. 2.12

Have Approach update your FoxPro and dBASE indexes, if any are available, by using the Add Index button to locate the indexes you want to keep updated.

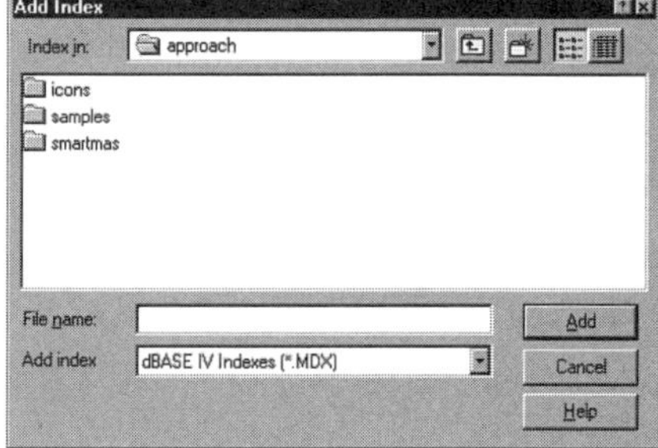

Fig. 2.13

From the Add Index drop-down list, you can choose from various file types, including dBASE IV (.MDX), dBASE III+ (*.NDX), FoxPro (*.IDX), and FoxPro compound indexes (*.CDX).*

5. Select the type of index you want to add from the Add Index drop-down list.
6. Select the file you want from the area in the center of the Add Index dialog box. The file name appears in the File Name text box.
7. Click Add to add the index to the list of indexes that Approach updates.

If you decide that you no longer want Approach to update particular indexes, you can remove them from the list. Follow steps 1 through 3 in the preceding steps, and then do the following:

1. Select the index you no longer need to have updated.
2. Choose Close Index.
3. Click OK to close the dialog box.

Enabling Approach to Update Paradox Indexes

In a Paradox database file, a primary index is built on the key field specified when the file is created. However, you can create additional secondary indexes for the file in Approach. Approach automatically maintains all secondary indexes for Paradox files.

To create a Paradox secondary index, follow these steps:

1. From the File menu, choose Open to open the Paradox database you want to work with.
2. Open the File menu again and choose User Setup and then Approach Preferences to open the Approach Preferences dialog box.
3. Select the Index tab (see fig. 2.14).

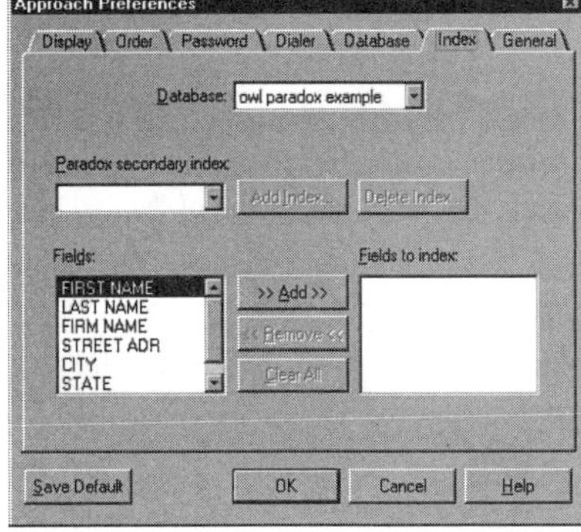

Fig. 2.14

To identify secondary indexes for a Paradox database, use the Index tab in the Approach Preferences dialog box.

4. Select the name of the new index file from the Paradox Secondary Index drop-down list, and add database fields to the index list by selecting each one and clicking the Add button (or double-click each field). Click the Add Index button.

   To remove a field from the Fields to Index list and place it back in the Fields list, click the field in the Fields to Index list and then click Remove. To move all fields back to the Fields list, click Clear All.

To delete a secondary index, select the index in the Paradox Secondary Index drop-down list and click Delete Index.

Modifying the Table Structure

You can modify the structure of a database at any time. For example, you can do any of the following:

- Add fields to the database
- Delete fields (which deletes all the data in those fields)
- Make fields longer or shorter
- Change the field type
- Change the field name
- Change the field options (on the Default Value or Validation page of the Field Definition dialog box)

The following sections discuss how to make specific changes to a database and the consequences of making certain changes.

Adding a New Field

To add a new field to the database, follow these steps:

1. From the File menu, choose Open to open the database.
2. Open the Create menu and choose Field Definition. The Field Definition dialog box appears.

> **Note**
>
> The Field Definition dialog box works exactly like the Creating New Database dialog box (refer back to fig. 2.3)—it even looks the same. The only difference between them is that the Template drop-down list found in the Creating New Database dialog box is replaced by a drop-down list that displays the names of all joined or "linked" databases in your application.

3. If necessary, scroll down to locate an empty line in the Field Definition dialog box. Type the new Field Name, Data Type, and the size and number of decimal places (if applicable).
4. If you prefer, choose Options and use the tabs to define the Default Value and Validation options. If you need to create a formula (Creation Formula, Modification Formula, or Formula Is True), click the Formula button to open the Formula dialog box.
5. After you finish defining all new fields, click OK to add the new fields to the database.

Note

After you create new fields, if the Show Add Field Dialog check box is selected on the General tab of the Approach Preferences dialog box, the Add Field dialog box appears on the current form. The Add Field dialog box displays only the fields you added to the database.

Modifying an Existing Field

To modify an existing field in a database, follow these steps:

1. From the File menu, choose Open to open the database.
2. Open the Create menu and choose Field Definition. The Field Definition dialog box appears.
3. If necessary, scroll down to the line in the Field Definition dialog box that displays the field you want to modify, and then click that line.
4. Change the name of the field (edit the Field Name column), the Data Type, or the size or number of decimal places (if applicable).
5. If you prefer, choose Options and use the tabs to define or modify the Default Value and Validation options.

When making changes to database fields that have data already in them, be aware of the following:

- If you shorten the size of a text or numeric field, the data that doesn't fit into the new length may be truncated and lost.
- If you decrease the number of decimal places for a numeric field, the data in the corresponding number of decimal places is lost.

Caution

Remember, if you change the type of data in any field except a text or number field, *all* data in that field is lost.

- If you change the field type from numeric to text, no data is lost.
- If you change the type from text to numeric, no data is lost—if the field contains only numbers. If any non-numeric characters are present in the field, however, those characters—and any characters after the first non-numeric character in the field—are lost.
- If you change any data-entry options, existing records aren't affected. For example, if you tell Approach to enter a value in a field automatically, only records created after you modify the field have the value entered. The existing records remain as they were.

- If you change or add a validation option, the validation is applied to new records only. Existing records are validated only if you display them one at a time and move the cursor to the validated field.

Viewing Your Data in a Worksheet

Approach creates and displays a default form (titled Blank Database) when you create a new database. This form displays all the information for a single record.

Besides the default form, you can view the database data in a worksheet. A worksheet displays the database data in a spreadsheet-like table (see fig. 2.15). Each field in the database is one column in the worksheet, and each record is one row. Approach automatically creates a worksheet titled Worksheet 1 when you create a new database. (For more information about using worksheets, see Chapter 14, "Using Worksheets and Crosstabs.")

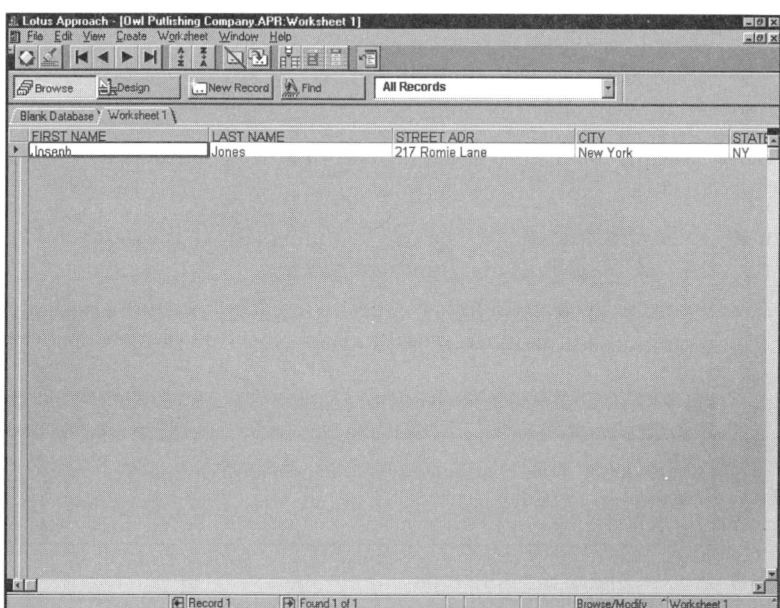

Fig. 2.15

Approach creates a default worksheet when you create a new database.

To switch from the current form to Worksheet 1, click the view tab called Worksheet 1. By using a worksheet, you can do the following:

- *Edit the database data.* Simply double-click the data item that you want to modify and then type your changes. When you move off the current row, Approach automatically saves the change to the database.
- *Add new records to the database.* Click the New Record SmartIcon and then type the data for the new record. When you move off the current row, Approach automatically saves the change to the database.

- *Change the width of a column in the worksheet.* Move the mouse pointer to the border between two columns. The mouse pointer turns into a double-headed arrow. Click and drag the border to change the column width.
- *Change the height of a row in the worksheet.* Move the mouse pointer over a row border. The mouse pointer becomes a double-headed arrow. Click and drag the border row to set the new height of the row.
- *Rearrange the order of the fields (columns) in the worksheet.* Click a field name at the top of a column. The column is highlighted and the mouse pointer becomes an open hand. Click and drag the column left or right to the new location.
- *Rearrange the order of records (rows) in the worksheet.* Click the button at the left end of the row you want to move. The row is highlighted and the mouse pointer becomes an open hand. Click and drag the row up or down to its new location.

Creating the Example Database

In this section, you create a database using the Owl Publishing example illustrated throughout this book. Follow these steps:

1. Open the File menu and choose New Database. The New dialog box appears. Select Blank Database from the list of SmartMaster names and click OK. Another dialog box named New appears.
2. You want to use a dBASE IV-type file, so leave the Create Type option as is.
3. Type **`Owl Publishing Company`** in the File Name text box.
4. Click Create. The Creating New Database dialog box appears.
5. Refer to table 2.1 at the end of this section to enter the fields into the Owl Publishing Company (.DBF) database. Enter the information from each row of the table into a row in the Creating New Database dialog box.

   For example, type **`FIRST NAME`** into the Field Name column on the first row. Because FIRST NAME is a text field, select Text from the Data Type drop-down list box. Click the Size column and then type **`25`** in this column to make this field 25 characters long. Press Tab to move to the next row.

   The Creating New Database dialog box should look like figure 2.16 after you enter the information in table 2.1. (Don't click OK yet, however, because you'll modify some fields next.)

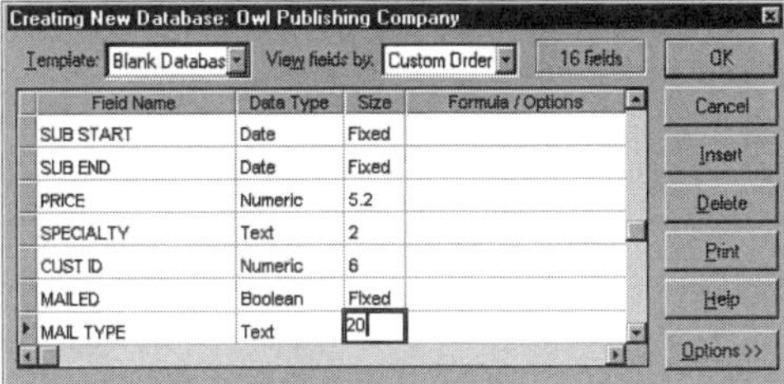

Fig. 2.16

All fields have been defined for the new database for the Owl Publishing Company.

6. Select the CUST ID field. (If the CUST ID field isn't visible in the list box, use the scroll bars to bring it into view.)
7. Choose Options. The Options section of the Creating New Database dialog box appears.
8. Choose the Serial Number Starting At option. Leave the default value of 1 for Serial Number Starting At and Incremented By.
9. Select the ZIP field.
10. Select the Validation tab.
11. Select Formula Is True. The Formula dialog box appears.
12. Enter the following formula in the Formula text box near the bottom of the dialog box (see fig. 2.17):

```
Length(ZIP)=0 or Length(ZIP)=5 or Length(ZIP)=10
```

> **Note**
>
> This formula ensures that the length is 0 (so that you can leave the field blank if you don't know the ZIP code), 5 (standard ZIP code), or 10 (ZIP+4 with a dash). The formula doesn't ensure that a dash is the sixth character in the ZIP+4.

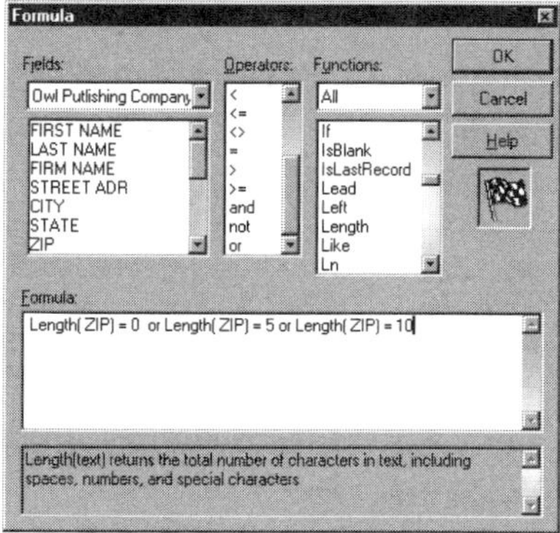

Fig. 2.17

Use the validation options to ensure that the ZIP code is correctly entered.

You can enter the formula by typing it or by choosing functions (Length), operators (or), and field names (ZIP) from the appropriate lists in the Formula dialog box.

> **Note**
>
> If the OK button in the Formula dialog box is dimmed or the flag has a red X across it, your formula is either incorrect or incomplete. Check your formula carefully.

13. Click OK in the Formula dialog box and the Creating New Database dialog box. Approach creates and saves the database Owl Publishing Company (.DBF and other physical files are created) and brings up the default Blank Database form for data entry.
14. Open the File menu and choose Save Approach File. Click Save in the Save Apr dialog box to save the Approach file with the same name as the previously created database.

Table 2.1 Fields in the Owl Publishing Database

Field Name	Data Type	Size
FIRST NAME	Text	25
LAST NAME	Text	35
FIRM NAME	Text	60
STREET ADR	Text	60
CITY	Text	25
STATE	Text	2
ZIP	Text	10
PHONE	Text	12
FAX	Text	12
NEWSLETTER	Text	40
SUB START	Date	
SUB END	Date	
PRICE	Numeric	5.2
SPECIALTY	Text	2
CUST ID	Numeric	6.0
MAILED	Boolean	Fixed
MAIL TYPE	Text	20

From Here...

In this chapter, you learned how to set up a database, including database design basics, selection of a file type, and construction of the database field. Approach's Default Value and Validation options were also discussed to show you how to customize the way a field works. You also learned how to use a worksheet to view your data in a simple list format. Finally, you tried out your new skills by building a sample database.

Now that you've set up your database, it's time to enter data. For more information, refer to the following chapters in this book:

- Chapter 3, "Building Data Input Forms," explains the basics of building forms.
- Chapter 4, "Enhancing Data Input Forms," details how to add fields, graphics, illustrations, and text blocks to forms.
- Chapter 5, "Working with Your Data," teaches you how to enter information into the various types of database fields.

CHAPTER 3

Building Data Input Forms

In this chapter, you learn the basics of creating Approach forms. You learn that you can view individual records in your database by using forms. You also become familiar with Approach's layout tools, which help you position and align objects on a form, group objects together, set up a grid to aid in object placement, and set the stacking order for overlapping objects.

In addition to forms, Approach lets you build reports, mailing labels (see Chapter 7, "Creating Reports and Mailing Labels"), and form letters (see Chapter 12, "Creating Advanced Reports"). Together with forms, these constructs are called *views* in Approach. Many of the techniques discussed in this chapter and in Chapter 4, "Enhancing Data Input Forms," can be used when building other types of views, especially reports.

In this chapter, you learn how to

- Create and use a default form
- Rename and delete forms
- Change the properties of a form, including colors and margins
- Use Approach's menus and tools in designing your forms
- Set the print and preview attributes for forms
- Work with styles to simplify and standardize form design

Working with Forms

We all work with paper forms every day—for example, writing checks, entering addresses in an address book, or applying for a job. Usually these forms have a name, such as *Check*, and several designated areas for you to put words and numbers, such as the date, payee name, and the amount of the check. These paper forms may be stored in a box or cabinet in some order, such as the check number, for reference purposes.

Similarly, on your computer you enter, edit, or view the data in your Approach database by using a form—an on-screen design that allows you to type the data you need into your database. Forms can contain many objects, such as database field objects, text blocks, graphics, and buttons.

Although you can use a worksheet to view multiple records at a time in a table format, it's often inconvenient to edit data in a worksheet. Most databases contain more fields than the worksheet can fit across your screen. As a result, you must scroll left and right to view the fields in a record. A form, however, lets you view a single record and fit all the field objects in the record on-screen at one time.

Tip

You can use reports to view and edit multiple records at once. For more information, see Chapter 7, "Creating Reports and Mailing Labels."

The first time you create or open an existing database, Approach automatically creates a default form (Form 1) so that all your fields can be displayed. However, you can easily build your own forms in Approach's Design mode.

Approach has tools that allow you to add field objects, graphics, and other objects to customize a form and make it more functional. You can change a form's size, color, default font, and many other properties. You can also change the way an object is shown on a form to make entering data easier.

Because forms are the normal way to work with your data, they must be convenient to use. You should group field objects that are commonly entered together, placing them on from one to five pages of a single form so that you don't overcrowd them. Approach also lets you create multiple forms that show the data in the database in different ways. You can display different fields from your database on different forms, and you can arrange field objects to focus attention on certain aspects of the data.

The forms you design are stored in an Approach file (*.APR or *.APT). To display forms you've already designed, you must open the Approach file they're stored in. If you make changes to forms, you must save those changes by saving the Approach file (open the File menu and choose Save Approach File).

The examples in this chapter are based on the Owl Publishing Company.APR file created at the end of Chapter 2, "Creating Database Tables." To reopen this .APR file, follow these steps:

1. From the File menu, choose Open.
2. Select Owl Publishing Company.APR from the list of files. You may need to adjust the folder and drive from which you're loading the file.
3. Click Open.

Using the Default Form

Approach automatically creates a default form under two circumstances: after you create a new database and save it by choosing OK in the Creating New Database dialog box, and when you open a database directly from the File menu by choosing Open. You can use the second method if the database wasn't created with Approach (and therefore has no Approach file containing a form) or if you created a database with Approach but didn't save the Approach file when you exited Approach.

The format of the default form is less than ideal, but at least you don't start with a blank screen. First, your database fields are laid out as field objects across the screen, left to right, as many as will fit. When Approach runs out of room, it places objects on the next row, and so on (see fig. 3.1). Second, all the fields in your database are included as objects on the default screen. Most of the time you don't want all the fields to be made visible on a particular screen! Finally, the labels for the objects on the form are your database field names. These labels may not be as descriptive as you'd like, and you're limited by the rules for naming fields in the database format.

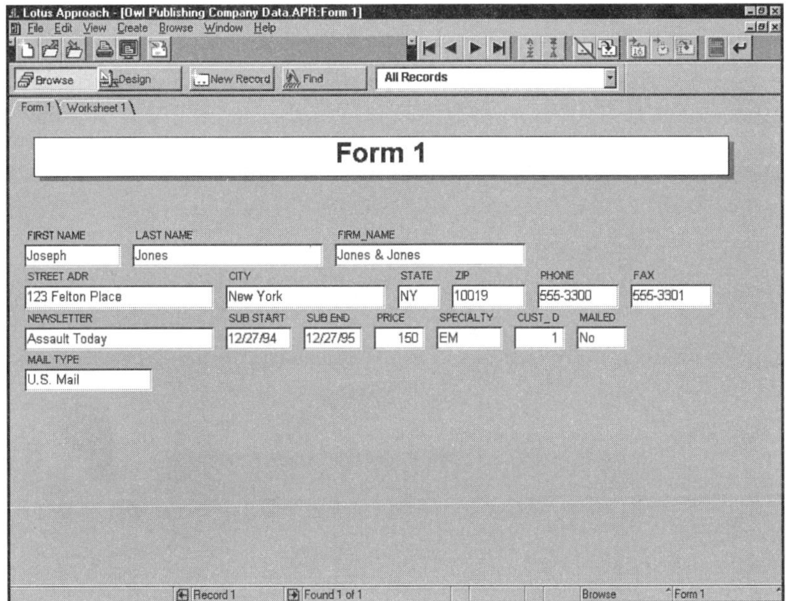

Fig. 3.1

Although the default form may be impractical for everyday use, use it as a starting point to set up a custom form.

The size of the default form is set automatically to the default paper size and orientation of your printer—usually 8 1/2 by 11 inches and portrait orientation. You can change these settings in Design mode, as discussed later in this chapter, to any setting allowed by your printer.

Tip

Forms for data entry work best if all the fields to be entered are on-screen as objects at the same time, even if this leaves large parts of the form page unused. If your database field objects won't all fit on one screen, break them into logical groups and create additional screen-sized form pages with buttons to get to them.

Approach lets you design the form you want easily by starting from the default form. Because all the fields in the database are visible, the default form is an excellent starting point for setting up a custom form. It's also an excellent form for entering some sample database records so that you can try out your new forms and reports.

Creating a New Form

You probably want to modify the default form simply because it's not a very effective form. You may also want to create a new form to achieve a custom layout, add custom text instructions to the screen, dress up the form with pictures and graphics, and add buttons to perform common tasks.

To create a new form, follow these steps:

1. With your Approach file open, switch to Design mode by clicking the Design button on the action bar.

   Tip

   Other methods to get into Design mode are choosing Design from the View menu or selecting Design from the status bar's current mode button. The shortcut is Ctrl+D.

2. Open the Create menu and choose Form. The Form Assistant dialog box appears (see fig. 3.2).

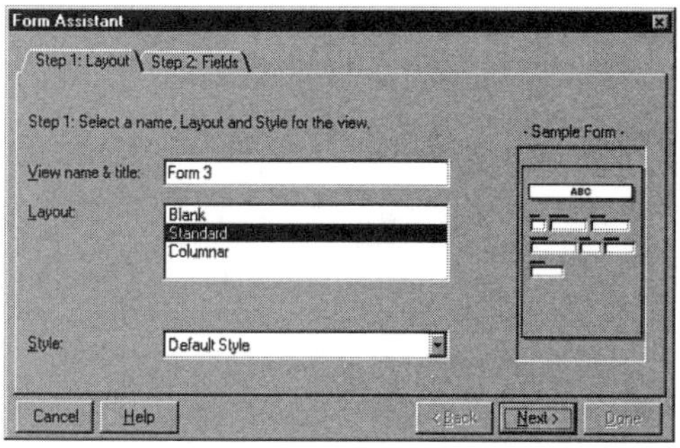

Fig. 3.2

The Sample Form section on the right side of the Form Assistant dialog box displays a preview of your form as you make your selections.

3. Type a name for the form into the View Name & Title text box. This name will be shown on the view tab and as the form heading text.
4. Select a Layout from the list. The Standard layout arranges the field objects horizontally across the page. A Columnar layout arranges the field objects vertically in columns. A Blank form provides an empty page for you to add your own field objects by using the various field tools. See Chapter 4, "Enhancing Data Input Forms," and Chapter 9, "Designing Advanced Forms," for more information on enhancing data input forms.
5. Select a named style from the Style drop-down list. A named style gives a form a set of InfoBox properties, such as a background color, text attributes, field object borders, and field object frames. Approach comes with a set of styles such as Default, 3D Look1, Chisel1, and Executive.
6. Click the Step 2: Fields tab or the Next button to move to the Fields page of the Form Assistant dialog box.
7. The Fields page contains two sections. The Database Fields list box lists all the fields for the current database. Click each field you want to add to the form as an object, and then choose Add after each selection to move each individual field to the Fields to Place on View list box. To select multiple fields, press the Ctrl key as you click and then choose Add. To select a range of fields, click the first field and then hold down the Shift key as you click the last field in the range.

Tip

You can also double-click single fields to add them to the Fields to Place on View list box.

Note

If you change your mind about a field, select it in the Fields to Place on View list box, and then choose Remove to remove the field from the list. You can also double-click the field in the Fields to Place on View list box to remove it from the list.

8. Click Done. The new form appears (see fig. 3.3). If you choose Standard Layout and Default Style, the field objects are laid out horizontally, just like on a default form.

Fig. 3.3

The new form displays the fields you selected and the title you entered in the heading and on the view tab.

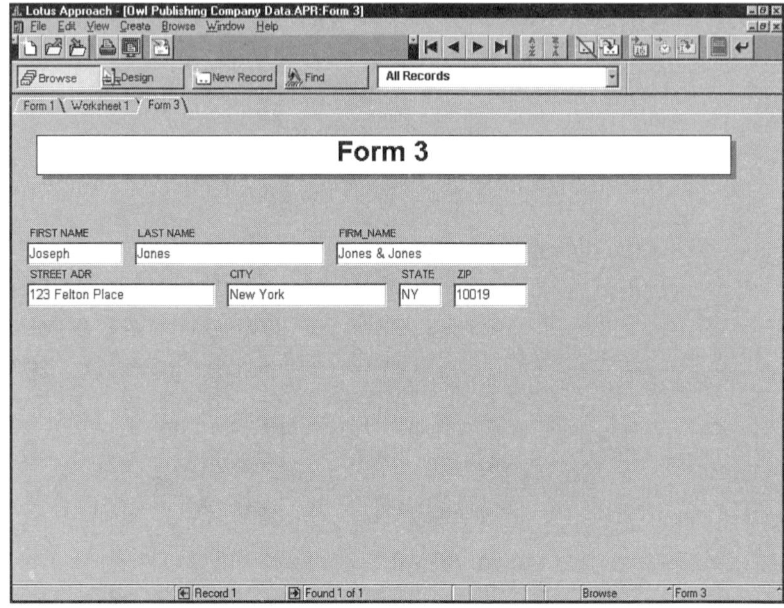

Changing the Name of a Form

When you create a new form, Approach gives it a default name, such as Form 3, if you don't provide another name for it at the time. After you create the form, you can change this name in the form's InfoBox to describe more clearly what the form does—for example, *Data Input* or *New Customer*. When Approach creates a default form for a new database, however, you don't have an opportunity to set the name of the form, but you can rename the default form just like any other form.

To rename a default form, follow these steps:

1. Switch to Design mode by clicking Design on the action bar.
2. If the form you want to rename isn't currently on-screen, choose the form from the view tabs across the top of the screen or from the status bar.
3. Open the Form menu and choose Style & Properties, or double-click a blank area of the form to bring up the InfoBox for the form. (You can also click the Change Properties SmartIcon.) Select the Basics tab in the InfoBox (see fig. 3.4).
4. Type a new name into the Form Name text box. Click the window's Close button to close the InfoBox. The form is renamed, and you can see the new name on the view tab. For the Owl Publishing example, rename the form to *Customer*.
5. Save the Approach file by opening the File menu and choosing Save Approach File, or by clicking the File Save SmartIcon.

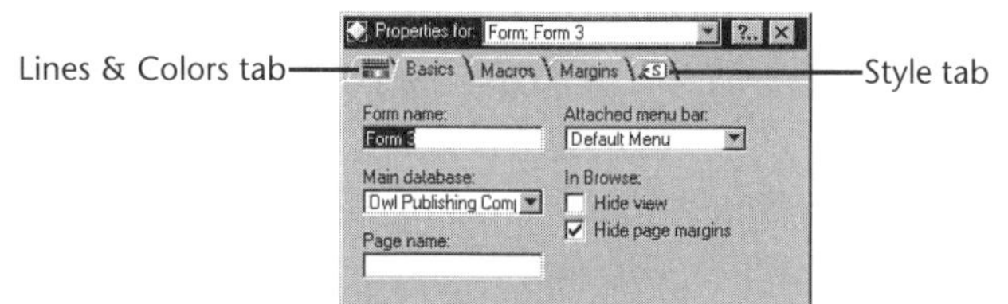

Fig. 3.4

A form's InfoBox lets you change the basic properties of your form.

Tip

You can also rename a form in Design mode by double-clicking the form's tab. Edit the text of the tab to change the name.

Changing the Basic Properties of a Form

Besides changing the name of a form, you can set other properties from the Basics tab of the form's InfoBox. You can choose a menu bar, whether the form is visible in Browse mode, and whether Approach displays the page margins. You can also change the main database and provide a page name if you plan to have more than one page in your form. To open the form's InfoBox, use steps 1 through 3 in the preceding section.

To hide the form in Browse mode, select the Hide View check box in the form's InfoBox. This will cause the form tab to disappear from the view tabs and the form name to not appear in the status bar list of views. To display a hidden form, select the Hide View check box again to turn it off. To hide the page margins, select the Hide Page Margins check box. This will cause the margin areas of your form to not appear on-screen. To display hidden page margins, select the Hide Page Margins check box again.

Note

The Main Database drop-down list in a form's InfoBox lets you change the database on which the form is based. The Main Database drop-down list is discussed in Chapter 9, "Designing Advanced Forms." The Attached Menu Bar option lets you select a different menu bar for the form. Menu bars are discussed in Chapter 17, "Customizing Approach."

Setting the Color and Line Properties of a Form

To select a named style for the entire form, choose the Style tab in the form's InfoBox and then one of the options from the Named Styles drop-down list. (For more information on creating named styles, see "Working with Named Styles" later in this chapter.)

Alternatively, you may set the attributes of the background and lines that Approach displays on a form by using other InfoBox tabs. To adjust these attributes, follow these steps:

1. Switch to Design mode by clicking Design on the action bar.
2. If the form you want to work with isn't currently displayed, choose the form name from the view tabs across the top of the screen or from the status bar.
3. Double-click a blank area of the form to bring up the InfoBox for the form. Select the Color tab in the InfoBox.
4. To select a frame style, click the Style drop-down list. A variety of frame styles are available, including raised and recessed 3D-look frames. Select the one you want.
5. Select a form background fill color or border color from the Fill Color or Border Color drop-down list. Approach displays a palette of available colors. Click the color you want to use. The rectangle marked with a `T` means transparent.
6. To select borders for the form's sides, use the check boxes in the Borders section of the InfoBox. Click the check boxes to place borders on the Left, Right, Top, and Bottom of your form.
7. To select a border width, click the Width drop-down list. Select a line width from the available thicknesses (1 point equals 1/72th of an inch).

Resizing the Form Page

First you need to decide how big your form page will be. This is set by opening the File menu and choosing Page Setup. At the top of the Page Setup dialog box, the current page is depicted. Set your paper size, source, and orientation based on how you would want your form to be printed, even if you don't plan to print it. The options in some of these fields are limited by your current printer selection, so you may want to verify which printer is current by clicking the Printer button.

Resizing the active area of the form on the page gives you more room to place field objects, graphics, and other objects. To resize the active area of the form on the page, click the margins tab in the form's InfoBox. Set your left, right, top, and bottom margins in inches, just like you would do on a paper form.

Duplicating a Form

You can copy a form so that you don't have to do all your work over again to create a similar form. To copy a form, follow these steps:

1. Switch to Design mode by clicking Design on the action bar.
2. If the form you want to duplicate isn't currently on-screen, choose the form from the view tabs across the top of the screen or from the status bar.

3. Open the Edit menu and choose Duplicate Form. Approach displays the duplicate of the form on-screen. You can change this duplicate without affecting the original—including changing its name.

> **Note**
>
> You should change the name of a form after you copy it. Approach doesn't allow two forms to have the same name and simply names the copy Copy of *xxxxx*, where *xxxxx* is the original form's name.

Deleting a Form

You can delete a form if you no longer need it. To delete a form, follow these steps:

1. Switch to Design mode by clicking Design on the action bar.
2. If the form you want to delete isn't currently displayed, choose the form from the view tabs across the top of the screen or from the status bar.
3. Open the Edit menu and choose Delete Form. Approach displays the confirmation alert dialog box. Click Yes to delete the form (Approach calls it the *current view* in the warning box).

Working with Objects

Approach lets you place various objects on your forms, including field objects, drop-down lists, graphics, and text. By placing objects on your form, you can customize the way the form looks and how it works. You also can resize and move objects. You have complete control over how and where objects appear on your form.

Selecting a Single Object

Before moving or resizing an object, you must select it. To select an object, switch to Design mode and click the item you want to modify. You can tell that the object is selected because four small black squares (called *sizing handles*) appear, one in each corner of the rectangle that surrounds the object. The sizing handles define the limits of the object selected (see fig. 3.5).

> **Note**
>
> The form shown in figure 3.5 has been magnified (using the magnification setting on the status bar) to show the sizing handles better.

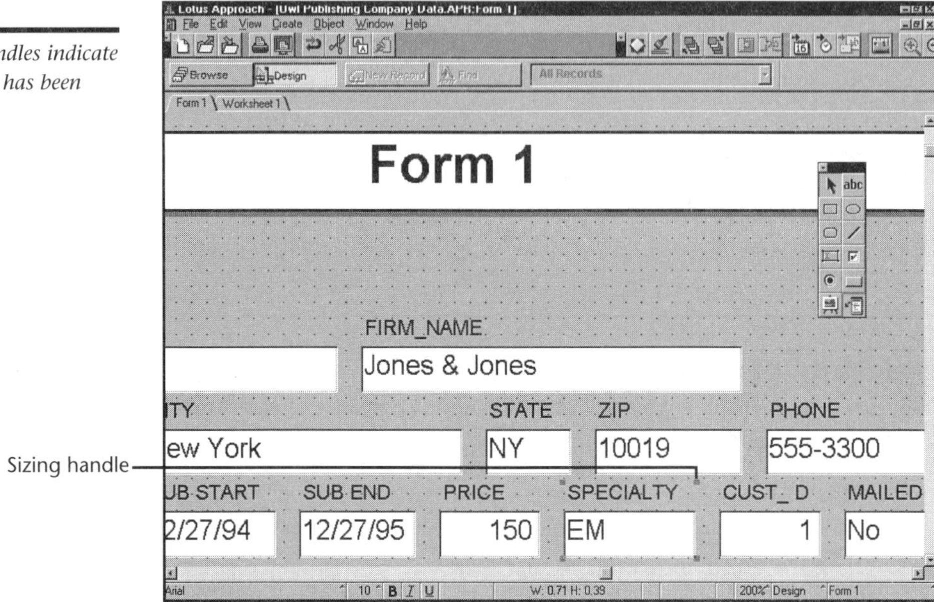

Fig. 3.5

The sizing handles indicate that an object has been selected.

Selecting Multiple Objects

You can select multiple objects in two ways. The first method is to move the mouse pointer to the upper left corner of the area that includes the objects you want, and then hold down the left mouse button and drag to the lower right corner of that area. All the objects that are completely included in the dragged rectangle are selected (see fig. 3.6).

> **Note**
>
> Be careful not to start your rectangle within an object, as it will cause only that object to be selected.

The second way to select multiple objects is to click the first object you want to select, hold down the Shift key, and then click the other objects you want to select. If you accidentally click an object you don't want, hold down the Shift key and click the object again to deselect it.

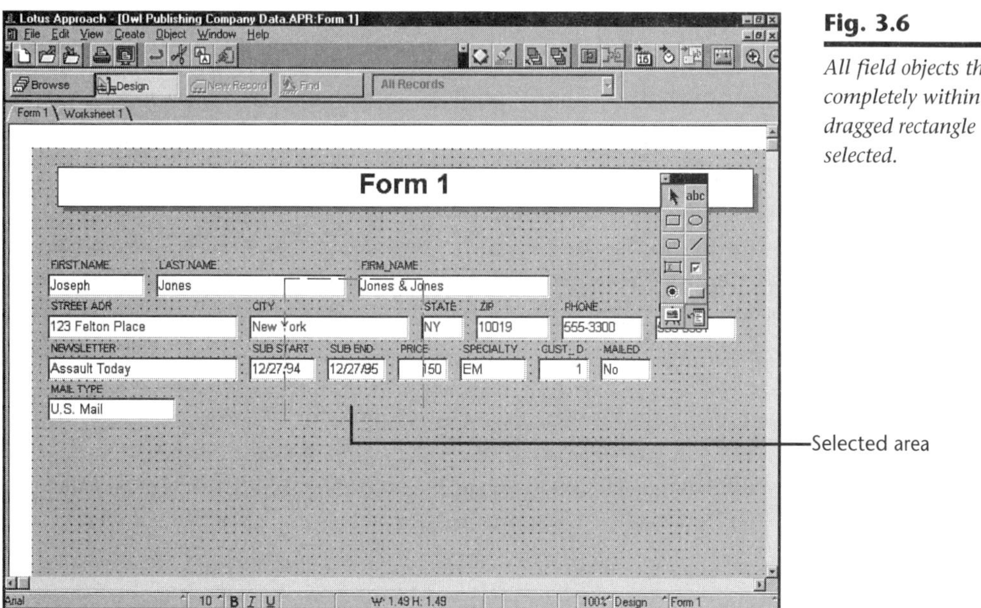

Fig. 3.6

All field objects that are completely within the dragged rectangle are selected.

Resizing On-Screen Objects

As in most Windows applications, after you select an on-screen object, you can resize it. Follow these steps:

1. Click one of the four handles at the corners of the selected object. (You can tell when the mouse pointer is positioned over one of the sizing handles because the pointer changes into a small, two-headed arrow.)
2. Hold down the left mouse button and drag the corner until the object is the size you want.

You can also adjust the size of an object using the object's InfoBox. In the object's InfoBox, click the Size tab, which looks like a rectangle with sizing arrows around it. Set the width and height on the Size page.

When sizing an object on a form, try to make the object just long enough to hold the maximum amount of information that the database field it represents will store. The object length will also depend on the font size you plan to use for that object on the form. Changing the object length doesn't change the database field size. If you make the form object too short, you won't be able to see all the information you type into the database field. On the other hand, if you make the form object too long, you waste screen space. Approach doesn't let you enter more characters on-screen than the length that was specified when the database field was defined.

You can adjust the length of the on-screen object that will contain the field data if you find that it's too long or too short. Follow these steps:

1. Switch to Design mode by clicking Design on the action bar.
2. Double-click a field object to bring up the InfoBox, and select the Font tab (marked az). Set the font you want for the information in that field object and the size. (See Chapter 4, "Enhancing Data Input Forms," for more details on changing the font.)
3. Click Browse on the action bar to switch back to Browse mode. (The InfoBox will disappear when the form is displayed in Browse mode.)
4. Type into the field object on the form the number of characters that the field it represents should be able to hold. If the FIRST NAME field can hold 25 characters, for example, click the FIRST NAME field object and type a text string of 25 characters (uppercase X works well as a place holder for this purpose).
5. If the on-screen object won't display all 25 characters entered into FIRST NAME, you must resize the object. To do this, return to Design mode.
6. To adjust the length of the field object, move the mouse pointer to one of the sizing handles; the pointer becomes a two-headed resizing arrow. Adjust the length in one of the following ways:
   - If the on-screen object was longer than the text string you typed, resize the object to make it shorter.
   - If the on-screen object wasn't long enough (the text string scrolled to the left as you typed the last few characters), resize the object to make it longer.

To make sure that you can see the data you entered in Browse mode when you're in Design mode, open the File menu and choose User Setup and then Approach Preferences to open the Approach Preferences dialog box. Select the Display tab, and make sure that the Data check box is set in the Show in Design section.

Memo-type database fields can have an unlimited length, and typing and editing text in a memo field object is much easier if the field object is more than one line deep. For memo field objects, use the sizing handles to stretch the object into a box that's as wide as your screen (and leave about a 1/4-inch margin on each side) and at least three or four lines deep (see fig. 3.7). When you type in a memo field object, the text scrolls up if you exceed the amount of space allotted for the object. Approach automatically wraps words in memo field objects. Approach also lets you display multiline text-type database fields in the same way.

The Data Input form in the Owl Publishing example has the default field layout. To practice resizing objects on a form, try resizing the FIRST NAME and LAST NAME field objects by following these steps:

1. Click Design on the action bar to switch to Design mode.
2. Click the FIRST NAME object near the top of the form, and drag the handle in the lower right corner to make the object shorter.

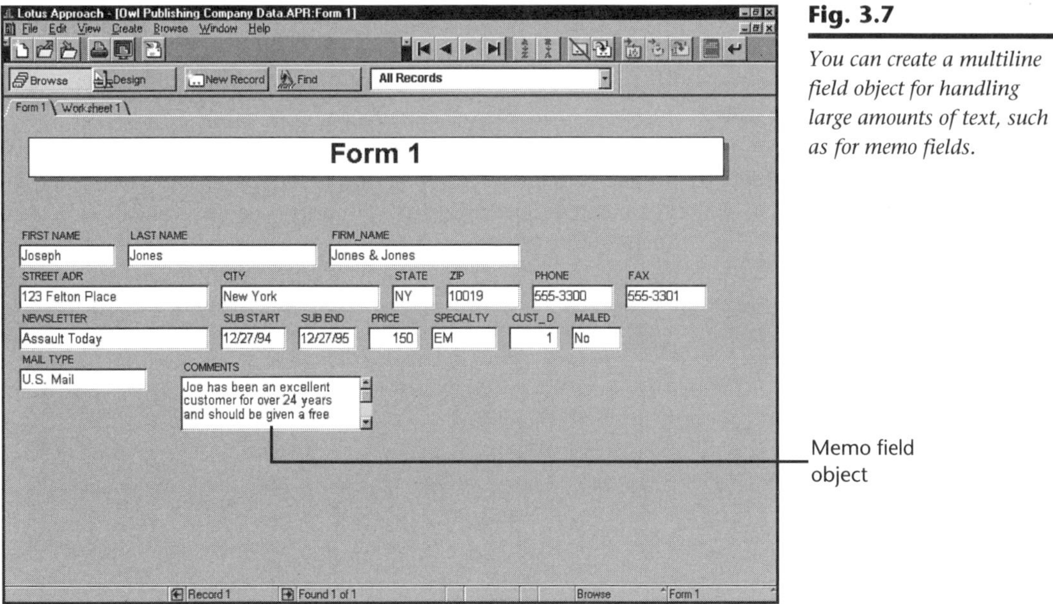

Fig. 3.7

You can create a multiline field object for handling large amounts of text, such as for memo fields.

3. Click the LAST NAME object and drag the sizing handle in the lower corner to make it shorter (see fig. 3.8).

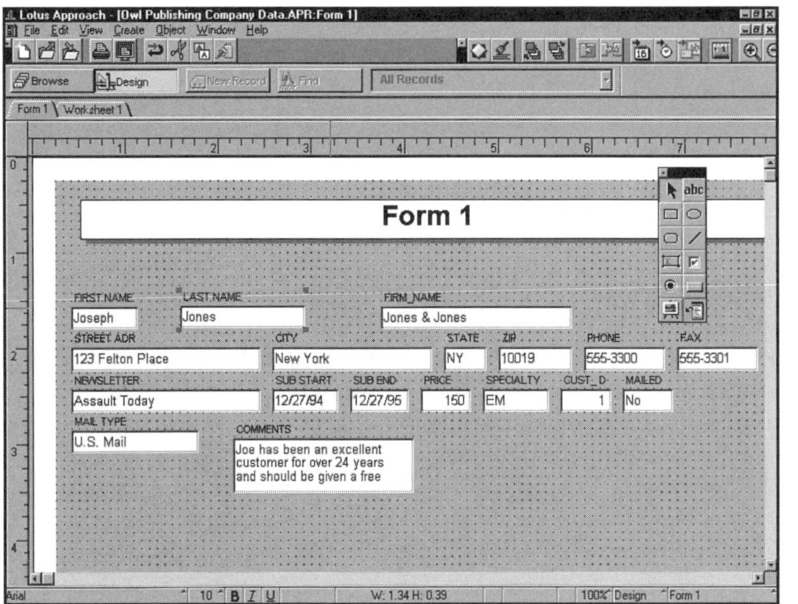

Fig. 3.8

The FIRST NAME and LAST NAME field objects have been shortened.

4. Open the File menu and choose Save Approach File. (By saving the file, you're saving the new form design as well.)

Moving Objects

Approach lets you move objects so that you can rearrange them on the form. To move a single object, select the object, click the object again (anywhere except over a sizing handle), and then drag it to its new location. When the mouse pointer is positioned over a selected object, it turns into a hand shape.

Tip

To move a selected object(s) a little bit at a time, use the arrow keys on the keyboard. Each time you press an arrow key, the object(s) moves one screen pixel in the direction of the arrow.

You can also relocate a single object by using the object's InfoBox. In the object's InfoBox, click the Size tab and type in new Top and Left displacements in inches from the margins.

You can also move multiple objects as a group. Select all the objects you want to move (see the earlier section, "Selecting Multiple Objects"). Then, making sure that the little hand pointer is visible, click any selected object and hold down the left mouse button to drag the whole group to its new location.

Suppose that you want to rearrange some field objects to make the layout of the Owl Publishing form more convenient. Moving the LAST NAME object to the right of the FIRST NAME object would help. To do this, follow these steps:

1. Click the LAST NAME object.
2. Move the mouse pointer anywhere inside the LAST NAME object. Hold down the left mouse button, and drag the object to the left, positioning it just to the right of the FIRST NAME object (see fig. 3.9).
3. Open the File menu and choose Save Approach File.

It's also a good idea to rearrange the objects on the Owl Publishing form so that they not only fit on one screen, but so that they're also more friendly and usable. Figure 3.10 shows a good example of a modified form. To make these changes, click and drag the objects into the positions shown. To make the objects fit on the same line, you may also need to shrink some of them, notably the STATE object. When you're through rearranging and resizing the objects, save your Approach file.

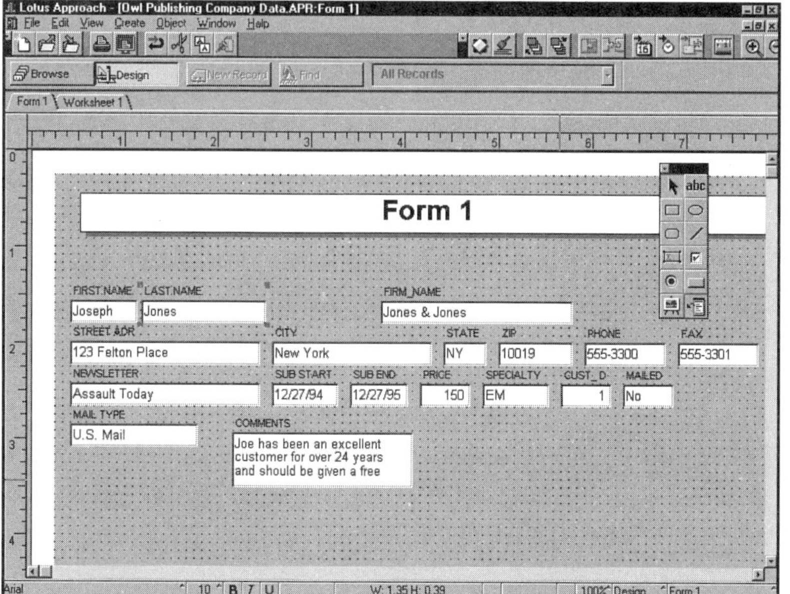

Fig. 3.9

After you move the LAST NAME object to the left, more space is available on the right side of the form.

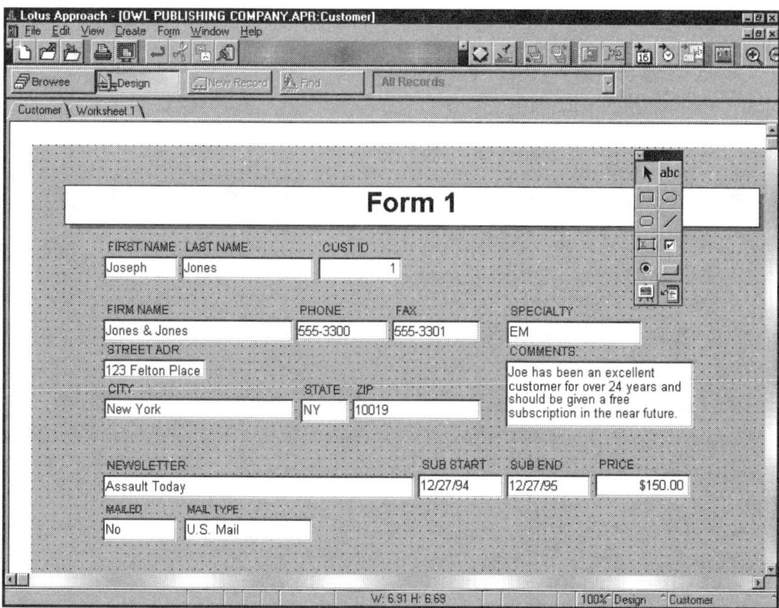

Fig. 3.10

The rearranged Owl Publishing form groups objects together logically, making data entry easier to do.

Cutting, Copying, and Pasting Objects

You can cut, copy, or paste objects on a form by using commands from the Edit menu. Cut removes the selected objects from the form and places them on the Windows Clipboard. Copy copies the selected objects to the Clipboard; the original objects remain unchanged on the form. Paste takes the contents of the Clipboard (placed there by Cut or Copy) and pastes them back on the form.

To use Cut or Copy, first select the objects you want to cut or copy, as explained earlier in the section "Selecting Multiple Objects." Open the Edit menu and choose either Cut or Copy.

To paste the contents of the Clipboard back onto a form, click the form at the position you want to paste, and then open the Edit menu and choose Paste.

The combination of Copy and Paste is useful for copying objects from one form to another in Approach. Follow these steps:

1. Open the form that contains the object(s) you want to duplicate. To open the form, select the form from the view tabs.
2. Select the object(s) you want to copy.
3. Open the Edit menu and choose Copy.
4. Switch to the form where you want to paste the object(s) by selecting the form's view tab.
5. Click the form at the place where you want the object(s) pasted.
6. Open the Edit menu and choose Paste.

Tip

You can also use Copy and Paste to duplicate an object on the same form so that you can make minor changes to the object or use it as a basis for another database field to be displayed in the same format.

Deleting Objects from a Form

To delete objects from a form, select the objects; then open the Edit menu and choose Cut, or press the Delete key.

Using Approach's Layout Tools

Approach has several tools to help you design your form exactly the way you want. They help you position objects on-screen more accurately and adjust their appearance. These tools are rulers, status bar dimensions, an alignment tool, a snap-to grid, a magnification tool, a grouping tool, and an object-stacking-order tool.

> **Note**
>
> To use these tools, you must be in Design mode.

Using Rulers

Approach provides a set of rulers—one across the top of the screen and one down the left side—to help you align objects on the page. As you move the pointer, a set of lines moves in the rulers, showing where the pointer is in relation to the measurements on the ruler.

To turn on the rulers, open the View menu and choose Show Rulers, or click the Show Rulers SmartIcon. A check mark appears next to Show Rulers on the menu. Figure 3.11 shows how the rulers appear on-screen.

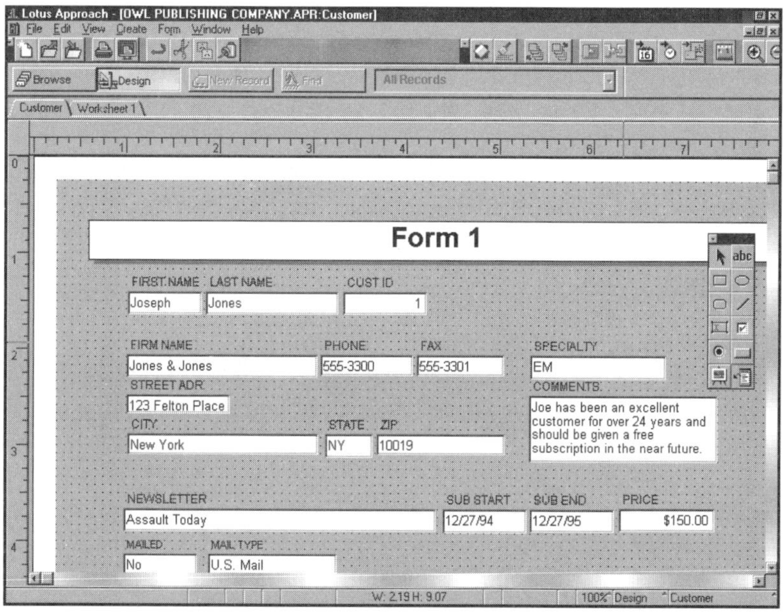

Fig. 3.11

To turn off the rulers, choose Show Ruler again to remove the check mark from the View menu.

Rulers are very handy for working with text objects, such as form headings. When you select a text object, additional information about the text object appears on the ruler:

- To adjust the size of the text object, click it and drag the sizing handles. You will see the movement as vertical and horizontal lines on the top and left ruler also move as you drag the sizing handles.
- The right margin for text in the text object is indicated as a blue arrowhead when you have selected the object for editing. This arrowhead faces to the left and is located just above the ruler line. Drag this arrowhead to reset the right margin. You can't, however, drag it to the right of the black arrowhead on the ruler, which is the indicator for the right edge of the text box.

- A tab is indicated as a small right-facing arrowhead with a vertical line to its right. These tab indicators are located above the ruler line. You can place multiple tabs for the text in the text object. To place a new tab, click above the ruler between the left and right edge of the text object. To move an existing tab, drag it to its new location. To delete a tab, drag it off the ruler.
- The left margin for text is indicated as a right-facing blue arrowhead with a line to its left. To adjust the overall left margin, click and drag the line and arrowhead to a new location. You can't drag the left margin past the left edge of the text object.

  The left margin arrowhead is split into top and bottom sections, which you can drag independently. To set a first-line indent, drag the top portion of the arrowhead to the right of the bottom portion. To set a hanging indent, drag the bottom section of the arrowhead to the right of the top portion.

Activating the Status Bar Dimensions

To position objects precisely, you can show on the status bar the exact position of your mouse pointer to 1/100th of an inch or centimeter, depending on the measuring units you're using on the ruler. These "grid" units are preferences you can set (see Chapter 17, "Customizing Approach"). The mouse position is displayed only when no objects are selected. As you move the pointer, the numbers change to reflect the new pointer position. The first number shows the distance of the pointer from the left side of the form. The second number shows the distance of the pointer from the top edge of the form.

If you select an object, Approach can display either the x- and y-coordinates of the upper left corner of the object or the height and width of the object (see fig. 3.12). To switch between displaying the left top x- and y-coordinates (the status bar displays `L:` and `T:`) and the width and height (the status bar displays `W:` and `H:`), click the dimension area of the status bar.

Using the Grid

Besides enabling you to align objects to each other, Approach has a grid to help you place objects. When the grid is turned on, an object's location is constrained to points on the grid. If you try to place an object so that it isn't on the grid, the object automatically moves to the nearest grid point. This feature helps you keep objects aligned on-screen.

If you try to resize an object with the grid turned on, Approach ensures that the adjusted edge is located on a grid point. If you try to size an object so that the adjusted edge isn't placed on the grid, that edge "snaps" to the closest grid point.

You have the options of snapping objects to the grid and viewing the grid. You can set these options independently. For example, you can snap objects to the grid, but not make the grid visible on-screen (an invisible grid); or you can view the grid (for alignment help) but not snap objects to the grid.

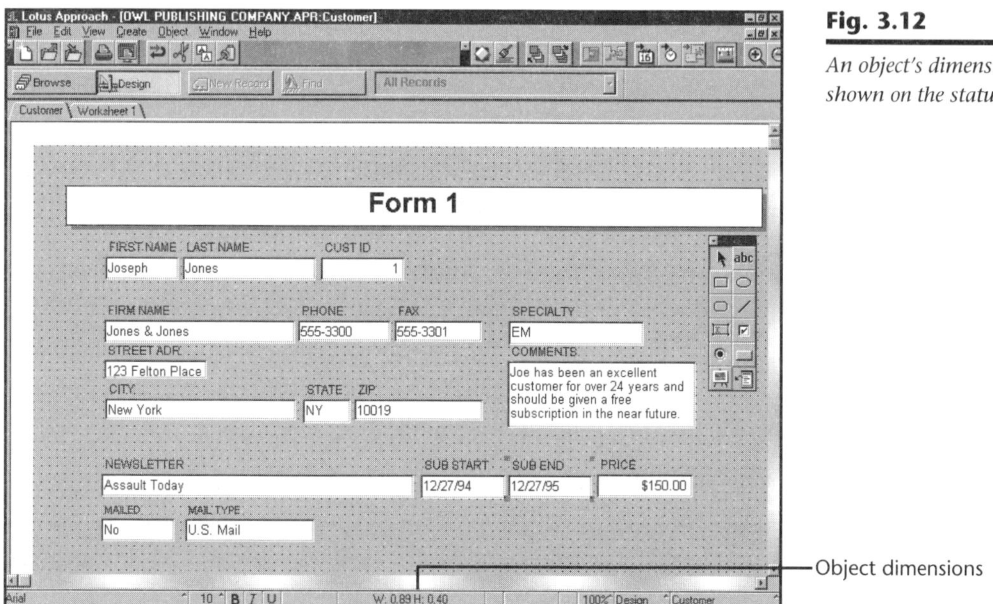

Fig. 3.12

An object's dimensions are shown on the status bar.

To snap objects to the grid, open the View menu and choose Snap to Grid. A check mark appears next to this menu item. To turn off the Snap to Grid, select this option again. To view the grid, open the View menu and choose Show Grid. A check mark appears next to this menu item, and the grid becomes visible. To hide the grid, select this menu option again.

Aligning Objects to the Grid. As you learned earlier in this discussion, you can use the grid to align objects in your forms. If you've turned off Snap to Grid and moved objects on the form, however, objects are no longer aligned to the grid. Approach therefore offers a feature that allows you to realign objects to the grid.

To align objects to the grid, follow these steps:

1. Switch to Design mode by clicking Design on the action bar.
2. Select the objects you want to align.
3. Open the Object menu and choose Align. The InfoBox for multiple objects appears.
4. Choose the To Grid radio button in the Align Selections section.
5. Select the other alignment options you want in the Horizontal or Vertical portions of the Object Alignment section. The selected objects will move on your form as you change your options. (See the following section for more information on alignment options.) The selected edge or center aligns to the nearest grid point. To align your selected objects' top edges to the grid, for example, choose the left button from the Vertical buttons of the Object Alignment section.

Aligning Objects to Each Other. Approach provides a powerful tool for aligning objects to each other that allows you to lay out a form quickly, and ensures that field objects and other objects are lined up without having to tediously align them by hand. You can align objects horizontally or vertically:

- If you align the objects vertically, you can choose to align their top or bottom edges or their centers. You can also have Approach space the objects evenly in the vertical direction.
- If you align the objects horizontally, you can choose to align their left or right edges or their centers. You can also have Approach space the objects evenly in the horizontal direction.

Follow these steps:

1. Switch to Design mode by clicking Design on the action bar.
2. Select the objects you want to align.

> **Tip**
>
> Remember, to select multiple objects, you click the first one, hold down the Shift key, and then click the others. Alternatively, you can drag a rectangle around the objects.

3. Open the Object menu and choose Align. The InfoBox for multiple objects appears (see fig. 3.13).

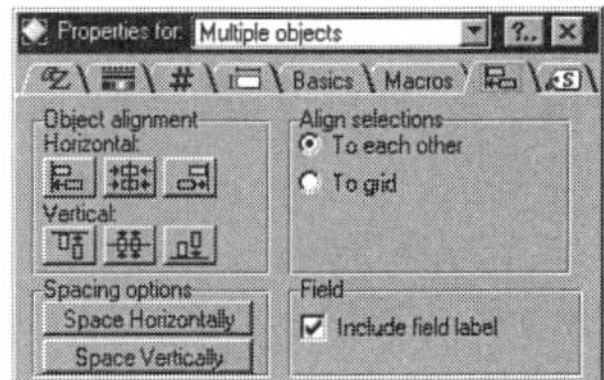

Fig. 3.13

Use the InfoBox for multiple objects to specify how objects should align.

The alignment page in the InfoBox is divided into four sections: Object Alignment, Spacing Options, Align Selections, and Field.

The Align Selections section contains two options. The To Each Other button aligns the selected objects to each other. The To Grid button aligns the selected objects to the grid. (See the preceding section, "Aligning Objects to the Grid," for details.)

To the left of the Align Selections options are the Object Alignment and Spacing Options sections.

To select the type of horizontal alignment you want, choose one of the following buttons:

- *Left button.* Approach aligns the left edges of all objects to line up with the left edge of the object farthest to the left.
- *Center button.* Approach aligns all objects so that their horizontal (left-to-right) centers are lined up.
- *Right button.* Approach aligns all objects so that their right edges line up with the right edge of the object that's farthest to the right.
- *Space Horizontally.* Approach distributes all the objects evenly between the object that's farthest to the left and the object that's farthest to the right.

To select the type of vertical alignment you want, choose one of the following options in the Object Alignment and Spacing Options sections:

- *Left button.* Approach aligns all objects so that their top edges line up with the top edge of the object that's highest on-screen.
- *Center button.* Approach aligns all objects so that their vertical (top-to-bottom) centers are lined up.
- *Right button.* Approach aligns all objects so that their bottom edges line up with the bottom edge of the object that's lowest on-screen.
- *Space Vertically.* Approach distributes all objects evenly between the highest and lowest objects.

On the Owl Publishing form, the CITY, STATE, and ZIP field objects are on the same line, so they should be aligned to each other. To align these three objects, follow these steps:

1. Click Design on the action bar to switch to Design mode.
2. Click the CITY object.
3. Hold down the Shift key and then click the STATE and ZIP objects.
4. Open the Object menu and choose Align. The InfoBox for multiple objects appears (refer to fig. 3.13).
5. Choose the left button from the Vertical buttons in the Object Alignment section. Notice how the objects move on your form (see fig. 3.14).
6. Open the File menu and choose Save Approach File to save the Approach file.

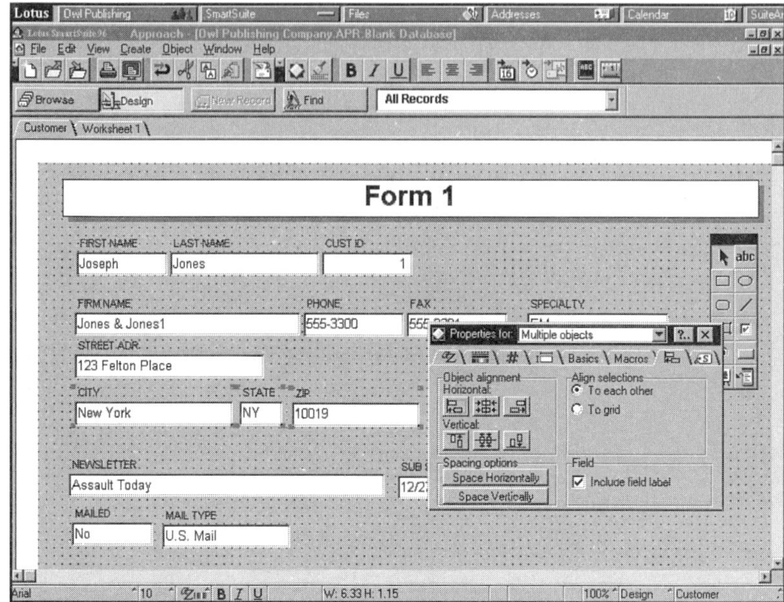

Fig. 3.14

The CITY, STATE, and ZIP field objects are aligned by their top edges.

Using Magnification

Displaying the form in a larger size helps you place objects precisely. Displaying the form in a smaller size allows you to see more of the form on-screen at once.

To make the form larger, open the View menu and choose Zoom In. Everything on the form appears larger, and you can't see as much of the form on-screen. If you want to view other parts of the form, use the scroll bars.

To make the form smaller, open the View menu and choose Zoom Out. Everything on the form appears smaller, and you can see more of your form on-screen. Each time you choose the Zoom Out command, the form halves in size, to a minimum of 25 percent of normal.

An alternate method for adjusting the amount of a form displayed on-screen is to use the magnification button in the status bar. When you click the magnification button, Approach lists the available magnifications in percentages. Select the magnification you want from this list. To return to the normal size, select 100% magnification from the status bar magnification list. This method is also available by opening the View menu and choosing Zoom To.

> **Note**
>
> If you've turned on the rulers, the measurements on them change size to reflect the new magnification of the form. One inch at 50% is shown as only about 1/2 inch wide on your screen, for example.

Grouping and Ungrouping Objects

Grouping objects on the form is helpful in several ways. By grouping objects, you can move, size, and set their properties as though they are a single object. This capability can save you a great deal of time.

For example, you can use the graphics tools in Design mode to construct a simple logo on the form. If you later decide to relocate this logo, however, you would have to make sure that all the portions of the logo were selected before you moved it; otherwise, you would leave pieces of the logo behind. If you needed to resize the logo, you would have to resize each graphic component individually.

After you group objects, however, you can click any part of the grouped object to display a single set of handles. You can then size or move this grouped object as you would any other object. Figures 3.15 and 3.16 help show the advantages of grouping objects.

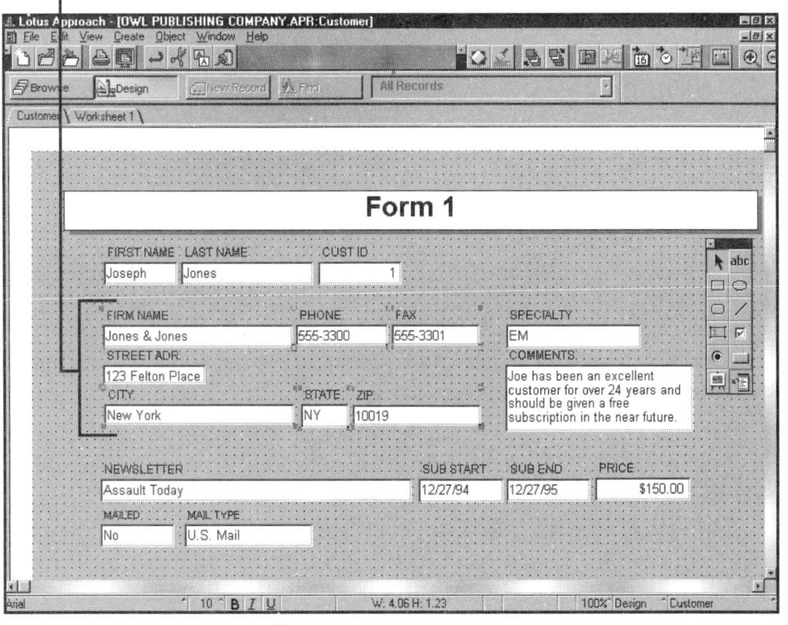

Fig. 3.15

Each object in this collection has individual sizing handles, making it difficult to size and move the objects together.

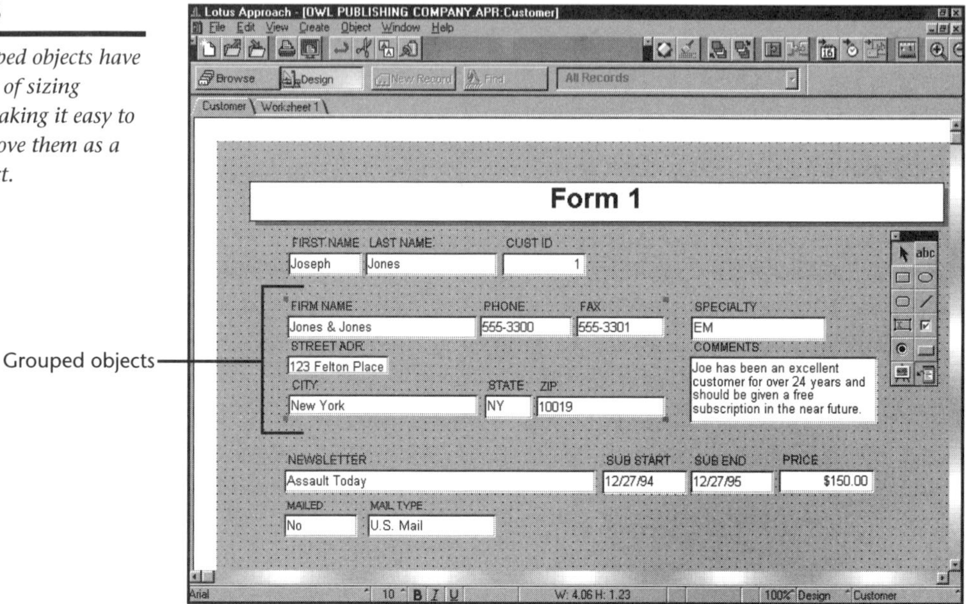

Fig. 3.16

These grouped objects have a single set of sizing handles, making it easy to size and move them as a single object.

Grouping Objects. To group objects, select the objects you want to include and then open the Object menu and choose Group. Alternatively, you can right-click within any of your selected objects and then choose Group from the shortcut menu. A single set of four handles appears on the boundary of the group.

> **Note**
>
> After you group several objects into a grouped object, you can group the resulting group with other objects.

Ungrouping Objects. To ungroup the objects, select the group and choose Ungroup from the Object menu or the shortcut menu. Approach separates the grouped object into its original objects or groups. If you combine a group with other objects, ungrouping leaves you with the original group and the objects. To separate the original group into its component objects, you must select that group and then open the Object menu and choose Ungroup again.

Stacking Objects

Another helpful layout feature is the capability to place objects on top of each other. Each object added to the screen is placed on its own layer, with more recently added objects being closer to the "top" layer. The most recently added object is on top, covering the other layers.

This stacking order affects how the objects appear on-screen and on the printout. If you have a form with objects on it and add a large box to the form, for example, the box covers up the objects because the box was added to the form after the objects.

> **Tip**
>
> The stacking feature is useful when you're designing your views. For example, you can place a large box on-screen and then place several objects inside that box to indicate that they're related.

Open the Object menu and choose Arrange. Approach has four commands on the Arrange submenu: Bring to Front, Send to Back, Bring Forward, and Send Backward. Use these commands to adjust the stacking order to get the effect you want.

To use any of these commands, you must be in Design mode. Click the object whose layer you want to modify, and use the following commands:

- To move an object behind all the others, use Send to Back. This command places all other objects in front of the object. Figure 3.17 shows a rectangle over the FIRST NAME and LAST NAME objects, and figure 3.18 shows the same rectangle after it's sent to the back.

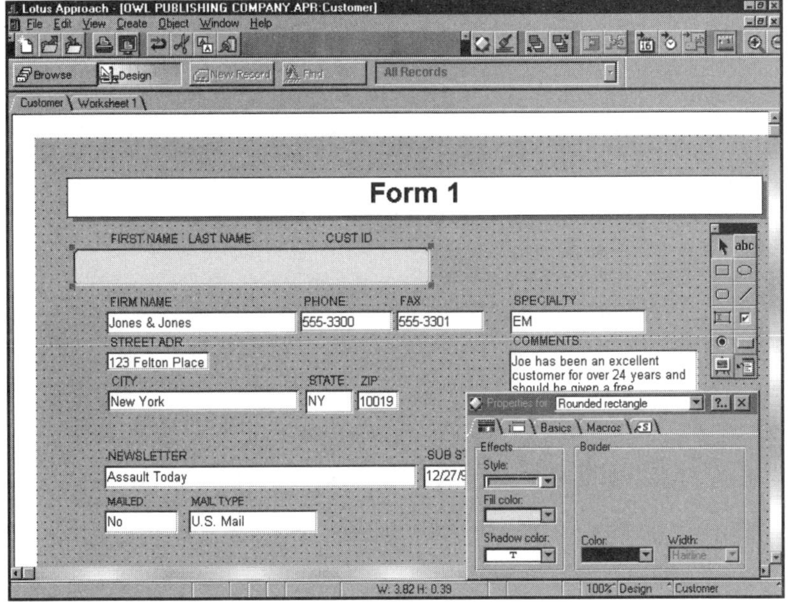

Fig. 3.17

Use Bring to Front to place an object in front of all others.

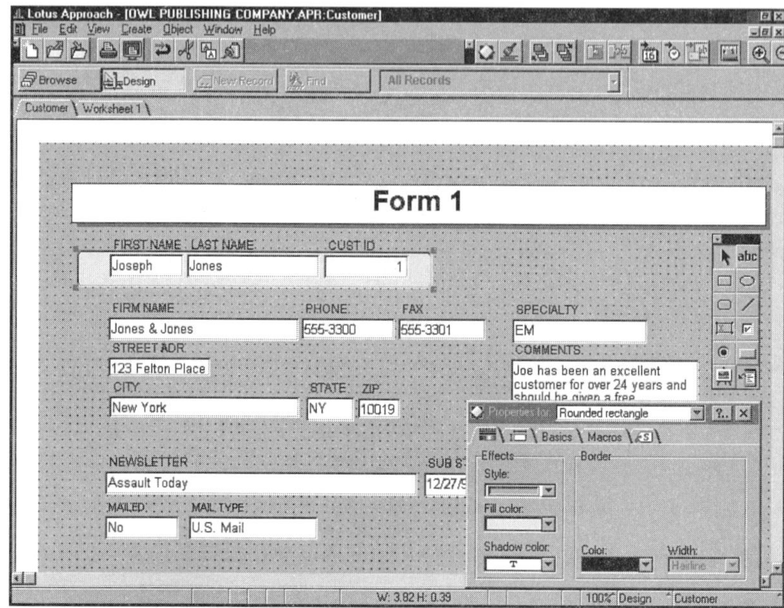

Fig. 3.18

Use Send to Back to move an object to the back.

- To move an object in front of all the others, use Bring to Front. This option places the object in front of everything else so that it's always visible.
- To move an object one layer forward, use Bring Forward.
- To move an object one layer back, use Send Backward.

> **Note**
>
> You can use the Bring Forward and Send Backward commands to adjust an object in relation to other objects. Adjusting an object by one layer, however, may not change how it looks in relation to another object, because the objects may not be next to each other in the stacking order. If so, execute the command several times until it has the desired effect.

Setting an Object's Print and Preview Attributes

You have the option to prevent an object from printing, show non-printing objects in Print Preview mode, and cause objects to relocate on the printout to close up the empty space on a form.

Preventing Objects from Printing

Normally, any object you place on a form is printed when you print the form and is displayed when you do a print preview. (See Chapter 7, "Creating Reports and Mailing Labels," for information on printing forms and reports.) But what if you don't want to print all the objects? For example, you may not want to print complex graphics because they may slow down the print speed considerably. Similarly, because buttons don't contain any useful information, you have no reason to include them on a printout (these buttons default to non-printing, by the way).

To prevent an object from appearing on a printout or a print preview, follow these steps:

1. Switch to Design mode by clicking Design on the action bar.
2. Open the InfoBox by selecting Object Properties from the shortcut menu or by double-clicking the object.
3. Click the Basics tab. Select the Non-Printing check box. The check box shows a check mark whenever you've selected an object that won't appear on a printout.

If you change your mind and decide to have the object appear on a printout, deselect the Non-Printing check box to remove the check mark.

Showing and Hiding Objects in Print Preview

If you decide to hide an object when you print the form, you may also choose to hide the object in Print Preview mode. By hiding the object in Print Preview mode, the on-screen form will look like the printed form. Approach still displays the object in Browse mode, so you can add data to a database field. Of course, certain types of objects (such as buttons to activate macros) don't make sense to hide because you can't use them if you can't see them.

To show an object in Print Preview mode, follow these steps:

1. Switch to Design mode by clicking Design on the action bar.
2. Open the InfoBox by selecting Object Properties from the shortcut menu or by double-clicking the object.
3. Click the Basics tab. Select the Show in Preview check box. The check box shows a check mark whenever you've selected an object that will appear in Print Preview mode. The Show in Preview check box is available only if you've also selected Non-Printing.

If you change your mind and decide to have the object not appear in Print Preview mode, deselect the Show in Preview check box.

Using Slide Up and Slide Left

When you enter data into a field object on a form , you can often leave blank spaces. Some empty space results if you don't enter data into all the objects on the form; empty space also appears when objects are much longer than the text they contain.

Blank space doesn't represent a major problem, but ugly printouts can result. You can tell Approach to move other objects and text or graphic objects on the form to close up the empty space when you print the form. Use Approach's Slide Up and Slide Left features, coupled with the Reduce Boundaries feature, to close up empty space.

If you cause an object to slide up, it moves up to fill an empty line. If you cause an object to slide left, it moves to the left to fill in any space left in an object that's much longer than its contents (see fig. 3.19). For Slide Left to work, however, the objects' bottom borders must be aligned. The quick way to align the objects is to select the objects you want to slide together, and then choose Object Properties from the Object menu to open an InfoBox. Then select the alignment tab and align the objects along the bottom to slide them left and along the left to slide them up.

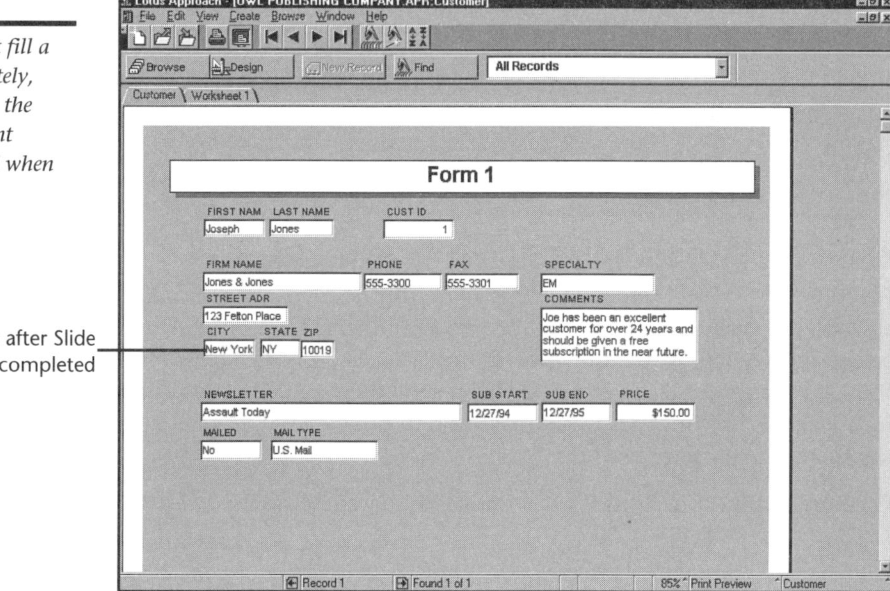

Fig. 3.19

When data doesn't fill a field object completely, Slide Left closes up the empty space in Print Preview mode (and when you print).

To access the Slide Up and Slide Left commands, switch to Design mode, select the objects you want, and display the InfoBox for multiple objects by choosing Object Properties from the Object menu. Select the Size tab. To set an object to slide left, click the Left check box under the When Printing, Slide heading. To set an object to slide up, click the Up check box in the When Printing, Slide heading.

Under normal circumstances, objects take up a specific amount of room on the form. Thus, the Slide Left and Slide Up features have no effect unless you allow Approach to adjust the size of any objects that contain blank space. To allow Approach to adjust the object size, select the Reduce check box on the Size page. The Reduce check box lets Approach shrink an object that contains empty space, potentially moving other objects left and up to fill in the empty space.

A related command is the Expand check box on the Size page. This check box enables Approach to increase the size of a screen object when the database field contains more information than can be displayed in the object on-screen. A good example of a use for the Expand check box is a memo database field with more text than Approach can display in the allotted on-screen object space. If you select the Expand check box, Approach will insert enough space in the printout to print the entire contents of the memo field.

> **Note**
>
> You won't be able to see the changes on the form unless you're in Print Preview mode or Design mode with field data showing. To enter Print Preview mode, click the Preview Smart-Icon or select Print Preview from the status bar. To show field data, open the View menu and choose Show Data. If the form is too small to read the text in Print Preview mode—and to see the effects of Slide Up or Slide Left—click the Zoom-In SmartIcon.

Working with Named Styles

InfoBoxes are useful for setting the properties of objects on-screen. From an InfoBox you can set the color, frame style, font, size, effects, label attributes, and many other properties of an object. However, it can be tedious to set all the properties for each new object you create. If you set an attribute (for example, the font) to different values for different objects, the effect can look haphazard instead of well planned. Using too many colors or fonts on a form is distracting. Ideally, you should establish a scheme of object attributes and stick to it throughout an Approach application.

Approach can help you choose a scheme of object attributes with a named style. *Named styles* are named sets of object attributes that you can easily apply to any new or existing object on a form. When you apply a named style to an object, the object takes on all the attributes of the named style that are appropriate for that object. For example, if you apply a named style to a rectangle, the rectangle border width and color, as well as the fill pattern and color, take on the attributes of the named style. Even though the named style may have text attributes as well, these aren't applied to the rectangle because a rectangle doesn't have any text.

Another advantage to named styles is that you can easily change the attributes of objects on a form. When you change the attributes of a named style, all the objects that use the named style automatically change to match the new style attributes. The exception is an object for which you've manually changed attributes using that object's InfoBox. The new style attributes don't override any manual changes you may have made. For example, if you change the typeface of a named style from Arial to Times New Roman, all objects that use that style will change their typeface except those objects for which you previously changed the typeface manually.

Attaching a Named Style

To attach a named style to an object, you must be in Design mode. Open the InfoBox by selecting Object Properties from the shortcut menu or double-clicking the object. Select the Style tab. From the Named Style drop-down list, select the style you want to use for the object. Approach supplies only one Named Style, the "default" style, which you can change.

Creating or Editing a Named Style

To create or edit a named style, open the Create menu and choose Named Styles. The Named Styles dialog box opens (see fig. 3.20). The buttons down the right side of the Named Styles dialog box let you Edit an existing style, create a New style, or Copy an existing style. Copying an existing style is very handy when you want to change just a few attributes and create a new style from the result.

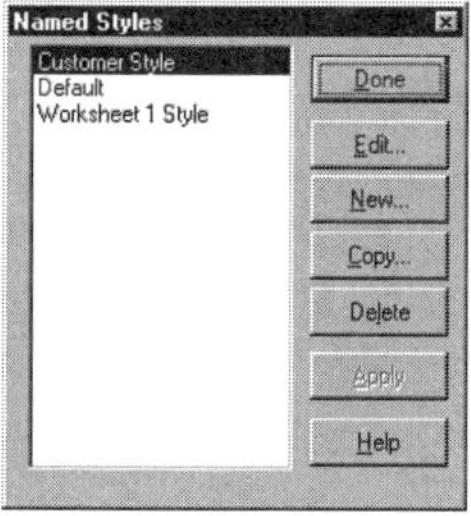

Fig. 3.20

Named styles help you standardize your design and facilitate later changes.

Once you choose Edit, New, or Copy from the Named Styles dialog box, the Define Style dialog box opens (see fig. 3.21).

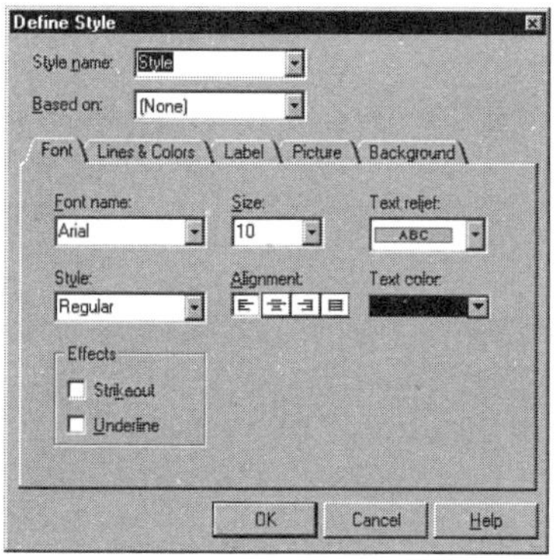

Fig. 3.21

A style sets all the properties of text, lines, pictures, fields, and labels.

The top portion of the dialog box lets you name and base your style on an existing style:

- To name your style, type a new name into the Style Name combo box. If you chose Edit from the Named Styles dialog box, Approach displays the name of the style you chose to edit instead of the Style Name combo box. If you chose Copy in the Named Styles dialog box, *Copy of* and the name of the copied style appears in the Style Name combo box.
- You can base your style on another style. To select a style on which to base your style, select the style from the Based On drop-down list.

The bottom portion of the Define Style dialog box looks much like an object's InfoBox. It has five tabs: Font, Lines & Colors, Label, Picture, and Background. Set the properties you want on each page. When you're done setting the properties on all the pages, click OK to return to the Named Styles dialog box.

You can set the following properties in the Define Style pages:

- *Font.* You can set the Font Name, Style, Effects (Strikeout and Underline), Size, Alignment, Text Relief, and Text Color.
- *Lines & Colors.* You can set the object Border Width from a drop-down list, and Border Color, Fill Color, and Shadow Color. You can choose a Frame and select on which sides you want the Border (Top, Bottom, Left, or Right). You can also set a text Baseline, make an object with this style Read-Only, and have the Borders Enclose a label.
- *Label.* In addition to setting all the attributes on the Fonts page, you can also set the Label Position in relation to a field object (Above, Left, Right, Below, or no label).
- *Picture.* The selections on this page tell Approach how to handle a picture that's too large or too small to fit in the space allocated for the picture on the form. If the picture is too large, you can have Approach Crop it or Shrink it to fit. You can also have Approach stretch a picture that's too small by checking Stretch If Too Small. Finally, you can allow the user to draw on a picture by using the mouse pointer. For more information on fields that can hold pictures (PicturePlus fields), see Chapter 10, "Using Advanced Field Types."
- *Background.* You can set the entire view's Border Color, Fill Color, Shadow Color, and Frame. You can also select the borders for the background by clicking the Top, Bottom, Left, or Right check boxes.

Deleting and Finishing with Named Styles

Use the Delete button in the Named Styles dialog box to delete a named style. (You can't delete the styles that come with Approach, however.) If you delete a named style that's used by an object, the attributes of the object don't change, but you do lose the ability to change the object's attributes by changing the named style.

When you're finished creating and editing named styles, click the Done button to exit the Named Styles dialog box.

From Here...

In this chapter, you learned the basics of building a form. You created a new form, renamed an existing form, and added various objects to a form. After you placed an object on a form, you could move and resize it. You used Approach's layout tools (such as the rulers and the grid) to position the objects more easily on the form. The alignment, grouping, and stacking tools allowed you to define precisely how the objects were displayed in relation to each other. You also learned to use Slide Up and Slide Left to control how objects look on a printout, and learned how to create and use named styles.

To learn more about creating forms, refer to the following chapters in this book:

- Chapter 4, "Enhancing Data Input Forms," discusses how to add additional items to your forms.
- Chapter 7, "Creating Reports and Mailing Labels," details how to create reports that display multiple records on a page. Unlike other database applications, Approach lets you enter data directly into reports.
- Chapter 14, "Using Worksheets and Crosstabs," shows how to modify and work with the spreadsheet-like worksheet.

CHAPTER 4

Enhancing Data Input Forms

In this chapter, you'll continue building and customizing your Approach forms.

You customize your forms while in Design mode. To work with forms you've already designed, you open the Approach file (.APR) you want to use. If you make changes to your forms, you must save those changes by saving the Approach file (choose Save Approach File from the File menu). Once you've laid out the structure of the database table (see Chapter 2, "Creating Database Tables"), you're ready to begin designing your data input forms.

In this chapter, you learn how to

- Place objects, such as database fields, on a form and customize how they look
- Change the data-entry format for a field, such as drop-down lists, check boxes, and radio buttons
- Change field data-entry order
- Change the format for date, time, numeric, and text fields
- Use text blocks, lines, and graphics to enhance your forms
- Import illustrations to enhance your forms

> **Note**
>
> All the techniques illustrated in this chapter can be used with other types of views, such as reports and mailing labels.

Adding and Creating Field Objects

Because field objects actually display your data, they're the most important part of any form. A form without fancy text and pictures can be boring, but a form without data is useless.

You can add field objects to a form at any time. You may want to add a field object to a form after the form is created; for example, you may have neglected to specify the field object when you first built the form. Alternatively, you can add a new field to the database and then show that field's content on your forms.

The following sections show you how to place field objects on a form as you design the form, and how to add field objects to the database as you're designing a form. The sections also provide an example of how to create a field in the database and add it to the Owl database form you created in Chapter 3, "Building Data Input Forms."

Placing Field Objects on a Form

You can place a field object on a form in two ways: by using the Add Field dialog box, or by using the menu or Draw Fields tool from the tools palette. To place a field object on the form by using the Add Field dialog box, follow these steps:

1. Switch to Design mode by opening the View menu and choosing Design, clicking Design on the action bar, or choosing Design from the status bar.
2. If the Add Field dialog box isn't visible (see fig. 4.1), open it by choosing Add Field from the Form menu or from any object's shortcut menu (right-click the field). You can also select the Add Field tool from the tools palette.

Fig. 4.1

Drag fields from the Add Field dialog box onto your form.

3. Select the name of the field you want to add to the form, and then drag it out of the Add Field dialog box. The mouse pointer turns into a grabbing hand, and the field name appears on a button attached to the mouse pointer.

   To add multiple fields to the form at one time, click the first field in the Add Field dialog box and then Ctrl+click the remaining fields. To select all the fields between two fields, click a field and then Shift+click another field.

Tip

To add a field to the database, click the Field Definition button. For more information on adding database fields, see "Creating New Field Definitions for the Form" later in this chapter.

4. Move the mouse pointer onto the form and release the mouse button where you want to add the field. Approach adds the field object to the form.

To place a field on the form by using the menu or Draw Fields tool, follow these steps:

1. Switch to Design mode by opening the View menu and choosing Design, clicking Design on the action bar, or choosing Design from the status bar.
2. Click the Draw Fields tool on the tools palette, or open the Create menu and choose Control and Field Box. The pointer turns into a crosshair shape.
3. Position the pointer at the upper left of where you want the field to start, hold down the left mouse button, and drag the pointer down and to the right to the location where you want the field to end. You can also click the form to position the field object in its default size.
4. Release the left mouse button. The InfoBox for database fields appears. The left side of the InfoBox displays a list of fields in the database.
5. From the list box, select the field you want to place on the form.

Tip

To create a new field in the database, click the Field Definition button. For more information on creating new database fields, see the following section.

6. If you like, minimize the InfoBox by double-clicking the InfoBox title bar, or close the InfoBox by double-clicking the Close button.

Note

The field InfoBox provides numerous other options for customizing the field objects on the form. After you know how to use these options, you may want to set them up immediately after choosing the field. You always can change them later, however.

Creating New Field Definitions for the Form

If the field you want to place on your form doesn't yet exist in your database, you must add a new field definition to it before you can place the field on the form you're designing. You can add a new field to the database by using either the field InfoBox or the Add Field dialog box. To add a database field by using the field InfoBox, follow steps 1 through 4 in the preceding steps to access the field InfoBox, and then choose the Field Definition button to open the Field Definition dialog box (see fig. 4.2). Add the new database field definition here, as discussed in Chapter 2, "Creating Database Tables."

Fig. 4.2

You can add a new field to your database while designing a form.

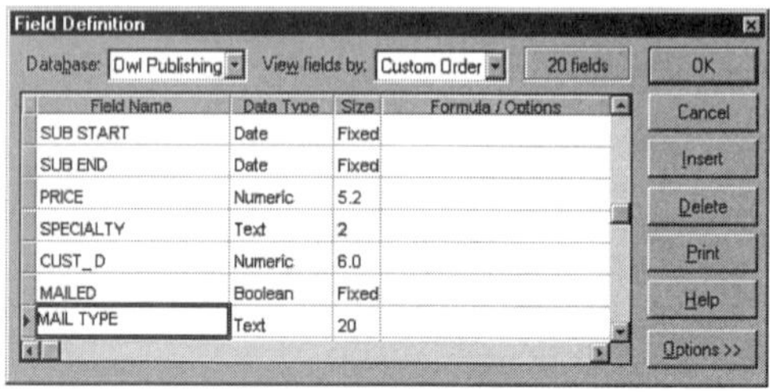

After adding the new database field definition, click OK to return to the InfoBox. The new field appears in the list of available fields, and you can place it on your form by using the Create menu or tools palette as discussed in the preceding steps. Depending on your settings in Approach Preferences, the Add Fields dialog box may also appear, displaying only the newly added fields.

Caution

You can modify any of the database fields while you're in the Field Definition dialog box—but remember that if you change the field type, you'll usually delete all the data in that field. You can, however, convert field types to text type without losing your data.

To add a database field by using the Add Field dialog box, open the Add Field dialog box by choosing Add Field from the Form menu. Click the Field Definition button to bring up the Field Definition dialog box. Enter your new field; then click OK to add the field to the database and return to the Add Field dialog box. If the Show the Add Field Dialog After Creating New Fields check box is checked in the General page of the Approach Preferences dialog box, the Add Field dialog displays only newly added fields when you return from the Field Definition dialog box. You can add the new database field to the form by dragging the field onto the form.

Adding a Field to the Sample Database and Form

When Owl Publishing sends out renewal notices, it wants to keep track of the number of notices sent out. Because the database doesn't contain a field for this purpose, you need to add one to the database and add a field object to the form so that it can be updated.

To create the new field, follow these steps:

1. Click the Design button on the action bar to switch to Design mode.
2. Open the Create menu and choose Control and then Field Box. The pointer changes to a crosshair shape.
3. Move the pointer next to the MAIL TYPE field, and drag the pointer to create a small rectangle where the new field is to be placed.
4. Release the mouse button. The field InfoBox appears.

5. Because the database field doesn't yet exist, choose Field Definition in the Basics page of the InfoBox.
6. Scroll down to an empty line in the Field Definition dialog box. Enter the new field information—for this example, type **`RENEW_NOTE`** for the field name, choose Numeric as the data type, and type **`2.0`** for the size (see fig. 4.3).

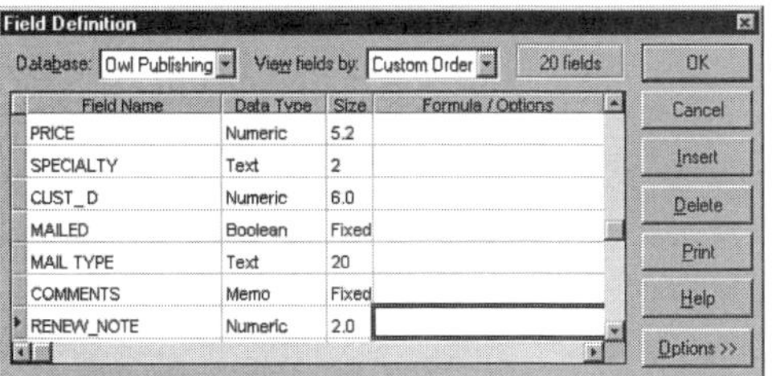

Fig. 4.3

Enter the specifications for the new field.

7. Click OK. The field InfoBox appears again, with the new field selected (see fig. 4.4). Depending on your settings in Approach Preferences, the Add Field dialog box may also appear. If it does, click its Close box.

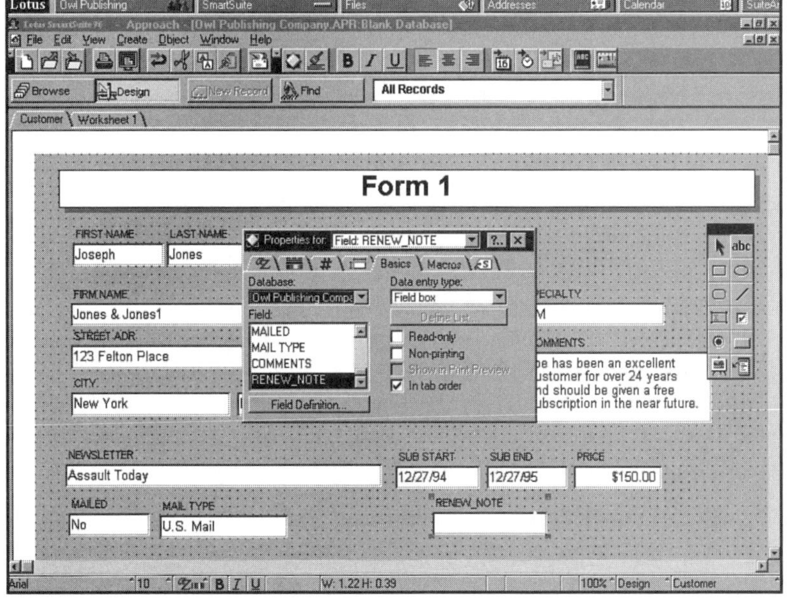

Fig. 4.4

The new field is added to the form.

8. Open the File menu and choose Save Approach File to save the changes to the form. (Approach automatically saves the changes to the database itself in step 7.)

Changing the Data-Entry Format for Fields

When you create a new form or place new fields on a form, the field objects appear as a Field Box data-entry type by default (little boxes into which you type information). Consider the data-entry form that you created for Owl Publishing in Chapter 3, "Building Data Input Forms." First, make sure that you're in Browse mode, and then click any field object. You can type information into that field.

It makes sense that most field objects appear in this default data-entry format. Field objects for database fields such as names and addresses really don't work in any other format. For convenience, however, some field objects can be represented other ways. Besides field boxes, your field objects can use standard Windows data-entry type controls such as drop-down lists, check boxes, and radio buttons to enter and view data on a form.

For example, if a database field will accept only one of a limited number of values, representing the field as a drop-down list containing those values is more convenient. You can use a drop-down list for a field object that records the method of payment, such as Cash, Credit Card, and Check. Placing these three choices into a drop-down list simplifies data entry considerably, because you simply select a value from the list rather than remember and type the acceptable values.

Adding a Drop-Down List Field Object to a Form

Approach provides two drop-down list formats: drop-down list and field box & list. You can choose any value from a drop-down list field object, but you can't type any other values. In a field box & list field object, on the other hand, you not only can select a value from the drop-down list, but you also can enter a value that isn't already displayed in the list. This type of list is called a *combo box* in Windows.

In the Owl Publishing example, the SPECIALTY field describes the legal specialties of Owl's potential customers. As Owl adds more and more newsletters, knowing what kind of law its potential customers specialize in will be important. Because the SPECIALTY field is limited to a small set of acceptable values, having it appear as a drop-down list on the form would be more convenient. That way, you can just select the desired value rather than type it each time.

To turn the SPECIALTY field object into a drop-down list, follow these steps:

1. Switch to Design mode by opening the View menu and choosing Design, clicking Design on the action bar, or choosing Design from the status bar.
2. Click the SPECIALTY field object on the form. (Use the scroll bars to make this field object visible on-screen, if necessary.)
3. Open the InfoBox by selecting Object Properties from the shortcut menu or by double-clicking the object. You can also open the InfoBox by selecting the object and clicking the Change Object Properties SmartIcon or by opening the

Object menu and choosing Object Properties. Click the Basics tab to display the Basics page.

4. The Data Entry Type drop-down list contains the various types of field object displays you can choose: Field Box, Drop-Down List, Field Box & List, List, Check Boxes, and Radio Buttons.

For this example, choose the drop-down list option. The Define Drop-Down List dialog box appears (see fig. 4.5).

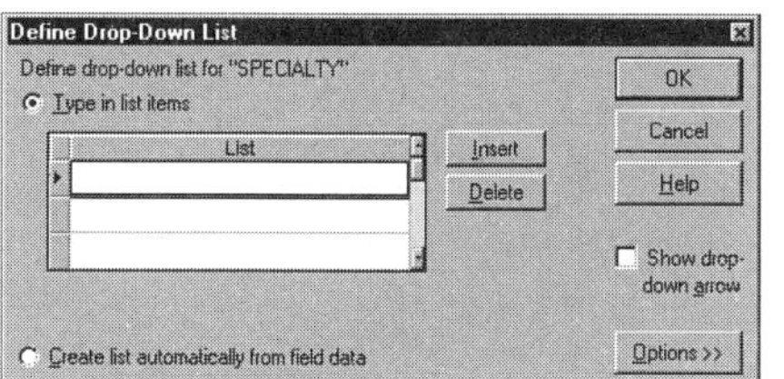

Fig. 4.5

Enter a list of acceptable values for your drop-down list.

> **Note**
>
> If you've never created a value list for this field, Approach automatically opens the Define Drop-Down List dialog box when you select Drop-Down List or Field Box & List from the Data Entry Type drop-down list in the InfoBox. Otherwise, you must click the Define List button in the InfoBox to open the Define Drop-Down List dialog box.

When you use the drop-down list or field box & list data-entry formats, you must specify the values that are to appear in the list. To add your own values to the value list, follow these steps:

1. In the Define Drop-Down List dialog box, select the Type in List Items radio button.

2. Type one value on each line of the list box. After you type each value, click the next line. If you have more values than can fit in the list box, use the scroll bar to move down to an empty line. You can also click any line and edit the value on that line.

   For the Owl Publishing example, type the following values into the list box: **`PF`**, **`PI`**, **`FM`**, **`EM`**, and **`CR`**.

> **Note**
>
> To remove a value from the list, select it in the list box and click Delete. The value is removed from the list. To insert a new value into the list, click a line and click Insert. The selected value moves down, leaving a blank line for you to enter a new value.

3. Click the Show Drop-Down Arrow check box to display a drop-down list arrow on the form field. If you don't click this check box, the drop-down list shows only the drop-down list arrow if you click the field or tab to it.
4. Click OK to close the Define Drop-Down List dialog box.
5. Switch to Browse mode to view your new drop-down list on the form (see fig. 4.6). To switch to Browse mode, click Browse on the action bar.

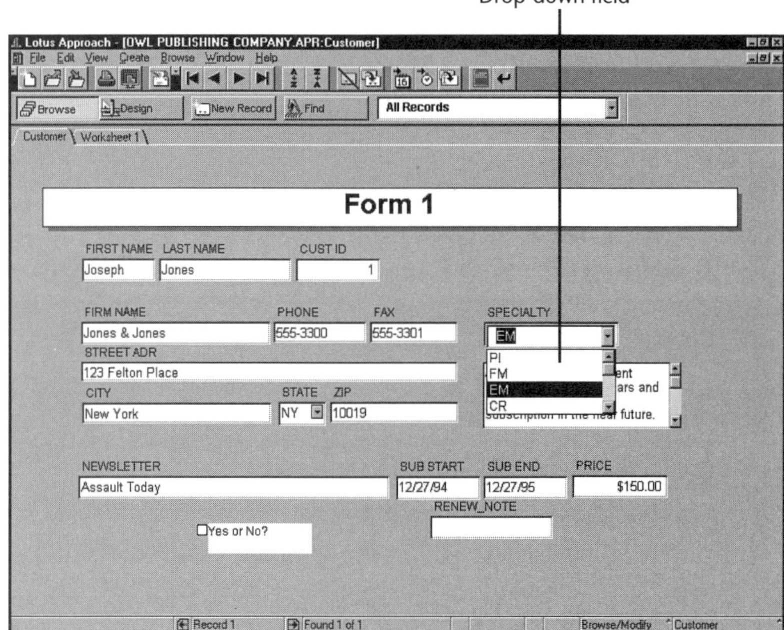

Fig. 4.6

The SPECIALTY field is formatted as a drop-down value list.

Reordering Values. If you like, you can rearrange the values in the list box of the Define Drop-Down List dialog box. In the Define Drop-Down List dialog box, follow these steps:

1. Click the button at the left end of the value you want to move in the list. A right-facing triangle appears in the highlighted button (refer to fig. 4.5).
2. Click in the text area of the line you want to move. Then move back to the triangle and click and hold down the left mouse button. The mouse pointer becomes an open hand.
3. Drag the value to the position you want it to have in the list. Approach indicates the proposed insertion point of the value in the list with a dark bar that appears between the two values where Approach will insert the moved value when you release the mouse button.

Tip

Typing a new value for a field where you've defined the list values explicitly for the field object doesn't automatically add that new value to the list that appears each time you use the field. If the new value is one you plan to use often, you can add it to the list of values assigned to the drop-down list box.

Using Values from a Field in the Database. If you've been entering values in a default format text field for some time and decide to convert the field object to a value list, remembering all the values that have been entered into the database can be difficult. In this case, Approach can create the value list from the values already entered in the field in the database (rather than have you manually enter a list of acceptable values in the Define Drop-Down List dialog box).

To create a value list from database fields already entered, follow these steps:

1. Switch to Design mode by opening the View menu and choosing Design, clicking Design on the action bar, or choosing Design from the status bar.
2. Click the field whose drop-down list or field box & list values you want to modify.
3. Open the InfoBox by selecting Object Properties from the shortcut menu or by double-clicking the object. You can also open the InfoBox by selecting the object and clicking the Change Object Properties SmartIcon, or by opening the Object menu and choosing Object Properties. Click the Basics tab to display the Basics page.
4. Select the Define List button. The Define Drop-Down List dialog box opens.
5. Select the Create List Automatically from Field Data radio button. The list box displays all the current values in that field in all records in the database. (Approach displays values only once—duplicate values aren't shown.)
6. Click OK to return to the form.

Note

If you choose the Create List Automatically from Field Data option with a field box & list field object, you get a list containing values that already have been entered in the field in the database, and you can add to the list by typing new values in the field box on the form. This combination allows any user of the database to add new values to the list. Also, unnecessary values are removed from the drop-down list when all occurrences of those values are removed from the database field itself.

Returning to the Owl Publishing example, the SPECIALTY field object on the form actually would be more useful as a field box & list data-entry type of object, with the values coming from the field in the database initially. This way, any values that need to be added to the list can be added simply by typing them in the field box part of the field object on the form. To accomplish this change, follow these steps:

1. Switch to Design mode by clicking Design on the action bar.
2. Select the SPECIALTY field.
3. Open the InfoBox by selecting Object Properties from the shortcut menu or by double-clicking the object. You can also open the InfoBox by selecting the object and clicking the Change Object Properties SmartIcon, or by opening the Object menu and choosing Object Properties. Select the Basics page by clicking the Basics tab.
4. Change the data entry type to field box & list. Then choose the Define List button in the InfoBox. The Define Drop-Down List dialog box opens.
5. Select the Create List Automatically from Field Data option.

> **Note**
>
> If you worked through the preceding steps, a list of the values already entered into this field in the database will replace the custom list of values you entered earlier in the Define Drop-Down List dialog box.

6. Click OK to close the Define Drop-Down List dialog box.
7. Switch to Browse mode (click Browse on the action bar) to view the converted field format.

   The SPECIALTY field object on the form is now a drop-down data-entry type of field object in which you can choose a value from the list or type a new value. The list shown in figure 4.7 has only a single value from one example record to show that the list can vary as the database fields change.

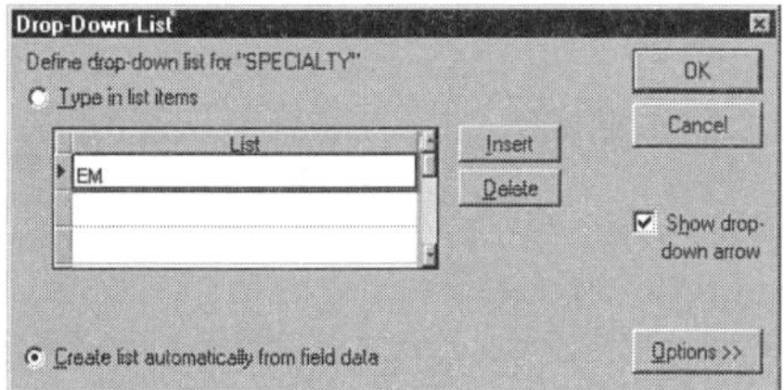

Fig. 4.7

The SPECIALTY field object is redefined as a field box & list data-entry type, with the list coming from the content of the database field.

8. Open the File menu and choose Save Approach File to save the changes to your form.

You can also create a value list from entries made in a field in another database with the selections available by clicking the Options button in the Define Drop-Down List dialog box. To do so, however, the other database must be linked to the current database. See Chapter 8, "Understanding Relational Databases," for a general discussion of relational links; see Chapter 9, "Designing Advanced Forms," for information on using this particular option with relational linked databases.

Restricting the Values in a Drop-Down List. When you create a list automatically from field data in the Define Drop-Down List dialog box, Approach normally makes all the previously entered values in the field available in the drop-down list. For example, if you have a field box & list field object that contains part numbers that your company orders from manufacturers, all the part numbers in the database are available in the drop-down list.

Approach lets you set criteria to limit the values that appear in the drop-down list. For example, you can set criteria so that only the parts available from a certain manufacturer are available in the drop-down list when you enter a record for that manufacturer. This capability helps limit mistakes but works best with a fairly static list of values. For example, it would be quite cumbersome to continually have to enter a part number that's already in your list (but not available in the drop-down list) because you're now buying a part from another manufacturer.

To display a subset of values in the drop-down list for a field object, follow these steps:

1. Switch to Design mode by opening the View menu and choosing Design, clicking Design on the action bar, or choosing Design from the status bar.
2. Open the InfoBox for the field object whose values you want to limit by selecting Object Properties from the shortcut menu or by double-clicking the object. You can also open the InfoBox by selecting the object and clicking the Change Object Properties SmartIcon, or by opening the Object menu and choosing Object Properties. Click the Basics tab to open the Basics page.
3. Select Define List. The Define Drop-Down List dialog box appears. Click the Options button to open the bottom portion of the dialog box.
4. Click the Filter the List Based on Another Field option. The Define Filter dialog box opens (see fig. 4.8).

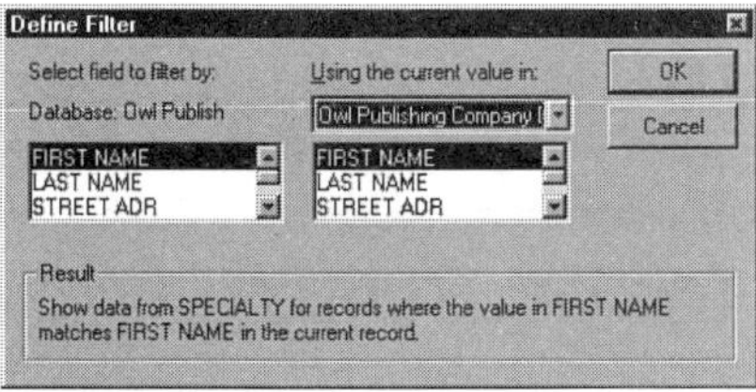

Fig. 4.8

The Define Filter dialog box creates limits on the values listed in a drop-down list.

> **Note**
>
> The first time you establish a filter by clicking the Filter the List Based on Another Field option, Approach automatically opens the Define Filter dialog box. To later modify an existing filter, you must click the Define Filter button.

5. Select the field to filter by from the list of database fields on the left, and make sure that the same field is selected on the right.
6. Click OK to return to the Define Drop-Down List dialog box. Values in the drop-down list are assembled only from database records in which the filter field you select matches the value of the filter field in the current record.

Caution

When you select the Filter the List Based on Another Field option in the Define Drop-Down List dialog box, Approach creates the list automatically from the field data. Thus, any typed list items are lost if you choose this option.

Setting Up Check Boxes

In addition to the field box and drop-down list formats already discussed, Approach offers a format in which field objects are displayed as check boxes.

A check box is simply a small square. Selecting (clicking) a blank check box places a check mark in it; selecting a check box already containing a check mark returns the box to its initial blank (off) condition. (You can also tab to a check box and press the space bar to select or deselect the check box.)

You can use check boxes to handle fields that accept only two values, such as Yes and No. If you have a field that indicates whether you've mailed a renewal flyer to a newsletter customer, for example, you can format that field for data entry as a check box field object. If the check box is blank, the flyer hasn't been mailed. When the flyer is mailed, the person doing the mailing clicks the check box to indicate that the flyer has gone out (see fig. 4.9).

Note

If your database field can have more than two values (such as Yes, No, and Maybe), you probably want to use a radio button field object type instead of a check box (see "Setting Up Radio Buttons" later in this chapter).

Note

You can define more than two values for a check box field object type. It will look like multiple check boxes but will act like radio buttons in that you can check only one of the boxes. If you want to be able to check more than one check box, you must define individual fields with each one as a check box type of field object on your form.

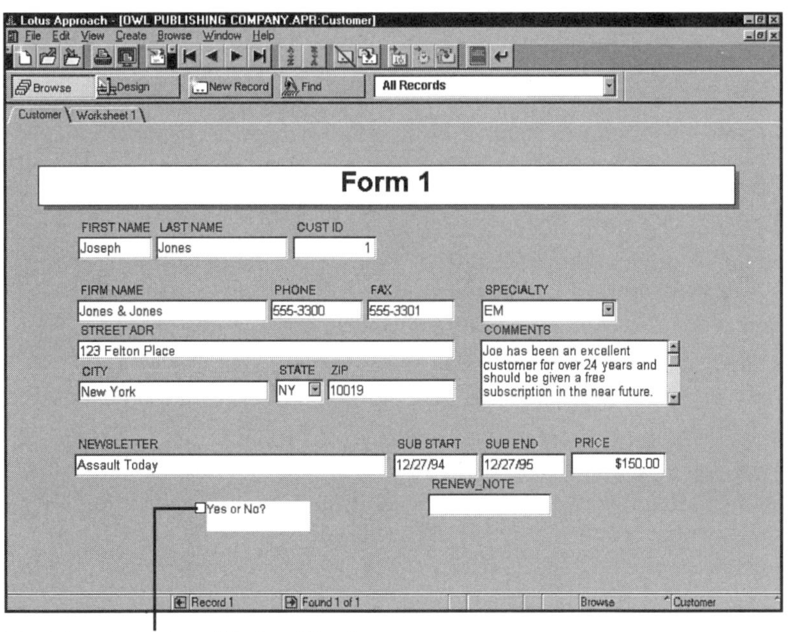

Fig. 4.9

Use a check box to indicate whether a condition is yes or no for a field.

Creating a New Check Box. To set up a check box, follow these steps:

1. Switch to Design mode by opening the View menu and choosing Design, clicking Design on the action bar, or choosing Design from the status bar.
2. Click the Draw Check box tool in the tools palette, or open the Create menu and choose Control and Check Box. The mouse pointer becomes a crosshair shape.
3. Position the pointer at the desired location for the new check box on your form. Click and hold down the mouse button while dragging the pointer diagonally to set the size of the check box. When you release the mouse button, the Define Check Box dialog box appears (see fig. 4.10).

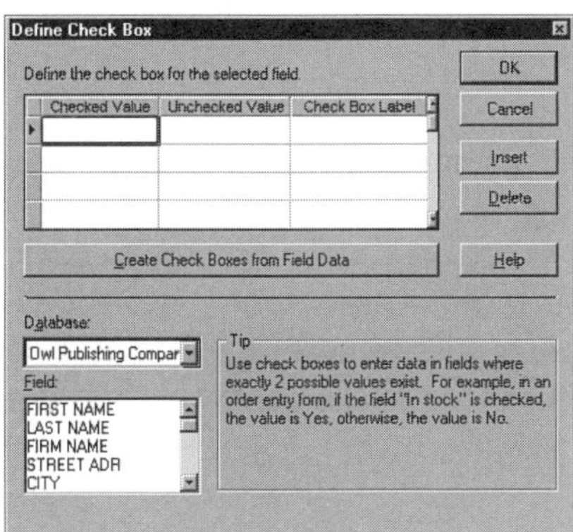

Fig. 4.10

Enter values to be represented by a check or no check.

4. Choose the field you want the check box to represent from the Field list box in the bottom left corner of the dialog box.
5. Enter a checked value, unchecked value, and check box label.

   The Checked Value column contains the value to be stored in the database field if the check box is checked. The Unchecked Value column contains the value to be stored if the check box isn't checked. If the check box field object represents a database field of type Text, the checked value and unchecked value can contain any text up to the maximum length of the database field. If the check box represents a database field of type Boolean (which is often the case), the values entered must be Yes/No. Any other values create an error condition.

   The Check Box Label is the text label that appears next to the check box object on the form. You can change the label here or in the InfoBox for the check box.
6. If you have more than one possible checked value for a single field, you can create a set of check boxes with different checked values. To insert a new value into the list, click the line above where you want to insert a value, and then choose Insert to insert a blank line. Fill in the checked, unchecked, and label values. To delete an existing value, click the line you want to delete and choose Delete.
7. After setting up the check box, click OK to return to the form.

> **Note**
>
> You can create multiple check boxes from a single field by filling in multiple lines in the Define Check Box dialog box. Multiple check boxes behave like radio buttons (see "Setting Up Radio Buttons" later in this chapter) in that only one check box can be selected at a time. However, unlike radio buttons, you can define an unchecked value. If you click another check box, Approach unchecks the previous check box. With multiple check boxes for one field, the checked value of the selected check box is stored in the database field.

Converting an Existing Form Field Object to a Check Box. Approach makes it simple to convert an existing form field object to a check box format. For example, you can convert the MAILED database field object from a field box to a check box on the form by following these steps:

1. Switch to Design mode by opening the View menu and choosing Design, clicking Design on the action bar, or choosing Design from the status bar.
2. Open the InfoBox for the field object you want to convert to check boxes by selecting Object Properties from the shortcut menu or by double-clicking the object. You can also open the InfoBox by selecting the object and clicking the Change Object Properties SmartIcon, or by opening the Object menu and choosing Object Properties. For this example, use the MAILED field object. Switch to the Basics page by clicking the Basics tab.

3. Select Check Boxes from the Data Entry Type drop-down list. The Define Check Box dialog box opens. (It looks like the Define Check Box dialog box shown in figure 4.10, except it's missing the field selection list.)
4. Enter the checked value, unchecked value, and check box label. For this example, enter **`Yes`** as the checked value, **`No`** as the unchecked value, and **`Mailed?`** as the check box label.
5. After setting up the check box, click OK to return to the form.

> **Note**
>
> If you want to modify the attributes of a previously defined check box, select the field object and display its InfoBox. On the Basics page, click the Define Buttons button to reopen the Define Check Box dialog box.

Reordering and Moving Check Box Sets. If you created a check box set with multiple checked values as described earlier in this chapter, they're automatically stacked vertically as a group of objects on your form. You may want to change the order or placement of these check boxes on your form, or even ungroup them and place each check box where it makes the most sense.

Reordering the check box values in the Define Check Box dialog box causes Approach to rearrange the order of the check boxes on the form within the vertical stack. From the Define Check Box dialog box, follow these steps:

1. Click the button at the left end of the value that you want to move in the list. A right-facing triangle appears in the highlighted button.
2. Drag the value to the position you want in the list (the mouse pointer changes to a hand shape). Approach indicates the proposed insertion point of the value in the list with a dark bar that appears between two values. Approach inserts the moved value when you release the mouse button.

You can also move groups of check boxes directly on the form. In Design mode, you can click and drag the group to move it, but you can't change the layout of the check boxes by resizing the group object (for example, you can't draw a wide rectangle and force the check boxes to line up next to each other on the form).

You can break up a check box into individual objects so that you can put each check box anywhere you want. To ungroup the check boxes, in Design mode click the set of check boxes and then open the Object menu and choose Ungroup. After you ungroup the check boxes, you can move them by using drag and drop as if the boxes were independent field objects.

Note

When check boxes are ungrouped, Approach no longer displays them in a single Define Check Box dialog box. Instead, each check box object has an InfoBox from which you can modify the checked value, unchecked value, and check box label by clicking the Define Buttons button in the Basics page to open the Define Check Box dialog box.

Once you've arranged the check boxes the way you want them, you may want to regroup them so you can work with the check boxes as a single object again. To regroup the check boxes, select the check boxes, open the Object menu, and choose Group. Remember, you can select multiple objects by dragging a rectangle around them or by holding down the Shift key and clicking on each object to be added to the group (see Chapter 3, "Building Data Input Forms").

Creating Check Boxes from Database Values. You can create a set of check boxes from data already entered into a database field. This is especially useful if you decide to convert a field object representing that field to a check box format.

To create a set of check boxes, click the Create Check Boxes from Field Data button in the Define Check Box dialog box. If the form field object was of any type except a drop-down list or a field box & list, Approach populates the checked value lines of the Define Check Box dialog box with the values in that database field. The check box label defaults to the checked value, but you can modify the label if you want.

If your form field object was previously a drop-down list or a field box & list type, Approach automatically creates the check boxes with the same values as the drop-down list without using the Define Check Box dialog box. The label on each check box corresponds to the drop-down list value.

Setting Up Radio Buttons

Another useful format for displaying and entering field data is as a group of radio buttons. A set of radio buttons for one database field is represented by a set of small circles with labels. Clicking one of the circles selects that button (the circle is filled in) and deselects all the other buttons in that set.

You can use a set of radio buttons to format a field object in which you can enter only one of a small number of mutually exclusive values, such as High, Medium, or Low (see fig. 4.11). You can select only one radio button at a time; selecting another button deselects the initially selected button. This exclusivity applies because the group of radio buttons actually controls the value that Approach places in a single field in your database—and a single field can contain only a single value.

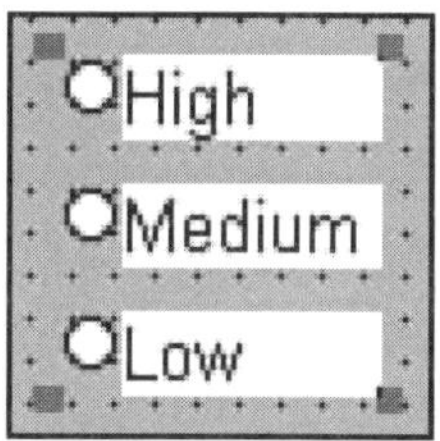

Fig. 4.11

Use radio buttons with fields that accept only one of a set of separate values.

Creating a New Radio Button Set. To create a field object as a set of radio buttons, follow these steps:

1. Switch to Design mode by opening the View menu and choosing Design, clicking Design on the action bar, or choosing Design from the status bar.
2. Click the Draw Radio Buttons tool in the tools palette, or open the Create menu and choose Control and Radio Button. The mouse pointer changes into a cross-hair shape.
3. Position the pointer at one corner of the desired location for the new set of radio buttons. Press and hold down the mouse button while dragging the pointer diagonally to set the size of the entire set of radio buttons. When you release the mouse button, the Define Radio Buttons dialog box appears (see fig. 4.12).

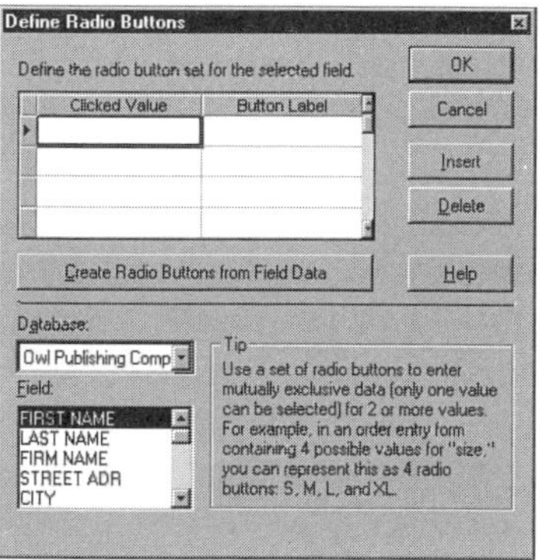

Fig. 4.12

After you position your radio box field object on the form, the Define Radio Buttons dialog box appears.

4. Choose the field you want the radio button to represent from the Database and Field list boxes in the bottom section of the dialog box.
5. Enter a clicked value and a button label.

   The Clicked Value column contains the value stored in the database field if you click the radio button associated with the button label you provided and select it (the circle is filled in). If the radio button represents a database field of type text, the clicked value can contain any text up to the maximum length of the field. If the radio button represents a database field of Boolean type (which is often the case), the values entered must be Yes or No. Any other values cause Approach to display all radio buttons as selected to tell you immediately that there's a problem.

6. To add another radio button to the set, you must insert a new value into the list. Click the line above where you want to insert a value and then choose Insert to insert a blank line to fill in with a new clicked value and label. To delete an existing value, click the line you want to delete and choose Delete.
7. After setting up the radio buttons, click OK to return to the form.

Converting an Existing Field to a Set of Radio Buttons. Approach makes it simple to convert an existing form field object to a radio button format. For example, Owl Publishing likes to track the way it sends individual renewal notices. The company sends renewal notices by one of three carriers: U.S. Mail, Federal Express, or UPS. You could use a drop-down list to represent these three choices, but for this example, radio buttons are used instead. To set up the buttons, follow these steps:

1. Switch to Design mode by opening the View menu and choosing Design, clicking Design on the action bar, or choosing Design from the status bar.
2. Select the field you want to modify. For this example, use the MAIL TYPE field.
3. Open the InfoBox for the field object you want to convert to a radio button type by selecting Object Properties from the shortcut menu or by double-clicking the object. You can also open the InfoBox by selecting the object and clicking the Change Object Properties SmartIcon, or by opening the Object menu and choosing Object Properties. Click the Basics tab to switch to the Basics page.
4. From the Data Entry Type drop-down list, select Radio Buttons. The Define Radio Buttons dialog box opens. (It looks like the Define Radio Buttons dialog box shown in figure 4.12, except that it's missing the field selection list.)
5. Enter the clicked values and button labels. For this example, enter **`U.S. Mail`** for the first clicked value and button label; **`Fed Express`** for the second clicked value and **`Federal Express`** for the button label; and **`UPS`** for the third clicked value and button label. When you're finished, the Define Radio Buttons dialog box should look like figure 4.13.

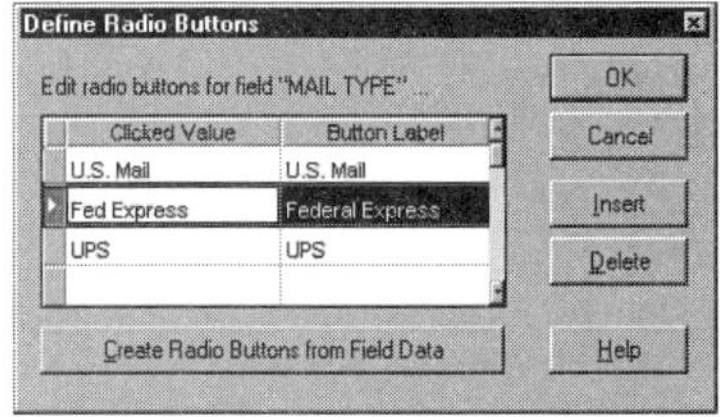

Fig. 4.13

This Define Radio Buttons dialog box is completed for the MAIL TYPE field object.

6. Click OK to return to the form with the new radio buttons in place (see fig. 4.14).
7. Open the File menu and choose Save Approach File to save the changes to your form.

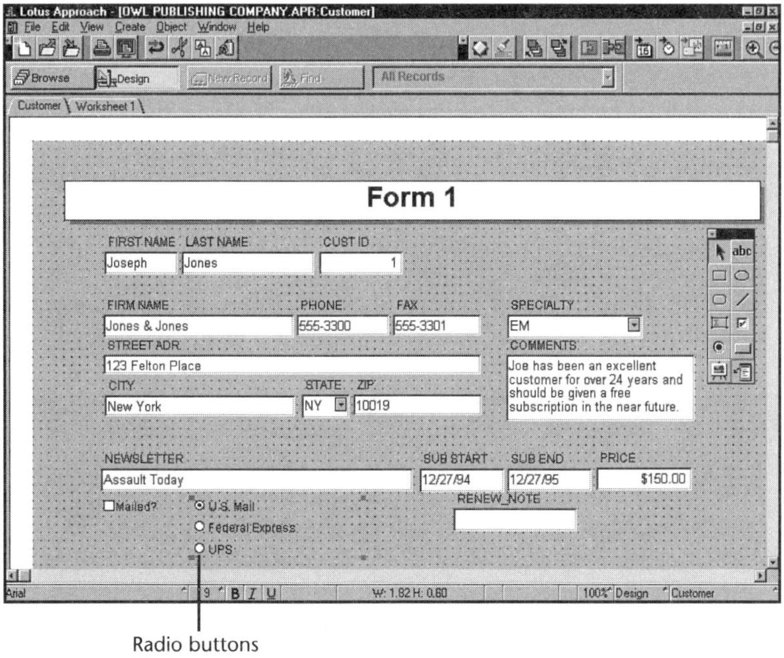

Radio buttons

Fig. 4.14

The finished radio buttons represent ways of sending out renewal notices.

To see the effects of your work, select the Draw Fields icon from the tools palette. Drag a field object rectangle on the form next to the new radio buttons. Select MAIL TYPE as the database field from the list of fields in the object's InfoBox. Return to Browse mode. Try clicking one of the radio buttons. Notice that the clicked value you assigned in the Define Radio Buttons dialog box now appears in the MAIL TYPE field on the form. The MAIL TYPE field object displays the value that's actually stored in the database when you click one of the associated buttons.

> **Note**
>
> To modify the attributes of a previously defined radio button field object, click the Define Buttons button in the radio button's InfoBox to reopen the Define Radio Buttons dialog box.

Reordering and Moving Radio Button Sets. A radio button field object consists of a set of radio buttons stacked vertically as a group of objects on your form. You may want to change the order or placement of these radio buttons on your form, or even ungroup them and place each one of the radio buttons separately.

Reordering the radio button values in the Define Radio Buttons dialog box causes Approach to rearrange the order of the radio buttons on the form. From the Define Radio Buttons dialog box, follow these steps:

1. Click the button at the left end of the value you want to move in the list. A right-facing triangle appears in the highlighted button.

2. Drag the value to the position you want in the list (the mouse pointer changes to a hand shape). Approach indicates the proposed insertion point of the value in the list with a dark bar that appears between two values. Approach will insert the moved value when you release the mouse button.

You can also move a group of radio buttons directly on the form. You can click and drag the group to relocate it, but you can't change the layout of the radio buttons.

You can break up a set of radio buttons into individual objects so that you can put each one anywhere you want. To ungroup the radio button group, in Design mode click the group and then open the Object menu and choose Ungroup. After you ungroup the radio buttons, you can move each one around the form independently.

Tip

Even when ungrouped, a radio button set still operates as one object on the form—selecting one radio button deselects all the others. Keep this in mind when moving the buttons independently so that the user of your form will not be confused. For example, you might arrange the radio buttons across the bottom of the screen rather than leave them in a stacked block, but they still are seen as a group by the user. You could also use color to keep them "grouped" in the eyes of the user.

When radio buttons are ungrouped, Approach no longer displays them in a single Define Radio Buttons dialog box. Instead, each radio button object has an InfoBox from which you can modify the Clicked Value and Button Label by clicking the Define Buttons button to open the Define Radio Buttons dialog box.

Once you've arranged the radio buttons the way you want them, you can regroup them so you can work with the buttons as a single object. To regroup, select the radio buttons and then open the Object menu and choose Group (Chapter 3, "Building Data Input Forms," explains how to select multiple objects).

Creating Radio Buttons from Database Values. You can create a set of radio buttons from data already entered into a database field. This is especially useful when converting a field object representing that field to a radio button format.

To create a set of radio buttons from database values, click the Create Radio Buttons from Field Data button in the Define Radio Buttons dialog box. If the form field object was of any type except a drop-down list or a field box & list, Approach populates the clicked value lines of the Define Radio Buttons dialog box with the values in that database field. The button label defaults to the clicked value, but you can modify the label if you want.

If your form field object was previously a drop-down list or field box & list, Approach automatically creates the radio buttons with the same values as the drop-down list without using the Define Radio Buttons dialog box. The label on each radio button corresponds to the drop-down list value.

Using Read-Only Fields on a Form

Defining a field object as "read only" on a form can often be helpful. If a field is in read-only format, the user can view the information in that field but can't change it. You can use this procedure, for example, when showing default text-formatted fields with their associated check boxes and radio buttons. That way, the set of buttons is used to enter values into the field, and the text-formatted field displays those values without enabling the user to type a value that isn't represented by a button.

Owl Publishing wants its employees to use the U.S. Mail, Federal Express, and UPS buttons to enter MAIL TYPE values. The employees must not be able to enter a value in the MAIL TYPE field object that displays the database value. To change a field object on a form to read only, follow these steps:

1. Switch to Design mode by opening the View menu and choosing Design, clicking Design on the action bar, or choosing Design from the status bar.
2. Select the field object you want to change—for this example, the MAIL TYPE field object.
3. Open the InfoBox by selecting Object Properties from the shortcut menu or by double-clicking the object. You can also open the InfoBox by selecting the object and clicking the Change Object Properties SmartIcon, or by opening the Object menu and choosing Object Properties. Click the Basics tab to open the Basics page.
4. Select the Read-Only check box. The field object selected is now set to read-only on the current form.
5. Open the File menu and choose Save Approach File to save the changes to the form.

Setting Field Object Properties

After you place your field objects on the form, you can adjust the order in which the cursor moves through the fields. You can modify how the data in a form field object appears by changing the color, font, background, shadow, frame, label attributes, and other properties of the object. This is easily done when each field object is placed on the form by using the InfoBox, or it can be done later.

If many of your field objects are going to be similar in appearance, you can use the Apply Format SmartIcon to copy an object's format (line, color, and text properties) to another object. Click the object whose format you want to copy, click the Apply Format SmartIcon, and click the object(s) to which you want to copy the format.

You can also select Fast Format from an object's shortcut menu to copy that object's format to other objects. Click other objects to which you want to copy the format; then reselect Fast Format from any object's shortcut menu to turn off Fast Format.

Note

You can't use the Apply Format SmartIcon to apply another field's format to a grouped set of radio buttons or check boxes. However, you can use the Apply Format SmartIcon to apply a format to individual radio buttons and check boxes.

Setting the Tab Order of Fields

When you're entering data in Browse mode, you can move from field to field on the form by pressing the Tab key. By default, Approach sets the tabbing order on a new form from left to right, top to bottom.

After you create the form with its initial fields selected, Approach doesn't modify the tab order of the fields when you rearrange the field objects on the form. If you later rearrange the field objects on the form, you may find that the cursor jumps all over the screen as you press Tab. Also, any new field objects you add to a form are placed at the end of the tabbing order, regardless of their location on-screen.

On the Owl Publishing data input form, pressing Tab doesn't move through the fields in a logical order. Approach, however, lets you change the tabbing order so that the cursor moves through the fields on the form in a more organized fashion. To change the tabbing order, follow these steps:

1. Switch to Design mode by opening the View menu and choosing Design, clicking Design on the action bar, or choosing Design from the status bar.
2. Open the View menu and choose Show Tab Order. A check mark appears next to the menu option.

   On the form, a small numbered box appears next to each field to indicate the field's tabbing order (see fig. 4.15). Also, the action bar shows OK, Cancel, Revert, and Clear Tabs buttons.
3. To adjust the tabbing order, click a numbered square, backspace over the number, and then type a new number. Alternatively, you can click Clear Tabs on the action bar or double-click the right edge of a numbered square to erase the numbers in all the squares, and then click the squares in the desired tabbing order. New numbers appear in the squares as you click them. If you want, you can go back to the original tab order by clicking the Revert button on the action bar.

   For this example, double-click one of the tab order boxes to erase all the numbers, and then click the tab order boxes in the order shown in figure 4.16.
4. After adjusting the tab order, choose OK on the action bar or open the View menu and choose Show Tab Order to turn off the tab order boxes. (The check mark next to the menu option disappears.)
5. Open the File menu and choose Save Approach File.

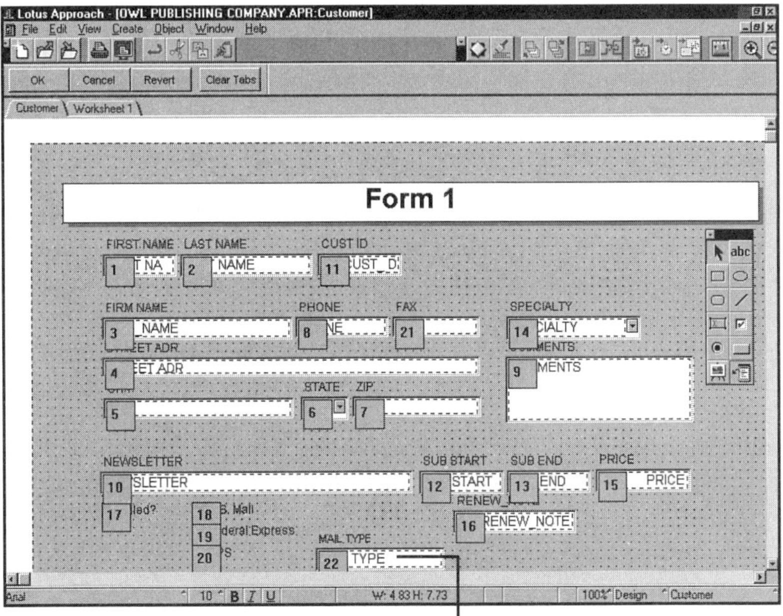

The MAIL TYPE field object is read-only, so it doesn't need to be in the tab order.

Fig. 4.15

The Owl Publishing form's tab order is indicated by numbered boxes.

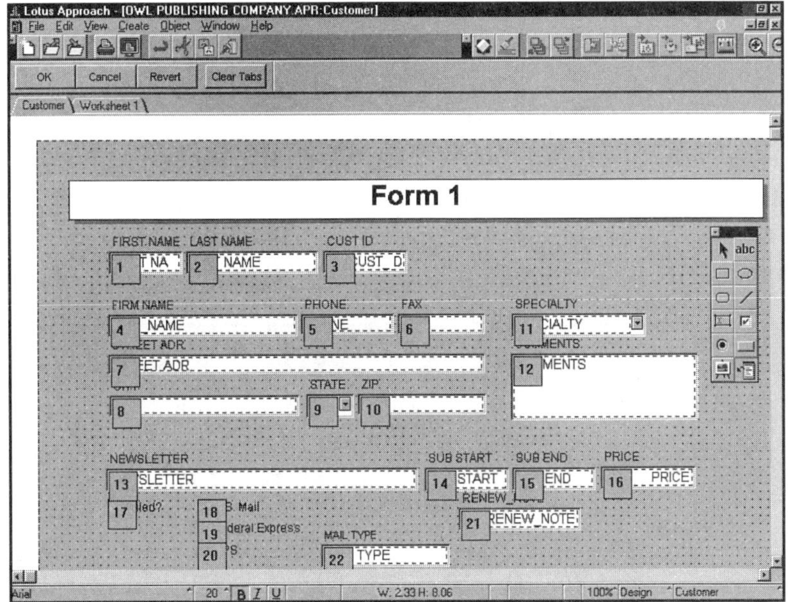

Fig. 4.16

The new tabbing order, represented by the new numeric order, has been set for the Owl Publishing Data Input form.

Excluding any object from the tab order is especially useful for objects you don't want the user to be bothered with. Text information and read-only field objects, as well as macro buttons, often aren't needed in the tab order, but they are accessible by clicking unless they are set to read-only.

To remove an object from the tabbing order, follow these steps:

1. Switch to Design mode by opening the View menu and choosing Design, clicking Design on the action bar, or selecting Design from the status bar.
2. Select the field object you want to exclude, or select several field objects to adjust multiple fields at once.
3. Open the InfoBox by selecting Object Properties from the shortcut menu or by double-clicking the object. You can also open the InfoBox by selecting the object and clicking the Change Object Properties SmartIcon, or by opening the Object menu and choosing Object Properties.
4. Click the Basics tab and deselect the In Tab Order check box. If you've selected multiple field objects to exclude, you'll need to select, and then deselect, the In Tab Order check box.

Adjusting the Appearance of Field Objects

You can format the values typed into or displayed from your database fields in field objects by changing font sizes and styles; text effects (for example, boldface and italic); and other properties such as text alignment, the relief effect (for example, raised or recessed lettering), and text color. You can emphasize a field object containing the most important data in a record, for example, by formatting the value it displays to appear in a large point size with boldface.

To format the appearance of the value in a field, follow these steps:

1. Switch to Design mode by opening the View menu and choosing Design, clicking Design on the action bar, or choosing Design from the status bar.
2. Select the field you want to modify, or select several fields to adjust multiple fields at once.

> **Tip**
>
> You can adjust the properties of multiple fields at one time by selecting the fields you want to modify and opening the InfoBox. The Settings For text box at the top of the InfoBox reads Multiple Objects.

3. Open the InfoBox by selecting Object Properties from the shortcut menu or by double-clicking the object. You can also open the InfoBox by selecting the object and clicking the Change Object Properties SmartIcon, or by opening the Object menu and choosing Object Properties.

4. Click the fonts tab (az) to move to the fonts page. Make sure the Data radio button is selected at the top of the page. Now, all the settings on this page affect the text that Approach displays in the field object (see fig. 4.17).

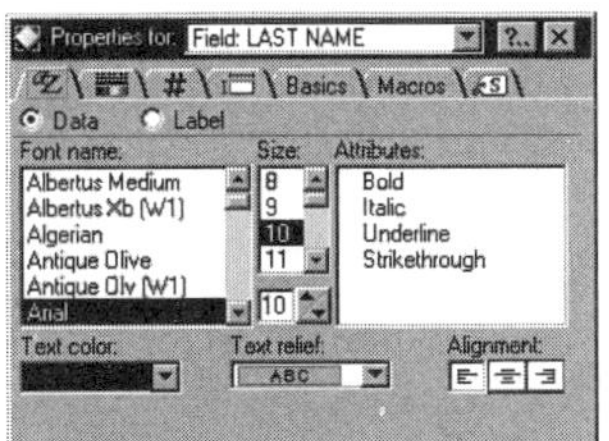

Fig. 4.17

The fonts page lets you assign font type, size, and styles.

> **Note**
>
> The settings for data on the fonts page don't affect the field object's label. For information on setting the attributes of the field label, see "Adjusting the Properties of Field Labels" later in this chapter.

5. Select the font you want to use from the Font Name list.
6. Select a style or effect from the Attributes list. Attributes include one or combinations of bold, italic, underline, and strikethrough.
7. Select the desired font size from the available point sizes in the Size list.

> **Tip**
>
> Fonts are measured in points. There are 72 points in one vertical inch. If you want a letter that's 1/2-inch tall, for example, set the size to 36 points.

8. Choose one of the following Alignment options to determine how the text will be aligned in the field:
   - The button on the left (the default) aligns text against the left edge of the field.
   - The middle button centers text in the field.
   - The button on the right aligns text against the right edge of the field.
9. If desired, select a text color from the color palette that Approach displays when you click the Text Color drop-down list.

> **Note**
>
> The T in the color palette stands for *Transparent*, or no color. Without a fill color, anything below an object in the stacking order shows through. To select an object with no fill color, you must click its border.

10. Select an option from the Text Relief drop-down list to change the look of your background and text. The default is two-dimensional or flat text on a flat background. The other options are to have the text "raised" or "recessed" relative to the background.

Adjusting Other Properties of Field Objects

In addition to adjusting font, size, style/effects, alignment, and color of field objects, you can change the background fill and shadow color, border weight and color, and frame style. You can also add borders to highlight a field object.

> **Note**
>
> For check box and radio button objects or groups, you can set only the fill color and shadow color as there is no border option. Instead, you can choose to change the relief of the little box or circle from a plain two-dimensional figure on the background to a "raised" or "recessed" appearance.

To adjust these properties, follow these steps:

1. Switch to Design mode by opening the View menu and choosing Design, clicking Design on the action bar, or choosing Design from the status bar.
2. Select the field objects you want to modify, or select several objects to adjust multiple objects at once.
3. Open the InfoBox by selecting Object Properties from the shortcut menu or by double-clicking the object. You can also open the InfoBox by selecting the object and clicking the Change Object Properties SmartIcon, or by opening the Object menu and choosing Object Properties. Click the color tab (with the colors on it) to move to the color page (see fig. 4.18).

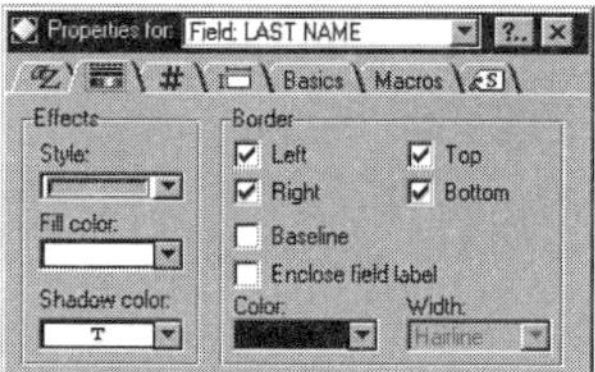

Fig. 4.18

Set colors and other graphical features from the color page.

4. Select the border width from the Width drop-down list. Available border widths range from hairline to 12 points (1/6 of an inch).
5. Select the border, fill, or shadow color from the Color, Fill Color, or Shadow Color drop-down lists. A color palette will appear. (The selection labeled T means transparent.)
6. Select a frame style from the Style drop-down list. The frame style specifies the format in which Approach draws the border around the selected field.

> **Tip**
>
> Some of the 3-D frame styles don't work well if the border is too narrow. If you want a 3-D frame style, select a border width of 3 points or greater.

7. Select the sides of the field on which you want Approach to draw borders by clicking the check boxes in the Border section. Besides drawing borders on the side of a field, you can add a text baseline by clicking the Baseline check box. A text baseline displays a line in the field object on which the text rests.
8. You can either include the label within the boundaries of the field object's border, or display the label outside the border. To include the label within the borders, check the Enclose Field Label check box.

Adjusting the Properties of Field Labels

You can adjust the properties of a field label using the field object's InfoBox. These properties include the font, size, attributes, alignment, text, color, relief, and position of the label text.

To adjust the label properties of a field, follow these steps:

1. Switch to Design mode by opening the View menu and choosing Design, clicking Design on the action bar, or choosing Design from the status bar.
2. Select the field object whose label you want to modify.
3. Open the InfoBox by selecting Object Properties from the shortcut menu or by double-clicking the object. You can also open the InfoBox by selecting the object and clicking the Change Object Properties SmartIcon, or by opening the Object menu and choosing Object Properties. Click the fonts tab to move to the fonts page.
4. Select the Label radio button at the top of the font page (see fig. 4.19). Adjust the label's font, size, attributes, alignment, color, and text relief as described earlier in "Adjusting the Appearance of Fields."

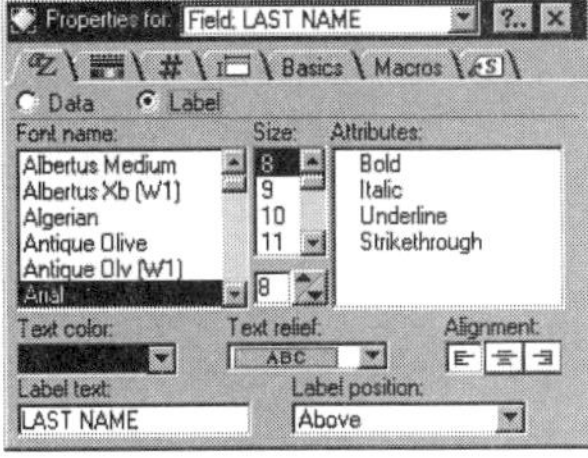

Fig. 4.19

Change the label properties from the font page.

5. If desired, change the text of the label by typing your changes into the Label Text box. The label text appears next to the field object on the form.

> **Note**
>
> If you select multiple field objects, you can't modify the label text. Also, if you select a grouped set of check boxes or radio buttons, you must click the Define Buttons button in the Basics page to open the dialog box (Define Check Boxes or Define Radio Buttons) that allows you to modify the check box or radio button labels.

6. Select the label position in relation to the field object from the Label Position drop-down list. You can locate the label above or below the field, or to the left or right of the field. You can also select No Label from this list to turn off the label display.

So far, the fields on the sample Owl Publishing data input form have been labeled by default, using the name of the field in the database. You can customize these field labels so that they're more descriptive and look less computer-like. Follow the preceding steps to format the labels to look like those in figure 4.20.

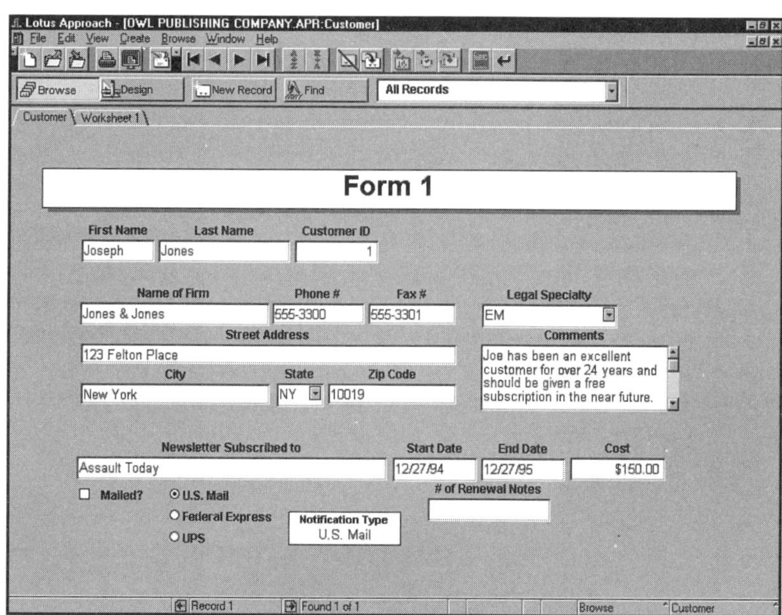

Fig. 4.20

The field labels on the Owl Publishing form are now centered above the fields and are more descriptive of the content.

Formatting the Display of Field Values

Approach can display the data you type into (or display from your database in your field objects) in a wide variety of formats. These formats affect the appearance of date, time, numeric, currency, and text values. You can change the display format of a field at any time. Changes affect the display format of new records and existing records on the form.

> **Note**
>
> The format changes discussed in this section affect only the appearance of the data. They normally don't modify how the data is stored in the database. However, if a text field is formatted as UPPER and Show Data Entry Format is on, Approach writes the data to the database in all uppercase (capital) letters.

To change the display format of field object values, follow these steps:

1. Switch to Design mode by opening the View menu and choosing Design, clicking Design on the action bar, or choosing Design from the status bar.
2. Select the field object you want to format. (When adjusting field object formatting, you can't select multiple field objects.)
3. Open the InfoBox by selecting Object Properties from the shortcut menu or by double-clicking the object. You can also open the InfoBox by selecting the object and clicking the Change Object Properties SmartIcon, or by opening the Object menu and choosing Object Properties. Switch to the format page by clicking the format tab (#), as shown in figure 4.21.

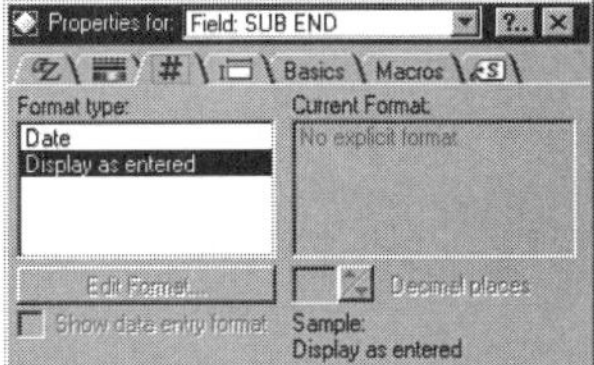

Fig. 4.21

For a field defined as a date in your database, the only format options allowed are Display as Entered and Date.

4. Choose one of the field formats from the Format Type drop-down list. Depending on the selection you make, Approach makes additional options available in the InfoBox. The format types are
   - Display as entered (default)
   - Currency
   - Date
   - Time
   - Numeric
   - Text

   (These formatting options are discussed in the following sections of this chapter.)
5. If you want Approach to display the data-entry format in the field object on the form as you enter data, check the Show Data Entry Format check box, if the Date format is selected. If this check box isn't checked, Approach doesn't display the selected format during data entry, but does reformat the field data once you move to the next field.

> **Note**
>
> The Show Data Entry Format check box is available in every format except Display as Entered.

Using the Display as Entered Setting

The Display as Entered selection displays the value in the exact way that you entered it. Use this button to disable any other format you've selected.

Using the Currency Setting

The Currency selection displays the list of countries for which formatting is provided. Select the country (Canada, Germany, Mexico, Netherlands, United Kingdom, or United States) and set the number of decimal places (default 0, maximum 8).

Going to the Owl Publishing example, you can format the Cost field object as a dollar amount. To do so, follow these steps:

1. Switch to Design mode by opening the View menu and choosing Design, clicking Design on the action bar, or choosing Design from the status bar.
2. Select the Cost field object.
3. Open the InfoBox by selecting Object Properties from the shortcut menu or by double-clicking the object. You can also open the InfoBox by selecting the object and clicking the Change Object Properties SmartIcon, or by opening the Object menu and choosing Object Properties. Click the # tab to move to the format page.
4. Select Currency from the Format Type list.
5. From the Current Format drop-down list, select United States. Also set the number of decimal places by scrolling the Decimal Places scroll box up to 2.
6. Open the File menu and choose Save Approach File.

The Cost field now displays numbers using the new format.

To precisely set up a unique format for your currency, select the Edit Format button in the InfoBox; the Edit Format Dialog Box appears. Edit your format code as discussed later in the section "Numeric Format."

Using the Date Format Setting

Approach offers you a lot of flexibility in setting up date display formats. You can represent dates as 05 Feb 1996; 2/05/96; Saturday, February 5, 1996; 2nd Quarter; and so on. After choosing the date selection, you can determine the order in which parts of the date are displayed, the format of each part, and the character that separates them. You even can specify your own date format string.

Choosing the Date Order. To select the order of appearance of the day, month, and year in a date field object, choose one of the 16 selections in the Current Format drop-down list: Day-Month-Year (common European format), Month-Day-Year (common American format), Year-Month-Day, or another format (see fig. 4.22).

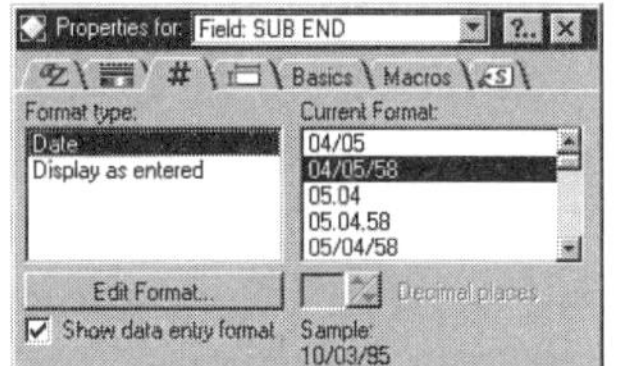

Fig. 4.22

You can select exactly how you want the date displayed.

Using Edited Date Formats. To use a date format other than those discussed in the preceding sections, choose the Edit Format button to display the Edit Format dialog box (see fig. 4.23). The Current Format shows the format you selected; the Format Code text box shows the code that resulted in the Current Format, and the Sample area shows the effect of any changes you make in the Format Code text box.

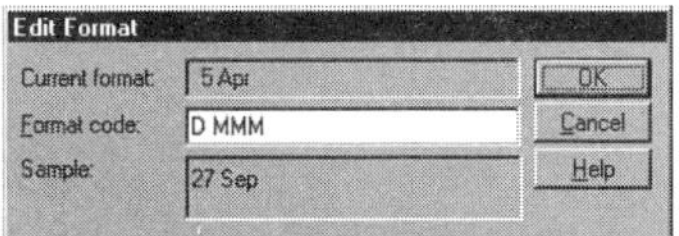

Fig. 4.23

The Edit Format dialog box lets you customize a field object's format at a very detailed level.

Each date format in the Current Format Codes list and the Format Code text box is divided into several parts. You can use the format code 444QuarterMMMMDDDDYYYY, which in practice may also include spaces and separator characters such as the slash (/) or dash (–), to illustrate what these parts mean:

- The numeric part of the date format entry (444) serves two purposes: it breaks the year into periods (in this case, quarters, indicated by the use of 4s) and indicates the place in the date format at which the period number (such as First) appears.
- The explanatory text part of the date format entry (Quarter) often indicates the type of period being used (such as Quarter); it can be used for any purpose you want, however.
- The month part of the date format entry (MMMM) indicates the month.
- The day part of the date format entry (DDDD) indicates the day.
- The year part of the date format entry (YYYY) indicates the year.

In Approach, the year can contain up to four periods. The value chosen for the numeric part of the date format entry indicates how many periods are to be used. Values from 2 to 4 are valid:

2: Semiannual (half a year)

3: Trimesters (thirds of a year)

4: Quarters (quarters of a year)

The chosen value can be repeated several times to change the appearance of the period number. A single-digit format entry (4) uses just the period number (2, 3, or 4); a two-digit format entry (44) uses the corresponding abbreviation (1st, 2nd, 3rd, or 4th); and a three-digit format entry (444) uses the full word (First, Second, Third, or Fourth). If you use a three-period year (rather than traditional quarters), entering 3 yields period numbers 1, 2, or 3; entering 33 yields period abbreviations 1st, 2nd, or 3rd; and so on.

The explanatory text part of the date format string allows you to sandwich text between the period and the year. This text is normally used to indicate the name of the periods into which you've broken up the year (such as Quarters) or to provide an abbreviation of the period (such as Q for quarters).

> **Note**
>
> The explanatory text can be any word that doesn't contain the letter D, Y, or M. Approach reserves these three characters for another type of date string (explained later in this section). If the text you want to use contains the letter d, y, or m, in lower- or uppercase, you must enclose the text in double quotation marks.

The final part of the date format string represents the year in one of two formats: YY and YYYY. Entering **YY** displays a two-digit year, ignoring the century (96). Entering **YYYY** displays the full year (1996).

If the date value is Dec. 27, 1996, for example, and you enter a custom date format of **444 Quarter YYYY**, the date displays as `Fourth Quarter 1996`.

> **Note**
>
> You can type the parts of the date format string in any order. The format string YYQ444 is valid, for example, and displays Dec. 27, 1996, as `96QFourth`.

You can also type a date format string that uses *d* to represent date, *m* to represent month, and *y* to represent year (dd/mm/yy, for example). The number of characters you use for each part of the date (date, month, and year) determines the display characteristics for that part. Table 4.1 shows the valid entries and their meanings.

Table 4.1 Date Format Characters in Month/Date/Year Format Strings

Character	Description
d	Displays day using minimum necessary number of digits
dd	Displays day using two digits (adds a leading zero to single-digit dates)
ddd	Displays day abbreviation (such as `Sat`)

Character	Description
dddd	Displays full day name (such as `Saturday`)
m	Displays month number using minimum necessary number of digits
mm	Displays month number using two digits (adds a leading zero to single-digit months)
mmm	Displays month abbreviation (such as `Feb`)
mmmm	Displays full month name (such as `February`)
yy	Displays year using two digits (no century)
yyyy	Displays year using four digits (includes century)

You can embed other characters as separators in the date string (such as – or /). You also can type the d, m, and y character strings in any order (mm/dd/yyyy or yy/mmmm/dd, for example). Character strings containing m, y, or d must be enclosed in double quotes (for example, "The Year of Our Lord "YYYY" A.D.").

Using the Time Format

The Time option lets you format a field object for 12- or 24-hour (military) time, choose a character to separate the different parts of the time, and specify values for Approach to use to designate morning times and afternoon times.

A Current Format list lets you choose how exact you want the time display to be (see fig. 4.24). The options vary from displaying time accurate to the hundredth of a second (**`2:03:45.23 h`**) to displaying just the hour (**`2 PM`**).

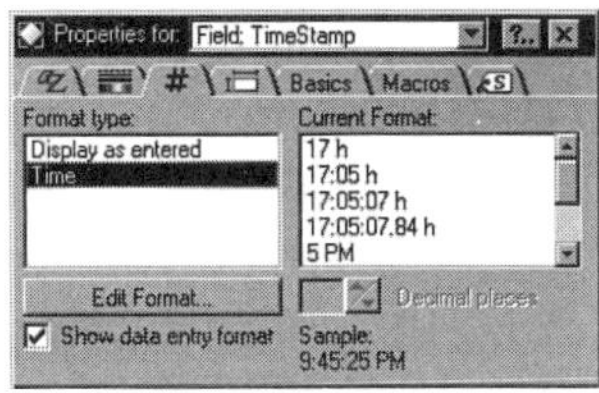

Fig. 4.24

Choose how much time to display from the Current Format list.

You can also choose the Edit Format button to select the formatting options you need.

To format the time for 12- or 24-hour time format, make the appropriate selection from the Time radio buttons. If you select 12-hour, Approach allows you to type the morning and afternoon time designators (AM and PM are the defaults) into the Time Suffix boxes. If you choose 24-hour, Approach lets you type a single designator (default is "h") into the Time Suffix text box.

Tip

You can leave the single time suffix blank, because time expressed on a 24-hour clock normally doesn't have a qualifier such as AM or PM.

Type the character you want to use to separate the various portions of the time (for example, to separate the hours from the minutes) into the Time Separator text box.

Using the Numeric Format

Choose Numeric from the Format Type list to format a numeric field object. You can use the Current Format list box to choose a common numeric format (see fig. 4.25). These formats include fixed, general, percent, percent with decimals, scientific, Social Security, telephone number, and ZIP code. You also can type your own custom format by selecting the Edit Format button to open the Edit Format dialog box. In the Format Code text box, use the characters detailed in the following sections.

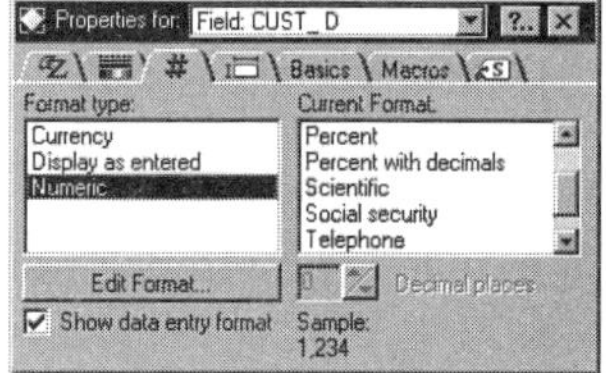

Fig. 4.25

Choose a numeric format from the list based on the type of data your field contains.

You can embed separator characters in a numeric format. Two useful numeric formats in the list box that use separator characters are the telephone number ((###)" "000-0000) and Social Security number (000-00-0000) formats.

The characters used to format numeric entries are zero (0), number or pound sign (#), decimal point (.), comma (,), semicolon (;), and percent sign (%). You can use quotation marks to embed special characters (such as spaces) in a format string.

Comparison operators, such as = and >, can also be used in a format string to check the number of digits entered and to choose a different format depending on the length of the data entered.

Zero. Zeroes (0) specify the number of decimal places to the right of the decimal point and the minimum number of digits to the left of the decimal point. Any unused placeholders to the left or right of the decimal point are shown as zeroes (with a 000 format, for example, the entry **9** appears as `009`).

Number Sign. Number or pound signs (#) also specify the number of digits on either side of the decimal point. With number signs, however, any unused placeholders remain blank (with a ###.# format, for example, the entry **9** appears as 9).

Decimal Point. The decimal point (.) specifies the location of the decimal point in a numeric string. With a format of #00.0#, for example, the numeric entry **9** is displayed as `09.0`.

Comma. The comma (,) specifies the presence of thousands separators (if zeroes or number signs enclose it). The number 9049, for example, when formatted as ##,##.#, is displayed as `9,049`.

> **Note**
>
> Notice that the actual location of the thousands separator in the string doesn't matter—Approach locates the thousands separator in the appropriate place.

Semicolon. The semicolon (;) separates a numeric format string into two separate parts. When a semicolon is used, the string to the left of the semicolon specifies the format for positive numbers and the string to the right of the semicolon specifies the format for negative numbers. The format ###.#;(###.#) displays negative numbers in the same general numeric format as positive numbers, but places them in parentheses. The number 9.2, for example, is displayed as `9.2`, but –9.2 is displayed as `(9.2)`.

Percent. The percent symbol (%) specifies that the number entered is to be multiplied by 100, and Approach displays a percent sign to the right of the resulting number. The numeric entry **.25**, formatted as ##.0%, appears as `25.0%`.

Comparison Operators. You can begin a format string with an integer and an equal sign (=), greater-than sign (>), or less than sign (<). The format string applies only to data that has the number of digits specified by the integer and the sign. For example, the format string =7 000-0000 applies standard phone-number formatting to a string of exactly 7 numbers.

You can combine multiple format strings that begin with an integer and =, >, or <. You must separate the multiple format strings with the vertical OR sign (¦). Suppose that a field has this format:

```
=7 000-0000¦<7 "x"######¦=10 (000)" "000-0000
```

If you enter a 7-digit phone number (for example, 5551212), Approach will display it as `555-1212`. However, if you enter less than 7 digits (for example, 12345), Approach will display the number as `x12345`. Finally, if you enter a 10-digit number (for example, **5105551212**), Approach displays it as `(510) 555-1212`.

Other Characters. You can embed any character other than those mentioned in the preceding sections as a symbol or separator in a numeric format string. One common character used is the dollar sign ($). The string $##0.00, for example, displays the number 8.45 as `$8.45`. If you use the format string $##0.00;($##0.00), the entry **8.45** appears as `$8.45`, but the entry **-8.45** would appear as `($8.45)`. This special display occurs because the right portion of the format string, used for negative numbers, has the symbols (,), and $ embedded in it. However, symbols other than currency, dashes, and parentheses must be enclosed in double quotes.

In similar fashion, the format (###)" "000-0000 displays the entry **5105551212** as a phone number: `(510) 555-1212`. A blank is embedded in the string between the) and the first zero.

Another useful numeric format, 000-00-0000, displays the entry **566849482** as a Social Security number: 566-84-9482.

Table 4.2 shows some common numeric formats and how they would represent some numbers.

Table 4.2 Examples of Number Formats

Format	5345.89	–43	1.2
#,##0.###	5,345.89	–43	1.2
#,#00.00;(#,#00.00)	5345.89	(43.00)	01.20
$#,##0.00	$5,345.89	–$43.00	$1.20
$#,##0.00;($#,##.00)	$5,345.89	($43.00)	$1.20

Returning to the Owl Publishing example, you can format the PHONE field without the parentheses by using the numeric format codes. To do so, follow these steps:

1. Switch to Design mode by opening the View menu and choosing Design, clicking Design on the action bar, or choosing Design from the status bar.
2. Select the PHONE field object.
3. Open the InfoBox by selecting Object Properties from the shortcut menu or by double-clicking the object. You can also open the InfoBox by selecting the object and clicking the Change Object Properties SmartIcon, or by opening the Object menu and choosing Object Properties. Click the # tab to move to the data format page.
4. Select Numeric from the Format Type list.
5. From the Current Format list, select the Telephone format.
6. Click the Edit Format button. The Edit Format dialog box appears.
7. Delete the parentheses from the Format Code and click OK.
8. Open the File menu and choose Save Approach File.

The PHONE field object now displays telephone numbers, using the new format.

Using the Text Format

You can set text formatting for a field object by selecting Text from the Format Type list. The Current Format list gives you choices for text formatting: ALL CAPITALIZED, all lowercase, First Capitalized, or Lead capitalized. First Capitalized capitalizes the first character of every word (good for fields that contain proper names). Lead capitalized capitalizes the first word in the text.

> **Note**
>
> The text isn't stored in the database field using the text formatting string to reformat it; the text usually is stored as entered by the user.

Working with Text Blocks

Approach allows you to add descriptive blocks of text to a form. You can use text blocks to give further details about the contents of a field; provide on-screen instructions; hold a page number, date, or time; or customize the form.

Inserting a Text Block

Text blocks often are used to place titles on a form. To create a title for the Owl Publishing form, follow these steps:

1. Switch to Design mode by opening the View menu and choosing Design, clicking Design on the action bar, or choosing Design from the status bar.
2. Click the existing Form 1 title and press the Delete key, or open the Edit menu and choose Cut. Approach removes the default title text box.
3. Click the Text tool on the tools palette, or open the Create menu and choose Drawing and Text. The pointer becomes an I-beam text cursor.
4. Place the I-beam at the upper left corner of the position you've chosen for the text block and then drag the pointer diagonally to the bottom right corner.

   For the Owl Publishing example, move the pointer to the empty area near the center top of the form. Click and drag an area about 2 1/2 inches long and about 1/2 inch high. (If not enough room is available in the area where you want to insert the text block, select and move fields on the form to create an empty space.)
5. Release the mouse button. The text block appears with a blinking cursor (see fig. 4.26).
6. Type the text into the text block. For this example, type **`Owl Publishing`** (see fig. 4.27).

   > **Note**
   >
   > The text wraps to the next line when it reaches the right edge of the text block.

7. Open the File menu and choose Save Approach File to save the changes to the form.

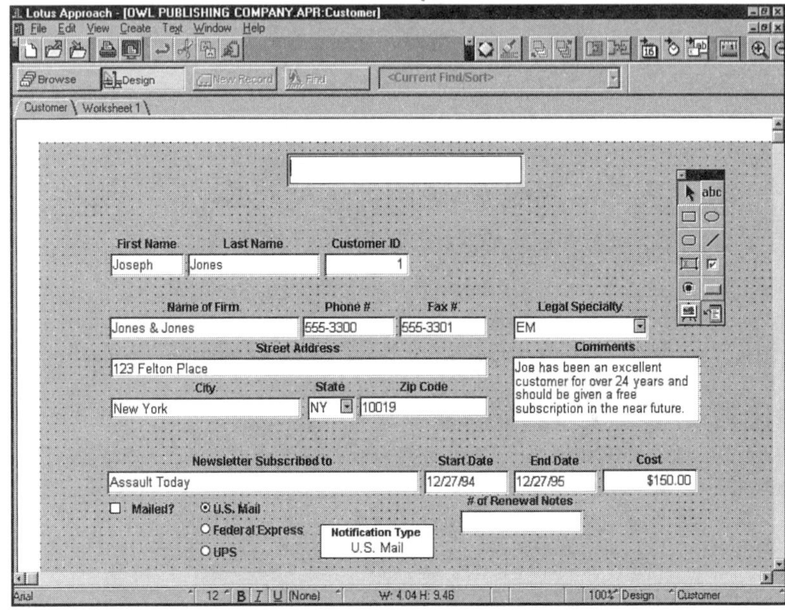

Fig. 4.26

A new text block has a blinking cursor in it, ready for you to enter its new contents.

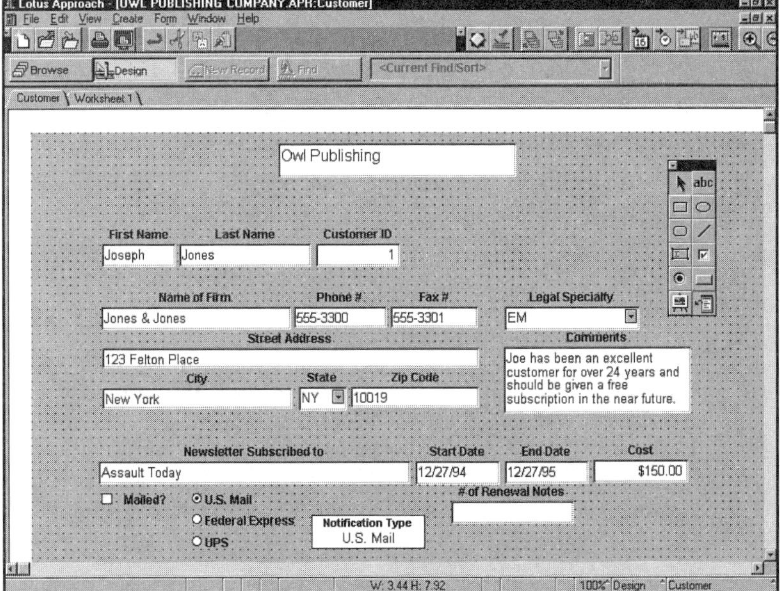

Fig. 4.27

The title block for the Owl Publishing form appears rather insignificant before further editing.

Editing a Text Block

You can edit the text in a text block. To switch to text-editing mode for the text block, select the Text tool from the tools palette and click the text block; or double-click the text block. Once you're in text-editing mode, you'll see the insertion point, a blinking cursor that indicates the place at which the next character you type will appear in the text. To move the insertion point in the text block, use the arrow keys or click at the desired insertion point.

> **Note**
>
> If you click a text block that's already selected (the sizing handles are visible), Approach places you in text-editing mode, in which you can modify the text in the text block (see the later section "Modifying Portions of Text in a Text Block"). To return to editing the properties of the text block, click somewhere else on the form and then click the text block again.

To select text with the mouse, drag over the desired characters. To use the keyboard, place the cursor next to the text you want to select, hold down the Shift key, and use the arrow keys to move the cursor over the characters to be selected.

After selecting text, you can cut, copy, or paste:

- To cut the text (removing it from the text block) and place it on the Windows Clipboard, open the Edit menu and choose Cut, or click the Cut SmartIcon.
- To copy the text to the Windows Clipboard (leaving the original text in its place), open the Edit menu and choose Copy, or click the Copy SmartIcon.
- To paste text that you've copied or cut, place the cursor at the desired insertion point; then open the Edit menu and choose Paste, or click the Paste SmartIcon.

To delete selected text, press Backspace or Delete.

You can also reposition the text in the text block by clicking and dragging the margin indicators and tabs that appear above the ruler line whenever you select a text block. Moving the left margin to the right, for example, would cause centered text to center to the right side of the text block between the new margin boundaries. If you used the Tab character in your text entry, the position of the tabs controls where these characters are placed. These controls appear only when you're showing the rulers while in Design mode.

Copying Text from Other Applications

You can also cut or copy text from another Windows application and paste it into the text block. Follow these steps:

1. Start the Windows application that contains the text you want to use.
2. Select the text in that application and place it on the Windows Clipboard. This task is normally accomplished by choosing the Cut (Ctrl+X) or Copy (Ctrl+C) option on the other application's Edit menu.
3. Switch back to Approach.
4. Select the Text tool and click the text block at the location where you want to insert the new text.

5. Open the Edit menu and choose Paste (Ctrl+V), or click the Paste SmartIcon to place the text into the text block.

Moving and Sizing Text Blocks

To resize a text block, click it to show the sizing handles. Drag any of the handles to adjust the size of the text block.

> **Note**
>
> If you've been typing into the text block, you must click elsewhere on the form first, and then click the text block to show the handles.

You can also resize a text block by using the text block's InfoBox. Click the Size tab to switch to the Size page of the text block's InfoBox. The Size tab has a box with sizing arrows on the top and left sides. Type the new width and height for the text block into the Width and Height text boxes using the units you have set for the ruler (inches or centimeters).

To move the text block, position the pointer inside the text block and when the little hand appears, click and drag the block to its new location. To adjust the location of the text block from the InfoBox's Size page, type the new location (according to the ruler in inches or centimeters) into the Top and Left text boxes.

Changing the Text Style of a Text Block

The title block entered earlier for the Owl Publishing form isn't quite right—it isn't centered, and the text is too small. It's easy to change the font, font style, size, alignment, or effects of the text in a text block by using the options in the Text Style dialog box. To modify the text block, follow these steps:

1. Switch to Design mode by opening the View menu and choosing Design, clicking Design on the action bar, or choosing Design from the status bar.
2. Open the InfoBox by selecting Object Properties from the shortcut menu or by double-clicking the text object. You can also open the InfoBox by selecting the text object and clicking the Change Object Properties SmartIcon, or by opening the Object menu and choosing Object Properties. Switch to the fonts page by clicking the fonts tab (az), as shown in figure 4.28. This fonts page is similar to the fonts page for fields discussed earlier in this chapter.
3. Make the appropriate changes in the InfoBox. You can change the font, size, attributes, alignment, and text color. You can also choose the line spacing (single, double, or triple space) from the Line Spacing buttons. For the Owl Publishing example, select Bold in the Attributes list box, 18 (or the nearest size your font offers) in the Size list box, and center from the Alignment buttons.

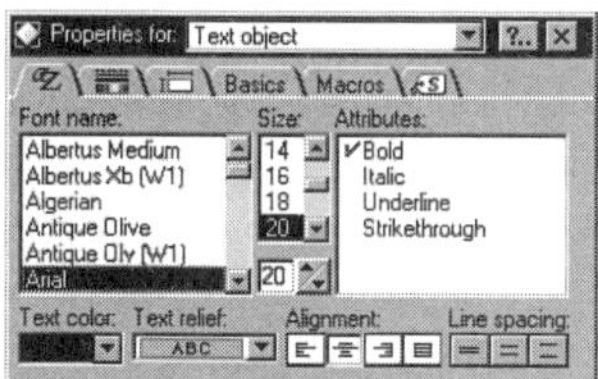

Fig. 4.28

You can easily change the font and style of a text block.

4. Open the File menu and choose Save Approach File to save the changes to the form.

Notice that the title block grabs your attention much more effectively now (see fig. 4.29). If necessary, resize the text block to see all the enlarged text.

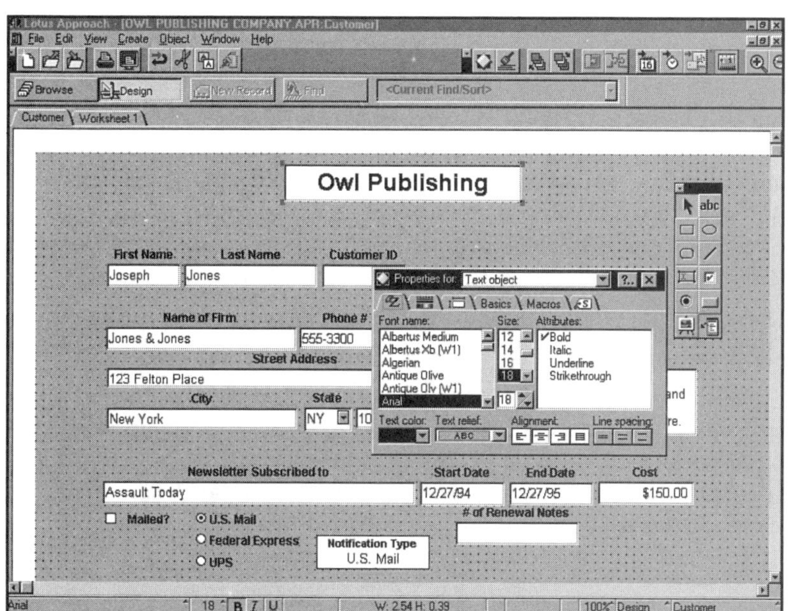

Fig. 4.29

The modified title block for the Owl Publishing form is much more effective in a larger type.

Modifying Portions of Text in a Text Block

You can modify selected portions of the text in a text block much as you would by using your favorite word processor. To do so, follow these steps:

1. Switch to Design mode by opening the View menu and choosing Design, clicking Design on the action bar, or choosing Design from the status bar.
2. To select a text block and enter text-editing mode, click the Text tool on the tools palette and then click the text block; alternatively, open the Create menu, choose Drawing and Text, and then click the text block. You can also select the text block by double-clicking it.

3. To select a portion of the text, click and drag the mouse pointer across the characters you want to modify.
4. Open the InfoBox by selecting Object Properties from the Object or shortcut menu or by clicking the Change Object Properties SmartIcon. The text editing InfoBox has a single page for changing the text attributes. The page is identical to the fonts page for text blocks discussed in the preceding section.

Tip

To use the shortcut menu for a text block, position the mouse pointer over the selected text when you press the right mouse button.

5. Adjust the font, size, attributes, alignment, color, and line spacing for the selected portion of the text in the text block.

Modifying Non-Text Properties of a Text Block

Careful selection of the colors and other properties you use in a text block can make the text block more effective. You can set the fill (background) and the pen (text) colors, border width and color, shadow color, and the frame style. For example, you can fill the title block on the Owl Publishing data-entry form to make it more attractive. To modify the other non-text properties of a text block, follow these steps:

1. Switch to Design mode by opening the View menu and choosing Design, clicking Design on the action bar, or choosing Design from the status bar.
2. Open the InfoBox by selecting Object Properties from the shortcut menu or by double-clicking the text block. You can also open the InfoBox by selecting the text block and clicking the Change Object Properties SmartIcon, or by opening the Object menu and choosing Object Properties. Select the color tab to move to the color page (see fig. 4.30).

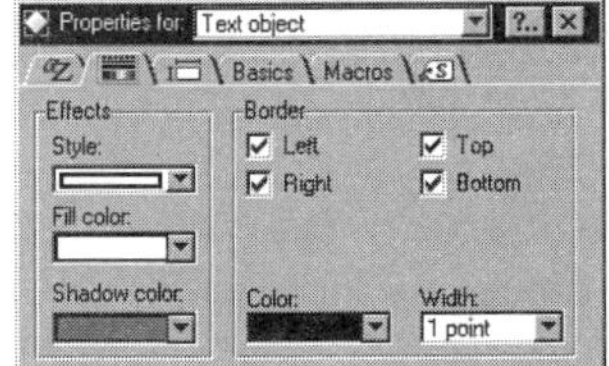

Fig. 4.30

Change colors and borders from the text block color page.

3. To set the border width, drop down the Width list and select the weight for the border. You can choose a border width from hairline to 12 point (1/6 of an inch).

4. To set the border color, drop down the color palette and select the color you want from among the available colors. Select T if you want a transparent (invisible) border.

> **Note**
>
> Text blocks always have borders—the only way to turn off the borders is to choose transparent (T) for the borders.

5. To set the fill color, drop down the Fill Color palette and select the color you want from among the available colors. For the Owl Publishing form, choose a lighter color that offsets the dark text.
6. To set the shadow color, drop down the Shadow Color palette and select the color you want from among the available colors.
7. To select a frame style, drop down the Style list and select the frame you want to use.
8. Open the File menu and choose Save Approach File to save the changes to the text block.

Inserting a Field into a Text Block

You can insert one or more fields into a text block so that the text of the block changes as the values in the field(s) change. Inserting a field into a text block is a way to display field information without allowing the user to edit the field.

To insert a field into a text block, follow these steps:

1. Switch to Design mode by opening the View menu and choosing Design, clicking Design on the action bar, or choosing Design from the status bar.
2. Click the Text tool on the tools palette or open the Create menu and choose Drawing and Text. The mouse pointer turns into an I-beam cursor.
3. Select the desired text block or create a new text block.
4. Move the insertion point to the left edge of the position in the text where you want to place the field.
5. Choose Insert and then Field Value from the Text menu or from the shortcut menu. The Add Field dialog box appears.
6. Select the field you want to place in the text block by clicking its name and then click OK. The name of the file and field appears in the text, enclosed in insertion symbols (<< and >>). If Show Data is selected, the field value appears instead of the insertion symbols.
7. Switch to Browse mode by opening the View menu and choosing Browse, clicking Browse on the action bar, or choosing Browse from the status bar. The value of the field for the current record appears in the text block (see fig. 4.31).

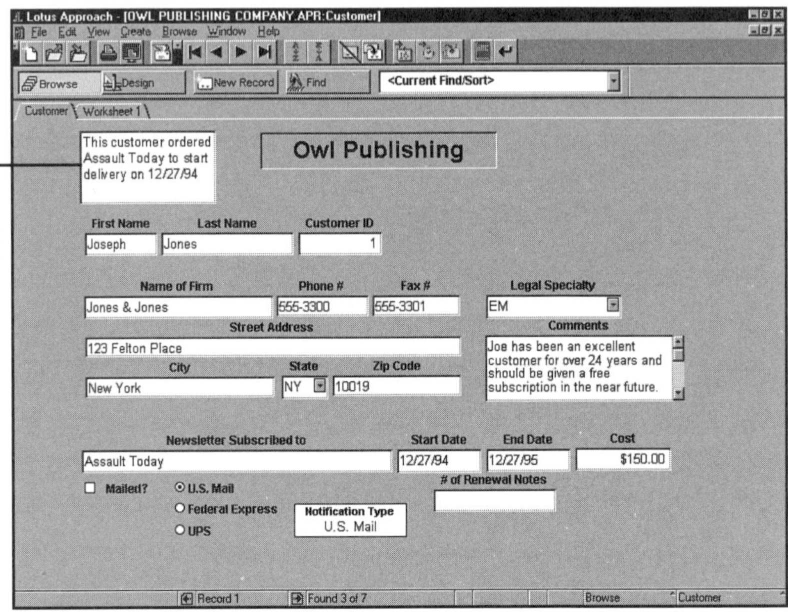

Fig. 4.31

The values of the inserted fields appear in the text block according to the database values for the current record.

A text box with two fields inserted (newsletter name and date)

> **Note**
>
> Summary-calculated fields don't show their results on the form in Browse mode. These types of fields display their results only in Preview mode.

Inserting a Date or Time into a Text Block

You can easily create a new text block that contains the date or time. To do so, follow these steps:

1. Switch to Design mode by opening the View menu and choosing Design, clicking Design on the action bar, or choosing Design from the status bar.
2. Open the Object menu and choose Insert. Choose Today's Date or Current Time from the submenu. You can also click the SmartIcon for Insert Today's Date or Insert Current Time.
3. Approach creates a new text block containing the requested value. You can type additional text into the text block and format the text, border, and background.

You can also insert the date or time into an existing text block. Owl Publishing, for example, wants to show today's date on its form. Follow these steps:

1. Switch to Design mode by opening the View menu and choosing Design, clicking Design on the action bar, or choosing Design from the status bar.
2. Click the Text tool on the tools palette or open the Create menu and choose Drawing and Text. The mouse pointer turns into an I-beam cursor.

3. Open the View menu and choose Show Ruler to display the rulers to help you place the text block.
4. Position the pointer at the desired location for the date, and then drag the pointer diagonally until the text block is the correct size. For this example, draw a text block about 2 inches long and 1/4 inch high in the upper left corner of the form, near the title block.
5. Type any text you want into the text block. For this example, type **`The date is:`** in the new text block. (If you want, you can skip this step and place the date in the form without any additional text.)
6. Choose Insert from the Text or shortcut menu, and then choose the item you want to insert (Date or Time) from the submenu. You can also click the SmartIcon for Insert Today's Date or Insert Current Time.

   For this example, choose Insert and then Date from the Text menu. The date code appears in the text block in Design mode (see fig. 4.32). When you switch to Browse mode, the actual date is displayed on the form (see fig. 4.33).
7. Open the File menu and choose Save Approach File to save your changes.

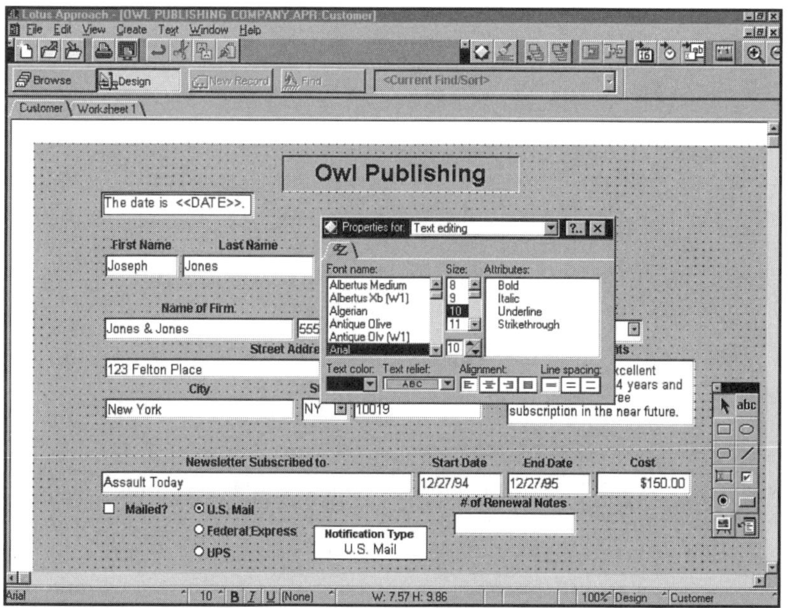

Fig. 4.32

The date field is inserted into a text block in Design mode with the insertion characters enclosing it.

Note

Changing the text block format—for example, changing the attributes to Bold—also affects the inserted field value.

Fig. 4.33

The current date appears in a text block in Browse mode.

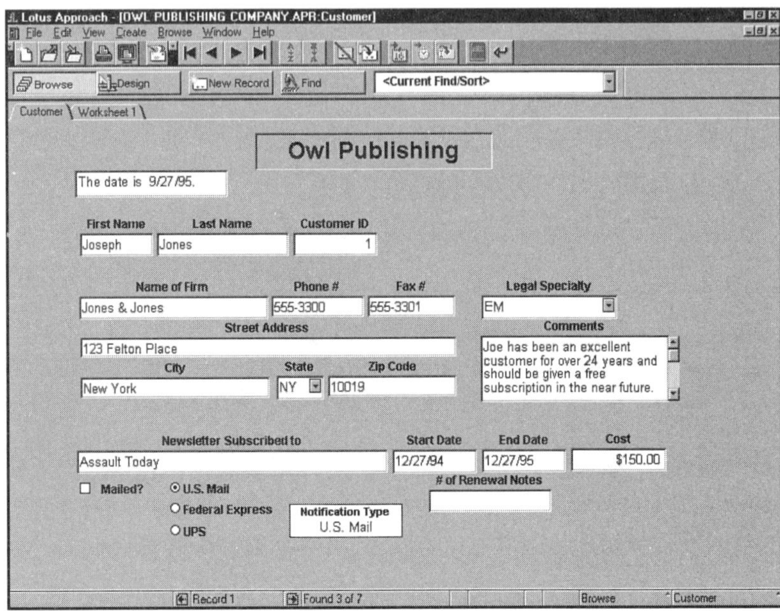

Using Graphics to Enhance Forms

Approach's simple graphics tools allow you to place shapes on your forms. These tools are available on the tools palette in Design mode. (If the tools palette isn't visible, open the View menu and choose Show Tools Palette.) You can use these drawing tools to draw squares, rectangles, rounded rectangles and squares, ovals, circles, and lines. When you click one of these tools, the pointer turns into a crosshair shape.

After you draw a graphics object, you can edit its fill color, drop shadow, and the width and color of its boundary line. You can also move and resize the graphics object.

Drawing Rectangles and Squares

To draw a rectangle or a rounded rectangle, choose the Rectangle or Rounded Rectangle tool. Position the pointer where the upper left corner of the rectangle should appear. Click and drag to the point at which you want the bottom right corner to appear, and then release the mouse button. The rectangle appears with sizing handles.

Tip

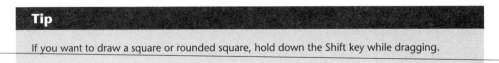

If you want to draw a square or rounded square, hold down the Shift key while dragging.

To add a rounded rectangle to the Owl Publishing form to box in the title, follow these steps:

1. Switch to Design mode by opening the View menu and choosing Design, clicking Design on the action bar, or choosing Design from the status bar.
2. Click the Rounded Rectangle tool.
3. Place the pointer on the upper left corner of the title box. The background fill color you added earlier makes this corner easy to find.
4. Hold down the left mouse button and drag the pointer to the bottom right corner.
5. Release the mouse button; the rounded rectangle appears (see fig. 4.34).
6. Open the File menu and choose Save Approach File to save the changes.

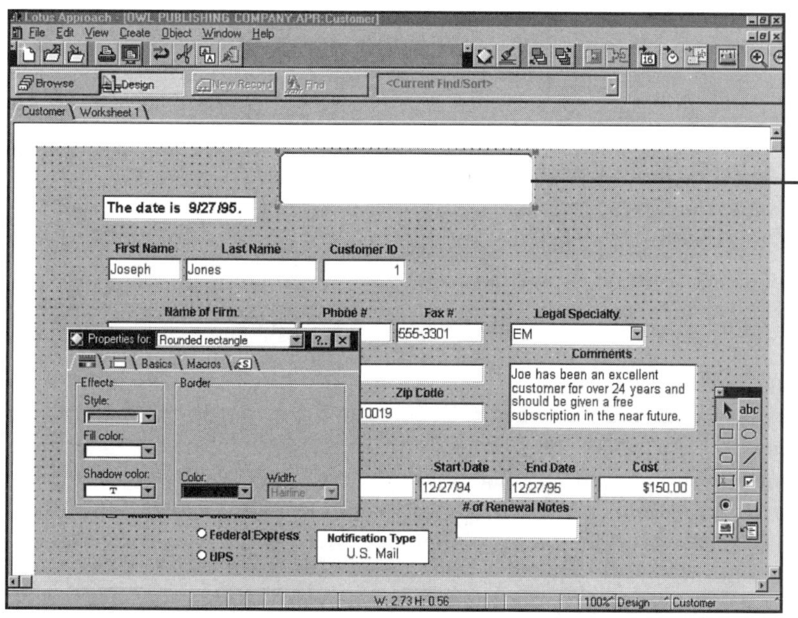

Fig. 4.34

Drawing a rounded rectangle around the title block covers the text temporarily.

Drawing Ovals and Circles

To draw an oval or a circle, choose the Oval tool. Position the pointer where you want the center of the circle or oval to appear. Click and drag diagonally until the oval or circle is the size you want, and then release the mouse button. The oval appears with sizing handles around its field object boundary, which appears as a rectangle surrounding the object.

> **Tip**
>
> If you want to draw a circle, hold down the Shift key while dragging.

Drawing Lines

To draw a line, choose the Line Drawing tool. Position the pointer where you want one end of the line to appear. Click and drag until the pointer reaches the other end of the line, and then release the mouse button. The line appears with sizing handles at either end.

> **Tip**
>
> If you hold down the Shift key while dragging, the line is constrained to 45-degree angles. It will shift around the starting point in 45-degree increments, easily helping you draw horizontal or vertical lines as well as other angled lines perfectly.

Moving and Sizing Graphics Objects

After you draw a graphics object on your form, you can modify its size and shape. To modify a graphics object, switch to Design mode and then select the object. Click any of the sizing handles that appear and drag to stretch the shape in the direction you want. You can also change the location from the size page of the InfoBox. To adjust the position of the graphics object, type the new location of the upper left corner of the object into the Top and Left text boxes.

To move a shape, click the shape's border (for a line, click the line) and drag the shape to its new location. For any filled shape (for example, a rectangle, rounded rectangle, or oval with a fill color other than transparent), you can click inside the shape and drag the shape to its new location. (The mouse pointer changes into an open hand shape when it's correctly positioned to move a shape.) You can also change the size from the size page of the InfoBox. To adjust the size of the graphics object, type the new width and height for the object into the Width and Height text boxes.

> **Tip**
>
> You can group graphics objects (including lines) into a single object to make moving and sizing them easier. To do so, select the objects and choose Group from the shortcut or Object menu.

Setting the Properties of Graphics Objects

You can adjust the border, fill, and shadow color for filled objects (for example, rectangles, rounded rectangles, and ovals) to make them stand out on a form. You can also adjust the border width and frame style.

To change these properties for filled graphics objects, follow these steps:

1. Open the InfoBox by selecting Object Properties from the shortcut menu or by double-clicking the graphics object. You can also open the InfoBox by selecting the graphics object and clicking the Change Object Properties SmartIcon, or by opening the Object menu and choosing Object Properties. Switch to the color page by clicking the color tab.
2. Select the border, fill, or shadow color from the Color, Fill Color, or Shadow Color palette. The T selection provides a transparent (invisible) color.
3. Select the border width you want from the Width drop-down list. The available widths are hairline to 12 points (1/6 of an inch).
4. Select a frame style for the border from the Style drop-down list.

To change the properties of a line, follow these steps:

1. Open the InfoBox by selecting Object Properties from the shortcut menu or by double-clicking the line. You can also open the InfoBox by selecting the line and clicking the Change Object Properties SmartIcon, or by opening the Object menu and choosing Object Properties. Switch to the color page by clicking the color tab.
2. Choose the line or shadow color from the Line Color or Shadow Color drop-down list palette.
3. Select a line width from the Line Width drop-down list. The available widths are hairline to 12 points (1/6 of an inch). To make the rounded rectangle around the Owl Publishing title block more distinct, select a 3-point line width.
4. Choose a line style from the Line Style drop-down list.
5. Choose Save Approach File from the File menu to save your work.

Working with Overlapping Objects

Because the rounded rectangle was the last object drawn in the Owl Publishing example, it completely covers the title text block. This is because it appears in a higher layer of the form than the title block and hides everything below it. To fix this problem, go into Design mode and select the rounded rectangle. Then open the Object menu, choose Arrange, and then choose Send to Back to move the rounded rectangle behind the title text block. Another solution is to choose a transparent fill color for the rounded rectangle so that the title block beneath it shows through.

If you haven't made the frame quite large enough, choosing Arrange and then Send to Back can cover part or all of the rectangle with the title text block. If you run into this problem, drag the sizing handles of the rectangle to make the object slightly larger.

If you used the Send to Back command, choose Arrange from the Object menu and then Bring to Front to restore the rectangle to its original layer.

To choose a transparent color fill, select the rounded rectangle. Open the InfoBox by selecting Object Properties from the shortcut menu or by double-clicking the rectangle. You can also open the InfoBox by selecting the rectangle and clicking the Change Object Properties SmartIcon, or by opening the Object menu and choosing Object Properties. Change to the Color page and open the Fill Color palette. From the available colors, select the box marked T (for Transparent) in the upper left corner of the palette. The title text now shows through, framed by the rounded rectangle border. Increase the border width to 4 points and set the border color to a deep blue (see fig. 4.35).

Also, just for fun, select and change the current date field to have a double border and black shadow so that it doesn't look like a data-entry field. Notice the difference this makes in figure 4.35!

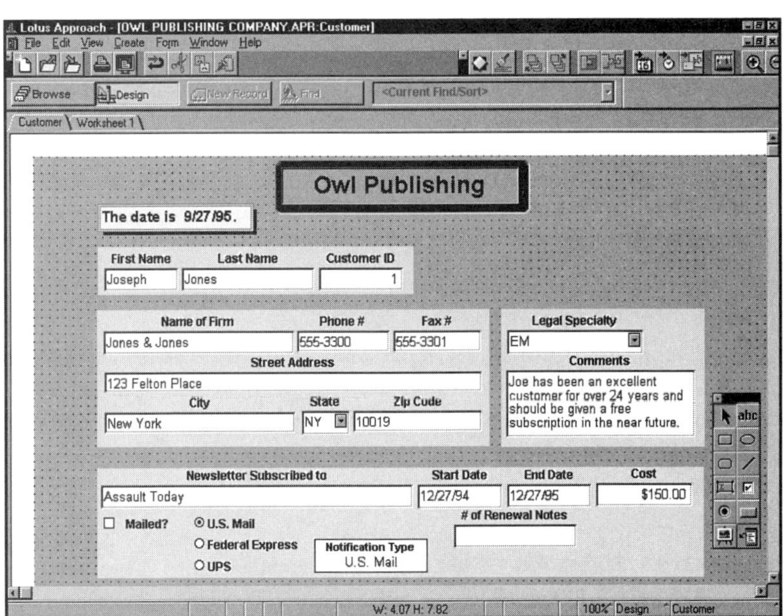

Fig. 4.35

The title bar now appears with its distinctive border frame.

Adding Illustrations to Forms

Approach also lets you place illustration files on your form, using several popular formats. To do so, you can use the standard Windows copy and paste operations, or you can paste an illustration directly from a file onto your form. The second option allows you to create and save an illustration with a drawing package and then import it into Approach. The following sections explain both methods for placing illustrations on a form.

Using Cut and Paste to Add Illustrations to Forms

To place an illustration on a form by using the standard Windows Clipboard cut, copy, and paste operations, follow these steps:

1. Start the application that contains the illustration you want to add to your form (or that you will use to create the picture).
2. Load or create the graphic and then select it.
3. Open the Edit menu and choose Cut or Copy to place the illustration on the Windows Clipboard.
4. Switch back to Approach.
5. Switch to Design mode by opening the View menu and choosing Design, clicking Design on the action bar, or choosing Design from the status bar.
6. Click the form at the location where you want to place the illustration.
7. Choose Paste from the Edit menu to place the illustration on the form.
8. Use the sizing handles to stretch or shrink the illustration, if necessary. You can also click in the picture and drag it to a new location. Use the size page of the InfoBox to set the location and size.

Pasting an Illustration onto a Form

To make the Owl Publishing form more attractive, you can put a logo in the upper right corner. The image used in this example is a .PCX file, but you can perform the same actions with any of the file types supported by Approach, including .BMP, .WMF, .TIF, .GIF, .TGA, .JPG, and .EPS files.

Choose a graphics file in any of the formats listed in the following steps. If you don't have a graphics file handy, create and save one by using Windows Paint.

To paste the illustration directly from a file, follow these steps:

1. Switch to Design mode by opening the View menu and choosing Design, clicking Design on the action bar, or choosing Design from the status bar.
2. Click the location where you want the illustration to appear. For the Owl Publishing example, click near the upper right corner of the form.
3. Open the Edit menu and choose Picture and Import. The Import Picture dialog box appears (see fig. 4.36).

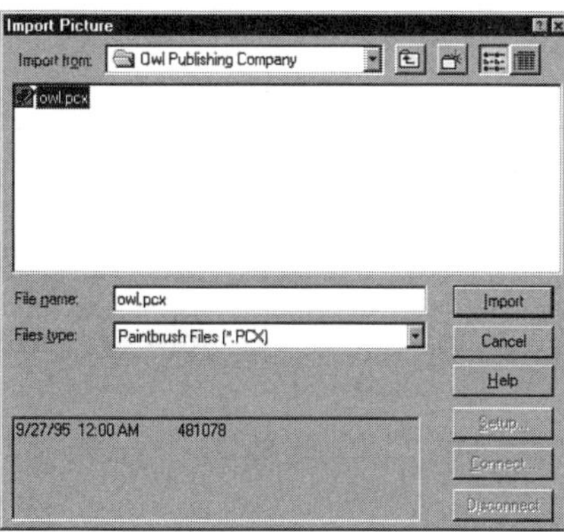

Fig. 4.36

The Import Picture dialog box lets you select any supported illustration file on your system for placement in an Approach view.

4. Use the folders and files box and the Import From drop-down list to select the folder and drive where your graphics file is stored.
5. From the Files Type drop-down list, select the file type of the picture you want to import.
6. Select the desired file from the folders and files list box below the Import From drop down list box.
7. Click OK. The illustration appears on your form.
8. Use the sizing handles to stretch or shrink the illustration, if necessary. You can also drag the picture to a new location, or use the size page of the illustration's InfoBox to type new values for the location and size.
9. Open the File menu and choose Save Approach File to save the changes.

Figure 4.37 shows what the finished form looks like with the owl logo added.

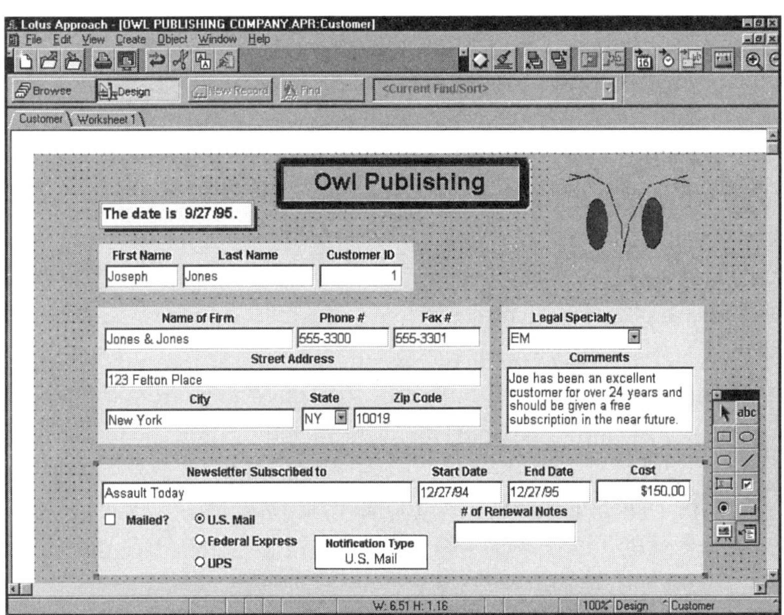

Fig. 4.37

An illustration of an owl's face, somewhat stylized, is pasted onto a form from a file.

From Here...

In this chapter, you learned to enhance your data-entry forms. You can now place text fields, radio buttons, check boxes, text blocks, and graphics on the form. You can adjust the color, border, shadow, and text attributes of these objects. You can also choose the display format for database field values on a form. You can edit the text in text blocks, adjust the properties of labels, and add illustrations from other applications to a form.

The concepts learned in this chapter apply to many other Design mode objects. For more information, refer to the following chapters:

- Chapter 7, "Creating Reports and Mailing Labels," explains how to use many of the techniques you learned in this chapter to build other types of views.
- Chapter 9, "Designing Advanced Forms," shows how to build more complex forms.
- Chapter 12, "Creating Advanced Reports," expands on Chapter 7 to show how to build advanced reports.

CHAPTER 5

Working with Your Data

As you work with your database, you'll spend the bulk of your time entering, finding, and sorting records. In this chapter, you learn how to create records and enter data into fields using Approach forms. This chapter focuses on the various types of field objects that Approach allows, and tells you how to enter data into each. You also learn how to move through your records and sort them in the order you want. After defining your database and laying out forms, you're ready to choose a form and to start entering data.

Note

You must use Browse mode to work with the data in your database.

In this chapter, you learn how to

- Access an Approach form for entering data
- Create, duplicate, update, and delete database records
- Enter data into the various field types, such as date and time fields
- Navigate through your database records by using the status bar, SmartIcons, and keyboard commands
- Sort your database records by using various criteria
- Spell-check your data by using Approach's built-in checker and dictionary

Accessing Forms

Because you can use Approach to create multiple forms, you need a way to switch between them. To switch from one form to another, click the form name you want from the view tab line. If you can't see the desired view tab because so many other view tabs are in the way, use the left and right arrows on the view tab line to scroll the tabs. You can also choose another form by selecting the form name from the button at the right end of the status bar. Clicking this button displays a list of available forms (as well as worksheets, crosstabs, reports, form letters, and mailing labels). Select the form you want from this list (see fig. 5.1).

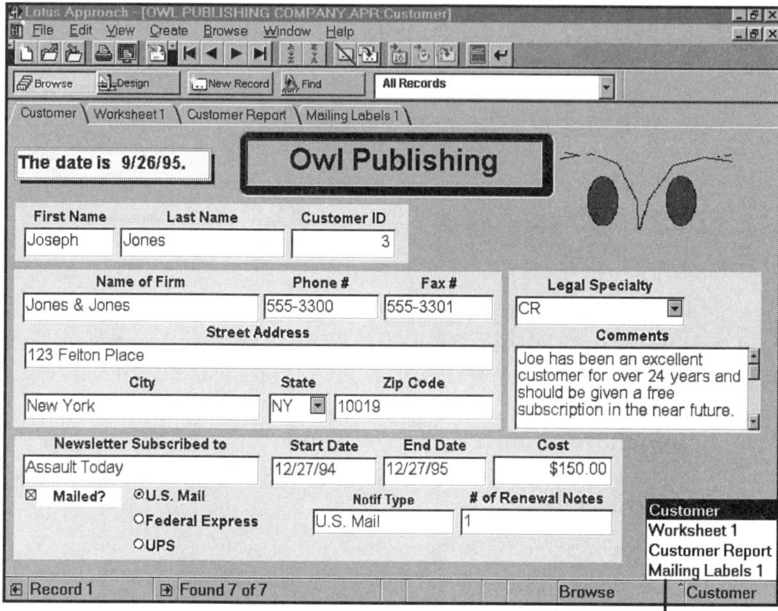

Fig. 5.1

Select a form by clicking the button on the far right of Approach's status bar.

Tip

If the view tabs aren't visible across the top of the screen, open the View menu and choose Show View Tabs.

Manipulating Records

Approach provides four ways to work with database records on a form. You can create a new record, duplicate an existing record, update an existing record, and delete an existing record.

Creating a New Record

After accessing the desired form, you can create a new record. To do so, click New Record on the action bar, press Ctrl+N, or open the Browse menu and choose New Record. Each time you create a new record, Approach presents you with a blank form in which to enter your data. When you've completed your data entry, save your record by clicking the Enter the Record SmartIcon or pressing Enter.

Duplicating a Record

Sometimes creating a new record is easier if you copy and modify an existing record. To do so, move to the record you want to copy by using the Record Forward or Record Backward SmartIcons (see "Navigating Through Your Records" later in this chapter for complete instructions), and then open the Browse menu and choose Duplicate Record. You can also click the Duplicate Current Record SmartIcon.

After you copy the record, make the necessary changes to the duplicate. Be sure to change any fields that were designated as Unique in the Validation section of the Field Definition Options dialog box. You can't duplicate the values contained in those fields (see Chapter 2, "Creating Database Tables," for details concerning this restriction). When you've completed your changes, save your record by clicking the Enter the Record SmartIcon.

Updating a Record

To update a record, move to the record you want to update and tab to or click the field you want to change. Type over the field contents, and Approach makes the change to your database. When you've completed your updates, save your record by clicking the Enter the Record SmartIcon.

Deleting a Record

To delete a record, move to the record you want to delete and click the Delete Record SmartIcon, or open the Browse menu and choose Delete Record. Approach asks whether you really want to delete the record. Choose No if you want to keep the record.

If your database uses a dBASE III+ or dBASE IV file type, deleting a record doesn't actually remove that record from the database file. The record is marked in a special way so that it no longer appears on-screen, but it remains in the database file and continues to take up space. To remove such records from the database file and recover the lost space, follow these steps:

1. From the File menu, choose User Setup and then Approach Preferences to open the Approach Preferences dialog box.
2. Click the Database tab to open the Database page.
3. Select the database name that needs space recovered. Click the Compress button in the dBASE and FoxPro Compression section of the Database panel. Click OK to execute the compression on the selected database.

Tip

You can also delete multiple records in Approach, but first you must perform a Find to generate a found set that includes all the records you want to delete (see Chapter 6, "Finding Records," for more information on this feature).

Moving Through Fields

On a form, the field object available for data entry has the focus. You can tell when a field object has the focus because the blinking text cursor appears in it. To move the focus to another field object, use one of the following methods:

- Move the mouse pointer to the field object you want and click it.
- Press Tab to move to the next field object in the tabbing order (see Chapter 4, "Enhancing Data Input Forms," for more information about setting the tabbing order). Press Shift+Tab to move to the previous field object in the tabbing order.
- If the Use Enter Key to Move or Tab Between Fields in Browse check box is selected in the General panel of the Approach Preferences dialog box, you can move between field objects by using the Enter key.

If the selected field object is a text-format field and has no database data showing in it, the cursor becomes a blinking insertion point, and you can begin typing your data.

Tip

To duplicate a value from the last newly created record, click the field object and choose the Duplicate Data from Previous Record SmartIcon, or open the Browse menu and choose Insert and Previous Value.

Entering Data into a Form

The process of entering data into a form is relatively straightforward. The data-entry technique used to enter data, however, depends on the format of the field object (text, check box, button, and so on).

Text Fields

To enter information in a text field object, simply type it. The length of the text to be entered can't exceed the length of the database field as specified in the Field Definition or Creating New Database dialog boxes. Approach warns you when you try to type more characters than the field can hold (see fig. 5.2). Most field objects on the Owl Publishing form (such as LAST NAME and FIRST NAME) are formatted as text field objects to display text database fields.

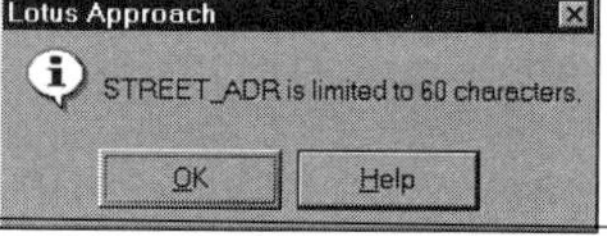

Fig. 5.2

Approach warns you when you type longer values than allowed.

Note

When you tab into a field object that already has data entered into it, the existing data will be selected for replacement (change color). If you only want to modify the existing data, use the mouse pointer to place the insertion point in the field where a change is needed, or press the End key to position your cursor at the end of the existing data in the field. Use the arrow keys to move left and right a character at a time. Whatever you type is inserted at the cursor. Use the Backspace or Delete key to remove any characters that are no longer needed.

If the Show Data Entry Format check box is selected in the Format page of a text field object's InfoBox, Approach displays the text you type in the specified format. If this check box isn't selected, the text takes on the specified format when you move to another field object.

The blinking insertion point indicates where the next character you type will appear. To move the insertion point, use the arrow keys or click the desired position.

Tip

Refer to Chapter 3, "Building Data Input Forms," for some tips on sizing form field objects to match the length of the fields in the database.

You can select text for replacement using either of the following techniques:

- Click and drag over the text you want to select.
- Use the arrow keys to position the blinking insertion point immediately to the right or left of the text you want to select, hold down the Shift key, and then use the arrow keys to select the text. You can also double-click a word to select just that word.

After you select text, you can delete it by pressing Delete or Backspace. You can also replace it by typing new text; whatever you type replaces the selected text.

You can cut or copy selected text to the Windows Clipboard by choosing Cut or Copy from the Edit menu. To place the contents of the Clipboard into the text at the insertion point, choose Paste from the Edit menu.

Numeric Fields

You can enter only numbers in numeric fields. (In the Owl Publishing database, numeric fields include COST and # OF RENEWAL NOTES.) Approach beeps when you try to enter non-numeric text into a numeric field if a data-entry format has been specified; otherwise, Approach warns you when you try to move to another field. If you mix numbers and letters, Approach warns you that the value entered isn't a number (see fig. 5.3) and refuses to accept the value.

Fig. 5.3

Approach warns you when you type a non-numeric value into a numeric field.

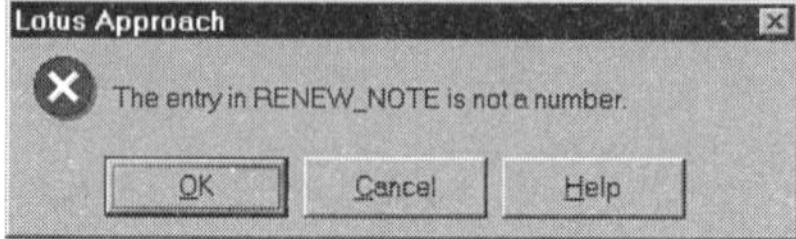

> **Note**
>
> If you need to mix numbers and letters, you must use a text-formatted field object. The exception to this rule is that you can create a numeric format string that includes non-numeric characters (for example, telephone numbers that contain parentheses).

The length of the number that you enter in a numeric field object can't exceed the database field length as specified in the Field Definition dialog box. Approach warns you that your entry is too long when you try to type more characters than a field can hold.

If the Show Data Entry Format check box is selected in the Format panel of a numeric field object's InfoBox, Approach displays the formatting characters and underlines to specify the maximum number of characters you can type (see fig. 5.4). If the check box isn't selected, Approach reformats the numbers you type into the correct format when you move to another field object.

Fig. 5.4

A numeric field object can display a line to indicate how many digits you can enter.

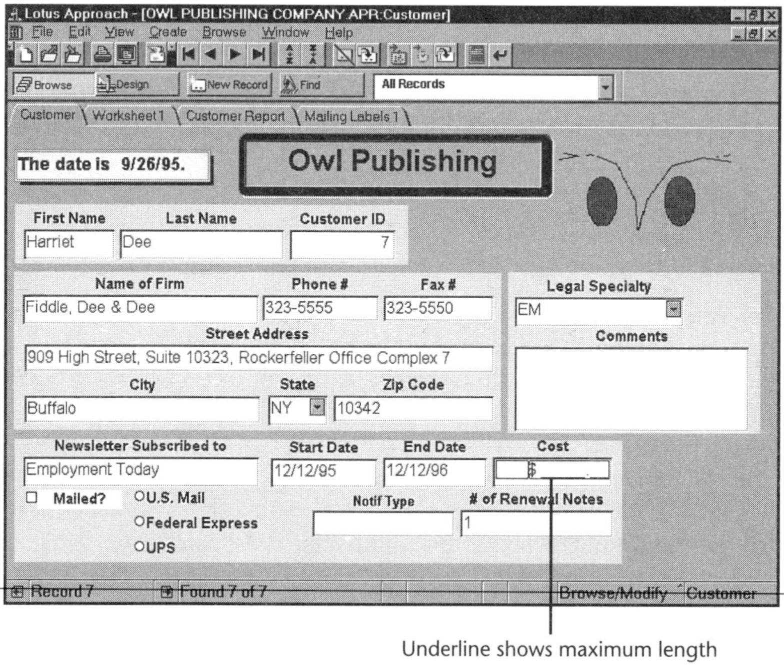

Underline shows maximum length

Date Fields

You must enter dates in the format set for short dates in the Windows 95 Regional Control Panel. If you select the standard U.S. short date format (mm/dd/yy), for example, you can enter up to 10 characters in the date field object, including the slashes and the full four-digit year. Approach displays the slashes for you—you don't need to type them unless you have the Show Data Entry Format check box deselected. When you select a date field object, the date in the database is displayed as numbers separated by slashes (for example, 12/27/94). When you leave the field object, the date is reformatted according to the display format options you've set for this field object. In the Owl Publishing database, SUB START and SUB END are examples of date field objects.

Tip

If the date you're entering is in the current month and year and there's no prior date displayed in the field object, you only need to enter the day. Approach will default the rest of the date for you. Or enter the month and day, and the year will default to the current year.

Time Fields

Time field objects can contain up to 12 characters, depending on the format you've set in the Windows Control Panel. You can type hour, minute, and second values into the field object, separating them with colons (HH:MM:SS). If you enter tenths or hundredths of a second, separate them from the whole second value with a decimal point (HH:MM:SS.00). You don't have to enter such a detailed time value, however; you can enter just the hour (HH) if you like, or the hour and minute (HH:MM).

You can also type **am** or **pm** after the time. If you enter the time in 24-hour format in a time field that uses the 12-hour format, Approach reformats the field in a 12-hour format and adds the AM or PM for you when you leave the field; you can enter a time such as **13:10** or **1:10pm**, for example. You can also specify a more exact time, such as **1:10:34pm**.

Caution

Approach will accept any number in the HH, MM, and SS parts of the time entered, and create a time out of it. 99:99:99 and 33:3 are both accepted during data entry, but the times generated aren't correct. Also, if you forget the colon and just type **330PM**, for example, you'll get a time displayed in the field, but not the time you expected.

If the Show Data Entry Format check box is selected in the Format panel of a time field object's InfoBox, Approach displays the formatting characters and spaces to specify the maximum number of characters you can type. If this check box isn't selected, Approach reformats the numbers you type into the correct format when you move to the next field object.

Tip

Time field objects are easiest for users to use if you specify the object with a time format but deselect the Show Data Entry Format check box. With this setting, users can enter **3:32pm**, for example, and Approach won't insist that they enter zeros to complete the seconds part of the date format before entering the am or pm. The user must, however, be sure to enter the colon(s), or the time will be incorrect.

Memo Fields

To enter information into a memo field object, type and edit it just like a text field object. Memo-type fields have no length constraints. You can use Enter to insert a carriage-return to end a line or paragraph. As you type, Approach scrolls the text automatically to make more room. You can move up and down through the text by using the arrow keys. If you type more text than the memo field object can display on the form, Approach provides a scroll bar to the right of the memo field object when you move to the next field, so you can scroll through the text.

Tip

If you're pressing Enter to move from field to field, press Ctrl+Enter to put a carriage return at the end of a memo field line. Pressing Enter ends your data entry and takes you to the next field.

Boolean Fields

When entering data in Boolean field objects, you're limited to a small set of clearly defined values. To indicate true or yes, enter **Y**, **Yes**, or **1**. To indicate false or no, enter **N**, **No**, or **0**. All other entries are interpreted as Yes or 1. Approach reformats the contents of Boolean fields to display as Yes or No, depending on your entry. The MAILED? field in the Owl Publishing database is an example of a Boolean field. However, a check box, not the actual Y/N, True/False values, indicates the value for this field on the form.

Drop-Down Lists

A drop-down list object provides a list of values to choose from. You can enter data into the field only by choosing values from this list. An arrow always appears next to the field object if the Show Drop-Down Arrow check box is selected in the Define Drop-Down List dialog box (accessed from the Define List button in the Basics panel of the InfoBox). If this check box isn't selected, the arrow appears only when you select the field object.

To choose a value, click the arrow next to the field object to drop down the list of values. A list of up to eight value choices appears (see fig. 5.5). If the list contains more values, a scroll bar also appears.

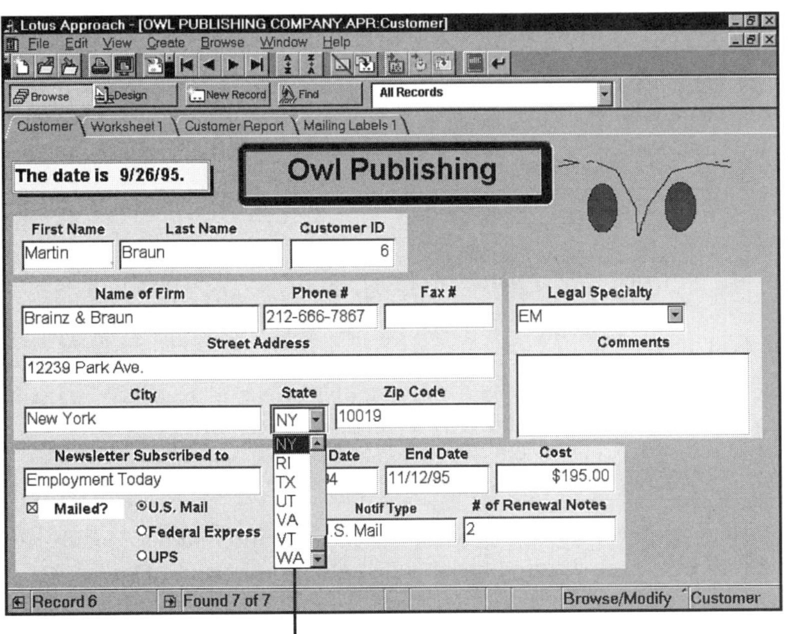

Fig. 5.5

The selection bar shows the value to be selected when you press Enter or Tab.

Drop-down lists can include any type of textual or numeric information. They're useful for selecting from a list of states, employees, ZIP codes, and so forth.

Use one of the following methods to choose a value from the list:

- Click the value.
- Move the selection bar to the value by using the arrow keys, and then press Enter (which makes the selection and enters the new or updated record) or Tab (which makes the selection and moves to the next field).
- In a long list of values, jump to the first value that begins with a certain letter by pressing that letter. This procedure is helpful if you've entered the values in the list in alphabetical order.

Field Box and List

A field box and list object allows you to choose a value from a drop-down list or to type a new value into the field box. An arrow appears next to the field box at all times if the Show Drop-Down Arrow check box is selected in the Define Drop-Down List dialog box (accessed from the Define List button in the Basics panel of the InfoBox). If the check box wasn't selected, the arrow appears only when you select the field.

To choose a value, click the arrow next to the field to drop down the list of values. A list of up to eight value choices appears. If the list contains more values, a scroll bar also appears. You can also type a new value into the field box and list. The SPECIALTY field in the Owl Publishing database is an example of a field box and list object.

> **Note**
>
> Within a field box and list object using typed-in values, you can't move to a value in the list by typing the first letter of the value. Your keystroke is interpreted as the first character of a typed-in value.

List Box

A list box field object provides a list of values from which to choose. You can enter data into the field only by choosing values from this list. A double arrow always appears next to the field object.

To choose a value, click the up or down part of the double arrow adjacent to the field object to move up or down the list of values. One value at a time is displayed. Tabbing out of the field object with a value showing sets that value as the current database field value.

List objects can include any type of textual or numeric information but are usually used for incremental values such as numbers or codes, where you want to be able to move up or down only one list entry at a time. They're useful for selecting from a list of sizes, quantities, colors, and so forth.

Check Boxes

Check boxes are useful when a field can have only one of two possible values (such as On/Off, Yes/No, or Satisfied/Unsatisfied). Check boxes have on and off values, which are set using the Define Check Box dialog box (discussed in Chapter 4, "Enhancing Data Input Forms"). Clicking a check box turns it on (a check mark appears in the box) and stores the on value in that field of the database. Clicking it again turns it off (the check mark disappears) and stores the off value instead.

In the Owl Publishing database, the MAILED? field is an example of a check box.

Radio Buttons

Radio buttons are useful when a field can have only one of a limited set of values (such as red, yellow, blue, or green). To choose from a set of radio buttons, click the button that corresponds to the value you want to enter. Clicking another button in the set selects that button and deselects the first one. In a set of three radio buttons denoting shipment methods in the Owl Publishing database, for example, you can choose only one of three options: U.S. Mail, Federal Express, or UPS.

Entering Sample Records

Owl Publishing has its first customer! You need to enter that customer's record into the database that you created in Chapter 2, "Creating Database Tables."

Note

Before trying the next example, delete any sample records you may have added. Also, make sure that the CUSTOMER ID field (a serial-number field whose value Approach sets automatically) starts with 1 for the records you enter. Otherwise, the records added in the following example will have a different customer ID number.

To reset the customer ID serial number, follow these steps:

1. Open the Create menu and choose Field Definition to open the Field Definition dialog box.
2. Click the CUST ID field in the Field Definition dialog box.
3. Click the Options button. The bottom portion (Default Value and Validation) of the Field Definition dialog box appears.
4. Make sure that a 1 is in the Serial number starting at the text box. If any other number appears, change it to 1. Then click the Serial number starting at the button.
5. Click OK to return to the form.
6. Click the Delete Record SmartIcon to delete any sample records you may have built.
7. From the File menu, choose Save Approach File.

To enter the first record of the Owl Publishing database, follow these steps:

1. Click Browse on the action bar, or open the View menu and choose Browse to switch to Browse mode.
2. Click the New Record button on the action bar.
3. Click the FIRST NAME field object in the form; then type **`Joseph`**.
4. Press Tab to move to the LAST NAME field object; then type **`Jones`**.
5. Type **`Jones and Jones`** for the FIRM NAME.
6. Type **`123 Felton Place`** for the STREET ADDRESS.
7. For the CITY, STATE, and ZIP CODE field objects, type **`New York`**, **`NY`**, and **`10019`**.
8. For the LEGAL SPECIALTY field object, type **`FM`**.

Note

You don't need to enter a mail type value (from the radio buttons) or # OF RENEWAL NOTES value for every record, because renewal notes aren't sent to companies with subscriptions that aren't about to expire.

9. For the NEWSLETTER SUBSCRIBED TO, type **`Assault Today`** as the newsletter name.

10. Enter a START DATE of **12/27/95** and an END DATE of **12/27/96**.
11. Enter a COST of **150.00**.
12. Press Enter.

Now you can practice entering some additional records into the database. (This way, you'll also have some records to experiment with later.) Table 5.1 shows values for more fields in the database. You won't place a value in every field, but you can enter values in the other fields, if you like.

> **Note**
>
> Remember to click the New Record button on the action bar before entering each new record. If you don't want to add another new record, press Esc to cancel the record—the previous record will still be saved. You can also press Tab from the last field object on a form to enter the record and move to the first field object on a new form to enter the next new record.

Table 5.1 Records for the Owl Publishing Database

First Name:	**John**	Newsletter Title:	**Assault Today**
Last Name:	**Roberts**	Sub Start:	**12/15/95**
Firm Name:	**Diddle & Diddle**	Sub End:	**12/15/96**
Street Address:	**217 Romie Lane**	Price:	**$150**
City:	**New York**	Renew Notes:	**1**
State:	**NY**	Mail Type:	UPS
Zip:	**10019**	Specialty:	PI
First Name:	**Marcy**	Newsletter Title:	**Burglary Made Simple**
Last Name:	**Pettis**	Sub Start:	**1/12/95**
Firm Name:	**Pettis and Co.**	Sub End:	**1/12/96**
Street Address:	**98 Snider Road**	Price:	**$175**
City:	**New York**	Renew Notes:	**0**
State:	**NY**	Mail Type:	
Zip:	**10023**	Specialty:	FM
First Name:	**David**	Newsletter Title:	**Assault Today**
Last Name:	**Green**	Sub Start:	**11/14/95**
Firm Name:	**Black and Blue, Inc.**	Sub End:	**11/14/96**
Street Address:	**1902 Christina Ave.**	Price:	**$150**
City:	**Buffalo**	Renew Notes:	
State:	**NY**	Mail Type:	
Zip:	**10342**	Specialty:	EM

First Name:	**George**	Newsletter Title:	**Burglary Made Simple**
Last Name:	**Kinder**	Sub Start:	**05/12/95**
Firm Name:	**Kinder & Garten**	Sub End:	**05/12/96**
Street Address:	**444 Yearling Ave.**	Price:	**$175**
City:	**Smallville**	Renew Notes:	**2**
State:	**NY**	Mail Type:	U.S. Mail
Zip:		Specialty:	EM

First Name:	**Martin**	Newsletter Title:	**Employment Today**
Last Name:	**Braun**	Sub Start:	**11/12/94**
Firm Name:	**Brainz & Braun**	Sub End:	**11/12/95**
Street Address:	**12239 Park Ave.**	Price:	**$195**
City:	**New York**	Renew Notes:	**2**
State:	**NY**	Mail Type:	U.S. Mail
Zip:	**10019**	Specialty:	EM

First Name:	**Harriet**	Newsletter Title:	**Employment Today**
Last Name:	**Dee**	Sub Start:	**12/12/95**
Firm Name:	**Fiddle, Dee & Dee**	Sub End:	**12/12/96**
Street Address:	**909 High Street**	Price:	**$195**
City:	**Buffalo**	Renew Notes:	
State:	**NY**	Mail Type:	
Zip:	**10342**	Specialty:	EM

Navigating Through Your Records

After you have a few records in your database, you must be able to page through them. You can use the SmartIcons, the status bar, or the keyboard to do so. The following sections discuss these different methods.

Using the SmartIcon Bar to Navigate Records

You can use the group of four arrow keys—often called *VCR buttons* because they resemble the controls on a VCR—that appear on the SmartIcon bar to move through your database:

- To move to the next record in the database, click the Next Record SmartIcon (with a right-pointing triangle).
- To move to the preceding record in the database, click the Previous Record SmartIcon (with a left-pointing triangle).
- To move to the first record in the database, click the First Record SmartIcon (with a left-pointing triangle and a vertical bar).
- To move to the last record in the database, click the Last Record SmartIcon (with a right-pointing triangle and a vertical bar).

Using the Status Bar to Navigate Records

The status bar also contains three controls that you can use to move through the database (see fig. 5.6):

- To move to the next record in the database, click the Next Record button.
- To move to the preceding record in the database, click the Previous Record button.
- To move to any record in the database, click the Record Number button. The Go To Record dialog box appears. Enter the appropriate record number, and then click OK.

Fig. 5.6

Navigation controls are available on the status bar.

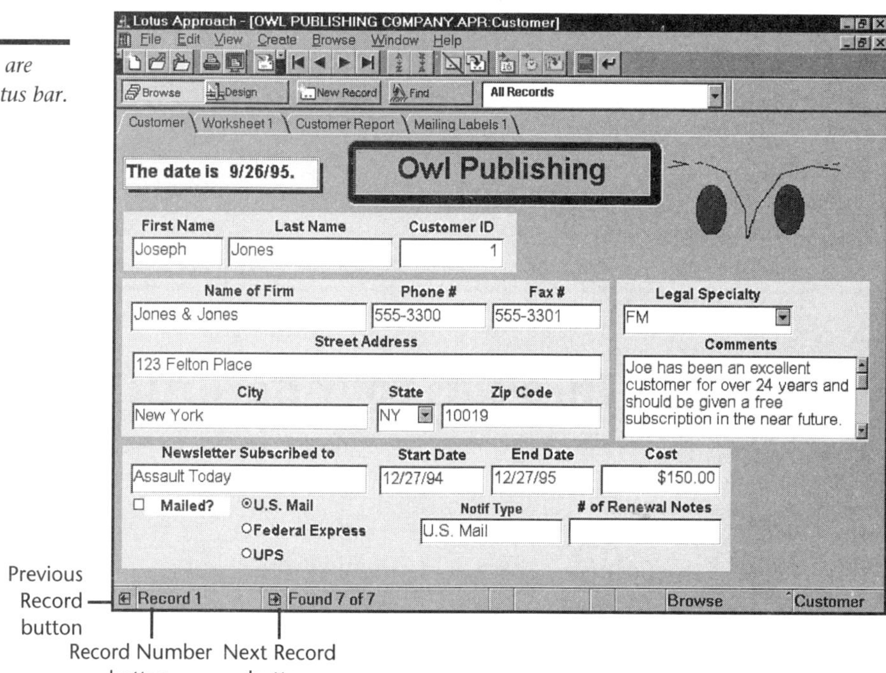

Using the Keyboard to Navigate Records

You can also use the keyboard to navigate through your records:

To Move To...	Press...
The next record in the database	Page Down
The preceding record in the database	Page Up
The first record in the database	Ctrl+Home
The last record in the database	Ctrl+End

Sorting Records

By default, Approach displays records in the order in which they were entered. This order may not always be the one you want. Rearranging the records in a certain order makes finding groups of similar records easier.

Tip

Descending order is especially helpful for date fields because the most recent date appears at the top of the list.

You can temporarily *sort*, or rearrange, the records based on the values contained in one or more database fields. You can also establish a default sort order for records. The default sort order is the order in which the records are displayed when no other (temporary) sort orders are in effect.

For any sort, the database field values can be sorted in ascending or descending order. In ascending order, the records are sorted from lowest value to highest value. Text values are sorted A-Z; numeric values are sorted low to high; dates and times are sorted earliest to latest. In descending order the opposite is true—the records are sorted from highest to lowest value.

After you sort your records, the new order affects how the records are viewed, updated, and printed. For example, if you sort the Owl Publishing database by newsletter names, all subscriptions for a particular newsletter appear together. If you sort by date instead, all subscriptions appear in chronological order.

Note

Except for the default sort order, all sort orders are temporary. If you perform a Find (as discussed in Chapter 6, "Finding Records,"), click the Show All SmartIcon, or close the Approach file, the records revert to their default sort order. However, you can establish a macro that recreates the sort order with the click of a button (see Chapter 13, "Automating Your Work," for more information about macros).

Sorting on One Field

The simplest type of sort is the single-field sort. As the name implies, you choose a single field in the database to sort the records on. For example, in the sample database, you can sort the database by firm name to get an idea of which firms are subscribing to which newsletters. To sort on one field, follow these steps:

1. Switch to Browse mode by clicking Browse on the action bar.
2. Open the Browse menu and choose Sort and Define. The Sort dialog box appears.

3. In the Database Fields list box at the left side of the dialog box, select the field you want to use for your primary sort field (the field by which the database is sorted). For Owl Publishing, select FIRM NAME from the field list.

   Your Sort dialog box should look like the one shown in figure 5.7.

Fig. 5.7

Setting up to sort records by FIRM NAME is done in the Sort dialog box.

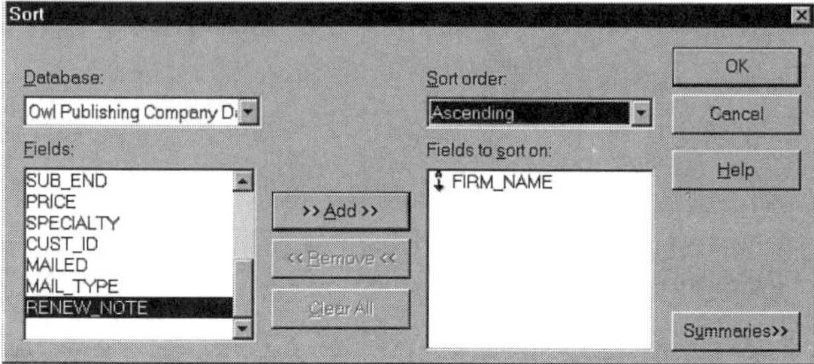

4. Click the Add button to move the field to the Fields to Sort On list box. A small icon indicating the sort order appears left of the field name, defaulting to Ascending order.

Tip

Rather than perform steps 3 and 4, you can double-click the field to move it to the Fields to Sort On list box.

5. Click the field name selected for the sort to select it, and then select Ascending or Descending from the Sort Order drop-down list to determine whether the database is sorted in ascending or descending order on that field. Use Ascending for this example. The icon left of the field name reflects the sort order (with a little A and down-arrow for ascending, or a little Z and down-arrow for descending).
6. Click OK to sort the records.

When you return to the form, try paging through the records. Now they appear in alphabetical order by FIRM NAME rather than in the order in which they were entered. Figure 5.8 shows the Worksheet view of the records in the database (see Chapter 14, "Using Worksheets and Crosstabs," for information on how to create worksheets). The records appear in their sorted order. If you want to return to the default order (the order in which the records were entered), open the Browse menu and choose Refresh Data.

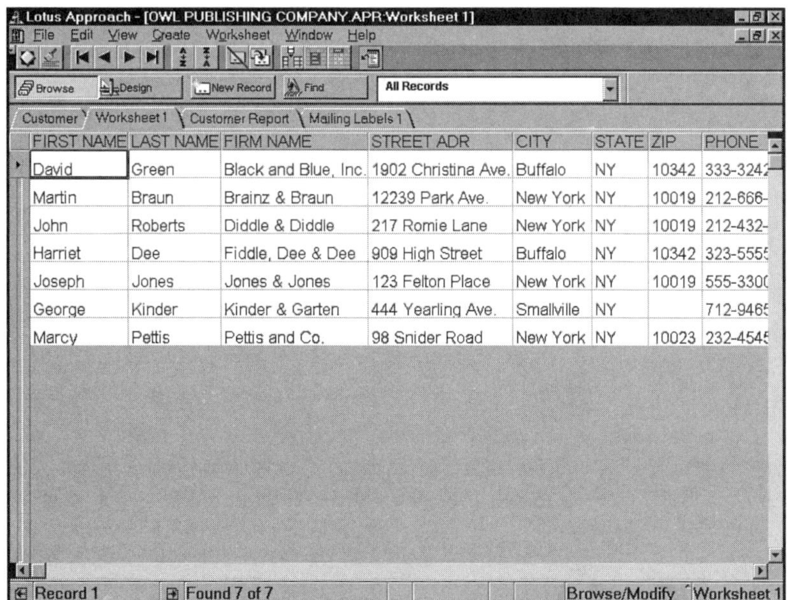

FIRST NAME	LAST NAME	FIRM NAME	STREET ADR	CITY	STATE	ZIP	PHONE
David	Green	Black and Blue, Inc.	1902 Christina Ave.	Buffalo	NY	10342	333-3242
Martin	Braun	Brainz & Braun	12239 Park Ave.	New York	NY	10019	212-666-
John	Roberts	Diddle & Diddle	217 Romie Lane	New York	NY	10019	212-432-
Harriet	Dee	Fiddle, Dee & Dee	909 High Street	Buffalo	NY	10342	323-5555
Joseph	Jones	Jones & Jones	123 Felton Place	New York	NY	10019	555-3300
George	Kinder	Kinder & Garten	444 Yearling Ave.	Smallville	NY		712-9465
Marcy	Pettis	Pettis and Co.	98 Snider Road	New York	NY	10023	232-4545

Fig. 5.8

The records appear in order in the Worksheet view.

There's another way to easily sort the records on a single field in ascending order. Simply click the field you want to sort; then open the Browse menu and choose Sort and Ascending, or click the Sort Ascending SmartIcon. To sort the records in descending order, click the field and open the Browse menu and choose Sort and Descending, or click the Sort Descending SmartIcon.

Sorting Records on Multiple Fields

You can sort your database on more than one field by adding more fields to the Fields to Sort On list box before clicking OK in the Sort dialog box. To do so, select additional fields in the order you want them sorted, clicking the Add button for each selected field to move it to the Fields to Sort On list. To establish the sort order for each additional field, use the Sort order list box and choose Ascending or Descending.

These newly added fields, called *secondary sort fields*, affect the sort order of the database within the order established by the primary sort field. In other words, the records are sorted first by the primary field; then, for all records with the same primary sort field value, the records are sorted by the first secondary field. If any records have the same values for the primary and secondary fields, they're sorted by the next secondary field, if any, and so on.

If the primary field in the Fields to Sort On list is NEWSLETTER (the newsletter subscribed to, in Ascending order), for example, and the secondary field is SUB START (the start date, in Descending order), the newsletter subscriptions are sorted in alphabetical order by the name of the newsletter. The first block of records includes all the entries for *Assault Today*, followed by a block of records for *Burglary Made Simple*, and so on. All the entries for *Assault Today* would be sorted by their subscription date, with the most recent subscriptions appearing first. All the entries for *Burglary Made Simple* would also be sorted by subscription date.

Figure 5.9 shows a list of some records that may appear in the new sort order.

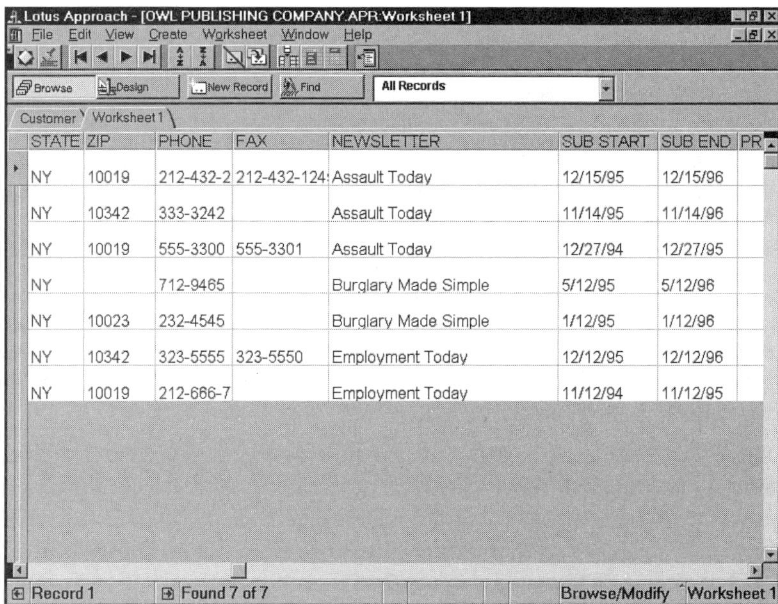

Fig. 5.9

Records are now sorted by newsletter name and subscription date.

If you decide that you don't want one of the fields in the Fields to Sort On list, select it and choose Remove or double-click the field. If you make a mistake and decide to start over, choose Clear All to erase all fields in the Fields to Sort On list box (which makes them available again in the Database Fields list).

After you set up the sort order the way you want it, click OK to sort the records. Although Approach is very fast, the program may pause while it sorts the records.

Setting the Default Sort Order

Approach lets you set the default sort order for a database. This default order is the order in which the records appear when no other sort order is in effect. To disable other sort orders and return to the default sort order, you can change views or open the Browse menu and choose Refresh Data.

To set the default sort order, open the File menu and choose User Setup and Approach Preferences to open the Approach Preferences dialog box. Click the Order tab to move to the Order page (see fig. 5.10). Select the database that you want to maintain the default sort order for from the Maintain Default Sort For drop-down list. Set the default order by using the Fields list and Fields to Sort On list. When you're finished setting up the sort order, click OK or the Save Default button.

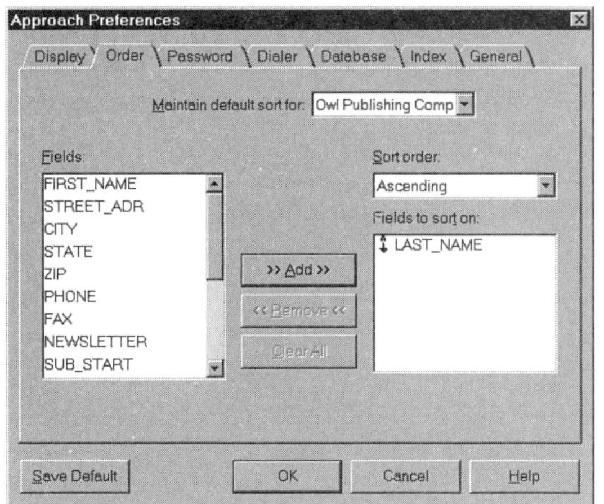

Fig. 5.10

You can set the default database sort order with the Approach Preferences dialog box.

Using the Spell Checker

Approach can check the spelling of text in your Approach files and databases. The text that Approach checks for you depends on which mode you're in:

- In Browse mode, Approach checks the spelling of data in all fields displayed, including memo fields, check boxes, radio buttons, and PicturePlus fields.
- In Design mode, Approach checks the spelling of text in field labels and text block objects, including text in the body of form letters. Approach also checks headers and footers on reports.

> **Note**
>
> The spell checker isn't available in Print Preview or Find modes.

Approach's spell checker compares the appropriate entries with the contents of a main dictionary and user dictionary. The main dictionary comes with Approach and can't be edited. The user dictionary is for words that aren't in the main dictionary. These words often include proper names and technical terms. You can add and delete words from the user dictionary at any time.

Running the Spell Checker

You must be in Browse or Design mode to run the spell checker. Follow these steps:

1. Select any text you want to spell check. If you don't select any text before running the spell checker, Approach checks all text.

   In Browse mode, you can select all or part of the text in a field. In Design mode, you can select text in a text object or an entire text object. If you select a text object, Approach checks all the text in the text object.

2. Open the Edit menu and choose Check Spelling (Ctrl+F2). The Spell Check dialog box opens (see fig. 5.11). Select the options you want for the spell check:
   - Click the Selection radio button to check the spelling of only the selected text or text object. The Selection radio button isn't available if you didn't select text before activating the spell checker.
   - Current Record (Browse mode) spell checks all the text in fields in the current record. Current View (Design mode) spell checks all the text in the current view (form, report, form letter, or mailing label).
   - Found Set (Browse mode only) spell checks all records in the found set. A *found set* is a special set of records that meet criteria you specify (see Chapter 6, "Finding Records," for more information on finds). After you specify the find criteria, Approach displays all records that match this criteria.
   - Selection Across Found Set (Browse mode only) spell checks the selected text in all records in the found set. This option isn't available if you didn't select text before running the spell checker.
   - Click the Memo Fields Only check box if you want to check only the text in memo fields. This is handy because you often type the bulk of the text you want spell checked into memo fields. Other fields also often contain proper names and technical terms that aren't in your dictionary.

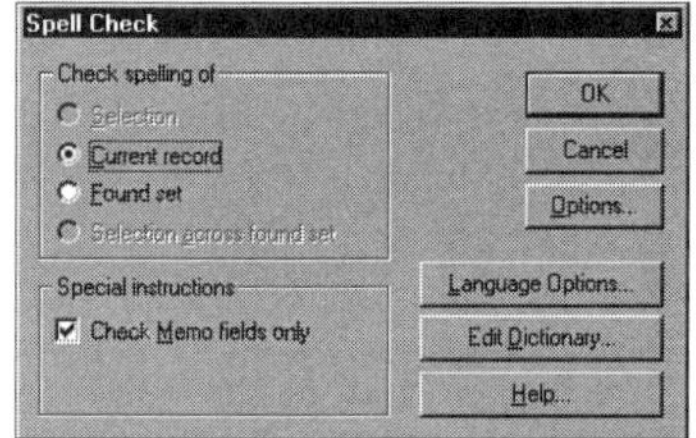

Fig. 5.11

The Spell Check dialog box lets you set the scope of the checking Approach will perform.

3. Click OK. Approach begins the spell check. If Approach finds a word that isn't in its dictionary, another Spell Check dialog box opens (see fig. 5.12). Approach displays the unknown word on a line at the top of the dialog box. If Approach doesn't find any unknown words, an alert box appears to inform you that the spell check is complete.

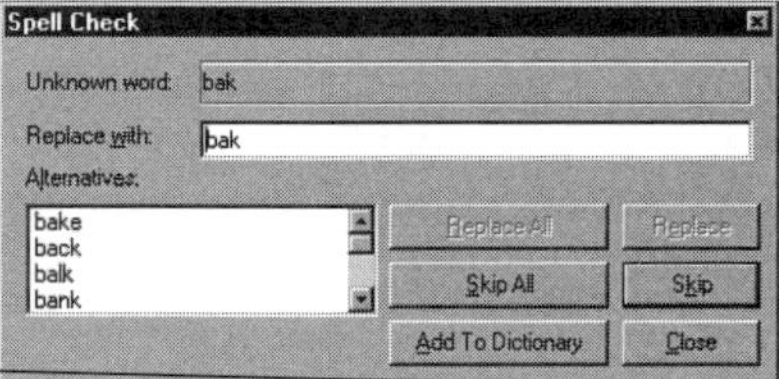

Fig. 5.12

Approach displays a word that may be misspelled along with a list of alternatives, if available.

4. For unknown words, Approach suggests possible replacements in the Alternatives list. To pick an alternative, click the word so that it appears in the Replace With text box. You can also type in a replacement word or edit one of the alternatives in the Replace With text box.

   To replace the word, click Replace or Replace All. Replace replaces this occurrence of the unknown word. If the word appears again later, Approach will question it again. Replace All replaces all occurrences of the word in the text you're checking.

   To skip a word, click Skip or Skip All. Skip skips this occurrence of the word. If the unknown word appears again later, Approach will question it again. Skip All skips all occurrences of the word in the text you're checking.

   To accept a word and add it to the dictionary, click Add to Dictionary. Approach won't question the word in future spell checks in any Approach file.

5. After you decide what to do with a questioned word, click OK in the Spell Check dialog box. Approach moves to the next unknown word. When Approach has completed checking the spelling, it displays an alert box to let you know that the spell check is complete.

Setting the Spell Checker Options

From the Spell Check dialog box shown in figure 5.11, the Options button presents another dialog box where you can specify different spell checker options, such as whether you want Approach to find repeated words. These options take effect when you click OK and become the new default for the spell checker. The following are some options you can select:

- *Check for Repeated Words.* This option finds words that appear twice in a row, such as *the the.*
- *Check Words with Numbers.* This option checks words that contain numbers, such as *Junior2.* The number must be included in the word in the dictionary, or Approach will flag the word as unknown.
- *Check Words with Initial Caps.* This option checks the spelling of words that begin with a capital letter, such as *Berlin.* Approach checks all words at the beginning of a sentence whether or not this option is selected.
- *Include User Dictionary Alternatives.* This option includes words from the user dictionary when Approach displays possible replacement words.

Editing the User Dictionary

The user dictionary contains any words that you've added to the main dictionary. The contents of the user dictionary are often proper nouns or technical terms that aren't found in a general-purpose dictionary. If you click Add to Dictionary when Approach displays an unknown word, the new word is added to the user dictionary.

You can edit the user dictionary to add or delete words from it. To edit the user dictionary, follow these steps:

1. Open the Edit menu and choose Check Spelling or click the Spell Check SmartIcon. The Spell Check dialog box opens.
2. Click Edit Dictionary. The Edit Dictionary dialog box opens (see fig. 5.13).

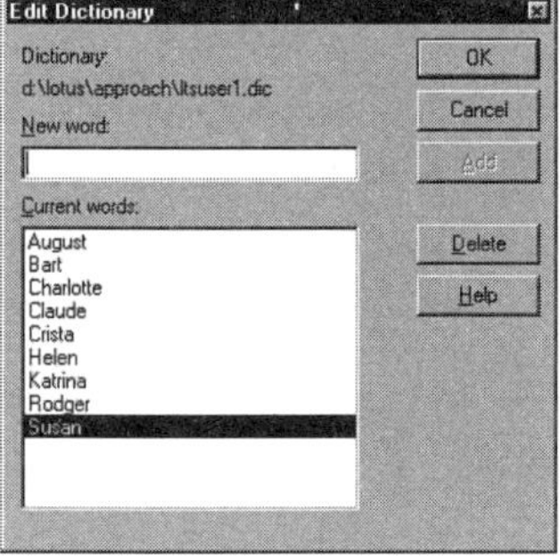

Fig. 5.13

Use the user dictionary to add words that aren't found in the regular dictionary.

3. To add a new word to the dictionary, type the word in the New Word text box. Click the Add button to add the word to the list of current words contained in the dictionary.
4. To delete a word, click the word in the Current Words list box, and then click Delete.

> **Tip**
>
> Once you click the Current Words list box, you can move the selection bar to pick a word using the arrow keys.

5. Click OK to save the changes, or Cancel to return to the previous version of the user dictionary.

From Here...

In this chapter, you learned how to enter data into the carefully crafted forms that you created with Approach. You also learned how to create, update, and delete records; move through fields on a form; enter data into fields and value lists; and use check boxes and radio buttons. You also explored the constraints for entering data into date, number, time, and Boolean fields.

After you entered several new records into your database, you moved from one record to another and sorted the records to look at them in a desired order. Finally, you learned how to spell check your work.

After you have data in your database, you can do quite a lot. For related information, see the following chapters in this book:

- Chapter 6, "Finding Records," shows how to locate specific data in your database.
- Chapter 14, "Using Worksheets and Crosstabs," discusses how to look at your data in a spreadsheet-like format and create special cross-reference reports called *crosstabs*.
- Chapter 15, "Creating Charts," shows you how to create a pictorial representation of your data.

CHAPTER 6

Finding Records

Computer-based database systems such as Approach excel at finding database records that match the conditions you define. In fact, this capability to locate information quickly is probably what persuades most people to switch to a computer for storing their records.

Suppose that your paper address book has a note on each page that indicates whether the person listed sent you a Christmas card last year. If you want to create a list of all those people, you would need to search through your address book by hand. With Approach, you can tell the computer to find and list this information for you.

If you have a business, you're probably creating multipart forms, such as invoices, so that you can file them by customer name and invoice number. Just think—if you had your invoices in an Approach database, you could find any invoice instantaneously, using any field value in the invoice or a related customer database. And you could get rid of those filing cabinets!

Approach has a powerful set of capabilities for locating information and making it available to you through an operation called *performing a find*. Other terms commonly used for this operation with computers include *searching* and *querying* your database. In addition to simple finds involving only one field at a time, Approach can handle some very sophisticated finds, such as finding everyone whose legal specialty is EM or PI and lives in Los Angeles.

New in Approach 96 are the Find Assistant and the presence on the action bar of the Named Find/Sort drop-down list, which dramatically increase the ease of use of Approach's power for novice and experienced database users. The new Find Assistant guides you through the process of finding, optionally sorting, and displaying a set of records that meet the conditions you define—and it confirms what it's going to do in English for you while you're defining your find criteria. Re-entering commonly used find criteria from scratch is also no longer necessary, as you can name and save any simple or complex find that you've created. What's more, these named finds are readily available from any view in your application just by selecting them from the action bar.

The found set consists of those records that meet your find criteria. After performing a find and obtaining the found set, you can perform operations on just the found records until you decide to return to using your entire database.

The more advanced functions, such as conditional finds (IF) and "sounds-like" finds, are discussed in Chapter 11, "Performing Advanced Finds."

In this chapter, you learn how to

- Set up and perform a find
- Perform finds for specific types of data, such as text, dates, and times
- Find a range of values or duplicate values
- Find blank or non-blank values
- Use multiple criteria for a find
- Modify or cancel a find
- Name and save your find criteria
- Perform, modify, or copy your named find criteria
- Hide or delete a found set of records

Setting Up and Performing a Find

To perform a find, Approach uses views, such as the data input forms you created in chapters 3 and 4, or you can use the Find Assistant, which is new in Approach 96. With either method, you can perform impromptu finds as needed, or create and save named finds for use at any time without re-entering your find criteria.

Using an Approach View

The first step in setting up a find by using a view is to decide which view you want to use. The form, report, worksheet, or other view you choose must display the database field(s) for which you want to specify your criteria.

After you decide which view to use, display the view on-screen and switch to Browse mode by clicking Browse on the action bar.

To create the find, you can select Find from the action bar or status bar, or you can press Ctrl+F. The view you selected clears, and none of your data is visible (see fig. 6.1). Approach displays the Find SmartIcon bar and replaces the action bar buttons with a new set of actions that assist you in performing the find.

Tip

You also can create a find by using the context-sensitive menu on the menu bar. For a form view, use the Browse menu; for a worksheet view, use the Worksheet menu. Other view types have their own unique context-sensitive menu name. All of these have Find on the menu, with Find, Find Assistant, Find Again, and Find All as submenu options.

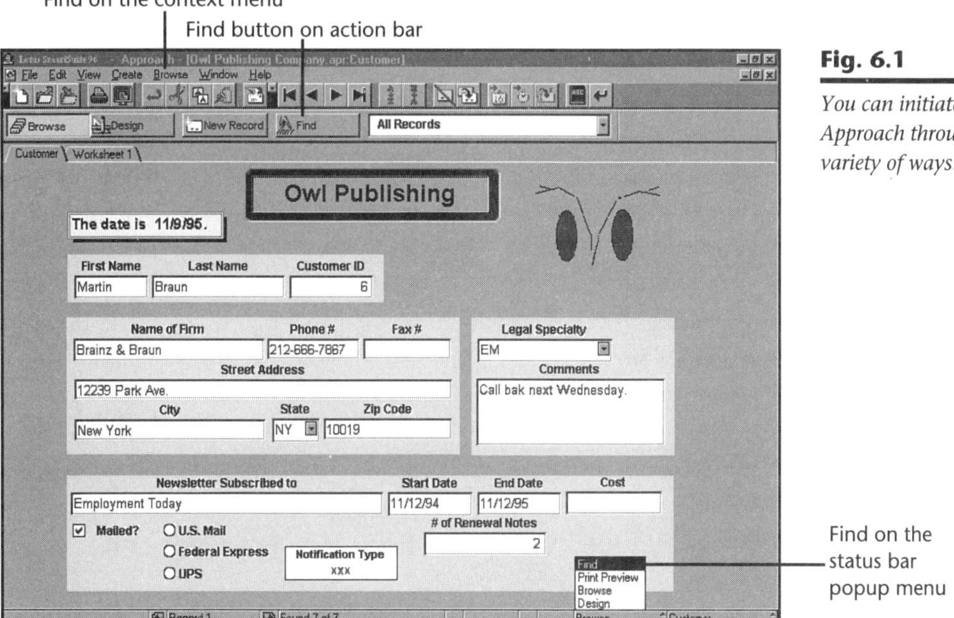

Fig. 6.1

You can initiate a find in Approach through a variety of ways.

Enter your find criteria within the field object that represents the desired database field on the form. You can enter find criteria for multiple fields in multiple field objects before executing the find. To enter the find criteria, follow these steps:

1. Click a field object (or move to it by using the Tab key) in which you want to enter find criteria.
2. Type the find criteria, including any find operators. You can type in a find operator (such as a question mark) or click the equivalent SmartIcon to place that operator in the criteria. (The following sections explain the Default Find set of SmartIcons and how to specify find criteria.)
3. When you're done entering the find criteria for all fields you want to include in the find, press Enter, click OK on the action bar, or click the Enter SmartIcon.

Figure 6.2 shows a situation in which you want to find all database records where the newsletter title is *Assault Today*. The text string *Assault Today* is the search criteria; the NEWSLETTER SUBSCRIBED TO field object represents the field being searched.

Approach processes your find criteria using all your database records, locates the records that meet your criteria, and creates the found set. The status bar at the bottom of the screen indicates how many total records in the database are in the found set (see fig. 6.3).

While the found set is active, use the arrow SmartIcons, the next and previous record buttons on the status bar, or the keyboard record navigation keys (Page Up, Page Down, Ctrl+Home, and Ctrl+End) to move through only the found set.

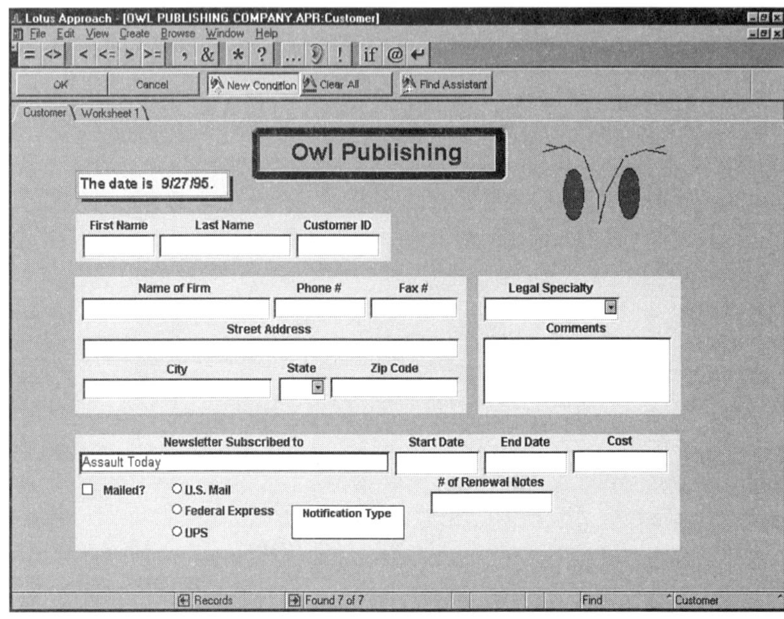

Fig. 6.2

Type your find criteria in the appropriate field object (the Newsletter Subscribed To text box object, in this example) where the database field is usually displayed.

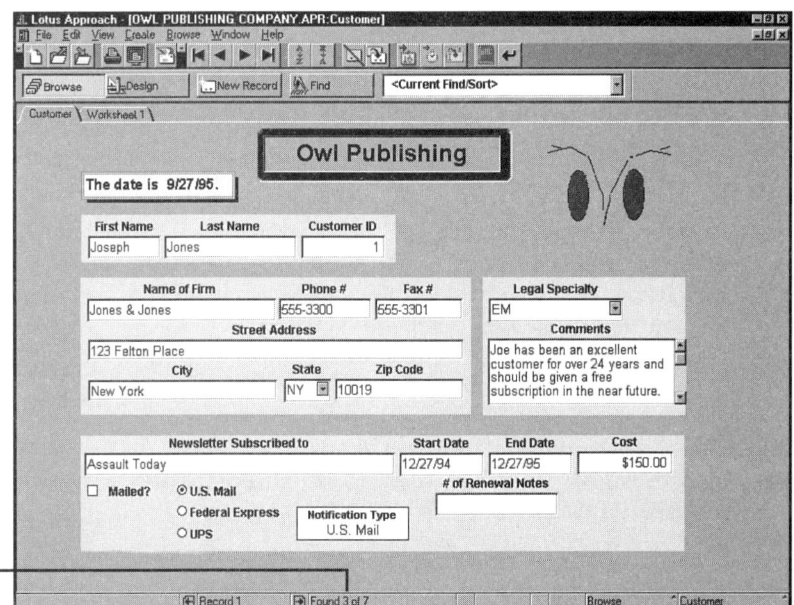

Fig. 6.3

The status bar shows how many records meet your criteria.

To return to the full set of records in your database, open the context-sensitive menu (for example, the Browse or Worksheet menu), choose Find, and then choose Find All (Ctrl+A). Or select the All Records option from the Named Find/Sort drop-down list on the action bar (this drop-down list is explained later in the section "Performing a Named Find"). The status bar now indicates that all records are available.

Using the Find Assistant

The first step in setting up a find by using the Find Assistant is to select and display the view on which you want the results of the find to be displayed. This view should display fields of interest for the database you want to search and may be any type of view.

The quickest way to activate the Find Assistant is to press Ctrl+I. Alternatively, open the context-sensitive menu (Browse, for example) and choose Find and then Find Assistant. The Find/Sort Assistant dialog box appears, displaying the Find Type page (see fig. 6.4).

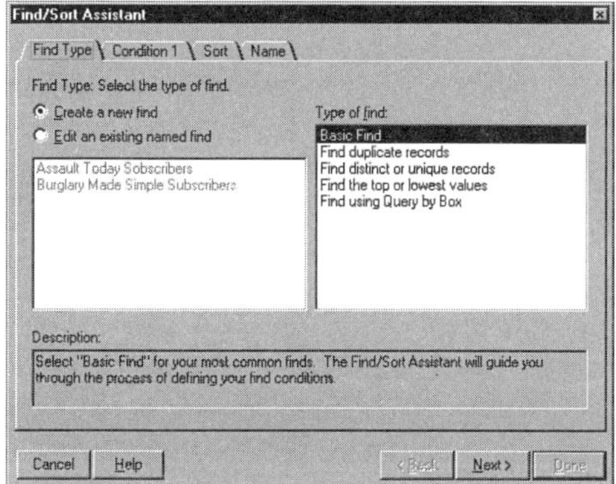

Fig. 6.4

The Find Assistant dialog box guides you step by step through setting up and performing a find.

The default on the Find Type page is to create a new find, and the type of find is a Basic Find. A Basic Find can involve one or more find criteria, or conditions. What's more, you can define an optional sort to display the found set in the order needed. To duplicate the find you just completed by using a view, follow these steps:

1. Select the Create a New Find radio button, if necessary.
2. Select Basic Find from the Type of Find list box; then click the Next button to see the Condition 1 page or click the tab for this page (see fig. 6.5).

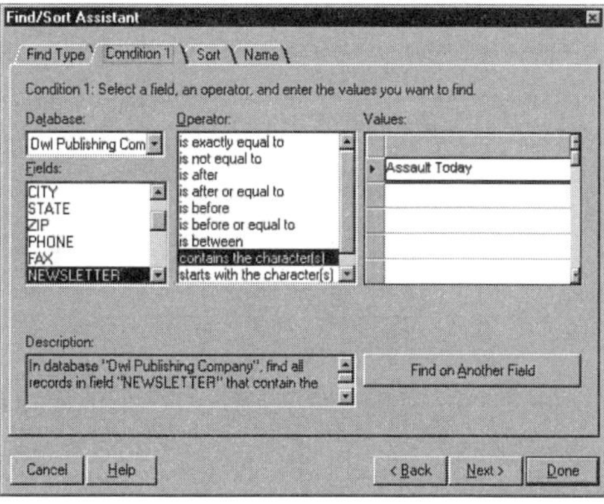

Fig. 6.5

The Find Assistant's Condition 1 page makes it easier to select the database and fields and to enter your Basic Find criteria.

3. Select the database from the Database drop-down list and the field name NEWSLETTER from the Fields list box.
4. Select the operator statement from the Operator list box. In this case, you want to find a record that "contains the character(s)" *Assault Today*.
5. Select the first empty line in the Values data-entry list and type **`Assault Today`** as your find criteria.
6. Click the Done button to perform the find. You should get the same results as shown earlier in figure 6.3.

Specifying the Find Criteria

When you enter your find criteria into a field object in a view, you can combine text and special find operators that modify how Approach interprets the text you've typed into the field object. These operators are symbols such as !, =, &, ?, and * and are described in table 6.1. Used with your text, find operators allow you to specify further searching operations for Approach.

While Approach is in Find mode on a view, find operators appear on the Default Find SmartIcon bar. Table 6.1 also shows these SmartIcons.

Table 6.1 The Approach Default Find Operators and SmartIcons

Operator	Description	SmartIcon
=	Finds exact matches (by itself, finds blank records).	=
<>	Field doesn't match; by itself, finds non-blank records.	<>
<	Less than.	<
<=	Less than or equal to.	<=
>=	Greater than or equal to.	>=
>	Greater than.	>
, (comma)	Separates multiple criteria in a single field (OR).	,
&	Combines criteria in a single field (AND).	&
*	Wild card for any number of characters.	*

Operator	Description	SmartIcon
?	Wild card for one character.	?
...	Within the range.	...
~	Sounds like.	
!	Case-sensitive.	!
IF	Conditional finds.	if
@	Field compared to result of following formula. Must be used with a comparison operator.	@
Enter	Perform the Find.	

Occasionally, your find criteria may contain one or more of the special find operator characters. To let Approach know that you want to use an operator character with your text criteria, you must enclose the text for the criteria in single quotation marks. For example, if you're looking for the phrase *& Dee* in the NAME OF FIRM field, you would type **`'& Dee'`** (enclosed in single quotation marks) in the NAME OF FIRM field object.

When you enter your find criteria by using the Find Assistant, you're selecting from sets of English phrases and moving through various pages (for example, the Condition 1 page shown earlier in fig. 6.4) to enter your find criteria. In this way, you can duplicate with the Find Assistant many of the finds possible when using a view and operators you type directly. The operators in table 6.1 for which the Find Assistant has no similar capability are ?, ~, !, IF, and @.

You can do five types of finds with the Find Assistant, as table 6.2 shows.

Table 6.2 Types of Finds Available with the Find Assistant

Type	Description
Basic find	Finds records based on the content of one or more database fields; can include AND and OR conditions
Find duplicate records	Finds records with duplicate values in one or more fields
Find distinct or unique records	Finds records with unique or distinct values in one or more fields
Find the top or lowest	Finds some specific number or percentage values of the records containing the highest or lowest values in numeric or calculated fields

(continues)

Table 6.2 Continued

Type	Description
Find using Query by Box	Lets you graphically create finds by using database fields, comparison operators, and AND/OR conditions

Note

When using the Find Assistant to enter find criteria, you don't need to include the single quotation marks around text entered in the Values data-entry box. Approach generates the proper syntax and even spells out the criteria you enter in the Description box to confirm that it understands what you want to find.

The next few sections discuss how to create and perform some of the finds possible in Approach by using the view method and the new Find Assistant. See Chapter 11, "Performing Advanced Finds," for information on performing more advanced finds.

Finding a Text String

To find all records where a field starts with a string of characters, type the text string into the appropriate field object in a view. Approach then finds all records in which the contents of that field start with the typed characters. For example, if you type **A** into the NAME OF FIRM field, Approach finds all records in which the firm name begins with the letter A.

Suppose that Owl Publishing wants to find the customer records for all subscribers to *Assault Today*. Follow these steps:

1. Switch to Browse mode by clicking Browse on the action bar.
2. Choose the form you want from the view tabs or the status bar. For this example, select the Customer form tab.
3. Open the Browse menu, choose Find, and then choose Find on the submenu (Ctrl+F); or select Find from the action bar or status bar.
4. In the NEWSLETTER SUBSCRIBED TO field object, type **Assault**.
5. Press Enter or click OK on the action bar.

Approach finds all records in which the newsletter title begins with the word *Assault*. This search is sufficient for finding all subscribers to *Assault Today* because no other newsletter title begins with that word. If Owl Publishing adds a new newsletter titled *Assault Monthly*, however, you need to revise the find criteria to **Assault T** to find only *Assault Today* subscribers.

With the Find Assistant, you can duplicate the preceding find by following these steps:

1. Switch to Browse mode by clicking Browse on the action bar.

2. Choose the form you want from the view tabs or the status bar. For this example, select the Customer form tab.
3. Open the Browse menu, choose Find, and then choose Find Assistant (Ctrl+I). The Find/Sort Assistant dialog box appears.
4. Select the Create a New Find radio button.
5. Select Basic Find from the Type of Find list box; then click the Next button to see the Condition 1 page or click the tab for that page (refer to fig. 6.5).
6. Select Owl Publishing Company from the Database drop-down list and the field name NEWSLETTER in the Fields list box.
7. Select the operator statement from the Operator list box. In this case, you want to find a record that "starts with the character(s)" *Assault*.
8. Select the first empty line in the Values data-entry box and type **`Assault`** as the find criteria.
9. Click Done to perform the find. The results appear, with the first record found displayed on your form.

Performing Case-Sensitive Finds. Approach isn't normally case-sensitive when searching dBASE- or FoxPro-formatted databases. In other words, if you type a string of characters into a field object in a view, the records are found whether the string appears in uppercase (capital letters) or lowercase. Typing **`dee`** into the NAME OF FIRM field, for example, finds all firm names that begin with *dee*—whether they're spelled *Dee*, *dEe*, or *DEE*. To find only those records that match the exact case of what you type, use an exclamation mark (!) in front of the text string. For example, to find only *dee* (and not *Dee*), type **`!dee`**.

Note

Paradox finds are usually case-sensitive. However, you can disable the default by using the Database page of the Approach Preferences dialog box. Click the Case Insensitive radio button to turn off Paradox case sensitivity except when you use the case-sensitive operator (exclamation mark, or !).

The Find Assistant can't perform case-sensitive searches because you can't enter the exclamation mark operator in the Values data entry box, and there's no case-sensitive type of find provided.

Finding an Exact Match. When you type a text string into a field object in a view to perform a find, Approach searches to find all records that begin with the text string. However, you can tell Approach to find only those records in which the value in the database field exactly matches the text string you entered. To do so, use an equal sign (=) in front of the text string. For example, if you type **`=Dee`** in the NAME OF FIRM field, you get a list of all records in which the firm name is just *Dee*—but not *Dee and Dee* or any other variation (see fig. 6.6).

Fig. 6.6

Use an equal sign (=) to find an exact match.

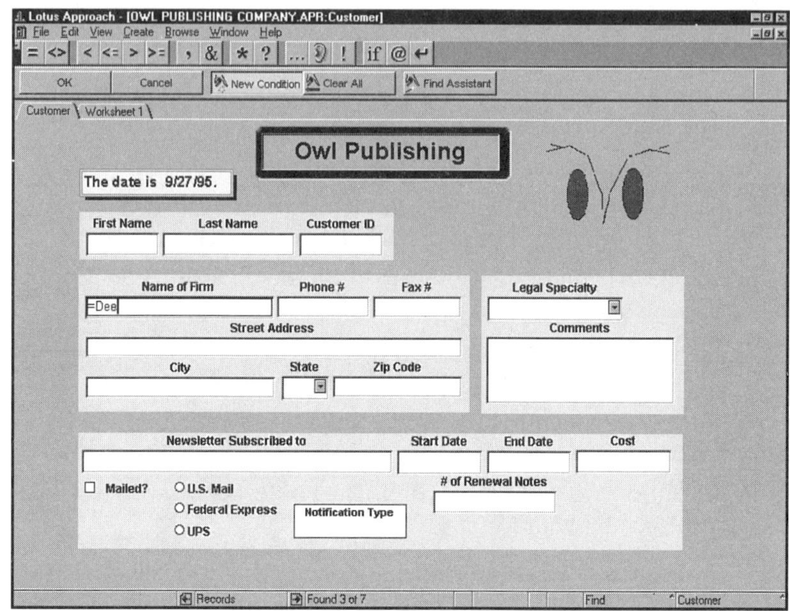

> **Note**
>
> This match isn't case-sensitive—you can still get variations such as *DEE* and *dEE*. Because you can't combine find operators such as ! and = in a single find criteria, you can't create an exact match and case-sensitive find with a single find criteria.

The Find Assistant can perform an exact match search by using the Basic Find type. Select the operator "is exactly equal to" on the Condition 1 page of the Find/Sort Assistant dialog box. In this example, type **dee** in the Values data-entry box to get the same results, and then click Done.

Using Multiple Find Operators to Find Records. You can use an ampersand (&) to combine find criteria for a single field when using a view. Suppose that you want an exact match of a text string. You can't combine the exact match symbol (=) with the match case symbol (!) unless you use the & symbol. This symbol connects both halves of the criteria. Therefore, to match the text string *Dee* exactly, you would enter **!Dee&=Dee** as the criteria in the field.

> **Note**
>
> *Don't* leave any spaces around the & symbol unless the string you're searching for includes a trailing space or a leading space.

The Find Assistant can't perform this particular multiple find operator search because it can't do case-sensitive searches.

Using Wild-Card Characters. With wild-card characters, you can use a view to search for text strings when certain characters vary or when you know only a portion of the text string. Suppose that you want to find all the firms where the firm name contains the name *Dee*. Because you aren't guaranteed that this name is the first word in the firm name, using the text search described in the preceding section may not find all occurrences. Therefore, you can use wild-card characters to tell Approach to look for the text string anywhere in the field.

Approach has two wild-card characters:

- The asterisk (*) is used to match any number of characters (including no characters). In the preceding example, you can find the firm(s) you're looking for by typing **`*Dee*`** as the criteria in the NAME OF FIRM field. This criteria shows any records in which the text string *Dee* appears anywhere in the firm name. If you enter a find criteria, such as **`Burg*`**, in the NEWSLETTER SUBSCRIBED TO field, a list of newsletters whose name begins with *Burg* appears.
- The question mark (?) is used to replace a single unknown text character. You can enter as many question marks as you want. To find a text string that's exactly four characters long and begins with B, for example, type **`B???`** as the criteria. To find a text string with any two characters, followed by the text *day* and two more characters, type **`??day??`** as the criteria.

You can combine * and ? in a single search criteria. For example, to find a string that begins with any single character, followed by the text string *day*, and followed by anything else, you enter **`?day*`** (see fig. 6.7).

The Find Assistant can't perform these types of wild-card searches because the wild-card characters are considered part of the text when entered in the Values data-entry box. Some finds that use the asterisk (*) can be accomplished by using the Basic Find type and the "starts with the character(s)," "contains the character(s)," and "ends with the character(s)" operators on the Condition 1 page of the Find/Sort Assistant dialog box.

Finding Numbers, Dates, and Times

Numbers, dates, and times work differently from text values. When you're using a view, finds on values typed into numeric, date, and time fields are always exact matches—you never need to use the = operator to specify an exact match with these types of fields.

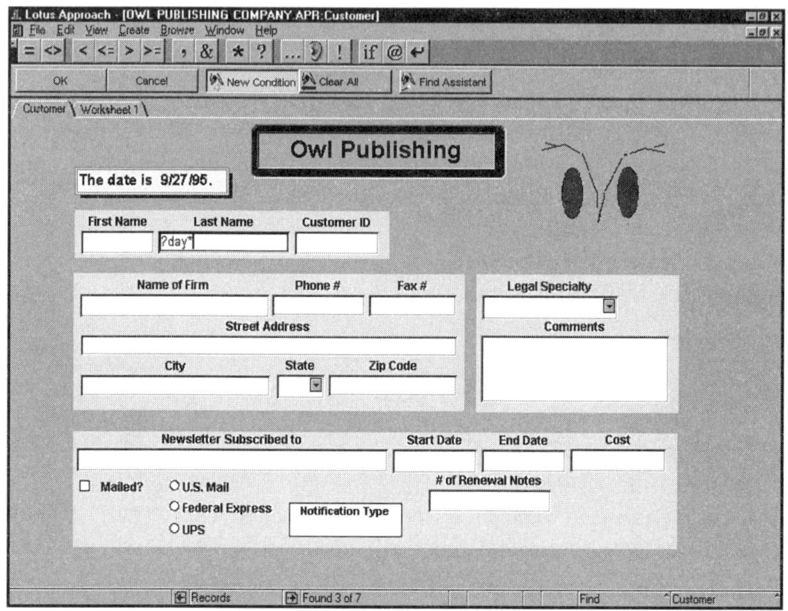

Fig. 6.7

You can combine wild-card characters for powerful searches.

Note

Make sure that the field into which you type your criteria is truly a numeric, date, or time field. Often, text fields are used to store numeric, date, or time values. The rules for finding values in text fields apply to these fields.

Using the text field search rules can actually be advantageous in certain circumstances. ZIP codes, for example, are assigned according to a system—codes starting with 9 are in West Coast states. If you want to send mail to customers in these states, you can use a simple criteria in the ZIP CODE field: 9. If the ZIP CODE field is numeric, you need more complex criteria.

The criteria for finding numbers, dates, and times is as follows:

- To find a number in a numeric or calculated field, type the number into the field object and press Enter.
- To find a date in a date or calculated field, type the date into the field object and press Enter. Type the date as numbers separated by a non-numeric character such as the slash character (for example, **12/31/94**). Entering the date in this format finds the date in any format.
- To find a time in a time or calculated field, use the hh:mm:ss syntax, using 24-hour (military) time or 12-hour time. Press Enter. Be sure to fill in zeroes for missing digits (for example, use **03** for 3 a.m.) and separate the portions of the time with colons. Entering the time in 24-hour or 12-hour format finds the time in either format.

See Chapter 10, "Using Advanced Field Types," for more information on calculated fields.

The Find Assistant detects the type of field you select for your find and displays an appropriate set of operators on the Condition 1 page (see fig. 6.8). You then enter your search criteria in the Values data-entry box, using the same rules as those listed in this section for finds using a view.

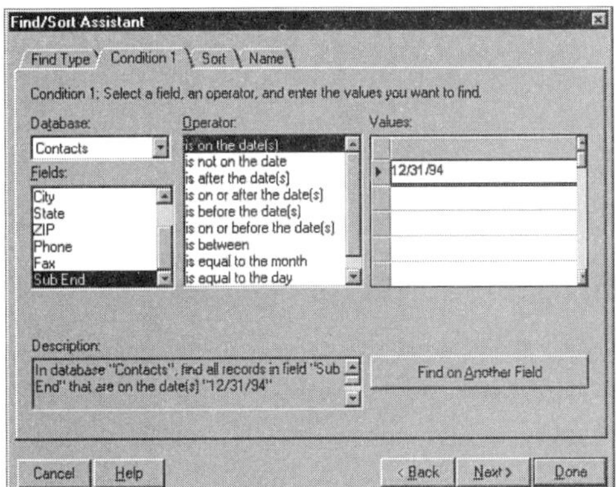

Fig. 6.8

Finds involving date fields are easily done using the date-oriented operators provided by the Find Assistant.

Entering Values in Check Box, Button, and Value-List Fields

While in find mode on a view, you can type your criteria into text, numeric, date, and time field objects as long as they aren't marked read-only. However, check box, radio button, list, and drop-down list fields don't allow you to type in values, even during a find. To enter the criteria for these field types, you must enter the value just as you would when filling in those values on a form, as follows:

- For check boxes, click the check box to indicate that you want to search for all instances in which the check box is marked. To search for all instances in which the check box isn't selected, click the check box twice—once to turn on the check box (an X appears), and again to turn it off (the check box is empty). Otherwise, the check box isn't used as part of the selection criteria.
- For radio button sets, click the button that represents the value for which you want to search.
- For list, drop-down list, and field box & list fields objects, either click the list to select the value you want, or type the value you want to search for. To search for a particular specialty on the Owl Publishing form, you can click the LEGAL SPECIALTY field and select the Specialty code you want. You can also type the code.

> **Note**
>
> Because you can't type values into check boxes or buttons, you can't use any of the special query operators (wild cards, ranges, OR, AND, and so on). If you need to use these operators to search check boxes or buttons, you must create another form in which these fields are formatted as default (text) field objects rather than as check boxes or buttons. You can also use an IF find, as discussed in Chapter 11, "Performing Advanced Finds."

The Find Assistant treats radio button and value-list types of fields the same as regular text fields. The values that they may contain aren't displayed automatically in the Values data-entry box in the Condition 1 page of the Find/Sort Assistant dialog box. Finds involving Boolean database fields, which are often displayed as check boxes on a form, are assisted as shown in figure 6.9.

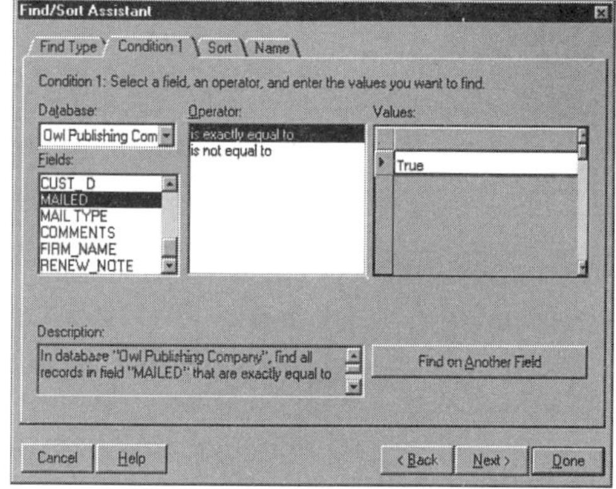

Fig. 6.9

The Find Assistant helps you in finds involving Boolean fields, which are often represented on forms as check box field objects.

Finding a Range of Values

Approach can find records in which fields are greater than a given value, less than a given value, or between two values (range). You can use text, numeric, and date and time fields in a range find.

When using a view to create a find, you enter the operators and comparison value(s) directly into the field object on the form. With the Find Assistant, you select the database field name and the appropriate comparison operator phrase in the Condition 1 page of the Find/Sort Assistant dialog box. Then you enter your comparison values in the Values data-entry box.

Finding a Greater-Than Value. To use a view to find all records that contain a value in a field that's larger than a comparison value, use the > (greater than) symbol, followed by the comparison value. To include records in the found set in which the fields also contain the comparison value, use the >= (greater than or equal to) symbol instead.

For example, to find all text values that don't begin with A (text values that begin with B, C, D, and so on), type **>Az** or **>=B**. To find a date later than 01/01/94, type **>01/01/94**. To find a number greater than or equal to 0, type **>=0**.

When you're using the Find Assistant with a Basic Find type, the Condition 1 page gives you different options for greater-than comparisons, depending on the database field type, as shown in the following table.

Field Type	> Symbol	>= Symbol
text	is after	is after or equal to
numeric	is greater than	is greater than or equal to
date	is after the date	is on or after the date
time	is after the time	is on or after the time

Finding a Less-Than Value. To use a view to find all records that contain a value in a field that's smaller than a comparison value, use the < (less than) symbol, followed by the comparison value. To include records in the found set that also contain the comparison value, use the <= (less than or equal to) symbol instead.

For example, to find all text values that are "less than Bob" (those that start with an earlier combination of letters in the alphabet, such as *Albert* or *Barb*) type **<Bob**. To find all dates earlier than 1994, use **<01/01/94** or **<=12/31/93**. To find all negative numbers, use **<0**.

When you're using the Find Assistant with a Basic Find type, the Condition 1 page gives you different options for less-than comparisons, depending on the database field type, as shown in the following table.

Field Type	< Symbol	<= Symbol
text	is before	is before or equal to
numeric	is less than	is less than or equal to
date	is before the date	is on or before the date
time	is before the time	is on or before the time

Finding a Value Between Two Values. To use a view to find all records that contain a field with a value that falls between two specified values, use an ellipsis (indicated by three periods, or ...) between the two values that define the range. To find records containing any date in 1994, for example, type **01/01/94...12/31/94**. In this example, records with fields containing a value of 01/01/94, any other date in 1994, or 12/31/94 are included in the found set.

Note

You must specify the range with the lower value on the left and the higher value on the right (12/31/94 is later than 01/01/94, and thus is a higher value). Approach can't find records if you fail to specify your ranges in this manner.

To find all records containing one of a range of numbers in a numeric field, type the limits of the range in that field. For example, to find all values between 1 and 10, inclusive, type **1...10**. If your range includes negative numbers, remember that negative numbers get smaller as the number value gets larger (–100 is smaller than –10).

Finding ranges of text works the same way. To find all records containing text strings that begin with letters in the first half of the alphabet, type **A...M** in the appropriate field.

Note

Only certain operators can be combined in a single criterion. You can combine multiple wildcard operators (such as **day?* or *??d*a**). You can also combine a single criterion with the & symbol. However, you can't combine any other operators in a single criterion. Thus, you can't use wild cards with the range find. Also, because you can't combine the ! operator with the range find, the find isn't case-sensitive.

Let's return to the Owl Publishing example for a moment. Suppose that Owl Publishing wants to find all records with subscription-end dates in 1995. Switch to Find mode by clicking Find on the action bar. Type **01/01/95...12/31/95** into the END DATE field object (see fig. 6.10) and press Enter.

After you finish inspecting the records that meet this criteria, open the Browse menu, choose Find, and then choose Find All to return to the entire database.

When you're using the Find Assistant with a Basic Find type, the Condition 1 page gives you a range-comparison operator, "is between," for all types of database fields. Repeating the example just done using a view, you would enter the date range as shown in figure 6.11.

After clicking Done, the same records you found before are available. Use the keyboard shortcut Ctrl+A to find all of your database records.

Using & to Find a Value Between Two Values. When using a view, you can combine the & symbol with the comparison operators (<, >, >=, and <=) to define a range search. Although using the & symbol involves more typing than using the ellipsis, you can be more specific about the limits on the range.

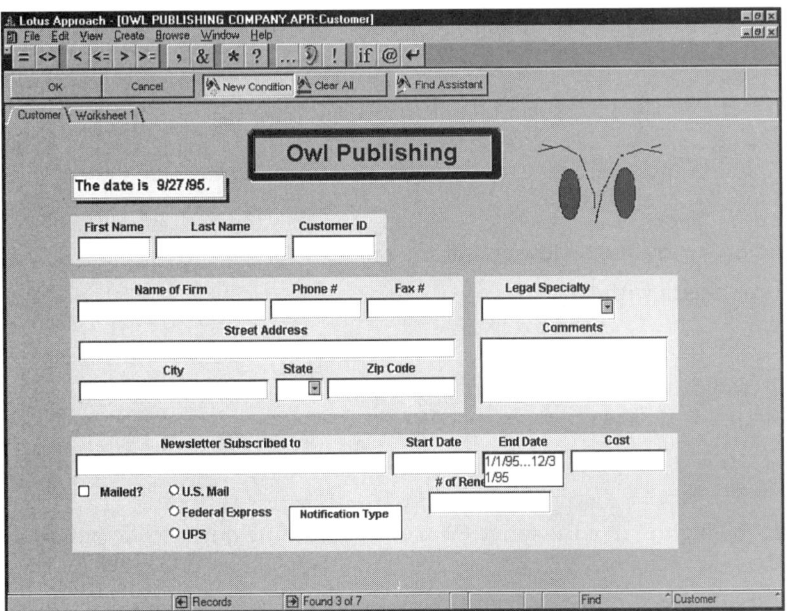

Fig. 6.10

Use the ellipsis to find records within a date range.

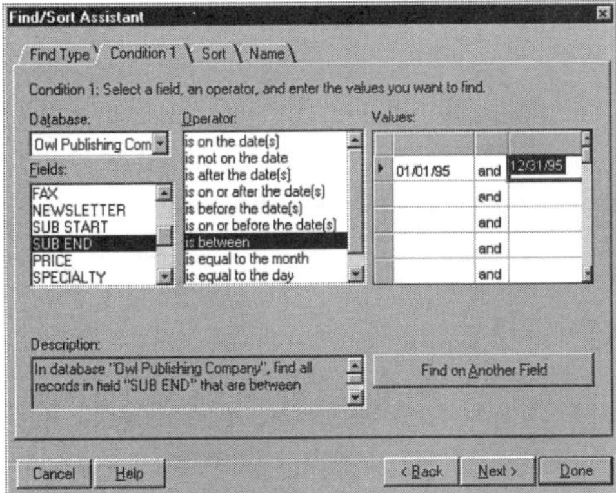

Fig. 6.11

Use the "is between" operator to find records within a date range with the Find Assistant.

> **Note**
>
> With the Find Assistant, you can duplicate the range searches described in this section by selecting the same field twice while using a multiple field AND find (described later in this chapter). You can't insert an & in a value entered in the Values data-entry box in the Find/Sort Assistant dialog box.

With the ellipsis, you must include the ends of the range in the found set. With the & symbol and comparison operators, however, you can specify the ends of the range without including those ends in the found set. That is, you can find all values between Ab and Mo, excluding those values (or including only one of them).

You can set up an & find by using a view in three steps:

1. Use the < or <= operator, as described earlier in the "Finding a Less-Than Value" section, to define the high end of the range.
2. Use the > or >= operator, as described earlier in the "Finding a Greater-Than Value" section, to define the low end of the range.
3. Join the two criteria with &.

For example,

- To find all records with text strings in a field between Ab and Mo but excluding those values, type **`>Ab&<Mo`** in the field object.
- To include the low end of the range (Ab) and everything up to Mo but excluding Mo, type **`>=Ab&<Mo`**.
- To include the high end of the range (Mo) and everything down to Ab but excluding Ab, type **`>Ab&<=Mo`**.
- To include both ends in the range and everything in between, type **`>=Ab&<=Mo`**. This syntax has the same result as using an ellipsis, but in this case is a lot more complicated to type.

> **Note**
>
> Remember, you can't use wild-card, case-sensitive, or exact-match operators in this type of range find using a view because these operators can't be combined with any other operators.

Finding Duplicate Records

In the process of entering large amounts of data, you can enter some records with duplicate data. Approach provides a way to find all the records with duplicate data in any combination of fields. You can select any fields on a form, including drop-down lists, radio buttons, and check boxes, although these types of fields will usually have values that duplicate other records.

To find duplicate records, follow these steps:

1. Switch to Browse mode by clicking Browse on the action bar.
2. Open the Browse menu, choose Find, and then choose Find Assistant on the submenu. The Find/Sort Assistant dialog box appears.
3. Select the Create a New Find radio button.
4. Select Find Duplicate Records in the Type of Find list. Click the Next button to see the Find Duplicates page (see fig. 6.12).
5. From the Fields list box on the left side of the Find Duplicates page, click the first field that you want to check for duplicates.

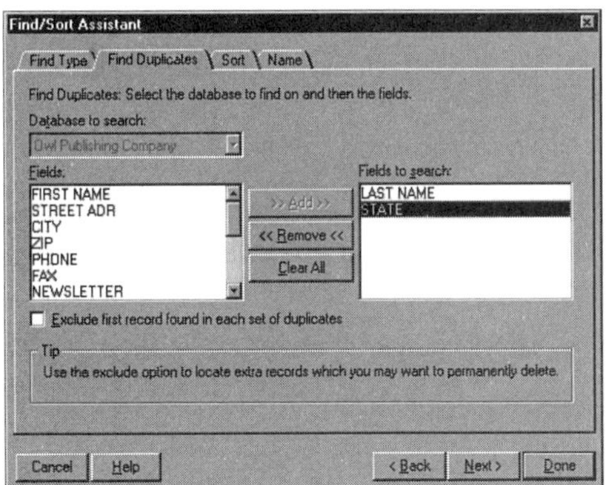

Fig. 6.12

When you're finding duplicate records, the Find/Sort Assistant dialog box provides a Find Duplicates page to enter your search criteria.

6. Click Add to move the field to the Fields to Search list box. (To remove a field from the Fields to Search list box, select that field and then click Remove.) You can also double-click a field to add or remove it.
7. Repeat steps 5 and 6 as needed to move all the fields that you want to check for duplicates to the Fields to Search list box. Only records that contain duplicates in all the specified fields are included in the found set.

> **Note**
>
> You must select the fields one at a time from the Fields to Search list box and move them by clicking the Add button. The Find Duplicates page doesn't let you select multiple fields at one time.

8. Near the bottom of the Find Duplicates page is a check box. If you check the Exclude First Record Found in Each Set of Duplicates check box, Approach excludes the first duplicate record from the found set. This is handy if the duplicates are errors that you want to delete but you want to leave one record of each set of duplicates in the database (see "Deleting the Found Set" later in this chapter).
9. Click Done to perform the find.

Finding Unique or Distinct Records

Finding unique or distinct records in your database is another function available to you through the Find Assistant. Use the preceding method for finding duplicates, but select the Find distinct or unique records option in the Find/Sort Assistant dialog box. Then enter your criteria on the Find Distinct page, which works just like the Find Duplicates page (refer to fig. 6.12).

This option is handy if you want to send a form letter, for example, to each unique customer in your customer database. You can also use this unique found set to create another database by exporting the found set.

Finding Blank Values in Fields

Finding records that contain blank or empty fields is important. These fields often represent data omissions. You may not have had the information that went into these fields, or the field is newly added and you need to fill in the information.

To use a view to find records that have a blank or missing value in a field, type an equal sign (=) into the field object on the form. The found set includes all records in which this field is blank or hasn't been filled in.

Owl Publishing suspects that not all their customers' addresses contain ZIP codes. To find these records for the company by using the Data Input form, follow these steps:

1. Switch to Find mode by clicking Find on the action bar.
2. Select the ZIP CODE field.
3. Type = and then press Enter. All records that have no ZIP codes are found.
4. After you finish inspecting the found record(s), open the Browse menu, choose Find, and then choose Find All to return to using the entire database.

When you're using the Find Assistant with a Basic Find type, the Condition 1 page has operators equivalent to the = symbol for each type of database field type. However, you can't enter an empty value in the Values data-entry box, making this type of find possible only when using a view.

> **Note**
>
> An *empty field* isn't exactly the same thing as a *blank field* in a database system. An empty field is said to have a *null value,* which indicates that the user hasn't supplied a value for this field in the database. A blank field indicates that the user entered blanks in this field. Boolean fields are empty until given a yes or no value by the user or by setting a default value during field definition.

Finding Non-Blank Values in Fields

Finding records containing fields that aren't blank is useful. Suppose that you want to send a large volume of mail. You don't want to generate mailing labels for customers for whom you don't have a complete address. By checking for non-blank fields, you can generate a found set of customer records with values in all the address fields.

By Using a view, to find a non-blank value in a field, switch to Find mode and type **< >** in the field object in which you want to search for non-blanks on the form. Click OK on the action bar to perform the search. The found set includes all records in which this field isn't blank.

When you're using the Find Assistant with a Basic Find type, the Condition 1 page has operators equivalent to the < > symbol for each type of database field type. However, you can't enter an empty value in the Values data-entry box, making this type of find possible only when using a view.

Using Multiple Criteria in a Single Field Object

You can find records in which the value in a field matches any of several different criteria. This type of find is called an *OR find* because the record will be part of the found set if the first condition is met OR the second condition is met OR the third condition is met (and so on). The record will be part of the found set if the field meets any of the criteria you type into the field.

Using a View with Multiple Criteria. To build a find with multiple criteria in a view, type the multiple criteria you want into the field object, and separate each part with a comma. Don't insert a space after the comma. If you want a list of all customers whose last name begins with A or J, for example, type **A,J** into the LAST NAME field object.

You can also use this technique with the = operator for full-string matches. To find the records of the last names *Abercrombie* or *Johnson*, for example, type **=Abercrombie,=Johnson**. There's no limit to the number of items you can add to this list.

OR searches on views can contain virtually any operators or combination of operators that are valid in each individual criterion:

- You can use wild cards in OR searches. For example, you can type ***Shell,A??n** to find any value in a field that ends in the word *Shell* or contains a 4-character value beginning with A and ending with n.
- You can use comparison operators such as > and <. For example, you can find all dates before 1994 or after 1994 (but excluding any dates in 1994) by typing **<01/01/94,>12/31/94** in the field.
- You can combine multiple criteria by using the & operator. For example, to find an exact match (including case) on *Dee* or any text strings beginning with C, type **!Dee&=Dee,C** in the field.
- You can combine all these operators into a complex find. For example, to find an exact match on *Dee*, all text beginning with C, or all text starting with E through Z, type **!Dee&=Dee,C,>=E** (for the last criterion, you can substitute **E...Z** for **>=E**).

Owl Publishing wants to find all the records with the names Roberts or Pettis in the LAST NAME field. To find specific records, follow these steps:

1. Switch to Find mode by clicking Find on the action bar.
2. Type **Roberts,Pettis** in the LAST NAME field object. Press Enter.
3. Only two records are now available—those for John Roberts and Marcy Pettis. Inspect them by using the VCR-like arrow buttons in the SmartIcon bar.
4. Open the Browse menu, choose Find, and then choose Find All to return to using the entire database.

Using the Find Assistant with Multiple Criteria. To use the Find Assistant to build a find with multiple criteria, type the criteria you want for a single field into the Values data-entry list box on separate lines. If you want a list of all customers whose last name begins with A or J, for example, use a Basic Type of find and click Next to go to the Condition 1 page. Select the LAST NAME database field, select the "starts with the character(s)" operator, and type **A** on the first line and **J** on the second line in the Values box. Click Done to perform the find. This method works when all of the comparisons use the same operator.

If you have multiple criteria with different operators, such as finding all customers whose last name begins with Dee, or C, or >=E, you must use the method described in the next section for multiple-field OR finds in different fields. When selecting the database fields in the Find Assistant, just select the LAST NAME field for every Condition type page.

Using Multiple Criteria in Different Fields

Approach can search for records in which find conditions have been specified in several different fields. Two different types of multiple field finds are available—an AND find and an OR find.

Setting Up a Multiple-Field AND Find. In a multiple-field AND find, a record is included in the found set only if the first criterion is satisfied AND the second criterion is satisfied AND the third criterion is satisfied (and so on). The record is included only if the fields in the record match all the criteria specified in the find.

By using a view, you can use any of the operators and techniques discussed previously on any of the fields, including an OR condition (multiple criteria in a field separated by commas). For example, to find all customers whose last names begin with A or C and who subscribe to the *Burglary Made Simple* newsletter, type **A,C** in the LAST NAME field and **Burglary Made Simple** in the NEWSLETTER SUBSCRIBED TO field (see fig. 6.13). Only those firms that meet both sets of criteria are included.

In this example, using a view, assume that Owl Publishing wants to mail some announcements about a new newsletter. The company wants to send the newsletter only to people who have full addresses in the database. At a minimum, the address must include the FIRST NAME, LAST NAME, STREET ADDRESS, CITY, STATE, and ZIP CODE. If any of these fields are blank, a mailing label isn't made for that subscriber.

To set up a multiple-field AND find to gather all the records in which these fields aren't blank, follow these steps:

1. Switch to Find mode by clicking Find on the action bar.
2. Type the criteria into the appropriate fields. For this example, type **< >** into the FIRST NAME, LAST NAME, STREET ADDRESS, CITY, STATE, and ZIP CODE fields (see fig. 6.14).
3. Click OK on the action bar.

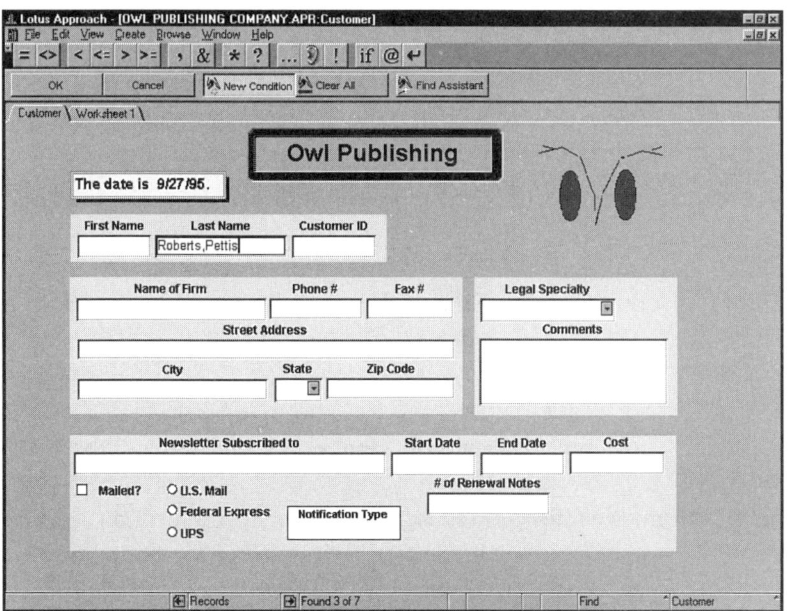

Fig. 6.13

Entering search criteria in multiple fields on a view is a powerful feature of Approach.

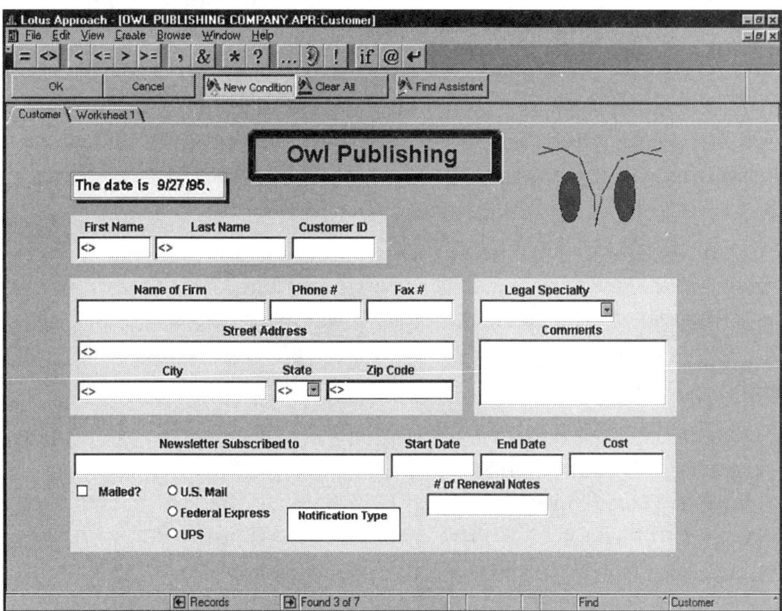

Fig. 6.14

Using < > in fields prevents a mailing label from being printed for incomplete addresses.

Approach begins its search, and the records with valid addresses appear in the found set. If you've been following the examples so far in this book, one record in the database is missing from the found set because it has a blank ZIP CODE field. (Remember? You entered George Kinder without a value for ZIP.)

By using the Find Assistant, you set up a multiple-field AND search using the Find on Another Field button on the Condition 1 page of the Find/Sort Assistant dialog box. For example, to find all customers whose last names begin with A or C and who subscribe to the *Burglary Made Simple* newsletter, enter the keyboard shortcut Ctrl+I to start the Find Assistant, and then follow these steps:

1. Select Basic Find from the Type of Find list box, and then click the Next button.
2. On the Condition 1 page, select the LAST NAME database field, select the "starts with the character(s)" operator, and then enter **A** on the first line of the Values data-entry box and **C** on the second line (finds names starting with A or C).
3. Click the Find on Another Field button. The Condition 2 page is displayed.
4. Select the Find Fewer Records (AND) radio button at the top of the page. Then select the NEWSLETTER SUBSCRIBED TO database field, select the "is exactly equal to" operator, and enter **Burglary Made Simple** on the first line of the Values data-entry box.
5. Click Done to perform the find. Only those firms that meet both conditions are included.

Setting Up a Multiple-Field OR Search. When you use a view to set up a multiple-field OR find, Approach uses more than one copy of the view so that you can specify each set of find criteria. You can use any technique detailed so far (including single-field OR conditions and multiple-field AND conditions) to fill out the view for each part of the find.

Each copy of the view is called a *request*. A record is included in the found set if the fields in the record match any requests specified in the find. The record is included if the first request is satisfied OR the second request is satisfied OR the third request is satisfied, and so on.

Suppose that Owl Publishing wants to find out which of its customers have subscriptions to *Burglary Made Simple* or to *Assault Today* that end in 1995. To set up a multiple-field OR find using a view with this criteria, follow these steps:

1. Switch to Find mode by clicking Find on the action bar. The form clears, and you're ready to set up a find.
2. Type the criteria for the first request into the first form. For the Owl Publishing example, type **Burglary Made Simple** into the NEWSLETTER SUBSCRIBED TO field and **1/1/95...12/31/95** into the END DATE field (see fig. 6.15). Notice that the text you type can be longer than the space provided on the form.
3. Open the Browse menu, choose Find, and then choose Find More. A new blank form appears.
4. Type the criteria for the second request into the second find form. For this example, type **Assault Today** in the NEWSLETTER SUBSCRIBED TO field and **1/1/95...12/31/95** into the END DATE field (see fig. 6.16).

   Repeat steps 3 and 4 to specify as many OR requests as you want. Records that meet any of the requests are included in the subsequent found set.

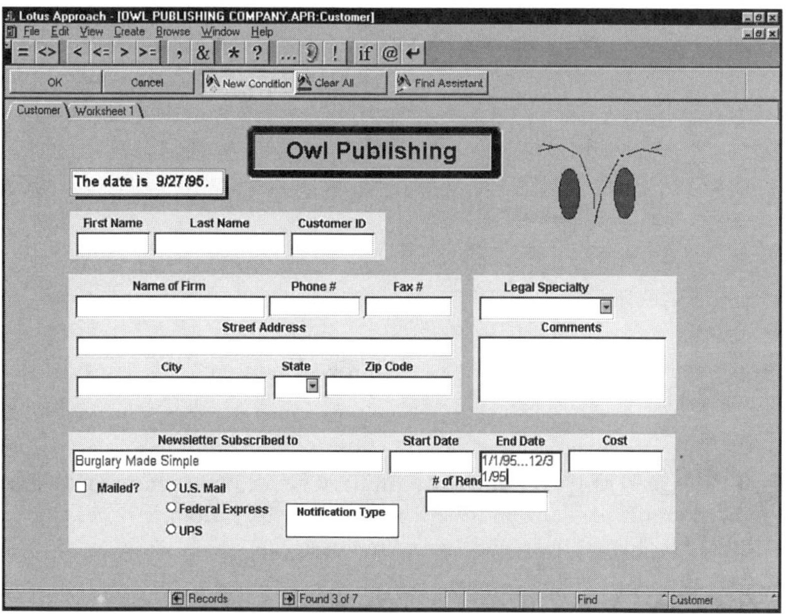

Fig. 6.15

Enter the first search criteria for OR searches.

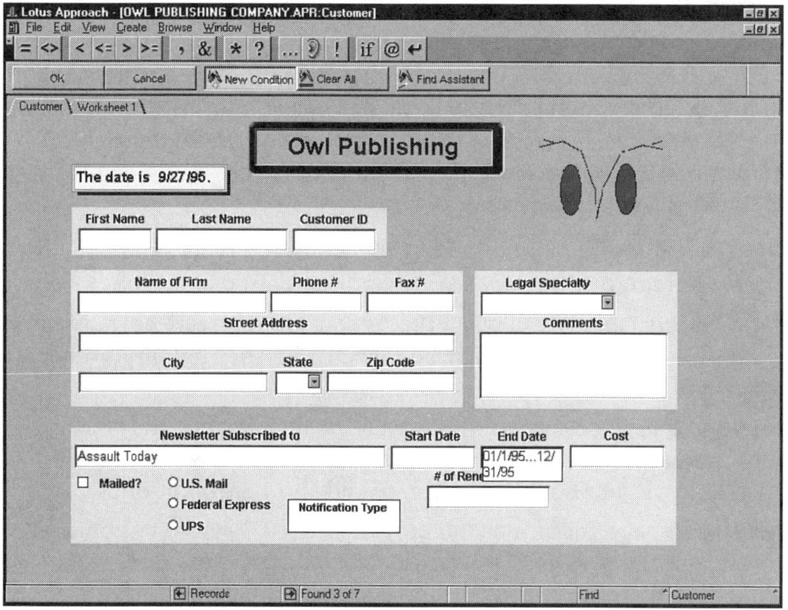

Fig. 6.16

Enter more unique find criteria for your OR search.

Tip

Move through multiple find request forms by using the next and previous record buttons on the status bar.

5. Click OK on the action bar after you finish specifying all requests to perform the find.
6. Use the VCR-like arrow buttons on the SmartIcon bar to move through the records in the found set to verify that the found set includes the records that match your criteria.
7. After you finish viewing the records, open the Browse menu, choose Find, and then choose Find All.

When you fill out each find request on a view in a multiple-field OR query, you can type a value into a single field or type values into multiple fields before moving to the next request. If you type multiple values into a single form before moving on to the next request, the find is evaluated in the following manner:

- For each request, records are included if they meet all the conditions on the find form—that is, an AND search is done on the database for the request.
- Approach builds the found set by joining the sets of records that satisfy each AND find on the individual requests.

With the Find Assistant, there's no direct equivalent to the multiple-field OR search using requests. But you can accomplish many of these types of finds by restructuring the search criteria. Take the case where Owl Publishing wants to find out which customers have subscriptions to *Burglary Made Simple* that end in 1996 or to *Assault Today* that end in 1995. Break the criteria up as follows:

1. Press Ctrl+I to start the Find Assistant, select the Basic Find type, and then click Next to see the Condition 1 page of the Find/Sort Assistant dialog box.
2. Select the SUB END database field, select the "is equal to the year" operator, and then enter **1996** in the Values data-entry box. Then click the Find on Another Field button to add a condition.
3. On the Condition 2 page, select the NEWSLETTER database field, the "is exactly equal to" operator, and enter **Burglary Made Simple** in the Values data-entry box. Click the Find on Another Field button to add another condition.
4. On the Condition 3 page, select the Find More Records (OR) radio button at the top of the page. Select the SUB END database field, select the "is equal to the year" operator, and then enter **1995** in the Values data-entry box. Click the Find on Another Field button to add another condition.
5. On the Condition 4 page, select the NEWSLETTER database field, select the "is exactly equal to" operator, and then enter **Assault Today** in the Values data-entry box.
6. Click Done to see the records that match these conditions.

Caution

When adding multiple AND and OR conditions with the Find Assistant, Approach evaluates the criteria set within a Condition page, followed by the ANDs across multiple Condition pages, and finally the ORs across multiple Condition pages. Be careful when setting up your finds using the Find Assistant because "a and b or c" *is not the same as* "a and b or a and c."

Finding the Top or Lowest Values

Finding records that contain values in the top or lowest range of values in your database can be very useful. Suppose that you want to find the top three customers according to their newsletter subscription value. You could sort the entire database high-to-low and view the records on a worksheet or report, but this would be inefficient. Finding the top 10 percent would require you to calculate how many 10 percent would be, and then sort the database for viewing.

The Find Assistant has a Find the Top or Lowest Values option with which you can locate a specific number or percentage of the highest or lowest values in your numeric or calculated fields. For example, using the Owl Publishing Company data, find the top three customers according to subscription value by following these steps:

1. Press Ctrl+I to start the Find Assistant. Select Find the Top or Lowest Values from the Type of Find list. Then click Next to see the Find Top/Lowest page of the Find/Sort Assistant dialog box (see fig. 6.17).

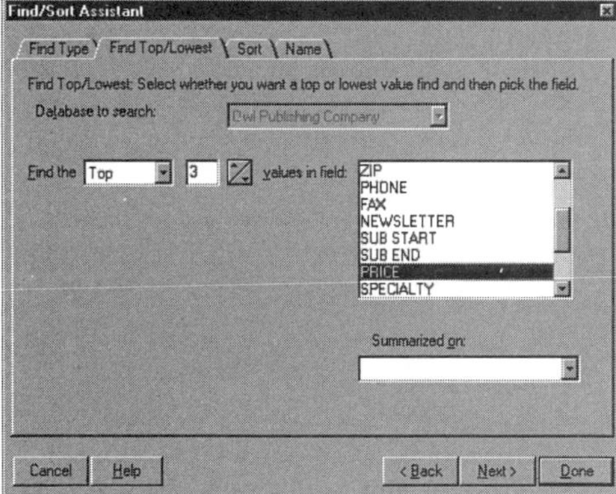

Fig. 6.17

Use the Find Top/Lowest page to locate database records that are in the top/lowest number/percentage on a numeric or calculated field.

2. Select the database from the Database to Search drop-down list and the PRICE database field from the Values in Field list box.

3. In the Find The drop-down list, select Top, and then set the spin box next to it from 10 down to 3.
4. Click Done to perform the find.

You'll see the records with the highest subscription value in the view from which you initiated the find. You can switch to Worksheet 1 view to see these records in a list format.

Performing a Find Using Query by Box

The Find Assistant lets you graphically create finds that can include AND and OR conditions. Because you see the find conditions displayed as a diagram on the Query by Box page of the Find/Sort Assistant dialog box, it's often easier to set up multifield or multicondition criteria with this facility.

Comparison operators are limited to =, < >, <, <=, >, and >=, regardless of the database field type you're using in your find.

Suppose that you want to find all *Assault Today* customers whose subscriptions expire after 1/1/95, or *Burglary Made Simple* subscribers whose subscriptions expire after 1/1/96. Follow these steps to do a Query by Box:

1. Start the Find Assistant by pressing Ctrl+I. The Find/Sort Assistant dialog box appears.
2. In the Type of Find list, select Find Using Query by Box. The Query by Box tab appears at the top of the dialog box; select this tab to see its associated page.
3. For each condition in your query, select a database in the Table drop-down list, a field name in the Field drop-down list, and an operator in the Operator drop-down list. Enter your comparison value in the Value text box. Then select And or Or to enter the next condition.

The example shown in figure 6.18 was created as follows:

Field Name	Operator	Value	Next Type
SUB END	>	1/1/95	And
NEWSLETTER	=	Assault Today	Or
SUB END	>	1/1/96	And
NEWSLETTER	=	Burglary Made Simple	Done

The find conditions entered using Query by Box show AND conditions grouped together in a box connected by OR conditions in a pointer-shaped box. This way, you can visually confirm that Approach will find the records that meet your criteria.

After you create some conditions, you can move them to change the logical relationship of the conditions displayed. To move a condition, position your mouse pointer over the condition; when the hand shape appears, click and drag the condition where you want it. For example, you could drag the last condition (`NEWSLETTER='Burglary Made Simple'`) from the second box to the first one and change the overall find condition. It would now find either newsletter that expired after 1/1/95 and any newsletter that expired after 1/1/96. Try creating the example query and move some of the conditions around to see how the relationships change.

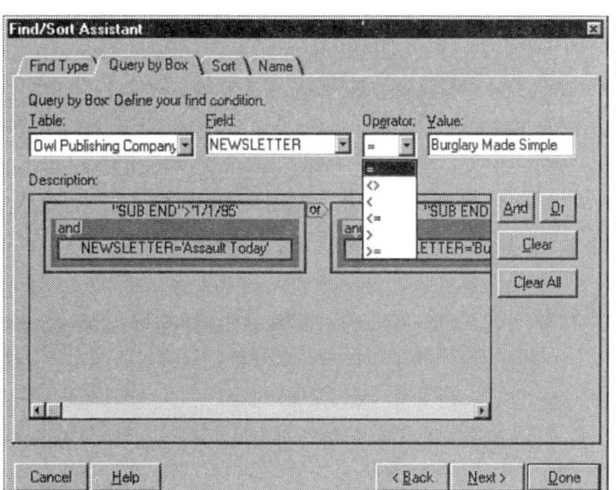

Fig. 6.18

Use the Query by Box page to find records by using AND and OR criteria on multiple fields.

Modifying Your Last Find

Setting up a find can take considerable time. Sometimes you may notice that the find you've constructed doesn't quite give you the found set that you want. You can modify your last find by opening the Browse menu, choosing Find, and then choosing Find Again (Ctrl+G). After your last find appears on-screen, you can edit any of its criteria and try again. You can also name your find and edit or perform it at any time (see "Naming and Saving a Set of Find Criteria" later in this chapter) or create a macro that lets you edit and perform any find you build (see Chapter 13, "Automating Your Work").

Canceling a Find During Creation

If you want to clear the find criteria you have entered on a view, click the Clear All button in the action bar.

If you decide that you don't want to perform a find that you've started to create using a view, press the Esc key or click the Cancel button on the action bar at any time to cancel the find. The previous found set is still active.

If you're using the Find Assistant, click the Cancel button or press the Esc key to close the Find/Sort Assistant dialog box.

Another way to cancel a find is to open the Browse menu, choose Find, and then choose Find All. If you cancel a find this way, the entire database becomes available.

Naming and Saving a Set of Find Criteria

If you've set up a find that you want to be able to use again without going through set up each time, you can give your find a name and save it. To do so, follow these steps:

1. Open the Create menu and choose Named Find/Sort. The Named Find/Sort dialog box appears (see fig. 6.19).

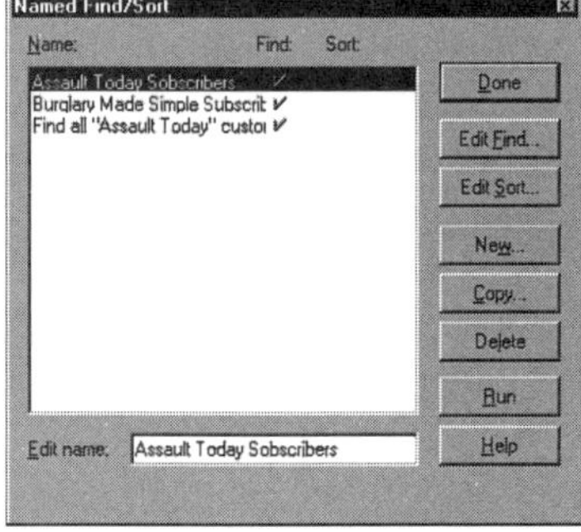

Fig. 6.19

Use the Named Find/Sort dialog box for saving frequently used criteria.

2. Click the New button and a dialog box will give you the option to use the Assistant, to use the View (current form), or to Cancel.
3. Click the View button; the current form appears in Find mode. Either enter your find criteria or, if you've just completed performing the find, click the Recall Last Find on the action bar to get the criteria filled in automatically.
4. Click OK on the action bar. The Name Find/Sort dialog box lets you enter a long, descriptive name for your find criteria. Click the Done button to complete the operation.

If in step 2 you had selected Assistant, the Find/Sort Assistant dialog box would now appear. Create your find by using the techniques you have learned in this chapter and click the Name tab. The Name page appears (see fig. 6.20). Enter a unique name for your find and click Done to save it.

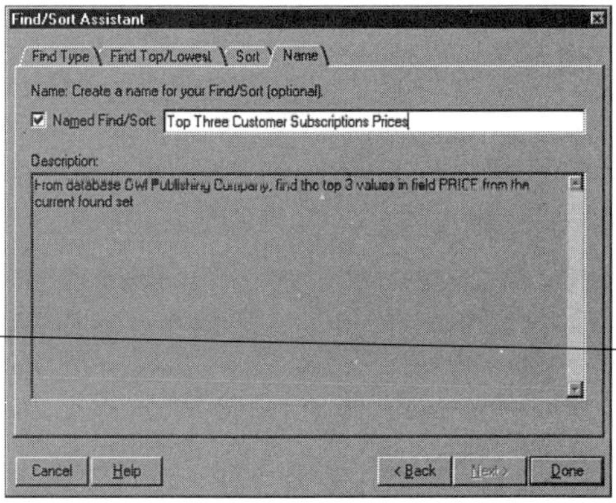

Fig. 6.20

Use the Name page in the Find/Sort Assistant dialog box to give your find a descriptive name.

Performing a Named Find

Names that you've given your named finds appear on the action bar in the Named Find/Sort drop-down list box (see fig. 6.21). To perform a named find, drop down the list and select the desired find name. Approach will perform the find and display the form and found set just as it would do if you entered the find criteria again.

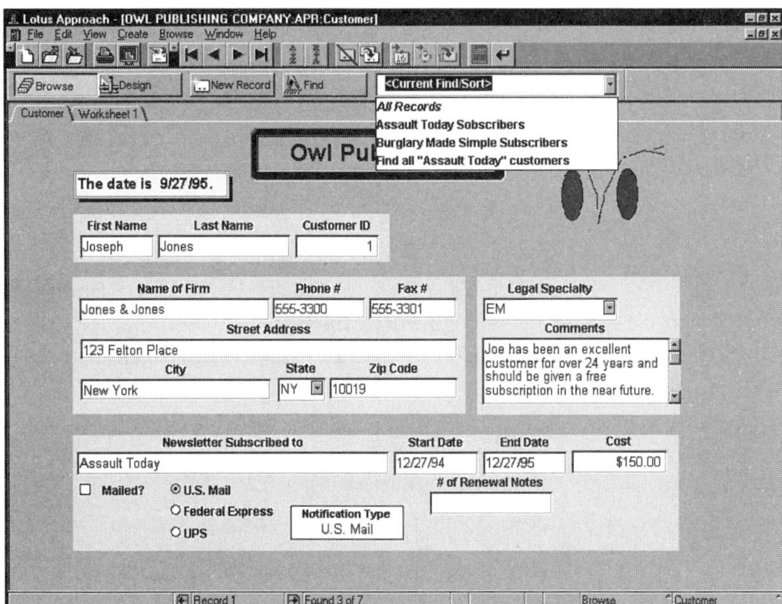

Fig. 6.21

Select a named find from the Named Find/Sort drop-down list on the action bar.

Modifying and Copying a Named Find

You may need to change your criteria in a named find if you discover your needs have changed. If you no longer need the original find, you can modify it. If you'll need the original find but need a similar one to address new conditions, you can copy the original and give it a new name.

To perform either of these operations, follow these steps:

1. Open the Create menu and choose Named Find/Sort. The Named Find/Sort dialog box appears (refer to fig. 6.19).
2. Select the name of the find you want to modify or copy from the Name list box, or type the name into the Edit Name text box at the bottom of the dialog box. To edit the find, click the Edit Find button; the original request view or the Find Assistant appears. To copy the find, click the Copy button; a dialog box will let you give the copy a name before going on to the view or Find Assistant.
3. Each criteria in your original or copied named find will be available for you to modify on a request form or in the Find Assistant. Click the next and previous record buttons on the status bar to find the request form you want to modify, if

you have multiple request forms in the current find. Alternatively, click the tabs in the Find/Sort Assistant dialog box to modify the conditions as needed.

4. Click OK on the action bar to save the updated find criteria when using a view. Click Done to save the updated find when using the Find Assistant.

Working with the Found Set

You can perform two especially useful operations on a found set—you can delete the entire found set, or you can fill a field with a value. These operations are in addition to your ability to navigate through the found set doing updates or reviewing a report that contains only the found set's records.

Deleting the Found Set

Opening the Browse menu and choosing Delete Found Set deletes all currently found records from the database. Deleting the found set is useful if you can create a find that gathers all the records you no longer need. If you no longer plan to send mail to firms with a specialty of EM, for example, you can write a find for all firms with that specialty and discard these records.

To delete the found set, follow these steps:

1. Perform the find that gathers the records you no longer want.
2. Open the Browse menu and choose Delete Found Set. Approach requests verification (see fig. 6.22).
3. When you click Yes, the records are discarded.

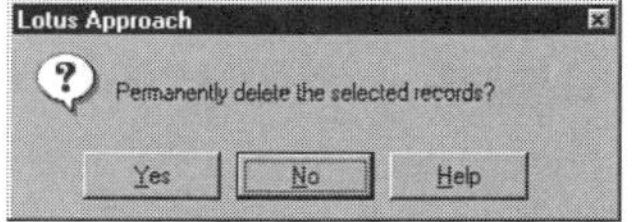

Fig. 6.22

You can delete a set of records that meet your find criteria.

Filling Fields in a Found Set

Approach can fill any field in a found set (or in the whole database) with a value. Opening the Browse menu and choosing Fill Field is useful if you just added a new blank field to a database, and the majority of the records have the same value in that field. You can fill the field with this value, and then go through and change only the few records with different values.

This operation is also handy if you create a find that gathers records with the same value in a field. You can then put the appropriate new value into this field. For example, you can create a find that gathers all firms located in Houston and Dallas. You then can fill the STATE field with TX, because both cities are in Texas.

To perform a fill field operation, follow these steps:

1. Switch to Browse mode by clicking Browse on the action bar.
2. If you're changing only the records in a found set, create and run a find that specifies the found set. Otherwise, fill field will use the entire database.
3. Open the Browse menu and choose Fill Field. The Fill Field dialog box appears (see fig. 6.23).

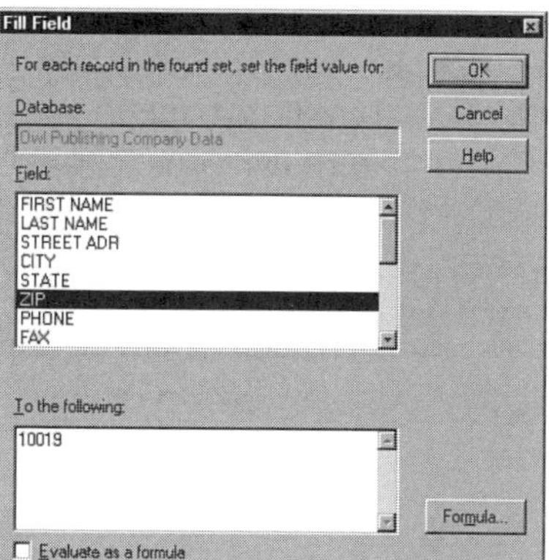

Fig. 6.23

While in Browse or Find mode, you can update a field using the Fill Field dialog box.

4. Select the field for which you want to enter a value. This field doesn't have to be empty, but the value you insert replaces any value in that field in the found set (or the entire database, if no current found set is active).
5. In the To the Following list box, type the value that you want placed in the field. Approach doesn't allow you to type a longer value than fits into the field. You can also create the value by building a formula, as described in Chapter 2, "Creating Database Tables," by clicking the Formula button on the Fill Field dialog box.
6. Click OK to insert the value into every record.

Hiding Records

With Approach, you can hide any records you don't want to work with. Hiding records makes them temporarily unavailable—it doesn't erase them.

Hiding records can be useful if you don't want to work with just a few records in the found set. Often, you create a simple find that retrieves not only all the records you want, but also a small number you don't want. Perhaps you could create a much more complex find that retrieves only the records you want, but hiding the few records you don't need is often simpler.

Note

Hidden records are still included in any finds you perform, because executing a new find undoes the Hide Records feature, making all records available to be found in the find. In other words, all records are available in any find.

To hide records, follow these steps:

1. Switch to Browse mode by clicking Browse on the action bar.
2. Move to the record you want to hide by using the Next Record or Previous Record SmartIcons, the record navigation keys on the keyboard, or the status bar buttons.
3. Open the Browse menu and choose Hide Record. The record is no longer available. You can also press Ctrl+H to hide a record.

Repeat steps 2 and 3 to hide all the records you don't want to work with. To make hidden records available again, open the Browse menu, choose Find, and then choose Find All.

From Here...

This chapter discussed how to find records that meet the find criteria you type into fields on a form or specify by using the Find Assistant. Special operators can be used to find the records you want. After this found set is obtained, you can perform operations on just those found records.

For more information on using Approach's find function, see the following chapters in this book:

- Chapter 7, "Creating Reports and Mailing Labels," shows you how to create reports and mailing labels, which can be very useful in displaying and using the results of a find.
- Chapter 9, "Designing Advanced Forms," shows you how to display the results of a find in a sophisticated form that includes multiple joined databases.
- Chapter 11, "Performing Advanced Finds," shows you how to perform even more powerful finds.

CHAPTER 7

Creating Reports and Mailing Labels

As powerful as Approach's forms are, they can't perform certain functions. A form can't present the information from more than one record at a time. A form also can't summarize information across multiple records in the database. Approach's powerful report builder, however, gets around the limitations of forms.

Approach also allows you to build mailing labels quickly and easily. You can set up custom mailing labels or use standard sizes from Avery. If you use standard size labels, Approach does all the work for you by setting sizes and margins.

If you're comfortable with designing forms, you should have no trouble designing reports and mailing labels; they work almost exactly the way forms work.

In this chapter, you learn how to

- Create blank, columnar, and standard reports
- Change the report name and basic specifications
- Set the number of columns in a report
- Delete or duplicate a report
- Add a header or footer to a report
- Customize a report with text, lines, boundaries, and more
- Use PowerClick reporting to organize and summarize your data easily
- Add a title page to a report
- Create a mailing label
- Delete or duplicate a mailing label
- Preview and print a report or mailing label

Understanding the Differences Between a Form and a Report

Reports present information in the database in ways that circumvent the limitations of forms. Consider the following report capabilities:

- Reports can show multiple records on a page. When you print a form, each page holds only a single record. In contrast, when you print a report, each page can hold the information from many records. You can adjust the size of the "body" box that holds each record to provide more or less room between records on a report.
- Reports can summarize information in different ways, without forcing you to re-enter the data. In the Owl Publishing database, for example, a report can summarize all firms that subscribe to a certain newsletter. If you kept a record of the salespeople who contacted specific firms to sell them newsletter subscriptions, you also can get a report of all sales, grouped by salesperson.
- Reports have formatting options that aren't available on forms. These options include title pages, headers, and footers.

In many ways, reports are also similar to forms. Consider the following traits:

- You can use reports as well as forms to input information. If you change a field in a report, these changes are stored in the database, just as if you changed the record on a form.

> **Note**
>
> Reports often don't include all the fields necessary to enter a record completely. If you enter records in this kind of report, they will be incomplete because information in some fields will be missing.

- You can customize fields on a report by using most of the options available on a form, such as specifying the data-entry format and display format.
- You can perform finds and sorts on a report.

Creating a Report

To create a report, follow these steps:

1. Open the Create menu and choose Report, or click the New Report SmartIcon. The Report Assistant dialog box appears (see fig. 7.1).
2. Type the name of the report in the View Name and Title text box.
3. Select a style from the Style drop-down list. The styles give the report a consistent look, such as shadowed, executive, chiseled, and so on.

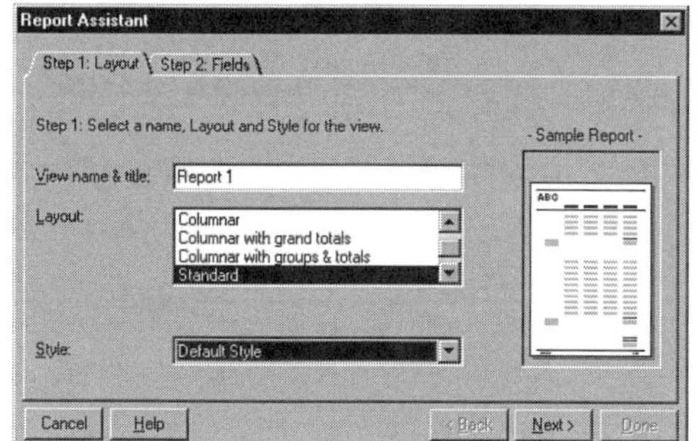

Fig. 7.1

The Report Assistant makes it easy to create a report.

4. Select the layout you want from the Layout list (see the following section, "Choosing the Type of Report").
5. For all reports except Blank and Summary-Only reports, select the fields to include on the report, as discussed in "Choosing Fields for the Report."
6. Click OK. Approach creates the report according to your specifications.

Choosing the Type of Report

The type of information needed in your report—data, summaries, special groupings and/or totals—determines the final report layout. Approach offers several different layouts that you can select from the Layout list in the Report Assistant dialog box: Blank, Columnar, Columnar with Grand Totals, Columnar with Groups & Totals, Standard, and Summary-Only. Summary reports (discussed in Chapter 12, "Creating Advanced Reports") summarize data across multiple records and place the results in various locations on the report. Blank, standard, and columnar reports are discussed in the following sections.

> **Note**
>
> If you have two or more joined tables in your database, another type of report tool is available—repeating panels. See Chapter 12 for more information on repeating panel reports.

Creating a Blank Report. To create a blank report, select Blank from the Layout list. A blank report opens a blank report template, with no fields or formatting present. You can use the techniques discussed in later sections to add fields, graphics, illustrations, text, headers, footers, and a title page to a blank report.

Creating a Standard Report. To create a standard report, select Standard from the Layout list. When you create this type of report, all fields you place on the report initially appear on lines across the report (see "Choosing Fields for the Report" later in this chapter). When no more room exists on a line, Approach moves down one line and continues placing fields on the report. This configuration is similar to the default forms that Approach creates (see fig. 7.2).

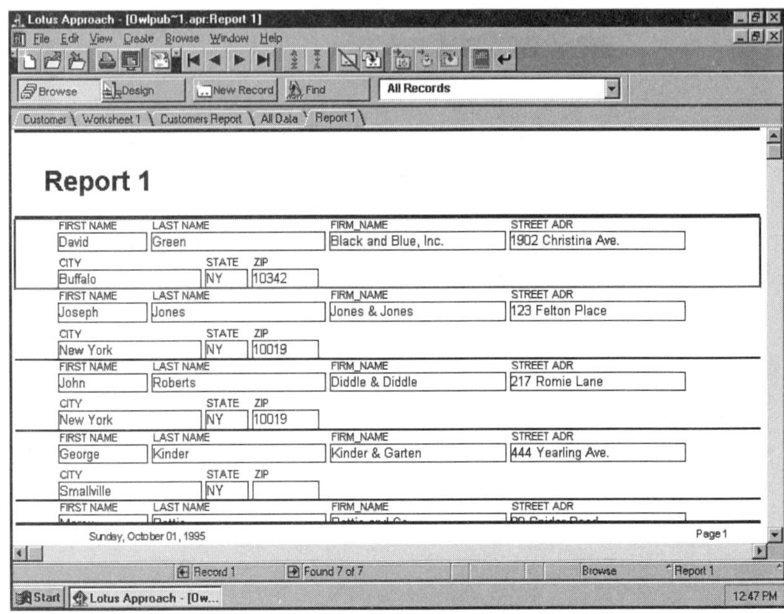

Fig. 7.2

A standard report, like the default form, contains fields across the page.

Creating a Columnar Report. To create a columnar report, select Columnar from the Layout list. In a columnar report, each record appears as a row in the report, and each field appears as a column. The name of the field appears as a column heading at the top of the column (see fig. 7.3).

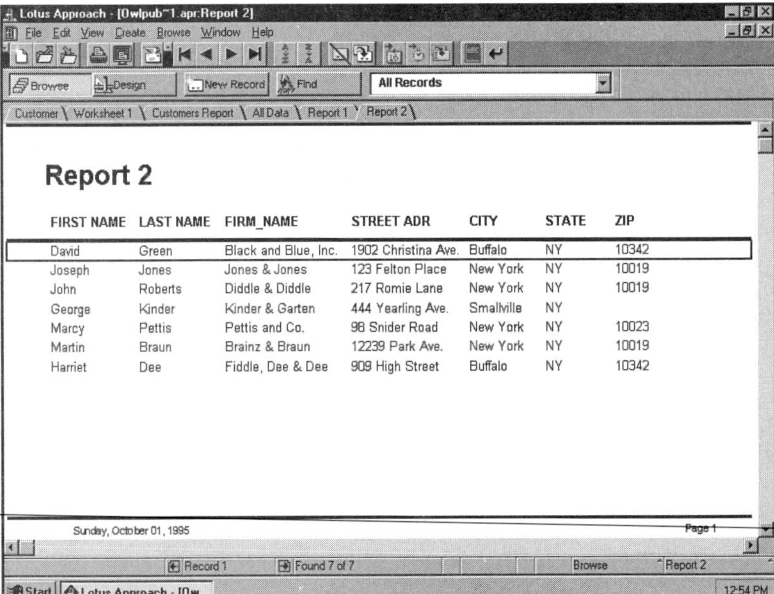

Fig. 7.3

A columnar report lists one record per row and a field in each column.

Selecting Columnar with Grand Totals from the Layout list generates a report similar to a regular columnar report, except that a calculation may be performed on one or more columns. Owl Publishing, for example, may need the total revenues from subscriptions listed in a report (see fig. 7.4).

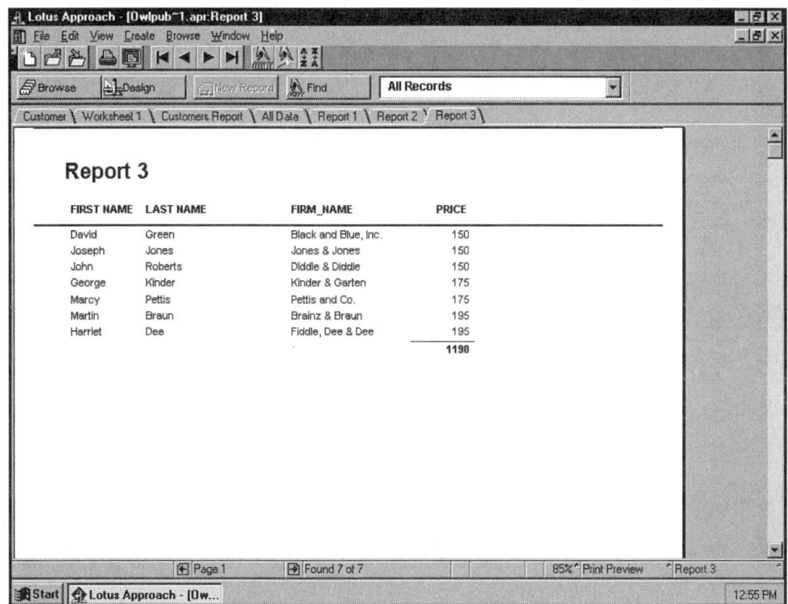

Fig. 7.4

A columnar report with grand totals performs a calculation on one or more columns.

Selecting Columnar with Groups and Totals from the Layout list takes the extra step of organizing and summarizing records by category before producing a grand total. In figure 7.5, for example, Owl Publishing's subscription revenues are further broken down by individual newsletter.

If your report doesn't start with groups or totals, don't worry. You can use PowerClick reporting to add these items later. For more information on this feature, see "Building Data Summaries with PowerClick Reporting" later in this chapter.

Note

When only field names (not data) are displayed in Design mode, the name of the column becomes a text item. You can move this text item independently of the column, and it has its own InfoBox.

If you include more columns in a columnar report than can fit across the page, Approach uses multiple pages (see fig. 7.6). You can see the page break as you scroll the display to the left and right. Approach doesn't try to keep all fields on one page; if the field is located at the right edge of a page, the column header and field text may be split across the pages. The best solution is to restrict columnar reports to one page by selecting fewer fields or choosing a smaller font.

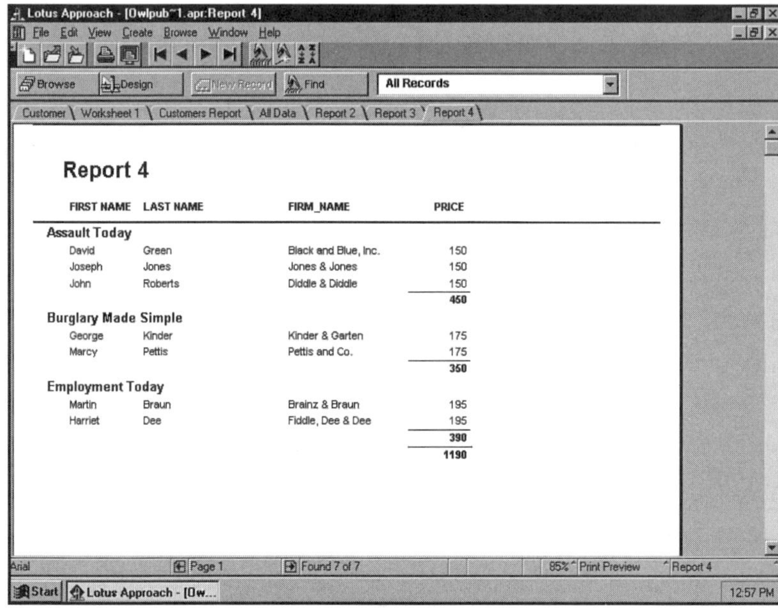

Fig. 7.5

A columnar report with groups and totals builds sub-summaries within similar categories.

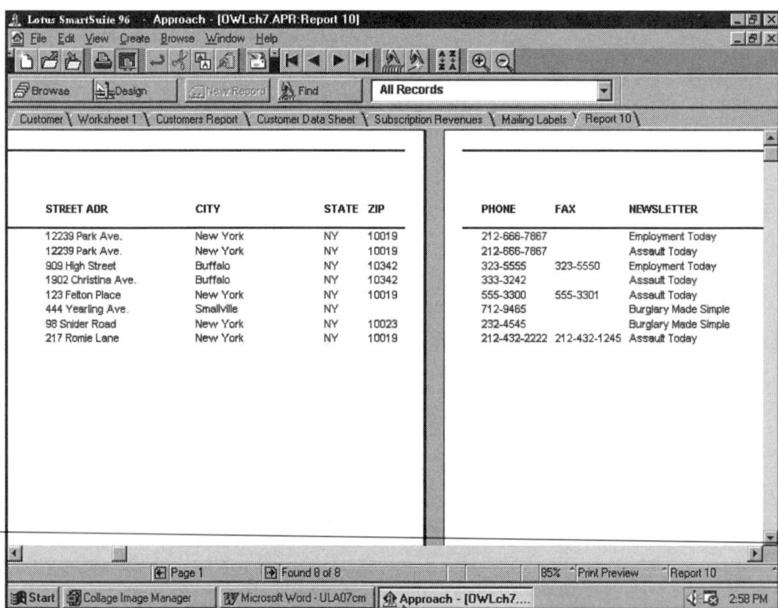

Fig. 7.6

A columnar report may sometimes break across pages.

Choosing Fields for the Report

For all reports except Blank and Summary-Only, you can choose the fields that Approach puts on the report. In the Report Assistant dialog box, click the Step 2: Fields tab or the Next button. The Fields list on the left side of the Fields page displays all the fields in the database. To add a field to the report, select the field in the Fields list and click Add. Approach moves the field to the Fields to Place on View list. You also can double-click the field to move it to the Fields to Place on View list.

Tip

To select multiple fields, click the first field and then Ctrl+click any other fields you want to select.

If you want to remove a field from the list of report fields, select the field in the Fields to Place on View list and click Remove. You also can double-click a field to remove it from the Fields to Place on View list.

You can return to the Step 1: Layout page by clicking its tab or by clicking the Back button.

Creating a Sample Report

Owl Publishing wants to create a columnar report that lists all its customers. This report will include only customer names and newsletter titles so that each record can fit on one row. Follow these steps to create a columnar report:

1. Switch to Design mode by opening the View menu and choosing Design, clicking the Design button on the action bar, or selecting Design from the status bar.
2. Open the Create menu and choose Report, or click the Create a New Report SmartIcon. The Report Assistant dialog box appears (refer back to fig. 7.1).
3. Type `Customers Report` in the View Name & Title text box.
4. Choose Executive from the Style drop-down list.

Tip

Approach is smart enough to remember what style and layout you last used.

5. Choose Columnar from the Layout list.
6. Click the Step 2: Fields tab to move to the Fields page.
7. In the Fields list, select FIRST NAME. Then Ctrl+click LAST NAME, FIRM_NAME, and NEWSLETTER.
8. Click Add. The fields appear in the Fields to Place on View list (see fig. 7.7).

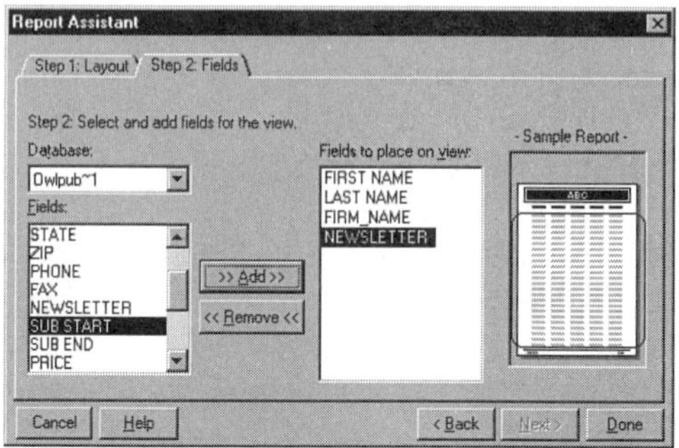

Fig. 7.7

Select the field names you want to add to your columnar report.

> **Tip**
>
> To save time, select fields for the Fields to Place on View list in the order you want them to appear in your report.

9. Click Done. The new report appears (see fig. 7.8). If the report shows data rather than the field names, choose Show Data from the View menu (remove the check mark) to show the field names rather than the data.

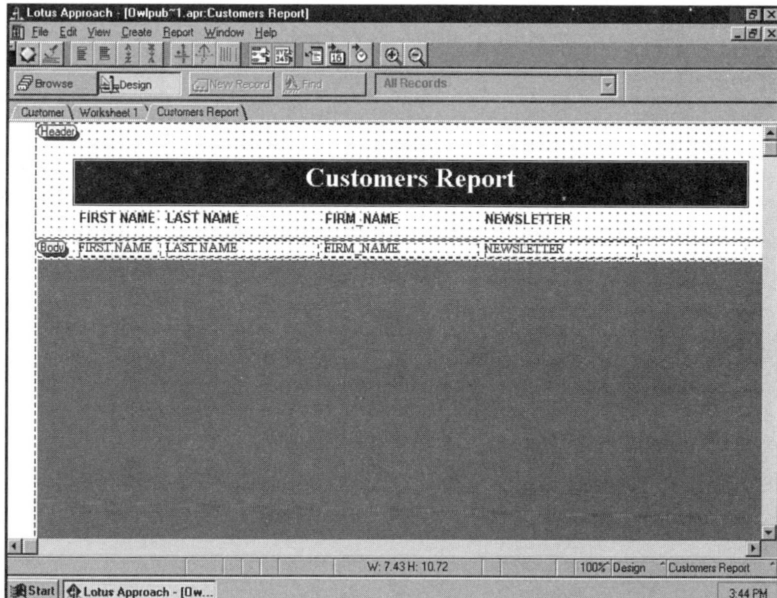

Fig. 7.8

The columnar report for Owl Publishing's customers is shown in Design mode, with Show Data turned off.

10. Switch to Browse mode to view the report (see fig. 7.9).
11. Open the File menu and choose Save Approach File to save the file.

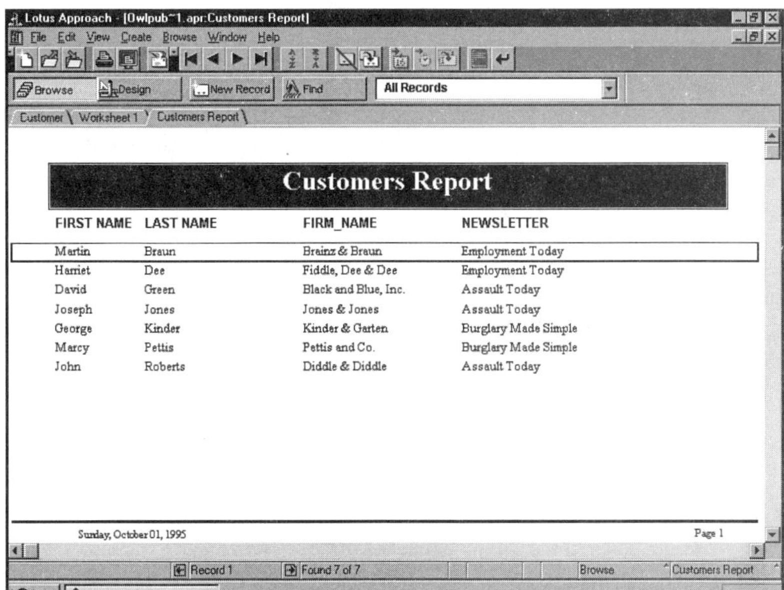

Fig. 7.9

Here, the columnar report is shown in Browse mode.

Owl Publishing also wants to create a standard report that includes all the information from the form. Follow these steps to create a standard report:

1. Switch to Design mode by opening the View menu and choosing Design, clicking the Design button on the action bar, or choosing Design from the status bar.
2. Open the Create menu and choose Report, or click the Create a New Report SmartIcon. The Report Assistant dialog box appears.
3. Type **`All Data`** as the name of the report.
4. Choose Shadowed from the Style drop-down list.
5. Choose Standard from the Layout list.
6. Click the Next button to move to the Step 2: Fields page.
7. Select FIRST NAME in the Fields list and click Add to move the field to the Fields to Place on View list. Continue clicking Add until all the fields from the database are available in the Fields to Place on View list. (The selection bar moves down the list of fields in the Database Fields list automatically as you click Add.)

Note

Don't get too enthusiastic when clicking the Add button! If you continue to click Add after you add all the database fields to the Fields to Place on View list, Approach returns to the top of the list and begins adding the fields to the Fields to Place on View list a second time.

8. Click Done. The new report appears (see fig. 7.10). If the report displays field data instead of the field names, choose Show Data from the View menu to turn off the field data.

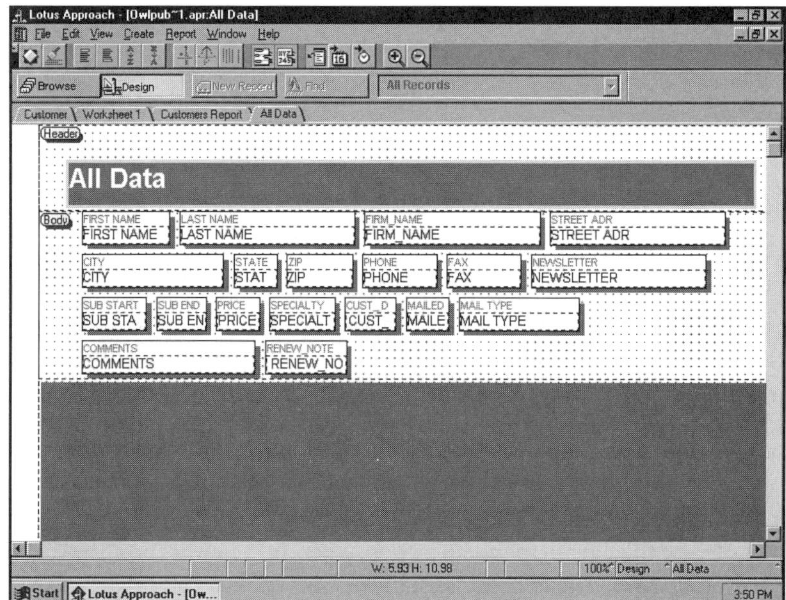

Fig. 7.10

You've created a standard report for Owl Publishing's customers (in Design mode, with Show Data turned off).

9. Switch to Browse mode to view the report (see fig. 7.11).
10. Open the File menu and choose Save Approach File to save the report.

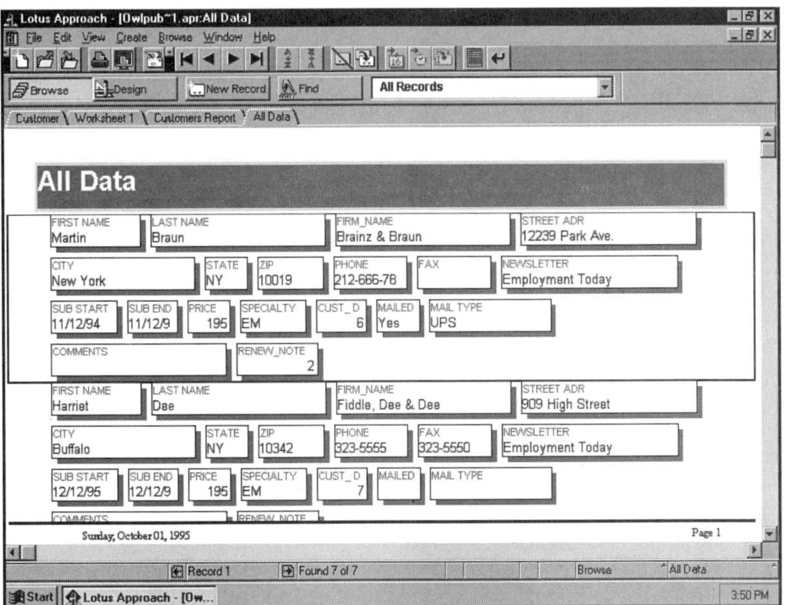

Fig. 7.11

Here, the standard report is shown in Browse mode.

Changing the Report Name and Basic Specifications

You can adjust many report properties from the report's InfoBox. You can change the name of a report, adjust the number of columns, and (if you prefer) keep each record together on a page. You make all these changes from the Basics page of the InfoBox (see fig. 7.12).

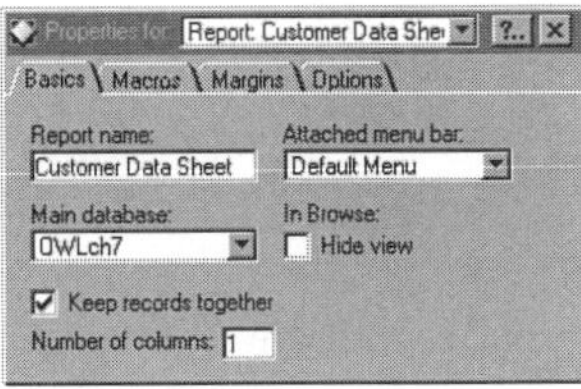

Fig. 7.12

You can make changes from the Basics page of the InfoBox.

To adjust the properties of the report, follow these steps:

1. Switch to Design mode by opening the View menu and choosing Design, clicking the Design button on the action bar, or selecting Design from the status bar.
2. If the report you want to modify isn't currently on-screen, click the tab for the report you want. You also can switch to the appropriate report by using the status bar.
3. Make sure that nothing on the report is selected (click a blank area of the report to deselect everything, if necessary).
4. Choose Report Properties from the Report menu (or the shortcut menu that appears when you right-click an object), or press Alt+Enter. The report InfoBox appears. Click the Basics tab.
5. To change the name of the report, type the new name in the Report Name text box.
6. To hide the report in Browse mode, click the Hide View check box. Approach won't display the report in the view tabs or the list of views in the status bar.
7. To change the number of columns, type the number you want in the Number of Columns text box. (See the following section, "Setting the Number of Columns," for more information.)
8. To keep each record together, select the Keep Records Together check box. When this check box is enabled, Approach doesn't split a record across different pages. If all the information about one record won't fit on the remainder of a page, Approach moves the record to the top of the next page.

Suppose that the report name for the Owl database standard report isn't descriptive enough. To change its name, follow these steps:

1. Switch to Design mode by opening the View menu and choosing Design, clicking the Design button on the action bar, or selecting Design from the status bar.
2. Select the All Data report by clicking the All Data tab or selecting the report from the status bar.
3. Open the InfoBox by choosing Report Properties from the Report menu or shortcut menu, or by pressing Ctrl+Enter.
4. Type **Customer Data Sheet** in the Report Name text box.
5. Open the File menu and choose Save Approach File.

Setting the Number of Columns

The Number of Columns text box in the report InfoBox allows you to set the number of columns you want printed in the report. By using more columns, you can place more information (sets of fields) on the page. If you specify more than one column, Approach prints your records from top to bottom in the first column, then moves to the second column, and so on.

> **Note**
>
> Using multiple columns is different from a columnar report. In a columnar report, Approach uses a single column for each field. Thus, a five-field report has five columns. When you create a multiple-column report, Approach repeats all the fields used in each column. Therefore, a columnar report with three fields, for which you specified two columns, actually contains six columns—the three field columns in the first report column, and the three field columns in the second report column. Approach's use of columns in these two contexts can be very confusing.

Using Multiple Columns in a Standard Report

If you're creating a standard report that has short fields and labels, you can see more records on each page if you use two or more columns (see fig. 7.13).

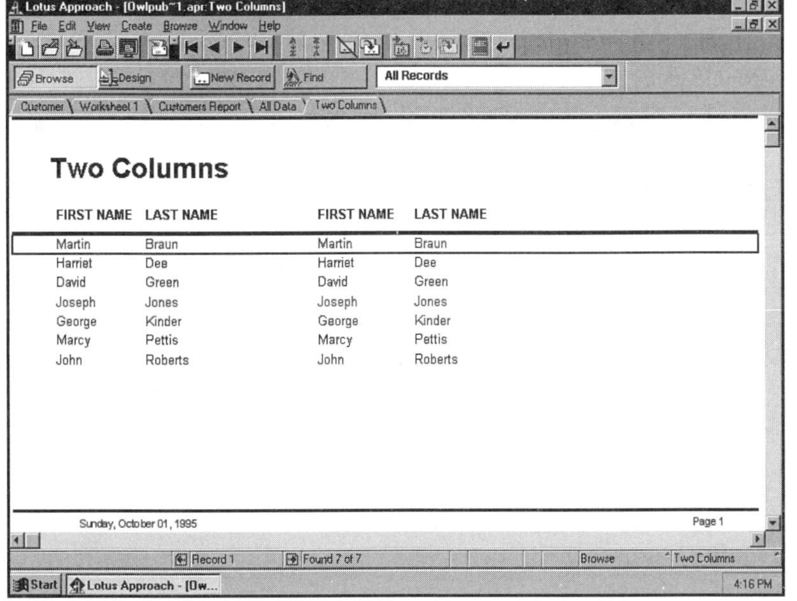

Fig. 7.13

Use multiple columns for your report to save paper.

Using Multiple Columns in a Columnar Report

In a columnar report, multiple columns are advantageous if your report includes only a few fields across the page. Each column contains all the selected fields for the report. Therefore, if you choose two fields and two columns for the report, four columns of data will appear on the report—the two fields selected in each of the two columns. With multiple columns, you can fit more records on the page (see fig. 7.14).

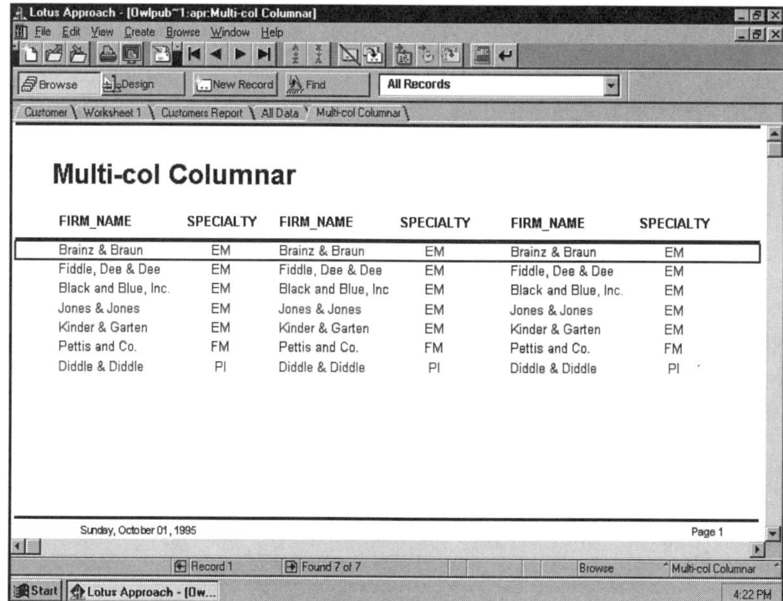

Fig. 7.14

You can also use multiple columns in a columnar report to fit more records on the page.

Viewing a Multicolumnar Report

You can view a multicolumnar report in several ways. To see the actual data in the report, use Print Preview or Design mode with field data showing (click the Show Data Instead of Field Names SmartIcon, or choose Show Data from the View menu, to display data instead of field names). You can't use Browse mode because all data is hidden in this mode. Approach displays the column borders if you're in Design mode with field names displayed instead of data (see fig. 7.15).

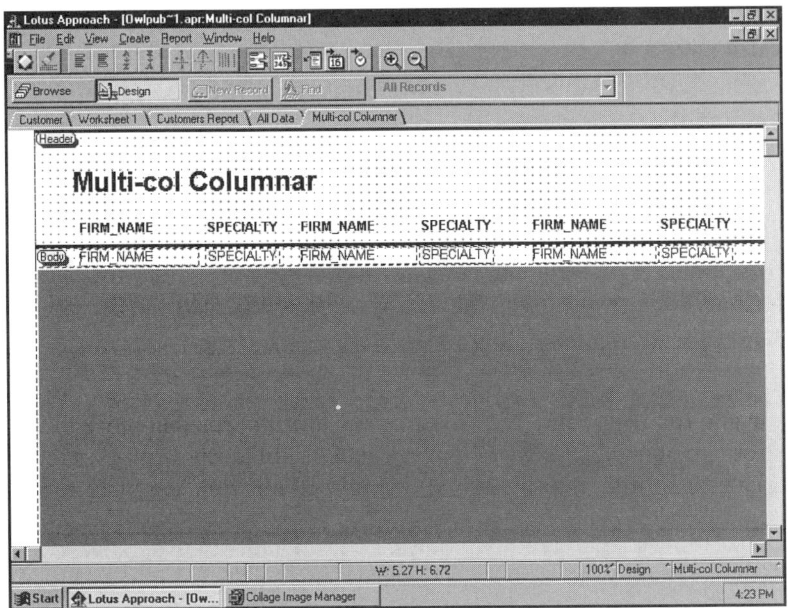

Fig. 7.15

When you view a multicolumn, columnar report in Design mode with field names displayed, a vertical dashed line shows the edge of each column.

Deleting a Report

You can delete a report that you no longer need. To do so, follow these steps:

1. Switch to Design mode by opening the View menu and choosing Design, clicking the Design button on the action bar, or selecting Design from the status bar.
2. If the report you want to delete isn't on-screen, choose the report from the view tabs or from the status bar.
3. Open the Edit menu and choose Delete Report. Confirm that you want to delete the report when Approach asks.

Duplicating a Report

Approach lets you duplicate an existing report to give you a head start in creating a report similar to one you already have. Making a duplicate is especially useful when you need to create complex mailing labels. To copy a report, follow these steps:

1. Switch to Design mode by opening the View menu and choosing Design, clicking the Design button on the action bar, or selecting Design from the status bar.
2. If the report you want to duplicate isn't on-screen, choose the report from the view tabs or from the status bar.
3. Open the Edit menu and choose Duplicate Report. The duplicate of your report appears on-screen. You can make changes (for example, change fonts, add and remove fields, or rearrange fields) to the duplicate without affecting the original.

Approach gives the duplicate report the same name as the original, except with the words *Copy of* in front of the name. If you duplicate the Customer Data Sheet report, for example, Approach names the duplicate *Copy of Customer Data Sheet.* Use the Basics page of the report InfoBox to change the name of the report, or double-click the report's tab and edit the name.

Customizing a Report

Approach lets you customize reports in many ways. You can add, remove, move, and size fields; specify the text attributes of fields and labels; change the text of a label; and add graphics. In fact, you can change reports in virtually all the ways you can modify forms!

Reports also have new elements that aren't present on forms. For example, you can add a header or footer to a report page and a title page for the report. Another new element is the body panel. On a form, each record occupies the entire form, but a report page can display multiple records. The rectangular portion on a report page that holds a single record is known as a *body panel.* As discussed in following sections, you may set various properties for body panels, such as color and border style.

Almost every change works the same way on reports as they work on forms. Therefore, whenever a function is the same for a form as for a report, only a summary of the function is covered in this chapter. For a more comprehensive discussion of each function, see Chapter 4, "Enhancing Data Input Forms."

Note

You must make all changes to a report in Design mode.

Adjusting the Attributes of a Body Panel

A body panel is the rectangular area on a report that surrounds the fields that make up a single record.

In Design mode, body panels appear differently, depending on whether you're displaying field names or field data, as in the following examples:

- If you're displaying field names, Approach shows you a single body panel with all the fields you included in the report from a single record (see fig. 7.16). If you select the body panel by clicking an area of the body panel in which no fields are present, Approach draws a heavy line around the body panel. All records in the report follow the format of this single record.

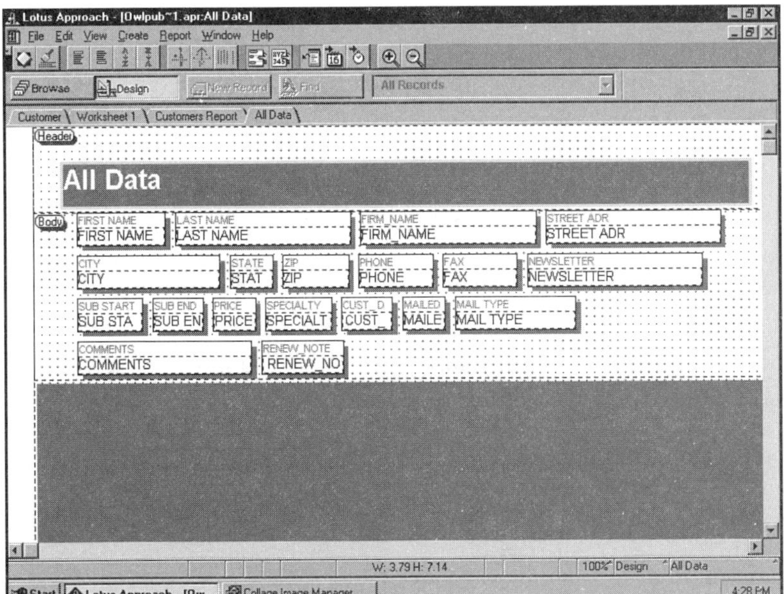

Fig. 7.16

Approach displays the field names when displaying a single body panel in Design mode.

- If you're displaying field data (by choosing Show Data from the View menu), Approach displays all the records in the database (see fig. 7.17). The layouts of all the records are identical. Changes you make to any record's body panel are reflected in all records. Displaying field data helps you see how a record will look in Browse mode as you adjust the record layout. But it can be confusing to see all the data while you're trying to modify the layout, however, and Approach's performance may slow when the data is displayed.

> **Note**
>
> To avoid confusion, it's probably best to make adjustments to a report with only the field names showing.

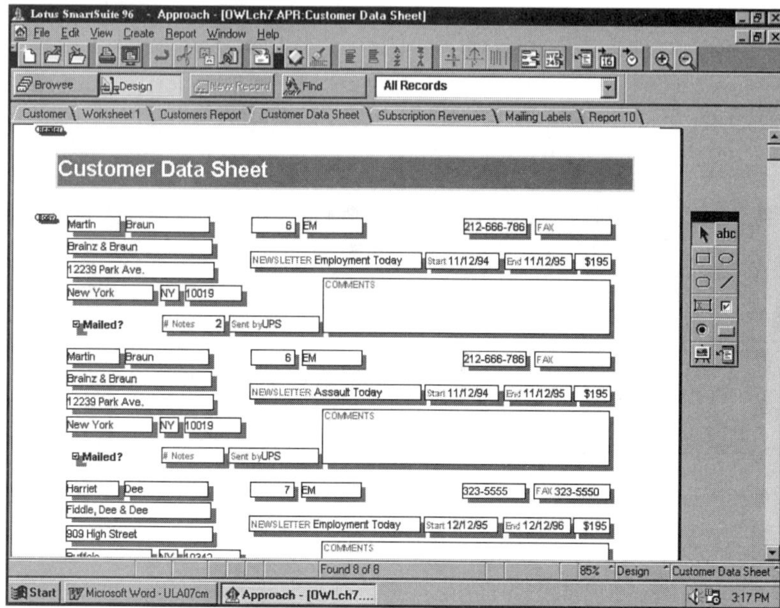

Fig. 7.17

When field data is shown in Design mode (with Show Data on the View menu turned on), Approach displays multiple records in body panels.

You can adjust the border and fill color of a body panel, and also the border width, frame style, and the sides of the body panel on which Approach displays a border. To adjust these properties, follow these steps:

1. Switch to Design mode by opening the View menu and choosing Design, clicking the Design button on the action bar, or selecting Design from the status bar.
2. Open the InfoBox for the body panel by double-clicking the body panel and choosing Report Properties from the popup menu, or choosing Report Properties from the Report menu.
3. Click the colors tab.
4. Select the border width from the Border Width drop-down list. Available border widths range from hairline to 12 points (1/6 of an inch).
5. Select the border and fill color from the Border Color and Fill Color drop-down lists. Select the box labeled T for transparent, or no color.
6. Select a frame style from the Frame drop-down list. The frame style specifies the format in which Approach draws the border around the body panel.
7. Click the check boxes in the Borders section (Left, Right, Top, and Bottom) to select on which sides of the body panel you want Approach to display a border.

Selecting, Resizing, and Moving Objects

You can select, resize, and move objects on a report by using the same techniques that you use on a form (see Chapter 3, "Building Data Input Forms"). You can select multiple objects with the mouse, resize objects by clicking and dragging the sizing handles, and move objects by clicking and dragging them. You also can cut, copy, and paste objects on a report.

To make the All Data report for the Owl Publishing database easier to use (and to practice modifying reports), try rearranging some fields. First, make sure that only field names are displayed on the report (choose Show Data from the View menu if data is displayed on the report). Then follow these steps:

1. Switch to Design mode.
2. Double-click the header rectangle to bring up the InfoBox for the report. Type **`Customer Data Sheet`** in the Report Name text box and close the InfoBox. The report name changes in the header and report tab.
3. Select the FIRST NAME field and drag one of the right sizing handles to the left to make the field smaller.
4. Select the LAST NAME field and drag it closer to the FIRST NAME field to close the gap.
5. Rearrange the rest of the report as shown in figure 7.18. Note that most of the field labels were turned off to save room. To turn off the field label, click the Label radio button in the font panel of the InfoBox, and then select No Label from the Label Position drop-down list.

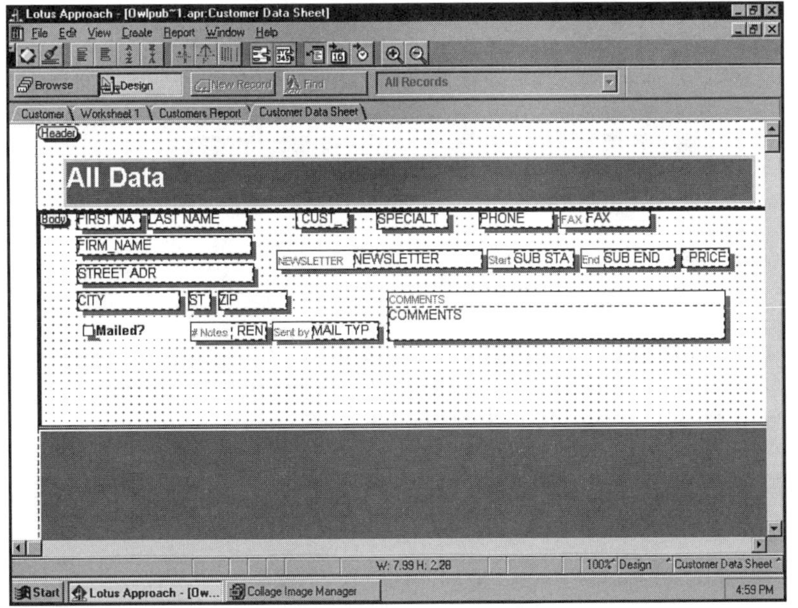

Fig. 7.18

The layout of the Customer Data Sheet report has been modified to hold additional information.

6. If you need to change the title of the report, click the text twice with the mouse, highlight the existing title, and type the new title.
7. Open the File menu and choose Save Approach File to save the file.

Adjusting the Boundary of a Record

If you rearrange the fields in a standard report so that they require less space, you end up with a great deal of blank space at the bottom of the body panel. To have Approach move up the next record to fill this space, you must adjust the boundary of the body panel in Design mode. If you don't adjust the boundary of the body panel, Approach shows and prints the report with blank space at the end of each record because the space allotted for each record wasn't changed (see fig. 7.19).

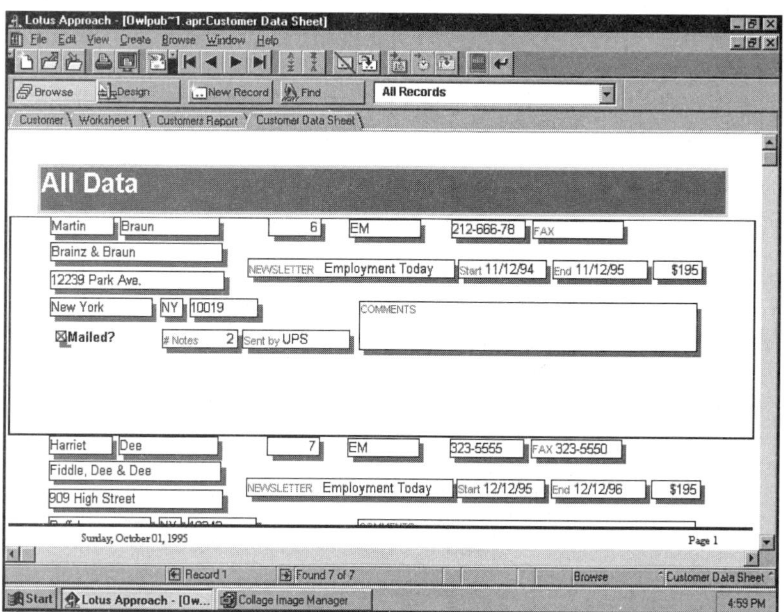

Fig. 7.19

This report has blank space at the end of each record.

To resize the body panel, move the mouse pointer over the bottom border of the body panel. The mouse pointer becomes a two-headed arrow. Drag the bottom border to change (shrink or increase) the size of the body panel.

> **Tip**
>
> To make sure that you click the bottom of the body panel (and not the bottom of a field in the body panel), Ctrl+click the bottom border.

To make better use of the space on the Customer Data Sheet report, Owl Publishing wants to adjust the record boundary to remove all the blank space between the records. To do so, follow these steps:

1. Switch to the Customer Data Sheet report by using the view tabs or the status bar.
2. View the report from Browse mode. Notice how much white space is between the records.
3. Switch to Design mode by either opening the View menu and choosing Design, clicking the Design button on the action bar, or selecting Design from the status bar.
4. To make the record boundary visible, click anywhere in the record *except* in a field. (You also can Ctrl+click anywhere in the record.) A black line appears around the panel (except at the bottom, where the line is gray). You must click and drag the gray bottom line to adjust the size of the body panel (see fig. 7.20).

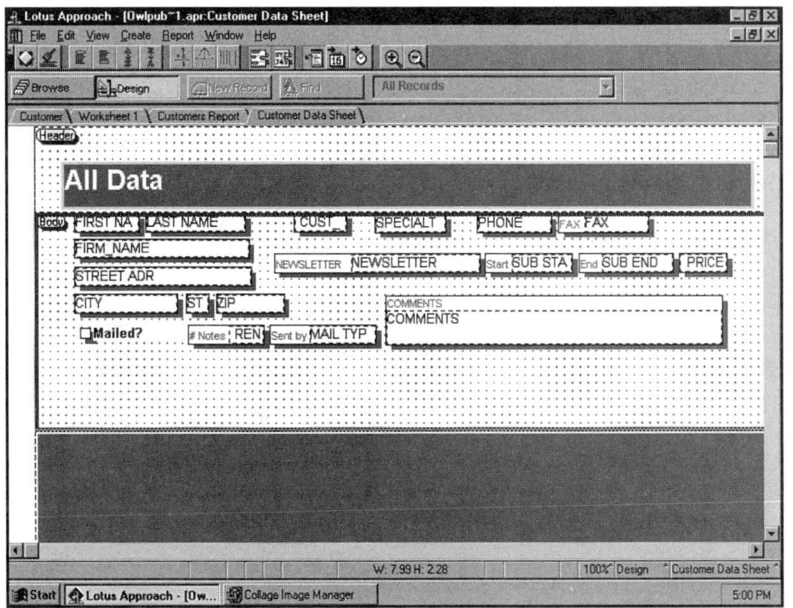

Fig. 7.20

The body panel shows the limits of the space that Approach uses for one record.

5. To adjust the body panel's size, drag the gray bottom border until it's just below the bottom line of fields.
6. Switch back to Browse mode. Notice that the wasted white space is gone.
7. Open the File menu and choose Save Approach File to save the file.

Figure 7.21 shows the resulting report, without excessive blank space between the records.

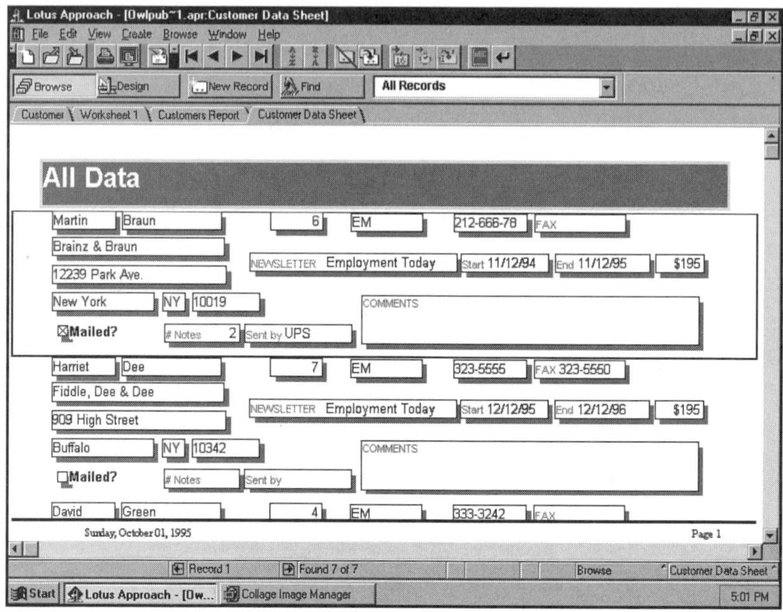

Fig. 7.21

Wasted space has been removed from the end of each record.

You may have a similar problem with columnar reports. If you shrink the font of the header line (which holds the labels for the columns) or the record body panel, the space used by these lines becomes partially empty. Click anywhere except in a field in the header line or the body panel to see the boundary, or Ctrl+click anywhere in the header or body panel. Drag the gray bottom border to close up the space on either line (see fig. 7.22).

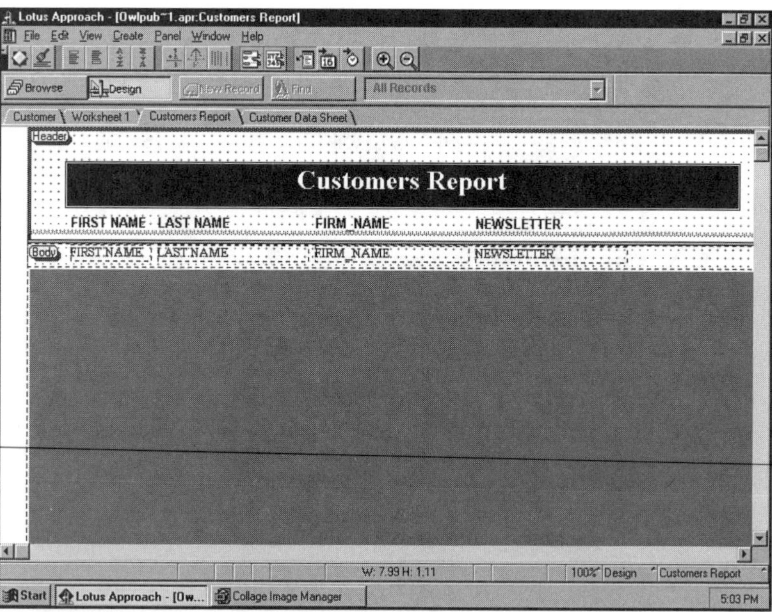

Fig. 7.22

Close up the space on the header line or the body panel in a columnar report.

Tip

You can also drag the body panel that holds the records to make it larger and to give more room to each record.

Working with Report Columns

Approach makes it easy to work with whole columns (a column and its header) on a columnar report. While you work with whole columns, you can move or resize a column and its header at the same time. Otherwise, the columns and headers behave like separate objects that you can move and resize independently.

To work with whole columns, you turn on columns and show data rather than field names. You must show data before Approach allows you to turn on columns. To show data, open the View menu and choose Show Data, or click the Show Data SmartIcon. To turn on columns, open the Report menu and choose Turn On Columns, or click the Columns SmartIcon.

When you first create a columnar report, Approach displays the columns in the order that you specified in the Report Assistant dialog box. By default, Approach sets the column and header width to the field width. However, you can reposition, resize, or delete a column and its header:

- To resize a column, click the column data. Approach highlights the column (see fig. 7.23). Move the mouse pointer over the right edge of the column, until it becomes a two-headed arrow. Drag the right edge of the column to make it larger or smaller.

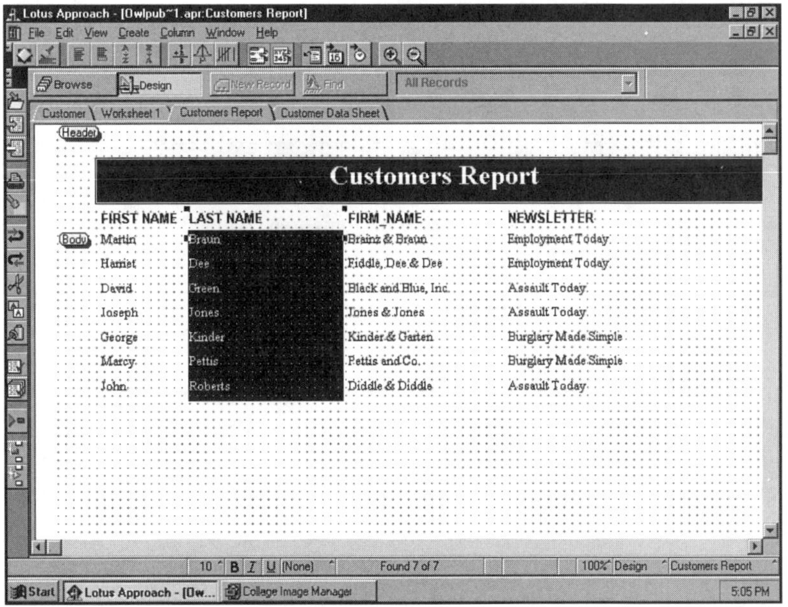

Fig. 7.23

You can resize only the right edge of a column.

- To move a column, click the column data to highlight the column. Then move the mouse pointer over the column, until it becomes a hand shape. Drag the column to its new position. Approach repositions other columns to move them out of the way and close up the gap left by the relocated column.
- To delete a column, click the column data. Approach highlights the column. Press Delete or choose Cut from the Edit menu. Approach then deletes the column and moves other columns to the left to close up the hole.

Using Slide Up and Slide Left

Reports and mailing labels often contain blank areas (see "Creating Mailing Labels" later in this chapter). These blanks occur for two main reasons: if some of the fields on the label aren't used, or if a field contains text that doesn't completely fill the field. For example, you can specify two address lines in your database to handle long addresses, but some records may leave the second line blank because it isn't needed. Or you may have left room for a long city field, but the city name for a particular record is short.

As with forms, Approach provides two special commands to close the gaps that result from these conditions—Slide Left and Slide Up. These check-box options are available from the dimensions page of a field or graphic object's InfoBox.

Slide Left closes any gap that appears when text doesn't completely fill a field. If the CITY and STATE fields are on the same line in the mailing label, for example, using Slide Left moves the STATE field to the end of the CITY field, leaving just one space between them.

Slide Up closes any gap that appears when a line isn't used. If the second address line on a label isn't used, for example, all the lines below it are moved up. Another good place to use Slide Up is for memo fields in which the entire field isn't filled with text. Approach moves up information below the partially empty memo field to fill the unused space.

> **Note**
>
> Slide Up and Slide Left don't work if fields overlap, if the bottoms aren't aligned, or if field boundaries touch.

Under normal circumstances, fields take up a specific amount of room on the form. Therefore, Slide Left and Slide Up have no effect unless you allow Approach to adjust the size of any fields that contain blank space. To allow Approach to adjust the field size, select the Reduce check box on the dimensions page of the InfoBox. The Reduce check box enables Approach to shrink a field that contains empty space, and potentially move other objects left and up (if you've enabled Slide Left or Slide Up for these fields) to fill the empty space.

A related command is the Expand check box on the dimensions page. This check box enables Approach to increase the size of a screen field and the body panel on the printout when the database field contains more information than can be displayed in the field. You must ensure that no other fields are present to the right of or beneath the field you allow to expand, because Approach will print over those fields. A good example of a use for the Expand check box is a memo field with more text than Approach can display in the allotted field space. If you check the Expand check box, Approach inserts enough space in the printout to fully print the contents of the memo field.

To cause a field or graphic object to slide left or up, follow these steps:

1. Switch to Design mode by opening the View menu and choosing Design, clicking the Design button on the action bar, or selecting Design from the status bar.
2. Click the field or graphic object.
3. Open the InfoBox for the field or object and click the dimensions tab.
4. Click the Left or Up check boxes in the When Printing, Slide section.

You won't see the changes on the report unless you're in Print Preview mode or in Design mode with field data showing. To enter Print Preview mode, click the Print Preview SmartIcon or select Print Preview from the status bar. To show field data in Design mode, choose Show Data from the View menu, press Ctrl+Shift+B, or click the Show Data SmartIcon. If the form is too small to read the text in Print Preview mode—and therefore, to see the effects of Slide Up or Slide Left—click the Zoom-In SmartIcon.

Using the Layout Tools

Approach has a number of tools to help you get the layout of a report just right. These layout tools work in the same way they work when you're laying out a form.

These layout tools include using the rulers, showing the screen coordinates of the mouse pointer or the selected object, and using the grid to align objects. You also can align objects in relation to each other, magnify objects so that you can place them more precisely, shrink objects so that you can see more of them on-screen, and group objects. Another handy layout tool is adjusting the way objects are layered on top of each other. Finally, you can prevent selected objects from printing or displaying in Browse mode. All these Approach features are discussed in detail in Chapter 3, "Building Data Input Forms."

Adding Fields to a Report

From Design mode, you can add fields to a report by using either the Draw Fields tool on the tools palette or the Add Fields dialog box. To add a field using the Draw Fields tool, follow these steps:

1. Click the Draw Fields tool. The pointer turns into a crosshair shape.
2. Drag a rectangle to define the location and size of the field. The field InfoBox appears.
3. From the Field list box, select the field you want to add. If the field you want doesn't exist yet, choose the Field Definition button to open the Field Definition dialog box. Add the field you want, and then choose OK to return to the field InfoBox. The new field will be selected in the field list.

To add a field from the Add Field dialog box, click the field you want to add and drag the field onto a body panel on the report. If you need to create a new field, click the Field Definition button to open the Field Definition dialog box. Add the field you want and click OK to return to the Add Field dialog box. You now can click and drag the new field onto the report.

Tip

You also can create a new field by copying an existing field (open the Edit menu and choose Copy) and then pasting that field back onto the report (open the Edit menu and choose Paste). Then double-click the copied field to display the InfoBox. Select the field you want from the field list, or create a new field by clicking the Field Definition button. Creating a field on the report in this way duplicates the attributes of the field you used to copy/paste.

Modifying the Report Field Display

You can change how a field is displayed on a report in all the same ways you can change the field display on a form. You can display fields as a drop-down list, field box and list, check box, and radio button. You also can set the values for a drop-down list (or field box and list) and set the on/off values for a check box, and the on value for a radio button.

To keep the user from entering something in a field, you can make it read-only. You also can adjust the order in which the user moves through the field by changing the tab order. Adjusting the tab order is useful because you can input data into a report, just as you can with a form.

You can change the font, size, effects, and color of the text entered into a field and the text of the field's label. You also can set the field background and shadow color, frame style, position of the field borders, and line width of the border.

You can move and resize fields by clicking and dragging or by using the dimensions page of the InfoBox.

Finally, you can change the display format of the field so that the entered data is displayed in the text, numeric, time, or date format you prefer.

Customizing Your Report

Blocks of text, graphics objects, and illustrations from graphics files add color and impact to a report. Adding these items to a report is handled in exactly the same way that you add them to a form.

The text tool, graphics tools, and copy/paste commands work in exactly the same way they work on a form. On a text block, you can change the text font, size, effects, and color, and also the text block fill and shadow color. You also can place a database field, the page number, time, or a date into a text block on a report. Finally, for graphics objects you can change the line color and weight, frame style, and also the fill and shadow color. You can move and resize text blocks and graphics objects by clicking and dragging or by using the dimensions page of the object's InfoBox.

On a report, you have the option of placing text blocks, graphics objects, and pictures from graphics files in headers and footers. By placing these items in a header or footer, you can ensure that they appear on every page of the report.

Working with Headers and Footers

Headers and footers are unique to reports and can be used to display the same information on each page. You can add text, graphics objects, OLE objects, database fields, and almost any other object that Approach supports to a header or footer. If you want the page number and date to appear on each page, for example, you can place these features in a text block in the header or footer.

If you set up a header, it appears at the top of every page. If you set up a footer, it appears at the bottom of every page. Figure 7.24 shows a sample report with a header and footer.

Note

When specified, a header or footer appears on every page of the report, including the first page. To suppress the header or footer on the first page of the report (or to use a different header or footer on that page), create a title page (see "Working with Title Pages" later in this chapter). By using a title page, you can make the first page different from the balance of the report.

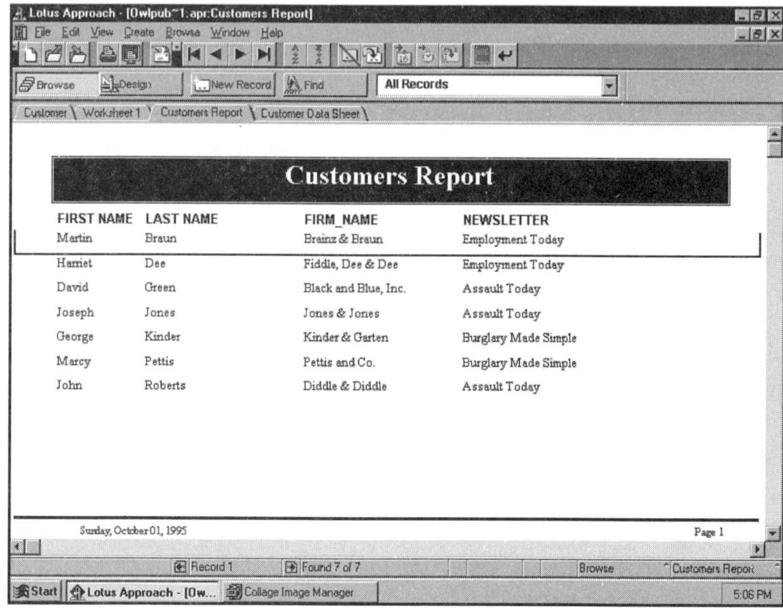

Fig. 7.24

A report with a header and a footer displays the same information on every page.

Adding a Header or Footer

To add a header or footer to a report, follow these steps:

1. Switch to Design mode.
2. If the report you want isn't on-screen, select it from the view tabs. You can also select the report from the status bar.
3. Open the Report menu; then choose Add Header to add a header or Add Footer to add a footer. When a header or footer is present in the report, these options show check marks in the menu.

After you insert a header or footer in your report, it appears on the page with a black box around it when selected in Design mode (see fig. 7.25). You must scroll down to the bottom of the page to see the footer.

> **Note**
>
> When you create a report with the Report Assistant (except a blank report), Approach always places a header and footer in the report. The default header contains a text block that holds the name of the report. The default footer contains a text block that contains the date and page number.

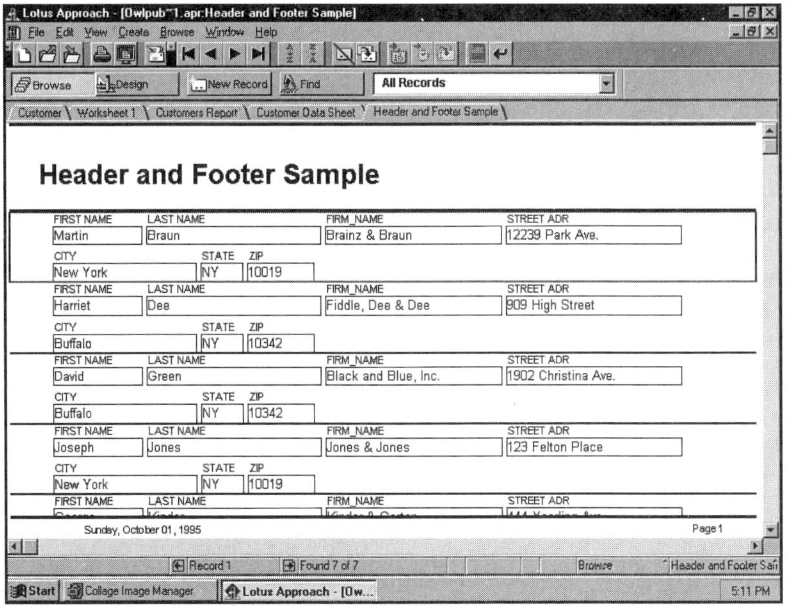

Fig. 7.25

The selected header or footer has a black boundary around it in Design mode, with the adjustable boundary displayed in dark gray.

Deleting a Header or Footer

To delete a header or footer from a report, follow these steps:

1. Switch to Design mode.
2. If the report you want isn't on-screen, select it from the view tabs. You can also select the report from the status bar.
3. To delete the header from the selected report, open the Report menu and choose Add Header. This action turns off the check mark, and the header disappears. To delete the footer, choose Add Footer from the Report menu. This turns off the check mark, and the footer disappears.

Resizing a Header or Footer

When you initially create a header or footer in Approach, it's approximately one text line high (about 1/4 inch). You may need to make the header or footer larger to accommodate more lines of text, graphics, or graphics files. To resize headers and footers, follow these steps:

1. Switch to Design mode.
2. If the report you want isn't on-screen, select the report from the view tabs or the status bar.
3. Scroll the report page until the header or footer area is visible (depending on which area you want to resize).

4. To select the header or footer area, click anywhere in the header or footer area *except* where an object is positioned. You also can Ctrl+click anywhere in the header or footer.

   When a header or footer is selected, a black border appears around three sides of the header or footer. One edge of the header or footer is gray. The gray edge is the bottom border of the header or the top border of the footer. The gray border is placed on the bottom edge of the header; you can resize the header only by stretching its bottom border down the page. The gray border is placed on the top edge of the footer; you can resize the footer only by stretching its top border up the page. (The gray border works just like the gray borders discussed previously in this chapter for resizing a report body panel.)

5. Move the mouse pointer over the gray border. The pointer becomes a two-headed arrow. Drag the gray border until the header or footer is the size you want, and then release the left mouse button.

Adding Objects to Headers and Footers

After you add a header or footer to a report, you can customize the header or footer to suit your purposes. Although initially a header or footer you add is empty, you can add text blocks, graphics drawn with the graphics tools, and illustrations (graphics files). You also can add all these objects to the default header or footer that Approach places on a report.

> **Note**
>
> If you add a database field (or a text block that contains a database field) to the header or footer, this field will contain the value from the first record on the page. In Browse mode, the field appears in the header or footer exactly as it appears in Design mode, with the label and database field name. However, the field displays its value in Print Preview mode.

You add objects to a header or footer in Design mode in the same way you place them elsewhere on a report. To add a text block to a header, for example, click the Text tool in the tools palette, and then click and drag to define the limits of the text block in the header.

After you add a text block, you can modify it in the following ways:

- Resize it by dragging the sizing handles or by using the InfoBox dimensions page
- Move it by dragging the text block to a new location or using the InfoBox dimensions page
- Customize it by selecting the text block, opening the InfoBox, and using the fonts or colors pages
- Insert a page number, time, or date into it (select the text block and choose Insert Date, Time, or Page # from the Object menu)

Now return to the Owl Publishing example for a moment. The company has decided to customize its Customer Data Sheet report by adding header and footer information. First, switch to Design mode and remove the default header or footer by opening the Report menu and choosing Add Header or Add Footer. To add a new header, follow these steps:

1. Select Customer Data Sheet from the view tabs or the status bar.
2. Turn on the rulers by opening the View menu and choosing Show Ruler.
3. Open the Report menu and choose Add Header. The header appears on the report.
4. Press Ctrl+L to bring up the tools palette, and then click the Text tool.
5. Move the mouse pointer into the header, and click and drag a text block about 1 1/2 inches long and 1/4 inch high. Locate the text block on the left side of the header.
6. Type **`Time:`** in the text block.
7. Open the Text menu and choose Insert and then Current Time to insert the current time into the text block (see fig. 7.26).

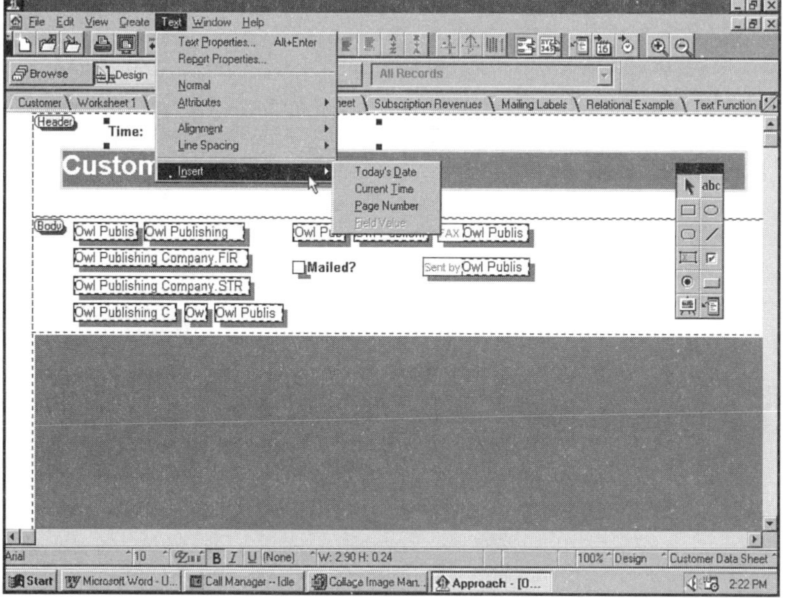

Fig. 7.26

You can place a field in a header or footer.

To add a footer, follow these steps:

1. Open the Report menu and choose Add Footer. The footer appears on the report.
2. Press Ctrl+L to bring up the tools palette, and then click the Text tool.

3. In the footer, drag a text block about 1 1/2 inches long and 1/4 inch high. Locate the text block in the center of the footer.
4. Type **`Page Number:`** in the text block.
5. Open the Text menu and choose Insert and then Page Number to insert the page number into the text block.
6. Click anywhere in the footer except in the text block to make the border visible. You can also Ctrl+click anywhere in the footer.
7. Drag the gray border up about 1/2 inch. This step increases the size of the footer.
8. Open the File menu and choose Save Approach File.
9. Switch back to Browse mode.
10. Click the Print Preview SmartIcon to view the report (see fig. 7.27).

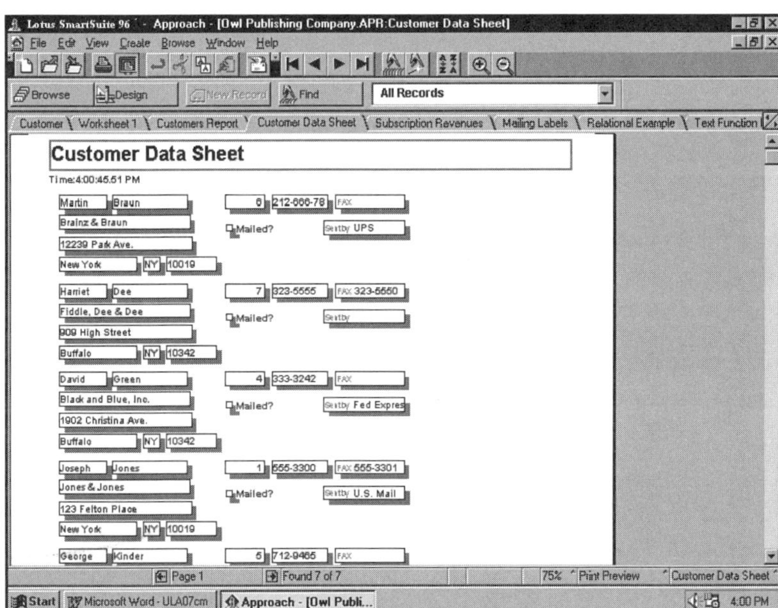

Fig. 7.27

You can select Print Preview to view a report.

Setting the Properties of a Header or Footer

You can set the properties of a header or footer from the InfoBox by following these steps:

1. Switch to Design mode.
2. Open the InfoBox by choosing Properties from the Panel menu or Panel Properties from the shortcut menu. Click the colors tab.
3. Select the border, fill, or shadow color from the drop-down list that Approach makes available when you click the Border Color, Fill Color, or Shadow Color drop-down lists. The box labeled T provides a transparent color.

4. Select the border width from the Border Width drop-down list. Available border widths range from hairline to 12 points (1/6 inch).
5. Select a frame style from the Frame drop-down list. The frame style specifies the format in which Approach draws the border around the selected field.
6. Click the check boxes in the Borders section (Left, Right, Top, and Bottom) to select on which sides of the body panel you want Approach to display a border.

Building Data Summaries with PowerClick Reporting

Approach allows you to customize a columnar report after it's created with the PowerClick reporting tool, an extremely powerful data-organization tool. By using PowerClick reporting, you can group data into easily recognized categories, perform calculations on columns, or add summaries and sub-summaries before and after data.

> **Note**
>
> PowerClick reporting works in Design mode with Show Data (on the View menu) turned on.

To use PowerClick reporting, click to highlight a column, and then select a Power-Click option from the Groups & Totals submenu off the Column menu. You can perform the following calculations on a column:

- Sum (total of all items in the column)
- Average (sum divided by number of column items)
- Count (of all the items in the column)
- Minimum (returns the lowest value in the column)
- Maximum (returns the highest value in the column)
- Standard deviation (of all items in the column)
- Variance (between items in the column)

Calculating Column Values with PowerClick Reporting

PowerClick reporting also can group records in a columnar report by values in a particular field. Summaries, such as totals, of the groups can lead or trail the category.

To display a total value for a column, follow these steps:

1. Switch to Design mode.
2. If the report you want isn't on-screen, choose it from the view tabs or the status bar.

3. Select the column that will display the calculation by clicking it.
4. From the Column menu, choose Groups & Totals, and then choose one of the submenu items (see fig. 7.28); or click one of the PowerClick SmartIcons.

A new AutoSum field will be created and displayed beneath the column. It can be formatted and used in other views just as any other field.

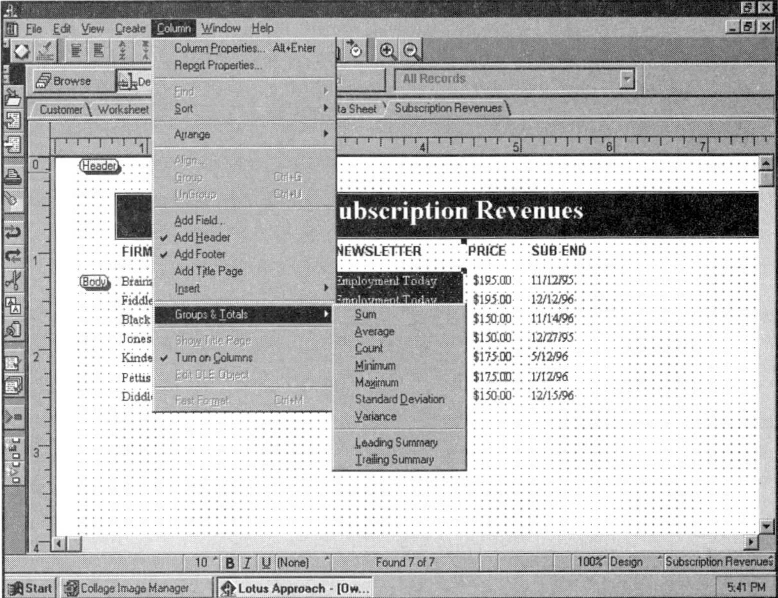

Fig. 7.28

PowerClick reporting helps you build summaries, groups, and grand totals into existing reports.

To summarize groups of records by category, follow these steps:

1. Switch to Design mode.
2. If the report you want isn't on-screen, select it from the view tabs or the status bar.
3. Click the column that will display the calculation.
4. From the Column menu, choose Groups & Totals and then choose Trailing Summary or Leading Summary.
5. Approach may ask to re-sort records into appropriate groups. Click OK to continue.
6. If Turn on Columns is checked on the Column menu, choose the item to turn it off.
7. Select the first entry in the column and drag it into the summary panel (the blank space before or after each group of records).

The column that contains each record should disappear, and a new, single entry will appear in the summary panel for each group of records.

Working with Title Pages

A report can have a title page that's different from the main pages of a report. Title pages are useful for displaying information that you want shown just once in the report, such as your name. A title page initially looks just like the report page. If the report page has a header or footer, the title page also contains one, but the header and footer on the title page are initially blank. You can customize anything on the title page (including the header and footer) independently of the report page.

Adding a Title Page

To add a title page to a report, follow these steps:

1. Switch to Design mode.
2. If the report you want isn't on-screen, select it from the view tabs or the status bar.
3. Open the Report menu and choose Add Title Page. A check mark appears next to this command on the Report menu.
4. To display the title page instead of the report layout page, choose Show Title Page from the Report menu. A check mark appears next to this command, and Approach displays the title page.

> **Note**
>
> After you choose Show Title Page from the Report menu, you're working with the title page. To switch back to working with the main page of the report, choose Show Title Page again to turn off the check mark. All changes you make to the title page are limited to the title page—they don't affect the main report page.

Deleting a Title Page

To delete a title page that you no longer need, open the Report menu and choose Add Title Page. If you change your mind, you can add the title page back again, but all customizing you did is lost.

Modifying a Title Page

When you initially add a title page, it looks exactly like the main page of the report, except that the header and footer are blank. The title page has the same field layout in the record, and all the properties of the fields, graphics objects, and body panels are preserved on the title page. You can make the following kinds of changes to customize a title page:

- *Add a header or footer to the title page.* These items can vary from the header or footer on the other pages of the report. You also can have a header or footer on the title page without the rest of the report having one.

- *Resize an existing header or footer.* If the title page already has a header or footer (because the report page contains them), modifying the header and footer on the title page doesn't affect the header and footer on the main page. Although the title page has a header or footer if the report page has one, the header or footer on the title page is blank—all objects added previously to the report header or footer do *not* appear on the title page header or footer.
- *Add objects to the title page, such as graphics, illustrations (graphics files), and text blocks.* You also can add page numbers, times, and dates to the text blocks.

> **Note**
>
> As with headers and footers on the report page, you can place a database field or a text block that contains a database field in a title-page header or footer. However, this database field will always contain the value of the field in the first record on the page. Also, the field value won't be visible, except in Print Preview or Design mode with field data showing.

The body panel, which contains the field layout for each record, is visible on the title page (see fig. 7.29). If you make no further changes to the title page, it will include records when you print it.

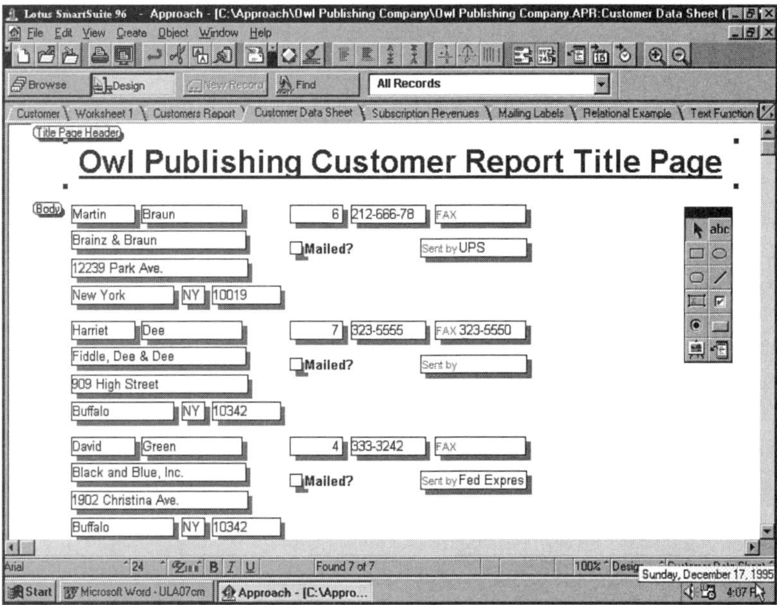

Fig. 7.29

A title page also can have a body panel, which can include records from the report.

The body panel that contains the record layout on the title page is the same one shown on the report page. If you make any changes to this layout (remove, resize, or move fields), all records in the report are affected. If you resize the body panel in the title page, the records in the rest of the report are also modified.

Setting the Number of Records on the Title Page

When you size the header and footer on the title page, all space remaining between the bottom of the header and the top of the footer is used to print records.

The number of records that show on the title page depends on how much room is between the header and the footer. If you want no records to print on the title page, size the header and footer so that the bottom of the header and the top of the footer meet. The record layout still shows on the page in Design mode and may make editing of title page text difficult (see fig. 7.30), but no records print on the title page.

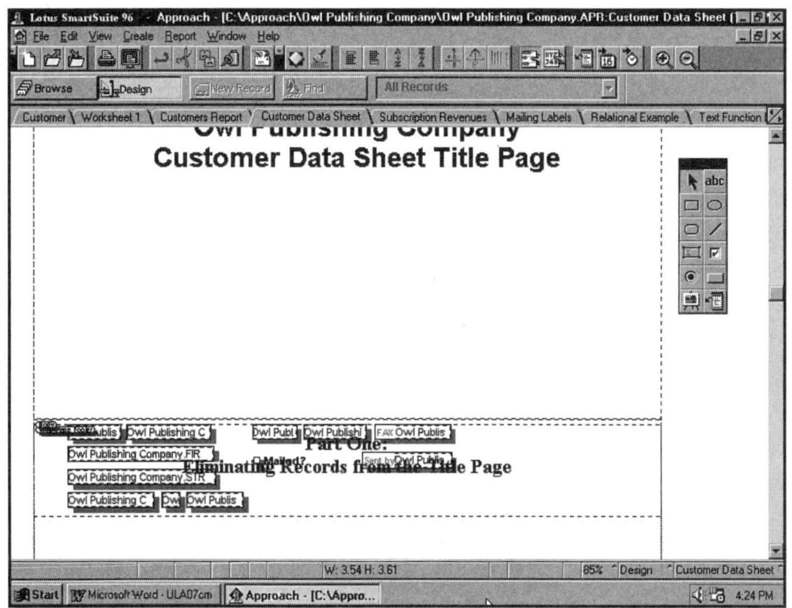

Fig. 7.30

This Design-mode title page includes a header, footer, and body panel.

To check this layout, switch to Print Preview mode or display field data in Design mode (choose Show Data from the View menu). Title pages can't be viewed in Browse mode.

In the Owl Publishing example, the company wants to add a title page—without records—to its main report. Follow these steps to add the title page:

1. Switch to Design mode.
2. Select the Customer Data Sheet report from the view tabs or the status bar. You should see the report page, showing the record layout.
3. Open the Report menu and choose Add Title Page, and then choose Show Title Page. The title page is now visible.

> **Note**
>
> Although the title page appears much like the main page, the text blocks in the header and footer are missing from this page.

Now, resize the header and footer so that no records print on the title page. Follow these steps:

1. Click in the header to show the black border with the gray bottom border.
2. Drag the gray bottom border down the page so that the header spans the upper half of the page. Notice that, as you make the header bigger, the record layout moves down the page to get out of the area taken by the header.
3. Scroll down the page until you can see the footer. Click the footer to show the black border and the gray top border.
4. Drag the gray top border up the page so that the top border of the footer meets the bottom border of the header. The footer overlays the record layout.

Next, to add a text block to the title page header, follow these steps:

1. If the rulers aren't on-screen, open the View menu and choose Show Ruler.
2. Press Ctrl+L to bring up the tools palette, and then click the Text tool.
3. Move the pointer into the header near the top of the screen, and drag a text block about 3 inches down from the top of the form. The text block should be about 3 inches long and 1/2 inch high.
4. Type **`Owl Publishing Company Customer Data Sheet Title Page`** in the text block.
5. Click the Pointer tool on the tools palette.
6. Drag the text block in the header so that it's centered on the page.
7. Double-click the text block to open the text InfoBox; or click the text block, open the Object menu, and choose Object Properties.
8. Click the fonts tab. Select Bold from the Attributes list and choose a larger point size (18 point works well) from the Size drop-down list.
9. Switch to Print Preview mode (click the Print Preview SmartIcon) to see the title page (see fig. 7.31).
10. Open the File menu and choose Save Approach File.

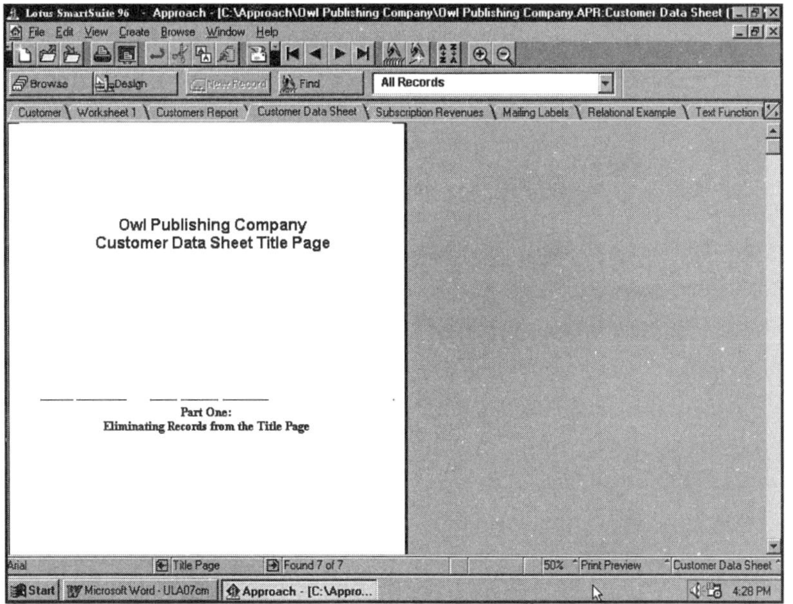

Fig. 7.31

The title page for the Customer Data Sheet report is now finished.

Note

The only item that appears on the title page is the text block you placed there. Because you left no room for records on the page, none appear.

Creating Mailing Labels

One of the most useful features of a database is its capability to generate mailing labels and other kinds of labels. If the database contains names and addresses, you can use these labels to mail information. If the database contains a list of the titles in your videotape collection, you can generate labels to place on the videotapes. A wide variety of labels is commercially available, and Approach can format information to fit on most of the popular sizes.

A mailing label is a special type of report, in which Approach provides extra help in setting the dimensions to match the common sizes of labels available. Because mailing labels also are a kind of report, you can modify mailing labels in most of the same ways in which you can modify a report. You can even enter data on a label. However, the information for fully specifying a record is rarely present in the limited space available on a label.

You can customize a mailing label in most of the same ways you can customize a form (see Chapter 4, "Enhancing Data Input Forms," for details). On a mailing label, you can do the following:

- Add, delete, and customize fields
- Customize the text format of a field
- Customize the display format of a field
- Customize the data-entry format of a field
- Add and customize field labels
- Draw graphics, using the graphics tools
- Paste or import illustrations (graphics files)
- Use all the layout tools (rulers, dimensions, grid, alignment, grouping, and so on) to place fields
- Add (and customize) text blocks

To practice using mailing labels, follow these steps to create labels for Owl Publishing:

1. Open the database from which you want to generate mailing labels and switch to Design mode.
2. Open the Create menu and choose Mailing Labels. The Mailing Label Assistant dialog box appears (see fig. 7.32).

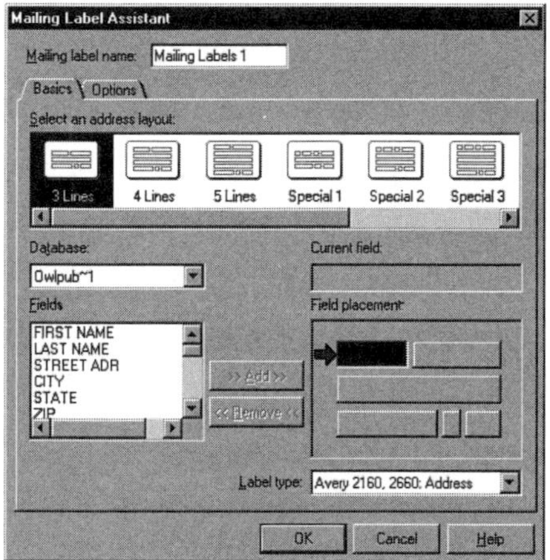

Fig. 7.32

Create mailing labels through the Mailing Label Assistant dialog box.

3. Make your choice in the Select an Address Layout scrolling list across the top of the dialog box. The address layout sets the template of the address label, including the number of lines of text and the general placement of the field placeholders. Approach will display the fields you choose to add in the Field Placement box on the right. For the Owl Publishing example, choose 3 Lines from the Select an Address Layout scrolling list.

Note

You aren't limited by the layout you choose in the Mailing Label Assistant dialog box. You can change the field layout on the mailing label by relocating and sizing fields, and adjusting the font size of the fields.

4. Approach displays one of the template placeholders in blue—this is the selected placeholder. When you add a database field to the template (as detailed in step 5), Approach adds the database field to the selected placeholder. To select where the next database field will be added to the template, click one of the placeholders in the template.
5. The database fields are listed in the Fields list. Select the fields you want on the mailing labels, using these selection methods:
   - To select one field, click it and choose the Add button, or double-click it. Approach adds the field to the template and advances to the next field in the template.
   - To select more than one field at a time, click the first field, Ctrl+click any other fields you want, and then click Add. Approach adds the database fields in the order in which they're listed in the Fields list.

Tip

To remove a field from the Field Placement box, click the field and choose Remove. You can also double-click the field to remove it.

For the Owl Publishing example, Ctrl+click the following fields: FIRST NAME, LAST NAME, STREET ADR, CITY, STATE, and ZIP. Choose Add. The selected fields move to the Field Placement box on the right side of the dialog box (see fig. 7.33).

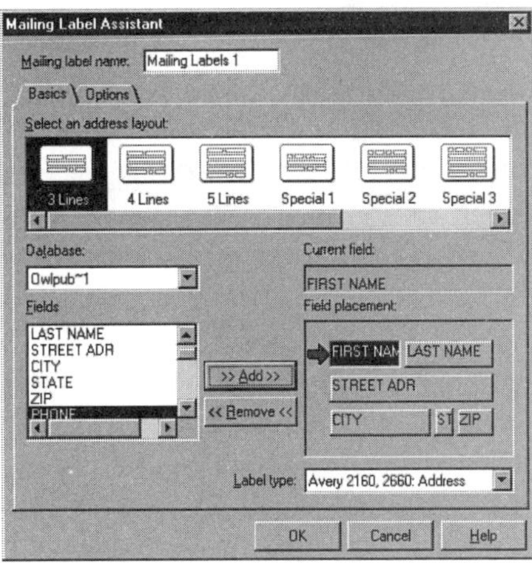

Fig. 7.33

Select the fields you want on Owl Publishing's mailing labels.

> **Note**
>
> If you select and move all fields to the Field Placement box at the same time, they're placed on the label in the order in which they were created. If you prefer a different order, add each field individually.

6. To specify a standard label, select the type of label you want from the Label Type drop-down list. For this example, select Avery 5161. This label is sheet-fed, with three labels across and 10 labels down (30 labels to a sheet). If you're using a tractor-feed printer, choose 5261.

   To specify a custom label, click the Options tab. For more information on specifying a custom label, see "Specifying Label Characteristics" later in this chapter.

7. Type the name of the mailing label report in the Mailing Label Name text box. For this example, leave it as the default name, Mailing Labels 1.
8. Choose OK. Approach creates the mailing label and displays it so that you can make any changes you want (see fig. 7.34).

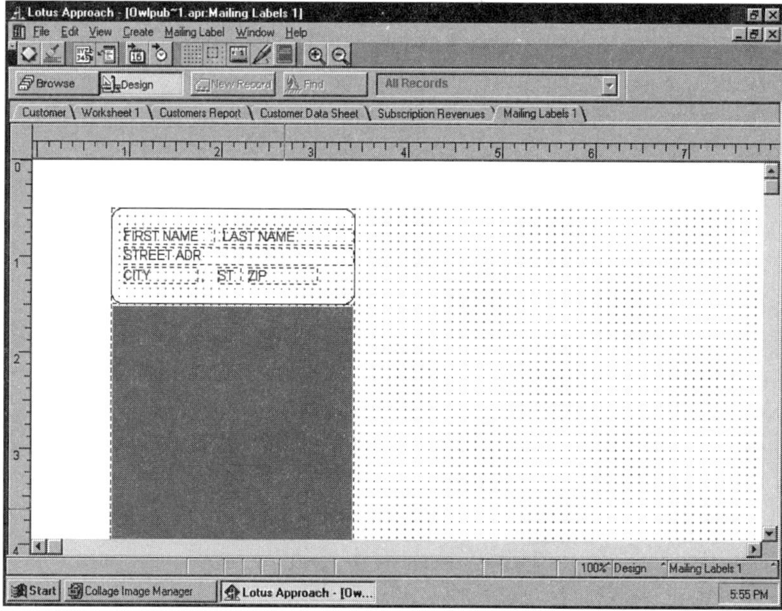

Fig. 7.34

This default mailing label is ready to be customized.

Note

Approach usually positions fields and adjusts spacing to match the format you selected. However, limited label space may cause Approach to place fields outside the boundaries of the label. You need to rearrange the fields so that they're all within the label (see the later section "Arranging the Fields on a Label"). You may also need to specify a smaller font size to fit all the information you want on the label. The rounded rectangle, which doesn't print, provides a guide to where the label edges are located.

Deleting a Set of Mailing Labels

If you decide that you don't need a set of mailing labels anymore, you can delete them by following these steps:

1. Switch to Design mode by opening the View menu and choosing Design, clicking the Design button on the action bar, or choosing Design from the status bar.
2. If the set of mailing labels you want to delete isn't on-screen, select the set from the view tabs or from the status bar.
3. Open the Edit menu and choose Delete Mailing Labels. Then confirm that you want to delete the mailing labels at the prompt.

Duplicating a Set of Mailing Labels

To give you a head start in creating a set of mailing labels that are similar to a set you already have, Approach allows you to duplicate an existing set of mailing labels. Making a duplicate is useful when you need to create complex mailing labels. To copy a set of mailing labels, follow these steps:

1. Switch to Design mode by opening the View menu and choosing Design, clicking the Design button on the action bar, or selecting Design from the status bar.
2. If the set of mailing labels that you want to duplicate isn't on-screen, select the set of mailing labels from the view tabs or from the status bar.
3. Open the Edit menu and choose Duplicate Mailing Labels. The duplicate of your mailing labels appears on-screen. You can make changes (for example, change fonts, add and remove fields, or rearrange fields) to the duplicate without affecting the original.

Approach gives the duplicate set of mailing labels the same name as the original with the words *Copy of* in front of the name. Use the Basics page of the report InfoBox to change the name of the report.

Specifying Label Characteristics

The Mailing Label Assistant dialog box provides two options for specifying the size and shape of the mailing labels—the Label Type drop-down list and the Options tab.

The Label Type drop-down list provides choices that include the common sizes of Avery labels. Because Avery is the most common brand of computer labels made, you have a good chance of finding your labels on this list. The list includes a wide variety of mailing labels, audio tape and videotape labels, floppy disk labels (5 1/4 inch and 3 1/2 inch), shipping labels, name badges, Rolodex cards, postcards, file-folder labels, and more. If you aren't using Avery labels, you may be able to use the Avery definition if your labels have the same dimensions as a supported Avery label.

The Options tab opens the second page of the Mailing Label Assistant dialog box so that you can specify custom dimensions for your labels (see fig. 7.35).

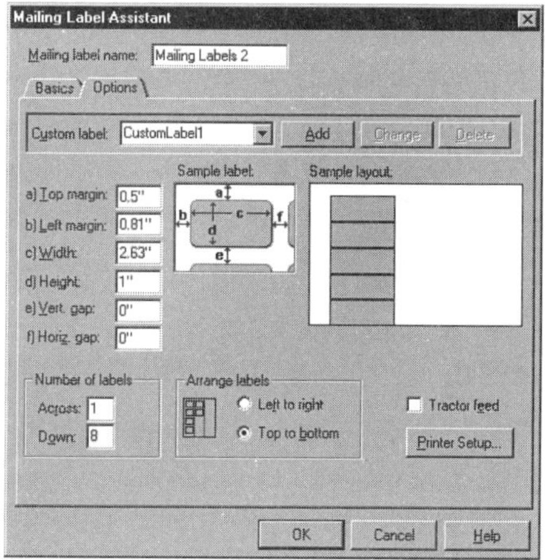

Fig. 7.35

Customize label dimensions through the Options page of the Mailing Label Assistant dialog box.

Tip

You can change the custom options of a mailing label in Design mode. To do so, click the Edit Label Options button in the mailing label InfoBox to open the Mailing Label Options dialog box. This dialog box is identical to the Mailing Label Assistant's Options page.

Type the name of your custom label definition in the Custom Label combo box. Click the Add button to add the custom label name to the list. You also can select a custom label name from the list, change the label specifications (as detailed in the following paragraphs), and click the Change button.

To delete a custom label definition, select the label from the Custom Label list and click the Delete button.

Enter the dimensions of your custom labels in the center section of the Options page. As you enter the dimensions, the Sample Layout section changes to give you an idea of how Approach will print the labels on the page. The label dimensions are as follows:

- *Top Margin*, the distance between the top line of labels and the top edge of the page.

> **Note**
>
> You don't need to enter top-margin measurements for tractor-fed labels.

- *Left Margin*, the distance between the left edge of the labels and the left edge of the page.
- *Width* of each label.
- *Height* of each label.
- *Vert. gap*, the vertical gap between labels on the page.
- *Horiz. gap*, the horizontal gap between labels on the page.

In the Arrange Labels section, choose the printing option you want. Left to Right tells Approach to print the labels in order of rows across the page. Top to Bottom tells Approach to print the labels in order by columns.

Set the balance of the label specifications across the bottom of the Options page:

- In the Number of Labels section, type the number of labels Across the page and the number of labels Down the page. The Sample Layout section adjusts to display your label layout.
- If you're using tractor-fed labels, choose the Tractor Feed check box. If you're using sheet-fed labels (labels used by laser or inkjet printers), make sure that the Tractor Feed check box isn't selected.

When you choose the Printer Setup button in the bottom right corner of the Options page, the Print Setup dialog box appears, and you can configure your printer with all its usual options.

Arranging the Fields on a Label

After you specify the label size and select the fields, you can size and arrange the fields on the label. You also may need to change the font and size of the fields so that all the information fits on the mailing label.

You perform these operations on mailing labels in the same way you perform them on forms or reports, by using the field's InfoBox. The following paragraphs summarize these actions:

- To size a field, select it and then drag the sizing handles until the field is the size you want. You also can use the dimensions page of the InfoBox.
- To move a field, select it and then drag the field to its new location. You can also use the dimensions page of the InfoBox.
- To change the font, size/effect, alignment, text color, and relief, select the field and choose the options you want from the fonts page in the InfoBox.
- To close up empty spaces when printing, select the Left and Up check boxes on the dimensions page of the InfoBox (see the earlier section, "Using Slide Up and Slide Left").
- Use the colors page in the InfoBox to set the border width, frame style, border color, fill color, shadow color, and the border location (left, right, top, and bottom).
- Click the Label radio button on the InfoBox font page to set the label font, style/effect, size, alignment, label text, position, color, and text relief. Usually, mailing labels don't use labels because of the limited space. To suppress a field's label, set the Label position to No Label.

Setting the Mailing Label Properties

Aside from the fields, a mailing-label design in Approach consists of three other parts: a rounded rectangle graphic, a body panel, and the mailing label background.

Approach uses the rounded rectangle to delineate the borders of each label. You can select the rounded rectangle by clicking anywhere in a mailing label except where there's a field. By default, the rounded rectangle is non-printing, but you can set it to print with the mailing labels by deselecting the Non-Printing check box on the Basics page of the rectangle's InfoBox. As with any other graphic object, you can adjust the border width, border color, fill color, shadow color, and frame from the colors page of the InfoBox. Of course, unless you plan to print the rounded rectangle, there's no point in adjusting its properties.

The body panel sets the boundaries of each label. The panel usually isn't visible because it's covered by the rounded rectangle discussed earlier. However, you can select the body panel by Ctrl+clicking anywhere in the mailing label. You can adjust the border width, border color, border location, fill color, shadow color, and frame from the colors page of the InfoBox. You can make the body panel visible by setting the fill color of the rounded rectangle to T (transparent).

Click between the labels in a mailing label layout to gain access to the mailing label's background. From the Basics page of the mailing label InfoBox, you can change the mailing label's name by typing a new name into the Mailing Label Name field box.

You also can use the colors page to set the border width and location, frame style, border color, and fill color. However, the properties of the colors page are always identical for the mailing labels and body panel.

Printing Records

You can tell Approach to print your currently selected form or report. If you sorted the records, they print in the current sort order. If you performed a find operation, only the records in the found set print.

Before printing, follow these steps to ensure that you print only what you need:

1. Switch to the form or report that you want to print. Approach prints the form or report that you're now using.
2. Choose the set of records that you want to print. Approach prints the current found set of records (or all records, if there's no found set).
3. Sort the records in the order in which you want them printed. Approach prints the records in the sort order you're now using.

Previewing the Printout

Before printing, you may want to see how the output will look, in case you want to make last-minute changes. The Print Preview feature shows how the report looks when printed.

If you formatted certain objects as non-printing or if you're using options such as Slide Up or Slide Left, what appears on the printout will differ from what appears on-screen. With Approach's Print Preview feature, you can check the report before wasting paper.

To preview a page, first make sure that you're in Browse mode. Click the Print Preview SmartIcon, select Print Preview from the status bar, or open the File menu and choose Preview. The previewed page appears on-screen at 75 percent of normal size. To see the previewed page in a larger size, simply click or select an alternate magnification from the status line.

To exit Print Preview mode, click the Print Preview SmartIcon again, select a different mode from the status line, or choose Preview again from the File menu.

Printing the Report

To print the form or report, open the File menu and choose Print. The Print dialog box appears (see fig. 7.36). The specifications for your printer are listed at the top of this dialog box. To change these specifications, click the Properties button. If you're printing multiple records on a page, the dialog box will ask you to list pages to be printed. If your report has one record per page, the dialog box will change to reflect individual records.

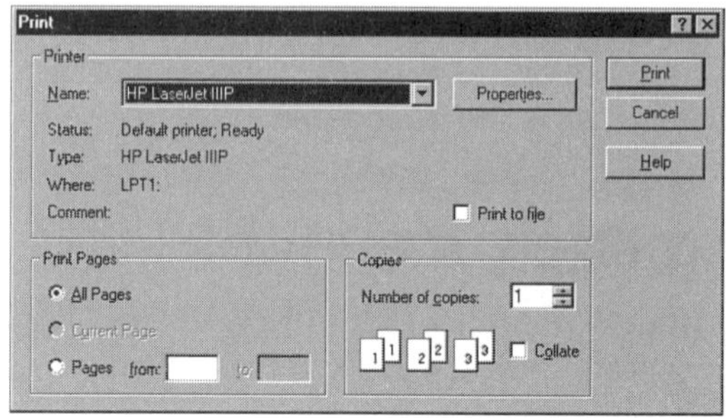

Fig. 7.36

Set print options through the Print dialog box.

Printing to the Printer. Before printing to your printer, you may want to set some options in the Print dialog box. If you're printing reports with multiple records on a page, click the appropriate radio button in the Print Pages section to set the pages you want to print:

- All Pages prints all the pages of the found set.
- Current Page prints only the current page of records within the found set.
- Pages From... To... prints the pages specified.

If you're printing reports with a single record per page, use the option buttons in the Records section to select specific records to print:

- All prints all the records in the current set.
- Current Form prints only the form page you have on-screen. This option is valid only for form letters and forms.
- Records From... To... prints only those records you specify, by number.

The Print dialog box also provides the following two options:

- In the Number of Copies spin box, specify the number of copies you need.
- Use the Collate check box to specify how you want multiple copies printed. If you leave this check box deselected, Approach prints multiple copies of the first page, followed by multiple copies of the next page, and so on. If you select Collate, Approach prints all pages of the entire first copy, all pages of the second copy, and so on.

Note

Choosing Collate considerably slows printing speed.

After you finish setting the options, click OK to print the information.

Printing to a File. Printing to a file saves a printed version of your document to a file. You then can print it later or transmit the report by modem. The saved file contains all the information necessary to send the file to the configured printer. A file saved in this format may not be readable on-screen.

Tip

To save a printed disk file in a format that you can read on-screen, reset your printer configuration to Windows' Generic/Text Only printer driver.

To print to a file, follow these steps:

1. Select the Print to File check box in the Print dialog box.
2. Click OK in the Print dialog box. The Print to File dialog box appears (see fig. 7.37).

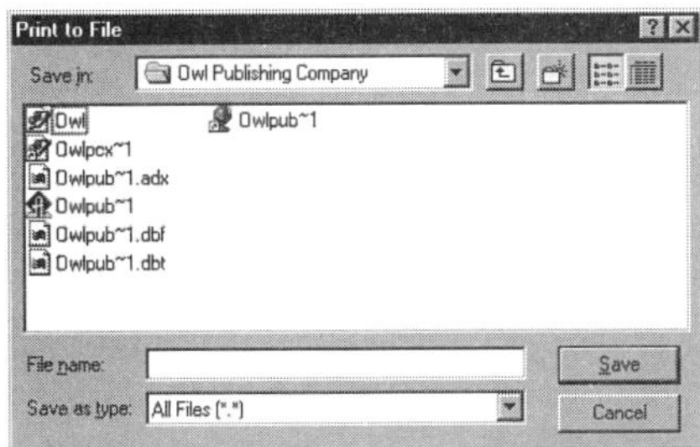

Fig. 7.37

The Print to File dialog box gives you more print options.

3. In the File Name text box, type the name of the file you want to print.
4. Use the Save In drop-down list to specify where you want Approach to save the file.
5. Click Save to save the printed file.

From Here...

As you've seen, reports are similar in many ways to forms, but they also have some important differences. You learned how to build a report, add fields to the report, and customize the format of those fields. You also saw how to "dress up" reports with graphics and text. You learned that headers, footers, and title pages—not available for forms—allow you to customize a report by adding items that appear on every page and to create a special first page. You learned that mailing labels are a special kind of report that allows you to create labels by using the data in your database and to place this data on commercial labels.

You can do much more with reports. For more information, refer to the following chapters in this book:

- Chapter 10, "Using Advanced Field Types," tells how to create more complex field types that can be very useful on a report.
- Chapter 12, "Creating Advanced Reports," continues the lessons learned in this chapter by discussing how to create reports that include summary information.
- Chapter 15, "Creating Charts," shows how to make colorful graphs and charts to include in reports.

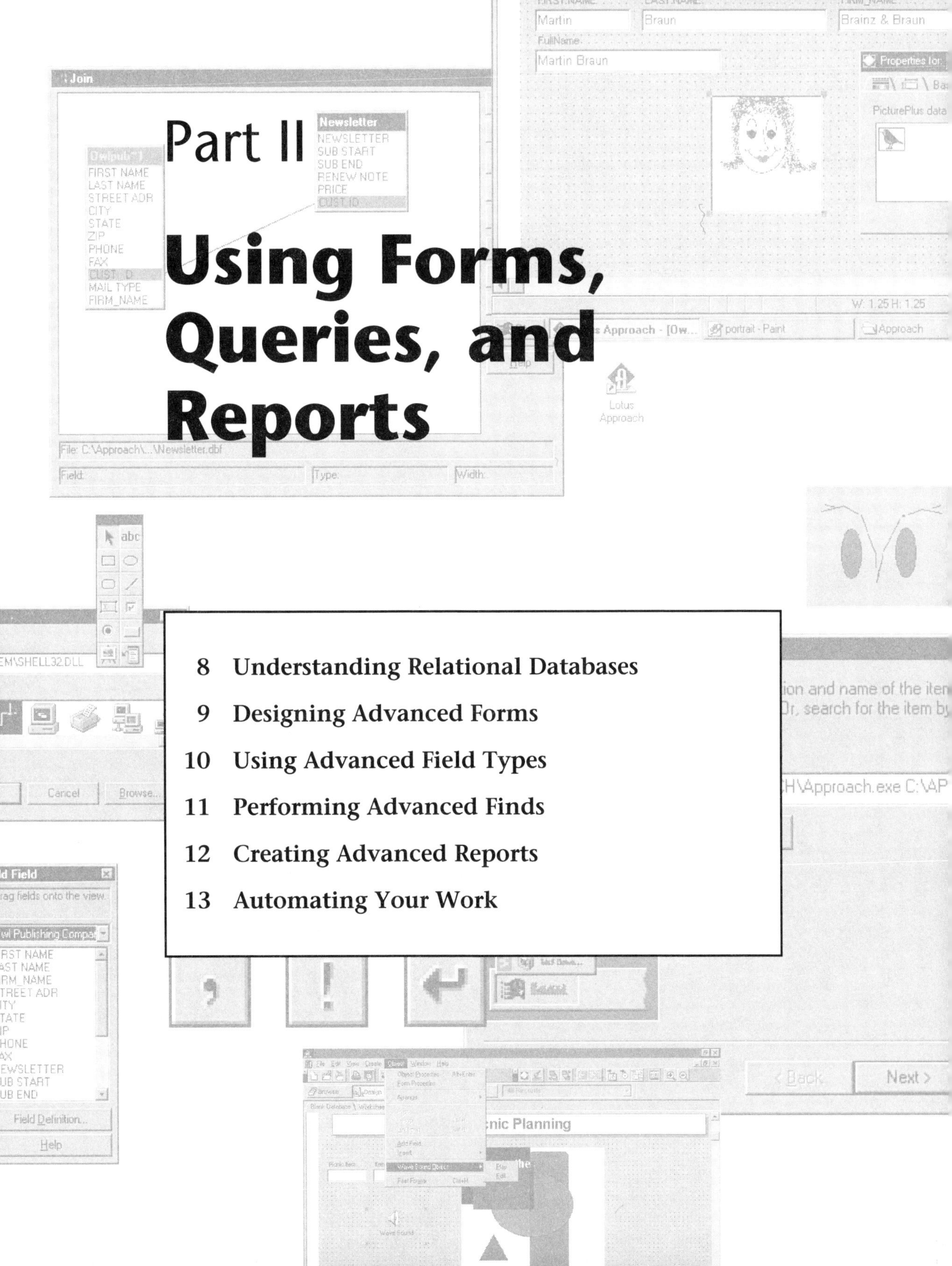

Part II

Using Forms, Queries, and Reports

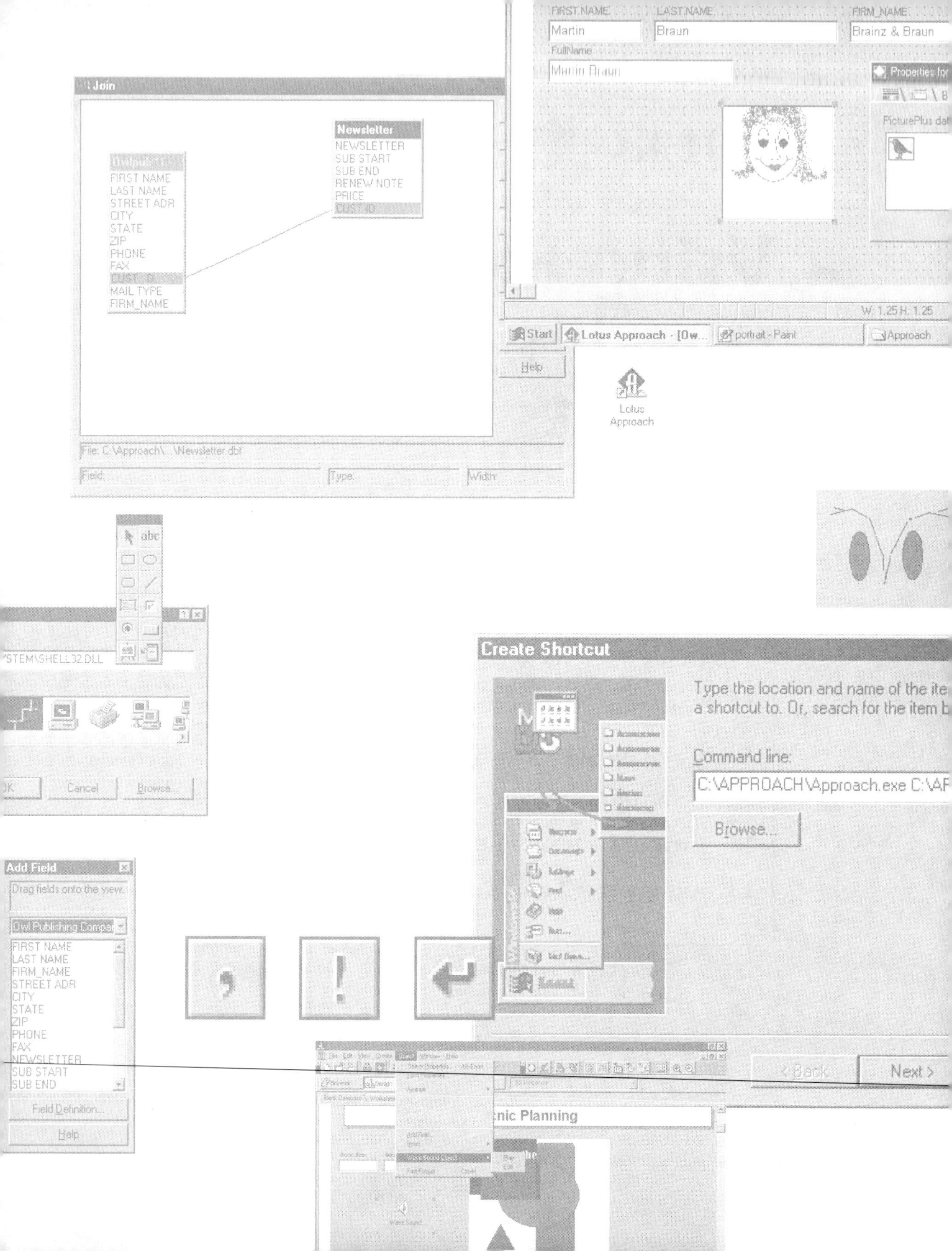

Join
Newsletter
NEWSLETTER
SUB START
SUB END
RENEW NOTE
PRICE
CUST ID
FIRST NAME
LAST NAME
STREET ADR
CITY
STATE
ZIP
PHONE
FAX
CUST_ID
MAIL TYPE
FIRM_NAME
File: C:\Approach\...\Newsletter.dbf
Field:
Type:
Width:
Help
FIRST NAME
LAST NAME
FIRM_NAME
Martin
Braun
Brainz & Braun
FullName
Martin Braun
Properties for
PicturePlus dat
W: 1.25 H: 1.25
Start
Lotus Approach - [Ow...
portrait - Paint
Approach
Lotus Approach
STEM\SHELL32.DLL
Cancel
Browse...
Create Shortcut
Type the location and name of the ite
a shortcut to. Or, search for the item b
Command line:
C:\APPROACH\Approach.exe C:\AF
Browse...
< Back
Next >
Add Field
Drag fields onto the view.
Owl Publishing Compar
FIRST NAME
LAST NAME
FIRM_NAME
STREET ADR
CITY
STATE
ZIP
PHONE
FAX
NEWSLETTER
SUB START
SUB END
Field Definition...
Help
cnic Planning

CHAPTER 8

Understanding Relational Databases

Up to this point, this book has discussed keeping all data in a single table. A database that stores everything in a single table is called a *flat file*. This chapter introduces a powerful new kind of database, called a *relational database*. You'll learn the advantages of a relational database over a flat-file database, as well as how to set up relational databases. You'll also completely rebuild the Owl Publishing database near the end of this chapter to make it relational.

In this chapter, you learn how to

- Distinguish flat-file databases from relational databases and the advantages of each
- Set up a relational link, including many-to-many, many-to-one, and one-to-one relationships
- Set up relational options
- Join aliased databases
- Set data-entry options for relational databases
- Establish security levels for users of your relational databases

Understanding the Disadvantages of Flat Files

The advantage of a flat-file database is that designing one is very straightforward. Keeping all your data in a single table, however, has some significant disadvantages, including wasting disk space, typing unnecessary data, and having to change data in multiple places.

Consider the Owl Publishing database. It includes customer information, such as names, addresses, and phone numbers. It also includes the name of the newsletter to which the customer subscribes, the price, and the subscription dates.

What would happen, however, if one customer wanted to subscribe to more than one newsletter? Handling such a situation with the current design would be very difficult.

You could create another record, complete with all the information about that subscriber (such as address, phone number, and so forth). The new record would also contain the information about the additional newsletter. Thus, if a person wanted to subscribe to three newsletters, that subscriber would have three separate records with three sets of customer information in the database (see fig. 8.1).

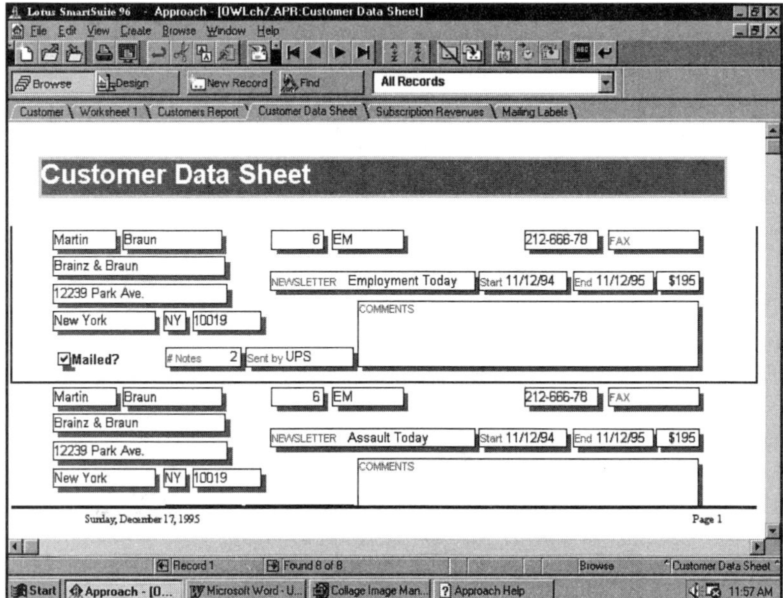

Fig. 8.1

A flat-file database requires redundant information for repeat customers, and could result in errors in billing.

Using multiple records in this situation presents the following problems:

- Information that's largely a duplicate of information stored in another record takes up quite a bit of disk space.
- Typing all those extra records takes a good deal of time. If Owl Publishing were a large publishing house, with hundreds of newsletters, would you want to retype all those addresses into the database?
- What if one of your larger customers changed addresses? Someone would have to go through the multiple records and change the address in each record.

You may have thought of a potential solution already—creating multiple sets of fields in the database (and on the form) for holding newsletter information. You can create, for example, the fields NEWSLETTER1, NEWSLETTER2, NEWSLETTER3, and so on to hold the title information. However, this "solution" presents some problems of its own:

- How many sets of fields do you make? If you create only a few sets, the day will come when you run out of fields. At that point, you'll have to create more sets of fields, revising the database and the form to hold them. If you create a large number of sets, you're wasting space in the database and on the form—and you can still run out of fields.

- How do you find information in a query? Suppose that you want to find all subscribers of a particular newsletter. The name of that newsletter may appear in the NEWSLETTER1 field on one record, in the NEWSLETTER3 field in another record, and so on. Approach allows you to find all records in which the contents of one field match your criteria *or* the contents of another field match your criteria. These queries become unwieldy, however, when you need to check the contents of a large number of fields.

These problems are difficult, and this example has considered only the case in which one set of data, the newsletter data, occurs multiple times. If another set of data also occurs multiple times (such as a firm with multiple entries in the SPECIALTY field), the problem quickly becomes unmanageable with a flat-file database.

Finding the Relational-Database Solution

The solution to this dilemma is to use multiple tables (databases)—that is, not to store all your information in a single table. For the preceding example, you could store the information about the customers (name, address, phone) in one table, and the newsletter subscription information (newsletter name, price, and subscription dates) in another table. Because the two tables must have a relationship that identifies which newsletter subscription information belongs to each customer, this type of database is called a *relational database*. Approach lets you build and use relational databases.

Setting Up a Relational Link

To create a relationship between two databases, you must join them. A *join field* describes how one or more fields in the first database relate to similar fields in the second database. It's usually best to use a unique ID value in each database, but you also can use a combination of fields that together uniquely identify a record in one of the databases. Because the join establishes the relationship between two databases, a join is also called a *relational link* between two databases. When you specify a record in one database, the value in the join field(s) of that database is used to find the matching record(s) in the other database. A join field is the only place in which information from one database should be stored in another database.

In the Owl Publishing example, the customer database would contain customer information such as name, address, phone, and so forth. One of the fields would be CUST_ID, which would contain a unique number that identifies a customer.

The Subscription database would contain information on subscriptions (newsletter title, subscription start date, subscription end date, and so forth). Clearly, you would need a field in the Subscription database to identify which customer the subscription belongs to. You would need the CUST_ID field in the Subscription database as well. The CUST_ID field would be the field that relates the two databases—the relational link.

> **Note**
>
> Relational fields don't have to have the same name in the two databases, but using the same name is helpful because it makes identifying the related fields easier.

When you identify a customer record in the customer database, Approach automatically has the value in the CUST_ID field. With this information, Approach can obtain the records with the matching value in the CUST_ID field of the subscription database.

Understanding the Advantages of a Relational Database

The advantages of a relational structure are significant:

- *You enter data only once.* The subscription information database doesn't contain the customer address information. Such information appears only in the Customer database. Even customers that subscribe to multiple newsletters have only a single record in the customer database. Thus, the customer's address is typed only once.
- *Data is stored only once.* The customer database contains the address information in a single record. If the customer moves, you need to change just a single record for that customer in the customer database to update all your address information for that customer.
- *You can enter an unlimited number of related records in the Subscription database.* If a customer subscribes to another newsletter, you only need enter the new subscription information in the subscription database with the CUST_ID for that customer.

Deciding When to Use a Relational Database

If you haven't used a relational database before, deciding when you should switch from a flat-file design to a relational design may be unclear. The answer is actually quite simple: Any time you need to store more than one occurrence of a piece of information, you need to think about using a relational design. In the Owl Publishing example, you found that you needed to store multiple occurrences of subscription information. Thus, you needed to build a new database to hold that information. If Owl Publishing decides that the company needs to keep track of multiple specialties (SPECIALTY), this information also would be a good candidate for a separate—yet related—database.

Deciding What a Related Database Should Contain

The related database should contain all the information that's directly connected to the subject of that database. The Owl Publishing subscription database, for example, would contain the newsletter title, subscription start date, subscription end date, and price because each quantity can occur only once for a given subscription. A subscription can have only one subscription start date. If the subscription start date changes (the customer renews the subscription), you enter a new record in the subscription database for this new subscription.

Using Information from Related Databases

After you build relationships between databases, you can place the information from related databases on the same form. The form is based on a "main" database, as discussed in Chapter 9, "Designing Advanced Forms." This form also can contain fields from related databases (called *detail databases*). When you change the data on a form for a field that comes from a detail database, the information in the detail database is updated automatically.

Understanding the Types of Database Relationships

Databases may be related to one another in three ways: many-to-one, one-to-one, and one-to-many.

Many-to-One Relationships

In a many-to-one relationship, a record in the primary database has no more than one matching record in another database, but a record in the other database matches more than one record in the primary database (see fig. 8.2).

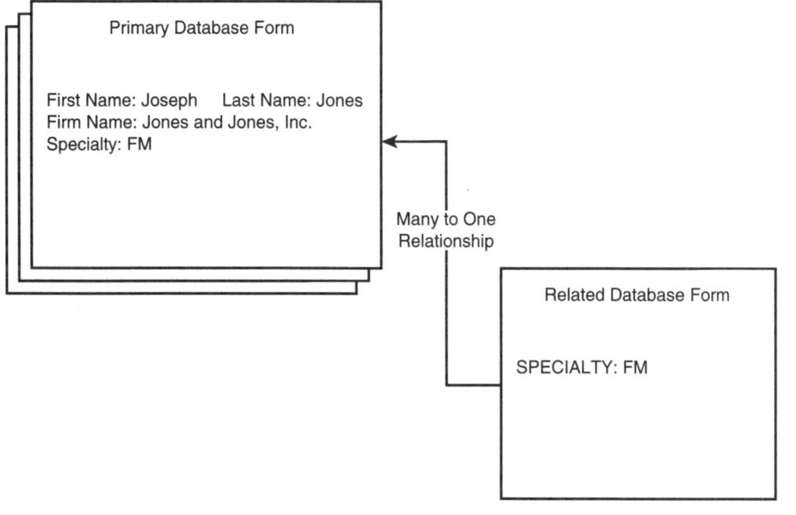

Fig. 8.2

In a many-to-one relationship, several subscribers may have a value of FM in the SPECIALTY field.

Many-to-one relationships are useful for performing lookups. When you enter the value for the relational field on your form, a lookup can retrieve other information about that value from the related database. You can then place this related data on your form (see Chapter 9, "Designing Advanced Forms," for information on how to set up a form this way). (A *lookup* essentially is a find operation that searches related databases instead of the primary database.) You don't have to type the data retrieved from the related database, nor do you need to store it in your primary database.

Suppose that you have a database that contains a field for the two-character SPECIALTY code. Each record in the Specialty database can also contain other data, such as a text field explaining what the code means. After your Customer and Specialty databases are related (by the SPECIALTY field in each database), the information in Specialty becomes available on the Customer form. Entering the SPECIALTY code (or choosing it from a list) on the Customer form establishes the matching record in the Specialty database. You then can place the text explanation from this record onto the Customer form—without having to type it (see fig. 8.3).

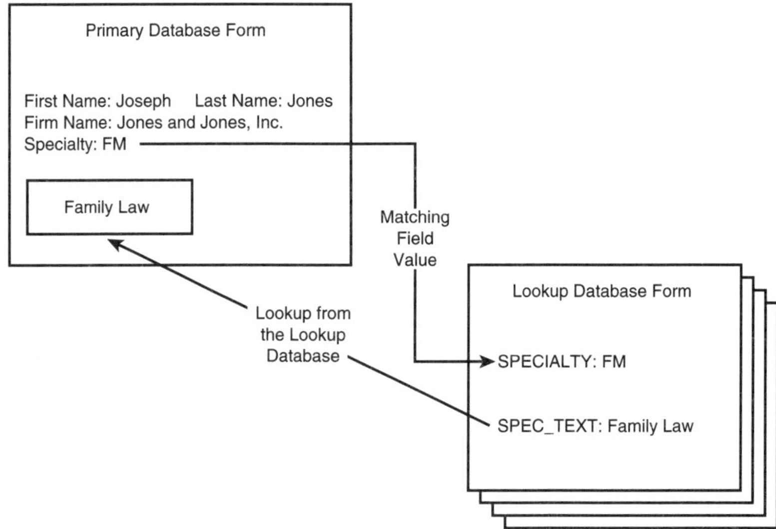

Fig. 8.3

Matching data in the SPECIALTY field is used to establish a relational link between the Customer and Specialty databases.

For a lookup to work properly, the linking field must come from the primary database for the form or report. In the preceding example, the SPECIALTY field displayed on the form must come from the Customer database (although the SPECIALTY field is present in both databases).

One-to-One Relationships

In a one-to-one relationship, a record in the primary database has no more than one matching record in another database. At first, you could include the field for this information in your primary database. However, there are some good reasons for occasionally using one-to-one relationships.

One good reason for setting up a one-to-one relationship is for security and confidentiality. You may have, for example, employee information that includes mailing address and salary. Clerical staff may enter the addresses, but the salary information is confidential. You could set up the address information in a database with its own form, and then set up another database that contains the salary information. The two databases can be joined by EMPLOYEE ID.

Chapter 9, "Designing Advanced Forms," shows how you can look up the employee address from the address database and place this information on the Salary form when working with the Salary database (see figs. 8.4 and 8.5).

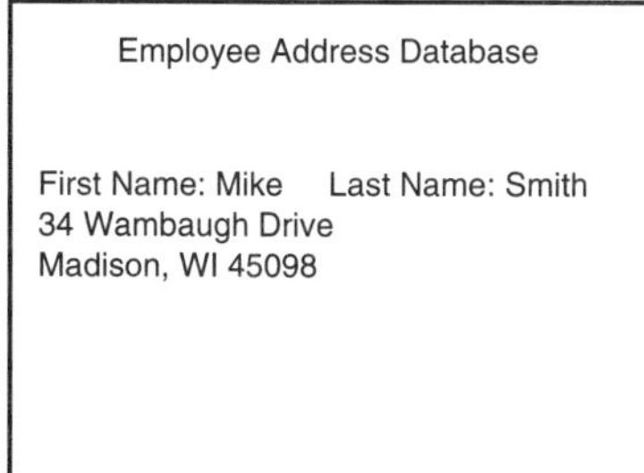

Fig. 8.4

An address is entered in the Employee Address view file.

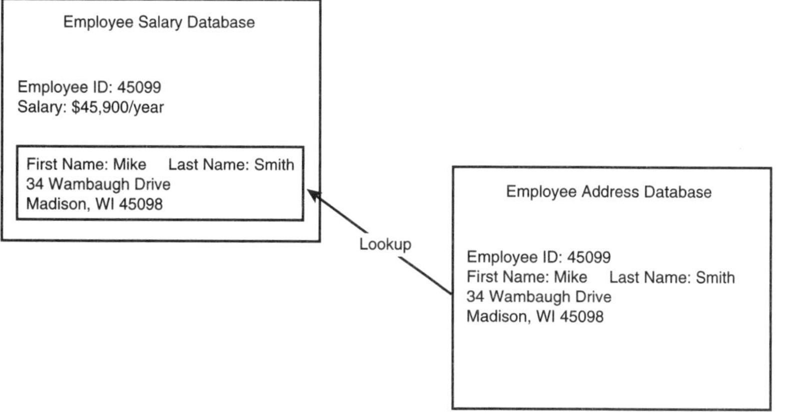

Fig. 8.5

The address is looked up and placed on the form in the Salary view file.

It's rare that you need to use one-to-one relationships in Approach. You could achieve the same results as in the preceding example by including the confidential data in the main database, but providing multiple Approach files. The Approach file used by the clerical staff would display only non-confidential fields, while another (password-protected) Approach file contains forms and reports that display all the data, including the confidential salary information.

One-to-Many Relationships

In a one-to-many relationship, a single record in the primary database can have many matching records in another (detail) database (see fig. 8.6).

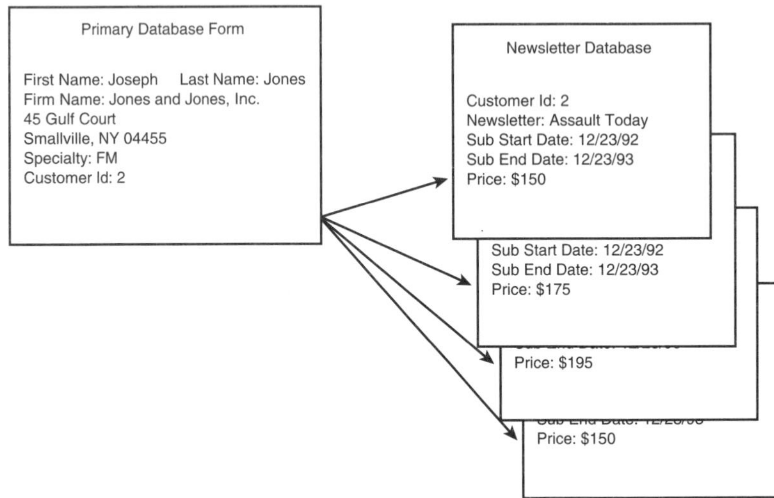

Fig. 8.6

In this one-to-many relationship, a customer can have a subscription to many different newsletters.

The newsletter example illustrates this relationship well. Each customer record in the Customer database can have many matching subscription records in the Subscription database. Approach lets you see these many records on a form in a repeating panel. (A *repeating panel* is a small table that displays records from a related database on a form.)

The field(s) that relates the two databases in a one-to-many relationship should identify each record uniquely in the primary database. Thus, using a unique customer ID works well. In contrast, if the values in the related fields aren't unique, strange things can happen. Suppose that you run a search for a customer whose last name is Brown. If you use LAST NAME as the related field, Approach finds the same set of matching records in the secondary database for everyone named Brown, which is clearly not correct.

Note

Although a single record in the primary database can have multiple related records in the secondary database, each record in the secondary database must match no more than one record in the primary database. For Owl Publishing, each customer record can have multiple subscription records, but each subscription record must be related to only a single customer record because the related field is the unique CUST_ID field.

Circumstances do exist, however, in which each record in the secondary database matches more than one record in the primary database. Suppose that you have a list of customers and a list of sales representatives. If each customer has multiple sales reps and each sales rep calls on multiple customers, you have a many-to-many relationship. Relational databases can't handle many-to-many relationships directly, although you can work around this limitation (as discussed in Chapter 16, "Exploring Advanced Database Relationships").

Joining Databases

Setting up the relational link between two or more databases is called *joining* them. To join two or more databases, you must do the following:

- Identify two or more databases to be joined.
- Identify the field(s) in each database to be the basis of the relationship.

After you define a join, it's stored as part of the Approach file. Any databases you open in the Join dialog box and join to other databases also are stored as part of the Approach file. Opening the Approach file opens all the joined databases and establishes any relational links you've defined.

Note

All databases you open in the Join dialog box must be joined to each other—that is, you must be able to navigate from any one database to any other database in the Join dialog box by traversing the join links. If you haven't set up the Join dialog box this way, the OK button will be dimmed.

You have considerable flexibility in how you join the databases. You could join multiple databases to one main database, for example, or you could join database A to database B, join database B to database C, and so on.

Note

Approach doesn't allow you to join two databases that are joined to the same database. If, for example, database A is joined to database B, and database B is joined to database C, you can't join database A to database C because A and C are joined to B. However, you may use database aliases to circumvent this limitation. See "Joining Aliased Databases" later in this chapter.

To join two databases, follow these steps:

1. Open the File menu and choose Open. From the Open dialog box, select the Approach file you want to open. Any databases used by the selected Approach file open automatically when you open the Approach file.

   Note

   The Approach file you open is the one that stores the relational information you define.

2. Open the Create menu and choose Join. The Join dialog box appears (see fig. 8.7). Any database associated with the Approach file opened in step 1 becomes visible in the working area of this dialog box, and a list of fields appears under the heading for each database.

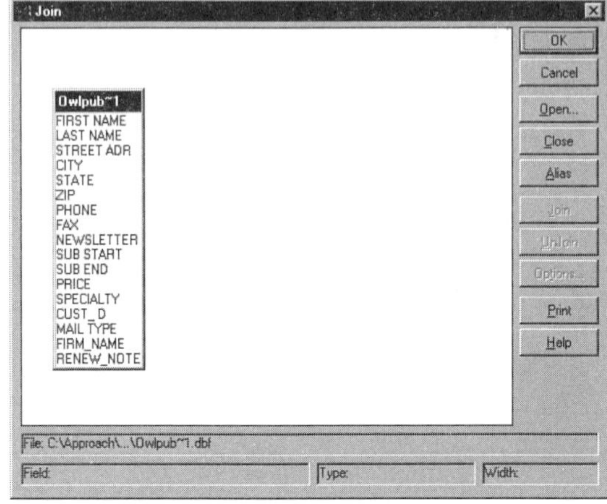

Fig. 8.7

You can click any field in a database in the Join dialog box. Approach displays the field name, type, and length at the bottom of the dialog box.

3. Choose Open to open a database you want to join to any databases already available in the Join dialog box. The Open dialog box opens (see fig. 8.8).

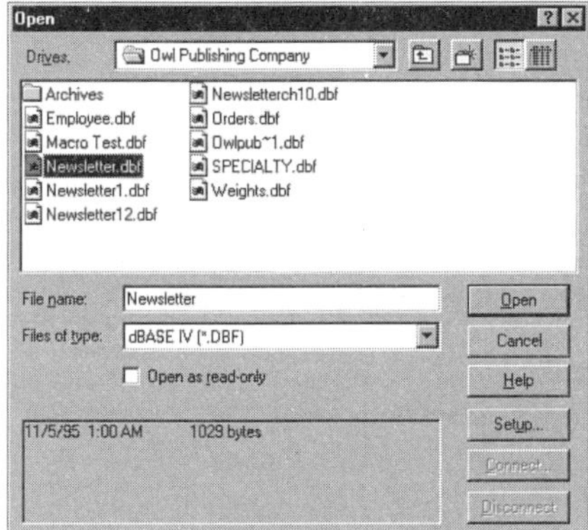

Fig. 8.8

Select a database that you want to join the main database to.

4. Select the database that you want to add to the Join dialog box from the file list near the top of the dialog box. The name of the database appears in the Name box.

> **Note**
>
> If the database isn't visible in the Open dialog box, use the Drives drop-down list and Files list to locate the file. If necessary, set the type of database file by using the Files of Type drop-down list.

5. Click Open. The database you selected in the Open dialog box now appears in the Join dialog box, with its list of fields (see fig. 8.9).

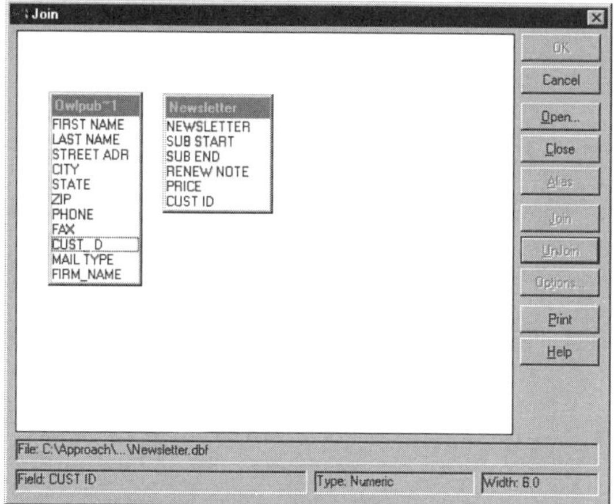

Fig. 8.9

Fields for both databases are displayed in the Join dialog box.

6. Select a database (such as the Owl Publishing database in fig. 8.9), and choose the field that will link this database to the newly opened database. The linking field may be a field already used to link to another database. Approach highlights the field name.

> **Tip**
>
> Approach lets you join databases of different types. For example, you can join a dBASE III+ database to a Paradox database.

7. Select a field in the newly opened database (the Newsletter database in fig. 8.9) that you'll use to link to the first database. Approach highlights the field name.
8. Click Join. A line appears between the databases, linking the fields selected in steps 7 and 8 (see fig. 8.10).
9. If you're going to join two databases in more than a single field, repeat steps 7 through 9 to establish the additional joins.

> **Tip**
>
> You can also establish a join between two databases by clicking a join field in the first database and dragging to the join field in the second database. When you release the left mouse button, Approach creates the join line. You can also use the click-and-drag method to create multiple-field joins between databases.

Rearranging the database boxes makes them easier to see and use. To rearrange the database boxes in the Join dialog box, drag them to new locations (see fig. 8.11). Approach redraws the join lines automatically and saves the new configuration in the Approach file.

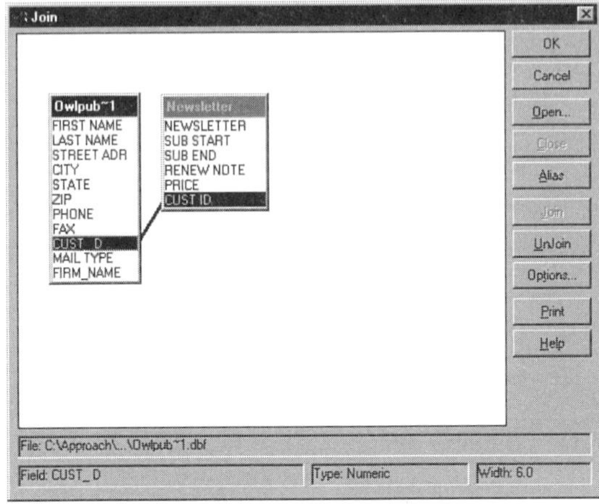

Fig. 8.10

The line between the two databases indicates that they're joined.

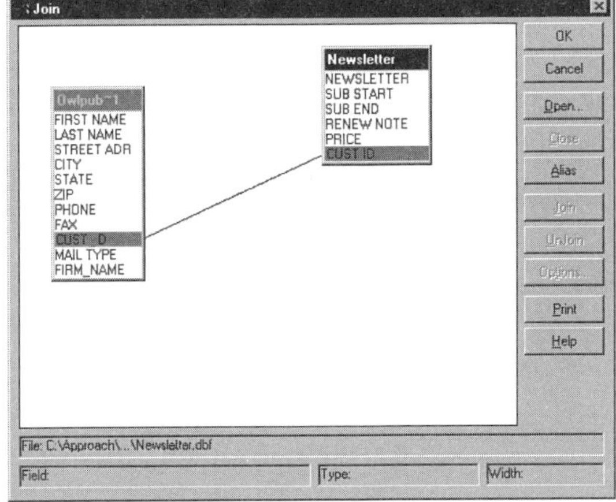

Fig. 8.11

You can rearrange the database boxes to make room for other joins.

You can print the join diagram by choosing Print. Click OK in the Print dialog box to create a printed version of your joins.

Joining Aliased Databases

One of the more difficult problems you face when designing relational databases is the need to occasionally join a database to itself. The classic example of this is the employee/manager relationship. At first glance, you might set this up with two databases. The Employees database contains a list of employees; the Managers database contains a list of managers. Each employee has one manager, but a manager may have many employees—a one-to-many relationship between a manager and his or her employees. Unfortunately for this scenario, managers also are employees and also reside in the Employees database. To handle this situation, you must join the Employees database to itself. In addition to other information, each record in the Employees database must contain two IDs: the employee's ID (EMPL ID) and the employee manager's ID (MGR ID). The values that go in the MGR ID field must be valid EMPL IDs.

To join a database to itself, you must create a "copy" of the database in the Join dialog box. The copy isn't an actual copy of the database, but only another instance of the same database called an *alias*. After you create an alias, you can set up a join between the alias and any database just as you would with any two databases. In the example discussed earlier, you would create an alias of the Employee table. This alias serves as the Managers table. You join the original Employee table and its alias using the relational link fields of MGR ID (Employee table) and EMPL ID (alias of Employee table). Because aliases are treated the same as any other joined databases, you can even create a form that displays a manager and all the manager's employees (see fig. 8.12).

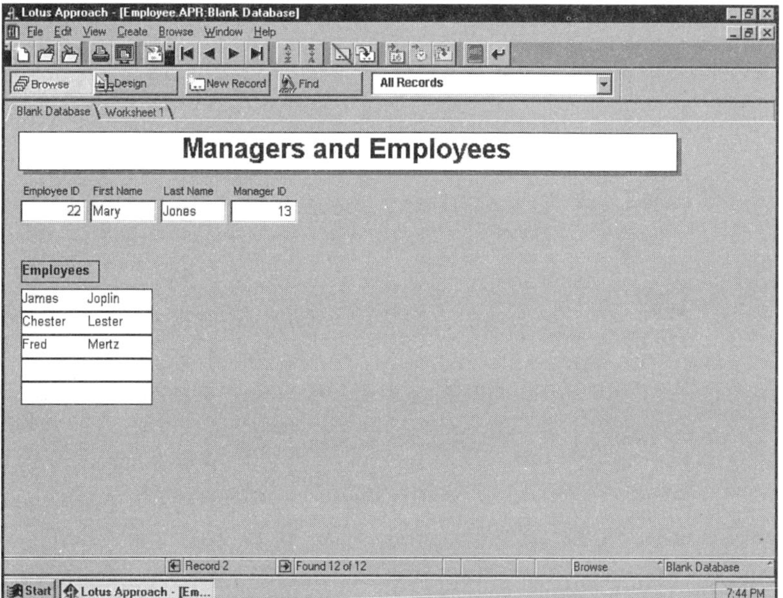

Fig. 8.12

By using an Employee database alias, you can display a manager and all that manager's employees.

To create an alias of a database in the Join dialog box, click the database you want and select Alias. Approach creates the alias and displays it in the Join dialog box (see fig. 8.13). You may create multiple aliases of a database. Approach appends a 1 to the original database name. The alias has the same name as the original database with a 2 (or 3, 4, and so on) appended to it—for example, EMPLOYEE:1 and EMPLOYEE:2. These numbers don't actually affect the database name; Approach just uses the numbers to distinguish between the database and its aliases.

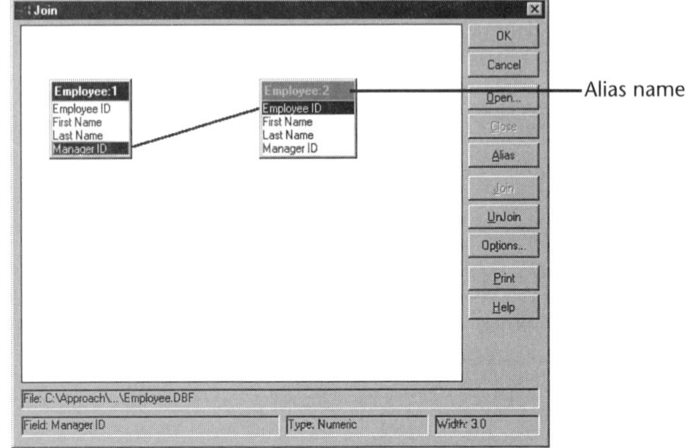

Fig. 8.13

For each alias, Approach appends a number (1, 2, 3, and so on) to the original database and its aliases.

Tip

Approach doesn't permit circular joins; however, you can avoid this limitation by using aliases. For example, if you join database A to B, and B to C, you normally couldn't join A to C. However, you *can* join A to an alias of C to achieve the same result.

Setting the Relational Options

After you join two databases, you can set some relational options that define certain features of the join. Many database relationships are structured so that adding a record in the first database automatically adds a record to the second database. If the Departments database is joined to the Employees database, for example, adding a new record to the Departments database also adds a new record to the Employees database, because a department must have at least one employee.

Sometimes, deleting a record in the second database makes sense when the matching record has been deleted from the first database. If a record is deleted from the Departments database, for example, you may want to delete all the employees in that department, but not if you'll be transferring them to another department. With the relational options, you can make these types of decisions.

To set the options for the relationship between two databases, follow these steps:

1. Open the Create menu and choose Join. The Join dialog box opens, displaying all the open databases and the relationships between them.
2. Click the line connecting the two databases for which you want to define the relational options.
3. Click the Options button. The Relational Options dialog box appears (see fig. 8.14). You can also double-click the join line to open the Relational Options dialog box.

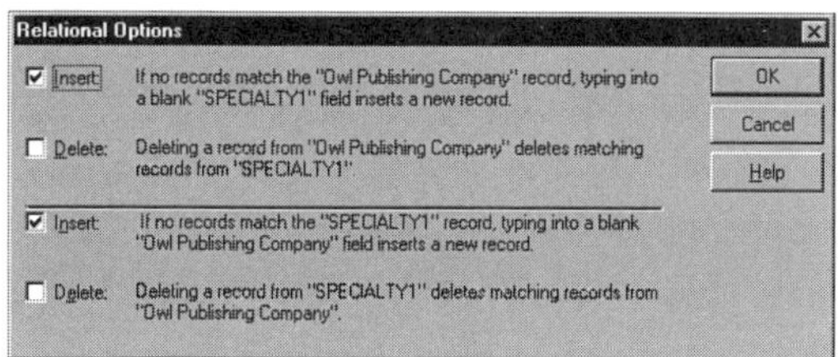

Fig. 8.14

You can control when records are created and deleted by setting relational options for your databases in the Relational Options dialog box.

4. Select one or more of the four check-box options that define the options you want to set. The two options above the line determine what occurs in the second database when you add or delete a record to the first database. The two options below the line determine what happens in the first database when you add or delete a record in the second database. These options are described as follows:

   - *Insert.* For a form based on the first database that also has fields from the second database on it, choose the Insert option above the line so that a record is added automatically to the second database when you add a record to the first database. Typing information into the fields on the form that come from the second database enters the typed information into the new record in the second database. Suppose the first form is based on the Owl Customer database and contains fields from the Newsletter (second) database. Use this option so that entering information in the Newsletter database fields on the form automatically creates a record for the newsletter in the second database. If you didn't use this option, you would have to go to a form based on the Newsletter database to create a new record for the newsletter (including the Customer ID). At that point, you then could see the information in that record on the first form.

     For a form based on the second database that has fields from the first database on it, choose the Insert option below the line so that a record is added automatically to the first database when you add a record to the second database. Typing information into the fields on the form that come from the first database enters the typed information into the new record in the first database.

   - *Delete.* When a form is based on the first database, choose the Delete option above the line so that all joined records in the second database are deleted automatically when you delete a record from the first database. Suppose that the first form is based on the Owl Customer database and contains fields from the Newsletter (second) database. If you use this option, when you delete the customer from the first database, all of that customer's Newsletter records are deleted from the Newsletter (second) database. If you didn't use this option, you would still have "orphaned" records in the Newsletter database (that is, the Newsletter database would have records that belonged to customers you had deleted).

When a form is based on the second database, choose the Delete option below the line so that all joined records in the first database are deleted automatically when you delete a record from the second database.

> **Caution**
>
> Be very careful about using the Delete option for databases joined in a one-to-many relationship. You normally don't want to delete a record from the "one" database when you delete a record from the "many" database. If the Departments database is linked to the Employees database, for example, you usually don't want to delete the Department record when you delete one of the Employees in that department. Similarly, you wouldn't want to delete a subscriber when that subscriber cancels just one of several subscriptions.

5. Click OK twice to close the Relational Options and Join dialog boxes.

Unjoining Databases

After you join two databases, you can unjoin them. Approach doesn't let you modify a join, however. If the wrong field joins two databases, you must unjoin the databases and rebuild the join. You can also unjoin two databases if you find that you no longer need the relationship between them.

Unjoining a database and closing it from the Join dialog box deletes all forms, reports, form letters, repeating panels, and mailing labels for which the database that you unjoined was the main database. (See Chapter 9, "Designing Advanced Forms," for information on assigning "main" databases for a form and on repeating panels.) The highlighted database box is closed when you click the Close button in the Join dialog box. Forms, reports, form letters, and mailing labels for which this database is the main database will be lost if you close it.

To unjoin a database, follow these steps:

1. Open the Create menu and choose Join. The Join dialog box appears.
2. Select the relationship line that you want to delete.
3. Choose Unjoin. The relationship line disappears.
4. Click the database(s) that has been unjoined and then click Close.
5. Click OK in the Join dialog box.

Setting Data-Entry Options for Related Databases

As you learned in Chapter 2, "Creating Database Tables," the Options button in the Field Definition dialog box lets you enter data-validation criteria for a field. If the criteria aren't met, Approach doesn't accept the value typed into the field.

When you set up relational joins that link one or more databases, additional options become available in the Validation page of the Field Definition dialog box. To set these options, follow these steps:

1. Open the Create menu and choose Field Definition. The Field Definition dialog box appears.
2. Click the Options button to open the lower section of the dialog box. Select the Validation tab to switch to the Validation page (see fig. 8.15).

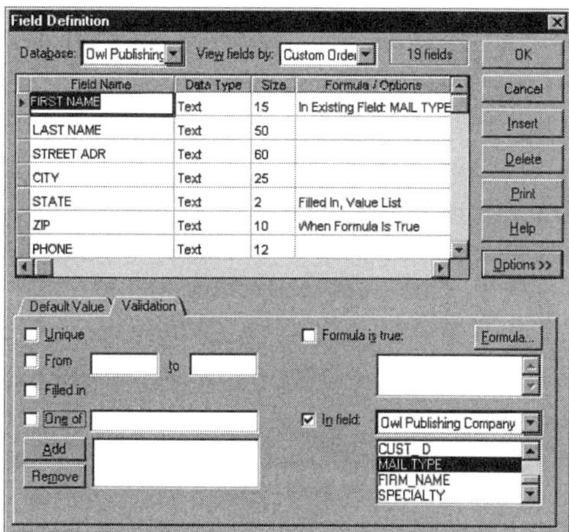

Fig. 8.15

In the Field Definition dialog box, the Database drop-down list shows other available databases.

3. When you're working with joined databases, more than one database is available for you to use. Select the database you want to work with from the Database drop-down list.
4. Select the field for which you want to modify the data-entry options in the Validation page.

In Field and Formula Is True are the validations that offer additional options when relational links have been defined. These validations are discussed in the following sections.

Using the In Field Option to Set Up a Validation List

The In Field option ensures that the value entered into a field is a value already entered into another field (called a *validation field*) in the same or in a different database. In Chapter 2, "Creating Database Tables," you learned how to select a validation field from the database in which your field is located. After you join a related database to your database, however, you can select the validation field from a related database.

Setting up the In Field option to validate against a field in another database is very useful. You can change the list of valid entries simply by adding or deleting a value in another database—perhaps a protected database to prevent the average user from changing its values. One interesting use for the In Field option in the Employee/Manager example would be to ensure that the value entered into the MGR ID field is a value that's already in the EMPL ID field.

To set up the In Field option to validate against a field in a related database, follow these steps:

1. Follow steps 1 through 4 in the preceding section to access the Field Definition dialog box and its Validation page.
2. Select the In Field check box.
3. Open the list box next to the In Field option for a list of all related databases. From this list, select the database you want to use.
4. Select the validation field from the field list just below the database name drop-down list.
5. Click OK to close the Field Definition dialog box.

Using Related Database Fields in Formula Is True

The Formula Is True option accepts a value typed into the field only if that value causes the formula to evaluate as true. If you choose the Formula button, the Formula dialog box opens to help you build a valid formula (see fig. 8.16).

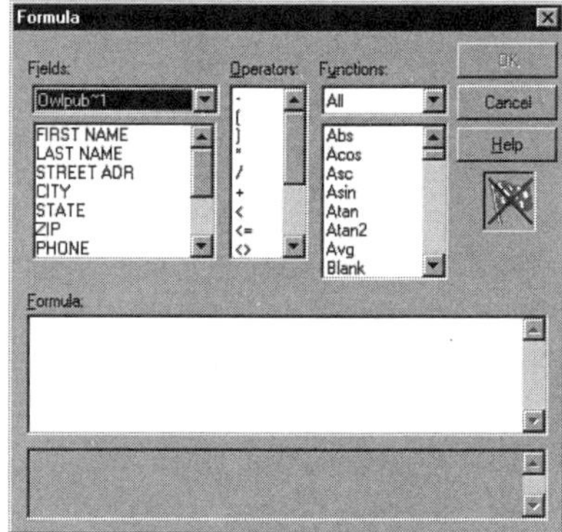

Fig. 8.16

You can use fields from joined databases in the Formula dialog box.

In Chapter 2, "Creating Database Tables," you learned how to include in the formula a field from the same database in which the validated field is located. After you join a relational database to your database, however, you can also select fields from related databases.

To include a field from a related database in the formula, follow these steps:

1. Follow steps 1 through 4 in the "Setting Data-Entry Options for Related Databases" section earlier in this chapter to open the Field Definition dialog box and its Validation page.
2. Select the Formula Is True check box.

3. Click the Formula button. The Formula dialog box appears.
4. From the drop-down list box just below Fields, select the database you want to use from the list of all related databases.
5. From the list box below the Fields option, select the field you want to include in the formula. The field appears in the Formula text box at the bottom of the dialog box.
6. Continue building the formula. (You can change databases at any time by repeating step 4.) Refer to Chapter 2, "Creating Database Tables," for information on how to use the Formula dialog box.
7. When the formula is complete, click OK to close the Formula dialog box.

> **Note**
>
> If the OK button is dimmed, a problem exists with the syntax of the formula. Correct the syntax and then click OK.

8. Click OK to exit the Field Definition dialog box.

Setting Up and Joining the Owl Publishing Databases

The Owl Publishing database that you used in Part I of this book served your purposes well, but it suffers from all the disadvantages of flat-file databases. Now, converting the Owl Publishing database application to a relational design is important so that you can do the following:

- Efficiently record the necessary information when Owl's customers subscribe to multiple newsletters.
- Perform data lookups so that you don't have to retype a great deal of information.

Building the Newsletter and Specialty Databases

The first step in revising the Owl Publishing application is to build two new databases to hold newsletter and specialty information. Follow these steps to build the Newsletter database:

1. Switch to Design mode.
2. Open the File menu and choose New. The New/Select a SmartMaster dialog box appears. Choose Blank Database and click OK.
3. Type **`Newsletter`** in the File Name text box and then click Create. The Creating New Database: Newsletter dialog box appears (see fig. 8.17).

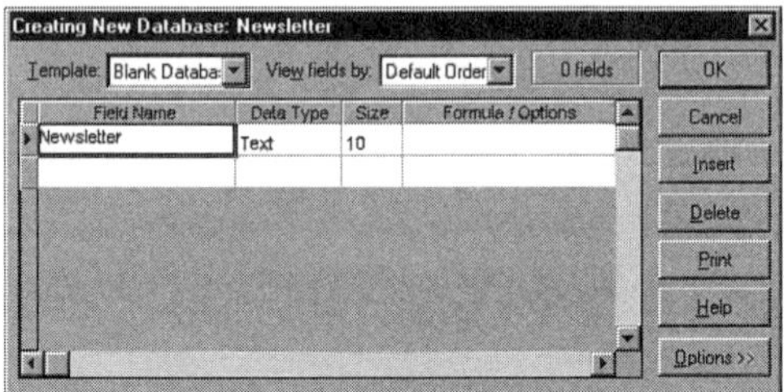

Fig. 8.17

The field definitions for the Newsletter database are defined in the Creating New Database dialog box.

4. By using the Field Name, Data Type, and Size columns in the following list, define the following fields for the Newsletter database:

Field Name	Data Type	Size
NEWSLETTER	Text	40
SUB START	Date	
SUB END	Date	
RENEW NOTE	Numeric	2
PRICE	Numeric	5.2
CUST_ID	Numeric	6

After you finish entering this information, the Creating New Database dialog box should look like figure 8.17.

5. Click OK to close the Creating New Database dialog box, create the database, and open the default form (see fig. 8.18). Change the text block in the title to *Newsletters*.

6. To enter the following records for the database, first click the New Record SmartIcon. Then type the information for one record and press Enter to save the record. Repeat this step for each record.

NEWSLETTER	SUB START	SUB END	RENEW NOTE	PRICE	CUST ID
Assault Today	12/15/93	12/15/94	1	150	1
Burglary Made Simple	1/12/93	1/12/94	0	175	2
Assault Today	11/14/93	11/14/94	0	150	3
Burglary Made Simple	5/12/93	5/12/94	0	175	4
Employment Today	11/12/92	11/12/93	2	195	5
Employment Today	12/12/93	12/12/94	0	195	6
Personal Injury for Profit	6/1/93	6/1/94	0	215	3
Burglary Made Simple	7/2/93	7/2/94	0	175	1
Personal Injury for Profit	8/4/93	8/4/94	0	215	4

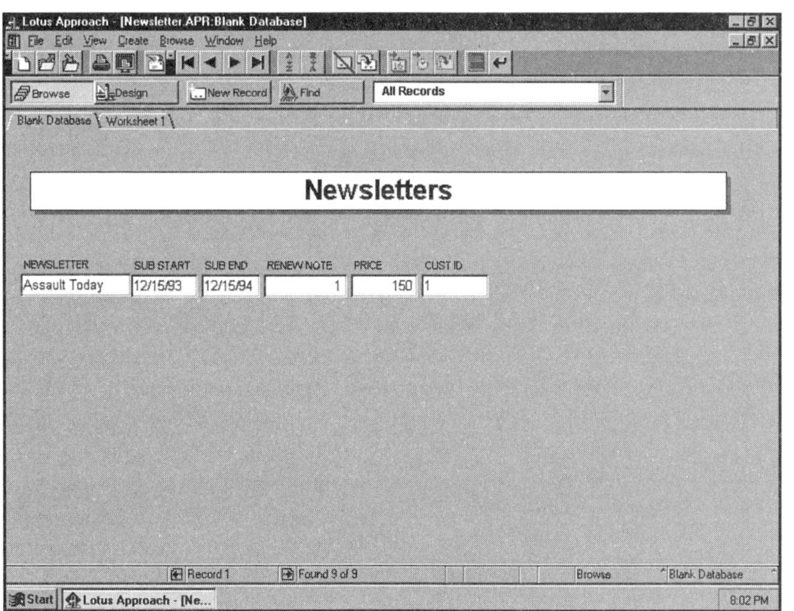

Fig. 8.18

The default form for the Newsletter database contains all of the fields from the database in the order in which you defined them, using the field names for the labels.

7. Open the File menu and choose Save Approach File. The Save Approach File dialog box appears.
8. Click OK.
9. Choose Close from the File menu.

The next step in revising the Owl Publishing application is to build a database to hold the information for legal specialties. Repeat the steps for building the Newsletter database, except use the data in tables 8.1 and 8.2 for defining the fields and entering the records. Call the file SPECIALTY.

Table 8.1 Field Definitions for the Specialty Database

Name	Type	Length
SPECIALTY	TEXT	2
SPEC TEXT	TEXT	20

Table 8.2 Record Data for the Specialty Database

SPECIALTY	SPEC TEXT
PI	Personal Injury
FM	Employment Law

(continues)

Table 8.2 Continued

RP	Real Property
CR	Criminal Law

Removing Information from the Owl Database

Because the information about newsletter subscriptions is now stored in the NEWSLETTER database, you no longer need the fields in the Owl Publishing database or those that display this information on the Customer form. You need to remove the fields from the Owl database and the Customer form. (In Chapter 9, "Designing Advanced Forms," you'll rebuild the Data Input form to add information from the SPECIALTY and Newsletter databases.)

Note

Just removing the fields from the form doesn't remove them from the database. Also, you aren't removing the Specialty field data from the form or the database because the SPECIALTY database is used only to validate the Specialty values and provide a description of the specialty code.

To clean up the Owl database and Customer form, follow these steps:

1. Open the File menu and choose Open. The Open dialog box appears.
2. Select Owl Publishing from the list of Approach files. If the file isn't visible, use the Directory list box and Drives drop-down list to move to the drive and directory in which the Owl Publishing.APR file is stored.
3. Click Open.
4. Switch to Design mode.
5. If the Customer form isn't on-screen, select it from the view tabs or the status bar.
6. Shift+click the following fields on the form: Newsletter Subscribed To, Start Date, End Date, Number of Renew Notes, and Cost.
7. Open the Edit menu and choose Cut to remove these fields from the form, or press the Delete key (see fig. 8.19).
8. Open the Create menu and choose Field Definition. The Field Definition dialog box appears.
9. Select each of the following fields and choose Delete after each selection to remove it from the database: NEWSLETTER, SUB START, SUB END, RENEW NOTE, and PRICE. Confirm that you want to remove the field each time Approach prompts you for confirmation.
10. Click OK.
11. Open the File menu and choose Save Approach File.

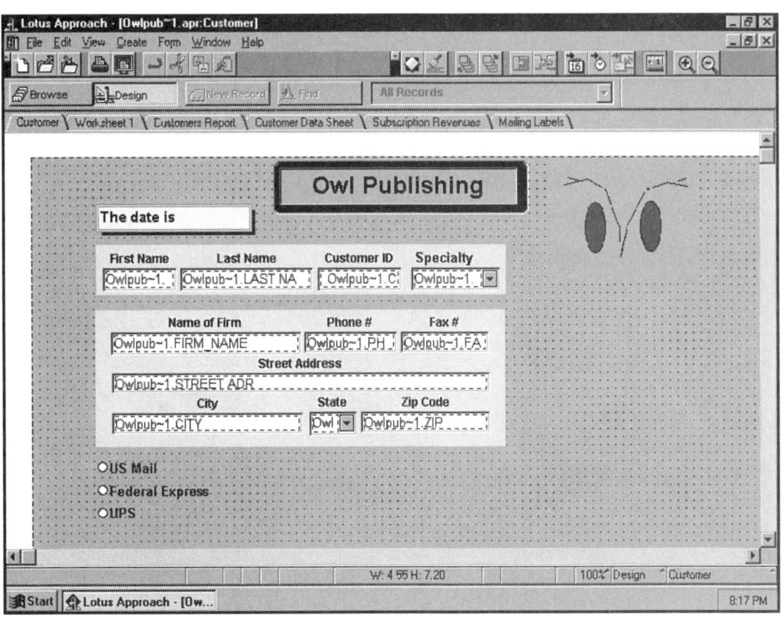

Fig. 8.19

The Owl Publishing form is without the newsletter fields.

Joining the Three Databases

The next step is setting up the relationships between the databases in the Owl Publishing application. To join the databases, follow these steps:

1. Make sure that the Owl Approach file is open and its form is on-screen.
2. Open the Create menu and choose Join. The Join dialog box appears, showing the Owl database (see fig. 8.20).

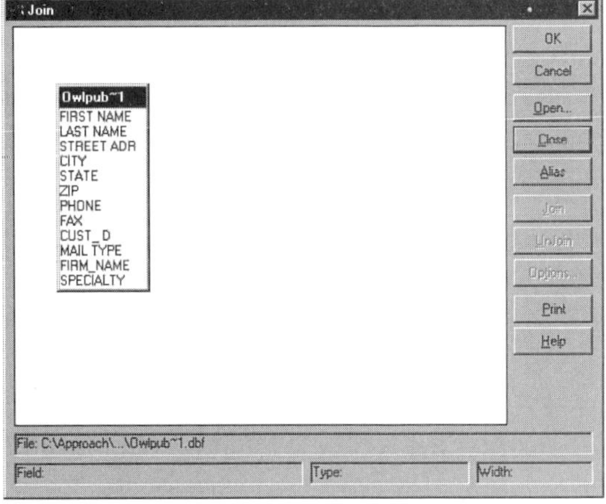

Fig. 8.20

The Join dialog box and the Owl database are ready to be joined.

3. Choose Open in the Join dialog box. The Open dialog box appears.
4. Select the Newsletter database from the list of available databases.
5. Click Open. The Join dialog box appears with the Owl Publishing and Newsletter databases listed.
6. Select the CUST_ID field in the Owl Publishing database box.
7. Select the CUST_ID field in the Newsletter database box.
8. Click Join. A line appears between the two databases, indicating that they're joined (see fig. 8.21).

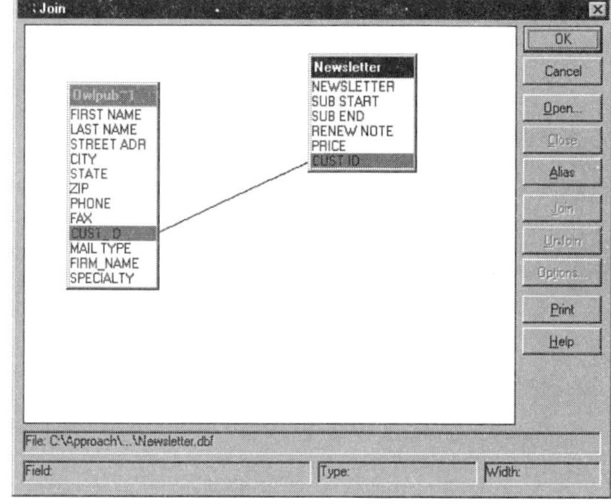

Fig. 8.21

The Owl and Newsletter databases are joined on the CUST_ID fields.

The join links the records in the Owl Publishing database (customers) with the newsletters to which they subscribe in the Newsletter database. The linking field is the CUST_ID field in both databases.

9. Choose Open in the Join dialog box. The Open dialog box appears.
10. Select the Specialty database from the list of available databases.
11. Click Open. The Join dialog box reappears, with the three databases listed.
12. Select the SPECIALTY field in the Owl Publishing database.
13. Select the SPECIALTY field in the Specialty database.
14. Choose Join. A line appears between the two databases, indicating that they're joined (see fig. 8.22).

You still have a few things left to do, so don't close the Join dialog box yet.

Setting the Relational Options for the Owl Databases

The final step in changing the flat-file Owl Publishing application into a relational design is to set the relational options. To join the relationship between the Owl database and the Newsletter database, you want the following relationships to be true (these are typical values for a one-to-many relationship):

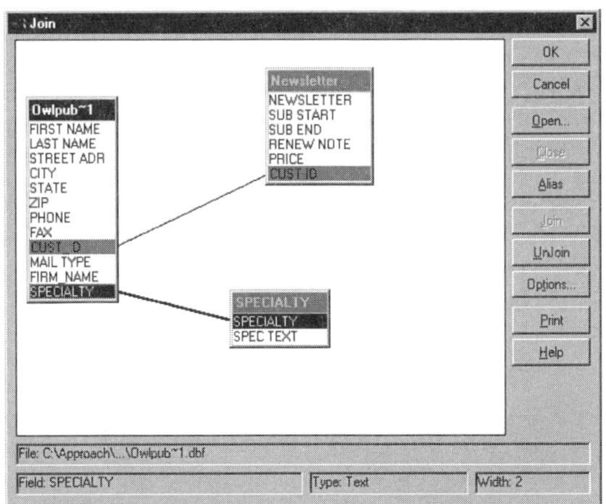

Fig. 8.22

The Owl and Specialty databases are joined on a field that facilitates a lookup of the long description of the legal specialty code for a customer.

- If you add a new record to Owl, add a matching record to Newsletter. This allows you to easily fill in information about the newsletter subscription for that customer.
- If you delete a record from Owl, delete all matching records from Newsletter. If you no longer have information about the customer, you don't need information about the newsletter subscriptions.
- If you add a new record to Newsletter for which no matching record exists in Owl, add a new record to Owl. Otherwise, there would be no customer for the newsletter to be attached to.
- If you delete a record from Newsletter, don't remove the matching record from Owl, because the record in Owl may match other records in Newsletter.

To set up these options, you should be in the Join dialog box. Then follow these steps:

1. Click the line joining Owl to Newsletter to select it.
2. Click the Options button. The Relational Options dialog box appears.
3. Check the Insert and Delete check boxes above the line and the Insert check box below the line (see fig. 8.23).
4. Click OK in the Relational Options dialog box to return to the Join dialog box.

The relationships between the Owl and Specialty databases are quite a bit different from the Owl to Newsletter database relationship, because the Specialty database is used as a lookup (many-to-one relationship). The following relationships therefore must be true:

- If you add a new record to Owl, don't add a new record to Specialty. A new customer doesn't necessarily need a new value of Specialty, because the values in Specialty are used for multiple customers.
- If you delete a record from Owl, don't delete the matching record in Specialty. A value in Specialty may be used by multiple customers.
- If you add a record to Specialty, don't add a new record to Owl. This new value of Specialty may not be used by any customer currently.
- If you delete a record from Specialty, don't delete the matching records from Owl. Even if you choose not to track a particular value of Specialty, that does not necessarily mean that you don't care about customers with this value of Specialty—these customers still have newsletter subscriptions.

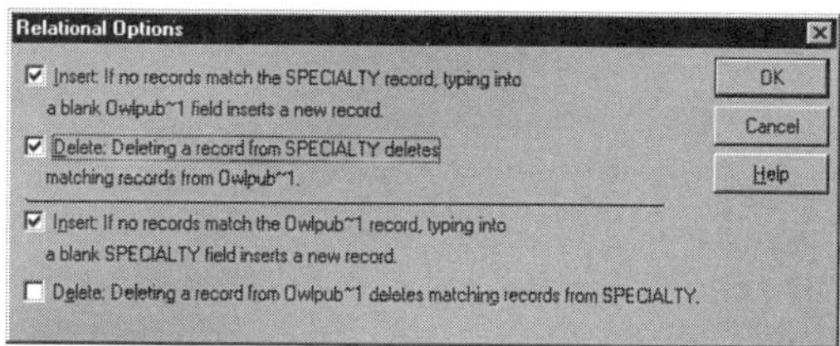

Fig. 8.23

Relational options are set between the Owl and Newsletter databases.

To set up these options, you should be in the Join dialog box. Then follow these steps:

1. Click the line joining Owl to Specialty.
2. Click the Options button. The Relational Options dialog box appears.
3. Select any checked boxes to uncheck them.
4. Click OK twice to exit the dialog boxes and to return to the Data Input form.
5. To save the Approach file, open the File menu and choose Save Approach File.

The next time you open this file, all three databases will be available. They also are linked as you've set them up in this example.

Establishing Security for Relational Databases

With flat-file databases, security is pretty simple. Either users have access to the database or they don't—a setup that you can establish with simple password protection on the database or on the Approach file used to access the database. You can even set up passwords on the database to allow read-only access or to allow changes to the data. And you can prevent users of your application from redesigning your screens by restricting updates to the Approach file. Setting up these simple password restrictions was discussed in Chapter 1, "Learning Approach Basics," in the section "Working with Files."

In relational database applications, however, having passwords on each database can become very cumbersome to manage and use. In the Owl Publishing application, for example, users could potentially be required to remember and enter three or more passwords to do their work!

To solve these more complicated types of security problems in earlier releases of Approach, the application designer would often resort to creating separate applications for different levels of user access. This method worked but resulted in additional complexities for the designer just to keep track of application changes and coordinating these changes across multiple versions of the Approach files and databases.

Approach 96 addresses these security issues with a new feature called *TeamSecurity*. Whether you're sharing your databases and applications across a network or you have several users that share a single computer, TeamSecurity helps provide security simply and efficiently for complex applications, as follows:

- A single password can provide access to multiple databases and views and have different user privileges specified for each database.
- You can assign groups of application users a single password for access to application views and databases, rather than a different password for each individual.
- You can select which views a user can have access to in the view tabs. For example, you might want to let a certain user have access to view the data-entry form and a worksheet, but not have access to certain forms and reports.
- Multiple passwords with different privileges can be set up for a single Approach application.

Designing Security for an Approach Application

In a small organization, the simplest thing to do is to assign each person a different user name and a unique password with the appropriate database and view privileges for your Approach application. To avoid confusion even in this situation, it would be advisable to have only one person with password assignment privileges and to have that person keep a secured list of current passwords in case someone forgets.

When many people use an Approach application, and groups of these users have similar access needs, it's simpler to assign and manage group names and passwords. Only one or two people should have password assignment privileges in this case, but you also may want to change the passwords for everyone periodically to maintain a high level of security. Large organizations generally have "password administrators" assigned to manage the changes needed and to keep everyone informed when the passwords change.

In either case, the passwords and user or group names need to be determined and tracked and access privileges reviewed any time new databases or views are added to the application. A simple form could be designed to facilitate this process, as follows:

1. List the database and view names down the left side of the page, because they're known and the users or groups are yet to be determined.

2. Across the top, list the user or group names as you determine them. Now you have a grid that can be filled in with check marks where privileges are granted.

The following table shows a sample grid for the Owl Publishing application.

Groups	Salesmen	Editors	Billing	Shipping	Reception
Databases					
Owl Publishing DB		X	X		
Newsletter DB	X	X	X	X	
Specialty DB		X	X		
Views					
Customer	X	X	X		X
Worksheet 1					
Customers Report	X	X	X		X
Customer Data Sheet	X				
Subscription Revenues		X	X		
Mailing Labels	X		X	X	

In this example, the Reception group has few privileges defined, as these users need to look up a customer only if they get a call or visitor to the office. Billing has the most privileges, as these users need to keep customer names and addresses current, correct bills, and mail notices. Also note that the Editors and Billing groups have the same privileges, except for mailing labels. Because this data doesn't need to be secure from changes by the Editors group, you can combine these two groups and give them one name and password.

As you can see, the more Approach applications that you develop and the higher the number of users or groups, the more complicated security and password administration can become. But nothing could be more important if you're putting financial or confidential information on your computer.

Setting Up Security for an Approach Application

After you determine your security needs, implementing the TeamSecurity for your application is very simple to accomplish. Open the application for which you are going to set up the security options and then follow these steps:

1. Open the File menu and choose TeamSecurity. The TeamSecurity dialog box appears (see fig. 8.24).
2. Click New. The Edit TeamSecurity dialog box appears (see fig. 8.25).

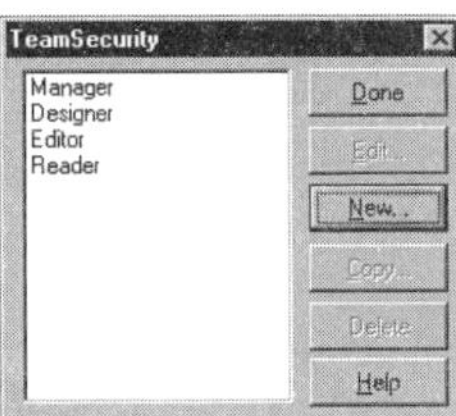

Fig. 8.24

The TeamSecurity dialog box lets you edit one of the suggested user or group names or define a new one.

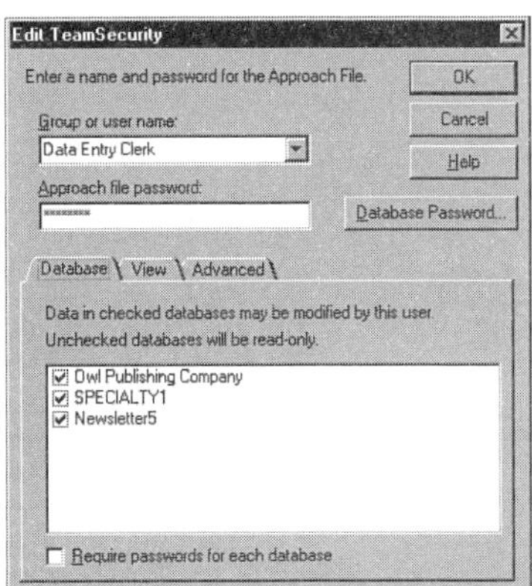

Fig. 8.25

The Edit TeamSecurity dialog box lets you customize separate privileges for each group.

3. Enter the name of a group or individual user in the Group or User Name text box. Remember that a group consists of a number of individuals who use the same name and password to access an Approach file. For example, the design for Owl Publishing calls for having a group called SALESMEN. So enter **SALESMEN** as the group name.
4. Enter a unique password (for example, **XXY123**) in the Approach File Password text box. (Don't forget to tell everyone in the SALESMEN group to use this unique password!) As you type the password, it will appear as asterisks, so be sure to type carefully.

> **Note**
>
> This password secures your database application (.APR). To secure the data itself, you must also enter a database password by clicking the Database Password button and using the Approach Preferences dialog box to define each database password. For more information about database passwords, see Chapter 1, "Learning Approach Basics."

5. On the Database page at the bottom of the dialog box, select the databases this group may modify and deselect those that should be read-only. Let the salesmen update the Newsletter database but not the databases containing customer or specialty data.

Tip

By default, TeamSecurity allows users to enter a single database to access all databases linked to your application. Optionally, you can select Require Passwords for Each Database on the Database page to override single-password access and require the group to enter a password for each database. You may want this for some groups, but not for the salesmen in this example.

Note

All groups must be given a password to enable TeamSecurity protection.

6. If you want to restrict users from using certain areas of your application, click the View tab to display the View page (see fig. 8.26).

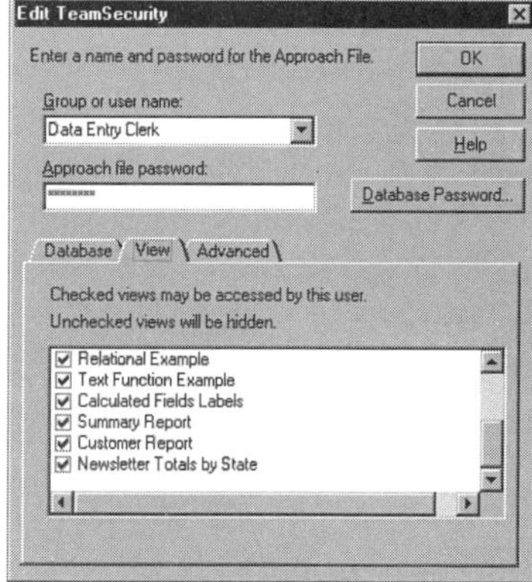

Fig. 8.26

The View page shows all the views selected initially. Deselect any views you don't want users to access.

7. Select which views the group may access and deselect which views should be hidden. For this example, deselect the Worksheet 1 and Subscription Revenues views, as the salesmen have no need to see this information.

Note

New views added after you define user or group privileges are available by default, so the application designer (or a password administrator) must edit privileges to hide the new view.

8. If the group needs to be able to modify the database application itself, click the Advanced tab (see fig. 8.27). Select whether the group has designer privileges for the Approach application and whether the group can change passwords. In this example, the salesmen can do neither, so don't select either check box.

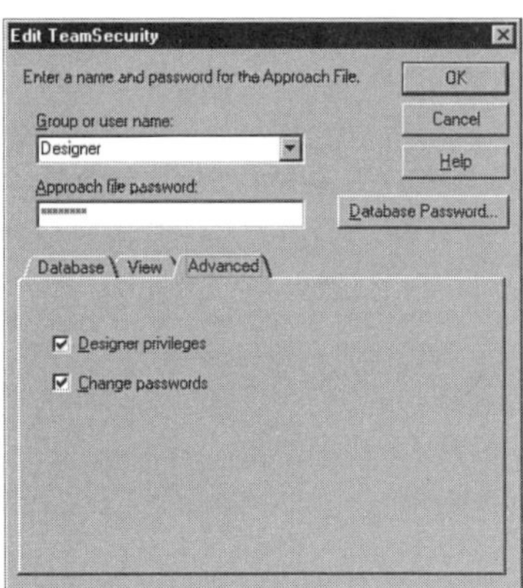

Fig. 8.27

Give designer and password-changing privileges with care—they could be used to keep you out as well!

> **Note**
>
> Any user having password privileges, which is the highest level of TeamSecurity, can also decide read-only and view privileges for other users. At this level of privilege, the group would also have access to Design mode for the Approach file.
>
> At least one user must be at the password privilege level of security, and you can have as many users at this level as you want. Once the Edit TeamSecurity dialog box is open, Approach won't let you define a password and exit the dialog box until someone is assigned password privileges in the Advanced tab. If no one is assigned password privileges, all users can potentially be locked out of the Edit TeamSecurity dialog box.

9. Click OK. The Confirm Password dialog box appears.
10. Confirm the password by entering it in the Retype Password text box exactly as it was entered previously.
11. Click OK to close the Confirm Password and the Edit TeamSecurity dialog boxes. The new group name you entered appears in the TeamSecurity dialog box.
12. If you want to add another group to your user list, click the New button again in the TeamSecurity dialog box. Otherwise, click Done to close the dialog box.

> **Tip**
>
> To save time when adding TeamSecurity groups, create and customize the first group, and then click the Copy button in the TeamSecurity dialog box for subsequent entries, modifying them as needed.

13. From the File menu, choose Save your Approach File to keep your security settings.

After you establish user groups and set passwords for each user class that will access your database application, close the Approach file. You won't be able to reopen it without entering a correct password first (see fig. 8.28).

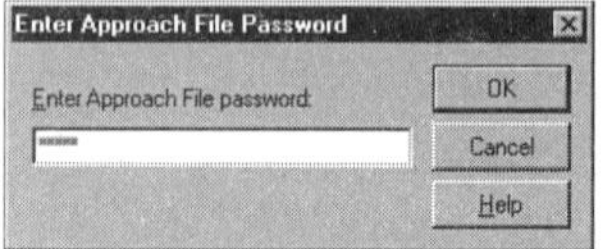

Fig. 8.28

When TeamSecurity is enabled, users must enter a password to open an Approach database application.

> **Tip**
>
> Because TeamSecurity makes it easy to hide database views from unauthorized users, design your Approach applications so that confidential data is collected on separate views. Restrict these views to special groups.

From Here...

After you begin to use Approach with relational databases, you begin to tap into its real power.

This chapter introduced how you can use Approach to develop a relational database. You learned how to set up relational links, including the options that specify how these links operate and the relationships that can exist between databases. This chapter also discussed using linked databases to provide a valid value list and to construct validation formulas. You then rebuilt the Owl Publishing example to turn it into a relational application. Finally, you began to define TeamSecurity to protect your data from unauthorized changes.

To learn more about using Approach with relational databases, refer to the following chapters in this book:

- Chapter 9, "Designing Advanced Forms," teaches you how to build forms that support one-to-many relationships using repeating panels.
- Chapter 12, "Creating Advanced Reports," teaches you how to create relational reports, as well as use options to summarize data across multiple linked databases.
- Chapter 16, "Exploring Advanced Database Relationships," teaches you how to design a many-to-many relational database.

CHAPTER 9

Designing Advanced Forms

Approach can build sophisticated forms that go beyond the capabilities of those discussed in Chapter 3, "Building Data Input Forms," and Chapter 4, "Enhancing Data Input Forms." If you link databases relationally, you can build powerful forms that draw information from multiple databases. A single form can contain fields from several related databases. Related database information can provide the values in drop-down lists, or be used to display multiple joined records on a form. You also can add objects from other Windows applications to a form.

In this chapter, you learn how to

- Add fields from related databases to a form
- Create and modify repeating panels
- Work with records in repeating panels
- Duplicate or delete records in a repeating panel
- Add a drop-down list, based on another field's values
- Add a description to a drop-down list
- Embed objects in an Approach form or report

Adding Fields from a Related Database

If databases are relationally linked, you can place fields from the linked databases on a single form. It doesn't matter when you place fields from a linked database—you can add them when you create the form, or you can add them later, when you use the Draw Field tool in the tools palette or the Add Field dialog box. After these fields appear on a form, you can edit them. By default, Approach updates the field in the linked database to reflect the new value you've entered.

The related information comes from another database. For example, you can display a customer's billing information on an invoice. The customer information is stored in a customer database, and the specific invoice information is stored in an invoice database. For each record in the invoice database, Approach finds the matching customer fields for this invoice, based on the customer's identification number (which also must be present in the invoice database).

Adding Relational Fields When You Create a Form

To add fields from multiple databases to a form when you create a form, follow these steps:

1. Open the Create menu and choose Form, or click the Create New Form SmartIcon. The Form Assistant dialog box appears (see fig. 9.1).

Fig. 9.1

The Form Assistant dialog box allows you to create new forms easily.

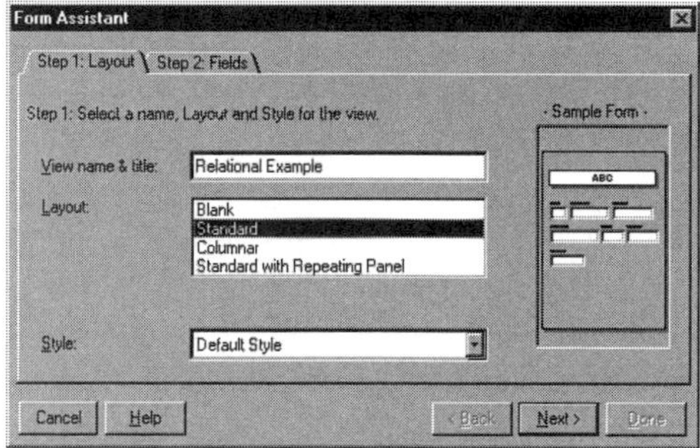

2. Type the name of the form into the View Name & Title text box, select a form style from the Style drop-down list, and choose a form layout from the Layout list. For any layout except Blank, click the Step 2: Fields tab or click the Next button to move to the Fields page.

> **Note**
>
> When working with multiple joined databases, a new layout appears in the Layout list: Standard with Repeating Panel. Working with this option is discussed in "Working with Repeating Panels" later in this chapter.

3. From the Database drop-down list, select the name of the database that contains the field(s) you want to add to the form (see fig. 9.2). The Fields list box displays the fields for the database.

Fig. 9.2

The Database drop-down list contains the names of all related databases in the view, or tabbed page, you're now using.

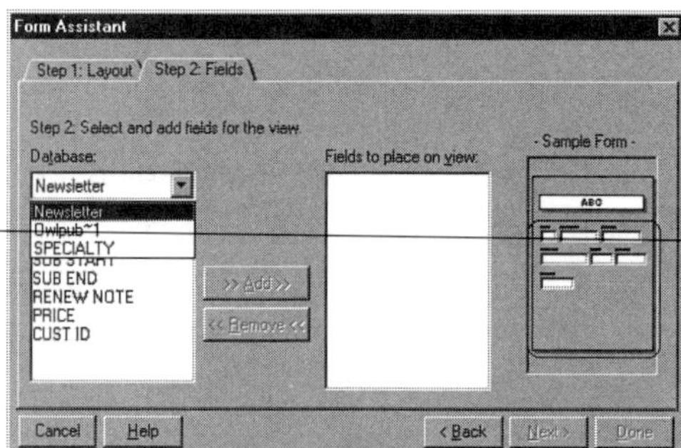

4. From the Fields list box, select the fields you want to add to the form.
5. Choose Add or double-click to move these fields to the Fields to Place on View list box.
6. If you want to add fields from another database to the form, repeat steps 3 through 5 to select another database and place the database fields on the form.
7. Choose Done. The Define Main Database dialog box appears. You can select the main database for the form from the Main Database drop-down list.

> **Note**
>
> When building a form based on related databases, the first database you add fields from is considered the "main" database for the form. The importance of the main database for a form is discussed in "Understanding the Main Database for a Form" later in this chapter.

> **Tip**
>
> You can return to a previously used database to add more fields to your view.

8. Click OK in the Define Main Database dialog box to create a form that contains all the fields selected in the Form Assistant dialog box. The fields are laid out in their default format (see fig. 9.3). Because the Approach file has joined databases, the fields are listed in the *Database.Field Name* format.

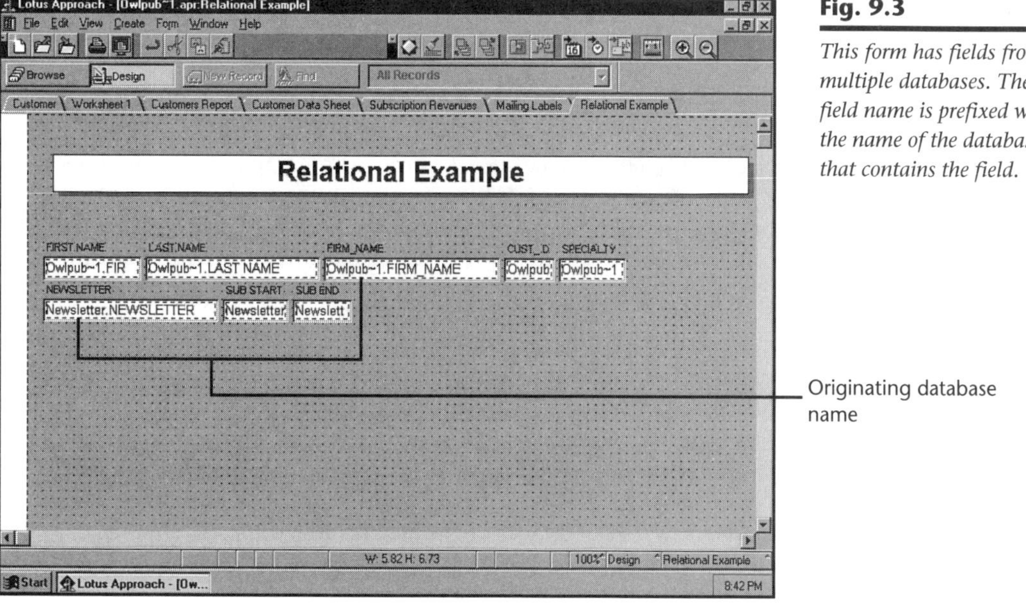

Fig. 9.3

This form has fields from multiple databases. The field name is prefixed with the name of the database that contains the field.

Adding Relational Fields to an Existing Form

To add a field from a linked database to an existing form, first select the form you'll be using from the view tabs or from the status bar. You can create a field on the form by using the Add Field dialog box or the Draw Field tool from the tools palette.

To add a field using the Add Field dialog box, follow these steps:

1. If the Add Field dialog box isn't showing, open it from the Form menu by choosing Add Field.
2. From the drop-down list near the top of the Add Field dialog box, select the database from which you want to add a field. All related databases are available in this drop-down list.
3. Approach displays the fields from the selected database in the field list. Select the field you want to add to the form and drag it onto the form.
4. If you want, you can customize the field by using the InfoBox to change the field font, size, style/effect, and color; label font, size, style/effect, and color; border width, location, and color; shadow color; size; data-entry type; and field display format.

To add a field by using the Draw Field tool from the tools palette, follow these steps:

1. If the tools palette isn't visible, press Ctrl+L or choose the View menu's Show Tools Palette option to display it; then select the Draw Field tool. The field InfoBox automatically appears. Drag a rectangle on the form to define where you want the field.
2. From the drop-down list on the left side of the InfoBox Basics page, select the database from which you want to add a field. The field list displays all the fields in the selected database.
3. Select the field you want to add to the form from the scrolling Field list box.

> **Note**
>
> If you create a field on the form by using the Draw Field tool, Approach sets the initial label text to the name of the first field in the form's main database. When you select another field, the field label will change automatically.

4. If you want, you can customize the field by using all the tools in the InfoBox, including field font, size, style/effect, and color; label font, size, style/effect, and color; border width, location, and color; shadow color; size; data entry type; and field display format.

> **Note**
>
> If you need to create a new field for the database before you can add it to the form, you can select the Field Definition button in the InfoBox or in the Add Field dialog box. You can also open the Create menu and choose Field Definition.

Owl Publishing wants to display the description joined to the two-digit specialty code stored in the SPECIALTY field. These descriptions are already stored (with the SPECIALTY field code) in the SPECIALTY database. Because of the relational link between these two databases, you need to add only the description field (SPEC TEXT) from the SPECIALTY database to the Customer form. The descriptive contents of that field then will appear every time you add a value for SPECIALTY to a record.

To add the new field from the related database, follow these steps:

1. Switch to Design mode by opening the View menu and choosing Design, clicking the Design button on the action bar, or choosing Design from the status bar.
2. If the Customer form isn't on-screen, select it from the view tabs or from the status bar.
3. If the Add Field dialog box isn't on-screen, display it by opening the Form menu and choosing Add Field. Select the SPECIALTY database from the drop-down list in the Add Field dialog box.
4. To see the rulers, open the View menu and choose Show Rulers.
5. Click the SPEC TEXT field in the Add Field dialog box and drag the field onto the form, just below the LEGAL SPECIALTY field box and list. Drop the field on the form.
6. Open the InfoBox for SPEC TEXT and click the fonts tab. Select No Label from the Label position drop-down list.
7. Click the sizing handles and shrink the SPEC TEXT field to one line. Drag it up just under the LEGAL SPECIALTY field (see fig. 9.4).

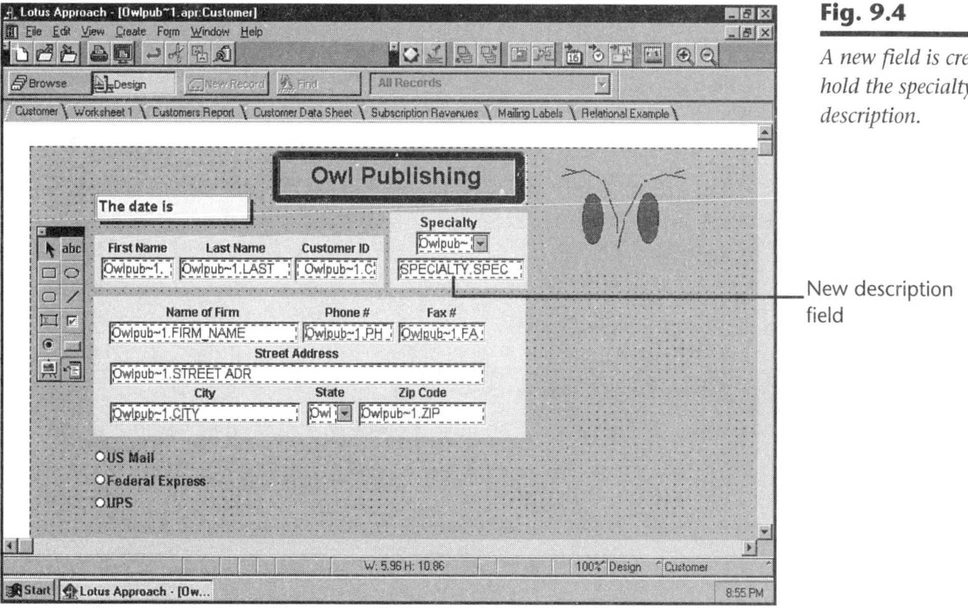

Fig. 9.4

A new field is created to hold the specialty description.

Switch to Browse mode. The description now appears on the form. If you modify the description on the form, it changes in the data SPECIALTY database where the data is actually stored.

Understanding the Main Database for a Form

A form always has a single database that's considered the "main" database. By default, the main database is the first database from which you add fields to a form when you create the form using the Form Assistant.

It's important to understand which database is the main database for a form. If you unjoin and close the database, all forms, reports, or repeating panels for which the unjoined database is the main database also are deleted. Also, the Insert and Delete options in the Relational Options dialog box operate only if the form used to add or delete a record in a database is based on that database (that is, that database is the main database for the form). The form must also contain fields from the joined databases.

In a report, you see each record from the main database once as a line item in the body of the report. You can write a report to list all of Owl Publishing's customers and group them by Newsletter using summary panels (see Chapter 12, "Creating Advanced Reports," for more information on grouping records). For a report that uses joined data, the report must be based on the database from which you want to display each record once.

In the Owl database example, you want to see all customers and their newsletter subscriptions. In this case, the main database must be the Newsletter database so that each newsletter is displayed only once. The report displays all the customers for each newsletter. If you base the report on the Owl Publishing database, you'll see each customer only once in the report, even if the customer subscribes to multiple newsletters (and should, therefore, appear multiple times—once for each newsletter to which he or she subscribes). In other words, when a report is based on two databases that have a one-to-many relationship, the main database must be the "many" database.

The main database for a form is the database whose name appears in the Main Database drop-down list in the form InfoBox. After you create a form, you can change the main database by selecting a new database from the list of related databases that Approach displays in the Main Database drop-down list.

Working with Repeating Panels

Because you need only a single field on the form to show the related value, placing a field on a form works well for lookups (many-to-one) and one-to-one relationships. In a one-to-many relationship, however, a single field can't show all the matching records in the joined database. To display the results of a one-to-many relationship on a form, Approach provides a repeating panel (see fig. 9.5).

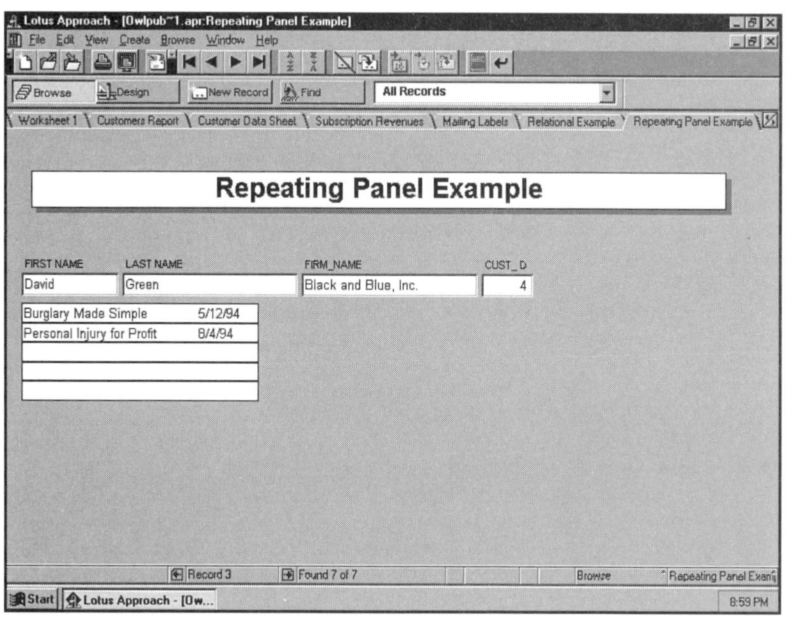

Fig. 9.5

A repeating panel displays multiple "many" records on a "one" form.

A repeating panel resembles a columnar-style report; each column is a field, and each row is a record. When designing a repeating panel, you specify the fields (columns) that will appear, and also how many lines the repeating panel will display. One matching record from the related database is displayed on each line. If more lines exist in the repeating panel than there are matching records, some lines remain blank. If more matching records exist than lines in the panel on which to display them, the repeating panel provides a scroll bar so that you can scroll through the extra records.

Understanding the Parts of a Repeating Panel

When viewed in Design mode, a repeating panel is comprised of three parts: the field bar, the data fields, and the body (see fig. 9.6).

The parts of the repeating panel are described as follows:

- The field bar—the first line at the top of the repeating panel—contains the data fields. It also sets the overall width of the repeating panel and the height of each record in the panel.

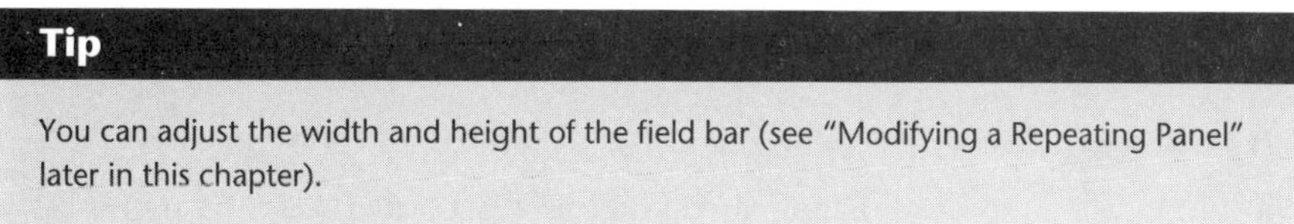
Tip

You can adjust the width and height of the field bar (see "Modifying a Repeating Panel" later in this chapter).

Fig. 9.6

The three parts of a repeating panel are displayed in Design mode.

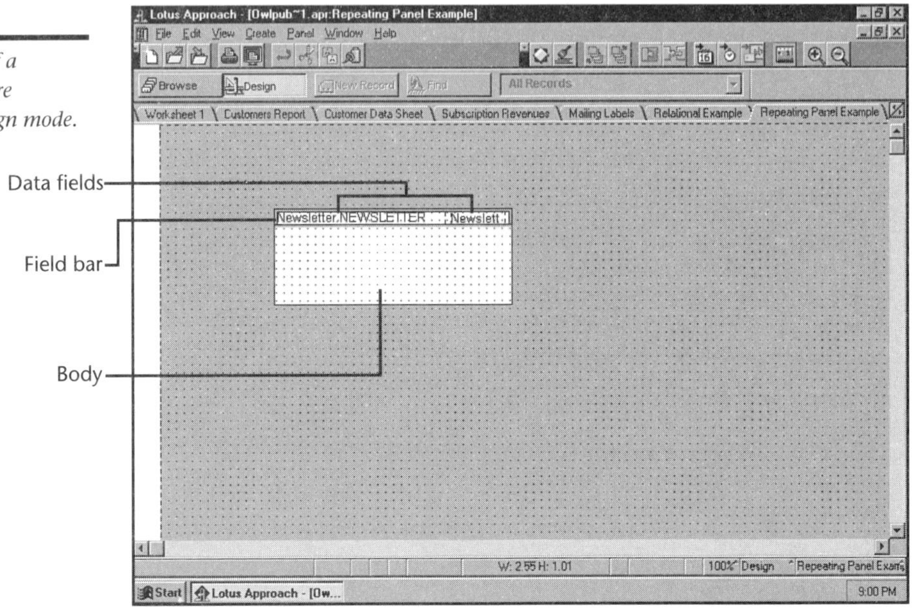

- The data fields are the fields from the related database. These fields are selected when you build the repeating panel, as described in the next section. The fields must reside within the field bar. You can add additional fields to the field bar (see "Modifying a Repeating Panel" later in this chapter).
- The body of the repeating panel is the portion of the panel that isn't taken up by the field bar. The body indicates the size of the panel on the form. In Browse mode, the entire body of the repeating panel is filled with rows of records; each row is the size of the field bar.

Creating a Repeating Panel

Before creating a repeating panel, make sure that you've built your database links as described in Chapter 8, "Understanding Relational Databases."

A repeating panel displays the many parts of a one-to-many relationship on a form. The database that represents the "one" side of the relationship must be the main database for the form to which the repeating panel is being added. If you assign the main database incorrectly for a form, Approach won't allow you to create a repeating panel based on the database you require. However, as noted previously, you can change the main database for a form.

A repeating panel must be based on a detail or "many" database.

You can create a repeating panel when you initially create the form, or you can add a repeating panel to an existing form.

Adding a Repeating Panel During Form Creation. To include a repeating panel on a form when you create the form, follow these steps:

1. Open the Create menu and choose Form. The Form Assistant dialog box opens. Type the form name into the View Name & Title text box. Select a form style from the Style drop-down list.
2. Select Standard with Repeating Panel from the Layout list.
3. Click Next or the Step 2: Fields tab to move to the Fields page. Select the fields you want from the form's main database in the Fields list and add them to the Fields to Place on View list. Don't select fields from the database that you'll use to create the repeating panel. You can select a field and click Add or double-click the field to add it to the Fields to Place on View list.
4. Click Next or the Step 3: Panel tab to move to the repeating panel page.
5. Select a database from the Database drop-down list. You must select a detail ("many") database.
6. Select the fields you want in the repeating panel in the Fields list and add them to the Fields to Place in Panel list.

> **Tip**
>
> Don't place the field that provides the relational connection into the repeating panel. When you create a new record in the repeating panel, Approach by default fills in the value of the connecting field in the related database. This process ensures that the new record in the repeating panel is associated with the current record in the main portion of the form and prevents wasted space in the repeating panel. Also, omitting the field prevents you from accidentally changing the join data, which causes the detail record to become unjoined from the main record and joined to a different main record.

7. Click Done to create the form with a repeating panel.

Adding a Repeating Panel to an Existing Form. To add a repeating panel to an existing form, follow these steps:

1. If the form to which you want to add the repeating panel isn't currently on-screen, select it from the view tabs or the status bar.
2. Open the Create menu and choose Repeating Panel. The Add Repeating Panel dialog box appears (see fig. 9.7).
3. Select a database from the Database drop-down list.

> **Note**
>
> The main database for the form doesn't appear in the list of available databases for the repeating panel. If the database you want for the repeating panel doesn't appear in the list, confirm that the form is based on the proper main database.

Fig. 9.7

In the Add Repeating Panel dialog box, select fields to include in your repeating panel.

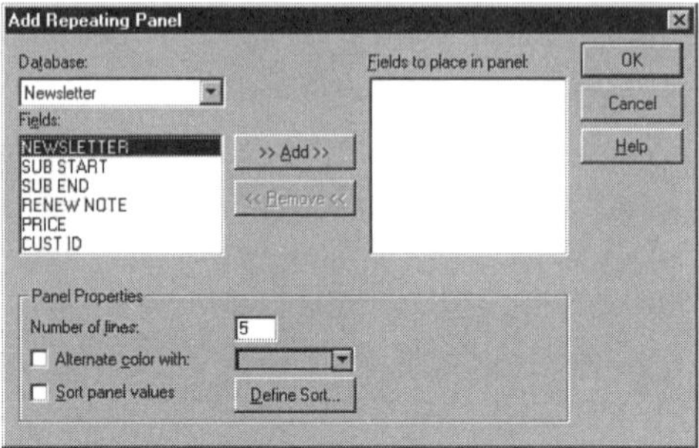

4. Select the fields you want in the repeating panel in the Fields list and add them to the Fields to Place in Panel list. Add the fields by double-clicking them or by selecting a field and clicking Add.

Tip

If you don't want a field in the panel, select the field in the Fields to Place in Panel list, and then choose Remove or double-click the field in the Fields to Place in Panel list.

5. In the Number of Lines text box, type the number of lines you want to appear in the repeating panel.
6. To make each record stand out, you can alternate the fill color of every other line in the repeating panel. Select the Alternate Color With check box. Then click the box to the right of the option and select the color you want to use from the color palette that appears.
7. To sort the values in the repeating panel, click the Sort Panel Values check box. To define the sort order, click the Define Sort button. The Sort dialog box opens. Select the fields to sort on in the Fields list and add them to the Fields to Sort On list. To add a field to the sort list, either double-click the field, or click it and then click Add. Select the Ascending or Descending radio button at the right side of the Sort dialog box.
8. Click OK to create the repeating panel.

Note

A repeating panel can contain only the fields for which it has room. The width of the page limits the width of the repeating panel. If you specify more fields than can fit in a full-page-width repeating panel, some fields won't appear in the repeating panel. These fields can be added later.

Owl Publishing wants to display the one-to-many relationship between the Owl Publishing database and the Newsletter database. The company will do this by placing on the Customer form a repeating panel that shows all the newsletters to which a customer in the Owl Publishing database subscribes.

To add a repeating panel to the Customer form, follow these steps:

1. If the Customer form isn't on-screen, select it from the view tabs or the status bar.
2. Open the Create menu and choose Repeating Panel. The Add Repeating Panel dialog box appears.
3. Make sure that the Newsletter database is displayed in the Database drop-down list box. If it isn't, select Newsletter from the drop-down list.
4. In the Fields list box, select the NEWSLETTER field. Then Ctrl+click the SUB START, SUB END, and RENEW NOTE fields.
5. Click Add to move the fields to the Fields to Place in Panel list box.
6. Click OK. The repeating panel appears on the Customer form (see fig. 9.8).

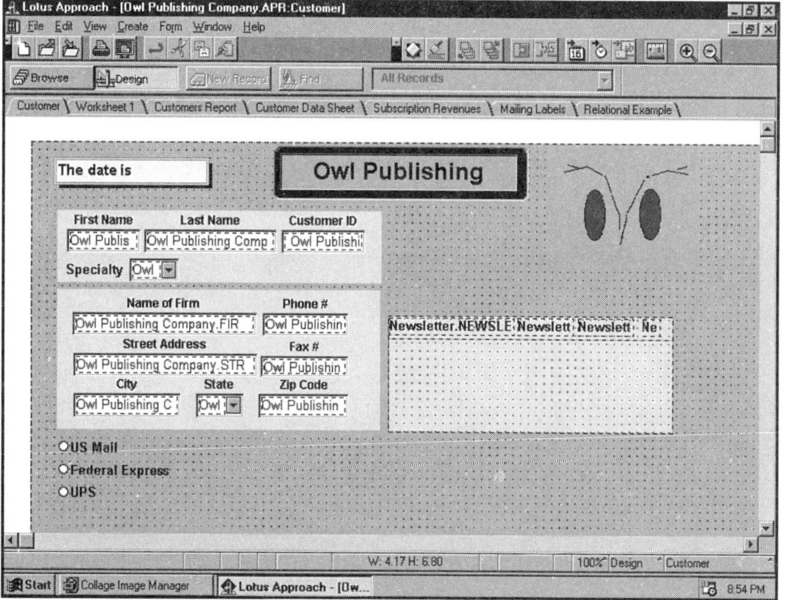

Fig. 9.8

This repeating panel records newsletter subscription information.

Modifying a Repeating Panel

After you build a repeating panel on a form, you can customize the panel in many different ways. You can

- Move the panel on the form
- Change the size of the panel

- Add or delete fields
- Change field sizes
- Specify borders, frame style, and data-entry formats for the fields
- Specify the fill, shadow, and border color of the panel
- Specify the fill and pen color of the fields in the panel
- Customize the font, size, style, effects, and alignment of the text in the fields

You must perform all customizing of the panel in Design mode. The customizing options are discussed in the following sections.

Moving a Repeating Panel. To move a repeating panel, click the body portion of the panel. A black border appears around the panel. Drag the repeating panel to its new location.

Changing the Size of a Repeating Panel. You can resize a repeating panel at any time. If you want to add fields to a repeating panel, for example, you need to widen the panel. If you remove fields from the repeating panel, you may want to shrink the panel to remove the empty gaps in the panel. Also, the fields can be resized, which may require resizing the panel.

To change the size of a repeating panel, you must change the size of the field bar. As you widen or shrink the field bar, the entire repeating panel changes width to match. You also can change the field bar's height. The field bar represents the height of each record in the repeating panel. If you make the field bar taller, the entire repeating panel grows in height, based on the specified number of records, as shown in figures 9.9 and 9.10.

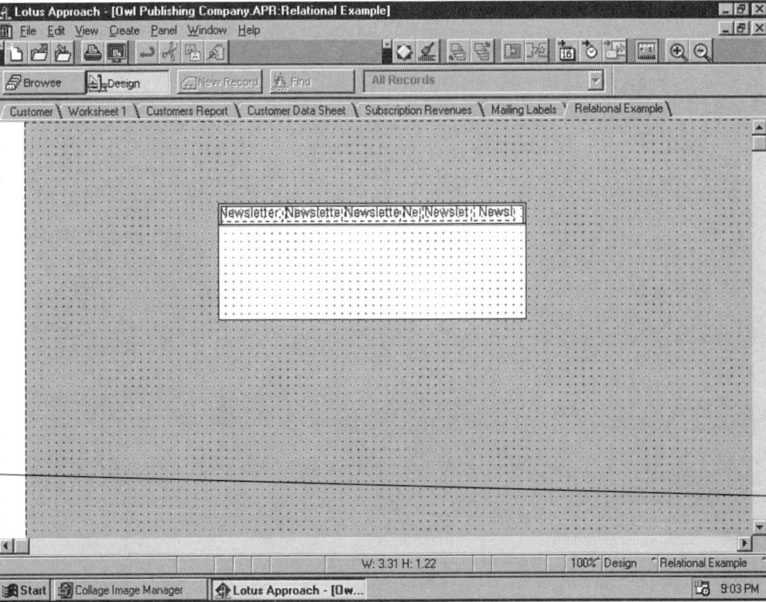

Fig. 9.9

The repeating panel must be large enough to contain the number of records specified.

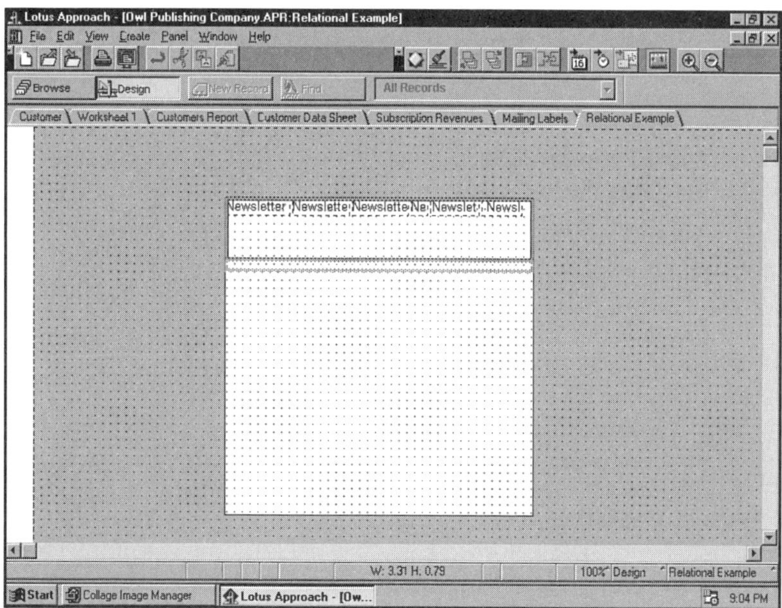

Fig. 9.10

Changing the size of the field bar causes the repeating panel to change size.

The first step in resizing the field bar is to select the repeating panel. Approach displays the field bar surrounded by a gray border. Move the mouse cursor over any edge of the field bar. The cursor turns into a two-headed arrow. Drag to change the size of the field bar (and also the entire panel). Dragging a side border increases or decreases the panel width. Dragging the top or bottom increases or decreases the panel height.

Changing the Options on a Repeating Panel. You can change the following repeating panel options from the Basics page of the InfoBox:

- Change the main database by making a selection from the Main Database drop-down list. However, the repeating panel *must* be based on the database for which you want to show all the records in the panel—you almost never would want to change the main database.
- Change the number of lines displayed in the repeating panel by typing the new number into the Number of Lines text box.
- Sort the values in the repeating panel by selecting the Sort Panel Values check box. Click the Define Sort button to open the Sort dialog box and define the sort order.

Changing the Other Properties of a Repeating Panel. You can change the fill, shadow, and border colors of a repeating panel. You can also select a border width and location, frame style, and alternate line-fill colors. You set these options from the colors page of the InfoBox:

- Select the border width for each row in the repeating panel from the Border Width drop-down list. Available border widths range from hairline to 12 point (1/6 inch).
- Select the border, fill, or shadow color from the drop-down list that Approach displays when you click the Border Color, Fill Color, or Shadow Color drop-down lists. The box labeled T indicates transparent.
- Select a Frame style from the Style drop-down list. The Frame style specifies the format in which Approach draws the border around each line in the repeating panel.
- Click the check boxes in the Borders section (for example, Left, Right, Top, and Bottom) to select which sides of each line you want Approach to display borders.
- If you want an alternate fill color on every other line, click the Alternate Fill Color check box.

Working with Fields in Repeating Panels. The field bar contains the fields displayed in the repeating panel. These fields work just like fields on the rest of the form. You can add, delete, move, resize, and change the characteristics of a field in a repeating panel.

Note

Because of the limited space in a repeating panel, you usually don't want to use field labels. Approach defaults to no labels for fields placed in a repeating panel when you create it. For any fields you add later, however, you may have to turn off the field labels by selecting No Label from the Label Position drop-down list.

To delete a field in the field bar, select the field and then click Delete, or open the Edit menu and choose Cut.

Tip

To test if fields are contained in a repeating panel, move the panel. If the fields move with it, they're contained in the panel.

To resize a field, select the field and then drag any of its sizing handles until the field is the size you want. You also can resize a field by using the dimensions page in the InfoBox.

To move a field, click inside it, and then drag the field to its new location. You can modify the order of fields in the field bar by rearranging the fields in this manner. You also can change the location by using the dimensions page of the InfoBox.

Note

After resizing or moving a field, make sure that the field is still fully contained within the boundaries of the field bar. If the field isn't fully contained, it doesn't appear in each of the multiple records in the repeating panel, as shown in figures 9.11 and 9.12.

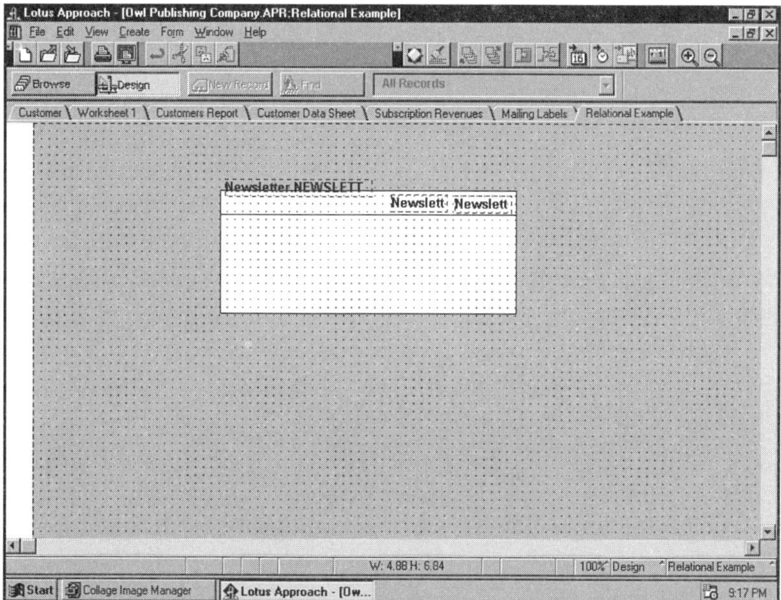

Fig. 9.11

This field isn't fully inside the field bar.

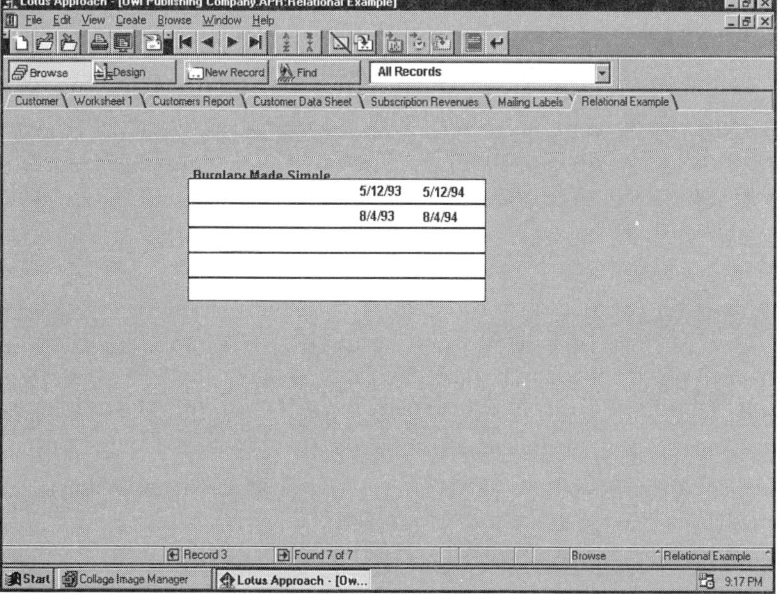

Fig. 9.12

A field that isn't fully contained doesn't appear in each record in the repeating panel.

Adding a Field to a Repeating Panel. To add a field to a repeating panel, make sure that the field bar is large enough to hold the new field. If the field bar isn't large enough, enlarge it as described earlier. You can drag a field from the Add Field dialog box into the field bar. You can also use the Draw Field tool in the tools palette. To use the Draw Field tool, follow these steps:

1. Click the tool.
2. Click and drag the new field rectangle inside the field bar.

> **Tip**
>
> You can copy an existing field and paste it in the panel, and then change the database and field from the InfoBox. The copied field retains the formatting characteristics of the original field.

3. From the field InfoBox, select the database and field you want to use. Make sure that you turn off the label by selecting No Label from the Label Position drop-down list on the fonts page.
4. If you want, you can further customize the text, colors, and border characteristics of the field using the InfoBox.

Adding Column Headings to a Repeating Panel. To identify the fields in a repeating panel, you can add column headings by placing text blocks above each column (see fig. 9.13). Use the Text SmartIcon to drag the text blocks above each column. Adding these headings should be the last step in the design of the repeating panel; add them after you define all the fields in the field bar and set the location and size of the fields.

Customizing the Owl Publishing Form. In the Owl Publishing example, the repeating panel you added previously to the Customer form needs to be customized to make it more useful. You need to perform the following tasks:

- Center the panel along the bottom of the form
- Make every other line a different color
- Add a new field to the repeating panel
- Add column headings to the repeating panel
- Change the field text color

To perform these tasks, follow these steps:

1. Switch to Design mode by opening the View menu and choosing Design, clicking the Design button on the action bar, or choosing Design from the status bar.
2. If the Customer form isn't on-screen, select it from the view tabs or the status line.

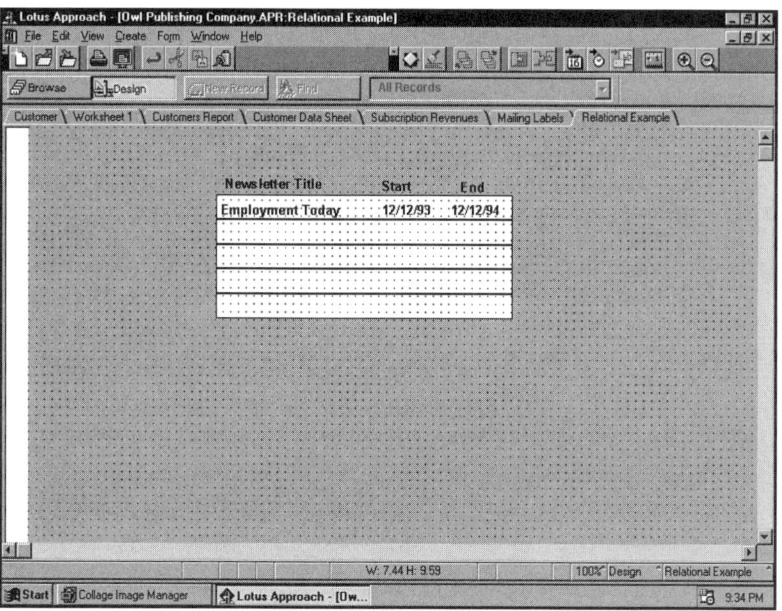

Fig. 9.13

You can add column headings to a repeating panel.

3. Rearrange the fields in the lower left corner of the form. Move the Mailed? check box and the notification type radio buttons up to the area just below the LEGAL SPECIALTY field.
4. Click the body of the repeating panel and drag it to the center in the lower portion of the Data Input form. Leave enough room above the repeating panel for column headings that you'll add later.
5. Click the body of the repeating panel. The field bar's gray borders become visible. Drag the right border of the field bar to make the repeating panel wider.
6. If the Add Field dialog box isn't visible, open it from the Panel menu (which appears on the menu bar when you've selected the repeating panel). Then choose the Newsletter database from the list of databases in the Add Field dialog box.
7. Select the PRICE field from the field list and drag it into the field bar of the repeating panel.
8. To customize the field, select the fonts tab in the InfoBox, click the Label radio button at the top left, and choose No Label in the Label Position drop-down list. If necessary, resize the field to fit into the field bar.

   In the Colors section, choose a Fill Color or select T (transparent). Also check to make sure that no borders are checked.

   After you finish, the repeating panel should look like figure 9.14.

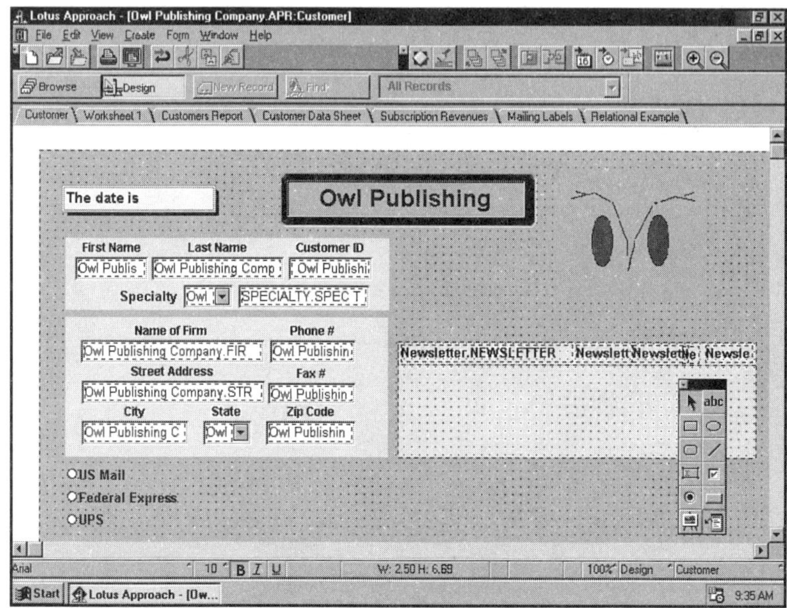

Fig. 9.14

A repeating panel was added to the Owl Publishing database.

9. Select the repeating panel by clicking its body. On the colors page of the InfoBox, click the Alternate Fill Color check box to alternate the colors on each line of the check box.

10. Select the Draw Text tool from the tools palette. Drag a rectangle over the Newsletter column. Type **`Newsletter`** in the text block.

Repeat this step for the other columns, using **`Start Date`**, **`End Date`**, **`# notes`**, and **`Price`** for the headings (see fig. 9.15).

Working with Records in a Repeating Panel

After you define the repeating panel on the form, you can add, delete, duplicate, and edit records in the panel, which is discussed in the following sections. The setting of the relational options (in the Relational Options dialog box), however, affects the technique for adding a record. For a reminder on how to change the Relational Options settings, see the next section. All record operations are performed in Browse mode.

Adding a Record to a Repeating Panel. When you add a record to a repeating panel, Approach enters the information you type into the related database (see fig. 9.15).

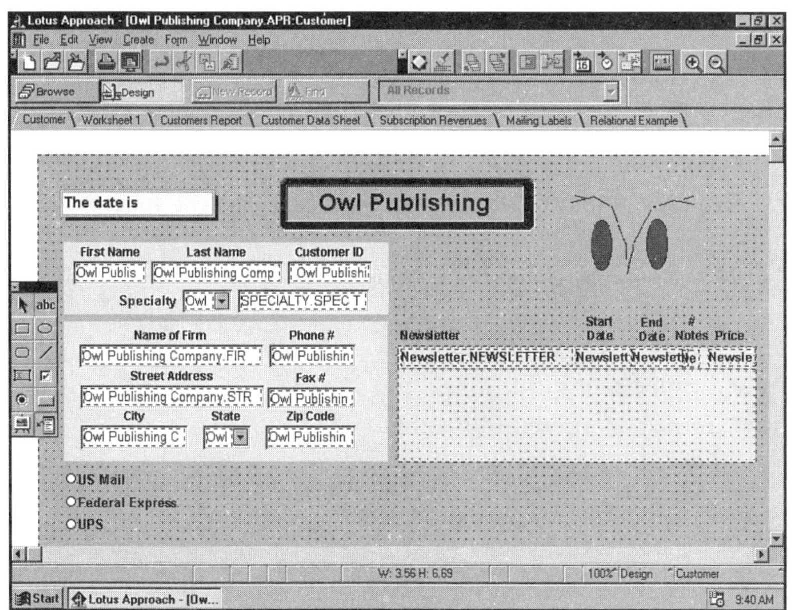

Fig. 9.15

Use column headings to identify each field.

You don't need to enter the value of the field in the related database that provides the relational connection. By default, Approach enters this value in the join field of the related database that matches the value in the join field in the main database, so that the record in the repeating panel is properly associated with the record in the main database.

The procedure for adding a new record to a repeating panel depends on the settings in the Relational Options dialog box (see fig. 9.16), found by choosing Join from the Create menu, and then selecting the line that links the related fields and clicking the Options button.

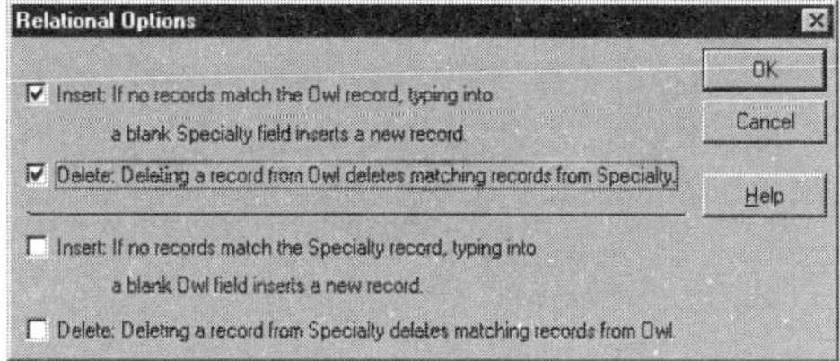

Fig. 9.16

The Relational Options dialog box controls how records are added.

If the first check box in the Relational Options dialog box (Insert) is checked, click the first blank line of the repeating panel, type values into the fields, and press Enter.

If all the lines in the repeating panel are full, scroll the lines up to display a blank line. Enter the new record in the blank line.

Note

Approach places a scroll bar next to the repeating panel after you fill all the lines in the repeating panel.

If the first check box in the Relational Options dialog box isn't checked, follow these steps:

1. Click any existing record in the repeating panel.
2. Create a new record by opening the Browse menu and choosing New Record; clicking the New Record button on the action bar; or pressing Ctrl+N. A blank line appears in the repeating panel.
3. Type the new information into the blank line.
4. Press Enter.

Adjusting Relational Options. If you need to change the relational options in the Relational Options dialog box so that you can add records to a repeating panel, follow these steps:

1. Open the Create menu and choose Join. The Join dialog box appears.
2. Choose the line linking the two databases on the form (one is the main database; the other is the repeating panel database).
3. Choose Options or double-click the join line. The Relational Options dialog box appears.
4. Click the Insert check box above the line.
5. Click OK twice to close the Relational Options and Join dialog boxes.

Duplicating a Record in a Repeating Panel. To duplicate records in a repeating panel, click any field in the record that you want to duplicate. Then open the Browse menu and choose Duplicate Record.

Deleting a Record from a Repeating Panel. To delete a record from a repeating panel, click the record you want to delete and then open the Browse menu and choose Delete Record. Approach asks for confirmation. Click OK to delete the record.

Editing a Record in a Repeating Panel. To edit the fields in a repeating panel, use the same methods as you would for editing fields on the main form:

- *Field box.* Type values into field boxes. Values can't exceed the length of the field in the database. To select the text in a text field, use the mouse pointer to click and drag the text. You can also select text by using Shift and the arrow keys. After the text is selected, you can delete, cut, or copy it.
- *Date or time fields.* Type valid dates or times into these fields.

- *Drop-down lists.* Click the drop-down list to display the value. Either click the value you want to use or select the value with the arrow keys.
- *Field box & list.* Select the field box & list to display the values, and then select the value you want to use. If the value you need isn't in the list, type it in.
- *Memo fields.* Type the values you want into a memo field. To select the text in a memo field, use the mouse pointer to click and drag the text. You can also select text by using Shift and the arrow keys. Once it's selected, the text can be deleted, cut, or copied. A memo field can be multiple lines, even in a repeating panel.
- *Check boxes.* Click the check box to place a check mark in the box. Click the box again to remove the check mark (leaving the box blank).
- *Radio buttons.* Click the button to select it. A selected button is filled in.

Transferring to Another Form from a Repeating Panel. A repeating panel displays records stored in a related database. Repeating panels often don't display all the fields in the related database. To edit these fields, you must switch to another form. Approach allows you to select a record in the repeating panel and switch to another form. If the form is based on the related database, all the information from the selected record may be displayed on the form. Then you can use the form to edit the record. To switch to another form from a record in a repeating panel, follow these steps:

1. Select the record in the repeating panel with which you want to work.
2. From the view tabs or the status bar, select the form to which you want to switch.

Owl Publishing wants to switch from a record in the repeating panel on the Data Input form to a form that displays the specific newsletter record. To make this switch, follow these steps:

1. Open the Create menu and choose Form. The Form Assistant dialog box appears.
2. Type **`Newsletter Input`** in the View Name & Title text box.
3. Choose Default Style from the Style drop-down list. Select Standard from the Layout list. Click the Next button to move to the Fields page.
4. Select the Newsletter database from the Database drop-down list.
5. Select the Newsletter field in the Fields list box. Ctrl+click the SUB START, SUB END, RENEW NOTES, PRICE, and CUSTOMER ID fields.
6. Choose Add to move the fields to the Fields to Place on View list.
7. Choose Done to create the default form.
8. Switch to Browse mode by opening the View menu and choosing Browse, clicking the Browse button on the action bar, or choosing Browse from the status bar.

9. Select the Customer form from the view tabs or the status bar.
10. Click any record in the repeating panel to make it the current record.
11. Select the Newsletter Input form from the view tabs or the status bar. Approach transfers the record to the Newsletter Input form.

The record you selected on the Customer form is now the current record in the Newsletter Input form.

Summing a Repeating Panel

Repeating panels hold multiple records. These records often contain numeric values. For example, on a main form that contains invoice information, a repeating panel can hold the individual line items that make up the invoice. One of the fields on a line may be the cost of the item. If the lines are summed, the result is the total cost of the items attached to the invoice.

With Approach, it's possible to sum a field in a repeating panel and to place the result on the form. To accomplish this action, you must add a field to the form to hold the result. This field contains a calculation that sums a field in the repeating panel (see Chapter 10, "Using Advanced Field Types," for more information on calculated fields).

To set up a sum for a field in a repeating panel, follow these steps:

1. Switch to Design mode by opening the View menu and choosing Design, clicking the Design button on the action bar, or choosing Design from the status bar.
2. Click the Draw Field tool from the tools palette.
3. Drag the area outside of the repeating panel where you want the summed field to be located. Approach creates a field on the form.
4. Click Field Definition in the InfoBox. The Field Definition dialog box appears (see fig. 9.17).

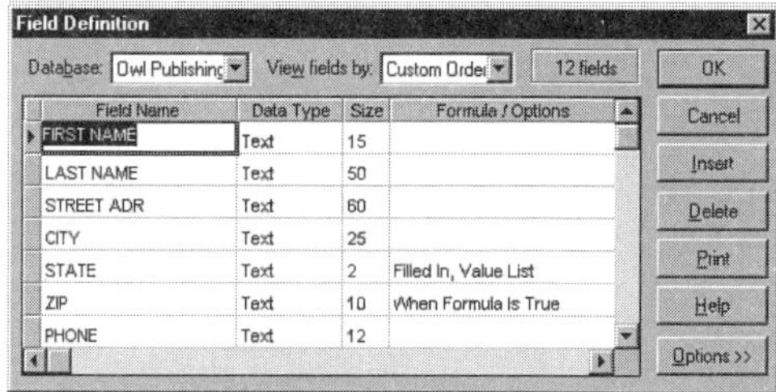

Fig. 9.17

Add calculated fields through the Field Definition dialog box.

> **Note**
>
> Because calculated fields are saved with the Approach file and not within a database, you don't have to select the database at this step, as you do when you're adding a new database field.

5. Find a blank line in the Field Definition dialog box. In the Field Name column, type the name of the new field that will hold the result of the calculation (for example, **Hold Sum**).
6. Select Calculated in the Data Type column. The Options section at the bottom of the Field Definition dialog box opens to display the Define Formula page (see fig. 9.18).

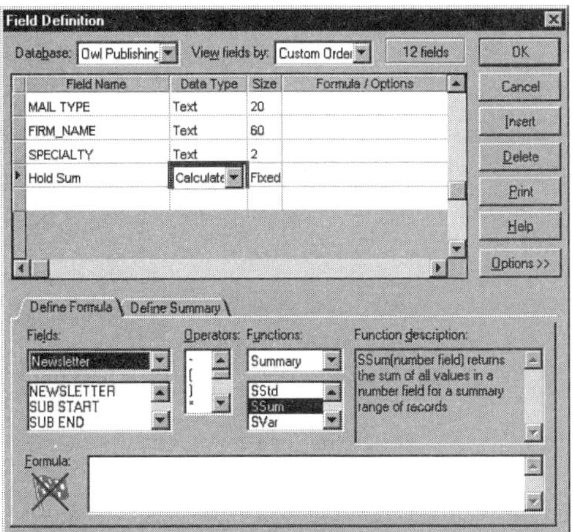

Fig. 9.18

The Define Formula page is found in the Field Definition dialog box.

7. Select the SSum function from the Functions list box so that it appears in the Formula list box near the bottom of the dialog box.

Tip

To reach the SSum function, use the scroll bars to scroll through the Functions list.

8. Make sure that the database displayed in the list box just below the Fields drop-down list is the database that provides the information in the repeating panel (that is, the Newsletter database). If it's not, select the correct database from the drop-down list. The list box displays the fields for this database.
9. Select the field on which you want to sum from the left-hand list box. (For this example, use the PRICE field.) The field appears between the parentheses, after the SSum function in the Formula list box.
10. Click the Define Summary tab to move to the Define Summary page. From the Summarize On drop-down list box, select the item that summarizes all the records in the appropriate database. (Here, select Summary of All Records in Newsletter.)

> **Note**
>
> Remember that this database must be the one that provides the information in the repeating panel. If the repeating panel is based on the Newsletter database, for example, the selection should read `Summarize on all records in Newsletter`.

11. Click OK to return to the form with the new calculated field. Adjust the text of the label by using the label page in the InfoBox. For this example, call the field **`Total Paid`**.

> **Tip**
>
> If the OK button isn't active, the formula you added is incorrect. Double-check the formula you added.

The new field appears on your form. As you page through the records in the main form, this field sums only the related records in the repeating panel (see fig. 9.19). The calculated field doesn't have the file name in front of it because the calculated field isn't attached to a database—it exists only in the Approach file.

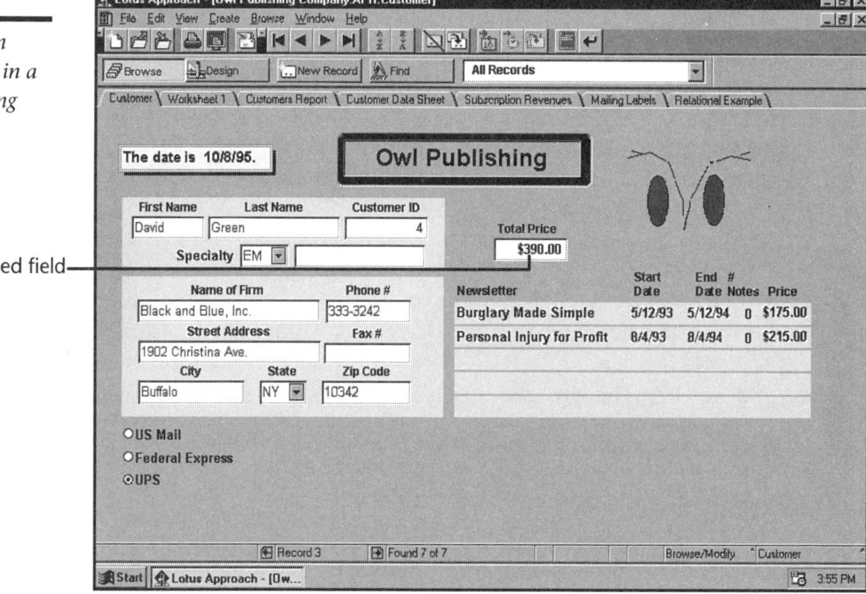

Fig. 9.19

This field on the main form sums the values in a column of the repeating panel.

Note

Summing a repeating panel is the only type of summary calculation where the value appears in Browse mode. Summary calculations based on other groupings display a value only in Print Preview mode.

Adding a Drop-Down List Based on Another Field's Values

When the display entry format of a field is set to drop-down list or field box & list, a drop-down list of values appears when you click the field. You can then select a value from the list. For a field box & list, you can also type a value.

Setting the data-entry format of a field to drop-down list or field box & list is appropriate if the list of possible values is relatively small. To select these data-entry format options, choose them from the Data Entry Type drop-down list in the Basics page of the field InfoBox.

To specify the values in the list, click the Define List button on the InfoBox Basics page. The Drop-Down List dialog box appears (see fig. 9.20).

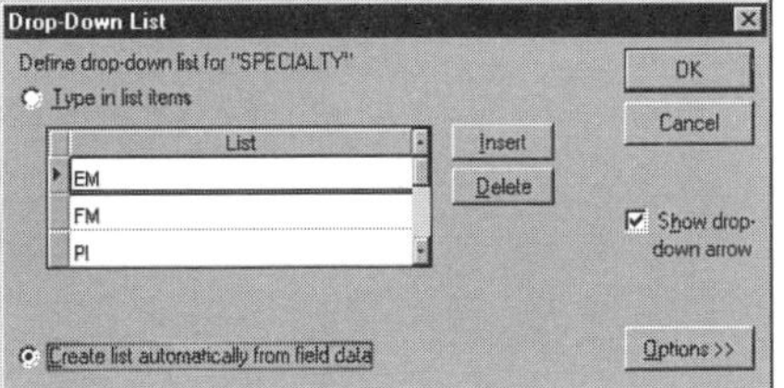

Fig. 9.20

The Drop-Down List dialog box allows you to specify the values for a drop-down list.

The values in the list can come from two different places:

- If you select the Type in List Items radio button, you can type the values into the Drop-Down List dialog box.
- If you select the Create List Automatically from Field Data radio button, Approach draws the values from the values already entered into a field. The default field that Approach draws the values from is the drop-down list field. You can draw the values from another field, however, either in the same or in a related database.

Because the Create List Automatically from Field Data option allows you to add valid values from another related database—perhaps a database that's protected from the average user—it's the most powerful of the options.

To draw a drop-down list from another database, join the database to your main database by opening the Create menu and choosing Join. After you create the join, follow these steps:

1. Switch to Design mode by opening the View menu and choosing Design, clicking the Design button on the action bar, or choosing Design from the status bar.
2. Select the field to be formatted as a drop-down list or field box & list.
3. Open the InfoBox by selecting Style & Properties from the shortcut menu or by double-clicking the object. You also can open the InfoBox by selecting the object and clicking the InfoBox SmartIcon, or by opening the Object menu and choosing Style & Properties.
4. If the data-entry format isn't a drop-down list or field box & list, choose the appropriate format in the Data Entry Type drop-down list in the Basics page of the InfoBox.
5. Choose Define List. The Drop-Down List dialog box appears.
6. Select the Create List Automatically from Field Data radio button.
7. Choose Options to open a new section in the Drop-Down List dialog box (see fig. 9.21).

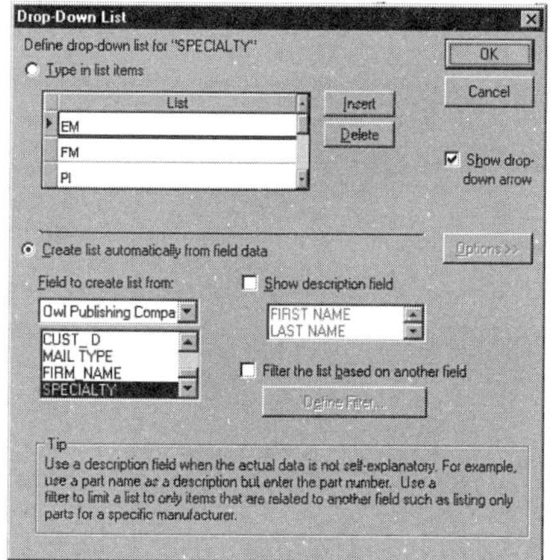

Fig. 9.21

The Drop-Down List dialog box provides some powerful options.

8. Select the database that contains the values you want to use for your drop-down list field from the Field to Create List From drop-down list box.
9. Select the field that contains the values you want to use for your drop-down list from the Field to Create List From list box. The List list box at the top of the dialog box displays the current values in the field you selected.
10. Click OK to close the Drop-Down List dialog box and to return to the main form.

The drop-down list in the main field is now drawn from the specified field in the linked database. If you change the contents of the field supplying the drop-down list, the drop-down list that appears when you click the main field also changes.

Now, here's a simple illustration of using a field in another database to supply the values for a drop-down list. A database called Items contains two fields: Item Number and Item Description. The Items database is joined to another database named Picnic. It also has two fields: Item Number and Quantity (see fig. 9.22).

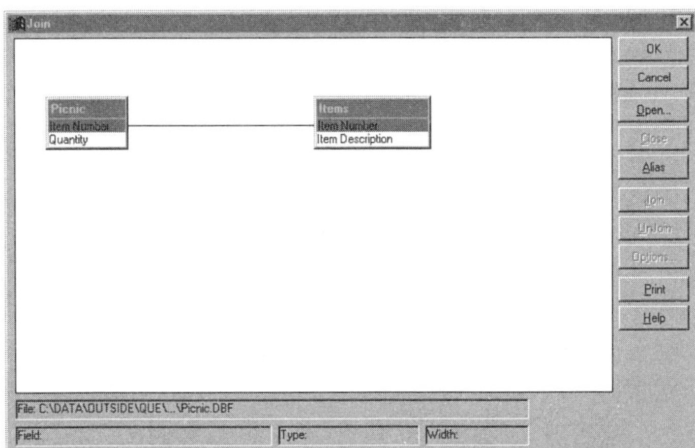

Fig. 9.22

The Items database is joined to the Picnic database by the Item Number field in each database.

By using the preceding steps, you set the data-entry format of the Item Number field in the Picnic database to a drop-down list in the field InfoBox. The drop-down list for the Item Number field in Picnic comes from the Item Number field in Items (see fig. 9.23).

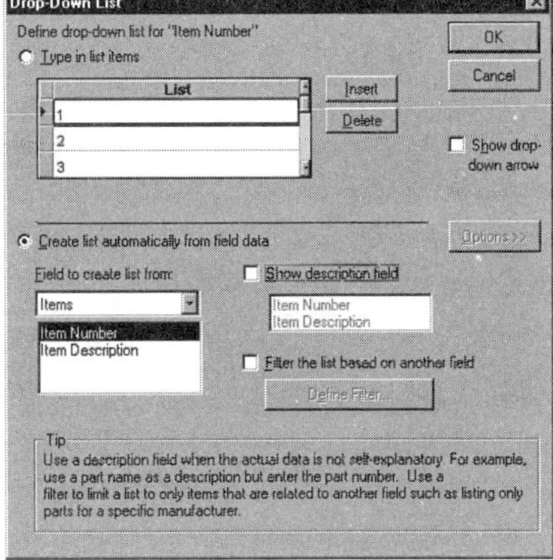

Fig. 9.23

The Drop-Down List dialog box shows that Item Number in Items is supplying the drop-down list for Item Number in Picnic.

When you click the Item Number field on the Picnic form, a drop-down list of values appears (see fig. 9.24). This list comes from the field Item Number in the Items database.

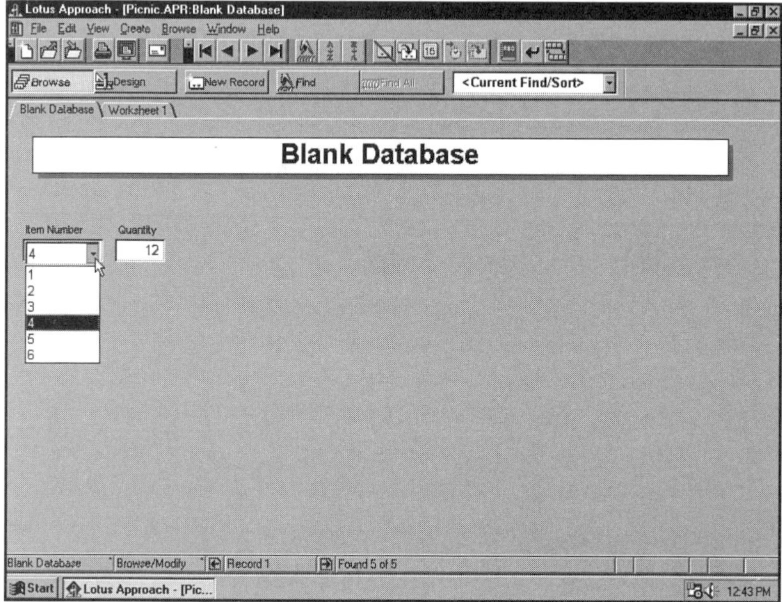

Fig. 9.24

The list of drop-down values comes from the Item Number field in the Items database.

Adding a Description to a Drop-Down List

Often, the information entered into fields in a database is in the form of alphanumeric codes—rather than long descriptive text, you simply enter a code that means the same thing. For example, the code `C` could be used for the text string *Catsup*. This practice dates back to the days when the only way information could be entered in a database was to type it. Codes were often used in place of text for the following reasons:

- Typing long descriptive phrases took much longer than typing codes.
- Ensuring that the text was typed accurately was difficult. If errors were inadvertently created, a text search might miss that record.
- Codes took up less room than text on-screen and on disk.

Deciphering a particular code can be difficult. When you click the Item Number field on the Picnic form, for example, a list of codes such as `00006` appears. What happens, however, if you don't remember that `00006` means Catsup?

Approach provides a mechanism to help you identify the codes. Rather than use codes, Approach displays descriptions in the drop-down list. When you select a description, Approach inserts the corresponding code into the field. In the preceding illustration, the drop-down list would contain descriptions such as Catsup or Hot Dogs. When you click the Catsup description, however, the code for Catsup (`00006`) will be entered into the field.

To use descriptions in place of codes, follow steps 1 through 9 in the preceding section, "Adding a Drop-Down List Based on Another Field's Values," to reach the point at which you've specified the database and the field that contain the drop-down list you want to use. To display the descriptions in the drop-down list rather than the codes, follow these steps:

1. From the Drop-Down List dialog box, click the Options button to access the additional options. Select the Show Description Field check box. The list box below this option then becomes available, showing a list of the fields in the same database in which the field that's providing the drop-down list is stored (see fig. 9.25).

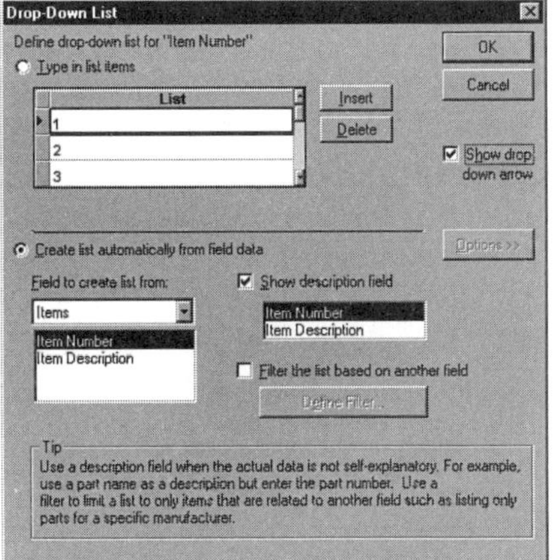

Fig. 9.25

Click the Show Description Field check box to see a list of available fields.

2. Select the field that contains the description you want to use. The List list box at the top of the dialog box displays the descriptions (see fig. 9.26).
3. Click OK to close the Drop-Down List dialog box and to return to the main form.

You now are using two fields from the linked database—the code (Item Number) field and the description (Item Description) field. The description field supplies the descriptions for the drop-down list that appears when you click the drop-down list field. The code field (in the same record) supplies the actual value that's entered in the drop-down list field on the main form, when you make a selection from the drop-down list.

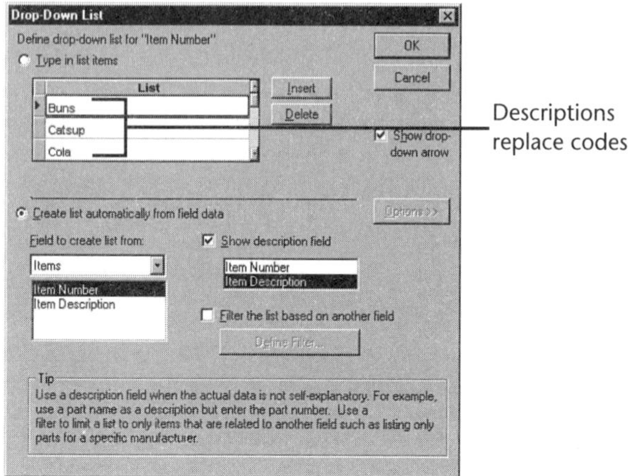

Fig. 9.26

The codes in the List box are replaced by descriptions.

Restricting List Values from a Related Database Field

In Chapter 4, "Enhancing Data Input Forms," you learned how to filter the values available in a record for a drop-down list based on a field. Briefly, you can specify a field that Approach uses to filter records (the *filter field*). The values in the drop-down list come only from records in which the value of the filter field matches the value in the filter field of the current record. For example, a drop-down list may contain the values in the Part field. You can filter the values available in the current record to just those Part fields for which the value in the Manufacturer field (the filter field) matches the value in the Manufacturer field of the current record.

In Chapter 4, you used a single database for matching—the field that contained the values and the filter field were in the same database. One difficulty with this approach is that you must build up a set of values in the single database before you set up the filter. If you don't create records before setting up the filter, you may end up with drop-down lists that contain no values.

After you join several databases, you can use a joined database to contain the drop-down list and match the filter field in the current database against the filter field in the joined database. The advantage to doing this is that you can create records in the joined database before starting to enter data into the current database. For example, you could build another database (Parts) that contains Parts and their Manufacturers, and use Manufacturer as the filter field. When you create an order in your Orders database (which is linked to your Parts database), you could use the Manufacturer with whom you're placing the order to filter the available Parts. To define a filter based on a related database, follow steps 1 through 9 in the earlier section "Adding a Drop-Down List Based on Another Field's Values" to draw the values in a drop-down list or field box and list from a related database. Then follow these steps:

1. Click the Filter the List Based On Another Field check box. The Define Filter dialog box opens (see fig. 9.27).

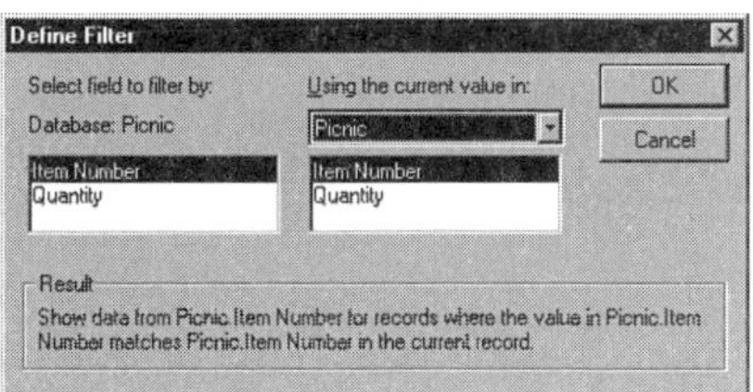

Fig. 9.27

Use a filter to limit the size of your drop-down list.

> **Note**
>
> The first time you click the Filter the List Based On Another Field check box, the Define Filter dialog box opens. To open the Define Filter dialog box after the initial opening, click the Define Filter button.

2. Select the database that contains the filter field from the Using the Current Value In drop-down list. All related databases are available in this list. The selected database must be the database that also holds the field containing the list of values.
3. Select the filter field from the list of fields in the database. Approach assembles the values in the drop-down list only from database records in the related database in which the filter field you selected matches the value in the filter field of the current database.

Embedding Objects

In Chapter 4, "Enhancing Data Input Forms," and Chapter 7, "Creating Reports and Mailing Labels," you learned how to paste objects created in other applications into a form or report. You can use these objects to create custom effects in the form or report. Approach also lets you embed an object directly in a form or report.

Embedding is a special technique that not only has all the capabilities of Paste but also makes editing the object much easier. With embedding, Approach "remembers" which application created the object that you placed on the form.

> **Note**
>
> The application that created the embedded object is known as the *server application* because it provides the information to Approach. Here, Approach is known as a *client application* because it informs server applications when information is needed, and then receives that information. Although this chapter discusses only using Approach as a client application, Approach also can be a server application.

When you need to edit an object that a server application provided, you can ask Approach to open the server application that created the object (see the later section "Editing an Embedded Object"). If your server application supports the latest version of object linking and embedding, OLE 2.0 (check the application's user manual), Windows 95 opens a special window, known as a *container*, to house the object. Approach's menus and tool palettes will expand to include components of the server application. This expansion permits you to create and edit objects from another application while never leaving Approach.

You then can use the server application to perform the editing. After you complete the editing, clicking outside the container returns you to a normal Approach screen. The object is then updated on the form or report.

By editing the object in the server application, you can use the application's tools to perform the changes. The tools in the server application usually are much better at modifying the objects you need than the tools built into Approach. You can embed a chart, for example, from a 1-2-3 worksheet. If you need to change the chart, it's easier to do this in 1-2-3 than in Approach. You also can create more complex graphics in a program such as Microsoft Draw than you can by using Approach's drawing tools, or you could add professional-looking backgrounds to your database by embedding Freelance Graphics SmartMaster templates in a form or report.

The Approach view file stores the object you choose to embed on a form or report. You can move the view file to another computer and the embedded object moves with it. However, if the other computer doesn't have the server application installed, the object can't be modified, although it still can be viewed and printed.

Embedding an Existing Object

You can embed an existing object several ways. If you don't need to modify the object before embedding it, you can choose the Create from File option from the Object dialog box under the Create menu. If you do need to modify the object before embedding it, you can cut and paste it from the active server application to Approach. You also can use the Create New option from the Object dialog box to start the server application, and then load the object so that it can be copied into Approach.

To embed an object that you don't need to modify first, follow these steps:

1. Choose the form or report into which you want to embed the object.
2. Switch to Design mode by opening the View menu and choosing Design, clicking the Design button on the action bar, or choosing Design from the status bar.
3. Click in the area where you want to insert the embedded object.
4. Open the Create menu and choose Object. The Insert Object dialog box appears (see fig. 9.28).

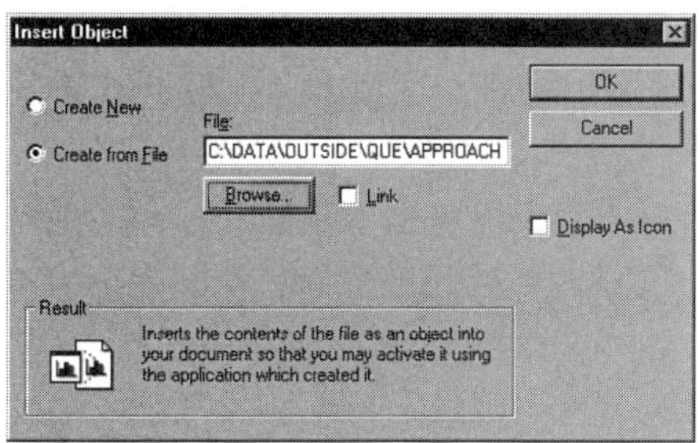

Fig. 9.28

You can embed an existing file by using the Insert Object dialog box.

> **Note**
>
> If you haven't clicked in the area in which you want to embed the object, Approach places it in the upper left corner of the workspace. From there, you can drag it into place.

5. Click the Create from File radio button. A File text box appears. Type the name of the file that you want to embed or click the Browse button to open the Browse dialog box and select a file from a list of files.
6. Click OK to return to the form or report. The embedded object appears on the form. You can edit the object (see "Editing an Embedded Object" later in this chapter).

> **Note**
>
> Older applications may not support OLE 2.0 conventions. In this case, Approach will launch the complete server application. Edit your object, and then select Update from the File menu to add your changes to the object in Approach. Choose Exit from the File menu to close the server application and return to Approach.

To embed an existing object through the server application, follow these steps:

1. Start the server application and load the file that contains the object you want to embed.
2. Select the object in the server application.
3. Open the Edit menu and choose Copy. The selected object is copied to the Windows Clipboard.
4. Switch to Approach.
5. Choose the form or report into which you want to embed the object from the view tabs or the status bar.
6. Switch to Design mode by opening the View menu and choosing Design, clicking the Design button on the action bar, or choosing Design from the status bar.

7. Click the form or report in the area where you want the object embedded.
8. Open the Edit menu and choose Paste. The object is embedded in the form or report.

As an alternative method of embedding an object that you need to modify, you can open the Create menu and choose Object. Follow these steps:

1. Choose the form or report into which you want to embed the object.
2. Switch to Design mode by opening the View menu and choosing Design, clicking the Design button on the action bar, or choosing Design from the status bar.
3. Click the area where you want to insert the embedded object.
4. Open the Create menu and choose Object. The Insert Object dialog box appears.
5. If it's not already selected, click the Create New radio button (see fig. 9.29). Select the type of object you want to create in the Object Type list box.

Fig. 9.29

You can create a new embedded object by using the Create New option in the Insert Object dialog box.

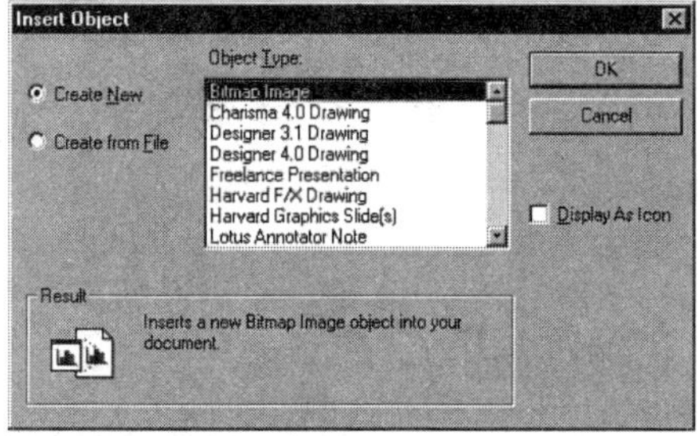

> **Note**
>
> Depending on which OLE server applications you've installed on your computer, your list of object types (as displayed in the Insert Object dialog box) may differ from the list shown in figure 9.29.

6. Click OK in the Insert Object dialog box. Approach opens the server application within a container in your workspace. It adds appropriate menus and tools to the Approach window, letting you modify the object as necessary. This is known as *in-place editing* (see fig. 9.30).
7. Load the file to embed. Use the server application's tools to edit the file before embedding it.
8. Click anywhere but in the object container to close the server application.

The embedded object appears in the form or report.

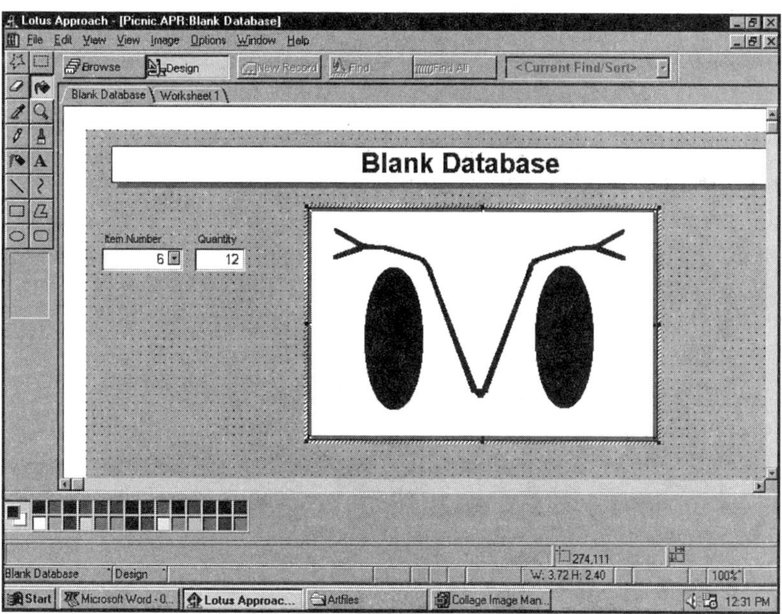

Fig. 9.30

By using OLE 2.0 server applications, you can edit an embedded object without leaving the Approach environment.

Embedding a New Object

The preceding steps show you how to embed an object that's already been created. To embed a new object, follow these steps:

1. In Approach, choose the form or report into which you want to embed the object.
2. Switch to Design mode.
3. Click the area where you want to insert the embedded object.
4. Open the Create menu and choose Object. The Insert Object dialog box appears.
5. Click the type of object you want to create in the Object Type list box.
6. Click OK. Approach opens the server application and provides a window in which you can create the object. The title of the window is the name of the Approach view file on which you're working, prefixed with the name of the server application.
7. Create the object you want to embed.
8. Click anywhere but inside the edited object's boundaries to close the server application.

The embedded object appears in the form or report.

Viewing an Embedded Object

Some embedded objects (for example, Microsoft Paint pictures) can be viewed in Approach. Other objects, however, display only the icon of the server application that created them (see fig. 9.31). Typically, these are objects that can't readily be displayed in a graphics environment. For example, how would you display the "picture" of a Sound Recorder sound?

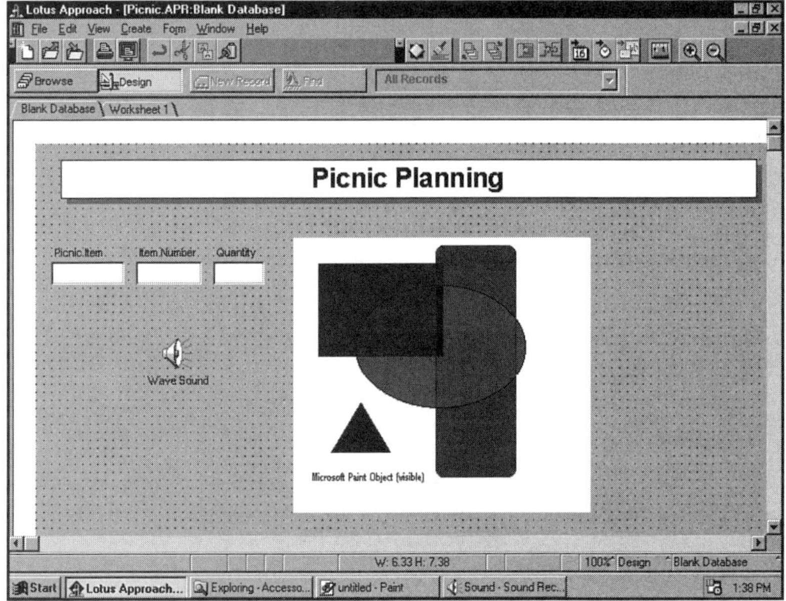

Fig. 9.31

Some embedded objects are visible in the form or report, but other objects display only the icon of the application that created them.

To view the objects that display only the server icon, double-click the icon. In Design mode, you also can select the appropriate menu item (which varies depending on the type of object) in the Object menu. If you embed a sound object in an Approach form or report, for example, you can listen to it by either double-clicking the icon or (in Design mode) by choosing Sound Object Play from the Object menu.

Working with Embedded Object Icons

As mentioned in the preceding section, some embedded objects can be viewed directly on an Approach form or report. These objects tend to be graphics files, such as a Microsoft Paint picture or a single frame from a video animation. If, however, space is tight on your report or form, you may not want to always display an embedded object. Instead, you can display the embedded object as an icon on the form. You also can change the icon from the default icon of the server application (for example, the microphone icon for Microsoft Sound) to another icon, and change the icon for embedded objects that always display as icons.

To show an embedded object as an icon on the form or report, select the Display As Icon check box in the Insert Object dialog box. The default icon of the server application appears just below this check box. Approach also displays a Change Icon button. To change the icon that Approach displays for an embedded object, follow these steps:

1. From the Insert Object dialog box, click the Change Icon button. (If the button isn't visible, click the Display as Icon check box first.) The Change Icon dialog box appears (see fig. 9.32).

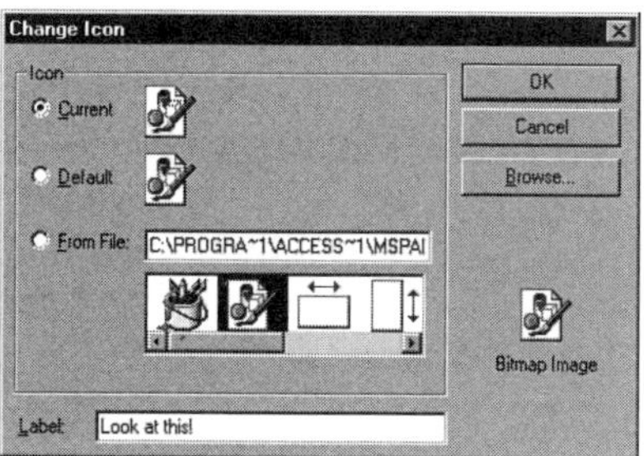

Fig. 9.32

Use the Change Icon dialog box to customize the appearance of icons and their labels.

2. Select the option for the icon you want. You can select the current icon, the default icon (the icon of the server application), or an icon from a file. If you select an icon from a file, you type the name of the file in the From File text box, or click the Browse button to select a file from disk. All icons contained in the typed or selected file are displayed in the area below the file name. Click the icon you want to use.
3. Type the label for the icon into the Label text box and click OK to return to the Insert Object dialog box. Click OK to place the embedded object on the form.

Editing an Embedded Object

To edit the contents of an embedded object, follow these steps:

1. Switch to Design mode.
2. Choose the form or report that contains the embedded object by using the view tabs or the status line.
3. Select the embedded object.
4. Select the command for editing the object from the Object menu or the shortcut menu. The server application that created the object opens on-screen and displays the object.
5. Use the server application to make the changes you want.
6. Click anywhere but inside the object's boundaries to close the server application.

The object is updated on-screen, as shown in figures 9.33, 9.34, and 9.35.

Fig. 9.33

To edit an embedded object, select it and choose the related edit command from the Object or shortcut menu.

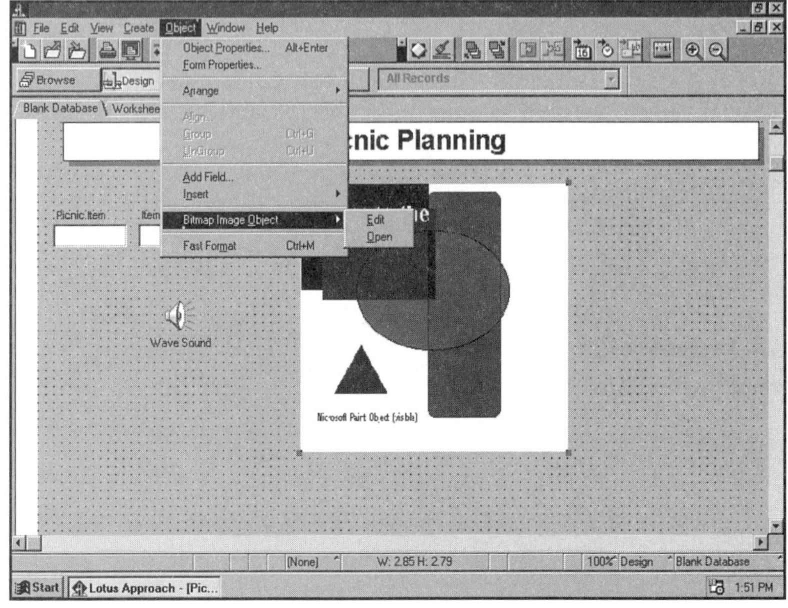

Fig. 9.34

The server application opens, and you can make changes to the object from within Approach.

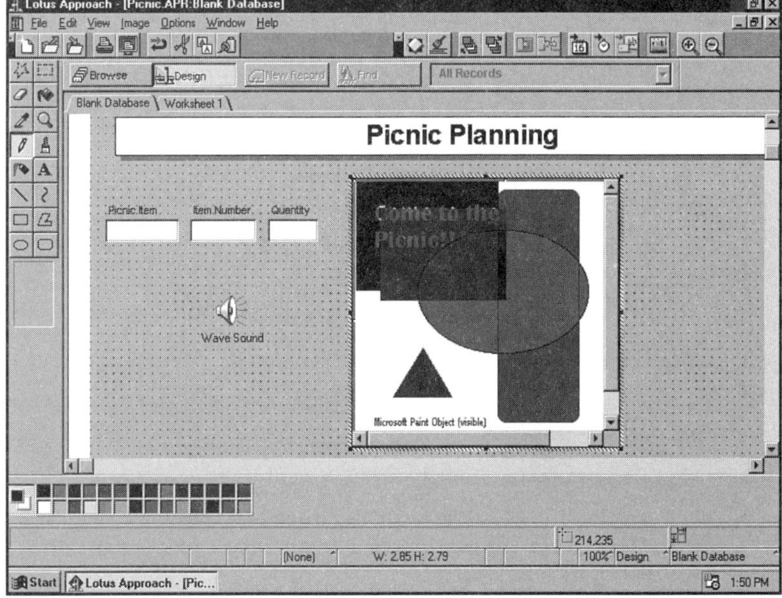

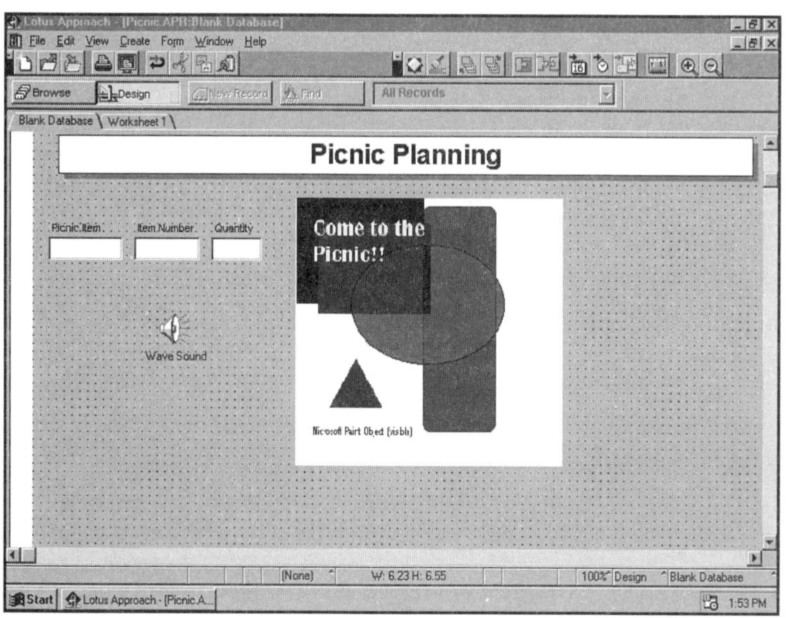

Fig. 9.35

When you click outside the object container, the embedded object is automatically updated.

When selecting a menu item to edit an embedded object, keep in mind the following:

- The menu item for editing an embedded object varies depending on the type of object. For objects that display their contents on-screen, the menu item displays the word *Object* and the name of the object (for example, Wave Sound Object), as shown in figure 9.36.

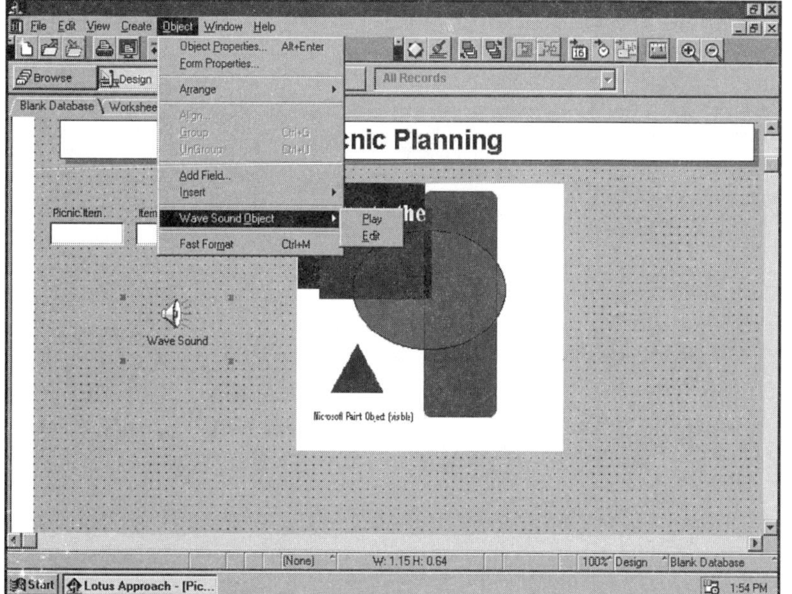

Fig. 9.36

Choose the item from the related Object menu for objects that display their contents.

- For most embedded objects, you also can double-click the object to open the server application. However, you can't use this technique if you use any kind of embedded sound or animation. Double-clicking a sound or animation application icon plays the sound or animation; it doesn't open the application.
- The embedded objects can't be activated or edited if the Approach file is moved to a system without the server application, or if the server application is removed from the system.

Approach allows you to edit embedded objects in Design mode:

- To move an embedded object, click and drag it to a new location.
- To resize an object, click and drag the sizing handles.

Note

By default, Approach scales the embedded object to fit into the space allowed for it on-screen. If you enlarge the boundaries of the object, Approach increases the size of the object to fill the new boundaries. If you make the boundaries for the object smaller, Approach shrinks the object to a smaller size so that it continues to fit in the allotted space.

From Here...

In this chapter, you learned how to create advanced forms that allow you to use relational databases. You also learned advanced techniques for defining forms, such as using repeating panels for showing the parts of a one-to-many relationship. You discovered that embedded objects can be used on a form to display objects that can't be created directly within Approach.

Now that you've mastered these skills, you'll also want to learn about advanced reports, how to use Approach as an OLE server, and how to combine its power with other Lotus products. For more information on these topics, see the following chapters:

- Chapter 12, "Creating Advanced Reports," tells you how to extend what you've learned to writing reports.
- Chapter 19, "Using Approach with Lotus SmartSuite 96," tells you how to combine Approach's power with other products in the SmartSuite. It also covers how to use Approach as an OLE server.

CHAPTER 10

Using Advanced Field Types

In addition to the field types (Boolean, date, memo, numeric, text, and time) discussed in Chapter 2, "Creating Database Tables," Approach lets you use more powerful fields. These advanced fields make it possible to perform calculations, store values temporarily, and place graphics and OLE (linked and embedded) objects in database fields.

In this chapter, you learn how to

- Define a calculated field
- Add a calculated field to an existing report or form
- Change the appearance of a calculated field
- Create a formula for a calculated field
- Use functions in a calculated field
- Create and add variable fields to existing reports or forms
- Change the appearance of a variable field
- Create and add PicturePlus fields to existing reports or forms
- Change the appearance of a PicturePlus field
- Add or remove an image or object to or from a PicturePlus field

Using Calculated Fields

Put most simply, a *calculated field* is a field that contains a formula. When you define the formula for the calculated field, Approach performs the calculation and displays the result in the field. You can define calculated fields when you first create a database, or you can add them later.

Unlike other field types, calculated fields don't belong to any one database in an Approach file. Instead, these fields reside in the Approach file. Calculated fields appear in the available field list for all databases in a view.

> **Note**
>
> Because calculated fields are part of the Approach file, the calculated field defined in one Approach file won't be available if you open the database(s) in another Approach file.

Parts of a Calculated Field

Calculated fields are constructed from four kinds of building blocks:

- References to field values
- References to constant values
- Operators (arithmetic, comparison, and Boolean)
- Functions

These items are detailed in the following sections.

References to Field Values. You can use the contents of fields in a formula for the calculated field. The fields that you use can come from the same database as the calculated field or from any relationally linked database.

> **Note**
>
> If the field name contains spaces, enclose the field name in double quotation marks (""). You also can select the field name from the list of fields, and Approach adds the database name or quotations as needed.

References to Constant Values. *Constants* are values you enter into a formula that don't change from record to record. You must observe certain rules when typing constants into a formula:

- Enclose text string constants in single quotation marks (for example, '**Approach**').
- Type date constants in the order *mm/dd/yy*, separated by slashes and enclosed in single quotation marks (for example, '**03/12/56**').
- Type time constants in the order of hours, minutes, seconds, and hundredths of seconds. Separate hours, minutes, and seconds with a colon (:). Separate seconds from hundredths of seconds with a decimal point. Enclose time constants in single quotation marks (for example, '**12:25:00.45**').
- Type Boolean constants as '**Yes**', '**yes**', '**Y**', '**y**', or '**No**', '**no**', '**N**', '**n**', (always enclose them in single quotation marks). You can also use **1** for Yes and **0** for No.
- *Don't* type numeric constants in scientific notation, such as $9.3*10^7$.

Arithmetic Operators. You can use arithmetic operators to build arithmetic equations in the formula for the calculated field. The arithmetic operators are multiplication (*), division (/), addition (+), subtraction (–), percentage (%), and negation (NOT).

Arithmetic operations are evaluated in the following specific order:

- Multiplication and division operations are evaluated first.
- Addition and subtraction operations are evaluated second.
- The percentage operation is third, followed by the negation operation.
- If any operations are on the same evaluation level (such as multiplication and division), they're evaluated from left to right in the formula.

You can modify the evaluation order of arithmetic operators by using parentheses. Approach always evaluates the contents of parentheses before evaluating other parts of the formula. Within a set of parentheses, the evaluation order occurs as described in the preceding list.

> **Note**
>
> In Approach, your formula can have multiple sets of parentheses. If Approach finds a problem with your formula, the OK button on the Formula dialog box will be inactive, and checkered flag will have a red × through it. Check to see that you have the same number of left and right parentheses. If the formula is unbalanced (the number of parentheses don't match), the formula isn't considered valid.

Comparison Operators. You can use comparison operators to compare two values or fields. The comparison operators include equal (=), greater than (>), less than (<), not equal to (<>), greater than or equal to (>=), and less than or equal to (<=).

Boolean Operators. You can use Boolean operators to connect parts, or clauses, of the formula. The Boolean operators are AND and OR.

The clause containing the AND operator evaluates as true only if both parts connected by the AND are true. For example, `5>6 AND 'A'<'B'` is false; although A is less than B, 5 isn't greater than 6. However, `5<6 AND 'A'<'B'` is true because both parts of the equation are true.

The clause that contains the OR operator evaluates as true if *either part* connected by the OR is true. For example, `5>6 OR 'A'<'B'` is true because A is less than B. However, `5>6 OR 'A'>'B'` is false because both sides are false.

You connect multiple clauses with combinations of ANDs and ORs. Clauses usually are evaluated from left to right (AND and OR have the same evaluation level). You can use parentheses, however, to modify this order. The result of each clause (true or false) then is used to evaluate the next clause.

As an example, look at the formula `5>6 AND 'A'<'B' OR 10<12`. This equation evaluates to be true. The first clause, `5>6 AND 'A'<'B'`, evaluates to false because 5 isn't greater than 6. The result (FALSE) is then used with `OR 10<12`. Because 10 is less than 12, this clause becomes FALSE OR TRUE, which evaluates as true.

Functions. Approach supports 86 functions that can perform various operations on text and numeric values. The value on which a function operates (known as an *argument*) can be a field or constant value. If a function uses multiple arguments, you must separate the arguments by using commas or the list separator in the Windows 95 Regional Settings control panel. The `Middle()` function, for example, returns a text string of a specified size from a specified position in another text string. It has the form `Middle(`*`text`*`, `*`position`*`, `*`size`*`)`. AND or OR can connect multiple functions in the same clause.

Creating a Calculated Field

As with all other field types, to create calculated fields you need to use the Field Definition dialog box. You can create a calculated field when you first define the database or add the field later.

Defining a Calculated Field for a New Database. When creating a new database, follow the steps detailed in the section "Designing a Database" in Chapter 2 to define the fields you need. Briefly, these steps are as follows:

1. Define the information you need to track. List all the database fields you think you may need.
2. Refine the list you built in step 1 to make sure that you have everything you need. Ensure that you aren't keeping extraneous information, and that you'll store fields in a format that will allow you to get your work done.

Then continue as follows:

1. Open the File menu and choose New Database. Select Blank Database from the window that appears and click OK. The New dialog box appears.
2. Type the database name in the File Name text box and select the file type from the List Files of Type drop-down list.
3. Click OK. The Creating New Database dialog box appears (see fig. 10.1).
4. Type the field name of the calculated field into one of the lines in the Field Name column.

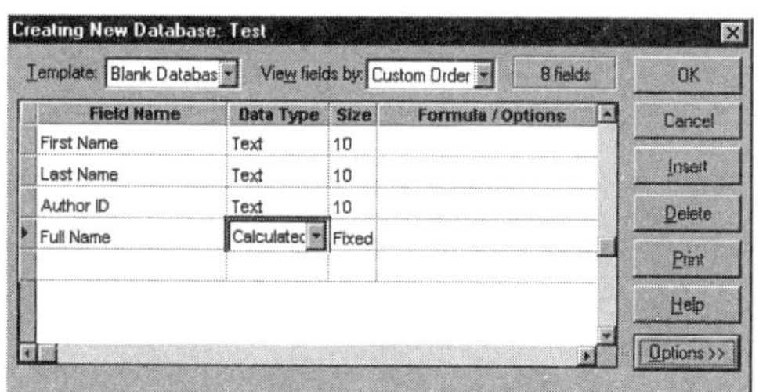

Fig. 10.1

You can add calculated fields from the Creating New Database dialog box.

5. From the Data Type drop-down list, select Calculated. The Creating New Database dialog box expands to display the Define Formula and Define Summary pages at the bottom. Use these pages to define the calculated field's formula (see fig. 10.2).

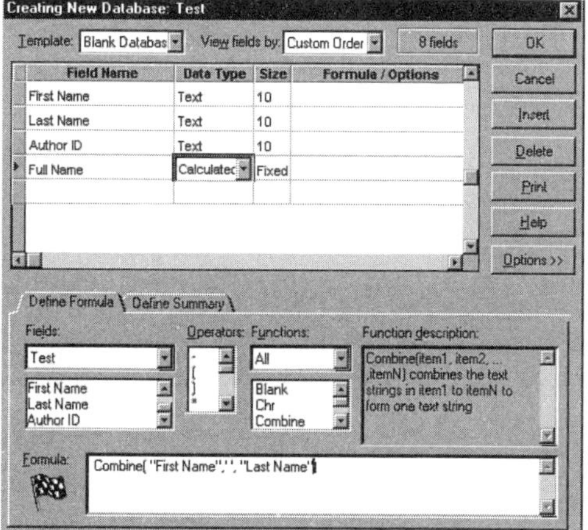

Fig. 10.2

The Define Formula and Define Summary pages let you build a calculated formula.

6. To define the formula you need, use the Fields, Operators, and Functions list boxes on the Define Formula page.

> **Note**
>
> If you're not sure what a specific function does or how to use it, click the function's name on the Define Formula page. An explanation appears in the Function Description box on the right side of the page.

7. When the formula is complete, click OK to close the Creating New Database dialog box.

> **Note**
>
> If you need to revise the formula, select the calculated field in the list of fields in the Creating New Database dialog box, and then click the Options button.

Adding a Calculated Field to an Existing Database. To define a calculated field in an existing database, follow these steps:

1. Switch to Design mode.
2. Open the Create menu and choose Field Definition. The Field Definition dialog box appears.
3. Type the field name on an empty line in the Field Name column. From the Data Type drop-down list, choose Calculated. The Field Definition dialog box expands to show the Define Formula and Define Summary pages. Use these pages to define the calculated field's formula.
4. To define the formula you need, use the Fields, Operators, and Functions list boxes on the Define Formula page.
5. When the formula is complete, click OK to close the Field Definition dialog box.

Adding an Existing Calculated Field to a Form or Report. After you define a calculated field, you can add it to an existing form or report just like you can any other field. Follow these steps:

1. Switch to Design mode.
2. Do one of the following:
   - Drag the calculated field onto the form from the Add Field dialog box.
   - Click the Draw Field tool from the tools palette, drag a rectangle to define the position and size of the calculated field, and select the calculated field from the field list on the Basics page of the field InfoBox.

> **Note**
>
> Calculated fields are displayed in italic text at the end of the field list in the InfoBox. If an Approach file has any variable fields, they're listed before calculated fields, in italics.

Changing the Appearance of a Calculated Field. You can change the appearance of a calculated field on a form or report just as you can change any other field by resizing, moving, changing the fill and pen colors, setting borders, and adjusting the attributes of the text for the contents of the field and the label.

To make changes to the field, switch to Design mode, and then perform any of the following procedures:

- To move the field, drag it to its new location or adjust the location from the dimensions page of the InfoBox.
- To resize the field, drag one of the sizing handles until the field is the size you want. You can also adjust the width and height from the dimensions page of the InfoBox.
- Select the border, fill, or shadow color from the popup boxes for each attribute. The box labeled T indicates transparent.
- Select the border width from the Border Width drop-down list in the colors page of the InfoBox. Available border widths range from hairline to 12 point (1/6 of an inch).
- To change the font, size, style/effect, color, alignment, or text relief of the data, move to the fonts page of the InfoBox and click the Data radio button at the top left.
- To change the label font, size, style/effect, color, alignment, position, text, or text relief, move to the fonts page of the InfoBox and click the Label radio button at the top left.
- Click the check boxes in the Borders section (for example, Left, Right, Top, and Bottom) of the colors page in the InfoBox to select which sides of the field you want Approach to display borders.
- Select a frame style from the Frame drop-down list on the colors page of the InfoBox. The frame style specifies the format in which Approach draws the border around the selected field.
- Use the Basics page of the InfoBox to keep the calculated field from printing or to prevent users from tabbing to it during data entry.
- If you created a named style for your fields, click the style page of the InfoBox to select the field style.

Creating a Formula

To build a formula for a calculated field, click the Options button of the Creating New Database dialog box (for a new database) or the Field Definition dialog box (when working with a calculated field in an existing database). For a calculated field, the extended portion of these dialog boxes displays the Define Formula page (refer back to fig. 10.2).

The Define Formula page is divided into five main sections: the Fields list box, the Operators list box, the Functions list box, the Formula text box, and the Function Description list box. The following sections describe how to use these sections, as well as the Define Summary page.

The Fields List Box. The Fields list box on the Define Formula page contains a list of all the fields in the database whose name appears in a drop-down list box that's just above the Fields list box. When you select a field in the Fields list box, it appears in the Formula text box at the bottom of the page.

Tip

Rather than select a field name from this list, you can type the field name into the Formula text box.

You can include fields in the formula from any other database that's contained in the current Approach file. You can switch to another database and view the fields by selecting it from the drop-down list box above the Fields list box. After you select the database name, the Fields list box displays the fields in that database.

Note

If a calculated field displays `<circular>` in Browse mode rather than a value, this means the field has a reference back to itself. This is known as a *circular reference*. Check the formula for the field or the fields it uses as references to find and correct the problem.

The Operators List Box. The Operators list box displays all the operators available for building a formula. These include arithmetic operators, comparison operators, Boolean operators, and parentheses for grouping expressions, as explained earlier in this chapter. To select an operator, you can select it from this list or type the operator into the Formula text box.

The Functions List Box. From the Functions list box, you can select from many powerful functions that Approach contains to build a formula. These functions include conversion, date, logical, time, trigonometric, string, financial, summary, mathematical, and statistical functions. To enter a function into a formula, select the function from the list box or type the function into the Formula text box.

Many functions operate on one or more values, or arguments. These values are entered between the parentheses that follow the function name. Functions can be field values or constant values. To enter a field value, select the field or type it. To use a constant value, you must type it. If a function uses multiple arguments, separate the arguments with commas.

Approach groups field-calculation functions into eight categories: Conversion, Date & Time, Financial, Logical, Mathematical, Statistical, Summary, and Text. You can view all functions, in alphabetical order, by choosing All from the drop-down list above the

Functions list box or, to save searching through long lists, choose one of the categories to restrict browsing to functions of one type.

> **Note**
>
> Approach gets various settings from the Windows 95 Regional Settings control panel that affects formulas. These settings include the default list separator (a comma in the United States), the default data format (*MM/DD/YY* in the United States), and the default time format (*HH:MM:SS.00* in the United States). If these settings were changed, enter the formula by using the current settings in this control panel.

The `Middle()` function, for example, returns a text string of a specified size from a specified position in another text string. It has the following syntax:

```
Middle(Text, Position, Size)
```

You can use functions as arguments in a function. To indicate whether the LAST_NAME field is blank, for example, you can combine the `If()` function with the `IsBlank()` function:

```
If(IsBlank(LAST_NAME),'Blank','Not Blank')
```

In this example, the `IsBlank()` function and its argument are used as the first argument in the `If()` function.

The Function Description Box. The Function Description box displays a short explanation of the function you select, along with its expected syntax—that is, which types of arguments must be included for the function to work correctly.

The Formula Text Box. The Formula text box displays the formula as you build it. At any time, you can edit the formula in this box.

> **Note**
>
> The formula flag in the bottom left of the box appears with a red × across it if the formula displayed in the formula area has an invalid syntax. Check the syntax of the formula and correct it where necessary. If you try to leave the dialog box without a valid formula in the Formula text box, an error message appears.

Now you can practice using the Formula text box to create a formula. For example, Owl Publishing's newsletters are always sold in one-year subscriptions; by knowing the start date of a subscription, you can calculate the end date. Calculating the end date saves time because then you don't have to enter the end date on each new subscription. To create a field that calculates the end date of a subscription, follow these steps:

1. Switch to Design mode. Open the InfoBox if it isn't open on the form.
2. Select the Customer form from the view tabs or the status bar.
3. Select the SUB END field in the repeating panel. (See Chapter 9, "Designing Advanced Forms," for information on using repeating panels on a form.)
4. Click the Field Definition button in the InfoBox. When you're defining a new calculated field, leave the old field (SUB END) in the database in case you make a mistake.
5. Scroll down the Field Definition dialog box until you reach an empty line. Click the empty line and type **SUB START** in the Field Name column.
6. Set the Data Type column to Calculated. The Define Formula page appears at the bottom of the dialog box.
7. Enter the following formula in the Formula text box (this formula is shown here as two lines, but you should enter it as one line):

```
NEWSLETTER."SUB START"+365.25+If(Mod(YEAR(NEWSLETTER."SUB START")
+1,4)=0,1,0)
```

   This formula calculates the date one year after SUB START and corrects for the extra day in leap years (see fig. 10.3).

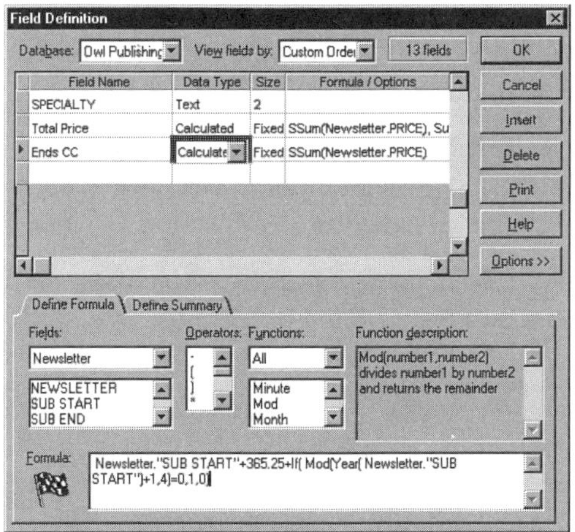

Fig. 10.3

The SUB START calculated field calculates the ending date for a one-year subscription.

Tip

Remember that fields, operators, and functions can be typed or selected from the lists within the Options section of the Field Definition dialog box.

8. Click OK to close the dialog box. Approach returns to the Customer form (see fig. 10.4).

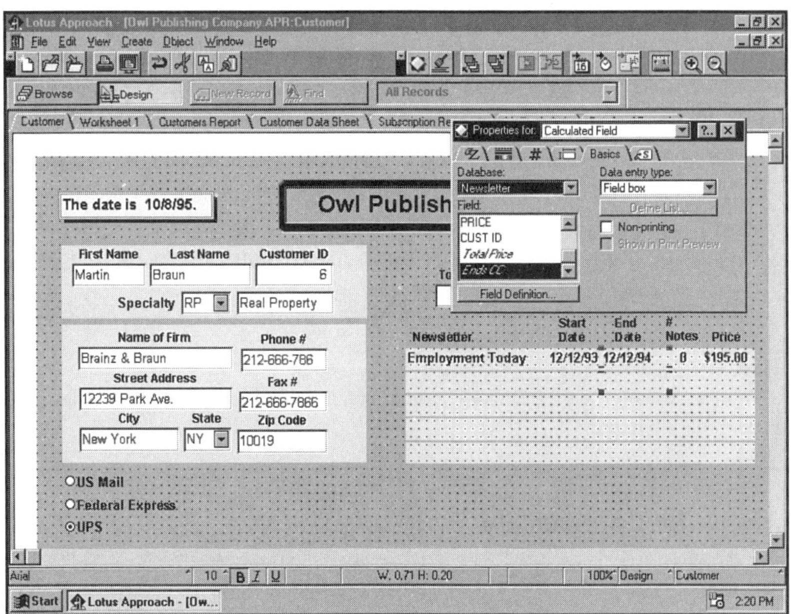

Fig. 10.4

The calculated subscription ending date is displayed in the repeating panel.

The Define Summary Page. For certain functions (known as *summary functions*), a calculated field can calculate and display a value that's summarized for the database in which the calculated field appears, for the summary panel in which the field is placed, or for all databases to which the field's database is relationally linked. You can select the summary option you want from the Summarize On drop-down list box on the Define Summary page.

The Summarize On options change depending on where you placed summary fields in your database applications. The three main options are All Records In (current database), Summary Panels Where this Field Is Placed, or All Records in All Databases:

- *All Records In (current database).* This option summarizes across all the current records in any one database, and it appears once for each database in a view file. Therefore, in your example this option appears three times: once for the Owl database (for example, Summarize on All Records in OWL), once for the Newsletter database, and once for the Specialty database. Use this option when the formula contains only fields located in a single database. Only the records now in use are summarized. Thus, if you're now working with a found set after performing a find, only the records in the found set are included in the summary calculation.
- *Summary Panels Where this Field Is Placed.* In Chapter 12, "Creating Advanced Reports," you learn to create summary panels on a report. A summary panel groups and summarizes records on the report by the value in a certain field. For example, you can create a summary panel to group and summarize information

by Specialty. The Summary Panels Where this Field Is Placed setting tells Approach to summarize on the same field that's used in the summary panel. This option is useful; you can create a single summary field (SUBTOTAL, for example) and reuse it in different summary panels, even on different reports.

- *All Records in All Databases.* This option summarizes across all the databases in the Approach file. Use this option if the formula contains fields from more than one database. It's especially useful for summarizing across records in a database that are related to the main database in a one-to-many relationship.

Note

The Summarize On drop-down list on the Define Summary page isn't available if the formula doesn't include a summary function.

Using Functions in Calculated Fields

Although calculated fields are often used to calculate and display mathematical results, Approach's functions give you considerably more power than just handling numbers. Approach lets you do the following:

- Use text functions to find characters within a string, combine fields, and split off portions of fields
- Use conversion functions to convert one type of data to another (for example, number to text)
- Use date functions to extract information about a supplied date (for example, the week of the year into which a particular date falls)
- Use logical functions to decide what calculations to perform based on the value of a field

If an argument is a constant (that is, not a reference to a field value), you must follow certain rules when typing the argument into the function:

- *Text string.* Enclose text strings in single quotation marks (**'ABCDEFG'**).
- *Date.* Type the date as numbers, separated by slashes and enclosed in single quotation marks (**'10/20/93'**).
- *Time.* Type the time as numbers and enclose it in single quotation marks. Separate the hours, minutes, and seconds with a colon (:), and separate the seconds from the hundredths of seconds with a decimal point. Use the AM or PM qualifier (**'10:20:34.02 AM'**). Any time value entered without a qualifier is taken as 24-hour time.
- *Numbers.* Don't enter numbers in scientific notation (as in $6.75*10^{-1/2}$). Numeric data can come from a numeric field or a text field that contains numeric data.

The following sections discuss some of Approach's more powerful functions, with examples that illustrate their use.

Working with Text Functions. You can manipulate the contents of text fields by using the functions `Left()`, `Right()`, `Length()`, `Middle()`, `Position()`, `Combine()`, and `Trim()`, as described in the following sections.

> **Note**
>
> In a text string, spaces are considered characters. It's important to take spaces into account when using functions that rely on factors such as position.

Left(). This function requires two arguments—a text string and a number (*n*):

```
Left(text,n)
```

The function returns the first *n* characters of the text string, counting from the left. If the text argument is the name of a text-type field, the value in that field is used in the function. For example, if the NAME field contains the value ABCDEFG, `Left(NAME,3)` returns ABC.

Right(). This function requires two arguments—a text string and a number:

```
Right(text,n)
```

The function returns, starting from the right, *n* characters of the text string. If the *`text`* argument is the name of a text-type field, the value in that field is used in the function. For example, if the NAME field contains the value ABCDEFG, `Right(NAME,3)` returns EFG.

Length(). This function requires a text string for its single argument:

```
Length(text)
```

It returns the length of the text string. If the *`text`* argument is the name of a text-type field, the value in that field is used in the function. For example, if the NAME field contains the value ABCDEFG, `Length(NAME)` returns 7.

Middle(). This function requires three arguments—a text string and two numbers:

```
Middle(text, start, size)
```

This function extracts a string of characters from the text string. The string of characters starts at the position given by *`start`*. If the *`text`* argument is the name of a text-type field, the value in that field is used in the function. If the number arguments are names of numeric fields, the values in those fields are used in the function. For example, if the NAME field contains the value ABCDEFG and the START field contains 3, `Middle(NAME, START, 3)` returns CDE.

Position(). This function requires three arguments—two text strings and a number:

```
Position(text, search, start)
```

`Position()` searches through the *`text`* string for the string of characters given by *`search`*. The search begins at the position given by *`start`*. If the *`search`* string of characters is found in *`text`*, `Position()` returns the character position at which the *`search`* string is found. If the *`search`* string isn't found, `Position()` returns zero.

If the *`text`* and *`search`* arguments are the names of text-type fields, the values in those fields are used in the function. If the *`start`* argument is the name of a numeric field or a text field that contains a number, the value in that field is used in the function. For example, if the NAME field contains the value ABC EFG, `Position(NAME,' ',1)` returns 4 because the first blank space in the contents of the NAME field is at position 4. Alternately, if the formula used for this value is `Position(NAME,' ',5)`, the value returned is 0 because the space is before the starting position given in the function.

Combine(). This function requires a list of text-type arguments:

```
Combine(argument list)
```

It links all the arguments in the list to form one text string. If the argument list includes field names, the function uses the values in the fields. Spaces and other text items are added in single quotation marks and separated by a comma.

For example, if the FIRST NAME field contains John and the LAST NAME field contains Doe, `Combine(FIRST NAME,' ',LAST NAME)` results in John Doe.

Trim(). This function requires a single text-type argument:

```
Trim(text)
```

It returns the supplied text with all leading and trailing spaces removed. If the argument is a text-type field name, the value in the field is used in the function. For example, `Trim('London ')` returns London (with no trailing spaces).

Spaces within the text string are ignored. For example, `Trim('Walnut Creek ')` returns Walnut Creek (with no trailing spaces). The space within the string remains unaltered.

Combining Text-String Functions. Approach lets you combine string functions to perform many complex string operations. You can extract single words from a field that contains multiple-word strings, for example. Therefore, if the FULLNAME field contains a person's full name (first and last name), setting up calculated fields that extract the first or last name from the full name is possible:

- Define the LASTNAME field, using the following formula:

  ```
  Right(FULLNAME,Length(FULLNAME)
  Position(FULLNAME,' ',1))
  ```

The second line of the formula finds the first blank in the full name (the blank between the first and last name). Subtracting this number from `Length(FULLNAME)` gives the length of the last name in the field. The `Right()` function uses this result to extract the last name from the full name string.

- Define the FIRSTNAME field using the following formula:

```
Left(FULLNAME, Position(FULLNAME,' ',1))
```

This formula takes any text from the FULLNAME field from the beginning of the field until the first space.

> **Note**
>
> The preceding example assumes that FULLNAME won't include more than two discrete words. Use of additional spaces, such as Robert L. Jones, could yield unexpected results.

You can use the `Combine()` function to combine the contents of fields for use in reports or mailing labels. You can combine, for example, the FIRST NAME and LAST NAME fields into a single calculated field:

```
Combine("FIRST NAME",' ',"LAST NAME")
```

You also can combine the CITY, STATE, and ZIP fields into a single field. The `Trim()` function removes any trailing spaces:

```
Combine(Trim(CITY),', ',Trim(STATE),' ',Trim(ZIP))
```

Building a calculated field in this manner ensures that no large spaces are left between the city, state, and ZIP code on a mailing label. You could also use the When Printing Slide Left check box on the dimensions page of the InfoBox to close up spaces between fields in a form, report, or mailing label.

> **Note**
>
> The preceding example assumes that ZIP is a text field. If ZIP is a numeric field, use the conversion function `NumToText()` to convert the ZIP value into a text value (see the next section, "Working with Conversion Functions"). The `Combine()` function then would look like the following:
>
> ```
> Combine(Trim(CITY),',',Trim (STATE),' ',NumToText(ZIP,'00000'))
> ```

Owl Publishing wants to create some mailing labels using the `Combine()` function so that the City/State line can include a comma. Follow these steps:

1. Use the techniques detailed in the earlier "Creating a Formula" section to create a calculated field named CITYSTATEZIP. The formula for this field is

   ```
   Combine(Trim(CITY),', ',Trim(STATE),' ',Trim(ZIP))
   ```

2. Use the techniques detailed earlier to create a calculated field named FULLNAME. The formula for this field is

```
Combine("FIRSTNAME",' ',"LASTNAME")
```

3. Open the Create menu and choose Mailing Label. The Mailing Label Assistant dialog box appears. Choose the 3 Lines label.
4. Type **`Combine Labels`** in the Mailing Label Name text box.
5. Select the Owl database from the Database drop-down list box.
6. Click the long center label field in the Field Placement diagram on the right side of the Mailing Label Assistant. Select the STREET ADR field in the Database fields list box and click Add.
7. Select Avery 5161 labels from the Label Type drop-down list.
8. Click the upper left label field in the Field Placement diagram. Select FULLNAME from the Database Fields list and click Add.
9. Click the bottom left label field in the Field Placement diagram. Select CITYSTATEZIP from the Database fields list and click Add.
10. Click OK to complete the mailing labels.

Figure 10.5 shows the labels in Design mode, when Show Data is chosen from the View menu. Notice that the labels are formatted exactly as you want.

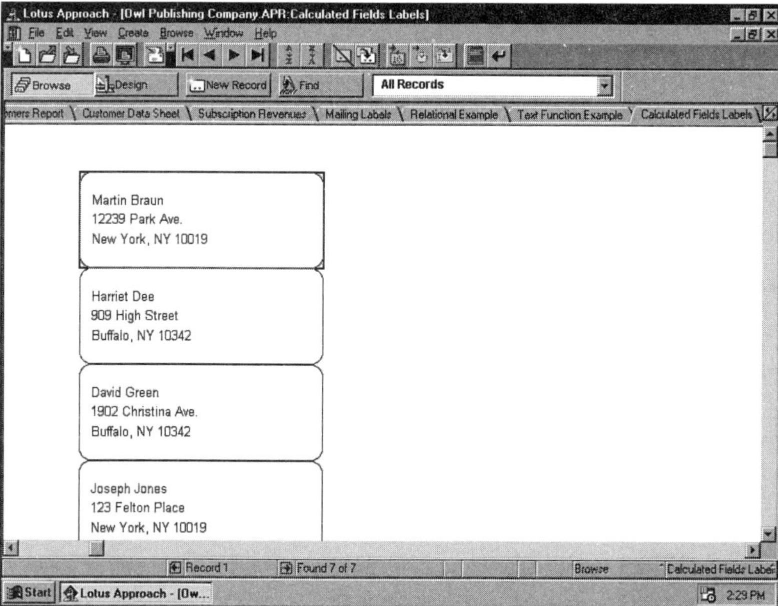

Fig. 10.5

The mailing labels are shown with calculated fields.

Working with Conversion Functions. To use functions that require a specific type of value, changing one type of value (such as numeric) into another type of value (such as text) is often necessary. You saw this in the preceding section, in which a number had to be converted to a string.

Approach supports the `DateToText()`, `NumToText()`, `TextToBool()`, `TextToDate()`, and `TextToTime()` conversion functions, as discussed in the following sections.

DateToText(). This function requires two arguments—a date and a text string:

```
DateToText(date,'text')
```

This function converts a date into a formatted text string. The date to convert is given by the *`date`* argument. If this argument is a field name, the value in the field is used in the formula. The *`text`* argument, enclosed in single quotation marks, supplies the format string for the date that determines how the converted date is displayed (see Chapter 4, "Enhancing Data Input Forms," for information on date formats). For example, `DateToText('3/22/96','MMMM DD, YYYY')` returns March 22, 1996.

NumToText(). This function requires two arguments—a number and a text string:

```
NumToText(number,'text')
```

This function converts a number into a text string. The number to convert is given by the *`number`* argument. If this argument is a numeric field or a text field that contains a number, the value in the field is used in the formula. The *`text`* argument, enclosed in single quotation marks, supplies the format string for the number that determines how the converted number is displayed (see Chapter 4, "Enhancing Data Input Forms," for information on numeric formats). For example, if the NUMBER field contains 8.45, `NumToText(NUMBER,'$00.00')` returns $08.45.

NumToWord(). This function requires two *`number`* arguments:

```
NumToWord(number,number)
```

This function converts a number into its word equivalent. The first *`number`* in the formula is the number to be converted. The second *`number`* argument describes how many decimal digits should be included in the word description. If this argument is less than the actual number of decimal digits, the number is truncated to that point. For example, if the NUMBER field contains 37.35413, `NumToWord(NUMBER,2)` returns *thirty-seven and thirty-five one hundredths*, and `NumToWord(NUMBER,0)` returns *thirty-seven.*

TextToBool(). This function requires a single text-type argument:

```
TextToBool(text)
```

This function returns No if the first character in the *text* argument is NO, no, N, n, or 0. If the first character in the *text* argument is any other character, this function returns Yes (for example, `TextToBool('Fred')` returns Yes). If the text argument is the name of a text-type field, the value of the field is used in the function.

TextToDate(). This function requires a single text-type argument:

```
TextToDate(text)
```

This function returns the date equivalent of the *text* argument, permitting it to be used in date functions (such as `WeekOfYear()`). Enter the text string in the format *mm/dd/yy* (any other format returns an error message). If the date *text* argument is the name of a text-type field, the value of the field is used in the function.

For example, `WeekOfYear(TextToDate('01/03/96'))` returns 1 (this date is in the first week of the year).

TextToTime(). This function requires a single text-type argument:

```
TextToTime(text)
```

This function returns the time equivalent of the *text* argument so that text can be used in time-oriented functions. For example, `TextToTime('10:30 PM')` returns 10:30 PM as a time value.

Enter the time string in one of the following formats:

- hh
- hh:mm
- hh:mm:ss
- hh:mm:ss.00

You can add AM or PM at the end of any of these text strings. If the text argument is the name of a text-type field, the value of the field is used in the function.

Working with Date Functions. Approach provides a wide range of functions for working with dates. By using these functions, you can extract information about a date or perform calculations using dates. Date functions include `Date()`, `Day()`, `DayName()`, `DayOfWeek()`, `DayOfYear()`, `Month()`, `MonthName()`, `Today()`, `WeekOfYear()`, and `Year()`.

All these functions require a single date-type argument. You can enter the argument as a constant or a date-type field name. If you enter the argument as a constant, you must use the format *mm/dd/yy* and enclose it in single quotation marks.

Date(). This function returns a date value corresponding to the numbers given as arguments:

```
Date(day,month,year)
```

For example, `Date(3,22,96)` returns the date value 3/22/96.

Day(). This function returns the day of the month from a date. For example, if the SUB END field contains 12/27/96, `Day(SUB END)` returns 27.

DayName(). This function returns a text string containing the name of the day, given the date. This function also can accept a number from 1 to 7 as the argument (1 is Sunday, 2 is Monday, and so on). For example, if the SUB END field contains 01/27/96, `DayName(SUB END)` returns Saturday.

DayOfWeek(). This function returns a number equal to the number of the day of the week (1 is Sunday, 2 is Monday, and so on). For example, `DayOfWeek('01/27/96')` returns 7 (Saturday).

DayOfYear(). This function returns a number equal to the number of days since January 1 of the year in the supplied date. For example, if the SUB END field contains 2/13/96, `DayOfYear(SUB END)` returns 44.

Month(). This function returns a number representing the month of the supplied date. For example, `Month('3/12/96')` returns 3.

MonthName(). This function returns a text string containing the name of the month in the supplied date. If, for example, the SUB END field contains 3/12/96, `MonthName(SUB END)` returns March.

WeekOfYear(). This function returns a number that represents the number of weeks since January 1 of the year in the supplied date. For example, `WeekOfYear('1/28/96')` returns 5.

Year(). This function returns a number that represents the year in the supplied date. The year returned is the full four-digit year (including century). For example, if the SUB END field contains 1/27/96, `Year(SUB END)` returns 1996.

Working with Logical Functions. Logical functions determine whether a given condition is true or false. These functions can be used with constants or, more likely, with field data. Logical functions also provide the opportunity for different values in a calculated field, based on how the contents are evaluated versus the condition given.

Blank(). This function tests to see whether a field is blank. If it is, this function returns a given value; if not, `Blank()` returns the field information. It needs two arguments—the field and the value:

```
Blank(field, value)
```

For example, `Blank("M INITIAL", 'NMI')` returns the text string NMI (no middle initial) if the MIDDLE INITIAL field is blank.

IsBlank(). This function tests to see whether a field is blank, and returns a Yes if it's blank or a No if it isn't. It needs just one argument, the field name:

```
IsBlank(field)
```

For example, `IsBlank(PAID)` equals Yes if the PAID field is empty.

`IsBlank()` also can be combined with NOT to evaluate when a field isn't blank. `NOT IsBlank(PAID)` would equal No if the PAID field were empty.

IsLastRecord(). This function tests to see whether the current record is the last one in the found set of records and returns a Yes if it is or a No if another record is after the current record. It needs just one argument, the field name: `IsLastRecord(field)`.

If(). One of the most powerful functions Approach offers is the `If()` function. With this function, you can test for a condition and perform calculations based on whether the condition is true or false.

The `If()` function requires three arguments—a condition and two values:

```
If(condition, truevalue, falsevalue)
```

The *`condition`* argument is a logical statement that must evaluate as true or false. Some examples follow:

- *Comparing the values in two fields: Field1>Field2.* If the contents of Field1 for the given record are greater than the contents of Field2, the result of this condition is true. Otherwise, the result of this condition is false.
- *Checking to see whether a field is blank.* The `IsBlank()` function determines whether a field is blank, as explained earlier. Its single argument is a field name: `IsBlank(field)` returns true if *`field`* is blank; otherwise, it returns false.
- *Comparing a date field to the current date.* The `Today()` function returns the date on the system clock. (It has no arguments, but you must still use parentheses.)

For example, you can compare the contents of the SUB END field to the current date with `SUB END>Today()`. This condition returns true if the date in the SUB END field is later than the current date. If the date in the SUB END field is earlier than the current date, however, the condition returns false.

- *Comparing two text strings.* The `Exact()` function compares two text strings. It uses two text-type arguments, which can be text fields: `Exact(`*`text1`*`, `*`text2`*`)`. `Exact()` returns true if the two text strings are exactly the same (including spacing and case). Otherwise, it returns false.
- *Checking to see whether multiple conditions are true using the AND and OR operators.* When multiple conditions are tested using AND, as in `Field1>20 AND Field2<100`, both formulas must be true to return a true response. If the OR operator is used, as in `DateField<Today() OR DateField>(Today()+30)`, either (or both) may be true to return the true response.

The *`truevalue`* and *`falsevalue`* arguments contain any value, including a constant, a calculation, or a field reference. `If()` returns *`truevalue`* if the condition evaluates as true; otherwise, it returns *`falsevalue`* if the condition evaluates as false.

Suppose that an employee database has a field (BIRTHDATE) containing the birthday of the employee. You can use a calculated field to compute the current age of the employee. The entire `If()` statement would look like the following:

```
If(IsBlank(BIRTHDATE),'No Date of Birth',
   Trunc(((Today()-Birthdate)/365.25),0))
```

The formula is built as follows:

1. It checks to see whether the BIRTHDATE field is blank by using the `IsBlank()` function. `IsBlank()` returns true if the BIRTHDATE field is empty. If a value is in the BIRTHDATE field, `IsBlank()` returns false.
2. If the BIRTHDATE field is blank, the formula returns the text string *No Date of Birth.*
3. If the BIRTHDATE field isn't blank, the formula use the following age formula to calculate the age:

```
Trunc(((Today()-BIRTHDATE)/365.25),0)
```

The `(Today()-BIRTHDATE)/365.25` clause returns a decimal number for the number of years that the employee has been alive (for example, 38.458). Because ages are counted in whole numbers, however, you need to remove the decimal portion of the age. The `Trunc()` function is used for this purpose. It requires two arguments: the number to truncate and a whole number that indicates how many decimal places the final result should have. The rest of the decimal places are discarded. In this example, you want no (0) decimal places.

> **Note**
>
> If you omit the number of decimal places for `Trunc()`, this function returns the number truncated to zero decimal places.

Nested If() Functions. You can place an `If()` function, using additional `If()` statements, inside the ***`truevalue`*** or ***`falsevalue`*** arguments. This is known as a *nested If,* because it nests within another `If()` statement. By nesting `If()` statements, you can test for multiple conditions. Consider the following simple one-level nest:

```
If(condition1,truevalue1,If(condition2,truevalue2,falsevalue))
```

If *`condition1`* in the outside `If()` statement is true, ***`truevalue`*** is returned. If *`condition1`* is false, however, the nested `If()` is executed as the false value. If *`condition2`* is true, *`truevalue2`* is returned. If *`condition2`* is false, *`falsevalue`* is returned. Realize that *`falsevalue`* could still be another `If()` statement, and so on.

Consider an employee database that records the date when an employee joined the company in a field named SERVEDATE. The number of years that an employee has been with the company could be calculated and displayed in a field named SERVE:

```
Trunc(((Today()-SERVEDATE)/365.25),0)
```

This company has a set of rules that determines the stock options for which an employee is eligible, based on the years of service: Basic, Supplemental, Plus, and Full. You can use a nested `If()` statement in a calculated field to calculate and display the stock option for which an employee was eligible, which is shown in the following example:

```
If(SERVE<=5,'Basic',If(SERVE<=10,'Supplemental',
  If(SERVE<=15,'Plus','Full')))
```

In this example,

- If the employee has five or fewer years of service, the condition in the first `If()` is true, and the text string *Basic* is placed in the calculated field.
- If the employee has more than five years of service, the condition is false, and the second `If()` is executed. If the employee has between six and 10 years of service, the condition of the second `If()` statement is true, and the text string *Supplemental* returns.
- If the employee has more than 10 years of service, the condition in the second `If()` is false, and the third `If()` executes. If the employee has between 11 and 15 years of service, the condition in the third `If()` is true, and the text string *Plus* returns.
- If this last condition is false (the employee has more than 15 years of service) the text string *Full* returns because it's the false result for the last `If()` statement.

Working with Summary Functions. Summary functions perform calculations across a range of records and display the value in the calculated field. Non-summary functions work within a single record.

As an example of a non-summary function, a sales commission might take the sales total for each record and calculate this value times a percentage to give a commission amount. Commission has one value per record in the database. A summary function calculates a value for a field over an entire group of records, such as the sum of all SALES TOTAL fields for the year 1995.

You use the summary functions with the Summarize On drop-down list on the Define Summary page of the Define Field dialog box. (For more information on the Summarize On drop-down list, see the earlier section "The Define Summary Page.")

The summary functions are as follows:

- `SAverage()` (summary average)
- `SCount()` (summary count)
- `SMax()` (summary maximum)
- `SMin()` (summary minimum)
- `SNPV()` (summary net present value)
- `SStd()` (summary standard deviation)
- `SSum()` (summary sum)
- `SVar()` (summary variance)

These functions are discussed in the following sections.

SAverage(). The summary average function has a single argument that must be a numeric field or a text field that contains numeric data: `SAverage(`*`field`*`)`. It calculates the average value for non-blank occurrences of the specified field for the current range of records. If the NUMBER field contained 2, 3, 4.3, and 6 in four records, for example, the `SAverage(NUMBER)` is 3.825 for that four-record group.

SCount(). The summary count function has a single argument that must be a field: `SCount(`*`field`*`)`. This function calculates the number of non-blank occurrences for any value in the specified field for the current range of records. Blank values aren't counted. If the NUMBER field contained 2, 3, 4.3, and 6 in four records, for example, the `SCount(NUMBER)` is 4 for that four-record group.

SMax(). The summary maximum function has a single argument that can be any type of field: `SMax(`*`field`*`)`. It returns the largest value in the field for the current range of records. If the NUMBER field contained 2, 3, 4.3, and 6 in four records, for example, the `SMax(NUMBER)` is 6 for that four-record group.

SMin(). The summary minimum function has a single argument that can be any type of field: `SMin(field)`. It returns the smallest value in the field for the current range of records. If the NUMBER field contained 2, 3, 4.3, and 6 in four records, for example, the `SMin(NUMBER)` is 2 for that four-record group.

SNPV(). The summary net present value function needs two arguments. The first is a field; the second is a constant—for example, `SNPV(shares,.05)`.

The SNPV returns the net present value of an investment based on a series of yearly cash flows (contained in the field) and a discount rate (the constant value). The discount rate is usually stated in percent (for example, 8 percent) but is entered into the formula as a decimal number (for example, .08). The periodic cash flows can be positive (income) or negative (investment).

The value in the field in the first record in the database represents the investment made in the first year. The value in the field in subsequent records represents the investment or income for subsequent years (for example, the second record is for year 2, the third record is for year 3, and so on).

For example, the PAYMENT field can have positive values of 6, 4.3, 2, and 3 in four records, one for each year. The interest rate is 8%. `SNPV(PAYMENT,.08)` is 13.035.

SStd(). The summary standard deviation function has a single argument that must be a numeric field or a text field containing a number: `SStd(field)`. It returns the standard deviation of the values in the specified field for the current range of records. The standard deviation is a measure of how widely dispersed the values are from the average value. If the NUMBER field contained 2, 3, 4.3, and 6 in four records, for example, the `SStd(NUMBER)` is 1.497 for that four-record group.

SSum(). The summary sum function has a single argument that must be a numeric field or a text field containing a number: `SSum(field)`. This function returns the sum of all the values in the specified field for the current range of records. If the NUMBER field contains 2, 3, 4.3, and 6 in four records, for example, the `SSum(NUMBER)` is 15.3 for that four-record group.

SVar(). The summary variance function has a single argument that must be a numeric field or a text field that contains a number: `SVar(field)`. It returns the variance of the values in the specified field for the current range of records. If the NUMBER field contains 2, 3, 4.3, and 6 in four records, for example, the `SVar(NUMBER)` is 2.242 for that four-record group.

Using Variables

A *variable* is a temporary holding place for data. It's useful for holding intermediate data and for passing results from one record to another. Variables are also useful in macros (see Chapter 13, "Automating Your Work," for examples of using variables).

When you store data in a variable field, this value is a single value that's available to every record in the database. Because it has only one value, the variable field will appear the same for every record in the database. Like a calculated field, the variable field is part of an Approach file and isn't stored in the database file.

Variable fields have a field type that determines the type of data they can store (such as Text, Date, Boolean, and so on). You can format variable fields like any other field; they can be formatted, displayed on a form or report, and used in calculations.

Creating Variable Fields

As with all other types of fields, to create variable fields you must use the Creating New Database or Define Field dialog box. You can create a variable field when you first define the database, or you can add it later.

Defining a Variable Field for a New Database. When creating a new database, follow the steps detailed in the "Designing a Database" section in Chapter 2 to define the fields you need. Then follow these steps:

1. Open the File menu and choose New Database. Select Blank Database from the window that appears and click OK. The New dialog box appears.
2. Type the database file name, select the file type, and click OK. The Creating New Database dialog box appears.
3. To define a variable field in the Creating New Database dialog box, type the name of the variable field into the Field Name column.

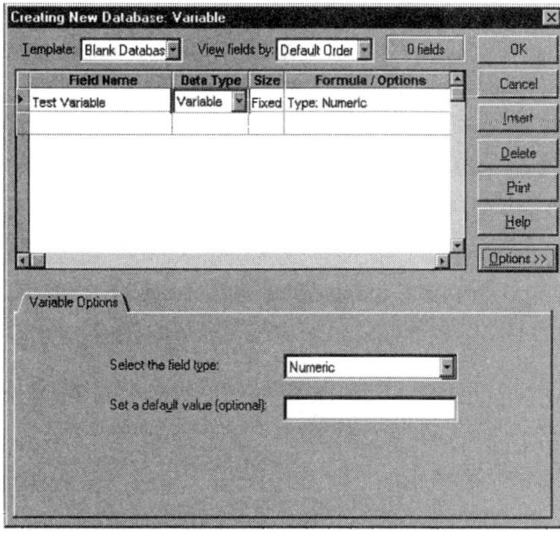

Fig. 10.6

A variable field, like a calculated field, is another data type.

4. Select Variable from the drop-down list in the Data Type column.
5. Click Options. The Creating New Database dialog box expands to display the Variable Options page (see fig. 10.6).
6. From the Select the Field Type drop-down list, select the field type. You can assign a field type of Boolean, Date, Numeric, Text, or Time.
7. If you want, you can set a default value for the variable field. To do so, type the default value for the variable field in the Set a Default Value (Optional) text box.
8. Continue designating fields for the database. When you're done, click OK in the Creating New Database dialog box to create the database.

> **Note**
>
> If you need to return to the Variable Options page, select the variable field in the list of fields in the Field Definition dialog box, and then click Options. Variable fields are displayed in field lists in italics. They're shown after "real" database fields and before calculated fields.

Adding a Variable Field to an Existing Database. To define a variable field in an existing database, follow these steps:

1. Open the Create menu and choose Field Definition. The Field Definition dialog box appears.
2. To define a variable field in the Field Definition dialog box, type the name of the variable field into the Field Name column.
3. Select Variable from the drop-down list in the Data Type column.
4. Click Options. The Field Definition dialog box expands to display the Variable Options page.
5. From the Select the Field Type drop-down list, select the field type. You can assign a field type of Boolean, Date, Numeric, Text, or Time.
6. If you want, you can set a default value for the variable field. To do so, type the default value for the variable field in the Set a Default Value (Optional) text box.

Adding an Existing Variable Field to a Form or Report

After you define a variable field, you can add it to an existing form or report just like any other field. Follow these steps:

1. Switch to Design mode.
2. Do one of the following:
    - Drag the variable field onto the form from the Add Field dialog box.
    - Click the Draw Field tool on the tools palette, drag a rectangle to define the position and size of the variable field, and select the variable field from the field list on the Basics page of the field InfoBox.

Changing the Appearance of a Variable Field

You can change the appearance of a variable field on a form or report just as you can change any other field by resizing, moving, changing the fill and pen colors, setting borders, and adjusting the attributes of the text for the contents of the field and the label.

To make changes to the field, switch to Design mode and then perform any of the following procedures:

- To move the field, drag it to its new location or adjust the location from the dimensions page of the InfoBox.
- To resize the field, drag one of the sizing handles until the field is the desired size. You also can adjust the width and height on the dimensions page of the InfoBox.
- Select the border, fill, or shadow color from the popup boxes for each attribute. The box labeled T provides a transparent color.
- Select the border width from the Border width drop-down list on the colors page of the InfoBox. Available border widths range from hairline to 12 point (1/6 of an inch).
- To change the font, size, style/effect, color, alignment, or text relief of the data, move to the fonts page of the InfoBox and click the Data radio button at the top left.
- To change the label font, size, style/effect, color, alignment, position, text, or text relief, move to the fonts page of the InfoBox and click the Label radio button at the top left.
- Select the check-box options in the Borders section (for example, Left, Right, Top, and Bottom) of the colors page in the InfoBox to select which sides of the field you want Approach to display borders.
- Select a frame style from the Frame drop-down list in the colors page of the InfoBox. The frame style specifies the format in which Approach draws the border around the selected field.
- Use the Basics page of the InfoBox to keep the calculated field from printing or to prevent users from tabbing into it during data entry.
- If you created a named style for your fields, click the style page of the InfoBox to select a field style.

Using PicturePlus Fields

A PicturePlus field can contain graphics and special objects called OLE (object linking and embedding) objects. OLE objects are objects created in other Windows applications that connect back to this application to be edited or updated. They include objects such as sound, charts, and written documents. With PicturePlus fields, you can include a wide variety of objects and information in your database. Approach provides quite a few ways in which you can add information to PicturePlus fields.

Unlike calculated and variable fields, PicturePlus fields are part of the database. However, the contents can be accessible only through Approach, and not through other applications that can read the same database format.

Creating PicturePlus Fields

As with all other types of fields, PicturePlus fields are created by using the Field Definition dialog box. You can create a PicturePlus field when you first define the database, or you can add it later.

Defining a PicturePlus Field for a New Database. To add a PicturePlus field to a new database, proceed as follows:

1. Open the File menu and choose New Database. Select Blank Database from the window that appears and click OK. The New dialog box appears.
2. In the New dialog box, type the database file name, select the file type, and then click OK. The Creating New Database dialog box appears.
3. Type the name of the PicturePlus field into the Field Name column.
4. Select PicturePlus from the Data Type drop-down list.
5. Click Options. The Creating New Database dialog box expands to display the PicturePlus Options page (see fig. 10.7).

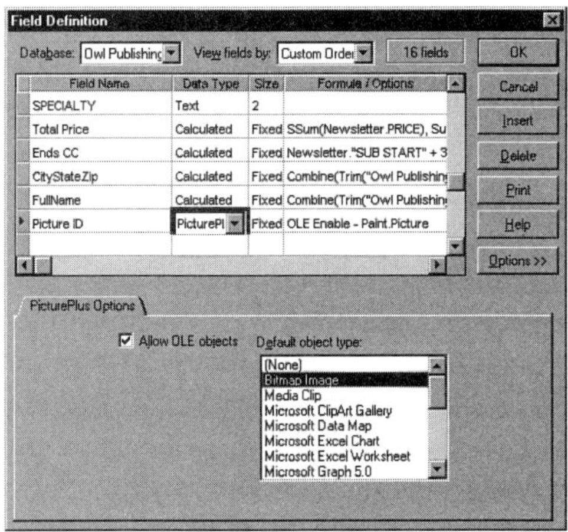

Fig. 10.7

The PicturePlus field can use OLE objects from other Windows applications.

> **Note**
>
> Approach can include file options for any available OLE server application, so your list may differ from the one shown in figure 10.8.

6. If desired, select Allow OLE Objects to set this option. When the check box is selected (the default), Approach lets you place OLE objects in the PicturePlus field, and the words `OLE Enable - (filetype)` appear in the Formula/Options column.

When the check box isn't selected, Approach allows you to place only graphics files in the PicturePlus field—it doesn't let you place OLE objects. The words `OLE disable` appear in the Formula/Options column.

7. If the Allow OLE objects check box is selected, choose the default OLE application from the Default Object Type list, or leave the setting at the default (None). This application opens when you double-click the PicturePlus field to place an object in the field (see "Adding an Object Using Embedding" later in the chapter).
8. Continue designating fields for the database. When you're done, click OK in the Creating New Database dialog box to create the database.

> **Note**
>
> To return to the PicturePlus Options page, select the PicturePlus field in the list of fields in the Field Definition dialog box, and then click Options.

Adding a PicturePlus Field to an Existing Database. To define a PicturePlus field in an existing database, follow these steps:

1. Open the Create menu and choose Field Definition. The Define Field dialog box appears.
2. Type the name of the PicturePlus field into the Field Name column.
3. Select PicturePlus from the drop-down list in the Data Type column.
4. Click Options. The Define Field dialog box expands to display the PicturePlus Options page.
5. If desired, select Allow OLE objects to enable this option. If the option is on, select a default OLE application from the Default Object Type list or leave this setting at the default (None), as described in the preceding section.
6. Click OK in the Field Definition dialog box.

Adding an Existing PicturePlus Field to a Form or Report. After you define a PicturePlus field, you can add it to any existing form or report. Follow these steps:

1. Switch to Design mode.
2. Do one of the following:
    - Drag the PicturePlus field onto the form from the Add Field dialog box.
    - Click the Draw Field tool on the tools palette, drag a rectangle to define the position and size of the PicturePlus field, and select the PicturePlus field from the field list on the Basics page of the field InfoBox. Unlike other types of fields placed on a form or report by using the Draw Field tool, Approach displays only PicturePlus fields in the field list.

Changing the Appearance of a PicturePlus Field

You can change the appearance of a PicturePlus field on a form or report just like you can any other field by resizing, moving, changing the fill and pen colors, setting borders, and adjusting the attributes of the text for the contents of the field and the label.

To make changes to the field, switch to Design mode and then perform any of the following procedures:

- To move the field, drag it to its new location or adjust the location from the dimensions page of the InfoBox.
- To resize the field, drag one of the sizing handles until the field is the size you want. You also can adjust the width and height from the dimensions panel of the InfoBox.
- Select the border, fill, or shadow color from the drop-down list that Approach makes available on the colors page of the InfoBox when you click the Border Color, Fill Color, or Shadow Color drop-down lists. The box labeled T indicates transparent.
- Select the border width from the Border Width drop-down list on the colors page of the InfoBox. Available border widths range from hairline to 12 point (1/6 of an inch).
- To change the font, size, style/effect, color, alignment, or text relief, make the appropriate selections from the fonts page of the InfoBox.
- To change the label font, size, style/effect, color, alignment, position, text, and text relief, make the appropriate selections from the Label section of the InfoBox's fonts page.
- Select the check-box options in the Borders section of the colors page in the InfoBox to select which sides of the field you want Approach to display borders (for example, Left, Right, Top, and Bottom).
- Select a frame style from the Frame drop-down list on the colors page of the InfoBox. The frame style specifies the format in which Approach draws the border around the selected field.

Changing the PicturePlus Options

You can set how Approach displays an image in a PicturePlus field when the image and the field aren't the same size. To set the PicturePlus options, you must be in Design mode, with the Options page of the PicturePlus field's InfoBox displayed (see fig. 10.8).

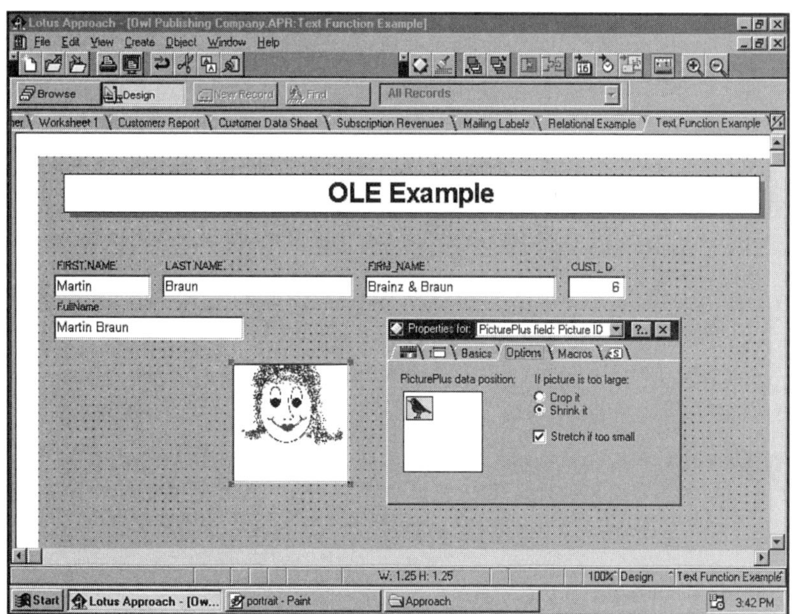

Fig. 10.8

You can set how the image appears in a PicturePlus field.

You can specify the following options for the PicturePlus field:

- Select Crop It if you want Approach to crop an object that's too large to fit into the field. A cropped object displays only as much of the image as will fit into the PicturePlus field frame.
- Select Shrink It if you want Approach to shrink an object that's too large to fit into the field. The object is reduced in size, proportionally, until it fits into the PicturePlus field. This can cause some distortion in the image.
- Select Stretch If Too Small if you want Approach to enlarge an object proportionally to fit in the PicturePlus field. If this check box is left blank, space shows around the edges of an object that's too small.
- Use the PicturePlus Data Position box to specify where the object appears within the PicturePlus field if the object doesn't fill the whole field. Nine positions are possible from a grid of three rows and three columns. Click a place in the box to indicate which of the positions you want, or drag the sample image.

Adding Images and Objects to a PicturePlus Field

After you place a PicturePlus field on a form or report, you can insert graphics images or OLE objects into the PicturePlus field. Because a PicturePlus field has a different value in every record, PicturePlus fields provide a mechanism for including images or OLE objects in each record.

You can insert a graphic image or OLE object into a PicturePlus field in two ways: by embedding the object and by linking the object. Embedding and linking are similar in that they allow you to easily edit the image or OLE object. They differ, however, in that they store the image file or OLE object file in different places. The following sections discuss the techniques for embedding and linking OLE objects.

Defining Object Embedding. Embedding is a special technique used for inserting information into a PicturePlus field. It not only works very much like Paste (you can even use Paste from the Edit menu) but also makes editing the object much easier. With embedding, Approach "remembers" which application created the object you previously placed on the form.

Embedded objects in a PicturePlus field can be edited or updated, just like embedded objects in an Approach file (described in Chapter 9, "Designing Advanced Forms").

Defining Object Linking. A linked object in a PicturePlus field is similar in many ways to an embedded object:

- You create the linked file in a server application, outside of Approach (Approach is the "client" application).

> **Note**
>
> For embedding and linking to work, the application providing the object must be a *server* application—that is, it must be specifically designed to take advantage of object linking and embedding. This is known as being *OLE aware*. Many (but not all) Windows applications can act as server applications. Although copying and pasting an image into an Approach PicturePlus field from a non-server application still is possible, the image isn't connected to the originating application. To modify this kind of image, you must open the originating application, load and modify the image, copy it in the originating application, and paste it into Approach.

- If the server application supports OLE 2.0, its tools are added to Approach to let you easily edit the object in place. If it supports an earlier OLE version, Approach opens the server application (see "Editing a PicturePlus Field Containing a Linked Object" later in this chapter). You then can use the server application to perform the edits. When the edits are complete, you can close the server application and return to Approach, automatically updating the linked object in the PicturePlus field.

Unlike an embedded object, linked objects aren't stored in the Approach database file. Instead, they're stored as normal files on disk. Because linked objects are stored as normal files, you can edit them by using the same server application that created them—even when Approach isn't running. If you link an Excel chart to a PicturePlus field on an Approach form, for example, you can open Excel and edit the chart.

If you do modify a linked file, the next time you open the Approach file to which it's linked, Approach can update the link, displaying the latest version of the file in the PicturePlus field. You can initiate this update automatically or manually, depending on the link options you set in Approach.

Linked files require more effort to set up and maintain than embedded files. Because you store a linked file separately from the Approach database file, however, you can link any given file to more than one Approach database file. You also can link the file to other Windows application files that support object linking. For example, you can link the same Excel chart to multiple Approach database files *and* to a Word for Windows document.

Linking a single file to multiple Approach databases (and other Windows application files) uses less disk space than embedding, in which the file must be stored in each application file to which it's linked. Also, if you update the single linked file, all Approach database files (and any other application files) to which the file is linked can be updated to reflect the changes.

Adding an Object Using Embedding. Approach offers the following five ways to embed an object in a PicturePlus field:

- Open the Edit menu and choose Paste.
- Open the Edit menu and choose Paste Special.
- Paste from an imported file.
- Drag-and-drop a file into a PicturePlus field.
- Open the Create menu and choose Object.

The following sections describe these methods.

Using Paste to Embed an Object. You can use Paste to embed an object in a PicturePlus field. By using this option, you can paste the entire object or only a portion of it into the PicturePlus field. To use Paste to embed an object, follow these steps:

1. Open the application from which you want to paste an object.
2. Load the file containing the object or create the object using the application.
3. Select the object (or portion of the object) you want to place into Approach.
4. Open the Edit menu and choose Copy.
5. Open Approach (or switch to Approach, if it's open already).
6. Switch to Browse mode.
7. Select the form or report you want from the view tabs or the status bar.
8. Click the PicturePlus field to select it.
9. Open the Edit menu and choose Paste. The selected object appears in the PicturePlus field (see fig. 10.9).

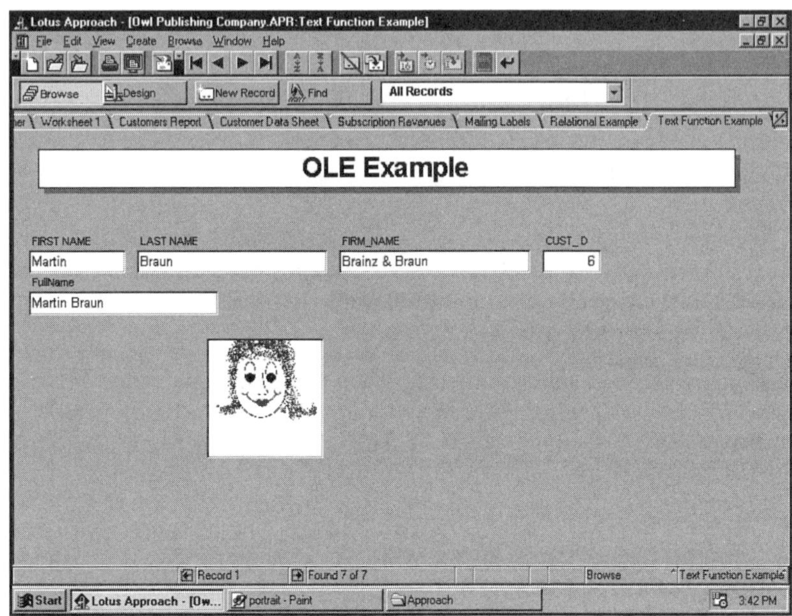

Fig. 10.9

After you use Paste, the embedded object appears in the PicturePlus field.

If the application providing the object isn't OLE aware, the Paste still works (for images only), but the image isn't connected to the originating application. To modify an image pasted into Approach from an application that isn't OLE aware, follow these steps:

1. Open the application that created the image.
2. Load the image (or copy it from Approach and paste it into the application).
3. Modify the image using the application's tools.
4. Copy it from the application and paste it back into the Approach PicturePlus field.

Using Paste Special to Embed an Object. You can choose Paste Special from the Edit menu to embed an object in a PicturePlus field. With this option, you can paste the entire object or only a portion of it into the PicturePlus field. Follow these steps:

1. Open the application from which you want to paste an object.
2. Load the file containing the object or create the object using the application.
3. Select the object (or portion of the object) you want to place into Approach.
4. Open the Edit menu and choose Copy.
5. Open Approach (or switch to Approach, if it's open already).
6. Switch to Browse mode.
7. Select the form or report by using the view tabs or the status bar.

8. Click the PicturePlus field to select it.

9. Open the Edit menu and choose Paste Special. The Paste Special dialog box appears (see fig. 10.10).

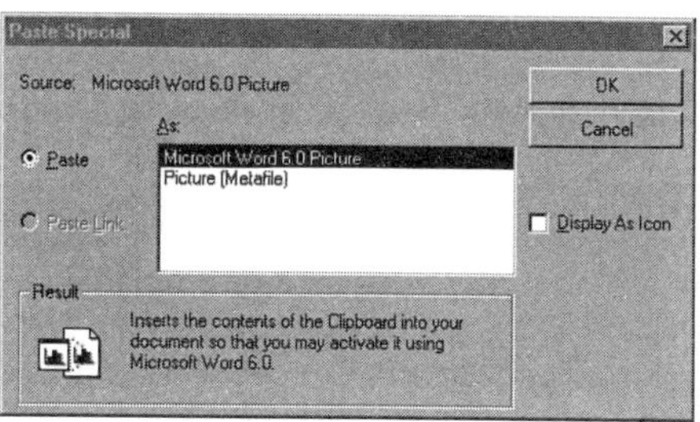

Fig. 10.10

Special paste options are available from the Paste Special dialog box.

10. The Paste Special dialog box displays a list of types of objects. Select the object type for the object you want to embed in the PicturePlus field.

> **Note**
>
> To maintain the connection between the object and the application that created it, you must select an object type in the Paste Special dialog box that includes the name of the server application (for example, Paintbrush Picture Object). For an image, if you select an option that doesn't include the application name (for example, Bitmap), the image is pasted into the PicturePlus field, but no connection to the application that created the object exists.

11. Click OK in the Paste Special dialog box to place the object in the PicturePlus field.

Using Picture Import to Embed an Object. You can choose Picture Import from the Edit menu to embed an object in a PicturePlus field. This option, however, allows embedding of an entire object only (that is, you can't embed only a portion of an image). Because Approach can recognize these image-file formats, you don't need a server application to be able to use these files in a PicturePlus field.

You also can embed an imported object by using Paste from File by following these steps:

1. Switch to Browse mode.
2. Select the form or report containing the PicturePlus field from the view tabs or the status line.
3. Click the PicturePlus field.
4. Open the Edit menu and choose Picture; from the submenu, choose Import. The Import Picture dialog box appears (see fig. 10.11).

Fig. 10.11

The Import Picture dialog box allows you to select the type of file you want.

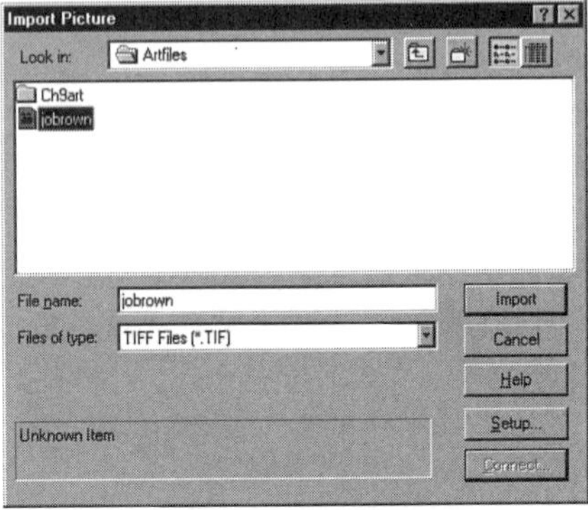

5. From the Files of Type drop-down list, select the type of file you want.

> **Note**
>
> Approach recognizes a number of file types. If you select a type that Approach doesn't recognize, it returns a `Sharing Violation` error, and the operation is unsuccessful. You can embed some of the unsupported file types, however, by using the Insert Object feature (see "Using Insert Object to Embed an Object" later in this chapter).

6. Adjust the location where you want to select the file by using the Look In drop-down list and the files list box in the center of the dialog box.
7. Select the file you want to embed. The file will appear in the File Name text box.
8. Click OK to embed the object in the PicturePlus field.

Using Drag-and-Drop to Embed an Object. You can use drag-and-drop to embed an object in a PicturePlus field. Drag-and-drop refers to locating a file in a directory, and then dragging the file name onto the Approach form and dropping it into the PicturePlus field. This option allows embedding of an entire object only. Again, you don't need a server application installed for compatible formats.

To embed an object using drag-and-drop, follow these steps:

1. Switch to Browse mode.
2. Select the form or report that contains the PicturePlus field from the view tabs or the status line.
3. Resize the Approach window so that it takes up as little room on-screen as possible, but with the PicturePlus field still visible.
4. Click the PicturePlus field to select it.
5. Open Explorer and size its window so that it's visible next to the Approach window.

6. Move to the drive and directory that contains the file you want to embed.
7. Select the file name in the Explorer window.
8. Drag the file name to the PicturePlus field (see fig. 10.12). Release the mouse button. The file appears in the PicturePlus window.

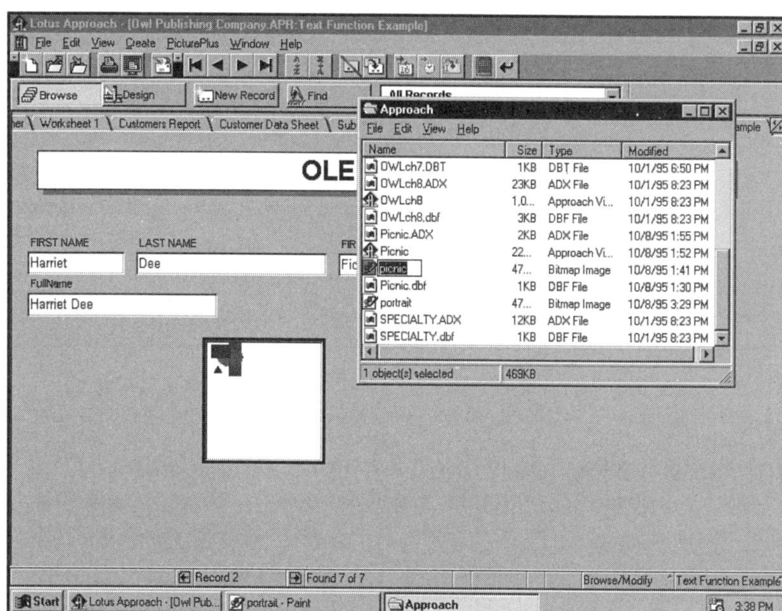

Fig. 10.12

Drag the file from Explorer and drop it in the PicturePlus field in Approach.

Using Create Object to Embed an Object. You can open the Create menu and choose Object to embed an object in a PicturePlus field. This option has advantages over the drag-and-drop and Paste from File methods. Because you must tell Approach what type of object you're embedding, you won't get `Sharing Violation` errors if Approach can't recognize the type of object. However, like drag-and-drop and Paste from File, you can insert only an entire object.

This method, like the others, starts by selecting the PicturePlus field the image will be inserted into. After that point, the steps are identical to those used in Chapter 9, "Designing Advanced Forms."

Editing a PicturePlus Field Containing an Embedded Object. To edit the contents of a PicturePlus Field, follow these steps:

1. Switch to Browse mode.
2. Double-click the PicturePlus field to open the source document.

> **Note**
>
> For most types of embedded objects, you can double-click the PicturePlus field to open the server application. You can't use this technique, however, if you're using any type of embedded sounds or animation. Double-clicking a sound or animation application icon plays the sound or animation; it doesn't open the server application.

3. Use the server application to make the changes you want.
4. Choose Update from the server application's File menu.

> **Note**
>
> Some server applications don't provide an Update command on the File menu. If this is the case, select Close from the File menu. When the server application asks whether you want to update the Approach file, click Yes.

5. Choose Exit from the File menu in the source (server) application. You're returned to Approach with the object updated on-screen.

Adding an Object Using Linking. Linking provides a link back to a file created within a server application. To link a PicturePlus field to an object file, you must meet the following conditions:

- Create and save the object file before you can link it to a PicturePlus field. If you haven't created the object file, open the server application and create a new object file. Be sure to save the new object file, however, before you try to link it to a PicturePlus field in Approach.
- Make sure that Approach and the server application are running at the time you create the link. After you create the link, you can close the server application.

To place a linked object into a PicturePlus field, follow these steps:

1. Open the server application. Load the file that contains the object you want to link to a PicturePlus field. If the object file doesn't exist, create one by using the server application and save the file.
2. In the server application, select the object (or portion of the object) you want to link to the PicturePlus field in Approach.
3. From the server application, open the Edit menu and choose Copy.

> **Note**
>
> Don't choose Cut—the link won't be created if you do. Also, leave the server application running because you haven't yet created the link.

4. Switch to Approach.
5. Select the form or report that contains the PicturePlus field from the view tabs or the status bar.
6. Switch to Browse mode.
7. Click the PicturePlus field.
8. Open the Edit menu and choose Paste Special. The Paste Special dialog box appears (see fig. 10.13).

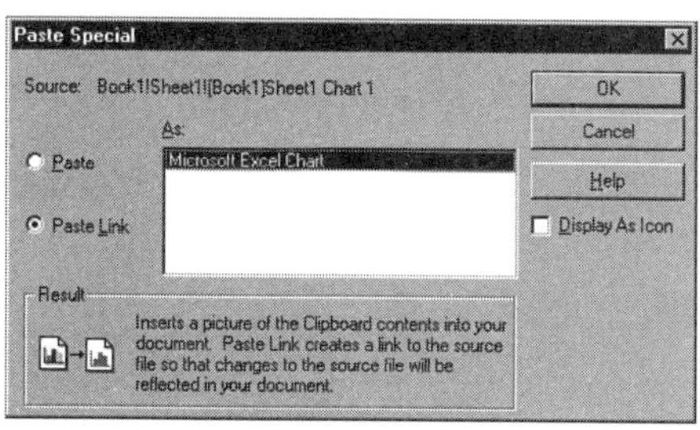

Fig. 10.13

Opening the Paste Special dialog box makes Paste Link available.

9. Choose Paste Link and click OK. The Paste Special dialog box closes, and the linked object is placed into the PicturePlus field.

Working with Established Links. After you establish a link between a server application and an Approach PicturePlus field, you can

- Set the update status of the link
- Delete the link
- Repair a broken link

The Links dialog box provides the tools to perform these tasks (see fig. 10.14).

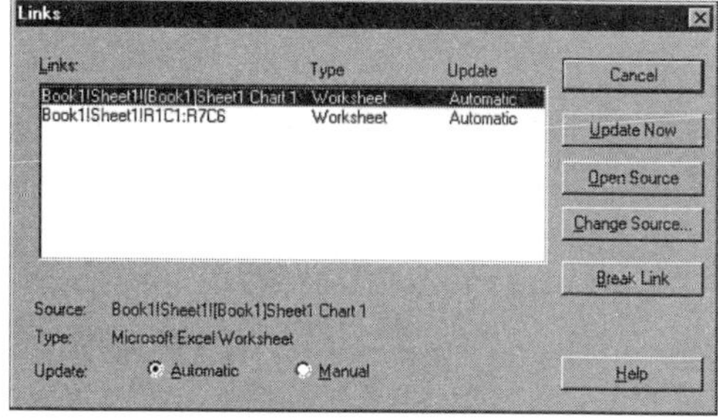

Fig. 10.14

You can modify links from the Links dialog box.

> **Note**
>
> The changes to links detailed in the following sections must be made in Browse mode. Although Approach allows access to the Links dialog box in Design mode, the Links dialog box is empty—no links are displayed. Therefore, to see links between server applications and PicturePlus fields, you must be in Browse mode and in the correct record.

Selecting the Link Status. A link can have one of two possible statuses—Automatic or Manual. These statuses determine how the link behaves when a change is made to the object file to which the PicturePlus field is linked.

If a link is automatic, it's updated when the Approach file is opened. Therefore, if at any time you used the server application to change the file to which the PicturePlus field is linked, the Approach file displays the latest version.

If the server application is open at the same time as Approach, a PicturePlus field with an automatic link displays the changes in the field as you make them in the server application. This occurs even if you don't save the file in the server application after you make changes. If you make changes in the server application and don't save the file, however, an automatic link becomes "out of synch" with the stored file until the next time you open the Approach file—that is, the contents of the PicturePlus field don't reflect the contents of the linked file on disk. This occurs because the PicturePlus field reflects the changes being made in the server application—but those changes weren't saved.

To bring the link back into synch with the stored file without closing and reopening the linked file, choose Update Now in the Links dialog box (see "Updating a Link" later in this chapter).

If a link is set to manual update, it isn't updated when the Approach file is opened. It also doesn't reflect changes made in the server application. To update the link and display the current version of the linked object, choose Update Now in the Links dialog box (see "Updating a Link" later in this chapter).

Setting the Link Status. To set the status of a link, follow these steps:

1. Select the form or report that contains the PicturePlus field for which you built the link.
2. Switch to Browse mode.
3. Click the PicturePlus field that contains the linked object.
4. Open the Edit menu and choose Manage Links. The Links dialog box appears with a list of the links established for objects in the database. Select the object in the chosen PicturePlus field.

5. Choose Automatic (default) or Manual.
6. Click OK.

Updating a Link. You should manually update a link for two reasons:

- To display the latest version of the object file in the PicturePlus field.
- To correct automatic links that get "out of synch" with the object file. This occurs if you make changes with the server application while Approach is open and don't save the changes in the object file.

To update a link so that the PicturePlus field displays the latest version of the object file, follow these steps:

1. Select the form or report that contains the PicturePlus field for which you built a link using the tabs.
2. Switch to Browse mode.
3. Click the PicturePlus field that contains the linked object.
4. Choose Manage Links from the Edit menu. The Links dialog box appears, listing the link for the object in the selected PicturePlus field.
5. Click the link and choose Update Now.
6. Click Close to return to the Approach form or report.

The PicturePlus field displays the latest version of the object file.

Deleting a Link. Approach allows you to break the link between an object and the server application. You can break a link in two ways. In the first method, use the Links dialog box; in the second method, use the Edit menu's Clear command.

To use the Links dialog box, follow these steps:

1. Select the form or report that contains the PicturePlus field for which you built the link.
2. Switch to Browse mode.
3. Click the PicturePlus field that contains the linked object.
4. Open the Edit menu and choose Manage Links. The Links dialog box appears. Click the link for the selected PicturePlus field.
5. Choose Break Link. The link disappears from the Links box.
6. Click OK.

If you break the link between an object file and a PicturePlus field by using the Links dialog box, the object remains in your PicturePlus field as it last appeared. All future changes you make to the file, however, aren't reflected in the contents of the PicturePlus field. You also can no longer edit the object, as described later in the section "Editing a PicturePlus Field Containing a Linked Object."

> **Note**
>
> If the object displays only the icon of the server application that created it, the graphic of the icon continues to be displayed in the PicturePlus field.

To use the Edit menu's Clear command, follow these steps:

1. Select the form or report containing the PicturePlus field for which you built the link.
2. Switch to Browse mode.
3. Click the PicturePlus field on the form or report.
4. Open the Edit menu and choose Clear. The object disappears from the PicturePlus field and the link is deleted.

Changing the Source of a Link. Changing the source of a PicturePlus field lets you specify a new application and file as the source for the PicturePlus field without going through the effort of opening the server application, loading or creating an object file, and using Paste Special from the Edit menu. Further, if you change the name of a linked object file or move it to a new location (for example, to a new directory or drive), Approach can't update the object because it won't be able to find the file. If a link is broken in this manner, you can reconnect it by telling Approach the new location or name for the file (for example, the new link source).

> **Note**
>
> When a link is broken, Approach gives you no warning when you open the Approach file or the form on which the PicturePlus field is located. However, if you try to edit the linked object, Approach gives you an `OLE Server Busy` error message.

To specify a new source, follow these steps:

1. Open the Approach file that contains the link whose source you want to modify.
2. Select the form or report that contains the PicturePlus field with the link whose source you want to modify.
3. Switch to Browse mode.
4. Click the PicturePlus field to select it.
5. Open the Edit menu and choose Manage Links. The Links dialog box appears. Highlight the object.
6. Choose Change Source. The Change Source dialog box appears (see fig. 10.15).

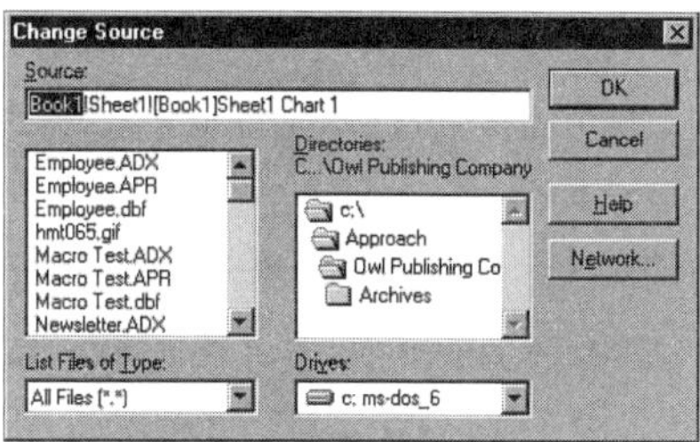

Fig. 10.15

The Change Source dialog box appears when you choose Change Source in the Links dialog box.

7. Select the file name from the list of files on the left side of the dialog box. Use the Directories list box and the Drives drop-down list to locate the object file you need. If necessary, use the List Files of Type drop-down list to display the correct file type.
8. Click OK to return to the Links dialog box.

> **Note**
>
> If you choose an invalid source (for example, a file that has no application associated with it), Approach warns you and gives you the opportunity to choose another source. If you insist on an invalid source, Approach establishes the link, but you can't open the source and edit the linked file. Approach continues to display the graphic from the last valid source.

9. Click the Update Now button if you want to update the PicturePlus field to show the latest version of the file for the reestablished link.
10. Click OK.

Editing a PicturePlus Field Containing a Linked Object. To edit a linked object, use the server application that created the object. You can do this from Approach or from the server application in Windows by opening the application and editing the file, just as you do with any other file created with that application.

To edit a linked object from Approach, follow these steps:

1. Switch to Browse mode.
2. Select the form or report that contains the PicturePlus field for which you built the link.
3. Click the PicturePlus field to select it.
4. From the PicturePlus menu, choose the object you want to edit. For example, to edit a Microsoft Drawing Object, choose Linked Drawing Object from the PicturePlus menu, and choose Edit from the submenu.

   You also can select the Open Source button in the Links dialog box.

> **Note**
>
> For most embedded objects, you also can double-click the PicturePlus field to open the server application. You can't use this technique, however, if you're using any type of embedded sounds or animation. Double-clicking a sound or animation application icon plays the sound or animation; it doesn't open the server application.

5. Use the server application to make the changes you want.
6. Choose Save from the File menu in the server application.
7. Choose Exit from the File menu in the server application. You're returned to Approach.

> **Note**
>
> If the link is an automatic link, the change is immediately displayed in the PicturePlus field. If the link is manual, you must use the Links dialog box to update the PicturePlus field (see "Updating a Link" earlier in this chapter).

Viewing an Embedded or Linked Object in a PicturePlus Field

Some embedded or linked objects display their contents in the PicturePlus field in Approach (see fig. 10.16). Typically, images from applications such as Paint and Draw are visible in the PicturePlus field on the form or report. Other objects, however, display only the icon of the server application that created them (again, see fig. 10.16). These objects include sound files, for which no way really exists to "display" the contents.

To view objects that display the icon of the server application, double-click the PicturePlus field. You also can click the PicturePlus field and select the appropriate menu item (which varies, depending on the type of object) from the PicturePlus menu. For example, if you embed a sound object in a PicturePlus field, you can listen to it by double-clicking the icon in the PicturePlus field, or by selecting the PicturePlus field, choosing Sound Object and then Play from the PicturePlus menu.

Removing an Object from a PicturePlus Field

To remove an object from a PicturePlus field, switch to Browse mode. Click the PicturePlus field, open the Edit menu, and choose Clear.

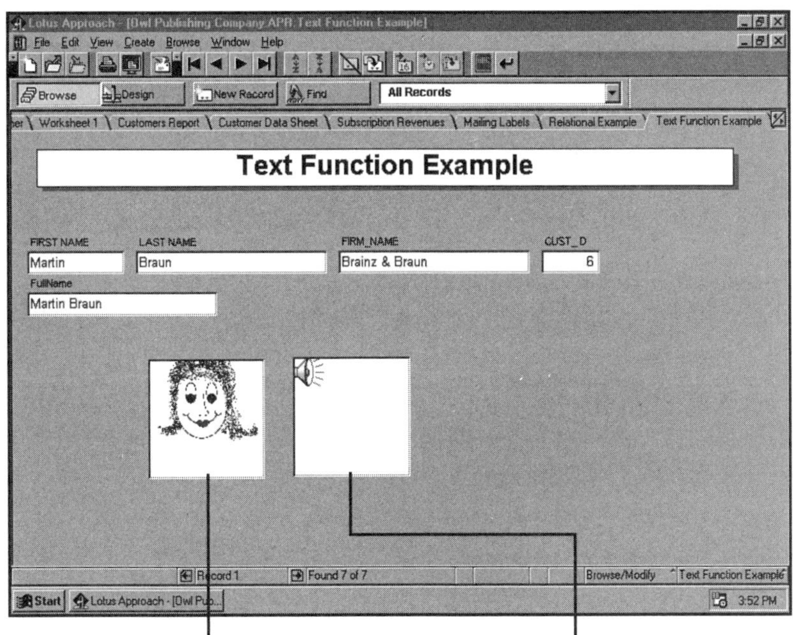

A visible image in a PicturePlus field

An icon image in a PicturePlus field

Fig. 10.16

Some embedded or linked images are usually visible in the PicturePlus field; others display only the icon of the server.

From Here...

Calculated and variable fields allow Approach to provide more information specific to your database. With the great variety of functions available, many tasks that might be difficult if you had to define your own formula become quite easy by using an Approach function.

For another method of including a greater range of information, use the PicturePlus field with linked or embedded objects. These objects can be stored within Approach but used in a variety of creative ways.

For more information on these advanced fields, see the following chapter:

- Chapter 12, "Creating Advanced Reports," shows you how to use calculated fields and variables to add powerful functions to reports.

CHAPTER 11

Performing Advanced Finds

Chapter 6, "Finding Records," discussed Approach's capability to find records that meet certain criteria. Most of the time, the methods discussed in Chapter 6 are sufficient to locate the records you need. In some cases, however, the Find Assistant can be used with more complex criteria. You also can create very powerful searches manually in Find mode, without the aid of the Find Assistant.

In this chapter, you learn how to

- Find records with fields whose contents "sound like" the criteria you typed
- Specify find criteria in a calculated field
- Find records with fields whose contents match the results of an `If()` statement, even if you can't type find criteria into those fields (for example, radio buttons)
- Find records with fields that contain the value in another field
- Find records based on the contents of a field in a related database

Performing a Sounds-Like Find

When searching for a text string, you may not always know exactly how to spell the text that you're looking for. In the Owl Publishing database, for example, you want to find the record for a customer with a first name of John or Jon. Approach lets you perform a "sounds-like" find.

This type of find selects records in which the text string sounds like what you typed in. A find in a STATE field for "Illinoise" would locate any records where the field searched contains the correctly spelled Illinois, and also any records with phonetically similar misspellings ("Illinoise"), such as the one used for the find criterion.

To perform a sounds-like find, follow these steps:

1. Switch to Browse mode.
2. Select the form or report you want to work with from the tabs or the status bar. For the Owl Publishing example, select the Customer form.

3. Click the Find button on the action bar; open the Browse menu and choose Find; or select Find from the status bar.
4. Select the desired field. For this example, select the FIRST NAME field.
5. Type ~ (tilde) in the find field or click the Sounds Like SmartIcon, and then enter the text that sounds like your find field. For this example, type **~Jon** (see fig. 11.1).

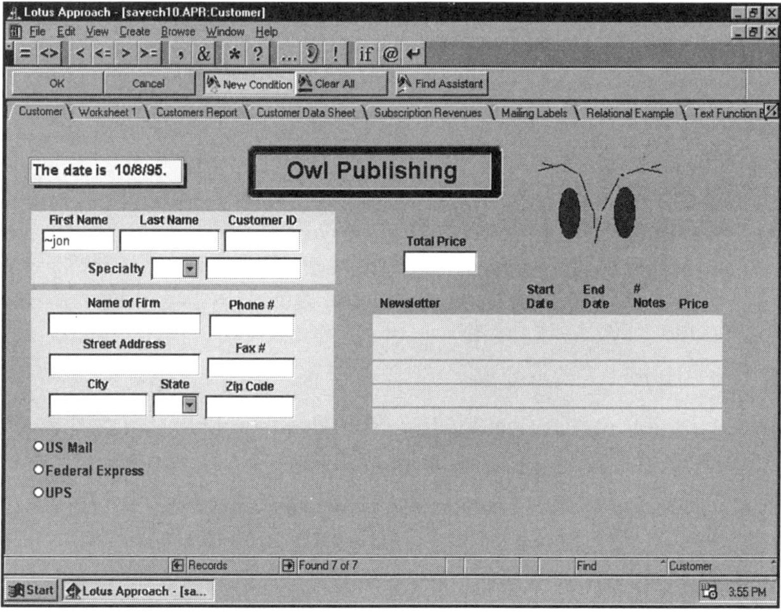

Fig. 11.1

A "sounds-like" find is performed on the FIRST NAME field.

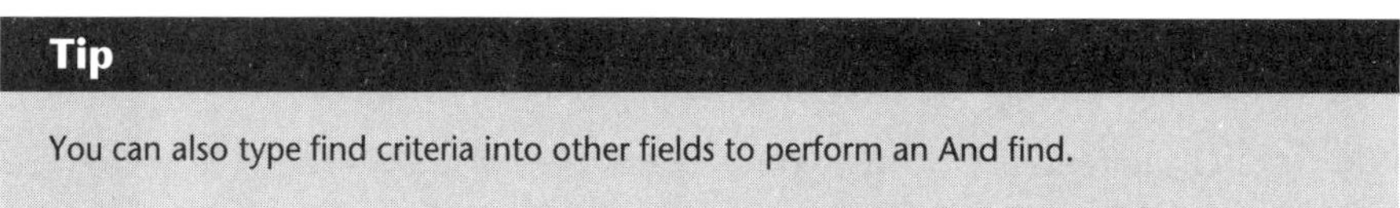
Tip

You can also type find criteria into other fields to perform an And find.

6. Click OK or press Enter. The record for John Roberts appears.

Finding on a Calculated Field

Calculated fields return the result of a calculation that you define when you create the field. Although you can't type a value into a calculated field in Browse mode, you can type find criteria into a calculated field.

By running a find on a calculated field, you can find values you may not be able to locate with Approach's standard find functions. For example, to find all records in which the combination of the first and last names exceeds a certain length would be very difficult using Approach's standard find functions. With a calculated field, however, you can create a formula using the `Length()` and `Combine()` functions to calculate the length of the combination of the two strings. This calculation could be handy for locating records for which you must use a larger mailing label. Use the following formula when defining the calculated field:

```
Length(Combine(FIRST NAME,LAST NAME))
```

With this calculated field, the find is simple to perform. For the find criterion, specify a number greater than the length you desire. If you want to find all combinations of the first- and last-name strings greater than 40 characters, for example, type **>40** in the calculated field.

Entering Criteria in Calculated Fields

Criteria entered in calculated fields are subject to the same rules as criteria entered in other types of fields. Thus, criteria entered in calculated fields can

- Reference constants and field values
- Use comparison operators (<, >, <>, >=, <=)
- Include a range of values
- Be case-sensitive
- Include wild cards
- Search for an exact match (=)
- Join multiple criteria
- Separate multiple criteria. Approach finds all records in which the value in the calculated field matches any of the criteria (an Or query).

Entering Find Criteria in a Calculated Field

To enter find criteria in a calculated field, follow these steps:

1. Switch to Browse mode.
2. Select the form or report you want to work with by using the view tabs or the status bar.
3. Click the Find button on the action bar; open the Browse menu and choose Find; or select Find from the status bar.
4. Type the criterion in the calculated field. You can also type your find criteria into other fields to perform an And find, or add additional find requests for an Or find.
5. Click OK or press Enter.

Using a Formula in a Find

You can use the Find Assistant to build a formula into any field during a find, or you can include a formula in a manual find. Approach compares the contents of the field with the result of the formula. If the comparison is true, the record is included in the found set.

> **Note**
>
> A formula used in a find must be preceded by a comparison operator (=, <, >, >=, <=, or <>) and the @ symbol.

Using Items to Build the Formula Find Manually

You can reference only the following items in a formula find:

Field names	Arithmetic operators
Functions	Constants

Field Names. The formula can reference other fields in the Approach file. Approach uses the value contained in the referenced field when it evaluates the formula. For example, if a variable field called REGION VARIABLE contained the value North, doing a find in the database field REGION for REGION VARIABLE would return a found set of all records where the REGION field matched North, the current value in the variable field. You might use this capability to allow the user to enter his find criteria on a special form you use just for finds. This special "find form" might contain just the variable field for the user to enter what he wants to search for. You then can run a macro that uses the contents of the field in a find.

Functions. You can include many of Approach's functions in formulas. Certain functions aren't appropriate, however, because they don't return a value. An example is the `Fill()` function, which fills one string, or group of text characters, with the contents of another string.

A common find performed with a function is `=@Today()` in a field that contains date values. This finds any records where the field used in the find contains today's date.

Arithmetic Operators. You can perform arithmetic operations as part of the formula. However, you can't use the multiplication operator (*) because Approach interprets it as the wild-card find symbol rather than as the multiplication operator. Because the formula already contains a comparison operator—the one needed at the beginning of the find—you can't include any other find operators in the formula. A find criterion can contain only one find operator.

An example of this could be a product-inventory system. To find records where the field containing the stock level, STOCK, is at least five units over the minimum stocking level stored in a second field named STOCK Minimum, you could do a find on

STOCK for `>@STOCK Minimum+5`. All records in the found set would be at a stock level at least five units above the minimum level.

> **Note**
>
> To search for a value in a field whose contents must match the result of a formula that includes a multiplication operation, you can compare the contents of the field to the contents of a calculated field that contains the formula (see "Searching for the Value in Another Field" later in this chapter).

Constants. You can include constants as part of the formula. When entering a formula, follow these rules:

- Enclose text-string constants in single quotation marks (for example, *'Approach'*).
- Type date constants in the order month/day/year, separated by slashes (for example, *03/12/56*).
- Type time constants in the order of hours, minutes, seconds, and hundredths of seconds. Separate hours, minutes, and seconds with a colon (:). Separate seconds and hundredths of seconds with a decimal point (for example, *12:25:00.45*).
- Type Boolean constants as 'Yes' or 'No' (enclosed in single quotation marks), or use the numbers 1 or 0.
- Don't type numeric constants in scientific notation.

Creating a Formula for a Find

To create a formula find, follow these steps:

1. Switch to Browse mode.
2. Select the form or report you want to work with by using the view tabs or the status bar.
3. Click the Find button on the action bar; open the Browse menu and choose Find; or select Find from the status bar.
4. Select the field for which you want to specify the find criteria.
5. Type the comparison operator followed by the `@` symbol (for example, type `<@` for a less-than comparison). Type the rest of the formula you want to use.
6. Click the OK button on the action bar or press Enter.

You can use the following example formulas in finds:

- To determine whether a field contains the current date, use `=@Today()`.
- To determine whether a field contains a date that's more than 30 days old, use `<@Today()-30`.
- To determine whether a field contains the name of the month given contained in the SUB START field, use `=@Monthname("SUB START")`.

- To determine whether a field other than LAST NAME contains the first letter in the LAST NAME field, use `=@Left("LAST NAME",1)`.
- If the FULL NAME field contains the first and last names separated by a space, use the following formula to determine whether a field contains the last name portion of the FULL NAME field:

  ```
  =@Right("Full Name", Length("Full Name") - Position("Full Name",' ',1))
  ```

- To determine whether a field is greater than or equal to the sum of a number and the contents of the numeric field NUMBER, use `>=@(75+Number)`.
- If the contents of the TextDate field is a text string in a date format, use the formula `<@TextToDate(TextDate)` to determine whether another date field contains a date less than the "date" in TextDate.

Searching for the Value in Another Field

You can enter criteria in a find field that compares the contents of the field with the contents of another field. The fields can be of any type except PicturePlus.

To construct the find, type a comparison operator and the name of the compared-to field into the find field. You can use any of the following comparison operators:

- Equal (=)
- Greater than (>)
- Less than (<)
- Greater than or equal (>=)
- Less than or equal (<=)
- Not equal (<>)

The found set returns all records in which the criterion evaluates to true.

By using a calculated field as the compared-to field, Approach allows you to compare the contents of the find field with the result of a formula. Follow these steps:

1. Add a calculated field containing the formula to the database (see Chapter 10, "Using Advanced Field Types").
2. Place the calculated field on the form. Now you're ready to specify the comparison between the find field and the calculated field.
3. Switch to Browse mode. To save this new calculated field, save the form by opening the File menu and choosing Save Approach File.
4. Select the form or report you want to work with by using the view tabs or the status bar.
5. Switch to Find mode by opening the Browse menu and choosing Find; clicking the Find button on the action bar; or selecting Find from the status bar.
6. Select the field for which you want to specify the find criteria.

7. Type the comparison operator followed by the @ symbol (for example, type =@ for an equals comparison).

> **Note**
>
> Without the @ symbol, Approach finds the field name rather than the field's contents for an exact match on a text string.

8. Type the name of the field whose contents you want to compare to the find field (see fig. 11.2). If you're comparing the contents of the find field to a calculated field, type the name of the calculated field.

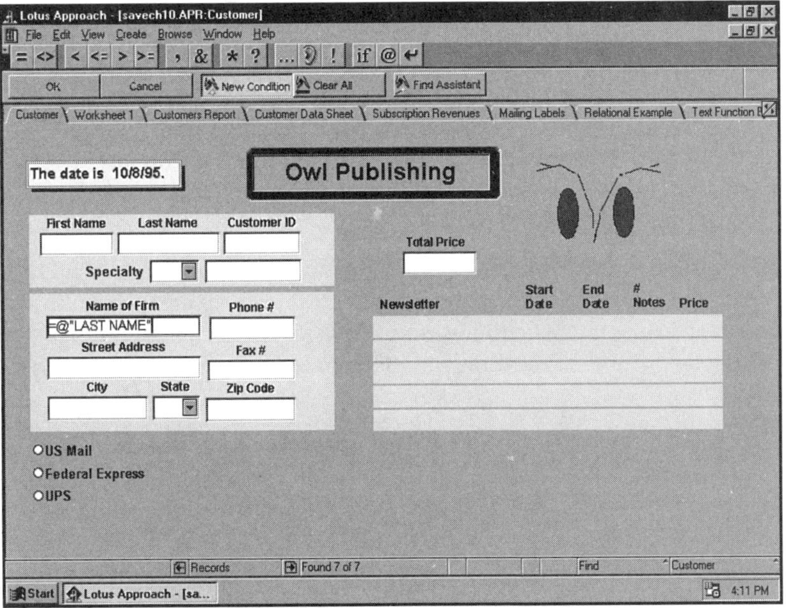

Fig. 11.2

Use =@ to find records in which one field contains the value in another field.

9. Click the OK button or press Enter.

You can also compare the contents of the find field to a formula by entering the formula into the field during the find (see "Creating a Formula for a Find" earlier in this chapter). Formulas entered directly into a field during a find, however, can't include the multiplication operator (*).

Using the *If()* Function in a Find

You can use the `If()` function in a find to retrieve all records in which the expression in the `If()` statement evaluates as true. To do so, type the `If()` function into any field on the form that accepts typed text during a find.

> **Note**
>
> You don't need to include in the expression the field into which you type the `If()` function. If you type `If("LAST NAME">='P')` into the First Name field, for example, all records in which the last name starts with any letter from P to Z are returned in the found set.

By using `If()` in a find, you can build complex criteria and perform finds you can't perform by using Approach's other find functions.

Using Items in an *If()* Expression

The expression in an `If()` statement can contain any of the following items, as explained in the next few sections:

Field names	Constants
Functions	Comparison operators
Arithmetic operators	Boolean operators

Field Names. Approach uses the value contained in the field when it evaluates the expression. For example, `If("LAST NAME"='Smith')` would return a found set where the LAST NAME field contained *Smith*.

Functions. Approach has 84 functions that perform various operations on text and numeric values. The value on which a function operates (called a *parameter*) can be a field value or a constant value. If a function uses multiple parameters, use commas to separate the parameters. Connect multiple functions in the same clause with And and Or.

Arithmetic Operators. The expression may contain the division (/), addition (+), and subtraction (–) arithmetic operators. An `If()` expression can't use the multiplication operator (*), however, because Approach interprets the asterisk as the wild-card find operator (see the workaround using calculated fields earlier in this chapter). Approach evaluates the arithmetic operations in the expression in a specific order:

- The division (/) operation is evaluated first.
- Addition (+) and subtraction (–) operations are evaluated second.
- If any operations are on the same evaluation level (such as addition and subtraction), they're evaluated from left to right in the formula.

You can modify the evaluation order of arithmetic operators by enclosing in parentheses the operation that you want performed first. Approach always evaluates the contents of parentheses before evaluating other parts of the formula. Within a set of parentheses, the evaluation order is as described in the preceding bulleted list.

To demonstrate this, consider the following two finds, again using Stock and Stock Minimum. The find `If(Stock Minimum=(Stock+5)/2)` would find all records where the minimum stocking level equals half of the sum of the quantity in the current stocking level plus five units. The find `If(Stock Minimum=Stock+5/2)` would find all records where the minimum stocking level equals the current stocking level plus 2 1/2 units.

Constants. You can use constants as part of the formula. Follow these rules:

- Enclose text string constants in single quotation marks (for example, *'Approach'*).
- Type date constants in the order month/day/year, separated by slashes (for example, *03/12/56*).
- Type time constants in the order of hours, minutes, seconds, and hundredths of seconds. Separate hours, minutes, and seconds with a colon (:). Separate seconds and hundredths of seconds with a decimal point (for example, *12:25:00.45*).
- Type Boolean constants as 'Yes' or 'No', with single quotation marks enclosing them, or the numbers 1 or 0.
- Don't type numeric constants in scientific notation.

Comparison Operators. Use comparison operators to compare two values or fields. The comparison operators are `=`, `>`, `<`, `<>`, `>=`, and `<=`.

Perhaps you're doing a company mailing and need to search for records within a range of ZIP codes, described by the first three digits of the ZIP code. This find can be done with an `If()` find and the `Left()` function. The find `If(LEFT(Zip,3)='940')`, for example, would return a found set of all records where the first three digits of the value stored in the ZIP field matched the find criteria, 940.

Boolean Operators. You can connect clauses in the `If()` statement with the And and Or Boolean operators, as follows:

- In an And clause, the clause evaluates as true when both sides of the And are true (for example, `5<6 And 'B'>'A'`).
- In an Or clause, the clause evaluates as true when either side (or both sides) of the Or are true (for example, `5>6 Or 'B'>'A'`).

Creating a Find Using the *If()* Function

To create a find using the `If()` function, follow these steps:

1. Switch to Find mode by opening the Browse menu and choosing Find; clicking the Find button on the action bar; or selecting Find from the status bar.
2. Select the form or report you want to work with using the view tabs or the status bar.
3. Select the field into which you want to type the `If()` expression.
4. Type the expression into the field (see fig. 11.3). You can also type find criteria into other fields to perform an And find, or add additional find requests for an Or find.

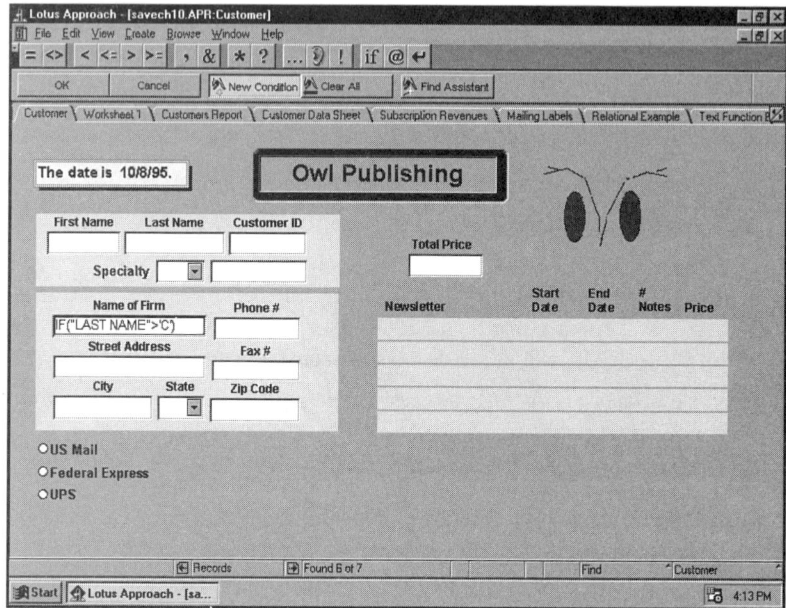

Fig. 11.3

You can put an `If()` *expression in any field that will accept text, such as the Name of Firm text box, even if that field isn't otherwise involved in the current find.*

5. Press Enter or click the OK button.

Using the *If()* Function to Perform More Complicated Finds

The `If()` function often can duplicate other find techniques. You can type a comparison formula such as **`If("LAST NAME">'P')`** into a field. Of course, you can perform the same operation by simply typing **`>P`** into the LAST NAME field. With the `If()` function, you can perform finds that can't be done with the normal find functions, however, as the following sections explain.

Using *If()* for Finds on Drop-Down Lists, Check Boxes, and Radio Buttons. One limit of Approach's "normal" find functions is that you can't type criteria into fields that don't accept typed text (that is, check boxes and radio-button fields). Standard finds that involve these field types are limited to a single value unless you resort to multiple finds (Find Mores). You can select a single value in a drop-down list field, for example, to find all records in which the field contains the value. Because a drop-down list field can't accept typed text, however, you can't specify multiple values (for example, all records in which the SPECIALTY field contains ED or RM).

You can type an `If()` function into any field on a form that accepts typed text. Thus, the `If()` function allows you to specify a find criteria for these types of fields that do include multiple values.

Now return to the fictitious company for a moment. Owl Publishing wants to find all the records in which UPS or Federal Express is used to send out renewal notices. Because these are buttons, you can't simply type the two values into the MAIL TYPE field. Instead, you can use an `If()` find, as follows:

1. Switch to Find mode by opening the Browse menu and choosing Find; clicking the Find button on the action bar; or selecting Find from the status bar.
2. Select the Customer form from the view tabs or the status bar.
3. Select the STREET ADR field.
4. Type **`If("MAIL TYPE"='UPS' OR "MAIL TYPE"='US Mail' OR "MAIL TYPE"='Federal Express')`** (see fig. 11.4).

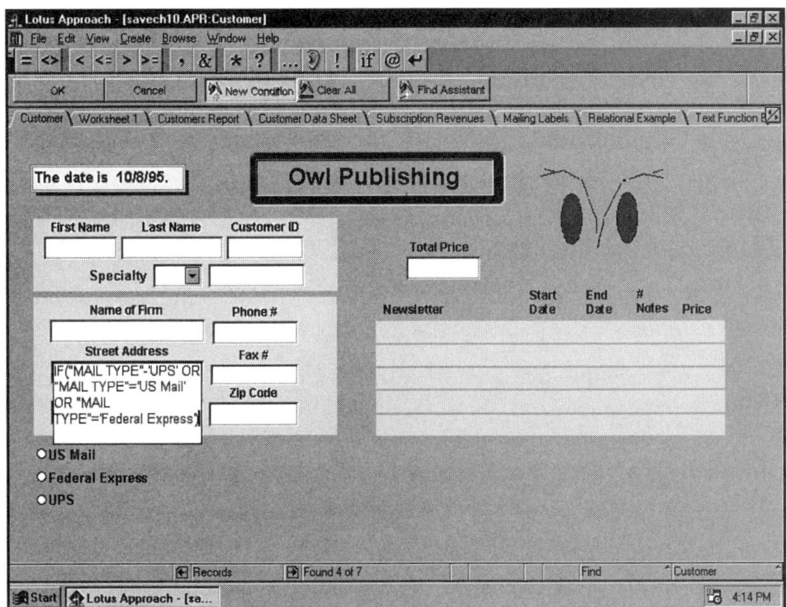

Fig. 11.4

Finding multiple values of a radio-button field is only possible if you use an `If()` *statement.*

5. Press Enter. All records with UPS, US Mail, or Federal Express are returned in the found set.

Using *If( )* to Compare the Values in Two Fields. Use the `If()` function to compare the contents of two fields, as shown below:

```
If(SALES92<SALES91)
```

This formula returns all records in which the value in the field SALES92 is less than the value in the field SALES91.

Using *If( )* to Evaluate a Formula. You can use the `If()` function to evaluate a complex formula. For example, to evaluate whether the result in the SUB END date is within 90 days of the current date, use

```
If ("SUB END"-Today()<=90)
```

The formula may contain many functions and multiple clauses connected by And and Or operators. If, for example, you want to see all records in which more than 90 days have passed since the date in INVOICEDATE, and a customer owes you money (BALANCEDUE is greater than zero), use

```
If (((InvoiceDate-Today())>90) And (BalanceDue>0))
```

Using *If( )* on a Field Not Displayed on the Current Form. You can use the `If()` function to find records where fields contain a matching criterion, even if that field isn't displayed on the current form. In mailing labels, for instance, you may not display the SPECIALTY field. You can find all records in which the SPECIALTY field includes the value RM from this field, however, by using the following formula in the STREET ADR (or any other text-type) field:

```
If(SPECIALTY='RM')
```

Finding on a Field in a Related Database

Forms and reports can include fields from related databases. These fields appear in the main body of the form/report or in a repeating panel (only on a form).

You can perform a find on a field in a related database as easily as you can perform a find on a field from the main database. As with fields from the main database, to perform a find, type your criteria into the fields from the related database. All the same find limits and capabilities apply to this type of find (see "Entering Criteria in Calculated Fields" earlier in this chapter). Multiple-field And finds can include related fields.

Exactly what the find returns depends on whether you type the find criteria into a related field in the main body of the form or report or into a repeating panel:

- If the related field is located in the main body of the form or report, the found set includes all records that match the criteria of the find. If a repeating panel is also in use, all related records in the repeating panel are returned as well.
- If the related field is located in a repeating panel and if the contents of the find field in any record in the repeating panel match the criteria, the found set contains the main record and the matching record from the repeating panel (see figs. 11.5 and 11.6).

Performing Finds in an Approach File with Related Files

When you use an Approach file that has related files, the find creates a found set within the database that the current form or report is based on. If you switch to a different form or report based on the same file, you'll still have the found set. If you switch to a form or report that's based on a different database, however, the data returns to an "unfound" state—that is, all records in the database on which the form or report is based are available.

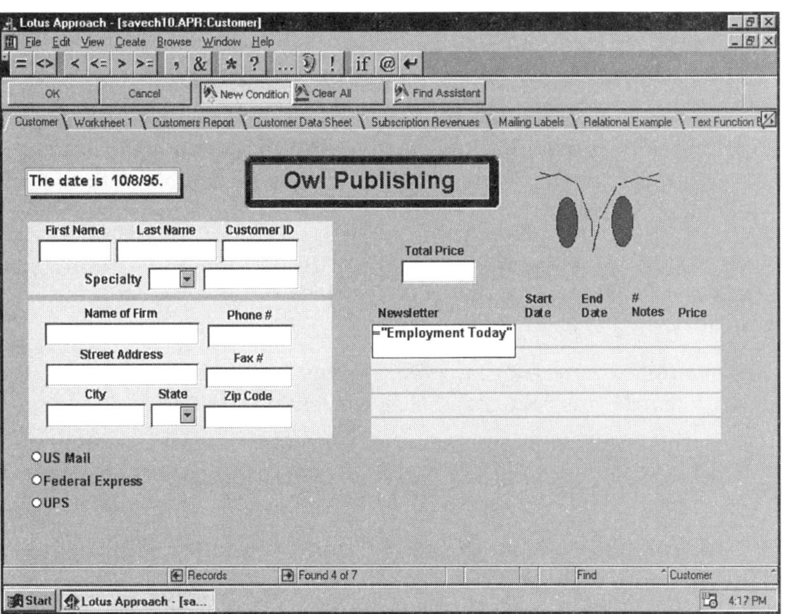

Fig. 11.5

Putting the Find criteria in the repeating panel will find all customers that have a newsletter subscription record that's for Employment Today.

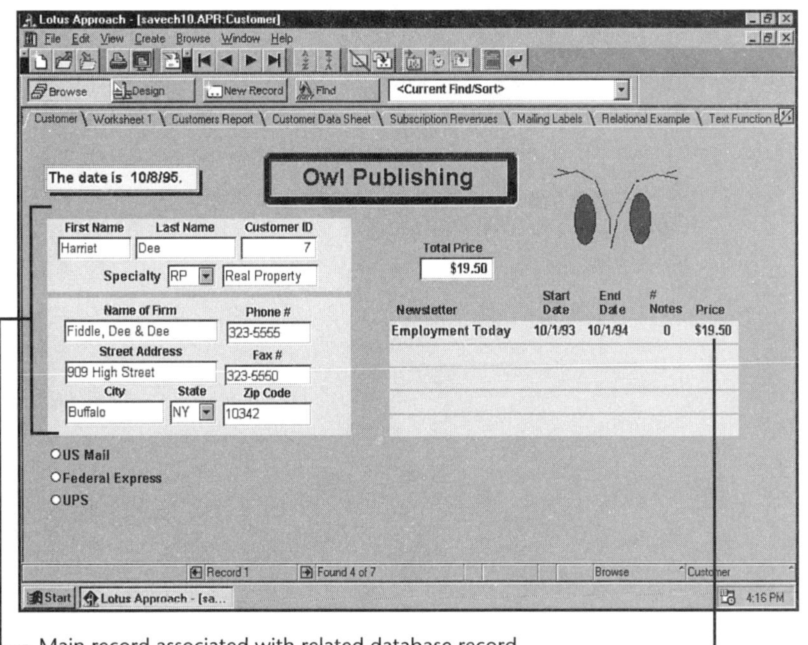

Fig. 11.6

The Find criteria returns the first main record and a matching related record with the other three matches available by using the Page Up and Page Down keys.

From Here...

As you've seen, Approach allows you to search for records using complex and powerful find criteria. The techniques covered in this chapter include finds with formulas, finds using the `If()` function, and doing a find with multiple criteria for a field that can't use standard text input. And, as before, these criteria can be combined further to create powerful And and Or finds.

After you know how to create complex finds, it's important to present the found information in reports, as well as show the results in crosstabs and graphs. For more information, see the following chapters in this book:

- Chapter 12, "Creating Advanced Reports," shows you how to create reports that include summary panels, use calculated fields, and build form letters.
- Chapter 13, "Automating Your Work," shows you how to create macros that use finds. With a macro, you can use predefined find criteria with the click of the mouse.
- Chapter 14, "Using Worksheets and Crosstabs," shows you how to display the results of a find in a worksheet or a crosstab report.
- Chapter 15, "Creating Charts," shows you how to display the results of a find in a variety of chart styles.

BARNES & NOBLE

STORE 2541 SPRINGFIELD, MO 417-883-2440

REG#02 BOOKSELLER#099
RECEIPT# 22529 08/25/97 2:38 PM

CUSTOMER COPY

S 0789702088 SE USING LOTUS APPROACH
1 @ 39.99 39.99

SUBTOTAL 39.99
SALES TAX - 6.1% 2.44
TOTAL 42.43
VISA PAYMENT 42.43
ACCOUNT# 4734290019823444 EXP 0599
AUTHORIZATION# 004393 CLERK 99

BOOKSELLERS SINCE 1873

stocking level plus five units. The find `If(Stock Minimum=Stock+5/2)` would find all records where the minimum stocking level equals the current stocking level plus 2 1/2 units.

Constants. You can use constants as part of the formula. Follow these rules:

- Enclose text string constants in single quotation marks (for example, *'Approach'*).
- Type date constants in the order month/day/year, separated by slashes (for example, *03/12/56*).
- Type time constants in the order of hours, minutes, seconds, and hundredths of seconds. Separate hours, minutes, and seconds with a colon (:). Separate seconds and hundredths of seconds with a decimal point (for example, *12:25:00.45*).
- Type Boolean constants as 'Yes' or 'No', with single quotation marks enclosing them, or the numbers 1 or 0.
- Don't type numeric constants in scientific notation.

Comparison Operators. Use comparison operators to compare two values or fields. The comparison operators are =, >, <, <>, >=, and <=.

Perhaps you're doing a company mailing and need to search for records within a range of ZIP codes, described by the first three digits of the ZIP code. This find can be done with an `If()` find and the `Left()` function. The find `If(LEFT(Zip,3)='940')`, for example, would return a found set of all records where the first three digits of the value stored in the ZIP field matched the find criteria, 940.

Boolean Operators. You can connect clauses in the `If()` statement with the And and Or Boolean operators, as follows:

- In an And clause, the clause evaluates as true when both sides of the And are true (for example, `5<6 And 'B'>'A'`).
- In an Or clause, the clause evaluates as true when either side (or both sides) of the Or are true (for example, `5>6 Or 'B'>'A'`).

Creating a Find Using the *If()* Function

To create a find using the `If()` function, follow these steps:

1. Switch to Find mode by opening the Browse menu and choosing Find; clicking the Find button on the action bar; or selecting Find from the status bar.
2. Select the form or report you want to work with using the view tabs or the status bar.
3. Select the field into which you want to type the `If()` expression.
4. Type the expression into the field (see fig. 11.3). You can also type find criteria into other fields to perform an And find, or add additional find requests for an Or find.

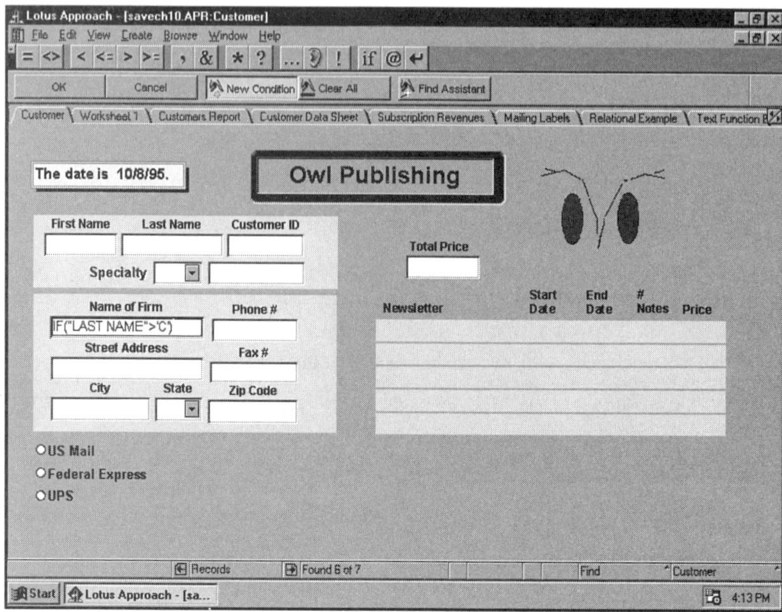

Fig. 11.3

You can put an `If()` *expression in any field that will accept text, such as the Name of Firm text box, even if that field isn't otherwise involved in the current find.*

5. Press Enter or click the OK button.

Using the *If()* Function to Perform More Complicated Finds

The `If()` function often can duplicate other find techniques. You can type a comparison formula such as **`If("LAST NAME">'P')`** into a field. Of course, you can perform the same operation by simply typing **`>P`** into the LAST NAME field. With the `If()` function, you can perform finds that can't be done with the normal find functions, however, as the following sections explain.

Using *If()* for Finds on Drop-Down Lists, Check Boxes, and Radio Buttons. One limit of Approach's "normal" find functions is that you can't type criteria into fields that don't accept typed text (that is, check boxes and radio-button fields). Standard finds that involve these field types are limited to a single value unless you resort to multiple finds (Find Mores). You can select a single value in a drop-down list field, for example, to find all records in which the field contains the value. Because a drop-down list field can't accept typed text, however, you can't specify multiple values (for example, all records in which the SPECIALTY field contains ED or RM).

You can type an `If()` function into any field on a form that accepts typed text. Thus, the `If()` function allows you to specify a find criteria for these types of fields that do include multiple values.

Now return to the fictitious company for a moment. Owl Publishing wants to find all the records in which UPS or Federal Express is used to send out renewal notices. Because these are buttons, you can't simply type the two values into the MAIL TYPE field. Instead, you can use an `If()` find, as follows:

1. Switch to Find mode by opening the Browse menu and choosing Find; clicking the Find button on the action bar; or selecting Find from the status bar.
2. Select the Customer form from the view tabs or the status bar.
3. Select the STREET ADR field.
4. Type **`If("MAIL TYPE"='UPS' OR "MAIL TYPE"='US Mail' OR "MAIL TYPE"='Federal Express')`** (see fig. 11.4).

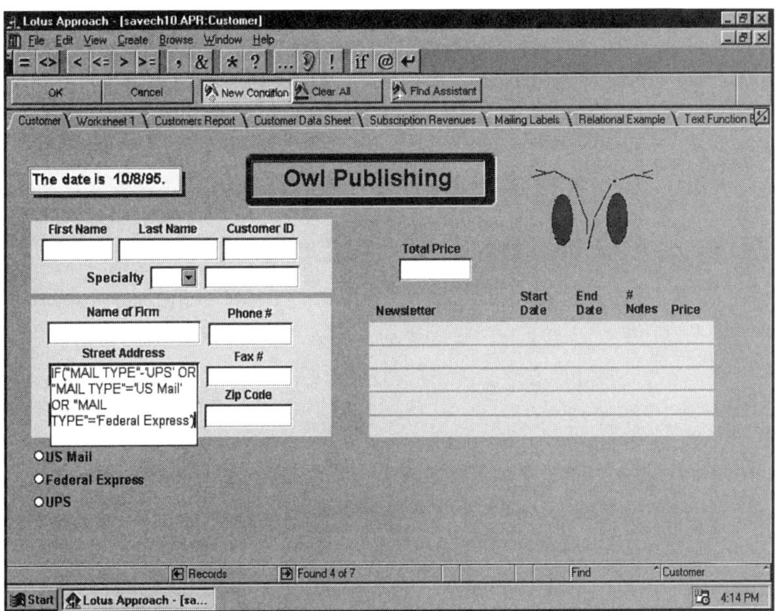

Fig. 11.4

Finding multiple values of a radio-button field is only possible if you use an `If()` *statement.*

5. Press Enter. All records with UPS, US Mail, or Federal Express are returned in the found set.

Using *If( )* to Compare the Values in Two Fields. Use the `If()` function to compare the contents of two fields, as shown below:

```
If(SALES92<SALES91)
```

This formula returns all records in which the value in the field SALES92 is less than the value in the field SALES91.

Using *If( )* to Evaluate a Formula. You can use the `If()` function to evaluate a complex formula. For example, to evaluate whether the result in the SUB END date is within 90 days of the current date, use

```
If ("SUB END"-Today()<=90)
```

The formula may contain many functions and multiple clauses connected by And and Or operators. If, for example, you want to see all records in which more than 90 days have passed since the date in INVOICEDATE, and a customer owes you money (BALANCEDUE is greater than zero), use

```
If (((InvoiceDate-Today())>90) And (BalanceDue>0))
```

Using *If( )* on a Field Not Displayed on the Current Form. You can use the `If()` function to find records where fields contain a matching criterion, even if that field isn't displayed on the current form. In mailing labels, for instance, you may not display the SPECIALTY field. You can find all records in which the SPECIALTY field includes the value RM from this field, however, by using the following formula in the STREET ADR (or any other text-type) field:

```
If(SPECIALTY='RM')
```

Finding on a Field in a Related Database

Forms and reports can include fields from related databases. These fields appear in the main body of the form/report or in a repeating panel (only on a form).

You can perform a find on a field in a related database as easily as you can perform a find on a field from the main database. As with fields from the main database, to perform a find, type your criteria into the fields from the related database. All the same find limits and capabilities apply to this type of find (see "Entering Criteria in Calculated Fields" earlier in this chapter). Multiple-field And finds can include related fields.

Exactly what the find returns depends on whether you type the find criteria into a related field in the main body of the form or report or into a repeating panel:

- If the related field is located in the main body of the form or report, the found set includes all records that match the criteria of the find. If a repeating panel is also in use, all related records in the repeating panel are returned as well.
- If the related field is located in a repeating panel and if the contents of the find field in any record in the repeating panel match the criteria, the found set contains the main record and the matching record from the repeating panel (see figs. 11.5 and 11.6).

Performing Finds in an Approach File with Related Files

When you use an Approach file that has related files, the find creates a found set within the database that the current form or report is based on. If you switch to a different form or report based on the same file, you'll still have the found set. If you switch to a form or report that's based on a different database, however, the data returns to an "unfound" state—that is, all records in the database on which the form or report is based are available.

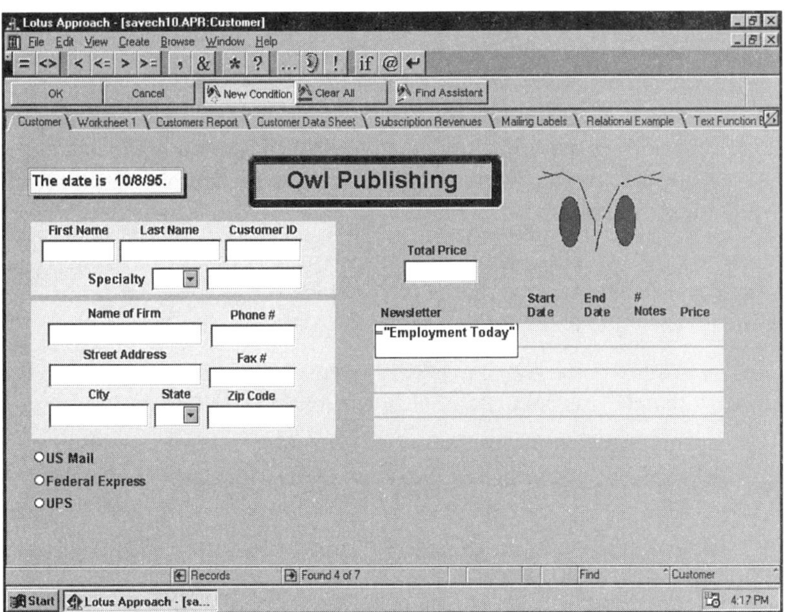

Fig. 11.5

Putting the Find criteria in the repeating panel will find all customers that have a newsletter subscription record that's for Employment Today.

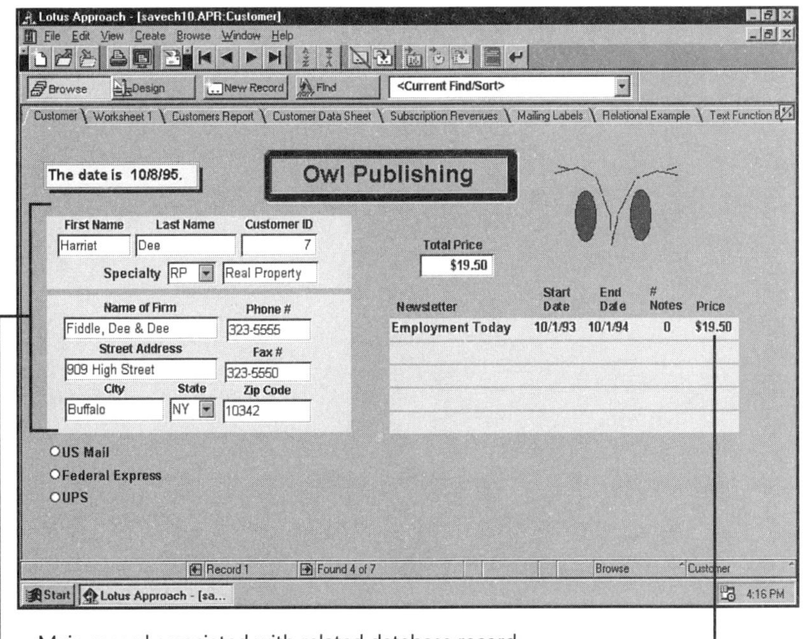

Main record associated with related database record

Record in related database returned by find

Fig. 11.6

The Find criteria returns the first main record and a matching related record with the other three matches available by using the Page Up and Page Down keys.

From Here...

As you've seen, Approach allows you to search for records using complex and powerful find criteria. The techniques covered in this chapter include finds with formulas, finds using the `If()` function, and doing a find with multiple criteria for a field that can't use standard text input. And, as before, these criteria can be combined further to create powerful And and Or finds.

After you know how to create complex finds, it's important to present the found information in reports, as well as show the results in crosstabs and graphs. For more information, see the following chapters in this book:

- Chapter 12, "Creating Advanced Reports," shows you how to create reports that include summary panels, use calculated fields, and build form letters.
- Chapter 13, "Automating Your Work," shows you how to create macros that use finds. With a macro, you can use predefined find criteria with the click of the mouse.
- Chapter 14, "Using Worksheets and Crosstabs," shows you how to display the results of a find in a worksheet or a crosstab report.
- Chapter 15, "Creating Charts," shows you how to display the results of a find in a variety of chart styles.

CHAPTER 12

Creating Advanced Reports

In Chapter 7, "Creating Reports and Mailing Labels," you learned how to print detailed records in standard or column format. In this chapter, you'll discover how you can use additional reporting features and calculations to organize and analyze your data.

In addition to reports, another type of view that's often printed is form letters. With the Approach Form Letter Assistant, you can quickly and easily create letters that include fields from your database.

In this chapter, you learn how to

- Create summary reports
- Create a Repeating Panel report
- Use PowerClick reporting to modify reports
- Add summary calculations to a report
- Modify the attributes of a report panel or object
- Create, edit, and print form letters

Understanding Summary Reports

The reports created in Chapter 7, "Creating Reports and Mailing Labels," were composed of different parts, or panels. The section that contains the fields displayed for each record is called the *body panel*. Also, the report can have a header, footer, or both.

Another panel that's available for use in reporting is called a *summary panel*. The summary panel is used to create various groupings of the data in the report.

> **Note**
>
> A summary panel is different from a body panel in that you can see a summary panel only in Print Preview or Design mode. If the report includes body and summary panels, you can see only the body panel in Browse mode.
>
> You can set Approach to display report summaries by default whenever you go to a report view. From the File menu choose User Setup, Approach Preferences, and the Display page. Then select Report summaries.

Summary panels, like body panels, can display field data. Generally, they aren't used to display all data in a record. Instead, summary panels often contain information specific to the current group. In the Owl Publishing database, for example, you might group the newsletter subscribers by state, using the summary panel to separate each state grouping. Because the current group's state would be the same for each record in the group, it can be displayed in the summary panel rather than in each record's individual body panel.

Summary panels are also used to display summary calculations. A *summary calculation* is a special calculation type that gives a value over a group of records or all records in a database. For example, in the Owl Publishing database you know which customers receive which newsletters, and you know the newsletters' subscription prices. You can create a summary calculation based on these customers' records that displays the total amount collected from all newsletter subscriptions.

If your report has a summary group based on a field value, such as a grouping by state, you can display the same summary calculated field you used for the grand total in the group panel. In this case, though, the value displayed in each state grouping would be the total amount collected for all newsletters in that state. Of course, the report can have a grouping by state and a grand total (see fig. 12.1).

You can set a summary panel to be displayed before (as a leading panel) or after (as a trailing panel) the records it's grouping. To display information before and after the group, you can define two panels for the same group—one leading and one trailing, as shown in figure 12.1. You can also define a panel to appear to the left or right of a detail record, rather than above or below, but this is less common. A report can have up to eight different summary panels.

You can set a summary panel to add a page break. For instance, there might be a new page after every trailing summary grouping by state. The page break occurs before a leading summary panel or after a trailing summary.

Three types of summary groupings are available:

- *All records.* This grouping creates a grand summary for whatever database is used for the report. For example, an all-records grouping might be used to show a sales total for a database based on the year's sales records.

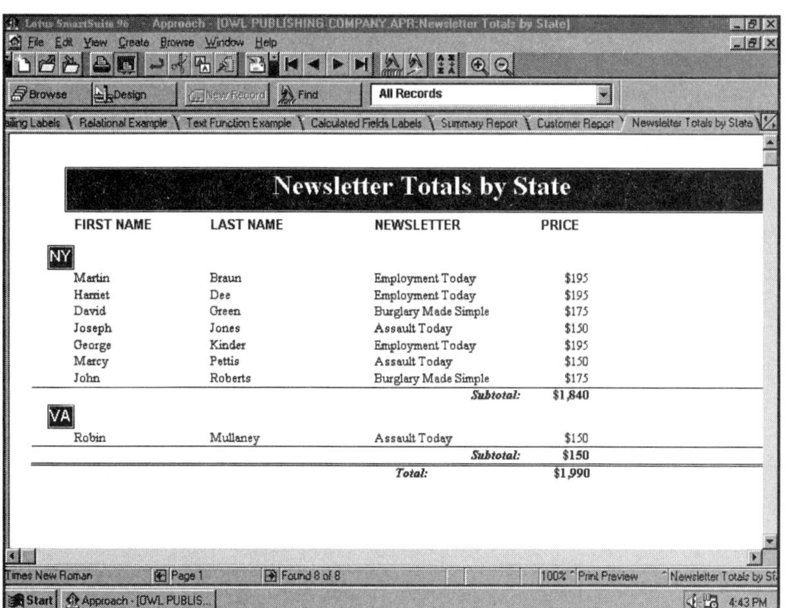

Fig. 12.1

This report shows newsletter customers grouped by state with a leading summary panel identifying the state, a trailing summary subtotal by state, and a grand total.

- *Records grouped by field content.* This grouping, one of the most common uses of a summary panel, allows you to group detail records by distinct values in a field. For example, you might group sales records by region to display regional totals, or you might group customers by ZIP code for a bulk mailing.

  New in Approach 96 is the ability to group records based on partial text field content or in numeric or date ranges when using the Report Assistant. This way, you can further subdivide ZIP codes or group records by quarter of the year, for example.

- *Every certain number of records.* This grouping displays a summary panel after a certain number of records. The number of records is set by the user. You might want to total every page or every 10 records, for example.

Creating Advanced Reports with the Report Assistant

The Report Assistant lists several different predefined report types. In Chapter 7, "Creating Reports and Mailing Labels," you used the Report Assistant to create blank, standard, and columnar reports. The remaining report types use summary panels. They can have—but don't necessarily include—a body panel. You can use these reports as-is after they're created, or you can customize them as needed.

The additional report types are as follows:

- *Columnar with Grand Total.* This report type is a columnar report with a trailing grand summary panel. One summary calculation can be defined for the grand summary panel.
- *Columnar with Groups & Totals.* This report type is a columnar report with leading and trailing summary panels for each group you define, and a trailing grand summary panel. You can later delete any leading or trailing summary panels that you don't need by going into Design mode on the report view. One summary calculation can be defined for the summary panels.

> **Note**
>
> The Columnar with Groups & Totals report type has replaced the Leading and Trailing Grouped Summary types that were in the Report Assistant in prior releases of Approach.

- *Summary Only.* This report has no body panel. It has a trailing summary panel grouped on a selected field and a grand summary. One summary calculation can be defined for the summary panels.
- *Repeating Panel.* This report is an easy way to print all records that appear in a repeating panel without running into the display limit of a repeating panel on a form. This report has a leading and trailing summary panel based on a field, and a trailing grand summary panel. One calculated field can be defined for the trailing summary panels.

> **Note**
>
> The Repeating Panel report, like the repeating panel for a form, is available only when you have files that are relationally joined in your Approach file.

You use several common steps to create advanced reports with the Report Assistant; however, a few differences still exist within the various types of reports.

The Columnar with Grand Total report has body and summary panels and is formatted as columns of data, one record per line, and grand totals for the column(s) you select. This report type is very simple to produce and also very similar to the report type described next.

The Columnar with Groups & Totals report also has body and summary panels and is formatted as columns of data, one record per line. You define grouping fields to create group totals. There are also grand totals for the column(s) you select. See the following section for instructions on creating this type of report.

The Summary Only report has, as the name implies, only summary panels. A smaller number of fields are usually displayed in this report type because it doesn't include detail records. See "Creating a Summary Only Report" later in this chapter for instructions on creating this report.

The Repeating Panel report lets you print data that's normally displayed on a form with a repeating panel, without the display restrictions of a repeating panel. This report is described later in the section "Creating a Repeating Panel Report."

Creating a Columnar with Groups & Totals Report

Suppose that you want a list of Owl Publishing's customers, grouped by each newsletter to which they subscribe. If a customer subscribes to more than one newsletter, that customer will be listed more than once. You also want to see the start date and stop date for each subscription and a summary calculation that determines the oldest start date for each newsletter.

To create a Columnar with Groups & Totals report, follow these steps:

1. Open the Create menu and choose Report. The Report Assistant appears with the Layout page on top (see fig. 12.2).

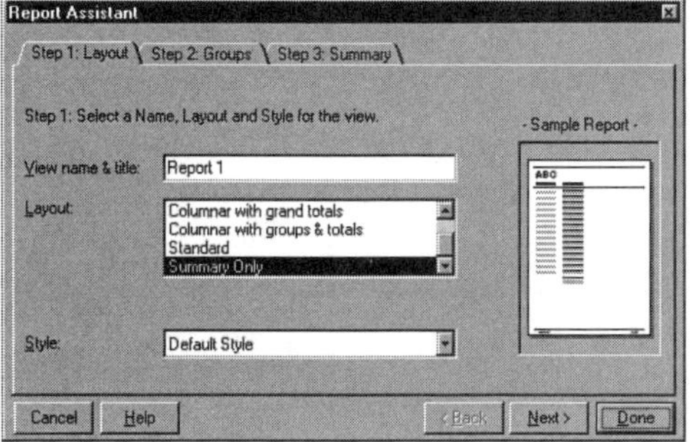

Fig. 12.2

The Report Assistant shows you a sample picture of the report as it will look based on the options you select on this page.

2. Type the report name, **`Newsletter Summary`**, into the View Name & Title text box.
3. Select Columnar with Groups & Totals from the Layout list box.
4. Choose B&W2 from the Style drop-down list.
5. Click Next to proceed to the Fields page (see fig. 12.3).
6. If the Database drop-down list doesn't show the database you want to add fields from, select the correct database. In this example, select the Owl Publishing database.
7. Choose the fields you want to add to the report from the Fields list box in the order in which you want them placed across the report left to right. To choose multiple fields, click the first field and then Ctrl+click any additional fields. In this case, select FIRST NAME and LAST NAME.

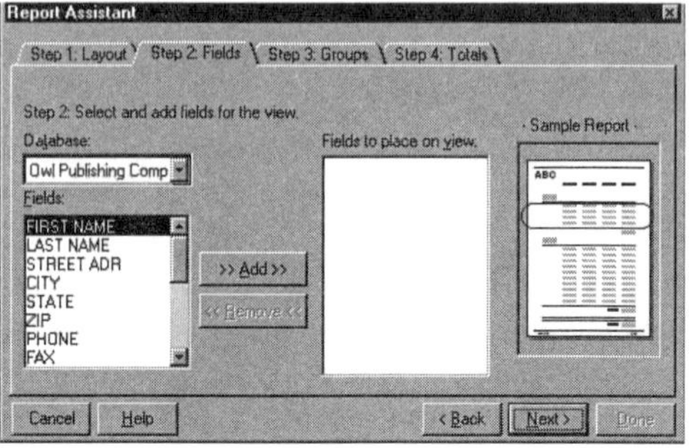

Fig. 12.3

The Fields page is where you select the fields to be displayed in the body of your report, as noted in the sample picture.

8. Choose Add to add the fields to the Fields to place on view list box.
9. Now add fields from the Newsletter database by repeating steps 6, 7, and 8. SUB START and SUB END are needed for this report.
10. Click the Next button to go to the third page, Groups (see fig. 12.4).

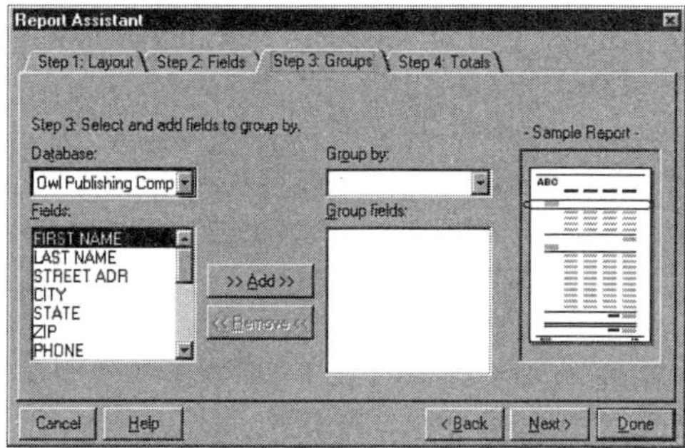

Fig. 12.4

The Groups page is where you select the fields to be used to group your records and how to group them.

11. Select the database from the Database drop-down list and the field(s) from the Fields list box; then click Add to move them into the Group fields list box. For this example, use the NEWSLETTER field from the Newsletter database to group the records. You can specify additional groupings, if you want.
12. Choose the NEWSLETTER field in the Group Fields list box, and then select the drop-down arrow for the Group By box. Because this field is a text field, you're given the default option to use the entire field for your groupings or to use the first one to five characters of the field. This is handy if you want to group together all the newsletters that start with the same three characters into one group, for example.
13. Click the Next button to go to the fourth page, Totals (see fig. 12.5).

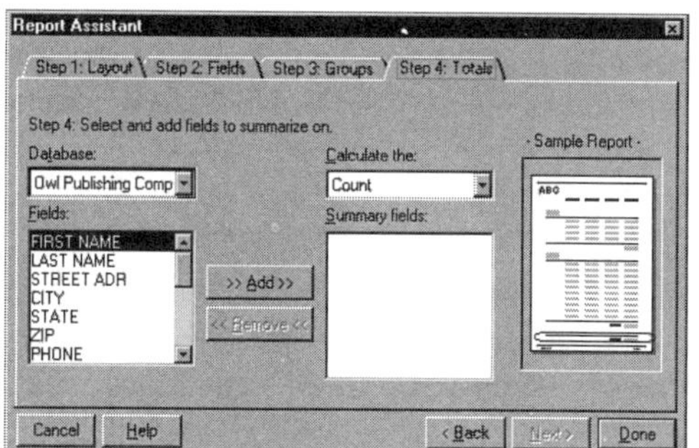

Fig. 12.5

The Totals page is where you select the field to be summarized and the type of calculation to be performed.

14. Select the database from the Database drop-down list and the field from the Fields list box that you want to use in your summary calculation. Use Add to move the field into the Summary fields list box. In this case, select the Newsletter database and the SUB START field.
15. Highlight the SUB START field in the Summary fields list box and then select the calculation type from the Calculate The drop-down list. Approach will create a calculated field using your field and the summary function you select, and put it on the report in the correct place.

    The following summary functions are available:

    Average — Standard Deviation
    Count — Sum
    Maximum — Variance
    Minimum

    For this example, select Minimum to find the earliest subscription start date for each newsletter grouping. More information about these summary functions can be found later in the section "Defining Approach Summary Functions."
16. Click Back to review your Report Assistant selections and to change any of them, if needed. Click Done when you're finished defining your report.
17. If fields from more than one relationally linked database are included in the fields page, the Define Main Database dialog box will appear. Choose the database name on which the report is to be based, which in this example is Newsletter because you're listing the start and stop date of each newsletter in the database.

You can see the completed report either in Design mode with Show Data on, or in Print Preview mode (see fig. 12.6). In Browse mode, only the header, footer, and body panel (containing selected fields from the current set of records) are displayed.

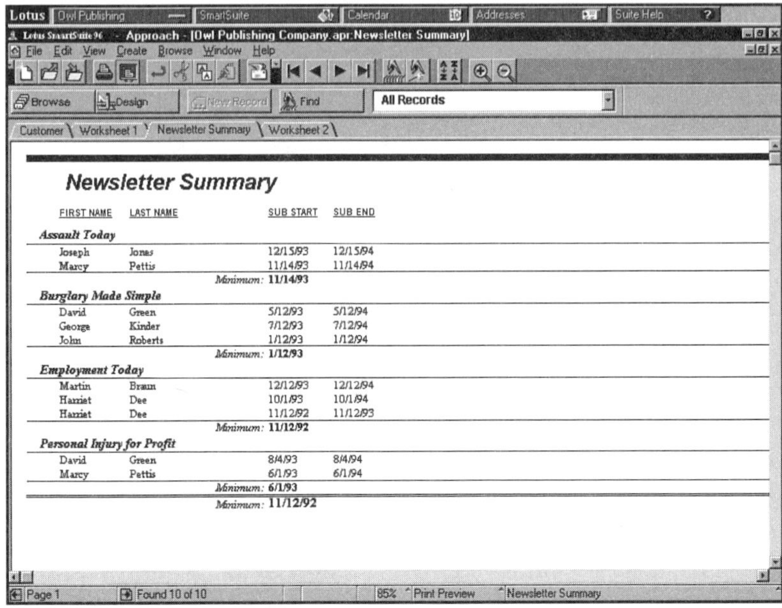

Fig. 12.6

The completed report shows customer subscriptions grouped by newsletter and with the earliest subscription date at the end of each group.

Each newsletter is a new group and automatically creates a leading summary panel with the newsletter name in it. Then the customer subscriptions are listed. The trailing summary panel shows the oldest start date for each newsletter. In the grand summary panel, the oldest subscription date in the database is shown. (Oldest date is retrieved by asking for the Minimum for the date; newest date would be the Maximum.)

Creating a Summary Only Report

The Summary Only report, as the name implies, contains no detail records. Instead, it contains only summary panels and usually summary calculations. It's another way to produce the newsletter report by the minimum subscription date. Rather than list each subscriber, though, the report lists each newsletter, its oldest subscription date, and the oldest overall date in a grand summary.

To create a Summary Only report, follow these steps:

1. Open the Create menu and choose Report. The Report Assistant appears with the Layout page on top (see fig. 12.7).
2. Type the report name—`Summary Report`—into the View Name & Title text box.
3. Select Summary Only from the Layout drop-down list.

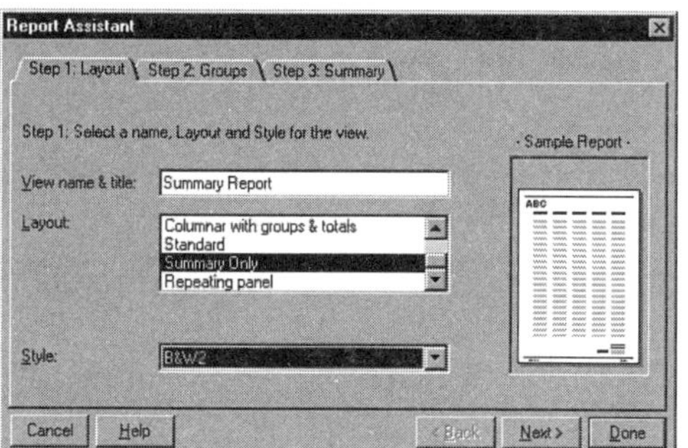

Fig. 12.7

Use the Layout page of the Report Assistant to make settings for a Summary Only report.

4. Choose B&W2 from the Style drop-down list.

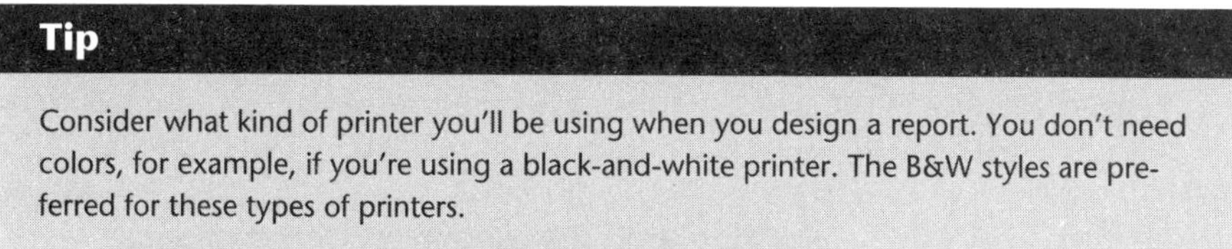

Tip

Consider what kind of printer you'll be using when you design a report. You don't need colors, for example, if you're using a black-and-white printer. The B&W styles are preferred for these types of printers.

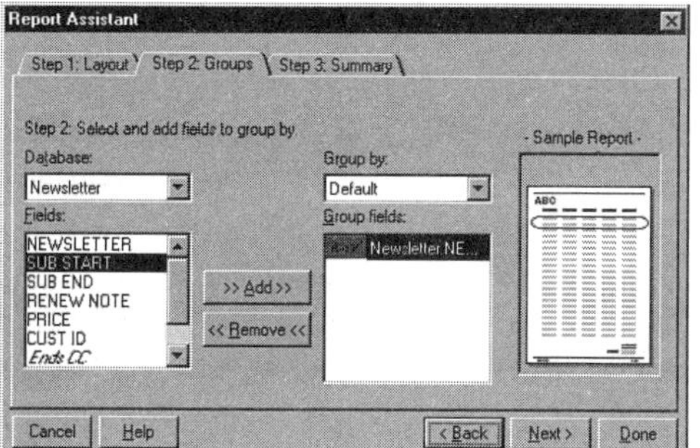

Fig. 12.8

The Groups page for the Summary Only report allows you to select the fields to group your report by and how to group them.

5. Click the Next button to proceed to the Groups page (see fig. 12.8).
6. Select the grouping field(s) on this page. To do so, first use the Database drop-down list and Fields list box to select the fields you'll be grouping the report by (from any joined database). Select NEWSLETTER from the Newsletter database as the field by which the records will be grouped.
7. The Group By drop-down list shows Default, which means to use the entire content of the NEWSLETTER field for the report groupings. New in Approach 96, you also have the option to use the Group By drop-down list to consolidate your groupings, if necessary. For example, you could group newsletters by only the first few letters in the NEWSLETTER field. You could also choose to group your newsletters by price and, if you have many different subscription prices for the newsletters, by price ranges rather than list each price as a separate group.

8. Click Next to move to the Summary page.
9. Define a summary calculation, if you want one, on the Summary page. First choose the database and field you want to summarize from the Database drop-down list and the Fields list box, and then select Add. The field name selected appears in the Summary fields list box. Choose the type of summary calculation you want from the Calculate The drop-down list, or double-click the summary icon to the left of a field name in the Summary Fields list box. Each selection in the Calculate The drop-down list can result in creating an Approach-calculated field using the selected summary function and the selected field. The following selections are available:

Average	Standard Deviation
Count	Sum
Maximum	Variance
Minimum	

   This report shows the oldest start date for each newsletter grouping. To show the oldest start date, select the minimum of field SUB START (see fig. 12.9).

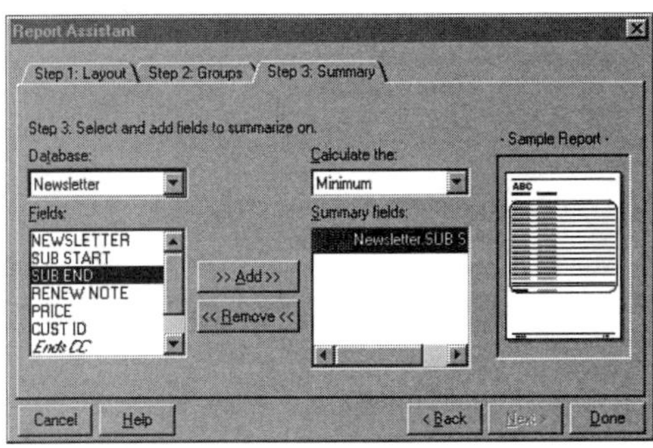

Fig. 12.9

Selecting Minimum for the summary calculation on the subscription start date field displays the oldest (earliest) date.

10. Click Back if you need to make any changes or adjustments in the Report Assistant. Otherwise, choose Done when you finish defining your report.

You can view the completed report either in Design mode, with Show Data on, or in Print Preview mode (see fig. 12.10). Because there's no body panel, Approach won't allow you to enter Browse mode when this report is the current view.

The Summary Only report can be useful for getting a quick overview. If more information is required, a similar report with detail information can then be constructed.

Creating a Repeating Panel Report

A repeating panel is a great way to show how many records from one database are joined to a main record in another database. An example of this is the main Owl Publishing customer information screen (see fig. 12.11). For this form, the main database is Owl Publishing, which contains customer records. The detail database, with one or more possible records per customer, is Newsletter.

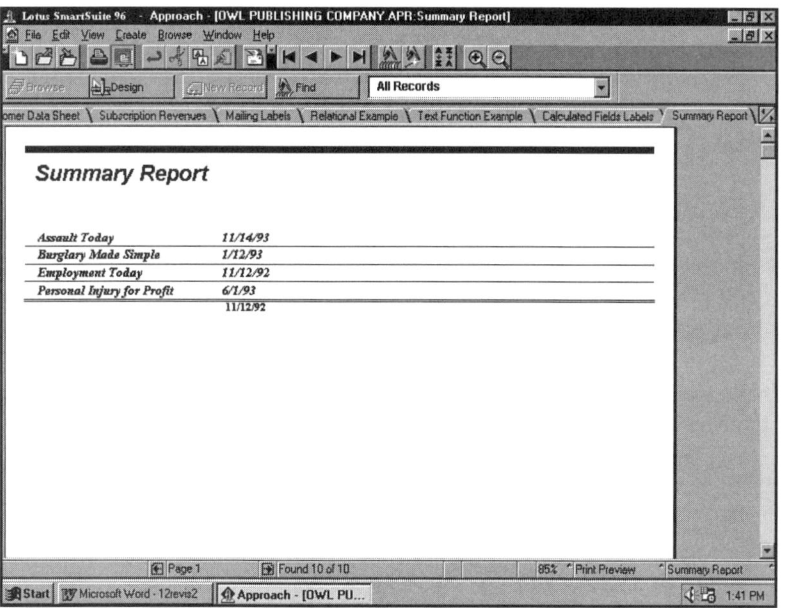

Fig. 12.10

The completed Summary Only report shows the oldest newsletter subscription date for each newsletter.

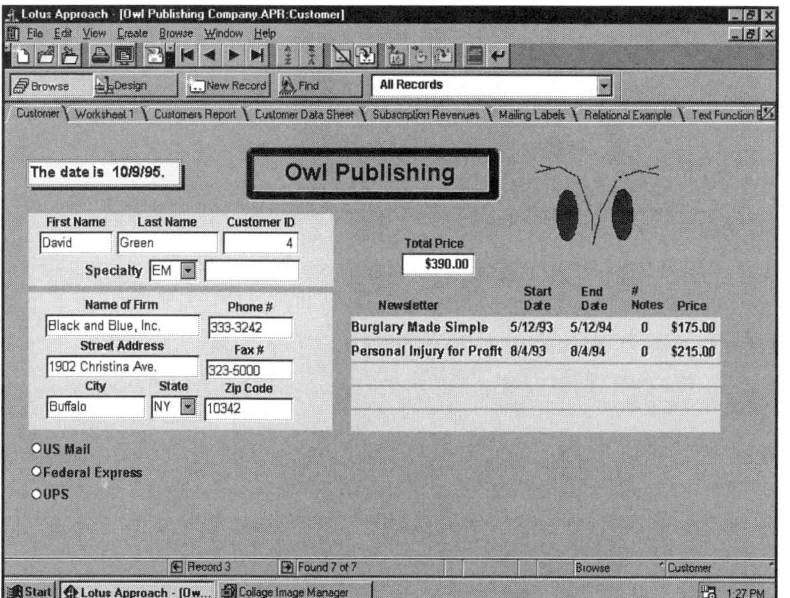

Fig. 12.11

The Owl Publishing customer form includes a repeating panel that lists all newsletters for each customer.

Note

Remember, a Repeating Panel report is an option only if you have joined databases.

Repeating panels are helpful in that they can display or be used to enter relational information. One problem, though, is that repeating panels that aren't in a Repeating Panel report are set to display only a certain number of records. You can view those records that aren't within the number shown by the repeating panel by scrolling through the panel.

The Repeating Panel report allows you to print all needed detail records, without any limits. The report is grouped by the same unique value that's used for the form, which in the example shown in figure 12.11 is the Customer ID. It also lists information from the detail database, Newsletter. Of course, this report might just as easily be used for any number of other one-to-many tasks, such as invoices or purchase orders.

To define a Repeating Panel report, follow these steps:

1. Open the Create menu and choose Report. The Report Assistant appears, with the Layout page on top (see fig. 12.12).

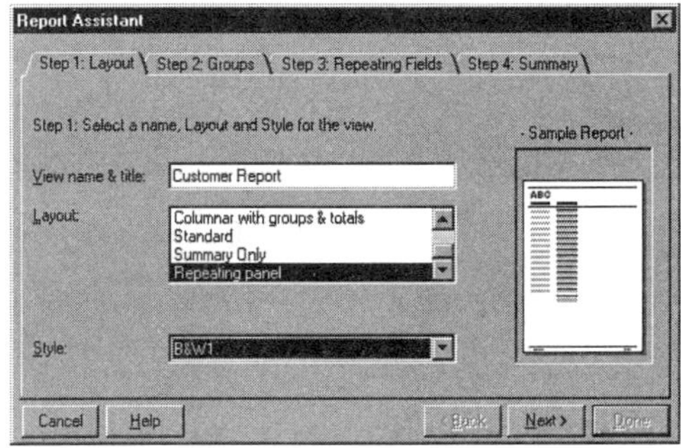

Fig. 12.12

A Repeating Panel report contains four steps, as shown by the four tabs in the Report Assistant.

2. Type the report name—**`Customer Report`**—into the View Name & Title text box.
3. Choose B&W1 from the Style drop-down list.
4. Select Repeating Panel from the Layout drop-down list.
5. Click the Next button to proceed to the next page, Groups (see fig. 12.13). This report will show subscriptions by customer, so choose FIRM_NAME from the Owl Publishing Company database.

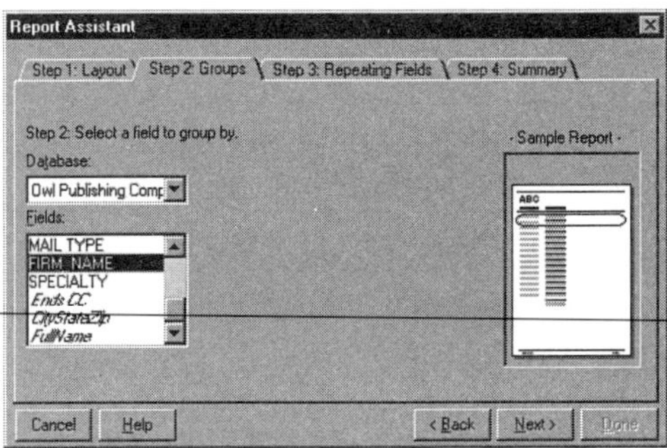

Fig. 12.13

Select a main field for the Repeating Panel report.

6. Click the Next button to proceed to the third page, Repeating Fields. Select the fields you want to appear in the repeating panel. If the Database option doesn't show the database from which you want to select the fields, select the database from the drop-down list.

   Choose the fields you want to add to the report from the Fields drop-down list. From the Newsletter database, select the NEWSLETTER, SUB START, SUB END, and PRICE fields to be repeating fields in the panel (see fig. 12.14). Click Add to add the fields to the list.

> **Tip**
>
> To choose multiple fields, click the first field and then Ctrl+click any additional fields.
>
> To remove a field from the Fields to Repeat list box, select the field and click Remove.

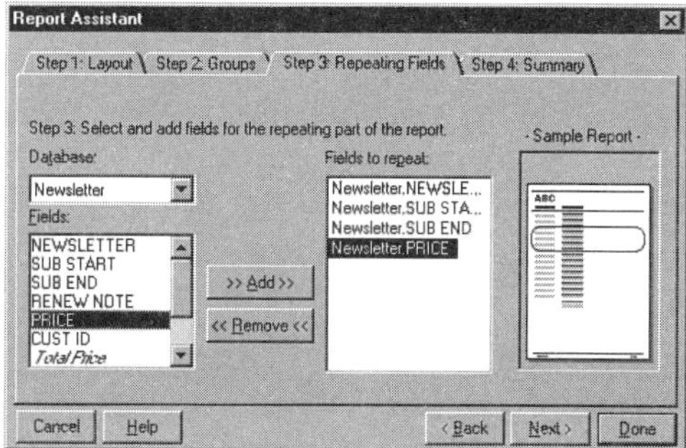

Fig. 12.14

Click Add to add Newsletter database fields to your repeating panel.

7. Click the Next button to continue to the fourth page, Summary (see fig. 12.15).

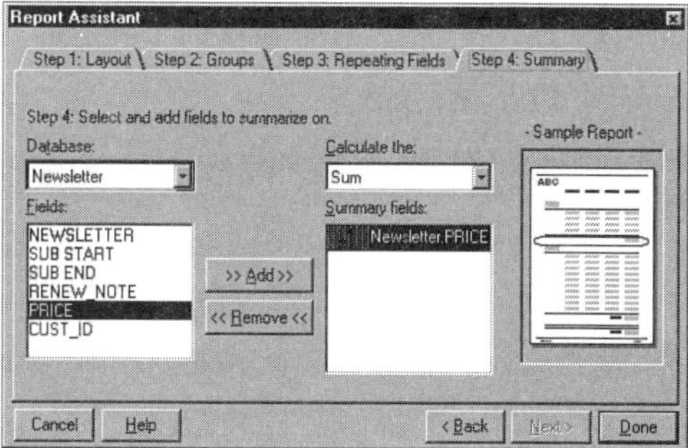

Fig. 12.15

The fields for the detail records are selected on the Summary page.

8. The optional Summary page allows you to define a summary calculation. Select the database field the calculation will use from the Database drop-down list and Fields list box. In this case, you'll want to summarize on PRICE in the Newsletter database. Use Add to add the PRICE field to the Summary Fields list box. Then

select Sum from the Calculate The drop-down list box to calculate the total price paid by each customer. This selection will create an Approach-calculated field using a summary function. The following selections are available:

Average	Standard Deviation
Count	Sum
Maximum	Variance
Minimum	

9. Click Back if you need to make any changes or adjustments in the Report Assistant. Otherwise, click Done when you're finished defining your report.

> **Note**
>
> If fields from more than one relationally linked file are selected in the Repeating Fields page, the Define Main Database dialog box appears, asking for the main database for the repeating fields section of the report. Select the database on which the repeating panel is based.

You can see the completed report either in Design mode, with Show Data on, or in Print Preview mode (see fig. 12.16). In Browse mode, only the header, footer, and repeating records are displayed.

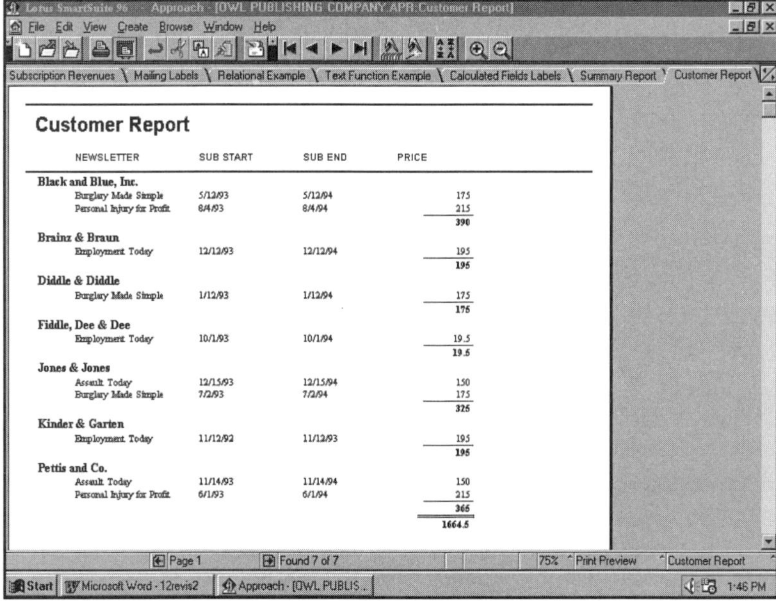

Fig. 12.16

The Repeating Panel report lists newsletters grouped by firm name and summarized by price.

Each listing of a firm name is a new grouping of the leading summary panel; after that is the repeating records for each grouping. The trailing summary panel lists the sum of the prices for each customer's newsletter subscriptions. In the grand summary panel, the total of all newsletter subscriptions is displayed. Other information can easily be added later in Design mode.

Modifying Reports

So far, the focus has been on creating reports through the Report Assistant. Although it will often produce the report you need, sometimes additional modification or customization is necessary to get the exact report you want.

Approach offers several features—such as show data, columnar editing, and PowerClick reporting—that make it easy to modify a report. To use these features, it's important to understand what they are and when they're available.

A simple columnar report is used to demonstrate these features. The report shown in figure 12.17 lists each Owl Publishing customer and his or her legal specialty. This report is based on the Owl Publishing database.

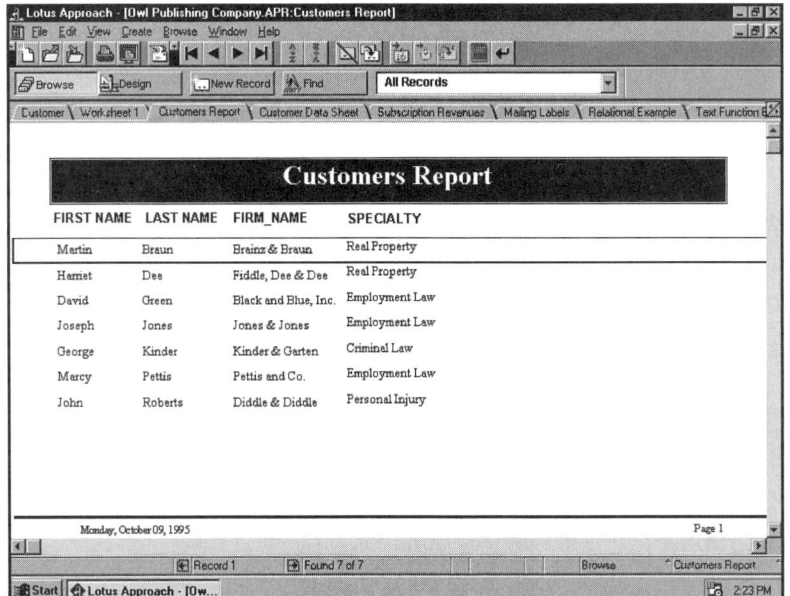

Fig. 12.17

A simple columnar report is shown just as it looks when created by the Report Assistant and before any customization.

Using Show Data

Show Data mode is a way to show actual data, rather than just report panels and objects in Design mode (see fig. 12.18).

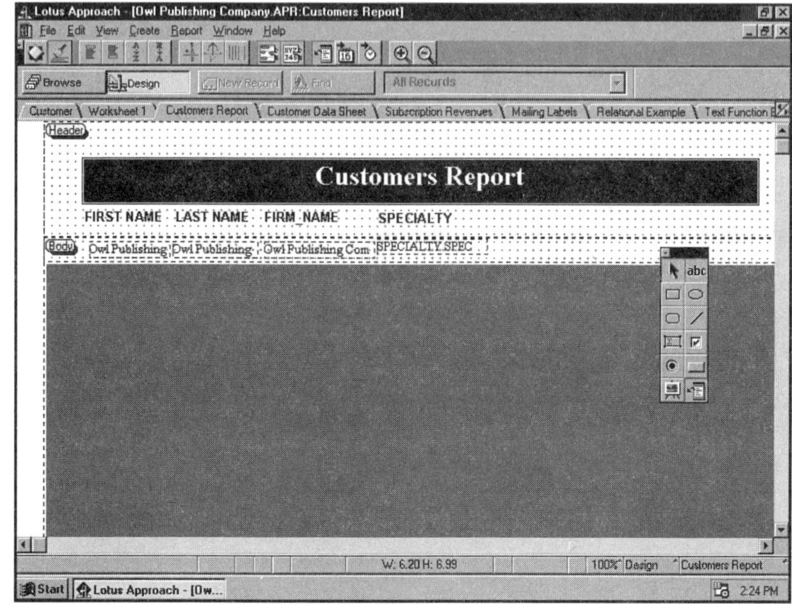

Fig. 12.18

The simple columnar report from figure 12.17 is shown here in Design mode with Show Data off.

To turn on Show Data, follow these steps:

1. Switch to Design mode, if you're not already there.
2. Open the View menu and choose Show Data.

To turn it off again, select the Show Data menu item again.

When Show Data is on, the report looks much as it did in Print Preview mode in figure 12.17, except that the panels and objects can be selected and manipulated in Design mode.

Working in Columnar Mode

When a report is in Design mode with Show Data on, the fields in the report can act as a single column. This way, you can select, resize, and move data, and get instant feedback on what the final result will look like.

To work in Columnar mode, follow these steps:

1. Switch to Design mode, if you're not already there.
2. Open the Report menu and choose Turn On Columns. When Columnar mode is on, the menu item will have a check mark in front of it, and the column manipulations SmartIcon bar will appear.

When you click a column, the entire column is selected (see fig. 12.19). After a column is selected you can

- *Resize it.* Click the right edge of the column to get the resize cursor. Drag it to the left or right to make the column narrower or wider.

- *Move it.* Click in the column and drag the column to the left or right to reposition it.
- *Delete it.* Click in the column to select it, and then open the Edit menu and choose Cut.
- *Copy it.* Click in the column to select it, and then open the Edit menu and choose Copy.

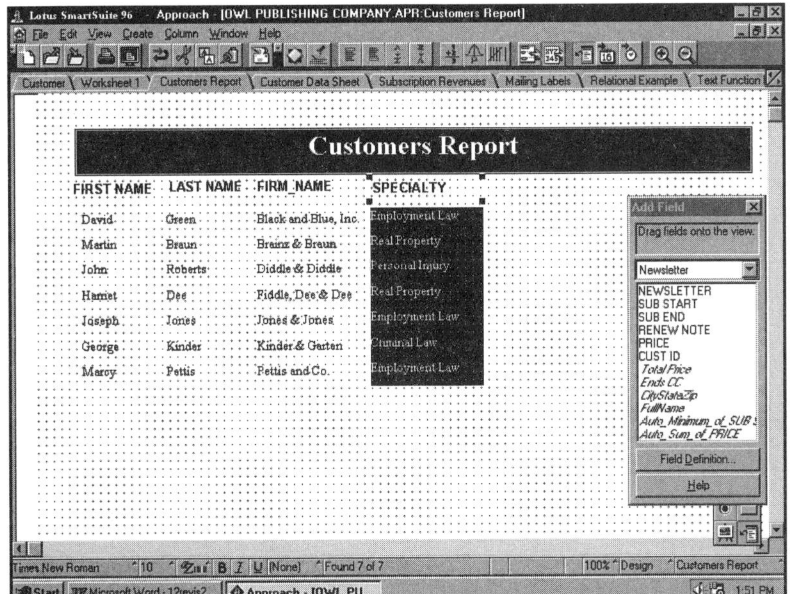

Fig. 12.19

The SPECIALTY field column is shown selected with Show Data on, and the field can now be resized more easily.

When a column is modified, the other columns move as needed. If a column is moved over an existing column, the existing column and any columns to the right of it moves to the right. This prevents one column from being placed over another.

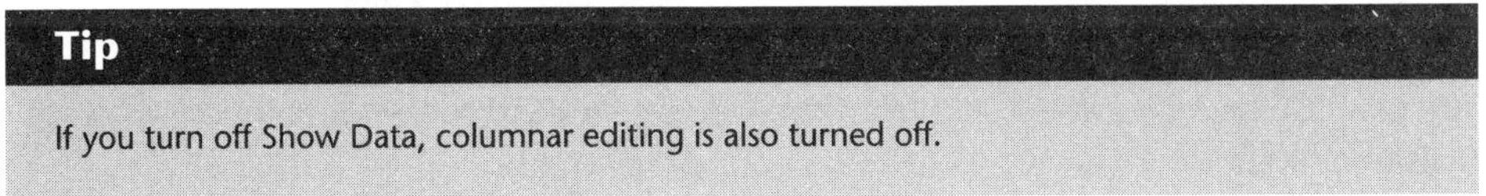
Tip

If you turn off Show Data, columnar editing is also turned off.

Adding a Field to the Report

The easiest way to add a field to a report is by dragging it from the Add Field dialog box. Follow these steps:

1. Switch to Design mode.
2. Open the Add Field dialog box by clicking the Add Field on the tools palette, or open the Report menu and choose Add Field. When the Add Field dialog box is open, the menu item will have a check mark in front of it.

3. In the Add Field dialog box, select the database for which you want the field listing. In this case, the report needs to list the newsletter to which each customer subscribes. Select the Newsletter database.
4. Select the field you want to add and drag it into the body of the report. For this example, select the NEWSLETTER field, drag it off the Add Field dialog box, and then release the mouse button when the field is positioned over the report (see fig. 12.20).

Fig. 12.20

You can drag-and-drop fields onto the report design.

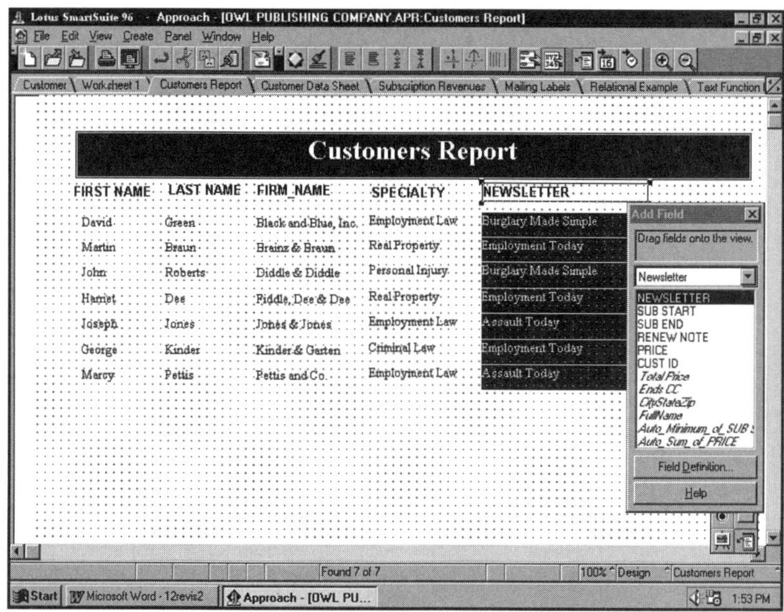

Tip

Close the Add Field dialog box by clicking the Close button in the top right corner.

You can also add the PRICE field from the Newsletter database to the report by using the same method.

Using PowerClick Reporting

You can use PowerClick reporting to quickly add summary panels or summary calculations to a report. A trailing grand summary with a calculated field can be added to a report in Design mode just by clicking the mouse.

To use PowerClick reporting to add a trailing grand summary, follow these steps:

1. Switch to Design mode.

2. Click the Trailing Summary SmartIcon. Because no fields are selected for grouping purposes, this creates a trailing grand summary. (If a field had been selected, this would be a trailing summary grouped by that field value.)
3. Click a field to select it.
4. Click the Sum SmartIcon to add the contents of the field and put a summary calculated field in the trailing grand summary. Count and Average SmartIcons are also available for PowerClick reporting use.

Figure 12.21 shows the sample report with a PowerClick summary added to the PRICE field.

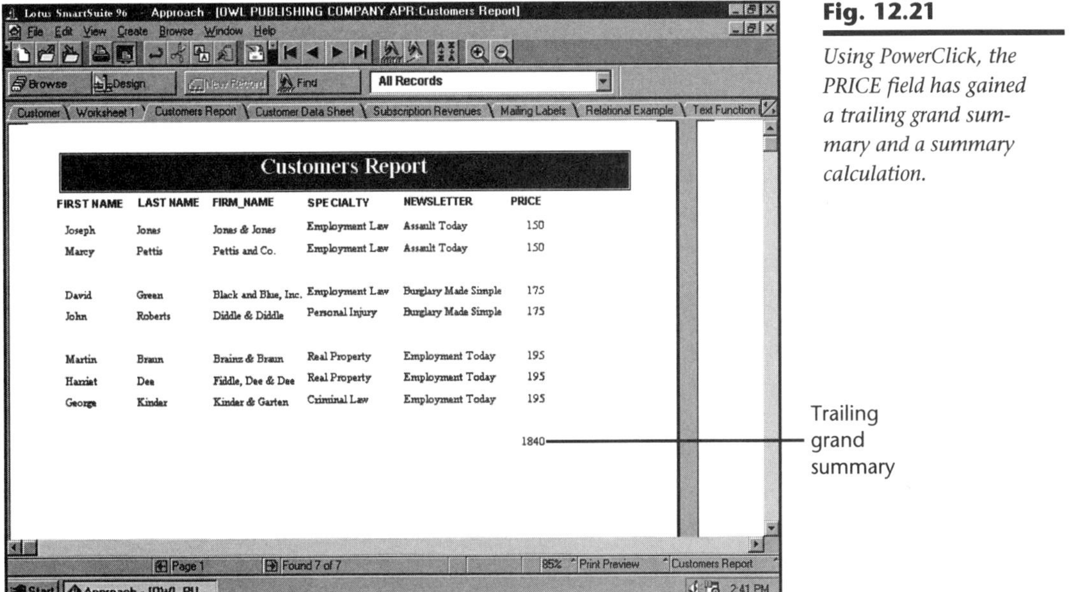

Fig. 12.21

Using PowerClick, the PRICE field has gained a trailing grand summary and a summary calculation.

With PowerClick reporting, you can add summary panels:

- The Leading Summary SmartIcon adds a leading grand summary panel if no fields are selected. If a field is selected, the summary panel groups over unique values in that field.
- The Trailing Summary SmartIcon adds a trailing grand summary panel if no fields are selected. If a field is selected, the summary panel groups over unique values in that field.

PowerClick reporting can also be used to add summary calculations. These calculations are described later in the section "Using Summary Functions in a Calculated Field."

Adding a Summary Panel

So far, you've learned how to add summary panels by using the Report Assistant and PowerClick reporting. You can also use the Summary dialog box to add a summary panel to a report (see fig. 12.22).

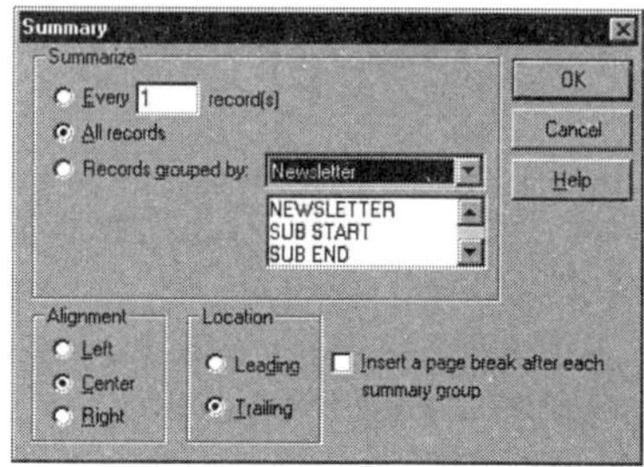

Fig. 12.22

The Summary dialog box shows the options available when you're adding a summary panel.

The Summary dialog box has these features:

- The Summarize section lists the various summarization options. A database can be summarized on Every (so many) Record(s), All Records, or Records Grouped By a specific field.
- The alignment—Left, Center, or Right—refers to the panels' placement with respect to a body panel. Center is used by the Report Assistant and PowerClicking. Left places a summary panel to the left of a body panel; Right places a summary panel to the right.
- The location, Leading or Trailing, tells the panel to display before or after the records it's grouping.

Tip

If you want leading and trailing panels on the same group, you need to define two panels.

Summary panels must be added in Design mode. To add a summary panel, open the Create menu and choose Summary. The Summary dialog box appears; adjust the summary options and click OK. The new summary is now added to the report.

Modifying Summary Options

The modification options for a summary panel are the same as the options when adding a new panel. You can adjust the summarize options, the alignment, or the location.

To modify a panel, follow these steps:

1. Switch to Design mode.
2. Double-click a summary panel to display an InfoBox, or click the InfoBox SmartIcon.

3. Click the Basics tab in the InfoBox to display the Summarize options (see fig. 12.23).

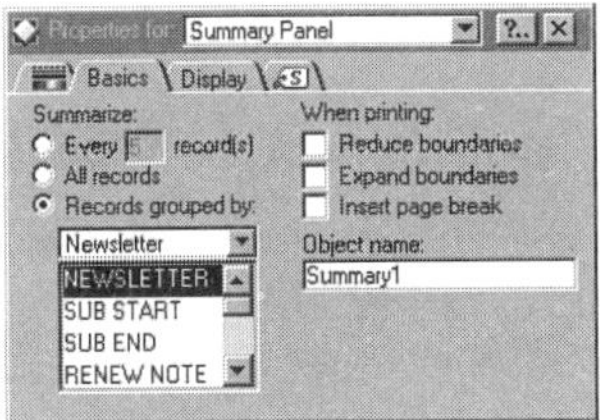

Fig. 12.23

The InfoBox for a Summary panel has a Basics page where you can change the Summarize options or the field that defines the summary grouping.

4. Click the Display tab in the InfoBox to set alignment and location options.

If you're working in Show Data when you do the modifications, you'll see any changes immediately. If Show Data is off, you'll see alignment and location changes immediately but not the actual data. New grouping options won't be apparent until you go to Print Preview mode or turn on Show Data.

Showing Panel Labels

Panel labels, located on the left side of the report panel, let you know the options for that panel. For example, figure 12.24 shows the panel labels for the header, a trailing summary grouped by newsletter, and two occurrences of the body panel.

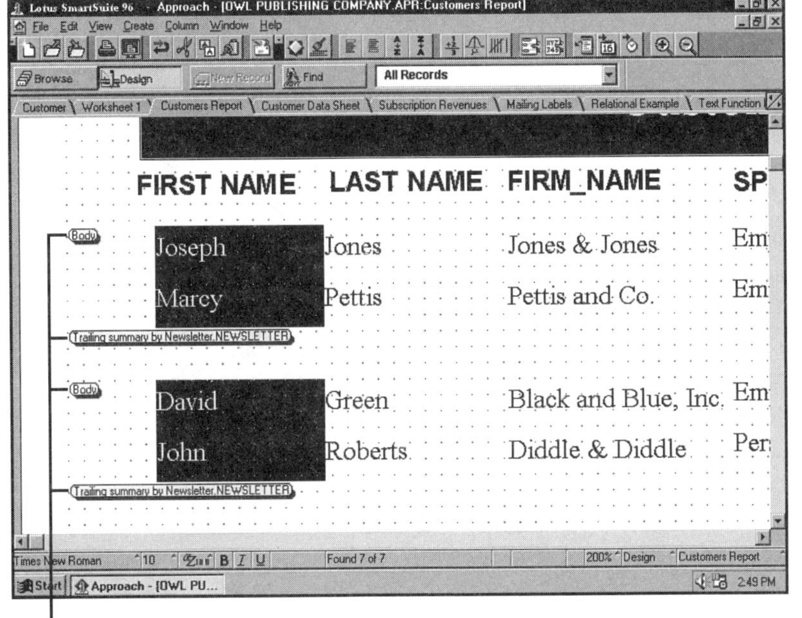

Fig. 12.24

Panel labels help clarify the various parts of your report's design.

Panel labels are controlled by a menu item and a SmartIcon. To toggle the panel labels on or off, open the View menu and choose Show Panel Labels, or click the Panel Labels SmartIcon. When panel labels are on, the menu item has a check mark in front of it.

Using Summary Functions in a Calculated Field

The Report Assistant and PowerClick reporting are two methods that have been used to define and add summary calculations. Each Assistant option and PowerClick SmartIcon can define a calculation using one of Approach's summary functions.

> **Note**
>
> If Show Data is turned off, each panel is displayed only once. If Show Data is turned on, a panel label is displayed multiple times.

> **Caution**
>
> Calculated fields using summary functions or any calculated fields based on a summary calculated field display a value only in Print Preview or Design mode with Show Data on. If your summary calculation is blank, check which mode you're in.

Defining Approach Summary Functions. Approach has eight summary functions. The following functions can be defined or modified either by the Report Assistant, by PowerClick reporting, or through the Field Definition dialog box:

- `SAverage()` The summary average function calculates the average value of the non-blank occurrences of the specified field for the current range of records.
- `SCount()` The summary count function calculates the number of occurrences of all non-blank values in the specified field for the current range of records. Blank values aren't counted.
- `SMax()` The summary maximum function returns the largest value in a field for the current group of records. It can use numeric, date, or time values.
- `SMin()` The summary minimum function returns the smallest value in the field for the current range of records. It can use numeric, date, or time values.
- `SVar()` The summary variance function has a single parameter that must be a field containing a numeric value. It returns the variance of the values in the specified field for the current range of records.
- `SNPV()` The summary net present value function needs two parameters. The first is a field, the second is a constant: `SNPV(Field, .05)`. The SNPV returns the net present value of an investment based on a series of yearly cash flows

(contained in the field) and a discount rate (the constant value). The discount rate is usually stated as a percentage (8 percent) but is entered into the formula as a decimal number (.08). The periodic cash flows can be positive (income) or negative (investment). The value in the field in the first record in the database represents the investment made in the first year. The value in the field in subsequent records represents the investment or income for subsequent years (the second record is for year 2, the third record is for year 3, and so on).

- `SStd()` The summary standard deviation function has a single parameter that must be numeric. It returns the standard deviation of the values in the specified field for the current range of records. The standard deviation is a measure of how widely dispersed the values are from the average value.
- `SSum()` The summary sum function has a single parameter that must be a field containing a numeric value. It returns the sum of all the values in the specified field for the current range of records.

Setting Summary Options. When a summary calculation is added to a summary panel through the Report Assistant or through PowerClicking, it's defined to evaluate its function depending on where it's placed. This means that the summary will evaluate the function over the current summary grouping.

For example, if a summary calculation is calculating the number of customers by using `SCount()` and is placed into a summary panel that's grouping by state, the calculated field will give the total number of customers for each state that displays in the report. If the calculation is also placed into a trailing grand summary, the field displayed in that panel will show the total number of customers in the database.

You can also define a summary field to evaluate over a defined report panel. This is done by using the Define Summary page in the Field Definition dialog box (see fig. 12.25). The panel you use needs to be from the same report in which the field will be used; otherwise, the field won't evaluate and will remain blank.

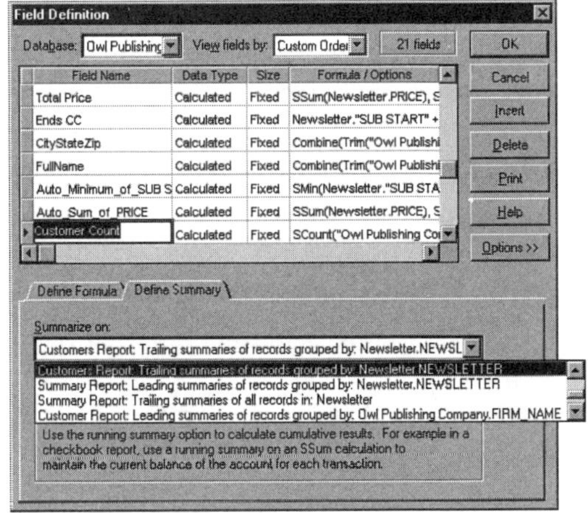

Fig. 12.25

A summary calculation can be controlled by where it's placed, or it can be attached to a specific summary panel.

To set or modify a summary calculation's options, follow these steps:

1. Open the Create menu and choose Field Definition.
2. Select the field name. The fields defined automatically have names such as AUTO SUM OF PRICE or AUTO COUNT OF CUSTOMER.
3. Click the Options button.
4. Click the Define Summary tab.
5. Select the new setting from the Summarize On list. This list includes defaults where the field is placed, summarized over each individual database, and summarized over all databases. It also has a selection for each summary panel defined in a report.
6. Click OK to save the settings.

A summary that's defined over a certain range can be used within summary panels that have a different grouping than the one for which the calculation is defined. For example, you might define a summary calculation as the SSum of sales for a company, summarized over a report's trailing grand summary. Then, within a regional summary, you can display the total of sales for that region with a Where Placed SSum of Sales. The same panel can also have the total sales company-wide as a comparison figure. If the company sales weren't defined as over the grand summary grouping, it would display the same value as the regional summary, because the two are summarizing the same field. By defining the company's sales over a specific group, it can be used anywhere within the report.

Defining a Running Summary. You can use a summary calculation based on a certain panel because the calculation can be used as a running summary. A running total or running count, for example, shows an updated value for each detail record in a report. Look at two examples of how a running total and a running count might be used:

- A running total can be used to show cumulative sales figures in a region. The regional sales report contains the sales of the current sales representative in each record. A running total showing the sales of the current representative summed with each representative from the region listed in the previous records can also appear in each record.
- A running count can be used to number each record in a report. The calculation with the summary count function appears in each record. As long as the field for which the running count is defined contains only non-blank values, each record has a new number.

The calculated field used for the running summary must be summarized over a set report panel. The running summary can't be defined as "where placed" in the Field Definition dialog box's summary options. If the summary panel is a grand summary, the running summary will evaluate its formula over every detail record in the report. If the summary panel is a grouping on a field, the running summary will evaluate for each record within a group and begin again for a new grouping.

For example, Owl Publishing wants to add a count of all customers to a report:

1. The running summary must be added in Design mode.
2. If there's no trailing grand summary in the current report, click the Trailing Summary SmartIcon to add one.
3. From the Create menu, choose Field Definition to open the Field Definition dialog box. Create a new field, named Customer Count, as a calculated field.
4. Click the Options button and select Summary from the Functions drop-down list. Choose SCount from the list box below it.

   Select a field that will be present in every record, such as CUST ID or LAST NAME. Double-click the field name in the list box to insert it between the parentheses in `SCount()`.
5. Click the Define Summary tab.
6. In the Summarize On list, choose the trailing grand summary for the current report—the Customers Report, in this case. Also, click the Make Calculation a Running Summary check box.
7. Click OK to close the Field Definition dialog box.
8. Place the Customer Count field into the Grand Summary panel you've chosen. If you want, add text to explain the field.
9. View the results in Design or Print Preview mode (see fig. 12.26). As a summary calculation, the running total won't display in Browse mode.

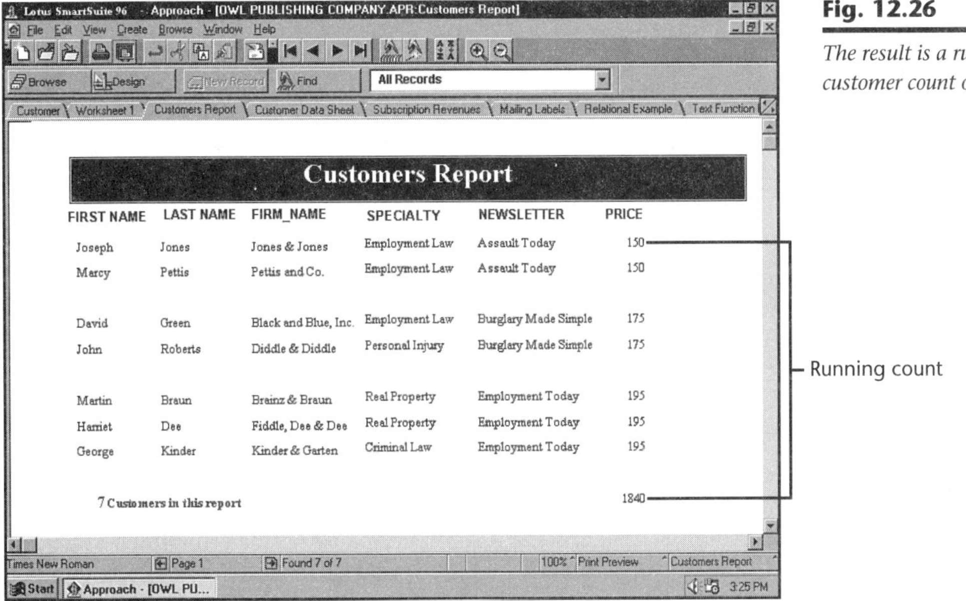

Fig. 12.26

The result is a running customer count on a report.

Reordering Summary Panels

Summary panels need to follow a certain order to display the groupings properly. In a leading summary, the largest group should be the top panel. In a trailing summary, the largest group should be the bottom panel.

For example, if your report has a leading group by region and within that group has a subgrouping by state, the region panel should be above the state panel. A leading grand summary, if present, should be above both panels. If the order isn't set properly, the report groupings will be incorrect. Rather than have state as a subgroup of region, region might appear as a subgroup of state—the opposite of the grouping you've tried to define.

To change the order of summary panels, click the panel and drag it up or down. You can change the order easily when Show Data is turned off. Also, this change is relative to the set location—leading or trailing. If the actual location needs to be changed from leading to trailing, for example, it's done through the InfoBox.

Modifying Panel and Object Attributes

Report panels and objects are like objects in a form or other view. They have attributes that can be set through the InfoBox. For example, you can select a panel and add a border around it or fill it with a color by using the Lines and Colors page.

You can resize a panel border by clicking it and dragging the resize cursor up or down. A border with a light gray color can be resized; borders with a darker gray can't be. Also, you'll get the resize cursor only when a border can be resized.

Similarly, you can modify or resize fields within a report panel. Make sure that the field is fully contained within the panel, though, or it won't display as expected. If necessary, a panel can always be resized to accommodate a larger field.

You can add features such as graphic objects, circles, and squares to any panel, just as you would add them to a form. You can also add pictures to a report panel by using the Clipboard or the Paste From File dialog box.

> **Note**
>
> The more objects you add to a report, the longer the report will take to format and print.

Removing a Summary Panel

A summary panel can be removed by clicking the panel to select it and pressing the Delete key. Objects within the panel are also deleted from the view, but not from the Approach file. For example, you can add a summary panel with a grouping by state, and include an `SCount()` calculation. If you select that panel and delete it, the panel and the calculation field object are removed from the view. The defined calculation remains in the Approach file and can be deleted, if it's not needed, by using the Field Definition dialog box.

Caution

Deleting a summary panel can't be undone. When you choose to delete a panel, make sure that it's the correct one. If you accidentally delete a panel that may be difficult to re-create, you can close the Approach file without saving and reopen it to return to your most recently saved version. This recovery option works best when you save your Approach file often.

Using Form Letters

A *form letter* is a document that combines text with the fields in a database. The text is the same in every letter, but the values in the fields change because each form letter is generated by using the fields in a different record. The letters are personalized by including unique information in the letter. A form letter to customers whose subscriptions are about to expire, for example, can include the subscriber's name, address, and the name of the expiring newsletter.

Approach can help you generate form letters using the fields in your database. An Approach form letter consists of blocks of text and database fields. You can create and edit text, add and rearrange fields, and change the style of text and fields. You can also change the format of fields. Before you print the form letters, you can perform a find to limit the form letters to just the found set of records.

Note

Unlike other Approach views, you can't modify the contents of fields inserted into text blocks on a form letter. However, you can insert fields into a form letter outside a text block that can be modified.

Creating a Form Letter

To create a form letter, follow these steps:

1. Open the Create menu and choose Form Letter, or click the Create Form Letter SmartIcon. The Form Letter Assistant opens to the Layout page (see fig. 12.27).

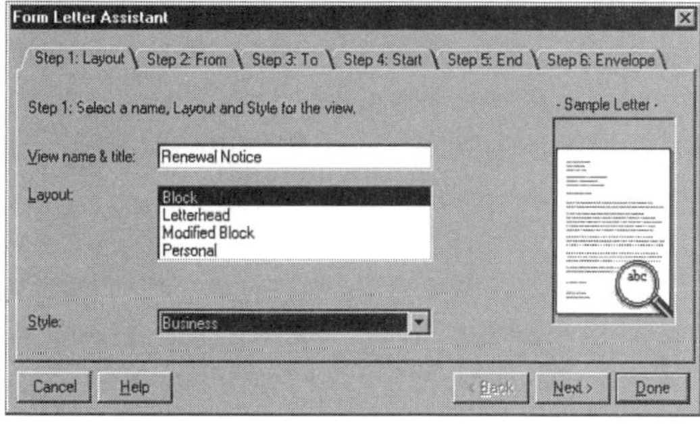

Fig. 12.27

The Form Letter Assistant offers several letter and layout styles.

2. Type the name of the form letter into the View Name & Title text box.
3. Select the letter style from the Layout list.
4. Select the style from the Style list to set properties such as background color and text attributes for your letter.
5. Click the Next button to continue to the second page, From (see fig. 12.28).

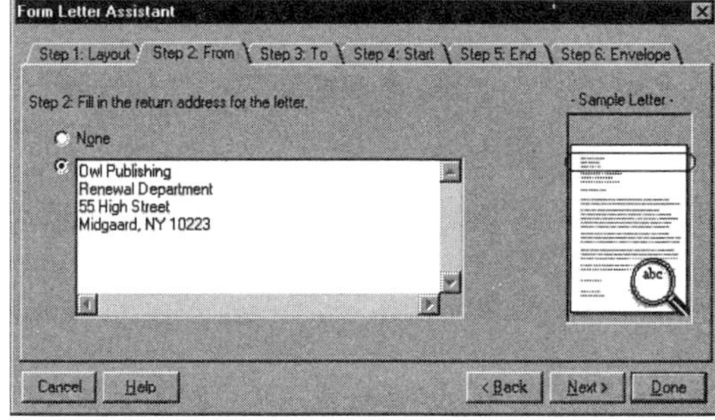

Fig. 12.28

The return address setting is saved for future form letters.

6. Enter the return address or select None. After you define a form letter, the return address section remains for the next time you use the Form Letter Assistant and can be modified as needed.
7. Click the Next button to go to the third tab, To (see fig. 12.29).

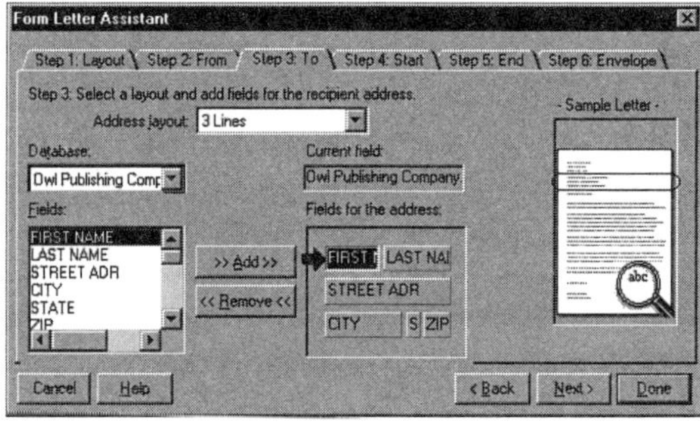

Fig. 12.29

Select database fields to use for the recipient address.

8. Adjust the number of lines for the address in the Address Layout drop-down list box. The Fields for the Address area shows where it expects fields to be placed.
9. Select a field and click Add to move the fields from the Database and Fields list boxes to the Fields for the Address area. A red arrow moves next to the placeholder that will be used for the field. If you keep clicking Add, the fields from the list box are added in the order entered.

Tip

To remove a field from the Fields for the Address area, select the field and choose Remove.

10. Repeat step 9 to add fields to the form letter from other databases.
11. Click the Next button to move to the Start page (see fig. 12.30).

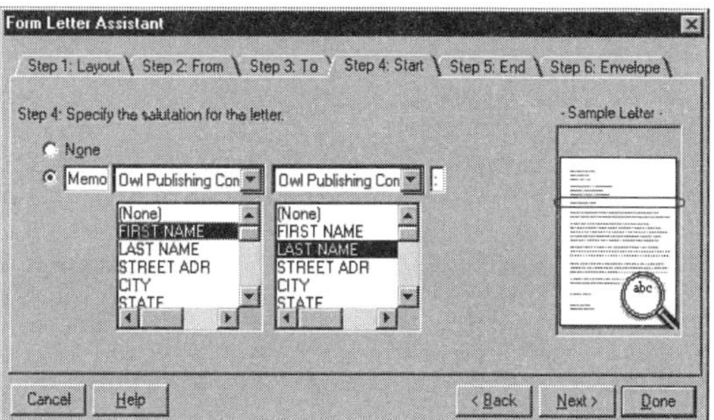

Fig. 12.30

Customize your salutation on the Start page.

12. Either select the None radio button to eliminate the salutation altogether, or select the second radio button (which is followed by a greeting field and two places to select database fields) to format your salutation. Either leave the greeting alone or type another one in that field box. Then choose one or two database fields to display in the salutation. Select (None) in the field list box to skip a field. You can also customize the punctuation by typing in the space provided.

Note

If you want to use an honorific (such as Mr., Mrs., or General) in the salutation, you should first create a separate field for it in your database application. Then select this field as the first included in the salutation.

After you create a form letter, the text entered for the salutation will remain until you change it. For this letter, type **`Memo to`** in the first blank, and then choose the fields FIRST NAME and LAST NAME from the Owl Publishing database. Leave the colon as the punctuation.

13. Click the Next button to continue to the next page, End (see fig. 12.31).

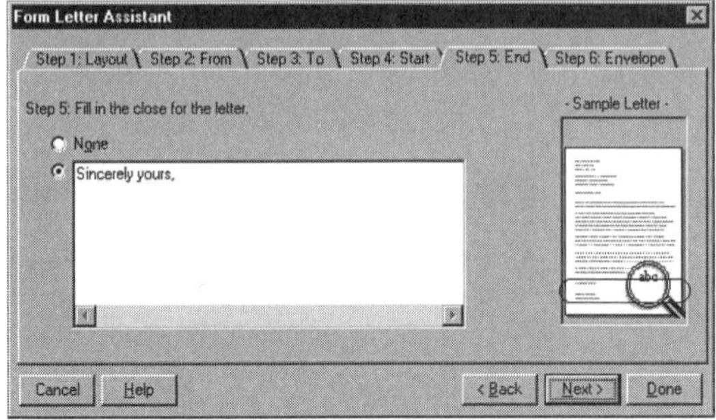

Fig. 12.31

Personalize the close of your letter.

14. On the End page, you can type a personalized closing in the text box or choose the None radio button to leave it blank. The closing that you use is available for future form letters until you modify it.
15. If you need envelopes now, click Next to go to the Envelope page (see fig. 12.32).

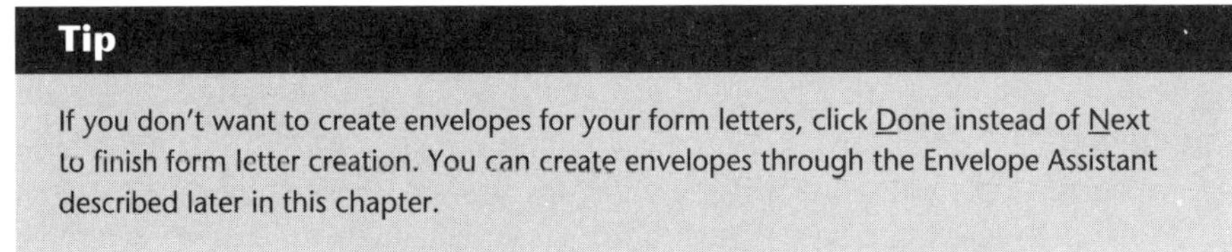

Tip

If you don't want to create envelopes for your form letters, click Done instead of Next to finish form letter creation. You can create envelopes through the Envelope Assistant described later in this chapter.

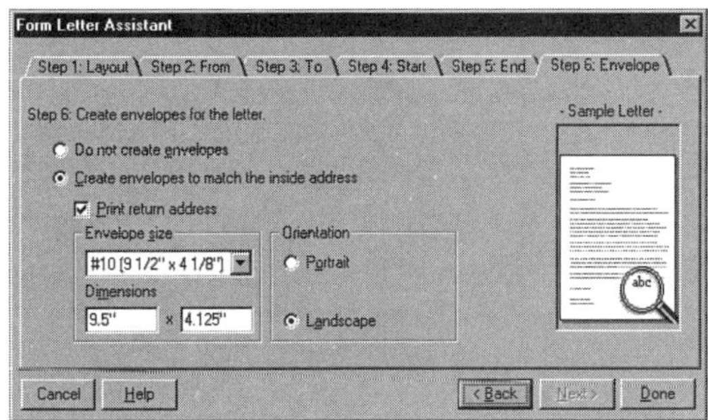

Fig. 12.32

By using the Envelope page, you can build an envelope for every customer record selected for a form letter.

You'll find the most common business envelope, a #10 with return address and customer address printed in landscape mode, is automatically selected. Make any changes needed.

16. Click Done to create the form letter and envelopes.

The new form letter appears. The fields you identified in the Create Form Letter dialog box appear on the form letter in insertion brackets (<< >>), as shown in figure 12.33.

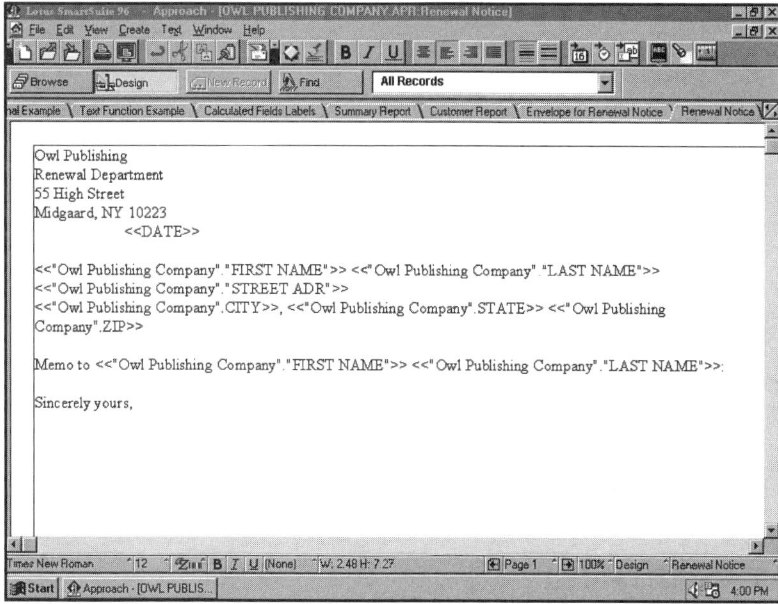

Fig. 12.33

A newly created form letter in Design mode contains your return address, the date, the To address, salutation, and closing text. It can now be edited like any other form in Design mode.

Creating Text in a Text Block

The newly created form letter consists of a single text block containing the fields that you identified in the Create Form Letter dialog box. The text block fills the entire form letter page. You can add and change text in this text block.

For example, you can add body text to the letter that was created for Owl Publishing by taking these steps:

1. The Text tool is selected immediately after creating the form letter. If it's not still active, select it from the tools palette. Open the Create menu and choose Drawing, and then select Text.
2. Click the form letter below the greeting.
3. Type the text—for example,

   We're sorry to inform you that your Owl Publishing newsletter subscription is almost expired. Please take a moment to renew your subscription.

4. View the letter in Browse or Print Preview mode to see how it will look when printed (see fig. 12.34).

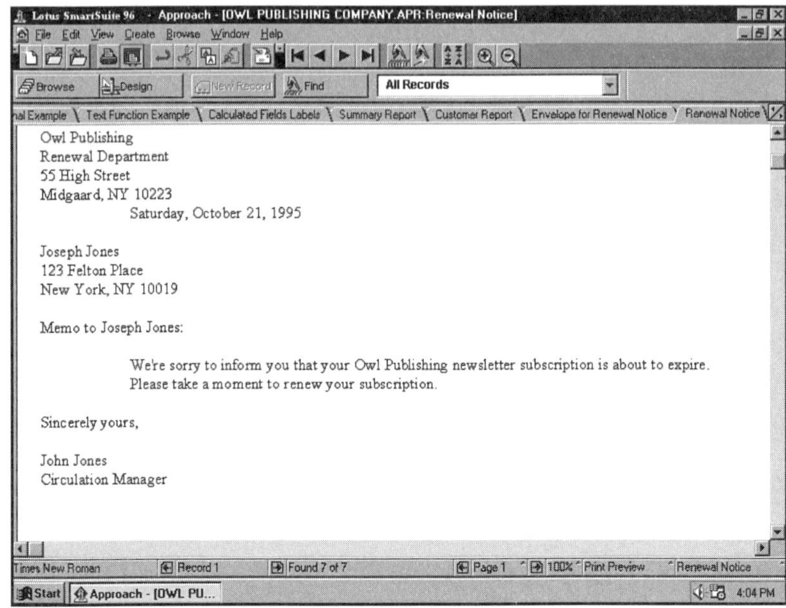

Fig. 12.34

Your personalized form letter is ready for printing.

Editing a Form Letter

The form letter is no different than any other Approach text block. The text attributes can be set in the InfoBox either by selecting the entire block for a global change, or by selecting text within the block to change a particular section of the text.

To insert new fields into the text block, follow these steps:

1. Choose the Text SmartIcon. Click in the form letter's text block where you want to add the new field.
2. Open the Text menu and choose Insert, and then choose Field Value.
3. Choose the field from the Insert Field dialog box. If necessary, change the database from the drop-down list. In this example, you might add the SUB END field to show the customer exactly when the subscription ends.

The field is inserted as a text object, like the other fields in the form letter, so it can't be used like a standard field object.

You can cut and paste text into the text block from elsewhere in the block or from another application, and add formatting such as italics or bold to individual words or letters in the text block. These attributes and others, such as alignment and spacing, are available by right-clicking anywhere in the main text block, from the Text menu, and in the text block InfoBox. Also, you can use logos or other graphics to modify form letters. Because these objects aren't text, they're placed on the form letter outside the main text block.

> **Note**
>
> A form letter can contain only one main text block, but it can be several pages long, depending on the space needed to hold all the fields and text in the text block and any other objects you may add. Consider this when deciding what field information you want to insert in your form letter. You can see how many pages will be used by looking at your form letter in Print Preview mode.

Printing the Form Letters

After you finish setting up your form letter, you'll want to print it. Approach prints one copy of the form letter for each current record. If you perform a find before printing the form letters, only the records in the found set are used to print the form letters.

To print the form letters, follow these steps:

1. Switch to Browse mode.
2. Choose the Form Letter from the list of forms and reports in the status bar or by its view tab.
3. If you want, use a Field On Another View to perform a find to locate the records for which you want to print the form letter.
4. Open the File menu and choose Print, or click the Print SmartIcon.
5. Click OK to print the form letters.

Printing Envelopes

You can create envelopes separately from form letters by using the Envelope Assistant. Follow these steps:

1. Open the Create menu and choose Envelope. The Envelope Assistant appears (see fig. 12.35). It has four tabs: Layout, From, To, and Printer.

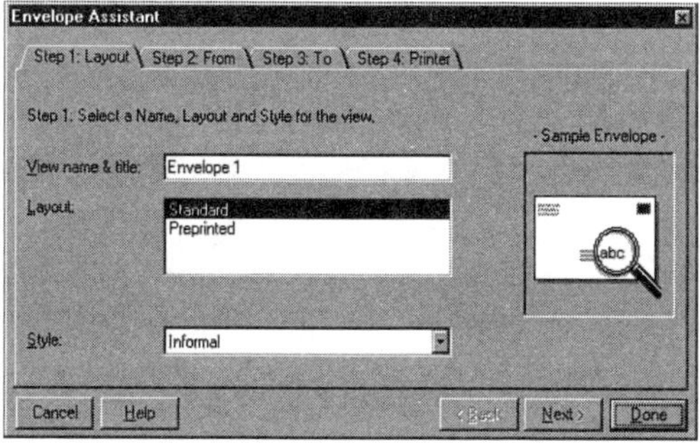

Fig. 12.35

Use the Envelope Assistant to create envelopes from the Owl Publishing customer list.

2. On the Layout page, you can note that Owl Publishing preprints its return address on envelopes, so choose Preprinted from the Layout list box. (Notice that the From tab disappears when you do this.)
3. Make any other choices needed in your envelopes, such as giving the view a name and selecting a style, and then click Next to go to Step 2 (now the To page). As you did with form letter envelopes previously, select the fields from the Owl Publishing Company database to complete the address.
4. Click Next to go to the Printer page. Select your envelope size and shape, and then click Done. An image of the printed envelope appears (see fig. 12.36).

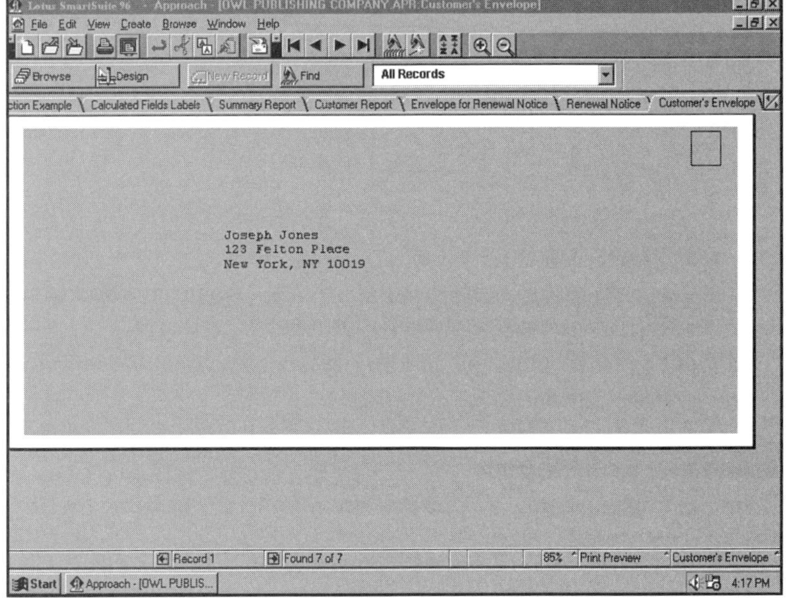

Fig. 12.36

The Envelope Assistant will build an image of the finished envelope. If you've chosen a Preprinted layout, a return address won't display.

From Here...

In this chapter, you learned how reports can give you greater control of data and display attributes than any other type of Approach view. You learned how to create and modify reports using report assistants and PowerClicking, and by adjusting panel and calculated field options.

You also learned that a form letter—while not nearly as complex in its construction as a report—is a specialized way to merge text and field information. You can use form letters to cover your basic mailing needs in Approach, rather than move your data to a word processing application.

For a quick way to work with or analyze the data in a database, consider using a worksheet or crosstab, or even a chart. To find out more, refer to the following chapters in this book:

- Chapter 14, "Using Worksheets and Crosstabs," describes how to use worksheets and crosstabs to display and analyze data.
- Chapter 15, "Creating Charts," shows how Approach data can be charted from the Chart Assistant or directly from a crosstab. You can place charts into report panels for a visual analysis of a field in the database.

CHAPTER 13

Automating Your Work

Approach's macro features help simplify your database work by automating routine activities. A *macro* is a series of operations that are saved by Approach under a macro name that you assign. When you want to perform those operations, you simply run that macro.

Approach macros are quite different from those you may have used before. Many other programs use the term *macro* to refer to a series of keystrokes that you record and play back whenever you want. By contrast, you create an Approach macro by selecting actions in a special dialog box—not by recording keystrokes.

Note

Approach macros automate many of the tasks commonly needed for database operation. Sometimes, however, you'll want more control over a database application than is possible with an Approach macro. LotusScript, a programming language that works with several Lotus products, should be used for those tasks. To help you determine whether you need LotusScript for your application, Lotus includes the manual *Using LotusScript in Approach* with the software. The *LotusScript Language Reference* is also included as help on your system if you install Help for Approach. Finally, the reference manual and the *LotusScript Programmer's Guide* are available by using a coupon enclosed in the Approach package.

Almost any series of operations you can perform yourself in Approach can be assisted or completely automated by a macro—or by a set of macros that you chain together. This means that you can use macros for a wide variety of operations. For example, you can use macros to create a menu-driven application that rivals the sort of product you would expect from a professional programmer.

In this chapter, you learn how to

- Create and use macros
- Assign commands to a macro
- Run a macro

- Edit or delete an existing macro
- Assign a macro to a button or object
- Attach macros to fields and views

After you create a macro, you or someone else can perform the operations embodied in the macro—no matter how complex—simply by running it. You can run a macro in any of the following ways:

- Make a menu selection
- Use a function key
- Click a special command button—or a graphics or text object—that you add to a form or report design
- Start or exit Approach
- Enter or exit a particular view
- Tab into or out of a particular field
- Change the value of a particular field

Creating a Macro

To help understand the concept of working with macros, you'll create a simple macro whose only purpose is to switch from the current view to another one. For example, if your Approach file contains 25 different views, you could use a macro to switch to the view named Worksheet 1.

> **Note**
>
> When you create a new macro, Approach stores it as part of the current Approach file.

To create a new macro, follow these steps:

1. Open the Approach file in which you want to create the macro.
2. Switch to Browse, Design, or Print Preview mode. (You can't define a macro in Find mode.)
3. Open the Edit menu and choose Macros. You'll see a dialog box similar to the one shown in figure 13.1.
4. Click the New button, and the Define Macro dialog box appears (see fig. 13.2). You use this dialog box to define the entire macro.
5. In the combo box labeled Macro Name, enter a unique name for the new macro. This can include a maximum of 29 spaces and special characters and will truncate any name entered that's longer than that limit. In this case, enter **`View, Switch to: Worksheet 1`**.

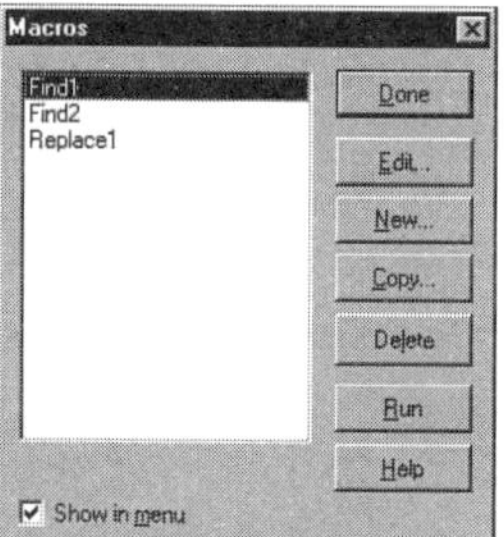

Fig. 13.1

Use the Macros dialog box to begin defining a new macro.

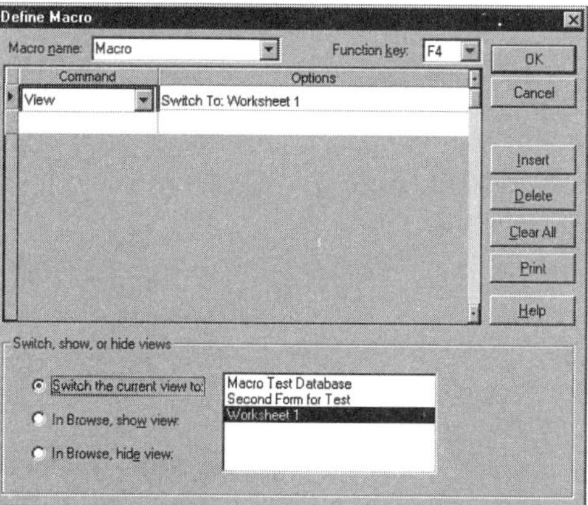

Fig. 13.2

Start defining your macro from the Define Macro dialog box.

Tip

In the Define Macro dialog box, you can drop down the Macro Name combo box to see what other macros have already been defined. Since the macro dialog boxes generally display only the first 24 characters of your macro names, you may want to restrict your names further so that they don't get confusing.

6. To assign a function key to this macro, select it from the Function Key drop-down list. Now you can begin to create the command for this new macro.

Note

You can assign any function key to a macro as long as that key isn't already assigned to another macro. Because the total number of function keys on your keyboard is limited, you may want to reserve them for functions common to many views in your Approach file, such as returning to your main menu view or spell checking the current view.

7. Click the down arrow in the column labeled Command. The list that appears extends across most of the dialog box and shows all the possible commands you can use within a macro (see fig. 13.3).

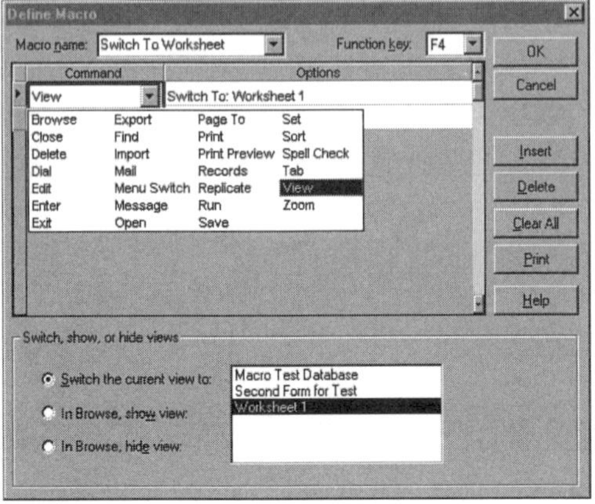

Fig. 13.3

Select a command to insert into the macro by clicking one of the commands displayed.

8. Click the command View (this command was already selected by default for a new macro, but the practice will do you good).
9. In the lower part of the dialog box, click the radio button labeled Switch the Current View To, and then choose the view labeled Worksheet 1. If this view doesn't exist in your current file, choose one of your favorites from the list. Note that the option you choose appears in the upper part of the dialog box in the right-hand column labeled Options.
10. To save the new macro, click OK and then click Done.

Your new macro consists of the single command you selected, which you can refer to as "View, Switch To: Worksheet 1." Each time you run the macro, this single command will be executed.

Now practice running this macro. Remember, the idea is that each time you run it, the macro will switch to the view you selected in step 9. Here's how to run your macro:

1. Switch to a view other than the one you selected in the preceding steps.
2. Make sure that you're in Print Preview or Browse mode. (You can't run a macro when Approach is in Design or Find mode.)
3. Open the Edit menu and choose Run Macro.
4. When the list of current macros appears, choose the one you just created. The macro runs, switching to the designated view.

Note

Each macro is saved as part of an Approach file, which you must save after creating a new macro. If you can't find a previously recorded macro, you probably didn't save the corresponding Approach file after creating the macro, or you're in the wrong Approach file.

Working with Macros

The preceding example describes the basic steps for creating a new macro. However, this simple macro consists of only a single operation—switching to a particular view. This is fine as a simple practice example, but in reality you can create macros consisting of many different operations.

The following sections describe how to create macros that consist of many different commands, and how to edit and save the macros you create.

Creating a New Macro

To begin creating a new macro, display the Define Macro dialog box by opening the Edit menu, choosing Macros, and then choosing New. Enter a unique name for the macro in the Macro Name combo box. You can optionally select a function key for the macro from the Function Key drop-down list. This function key will then be reserved so that whenever you press it, the macro will run.

Entering Commands. You build a macro by selecting the commands for it. When you choose a new command, it becomes part of the list in the Command column in the Define Macro dialog box. The order in which the commands appear on-screen (top to bottom) is the order in which they will execute each time you run the macro. For example, the macro shown in figure 13.4 consists of the following three commands:

Records, First

View, Switch To: Worksheet 1

Zoom, In

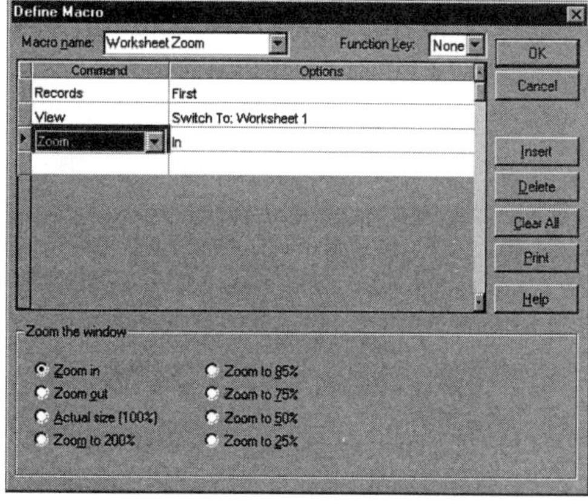

Fig. 13.4

This macro consists of three commands, which will go to the first record in the database, switch to the Worksheet 1 view, and then zoom in on the data on-screen.

You can insert each new command anywhere in the current list of commands—at the bottom, in the middle, or at the top. You can order the commands any way you want, provided that they make sense. For example, you can create a macro consisting of the following two commands in this order, but they don't make any sense because you can't move past the last record in a database file:

- *Records, Last Record.* This command moves Approach to the last record in the current database file.
- *Records, Next Record.* This command moves Approach to the next record in the database file.

To enter a new command in the Define Macro dialog box, follow these steps:

1. In the Command column, select where you want to insert the new command:
    - To enter a command at the bottom of the current command list, click the first blank line below the last command. For example, in figure 13.4 you would click immediately below the command Zoom, In.
    - To enter a new command before an existing one, click that existing command, click the Insert button, and then click the new blank command space to highlight it and see the drop-down arrow for that field.
2. Click the drop-down arrow that appears, and you'll see the entire list of available commands. A description of each available command is listed later in this chapter.
3. Click the command you want to insert.
4. If any options are associated with this command, they'll appear at the bottom of the dialog box. Select the one you want for the command. For instance, in figure 13.4 the Zoom In option is selected.

Repositioning and Deleting Commands. As you build a new macro, you may find errors as you recheck your work. To correct them, you can do the following:

- Edit an existing command, either by selecting new options for it or by replacing it with another command.
- Delete a command.
- Rearrange the order in which the commands appear.

These important features allow you to correct errors before they become big problems.

To edit an existing command in the Define Macro dialog box, follow these steps:

1. Click anywhere on the line displaying that command.
2. Change the options at the bottom of the dialog box.
3. To replace the command with another one, click it in the Command column, pull down the list of commands, select the new command, and then select its options.

To move a command from one location in the command list to another, follow these steps:

1. Click the row marker at the far left end of the command you want to move so that the entire line is highlighted (see fig. 13.5).

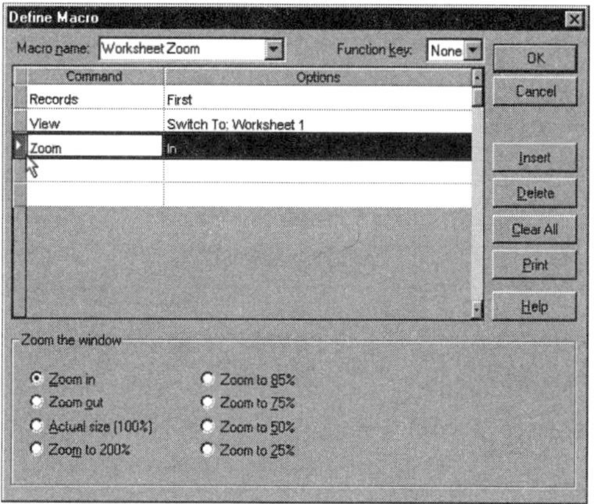

Fig. 13.5

To move a command, first click its row marker.

2. When the little hand replaces the mouse pointer, hold down the mouse button and drag the row marker up or down to where you want to reposition it (see fig. 13.6). Notice the heavy guideline that appears. This line indicates the upper boundary of the new position for the command.
3. When the command is where you want it, release the mouse button.

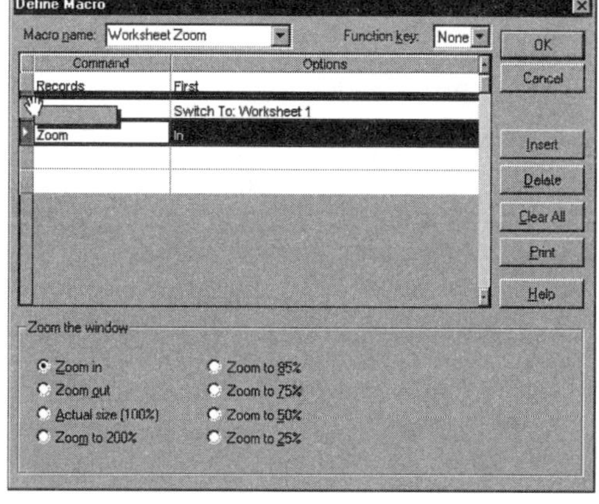

Fig. 13.6

Reposition a command by dragging and dropping it.

If you need to delete a command, follow these steps:

1. Click the row marker for the command you want to delete so that the entire line becomes highlighted, or click anywhere in that row.
2. Click the Delete button.

Note

If you accidentally delete a command, you can recover—provided that you don't mind losing all your unsaved current work—by clicking the Cancel button. Approach then displays a confirmation message that gives you the opportunity to save all your macro changes, undo all your current changes, or continue editing the macro.

Editing and Deleting an Existing Macro

You can edit an existing macro by repositioning, modifying, and deleting existing commands and by adding new ones. These operations are identical to those described in the preceding sections.

To edit a macro, first select it from the list of current macros, and then make your changes, as follows:

1. Open the Edit menu and choose Macros.
2. When the list of macros appears, double-click the name of the macro you want to edit. Alternatively, you can click the macro name and then click Edit. The Define Macro dialog box appears.
3. Make whatever changes to the macro you want, using the techniques described in the preceding sections.
4. To save your changes, click OK and then Done to exit the Macros dialog box.

You can easily delete a macro that's no longer needed by following these steps:

1. Open the Edit menu and choose Macros.
2. Click the name of the macro.
3. Click the Delete button.
4. When Approach asks you to confirm the deletion, choose Yes (unless you suddenly change your mind, in which case you should choose No).

Saving Your Macros

Each macro you edit or create is part of the Approach file that's now open. When you save the Approach file, the macros you've edited or created are also saved. From another point of view, if you create a new macro and then later exit the Approach file without saving it, your macro will be lost.

Note

Each macro is restricted to the Approach file in which you created it. Consequently, if you create a macro for file A, you can't use it directly with file B. Instead, you'll have to open file B and then re-create the macro from scratch.

Looking at the Available Macro Commands

When building new macros, you can choose from 27 different major types of macro commands. These are referred to as "major" commands because many of them have several options from which to choose. A few commands offer you virtually unlimited choices. Consequently, you have at your disposal a gigantic variety of different commands, offering endless possibilities for automating your work.

The following sections briefly describe the 27 major command types. They are listed in the order in which they appear in the Define Macro dialog box.

Browse. Browse switches from the current view mode to Browse mode. This command is of limited value by itself because you can use a macro to switch to Browse only from Print Preview mode. It's used most often when switching to a form view from a report or other view that's commonly shown in Print Preview mode.

Note

Remember that you can't run a macro from Find or Design mode.

Close. This command closes the current Approach file but doesn't exit Approach. If you've made any changes since the last time you saved your Approach file, Approach asks whether you want to save them now.

Delete. This powerful—but extremely dangerous—command gives you the option of deleting either the current record, the current found set, or any particular file on your computer. To make the command even more potentially lethal, you can turn off Approach's standard dialog box that warns you of an impending deletion and gives you an option not to delete the file or records.

Caution

Be very careful when using this command. If you use the Delete command incorrectly, you can wipe out part or all of an Approach database.

Dial. This command dials the telephone number contained in the field you specify, and for the record that's current when the macro runs. Approach uses whatever dialup settings are now in effect.

Note

For information on customizing the autodialer feature of Approach, see Chapter 17, "Customizing Approach."

Edit. By using the Edit command, you can select a radio button option to do any of the following:

- *Cut.* Remove the current selection (for example, whatever you now have highlighted on-screen) to the Windows Clipboard. This is equivalent to opening the Edit menu and choosing Cut.
- *Copy.* Copy the current selection to the Clipboard (equivalent to opening the Edit menu and choosing Copy).
- *Paste.* Paste the Clipboard contents to the current position of the text cursor (equivalent to opening the Edit menu and choosing Paste).
- *Select All.* This option is equivalent to opening the Edit menu and choosing Select All, and it's effective only when a worksheet is displayed in Browse mode.
- *Open Paste Special Dialog and Wait for Input.* This option displays the Paste Special dialog box. The macro—when it runs—pauses when the Paste Special dialog box is displayed, so that you can make your selection there.

Enter. The Enter command is equivalent to pressing Enter or clicking the Enter icon. Its main use is to accept the record now being entered or edited. Especially when entering new records into your database, you need to use Enter in your macro before switching to other views in order to save the data you have typed in so far.

Exit. This command exits Approach, unlike the Close command which just closes the currently opened Approach file. If you've made any changes since the last save, Approach asks whether you want to save them.

Export. The Export command automatically performs an export operation, using the set of options you select when creating the macro. Alternatively, you can set this command to pause the macro when it runs, displaying the Export Data dialog box for user input.

Find. The Find command performs a preset find operation using the options you specify when creating the macro. You can enter a new find operation or select from a list box of Named Find/Sort operations. Alternatively, you can set up this command by using Go to Find and wait for input to pause the macro when it runs, displaying the Find screen for user input. Other command options include Find Again, Go to Find Assistant and Wait for Input, Find All Records, and Refresh the Found Set. If a stored find is run, you have the option to choose Run a Macro If No Records Are Found and select the macro name from the drop-down list.

Import. The Import command performs an import operation using the options you select when creating the macro. Alternatively, you can set the command to pause the macro when it runs, displaying the Import Data dialog box for user input.

Mail. The Mail command displays the TeamMail dialog box, pausing the macro for user input. Alternatively, you can set this command to send mail automatically, using the TeamMail options you select when creating the macro.

Menu Switch. This command switches to another menu, which you specify when creating the macro. You can also go to the Customize Menu dialog box to create a custom menu from here directly. (Custom menus are discussed in Chapter 17, "Customizing Approach.")

Message. The Message command displays a dialog box with the message you set up as part of the command. The dialog box title can be up to 31 characters long, and the message text can be multiple lines of information with embedded field data. Field names for all types of fields must be specified in the text area as in the following examples: `<<MAILED>>`, `<<"LAST NAME">>`, `<<NEWSLETTER.Newsletter>>`, `<<"Calc amt due">>`.

New in Approach 96 is the ability to define one or two buttons in the dialog box with your own labels and attached macros of your own making, or to run the "Continue" or "Stop" build-in actions. The default is "OK" for the button label and "Continue" for the action. This very desirable feature lets you involve the user more directly in the flow of logic in your application instead of merely informing them that something has happened or is incorrect. Button labels can be up to 16 characters long.

Open. This command opens a file, which you select when creating the macro. Alternatively, you can use this command to pause the macro when it runs, displaying the File Open dialog box for user input.

Tip

You normally don't use the Open command to open databases, as they are automatically opened by Approach when your application is loaded. You can, however, open any file on your computer and run the associated application—including opening another Approach .APR-type file. This is very useful when you have several Approach applications used by the same people and want to provide macro buttons to move between the applications seamlessly.

Page To. Page To switches to a different page of a multipage form. When the macro runs, it goes to the specified page (first, last, previous, next, or a particular page number). Because this command doesn't change the current record, use the Records command to switch to a different record in the database.

Print. The Print command performs a print operation when the macro runs, using the print options you select when creating the macro. Alternatively, you can set the command to pause the macro when it runs, displaying the Print dialog box for user input.

Print Preview. This command switches to Print Preview mode.

Records. This versatile command has several options. You can use it to go to a particular record in the current Approach file, such as the first record, last, next, and so on. Alternatively, you can set up this command to create a new record, hide a record, or duplicate an existing record.

Replicate. This command option replicates a Notes database, using the options you establish when creating the macro. Alternatively, you can use the command to pause the macro when it runs, displaying the Replicate dialog box for user input.

Run. This powerful command runs a macro you specify. You can include If/Else conditions so that the macro you choose runs only if certain conditions exist. You can also use the Run command to run the current macro again—starting from the top. This feature provides the mechanism for creating looping macros. This command can also run another macro, and then return to the original macro to continue running it.

Save. This command saves the current Approach file. Or you can set the command to pause the macro when it runs, displaying the Save As dialog box for user input.

Set. This command sets the value of the field you specify to a particular value that you also specify. The value can be a constant such as a number or text string, or you can specify a formula. The formula is defined using the Formula dialog box, in which you specify field names, operators, and functions in the same way you defined calculated fields in Chapter 10, "Using Advanced Field Types." Using the Set command with Approach's built-in `If()` function allows you to selectively set field values under specific conditions.

Sort. The Sort command performs a sort operation, using the options you select when creating the macro. Or you can use this command to pause the macro when it runs, displaying the Sort dialog box for user input. Summary fields and groupings can optionally be specified by clicking the Summaries button.

Spell Check. This command opens the Spell Check dialog box, pausing the macro for user input. This way, you can check the spelling of data in the current record or found set, including text in memo fields. The spell checker is discussed in detail in Chapter 5, "Working with Your Data."

Tab. This command moves the cursor to a specific tab number in the current view's tab order. When creating the macro, you must specify the tab number to go to. This command doesn't tab forward from the current field, but starts with the field in tab position 1 and proceeds from there.

View. The View command switches to the view you choose in the current Approach file. This could be a form, a worksheet, or any other type of view. Another option for this command lets you hide a view or show a view that was previously hidden. This would let you prevent a user from getting to a particular view until you have determined that the user needs to do so, and then show it and switch to it, if appropriate, with a second View command.

Zoom. The Zoom command either zooms in, zooms out, or switches the magnification of the current view to the actual size. Whatever part of the current view shown on-screen is zoomed, and you can scroll to other parts of the view from there.

Running Macros

After you create a macro, you can set it up to run in several different ways:

- Press the function key—if any—that you've assigned to the macro.
- Open the Edit menu and choose Run Macro, and then select the macro from the displayed list.
- Click the macro name from the Macros dialog box and then click the Run button.
- Click a button or other object to which you assigned a macro.
- Set it up as part of another macro (using the Run command) or within a LotusScript application.

Tip

If your macro fails to run, make sure that you're not in Design or Find mode, because no macros will ever run there. If your macro runs incorrectly, you'll have to try tracking down the problem—perhaps on a step-by-step basis. At critical points in your macro, add Message commands temporarily to display useful field contents and to inform you as to what the macro is doing. These messages may tell you what data is incorrect or why the macro is doing strange things. As a last resort, make a copy of the entire macro to save it, try deleting every command in the macro except the first one, and then run it. If it does what you expect, add another command and run the macro again until you find the troublesome command(s).

You can also have a macro run automatically under any of the following circumstances:

- Opening or closing a particular Approach file
- Tabbing into or out of a specific field
- Changing the value in a specific field
- Switching into or out of a particular view

Using Open and Close Macros

You can create a macro that runs automatically each time you open a particular Approach file. To accomplish this, open the Approach file you want, create the macro, and assign it the name Open. Similarly, if you assign the name Close to a macro, it will automatically run each time you close its associated file.

Because each macro is saved as part of the Approach file that's open when you create it, you can create a separate pair of Open and Close macros for each of your Approach files.

Attaching Macros to Field Objects

You can assign up to three macros to a particular field object in a view:

- A macro that runs whenever you tab into the field. For example, for certain fields you might want to display a message indicating that the fields need to be updated periodically and listing the rules for updating them.
- A macro that runs whenever you tab out of the field. For example, you may want to perform special calculations on a field to verify its value or to look up data in a related database for which this field is the key.
- A macro that runs whenever you change the value of the field. For example, you could display a message telling the user that the value entered isn't allowed, or to confirm that the value is to be added to the database.

Note

You can assign a macro to a field object on a particular view only in Design mode. Also, this technique won't work for worksheet or crosstab views because macros can't be attached to fields in those types of views.

To assign one or more of these types of macros to a field object, follow these steps:

1. Switch to a Form view, and then switch to Design mode.
2. Double-click the field object you want to use so that its InfoBox appears.
3. Click the Macros tab in the InfoBox (see fig. 13.7).

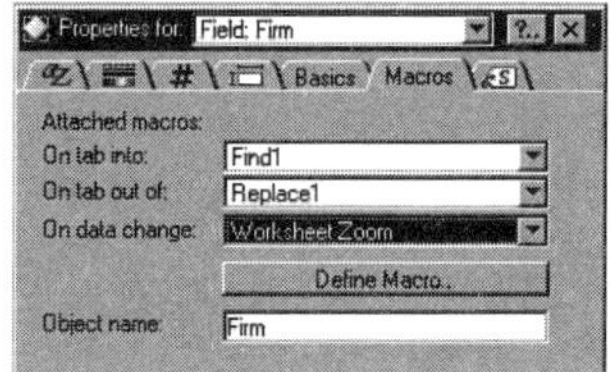

Fig. 13.7

Use the InfoBox to attach macros to a field object in a view.

4. If you haven't yet created one or more of the macros, choose the button labeled Define Macro, and then build the macro or macros. When you're finished, exit the Macros dialog box by choosing Done.
5. Assign the macros you want by using the appropriate drop-down lists in the InfoBox. You can assign the same macro to multiple conditions; for example, you may want to have a macro run when the content has changed or when the field is tabbed out of.

If you want to detach a macro from a field, follow the preceding steps, but choose the blank item in the corresponding drop-down list box.

Attaching Macros to Views

You can attach a macro to a particular view so that it runs whenever you switch to that view. You can also attach another macro that runs whenever you switch out of the view. To set up one or both of these macros, follow these steps:

1. Switch to the view you want, and then switch to Design mode.
2. Display the InfoBox for this view (the easiest way is to click the InfoBox icon or double-click a blank part of the form).
3. Click the Macros tab (see fig. 13.8).

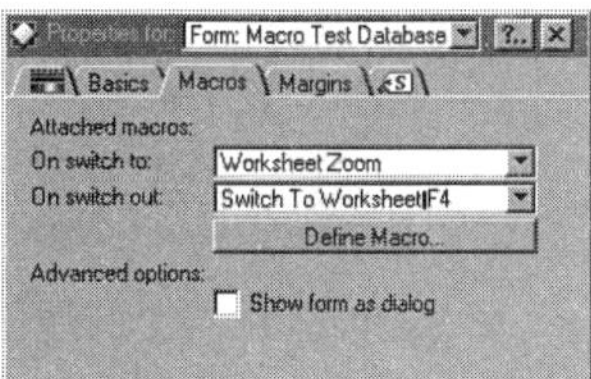

Fig. 13.8

Use the view's InfoBox to attach macros to a view.

4. If you haven't yet created one or both of the macros, click the Define Macro button, and then build the macros. When you're finished, exit from the Macros dialog box by clicking Done.
5. Assign the macros you want by using the appropriate drop-down lists.

If you want to detach a macro from a view, follow the preceding steps, but choose the blank item in the corresponding drop-down list box.

Running Macros with Buttons and Objects

You can attach a macro to a text or graphic object you create within Approach. You can then run the macro simply by clicking the object.

You can also create a macro button and attach it to a macro; clicking the button runs the macro. You can create the macro first and then create the button and attach the macro, or you can create the button and the macro at the same time.

Text and Graphics Objects. You can attach a macro to any text or graphic object you've already created on a form. This handy feature allows you to create highly customized objects to use as buttons for running macros. For instance, you could create a macro that prints the current view, and then attach it to a graphic object in the shape of a printer (see fig. 13.9). When you click this object, Approach prints the view.

To attach a macro to a text or graphic object that you've already created, follow these steps:

1. Switch to the view containing the text or graphic object.
2. Switch to Design mode.
3. Click the object you want to use.
4. Display the InfoBox for the object, and then click the Macros tab (see fig. 13.10).
5. If you haven't yet created the macro, choose the Define Macro button; then build the macro. When you're finished, exit the Macros dialog box by clicking Done.

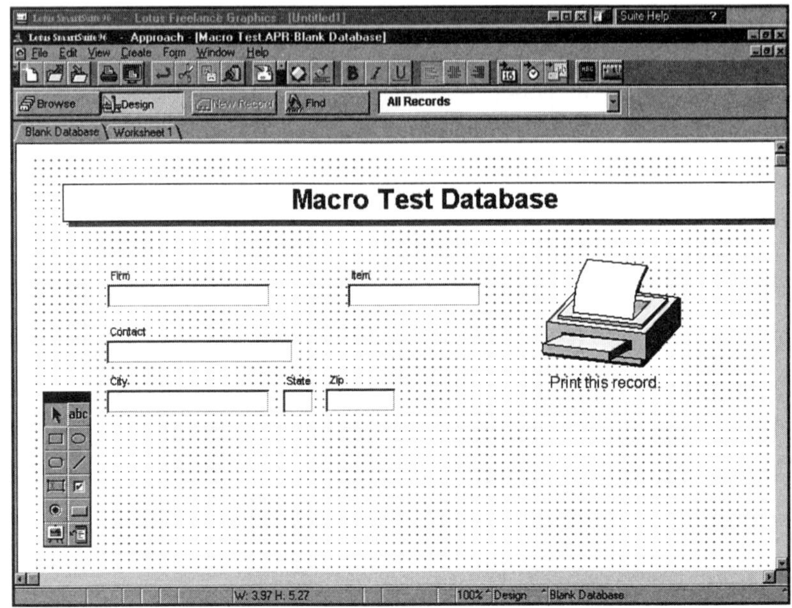

Fig. 13.9

You can create highly customized graphic objects as macro buttons.

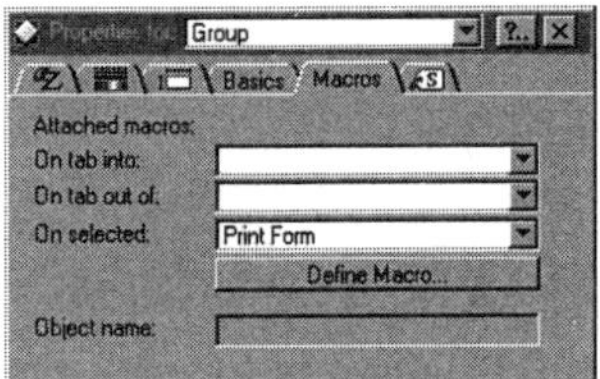

Fig. 13.10

Use this InfoBox to attach a macro to a text or graphic object.

6. By using the On Tab Into, On Tab Out Of, or On Selected drop-down list boxes, select the macro you want to attach.

Macro Buttons. You can create a standard macro button on any of your forms or reports, and then attach a macro to the button. When you click the button, the macro runs. A macro button looks exactly like the buttons on the action bar, and you can add your own descriptive text to the button so that a user will have no doubt as to the button's purpose.

Follow these steps to create a macro button and assign it to a particular macro:

1. Display the form or report you want to use.
2. Make sure that you're in Design mode.
3. Display the tools palette (either click the Show Tools palette icon, or open the View menu and choose Show Tools Palette).

4. Click the Button icon on the tools palette, and then click where you want the button to appear on the form or report. If necessary, drag the button to exactly where you want it.
5. Double-click the new button to display its InfoBox. Then click the Basics tab (see fig. 13.11).

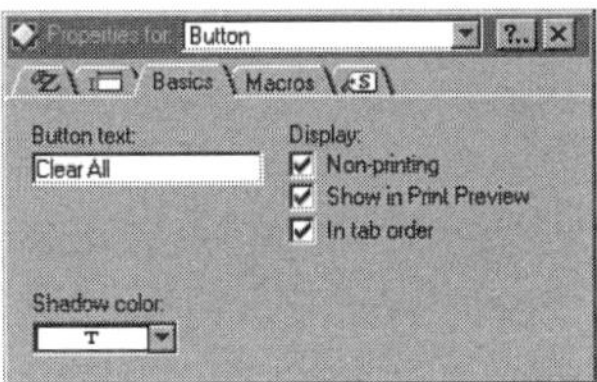

Fig. 13.11

Enter the text for a macro button. You can resize the button if your text doesn't fit in the initial button drawn on the view.

6. Enter the text that you want to appear on the button. The text won't wrap to additional lines but is restricted to one line.

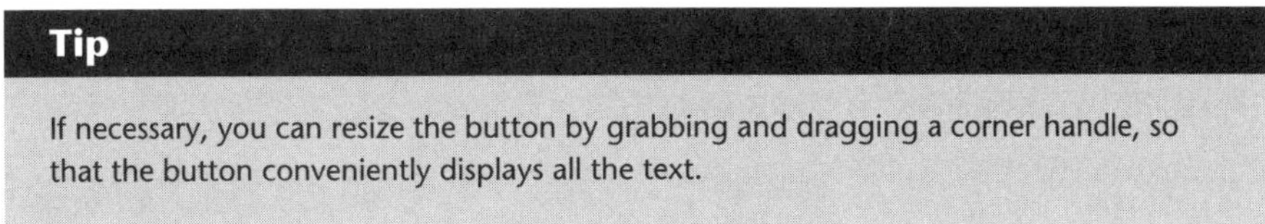

Tip

If necessary, you can resize the button by grabbing and dragging a corner handle, so that the button conveniently displays all the text.

7. If you want the button to appear in Print Preview mode, choose the Show in Print Preview option.
8. Click the Macros tab (see fig. 13.12).

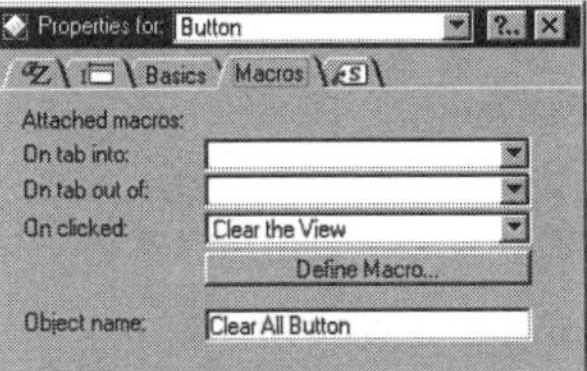

Fig. 13.12

Select the macros for the button from the list boxes based on the conditions desired for the macro to run.

9. If you haven't yet created the macro for this button, choose the Define Macro button, and then create the macro. When you're done, exit the Macros dialog box by choosing Done.
10. From the On Clicked drop-down list box in the InfoBox, select the macro you want to assign to the macro button.

You can easily delete a macro button you no longer want to appear in a view. Select the view, switch to Design mode, click the button, and then press Delete; or open the Edit menu and choose Cut. Notice that the macro that was attached to the button isn't deleted; it remains part of the associated Approach file so that you can use it again.

Looking at Some Macro Examples

The best way to learn how to create macros is to study as many different examples as possible. The following sections present several types of macros that you can use most effectively by reproducing and running them on your own computer.

To duplicate each example in the following sections, begin in the same way—by opening the Edit menu and choosing Macros. When the Macros dialog box appears, click the New button so that the Define Macro dialog box appears.

Sorting Records

Frequently you may want to work with a group of records that are sorted into a particular order. For instance, you might want to perform a weekly operation that requires sorting a file of order records by state, and then for each state by city.

To create a macro to perform this particular type of sort operation, fill in the Define Macro dialog box as shown in figure 13.13.

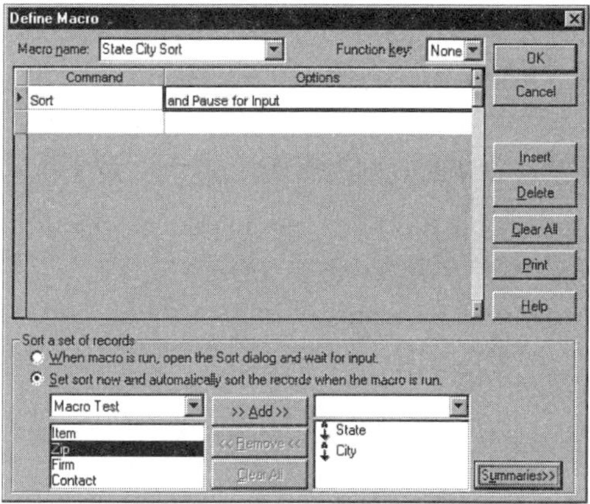

Fig. 13.13

Use this macro to perform an automatic sort.

As a review, let's go through the steps for accomplishing this:

1. In the Macro Name text box, enter a new name for this macro.
2. In the Command column, pull down the list of commands and then click Sort.
3. In the lower part of the dialog box, choose the Set Sort Now and Automatically Sort the Records When the Macro Is Run option, and then copy the STATE and CITY field names from the left list box to the right one.
4. When you're done, click OK.

Replacing Field Values

You can use macros in many ways to automatically replace the contents of one or more records. As a simple example, figure 13.14 shows a macro that replaces the NUMBER OF ITEMS field of the current record with zero.

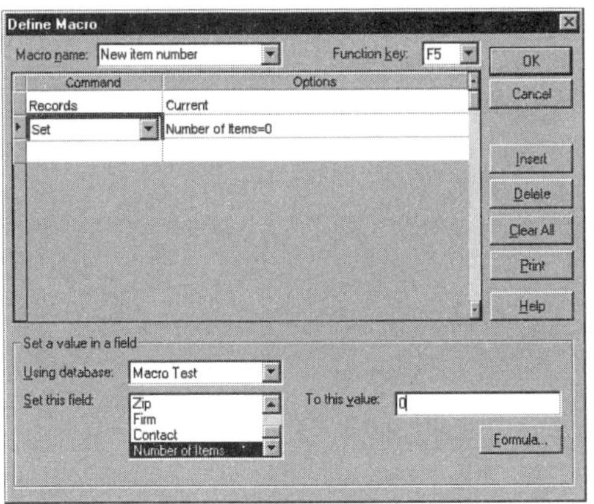

Fig. 13.14

Use this macro to replace a field value in the current record.

This macro consists of two commands:

- *Records, Current.* When you set up this command, choose the Current Record option at the bottom of the dialog box. The complete command tells Approach to set up the current record (whichever one you now have selected when the macro runs) for modification.

Tip

When using a macro to modify a record, use the Records command to select that record.

- *Set, Number of Items=0.* As part of this command, you choose the NUMBER OF ITEMS field and the value 0. When the macro runs, this command sets the NUMBER OF ITEMS field to a value of zero.

For each of the remaining macro examples, you'll see a figure similar to 13.14, listing the commands that make up the macro. For each command, the entry in the Options column indicates the corresponding options you should select at the bottom of the Define Macro dialog box.

A Looping Example: Replacing a Field Value for All Records

One of the most powerful features of the macro language is its capability to perform loops, whereby a macro is repeated over and over—each for a different record.

To illustrate how a looping macro works, let's expand on the previous example by creating a macro that sets the NUMBER OF ITEMS field to zero *for every record in the database file*. This macro is shown in figure 13.15.

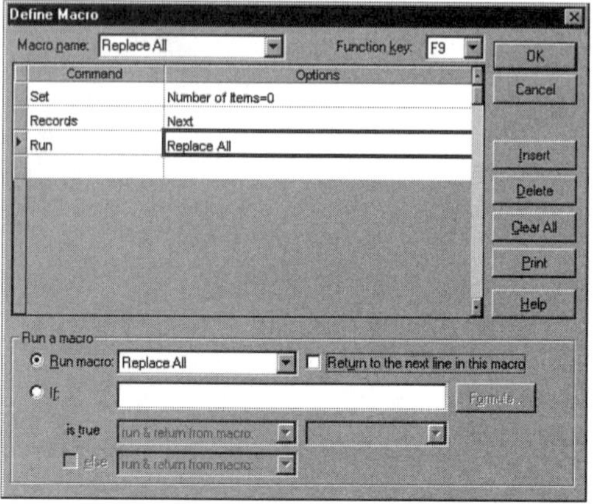

Fig. 13.15

You can use macros to replace a field value in all records.

Let's go through the different commands that make up this macro:

- *Set, Number of Items=0.* This command replaces the value of the NUMBER OF ITEMS field to zero in the current record.
- *Records, Next.* This command moves to the next record in the current database file.
- *Run, Replace All.* Use this command to cause the macro to loop. To accomplish this, you select the Run Macro option, as shown in figure 13.15. By using this option, you select the name of the macro you want to run—in this case, the name of the current macro. In other words, when the Run command in this macro executes, the macro runs itself again! Therefore, the three commands that make up the macro repeat themselves—including the Run, Replace All command, which then repeats the macro again, and so on.

Here are some important points to note about this macro:

- Each time the macro repeats itself, the NUMBER OF ITEMS field of a different record is modified because of the command Records, Next, which moves to the next record in the database file.
- The macro automatically stops running when there are no more records in the current database file. This is a handy feature that simplifies your programming a great deal.
- The macro doesn't automatically begin at the first record in the database file. Instead, it starts with whatever record you happen to have selected when you run the macro. To make the macro modify every record in the file, you must manually click the first record in the file SmartIcon before running the macro.

Tip

An improvement on this macro would be to have it begin by automatically jumping to the first record in the file. You'll see how to accomplish this in the next example.

Setting Up Another Looping Example

The problem with the previous macro example is that before you run it, you must remember to go to the first record in the database file; otherwise, not every record will be modified. You can eliminate this shortcoming by creating a second macro that

- Jumps to the first record in the current database file
- Runs the macro "Replace All" (the one in the previous example)

Figure 13.16 shows the two commands in this macro. The Records, First command causes Approach to jump to the first record in the current database file. Then the Run, Replace All command tells Approach to run the macro named Replace All. As described in the previous example, this macro then replaces values in the NUMBER OF ITEMS field, starting with the current record (which is the first one, in this case).

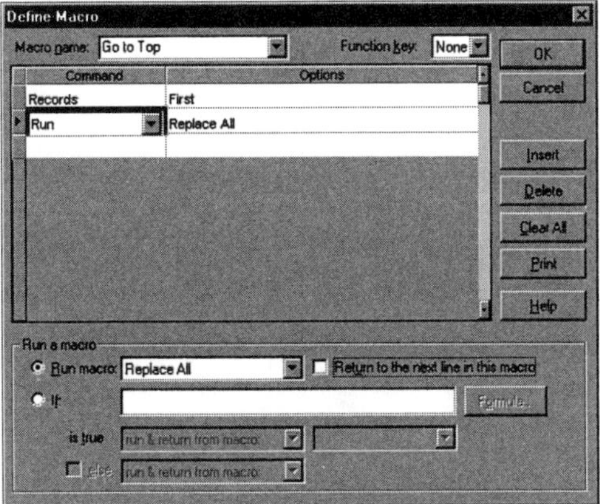

Fig. 13.16

Use this macro to go to the first record and begin a looping macro.

Note that in this new two-macro set, you run the macro Go To Top, which does its setup, and then run the macro Replace All.

Finding a Group of Records

As you work with Approach database files, you'll often need to locate particular groups of records. For example, you might want to view only those records for a particular city or for a particular salesperson.

Approach offers two different types of macro techniques for finding groups of records. With the first, you preselect the search conditions you want to use so that whenever you run the macro, it locates the records satisfying just those search conditions.

With the second method, you set up a macro so that each time it runs, it pauses with the Find dialog box or Find Assistant displayed, so that you can enter whatever search conditions you want. After you do, Approach will first find and display the records satisfying your search conditions and then resume running the macro.

Presetting a Group of Find Conditions. Figure 13.17 shows a macro in which you preset a group of find conditions.

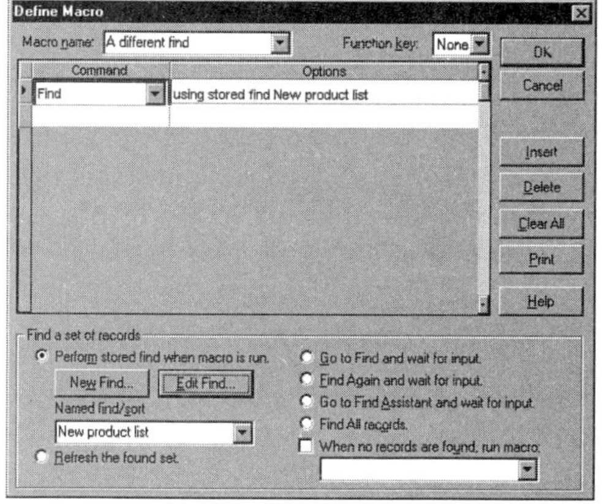

Fig. 13.17

You can use this macro to preset a group of find conditions.

To create this macro, follow these steps:

1. Open the Edit menu and choose Macros. Next, click the New button to display the Define Macro dialog box.
2. Enter a name for the new macro.
3. Pull down the list of commands, and then choose the Find command.
4. Choose the Perform Stored Find When Macro Is Run option, and then click the New Find button.
5. When the Find screen appears (see fig. 13.18), fill in the find conditions you want. The Find screen will be the view you have displayed when you started to create this macro.
6. Press Enter to return to the Define Macro dialog box.
7. Click OK to save the new macro.

The single-command macro shown in figure 13.17 is useful as an example, but in practice you'll probably want to incorporate the Find command as part of a larger macro. You'll see some examples later in this chapter.

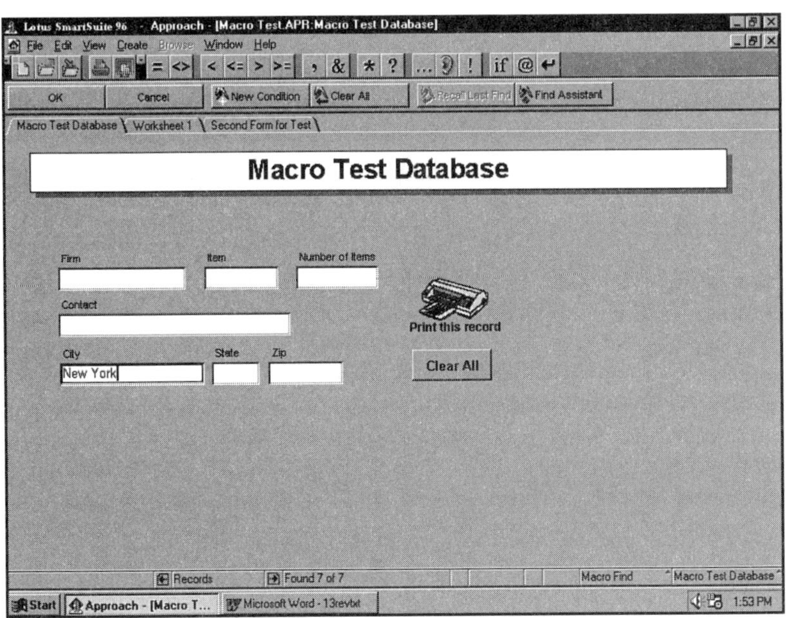

Fig. 13.18

Enter the find conditions you want to preset.

Pausing for Input. Rather than pre-set a group of find conditions within a macro, you can create a macro that pauses during execution, so that you can enter the conditions at that time. Figure 13.19 shows an example of this type of macro.

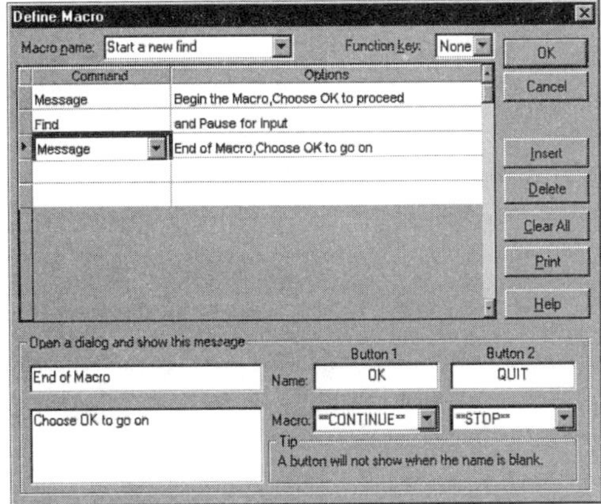

Fig. 13.19

This macro pauses for the user to input a set of find conditions.

Here's an explanation of the commands in this macro:

- *Message, Begin the Macro, Choose OK to Proceed.* Displays a message for the user.
- *Find, And Pause for Input.* Displays the Find screen, pausing for user input. When the user finishes entering find conditions, Approach finds and displays all records matching the find conditions, and then resumes running the macro.

- *Message, End of Macro, Choose OK to Go On.* Displays another message for the user.

The message commands here are for illustration purposes only. In practice, you might use other commands with this type of Find command, to sort the records into a particular order or to display the found set on another view, for example.

Modifying a Group of Records (1)

A common database operation involves modifying a particular group of records within a database. For instance, you might want to delete them or modify the contents of specific fields. Suppose that you've hired a replacement salesperson to cover the San Francisco territory. To reflect this change in your Orders file, you'll need to change the SALESPERSON field for those records dealing with clients in San Francisco.

> **Note**
>
> This is the first of two different example macros for accomplishing the same operation—namely, modifying the San Francisco records to reflect a new salesperson. These macros illustrate an important point: There's usually more than one way to write a macro to perform a particular set of operations.

Figure 13.20 shows how a macro can accomplish this operation. This is a looping macro, similar to the one described earlier. Here's a synopsis of the commands it uses:

- *Set, Salesperson=IF(City = 'San Francisco', 'Caparelli', Salesperson).* This rather complicated command conditionally changes the value of the SALESPERSON field for the current record. The Set command includes in a formula for Salesperson the built-in function `IF(Condition, Value 1, Value 2)`, which has the following meaning:
    - IF the value of `Condition` is true, use the value `Value 1`.
    - OTHERWISE use the value `Value 2`.

  In the current context, the Set, Salesperson... command has the following meaning: If the value of the CITY field for the current record is San Francisco, set the SALESPERSON field to Caparelli (the new salesperson); otherwise, set the SALESPERSON field to itself—in other words, don't change it.
- *Records, Next.* Go to the next record in the current database file.
- *Run, SF Salesperson.* Run this macro again.

As in the previous looping example, before running this macro you would click the first record in the file. Or you could create a second macro, similar to the Go To Top macro described earlier, which would jump to the top of the file and then run the SF Salesperson macro.

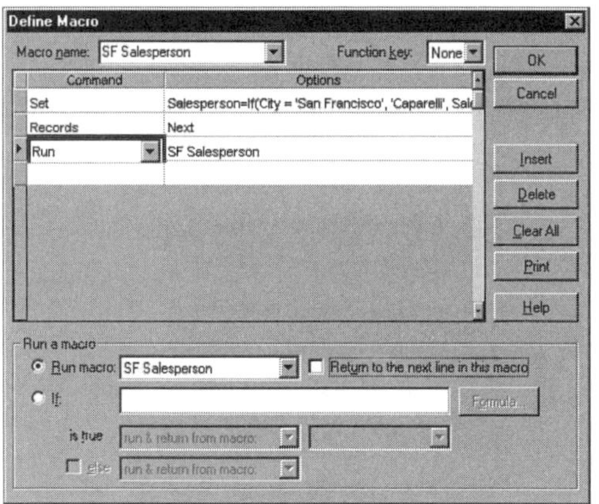

Fig. 13.20

You can use this macro to modify a particular set of records.

Modifying a Group of Records (2)

The previous example illustrated a macro that used a formula containing the built-in conditional `IF()` function to modify a particular group of records. Figure 13.21 shows another approach to the problem.

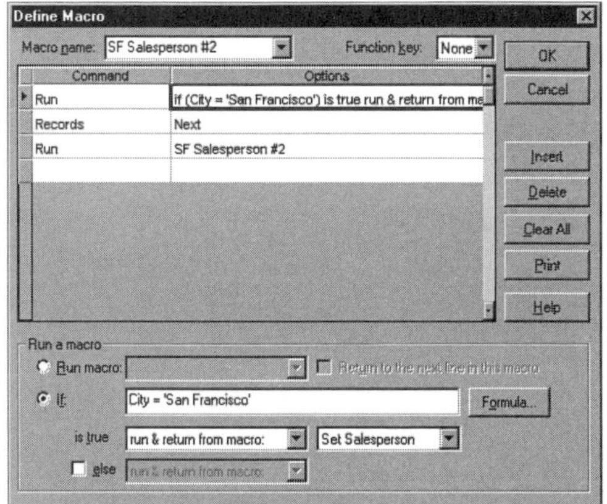

Fig. 13.21

You can define another macro for modifying a particular group of records.

Here's an explanation of the commands:

- *Run, IF(City = 'San Francisco') Is True Run & Return from Macro: Set Salesperson.* This is a new variation on the Run command. When this command executes, the macro Set Salesperson will be run only if the value of the CITY field in the current record is San Francisco.

  The Set Salesperson macro changes the value of the SALESPERSON field (see fig. 13.22).

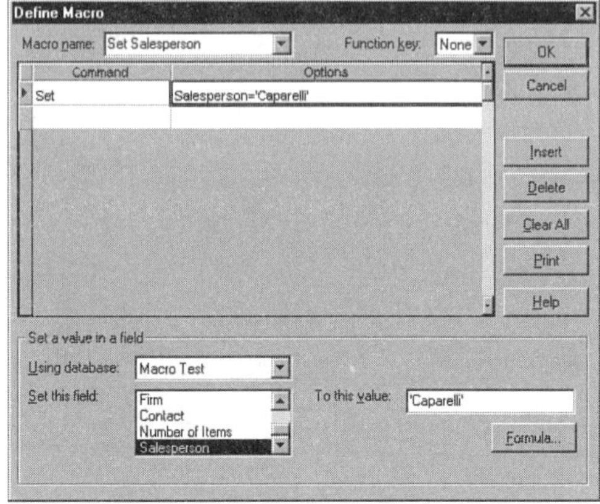

Fig. 13.22

This Set command, used in the Set Salesperson macro, replaces the value of the SALESPERSON field for the current record.

- *Records, Next.* Jumps to the next record in the current database file.
- *Run, SF Salesperson #2.* Runs the current macro again, thus creating a loop that will process every record in the file (provided that you move to the first record before running this macro).

The Set Salesperson macro is a separate macro you must create before building the SF Salesperson #2 macro. Its only purpose is to modify the value of the SALESPERSON field in the current record. Figure 13.22 shows this one-command macro.

Using Macros to Create a Multi-Screen Data-Entry Form

Suppose that you want to create a new data-entry form, but there isn't enough room on one screen for all the field objects you want to include.

> **Note**
>
> New in Approach 96 is the ability to create a form with as many as five pages spanning multiple screens. However, these pages must all be based on the same main database because they are all part of one view. The macro approach lets you specify different main databases to each page of your "form" and also validate conditions to control the movement from page to page, if necessary.

To solve this dilemma, you can create a second form to display the remaining fields. As far as Approach is concerned, your second form is completely unrelated to the first one; only you know that there's a logical connection between the two. Whenever you enter new records or modify existing ones, you can switch from one form to the other as needed.

To simplify the process of switching back and forth between the two forms, you can use macros linked to command buttons on the forms. To switch from one form to the other, you simply click the appropriate button on either form.

To illustrate how this works, figure 13.23 shows the two screens that make up the complete data-entry form for a Customers database file. For the user's convenience, the two forms are labeled Page 1 and Page 2.

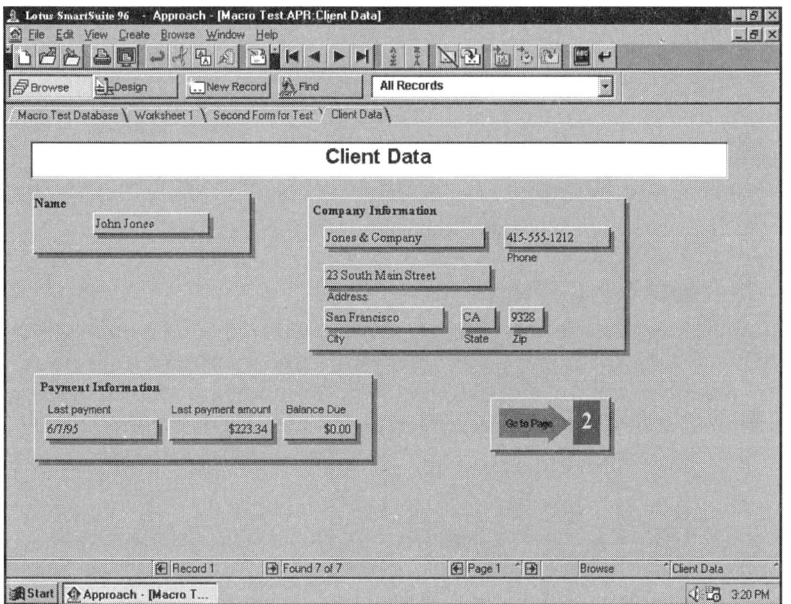

Fig. 13.23

A macro allows you to jump to a second screen for further data entry.

Notice that the bottom of the first screen displays a macro button labeled Go To Page 2. This button is attached to a macro whose only purpose is to switch to the other page. Consequently, when you click this macro button, the macro switches to page 2. Similarly, the second screen displays a macro button that, when clicked, switches to the first page.

> **Note**
>
> The arrow and large number 2 on the macro button in figure 13.23 aren't actually part of the button, although it appears to be so. Instead, they are graphics objects imported from a separate software package and positioned directly on top of the button.

Here's an outline of the steps you follow to create this two-page data-entry form—including the macro buttons:

1. Create the two separate forms, naming them Form 1 and Form 2 (or other names, if you want). Set up each form with the fields you want.
2. Create a new macro with the name Go To Form 2. It should consist of the following single command: *View, Switch to Form 2.*

3. Create another new macro, with the name Go To Form 1. It should consist of the following single command: *View, Switch to Form 1.*
4. Switch to Design mode in Form 1.
5. Create a macro button, placing it somewhere convenient on the form. Place the text *Go To Page 2* on the button.
6. Attach the Go To Form 2 macro to this new macro button.
7. Switch to Form 2.
8. Create a macro button, placing it somewhere convenient on this form. Place the text *Go To Page 1* on the button.
9. Attach the Go To Form 1 macro to this macro button.

Creating a Master Menu Form

By using the techniques described in this chapter, you can easily create an impressive Approach form that acts as a "main menu" to other forms and reports. You—or the staff in your office—can then use this menu to perform various operations. You can even automate Approach to display this menu each time a user opens the Approach file of interest.

Figure 13.24 shows this type of menu, which is labeled *Welcome to the Customers Database* and consists primarily of a group of macro buttons. Each button is attached to a macro that performs a particular operation or set of operations. For instance, clicking the first button would run a macro that switches to a data-entry form for adding new records.

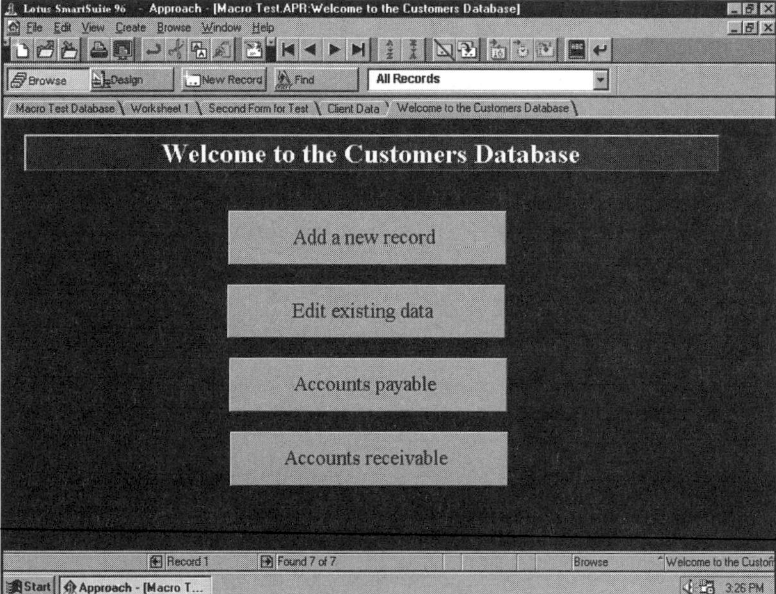

Fig. 13.24

Use this menu form to select other database activities.

Here are a few tips you might want to incorporate into your own menus:

- You can spruce up your menus by tastefully adding text and graphic objects. If you have access to a clip-art software package, browse through it for images that you might want to use.
- By creating menus as described in this section, you can create a set of multi-tier menus. The main menu would contain a set of buttons, each of which would lead to a secondary menu. The options there could lead to other menus or to specific views and tasks.
- You can have Approach automatically display a menu each time you open a particular database file. To accomplish this, create a new macro as part of that file, naming the macro Open. This macro should consist of the single command View, Switch to *Menu*, where *Menu* is the name of the form containing the main menu for the database file. Because the name of the macro is Open, it will automatically run each time you open the Approach file, thereby displaying the main menu for the database.

From Here...

This chapter has presented the basic tools you can use to create and run your own macros. By using the techniques described in this chapter, you can use macros to automate and simplify your work with Approach. Many other chapters can expand your knowledge of parts of Approach you can use with macros. Refer to the following chapters in this book for more information:

- Chapter 4, "Enhancing Data Input Forms," describes how to add graphics and text objects to your forms.
- Chapter 6, "Finding Records," explains how to search for groups of records.
- Chapter 11, "Performing Advanced Finds," describes advanced query operations that lend themselves to automation.
- Chapter 12, "Creating Advanced Reports," describes techniques for creating reports you can then control with macros.

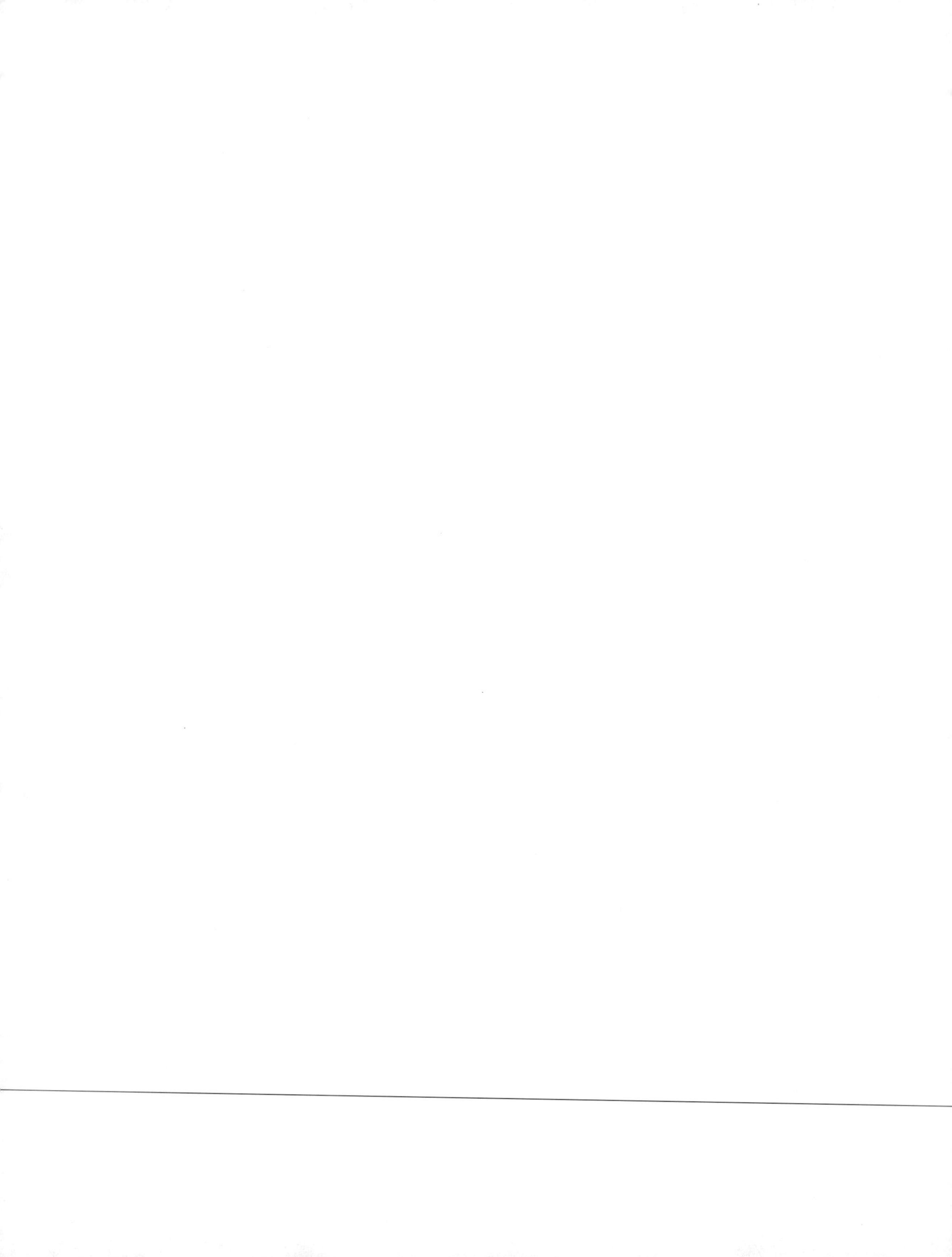

Part III

Getting the Most from Approach

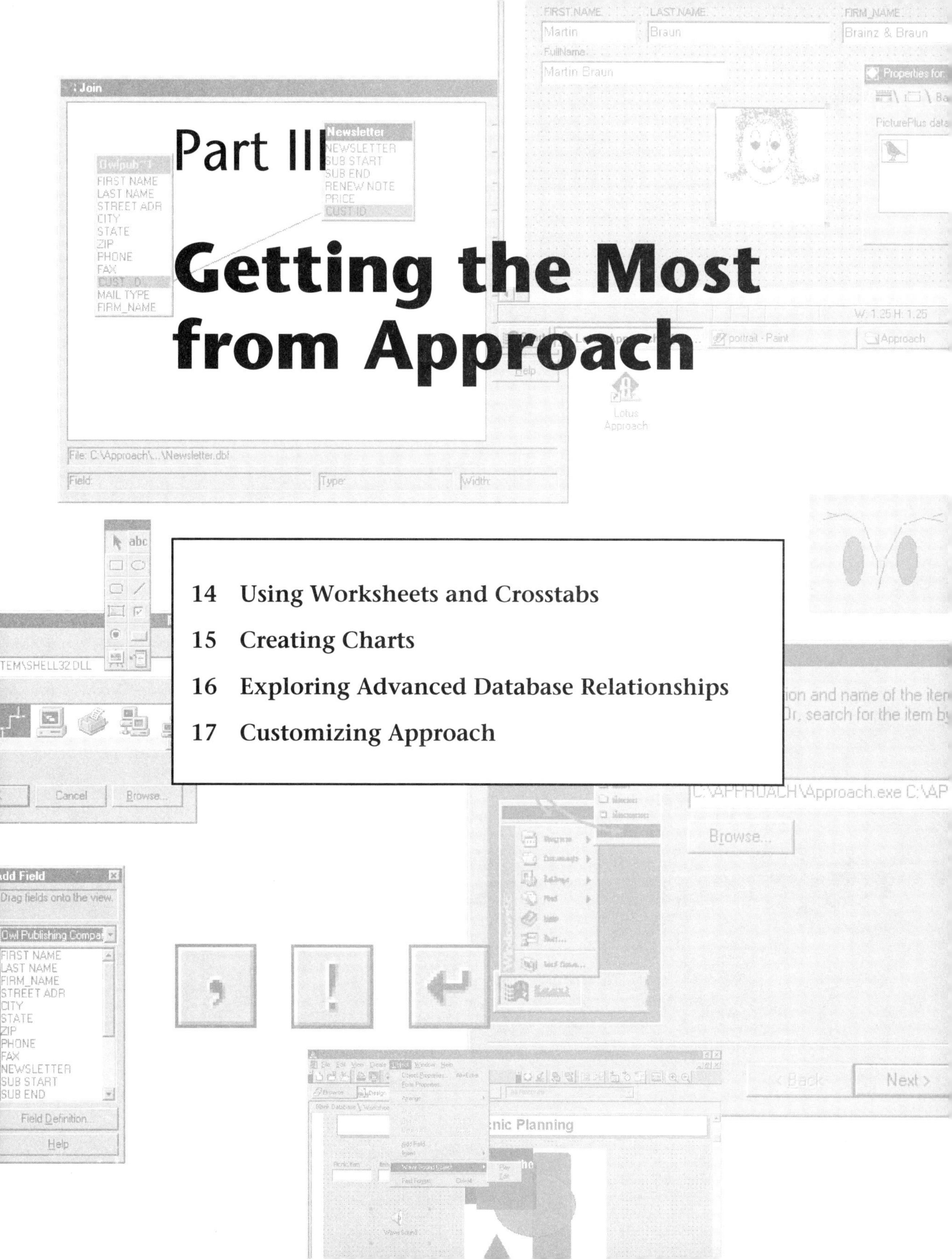

14 Using Worksheets and Crosstabs

15 Creating Charts

16 Exploring Advanced Database Relationships

17 Customizing Approach

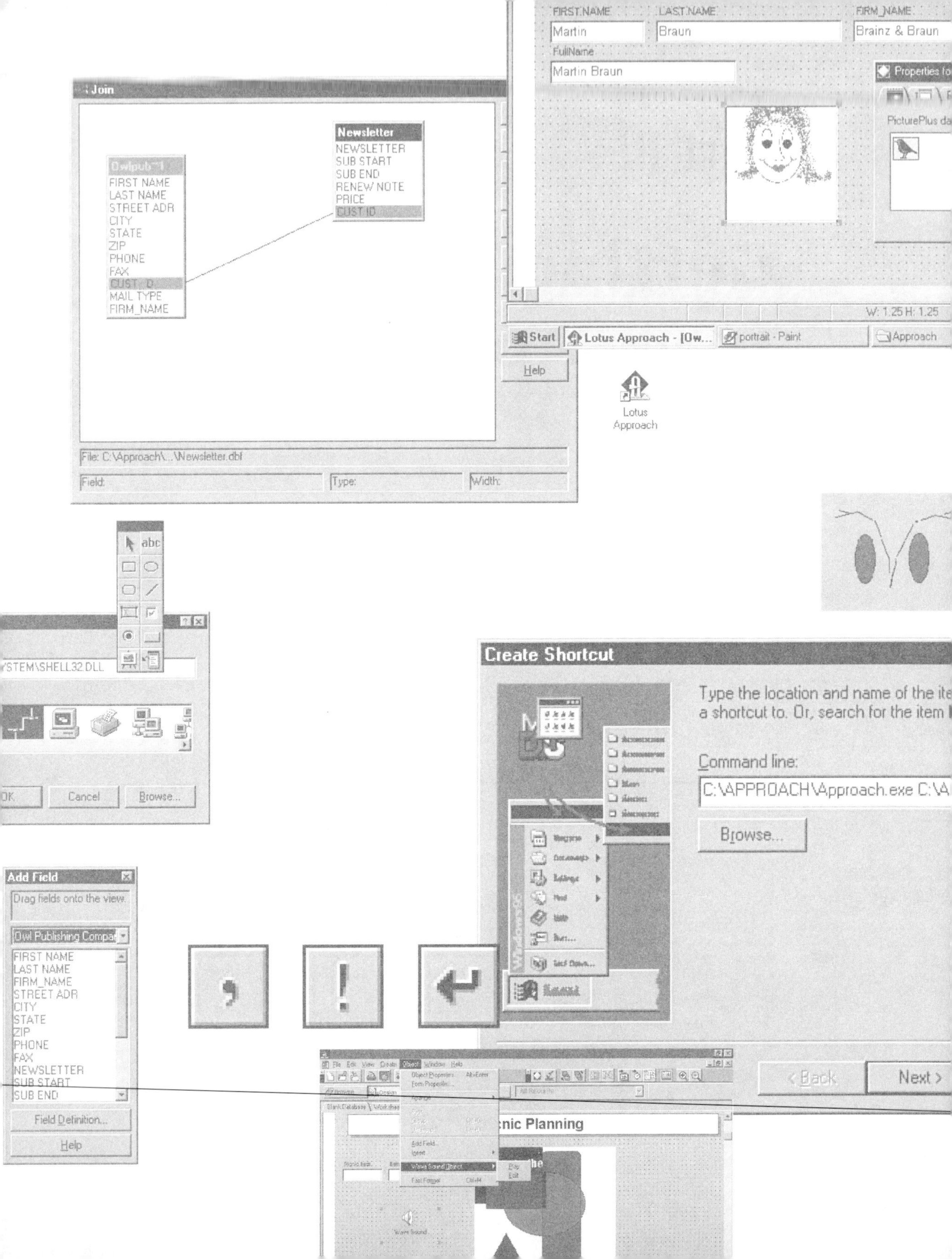

FIRST NAME
LAST NAME
FIRM_NAME
Martin
Braun
Brainz & Braun
FullName
Martin Braun
Join
Newsletter
NEWSLETTER
SUB START
SUB END
RENEW NOTE
PRICE
CUST ID
FIRST NAME
LAST NAME
STREET ADR
CITY
STATE
ZIP
PHONE
FAX
MAIL TYPE
FIRM_NAME
PicturePlus
W: 1.25 H: 1.25
Start
Lotus Approach - [Ow...
portrait - Paint
Approach
Help
Lotus Approach
File: C:\Approach\...\Newsletter.dbf
Field:
Type:
Width:
abc
STEM\SHELL32.DLL
OK
Cancel
Browse...
Create Shortcut
Type the location and name of the ite
a shortcut to. Or, search for the item
Command line:
C:\APPROACH\Approach.exe C:\A
Browse...
Add Field
Drag fields onto the view.
Owl Publishing Compar
FIRST NAME
LAST NAME
FIRM_NAME
STREET ADR
CITY
STATE
ZIP
PHONE
FAX
NEWSLETTER
SUB START
SUB END
Field Definition...
Help
< Back
Next >
nic Planning

CHAPTER 14

Using Worksheets and Crosstabs

Although looking at a record in a form view is often best, Approach worksheets and crosstabs allow you to see the "bigger picture" of your database. By using worksheets, you can display and edit information in a convenient tabular format. A crosstab view also appears as a table, but unlike a worksheet, it displays summaries of database information rather than data from individual records.

In this chapter, you learn how to

- Create a worksheet
- Select the data to be used in a worksheet
- Customize the worksheet's appearance
- Add, edit, or delete data from a worksheet view
- Create a crosstab view
- Adjust crosstab row height and appearance
- Add and delete crosstab fields
- Add and delete summary rows and columns

Using Worksheets

The Approach worksheet view gives you a two-dimensional, columnar picture of the information in your database. Each row in a worksheet displays the information from a single record, and each column contains values for a single field. Worksheets are very handy because they can display a large amount of database information on-screen.

> **Note**
>
> The examples in this chapter are based on the Orders database shown in figure 14.1.

Fig. 14.1

A worksheet displays a columnar view of a database.

Instrument	NumItems	Salesperson	Client
Violin	5	Jones	Classic Sounds
Viola	10	Jones	No Strings
Violin	15	Harris	Classic Sounds
Viola	5	Jones	Sounding Goods
Cello	25	Harris	No Strings
Viola	5	Peters	Classic Sounds
Cello	20	Peters	Classic Sounds
Viola	5	Jones	Sounding Goods
Viola	25	Harris	No Strings
Violin	10	Peters	Good Works
Cello	5	Harris	Good Works

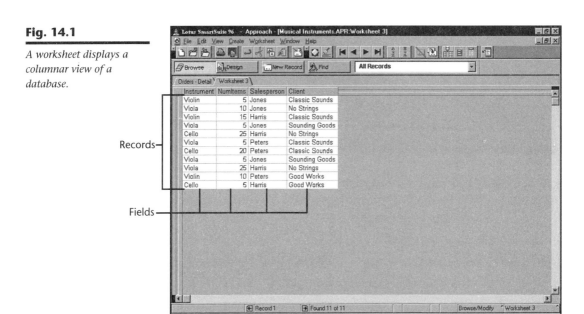

Figure 14.1 shows an example of a worksheet. The data displayed in this worksheet are sales figures from an Orders database for a musical instrument dealer. Each record in this database represents a single order placed by a customer. The following database fields are displayed in the worksheet:

Field	Contents
INSTRUMENT	Type of instrument sold
NUMBER OF ITEMS	Number of instruments sold in this order
SALESPERSON	Name of salesperson making the sale
CLIENT	Name of client buying the instruments

The top row of a worksheet contains column labels, which by default are the names of the fields. You can modify these labels to be more descriptive. Each remaining row in a worksheet shows the information from a single record.

A worksheet is particularly useful for working with data on-screen because it offers a number of techniques for easily selecting the data you want to view. For example, you can quickly add a new field to a worksheet simply by dragging and dropping the name of the field onto the screen. Similarly, you can easily delete a field from a worksheet by dragging the column out of the worksheet or by highlighting the column and pressing the Delete key.

Because a worksheet displays a relatively large amount of data at one time, it's a convenient platform for browsing and editing. Moreover, you can split the screen into two or four panes, each of which can display a different part of a worksheet. This can be extremely useful when working with large worksheets.

Approach allows you to display worksheet data sorted by the values of one or more fields. By using standard searching operations, you can display any desired subset of records. Also, you can use a worksheet as a platform for editing, adding, and deleting records.

Note

Each time you use Approach to create a new database, a new worksheet, named Worksheet 1, is automatically created that contains every field in the database.

You can create as many different types of worksheets for a database as you want, each with its own group of fields. After creating a worksheet, you can customize its appearance by adjusting row and column dimensions, by assigning custom colors to the background and border of different groups of cells, and by formatting the data that's displayed on the worksheet.

You can use a worksheet to browse through a database. You can also edit the contents of the database by adding, deleting, and modifying records.

Creating a New Worksheet

Approach automatically assigns a name—something like Worksheet 1—to a new worksheet, and it assigns the field names as column labels. However, you can modify these names later, if you want.

To create a new worksheet, follow these steps:

1. Open the Create menu and choose Worksheet. The Worksheet Assistant dialog box appears (see fig. 14.2). Check the drop-down list box labeled Database to make sure that it lists the database containing the fields you want in your worksheet. If it doesn't, select the correct database.

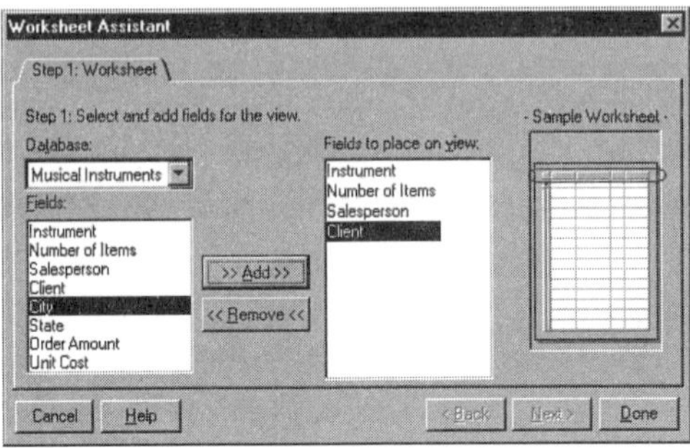

Fig. 14.2

Select the fields to appear in the new worksheet.

The list labeled Fields displays the fields in the current database. The list on the right, labeled Fields to Place on View, will display the fields you've selected to be part of the worksheet.

2. Choose the fields you want to appear in the worksheet. To copy a field from the Fields list to the Fields to Place on View list, either double-click the field or click it once and then click the Add button.

   If you change your mind while working with this dialog box, you can delete a field from the Fields to Place on View list either by double-clicking it or by clicking it once and then clicking the Remove button.

3. When you've finished selecting the fields, click the Done button. Approach creates and displays the new worksheet, switching to Browse mode.

Elements of a Worksheet

Each worksheet contains various standard elements, as shown in figure 14.3.

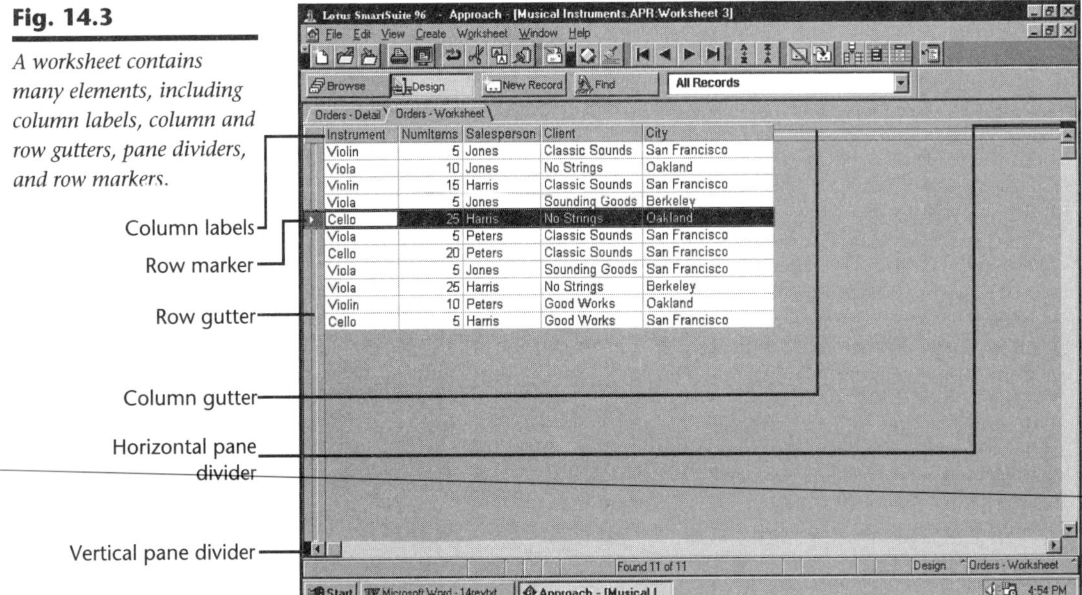

Fig. 14.3

A worksheet contains many elements, including column labels, column and row gutters, pane dividers, and row markers.

These worksheet elements include the following:

- *Column labels* (also called *headers*). Each column is headed by a label. Initially, Approach uses field names for these labels; however, you can change these labels to be more descriptive.
- *Column gutter.* This narrow horizontal band contains all the column labels.
- *Row gutter.* This is a narrow vertical band at the left edge of the worksheet. Clicking the row gutter selects an entire row.
- *Row marker.* This marker appears next to the row containing the cell or cells now selected. If more than one row is selected, the marker appears next to the topmost selected row.
- *Pane dividers.* You can use these markers to divide the screen into two or four worksheet panes for viewing different parts of the worksheet simultaneously.

Basic Worksheet Operations

You can perform many different operations on the cells and column labels of a worksheet, including the following:

- Customize the background color and borders of the selected cells and labels
- Customize the font, alignment, and format of the selected cells and labels
- Copy the selected cells and labels to the Windows Clipboard

To enhance your ability to manipulate a worksheet, you can display two or four worksheet panes, each of which can contain a separate view of the worksheet. You can resize the panes and navigate within each pane independently by using the associated horizontal and vertical scroll bars.

> **Note**
>
> When you're creating or using a worksheet, there are two reasons for switching to Design mode. First, some of Approach's functions work only in Design mode, so you may as well save yourself the trouble of having to switch back and forth between Browse and Design modes. The second reason is that you must be in Design mode if you're using a password with a worksheet. You can use passwords to limit access to your database and Approach view files by using the program's TeamSecurity feature (refer to Chapter 8, "Understanding Relational Databases").

Selecting Cells and Labels. To perform any type of operation on a group of cells or labels, you must first select them. You can select individual cells or labels, groups of cells, one or more rows, or one or more columns—with or without the labels. You can also select the entire worksheet—with or without the column labels.

When you select a single cell, it becomes outlined with a heavy border. When you select a group of cells, the left-most cell is outlined and the rest are highlighted, as shown in figure 14.4.

Fig. 14.4

Use the mouse to select a group of adjacent cells.

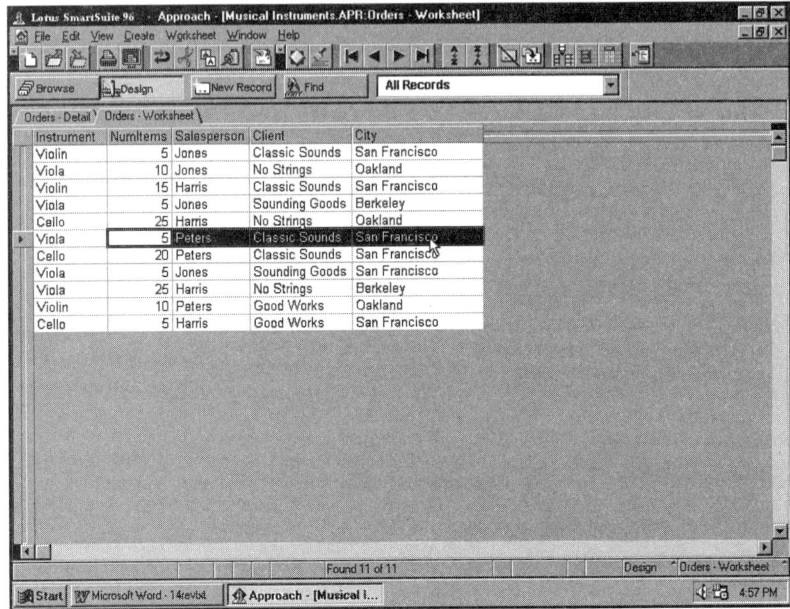

Table 14.1 lists the operations you can use for selecting various combinations of cells and labels.

Table 14.1 Selecting Cells and Labels in a Worksheet

To Select	Operation
A single cell	Click the cell with the mouse or use Tab, Shift+Tab, and the arrow keys to move from one cell to another.
A group of adjacent cells	Use the mouse to click the first cell; then hold the left mouse button down and drag the mouse left, right, up, or down to select the other cells you want.
An entire row of cells	Move the pointer to the left end of the row until it changes to a right arrow; then click (see fig. 14.5). When the row is selected, the row marker appears.
Two or more adjacent rows	Move the pointer toward the left end of the row until its shape changes to a right arrow. Then hold down the left mouse button, and drag the pointer up or down to select the other rows. Or select the first row of cells by clicking in the row gutter. Then hold down the Shift key, move to the last row you want to select, and click in the row gutter again.
An entire column of cells, including the column label	Click the label for that column (see fig. 14.6).

To Select	Operation
A column of cells, not including the column label	Click the label for that column and then click the Select Column Cells icon; or fromthe Worksheet menu choose Select and then Cells Only. Diagonal slashes will appear over the column label, indicating that it's not selected.
A column label	Click the label and then click the Select Label icon; choose Select and then Header Only from the Worksheet menu; or click the label twice.
A column label	Triple-click the label for editing.
Two or more adjacent columns	Select the label for the first column, hold down the mouse button, and drag across the labels for the other columns. Or click the label of the first column you want to select, and then Shift+click the label of the last column to select. If you want to exclude the labels from the selection, click the Select Column Cells icon.
Two or more adjacent column labels	Select those columns and then click one of the labels; or click the Select Label icon.
The entire worksheet, including labels	Click the upper left corner of the worksheet.
All the column labels	Click twice in the upper left corner of the worksheet.

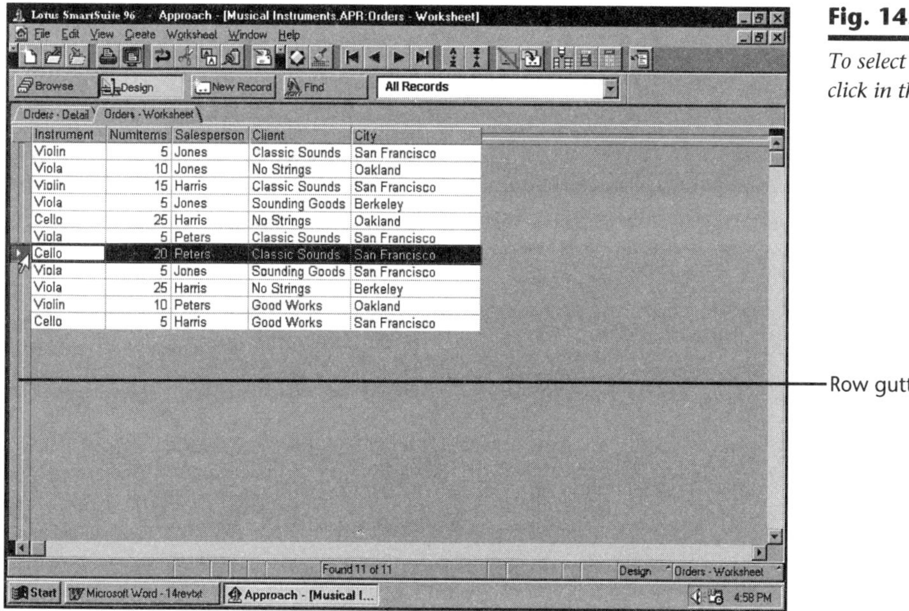

Fig. 14.5

To select a row of cells, click in the row gutter.

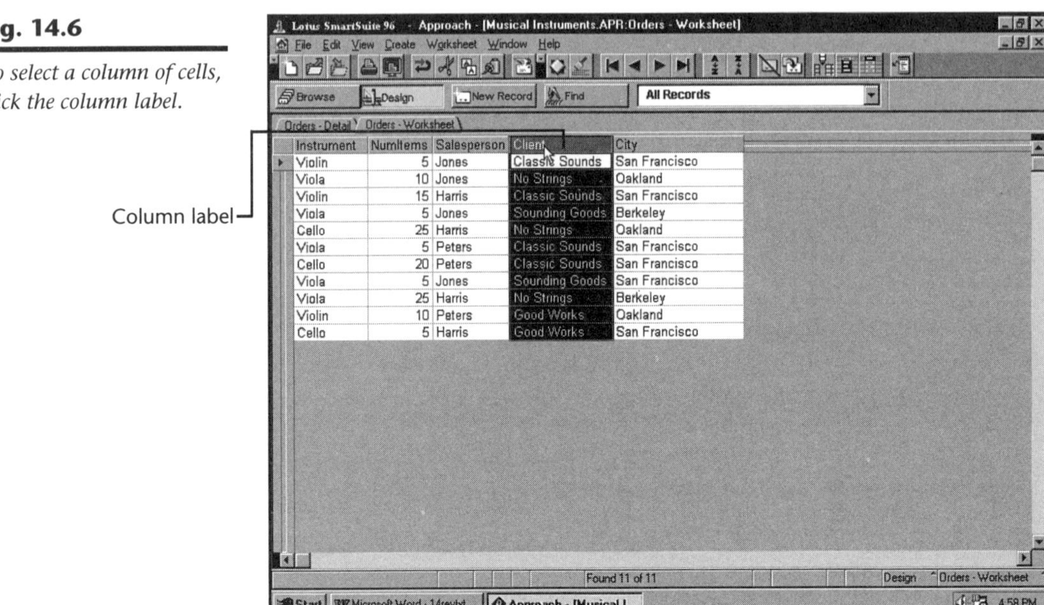

Fig. 14.6

To select a column of cells, click the column label.

Using Multiple Panes. When working with large worksheets, you probably won't be able to see all the data at once. However, you can display two different views of a worksheet, each in its own pane and with the panes arranged vertically or horizontally. You can then scroll each view somewhat independently, using the horizontal scroll bar and the two sets of vertical scroll bars.

You can also display four views of a worksheet, each in its own pane (see fig. 14.7). In this situation, Approach supplies four sets of scroll bars—two vertical and two horizontal—which you can use to scroll within each of the four panes.

If the same cells are shown in two or more different panes, and if you select those cells in either pane, they're also shown as selected in the other panes. Similarly, when you make a change to the worksheet in any pane, that change is reflected automatically in the other panes.

To display two panes arranged horizontally, drag down the horizontal pane divider (refer back to fig. 14.3 to find the pane dividers). Or, to display two panes arranged vertically, drag the vertical pane divider (located at the left end of the horizontal scroll bar) to the right.

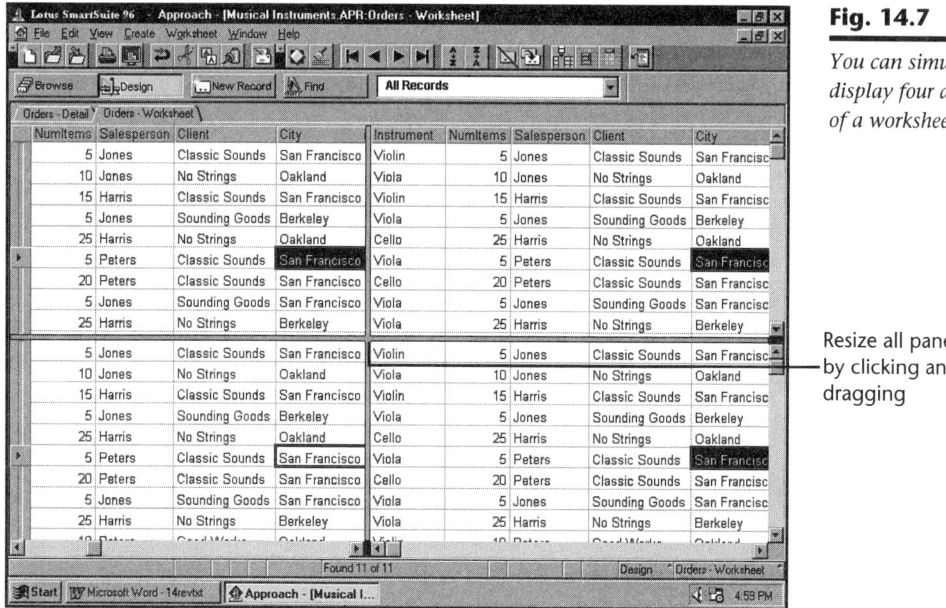

Fig. 14.7

You can simultaneously display four different parts of a worksheet.

To display four panes, as shown in figure 14.7, use the vertical and horizontal pane dividers. To readjust the size of the panes, use the mouse to reposition the pane dividers or the divider bars separating the panes. You can also resize all four panes at the same time by dragging the intersection of the two divider bars.

Selecting the Data to Appear in a Worksheet

When you first create a new worksheet, you select the fields to be included. However, you can modify the worksheet later by adding new fields, deleting those you no longer need, or by rearranging and resizing the columns within the worksheet. You can also add new columns for displaying calculations that are based on the information in the database.

Adding New Fields. To add a new field, first display the Add Field dialog box (see fig. 14.8). You can use this box to select the new fields for the worksheet.

Fig. 14.8

Insert a new field by dragging its name onto the worksheet.

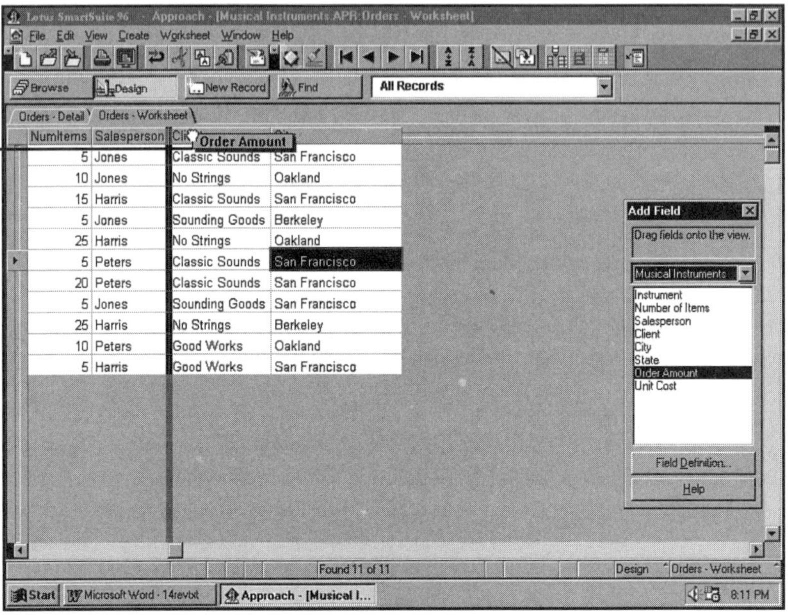

New field being placed

Then to add one or more fields to a worksheet, follow these steps:

1. Display the Add Field dialog box by opening the Worksheet menu and choosing Add Field. The Add Field dialog box appears.
2. In the Add Field dialog box, click the name of the new field, then drag it onto the worksheet. As you drag the field name, a dark vertical line appears to the left of where the new field will appear (see fig. 14.8). If necessary, you can reposition the field later.

Deleting Fields. To delete a field from a worksheet, follow these steps:

1. Click the label for that column, and then release the mouse button.
2. When the pointer changes to the shape of a hand, click the column label again, hold down the button, and begin dragging the hand up. As you do, the hand changes to the shape of a wastebasket with an arrow pointing into it (see fig. 14.9). Continue dragging the icon up and off the worksheet.

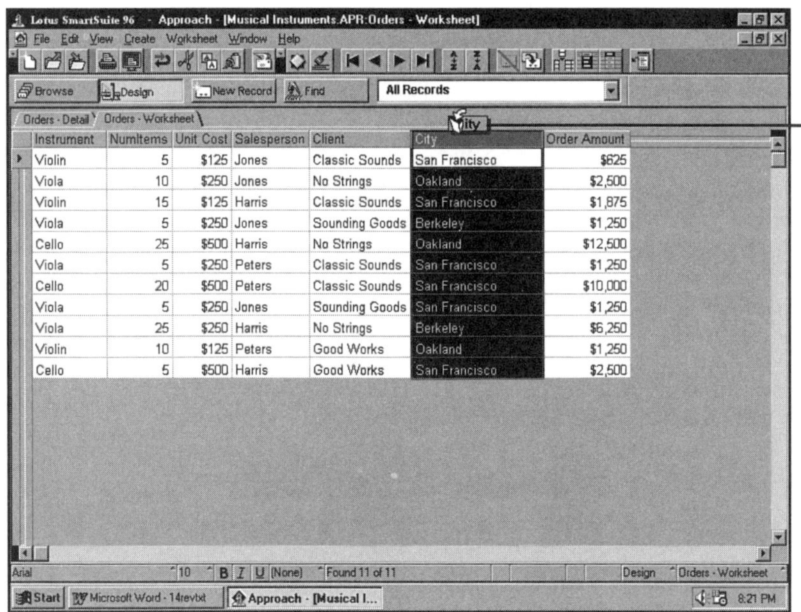

Fig. 14.9

Use the mouse to drag a field off the worksheet.

Rearranging the Fields. When you create a new worksheet, the columns are arranged in the order in which you originally selected the corresponding fields. However, you can easily rearrange the columns at any time.

To move a column from one position to another, follow these steps:

1. Click the label for that column, and then release the mouse button.
2. When the pointer changes to the shape of a hand, click the column label again, hold down the button, and drag the column left or right to the new position on the worksheet.

Inserting Special Calculations. You can enhance your worksheets by including special calculations based on values in the database. Suppose that a worksheet contains the fields NUMBER OF ITEMS SOLD and PRICE PER ITEM. You can insert a special column that displays the product of these two fields.

Adding a special calculation to a worksheet requires two steps. First, you create a new blank column where you want the calculations to appear; then you insert a formula into that column. Approach automatically applies the formula to every record in the worksheet.

When building a calculation, you can use any of Approach's built-in functions, or you can use standard arithmetic operators to create simple calculations.

Note

Approach contains a large repertoire of useful built-in functions. To review these functions, display the Formula dialog box shown in figure 14.10. Open the Worksheet menu and choose Add Field, click the Field Definition button, click the Options button, and then click the Formula button.

To insert a formula into a new column, follow these steps:

1. Select the column that's just to the left of where you want to insert the new column.
2. Open the Worksheet menu and choose Add Column. The new column is created and selected, and the Formula dialog box appears (see fig. 14.10).

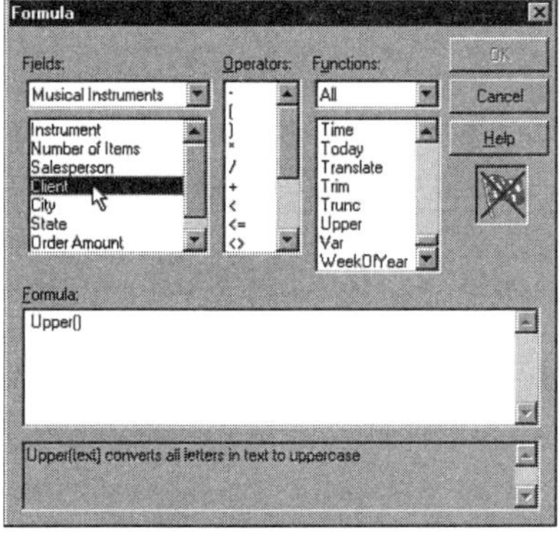

Fig. 14.10

Use the Formula dialog box to add a calculated field to your worksheet.

3. In the Formula box at the bottom, enter the formula you want to use. To use one of Approach's built-in functions, double-click its name in the Functions list box, and then add the values you want to use within the function's parentheses. Similarly, you can add fields and arithmetic or logical operators by clicking their names in the Fields and Operators lists. You also can type these values directly into the Formula box.

   For example, to display the CLIENT field values in all uppercase, double-click Upper in the Functions list. Approach places the cursor between the parentheses so that clicking Client in the Fields list automatically places the field in the right part of your formula.
4. Click OK. Approach calculates the formula for every record in the worksheet and displays the results in the new, unlabeled column.

Customizing the Worksheet Appearance

Approach offers a great deal of flexibility in customizing the appearance of your worksheets. You can do the following:

- Adjust row and column sizes
- Edit column labels
- Customize cell background and border colors
- Control the formatting of cell contents

Adjusting Row and Column Sizes. You can adjust the width of individual columns to accommodate extra long data values or improve the appearance of your worksheet. You can also control row heights. For instance, this might be necessary to accommodate text whose font size you've increased. Any change you make to the height of a row is automatically applied to every row in the worksheet, but column changes apply only to the columns you've selected.

To change the width of an individual column, follow these steps:

1. Click the column gutter at the right edge of the column you want to adjust until the pointer takes the shape of a double arrow (see fig. 14.11).

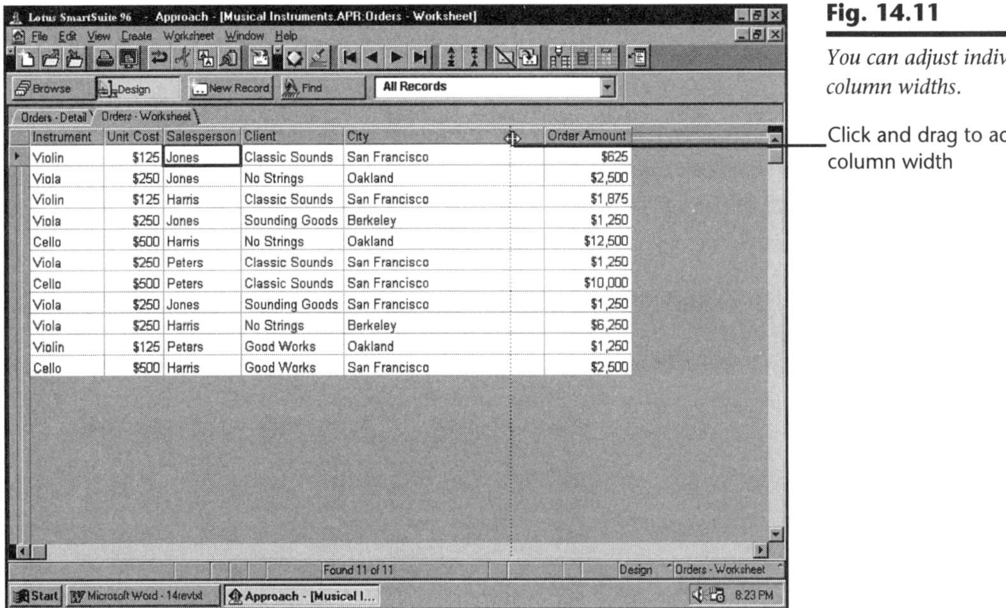

Fig. 14.11

You can adjust individual column widths.

2. Holding down the mouse button, drag the mouse right or left to resize the column.
3. Release the button when the column is the size you want.

Tip

To insert extra space between columns, insert a blank column and adjust its width.

Follow these steps to adjust the row height:

1. Click the row gutter at the bottom of any row until the pointer takes the shape of a double arrow.
2. Holding down the mouse button, drag the mouse up or down to resize the row.
3. Release the button when the row is the size you want.

Caution

If you reduce the row height too much, the entire worksheet disappears! If this happens, simply choose Undo from the Edit menu to make the worksheet reappear. Or move the pointer to the upper left corner of the worksheet (at the top of the row gutter). When the pointer changes to a double arrow, drag it down approximately one-half inch. The worksheet reappears, and you can readjust the row heights—this time more carefully.

Changing Column Labels. When you create a new worksheet, Approach assigns field names to the column labels. However, you can change any of these labels to improve the clarity of the worksheet.

To modify a label, follow these steps:

1. Click the label you want to edit three times. The entire label is highlighted and the text cursor appears.
2. To enter an entirely new label, just begin typing; the original label is replaced by whatever you enter. Or you can click the label a fourth time to position the text cursor, and then edit as you would any text.

Customizing the Cell Appearance. You can customize the appearance of a table so that different columns and labels stand out in different ways. For example, you can alternate the background colors of different columns or assign special fonts to the labels.

Note

You can customize one or more groups of columns, but you can't customize individual rows or cells.

You can customize any of the following groups of cells:

- A single column
- A group of columns
- One or more column labels
- The entire worksheet

To customize one or more columns, with or without their labels, you must first select the cells. Then you can apply any of the changes described in the following sections.

Displaying the InfoBox. By using the InfoBox, you can customize the selected cells. Unlike many other dialog boxes, the InfoBox remains on-screen until you close it. This means that you can customize one group of cells, switch to the Approach window and select another group of cells, and then return to the InfoBox to customize the new group.

Tip

To quickly switch between customizing worksheet components and the entire worksheet, click the down arrow next to the title on top of the InfoBox and click the worksheet name that appears in the drop-down box.

You can use any of the following methods to display the InfoBox:

- Click the InfoBox icon.
- Open the Worksheet menu and choose Worksheet Properties.
- Press Ctrl+E.
- Click the worksheet anywhere with the right mouse button and choose Worksheet Properties from the menu that appears.

The contents of the InfoBox change depending on which part of the worksheet is selected. For example, if the entire Salesperson column is highlighted, the InfoBox title will read `Properties for: Column: Salesperson` (see fig. 14.12). On the other hand, if only a single cell is highlighted, the properties for the entire worksheet are described (see fig. 14.13).

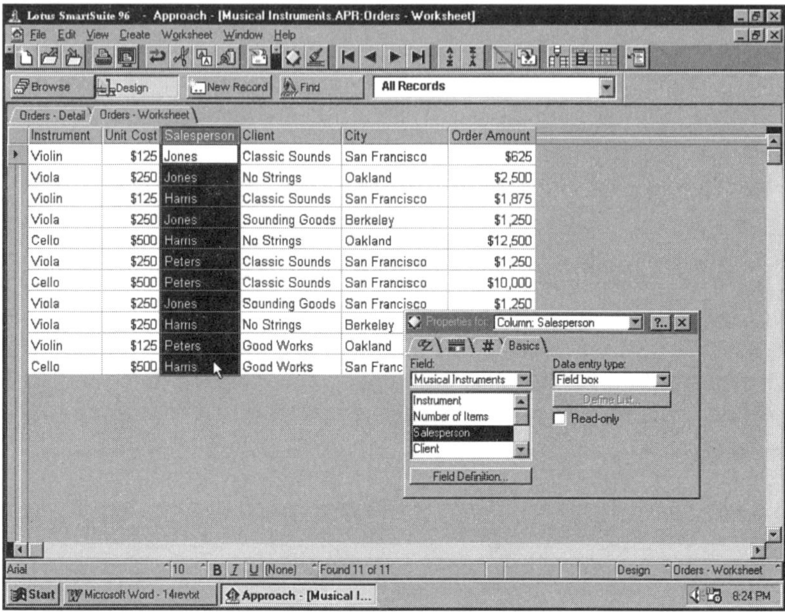

Fig. 14.12

Selecting a column causes the properties for that field to appear in the InfoBox.

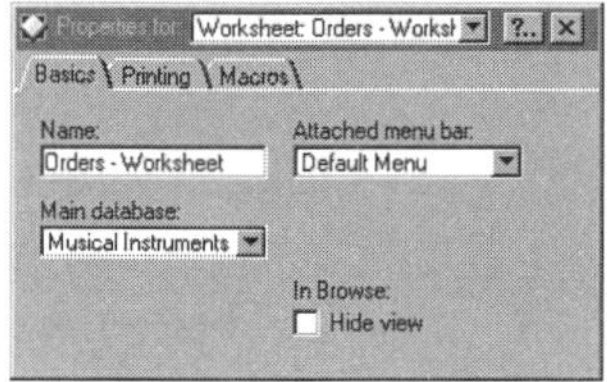

Fig. 14.13

When the InfoBox is on-screen, selecting a single cell brings up the properties of the entire worksheet.

To make a selection from the InfoBox, follow these steps:

1. Select the group of cells you want to customize.
2. Click the appropriate tab at the top of the InfoBox.
3. Make your choices from the options that appear.

Tip

The options described in this and the following two sections aren't available for single cells, single rows, or groups of rows.

Setting Font, Color, and Alignment. You can control the appearance of data within one or more columns by adjusting their font, style, color, size and alignment. To make these changes, follow these steps:

1. Click the column label to select the entire column. If you want to exclude the column label from your changes, click the Select Column Cells icon.
2. Click the fonts tab at the top of the InfoBox (see fig. 14.14).

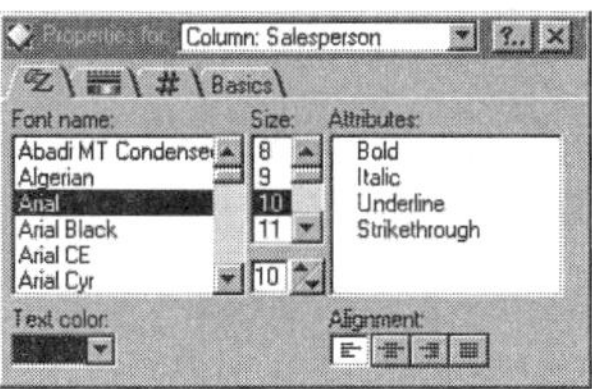

Fig. 14.14

Use this part of the InfoBox to control the appearance of text.

3. Make your choices for font, style, color, size and alignment.

Setting Cell Fill and Border Colors. To choose colors for the cell fill and borders, follow these steps:

1. Click the column label to select the entire column. If you want to exclude the column label from your changes, click the Select Column Cells icon.
2. Click the colors tab at the top of the InfoBox (see fig. 14.15).

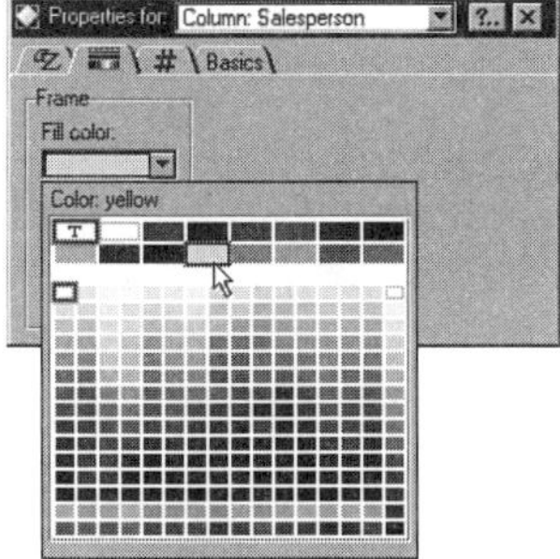

Fig. 14.15

Use this page in the InfoBox to customize cell colors and borders.

3. Make your color choices from the drop-down boxes that appear when you click the Fill Color and Border Color blanks.

Formatting Data. You can control the format of the data in a worksheet. The options available to you depend on whether you're formatting text, numeric, date, or time information.

To format the data in all the cells of one or more columns, follow these steps:

1. Select the entire column or columns, and then exclude the column labels.
2. Click the third tab at the top of the InfoBox (see fig. 14.16).

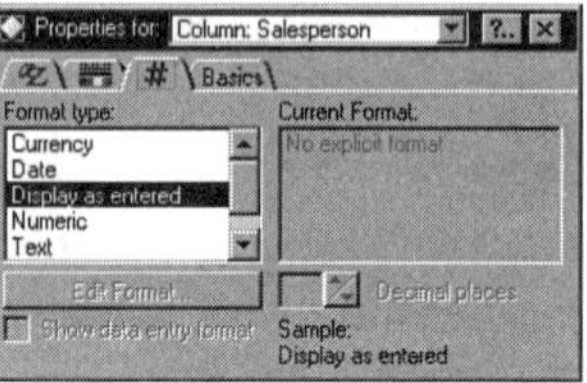

Fig. 14.16

Use the InfoBox to control how text is formatted.

3. In the drop-down list box labeled Format Type, select the type of data displayed in the column.
4. A new set of list boxes appears, depending on the type of data you select. By using these list boxes, select the type of formatting you want.

Changing Field Basics. The InfoBox also lets you change the field information of a worksheet column. You can rename your worksheet, choose another field for that column, add a drop-down list, or make your column read-only. To make these changes, follow these steps:

1. Click the column label to select the entire column. If you want to exclude the column label from your changes, click the Select Column Cells icon.
2. Click the Basics tab at the top of the InfoBox (see fig. 14.17).

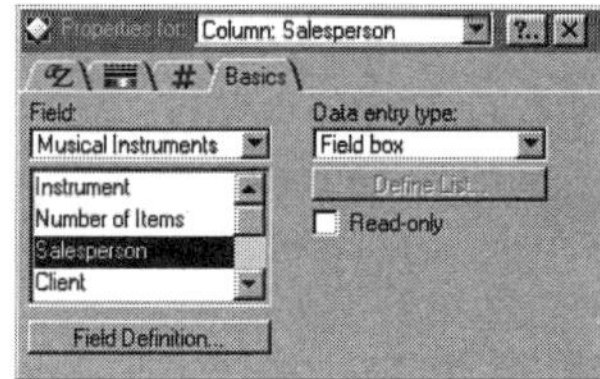

Fig. 14.17

Use this part of the InfoBox to control column fields.

3. Make your choices from the selections shown.

Customizing the Worksheet Settings

Several settings are associated with each worksheet, and you can adjust these settings to control various aspects of the worksheet. These settings include the following:

- The worksheet name
- Parameters that control how a worksheet appears when printed
- Macros that execute when you select or deselect a worksheet

These settings are all accessible via the InfoBox for the worksheet, which you can display by using any of the methods described earlier. When the InfoBox appears on your screen, click any single worksheet cell—except a column label—and the InfoBox changes to look like figure 14.18.

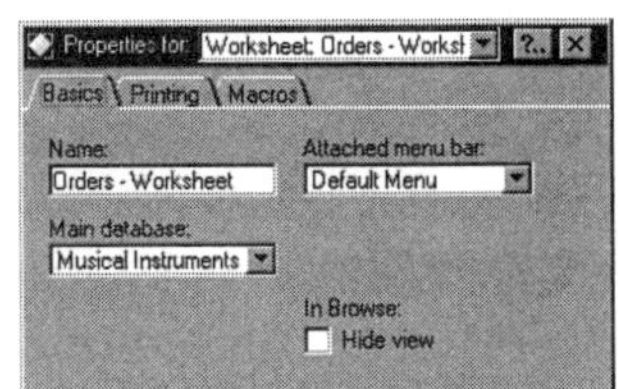

Fig. 14.18

Use this InfoBox to choose the worksheet settings.

To change a worksheet name, click the Basics tab in the InfoBox, and then enter the new name in the Name text box.

You can control certain aspects of how a worksheet appears when printed. To make these selections, click the InfoBox's Printing tab and then choose the print options you want.

You can attach two macros that will execute whenever you switch to or from a worksheet. To specify these macros, click the Macros tab of the worksheet's InfoBox, pull down each macro list, and make your selection. Note that you can select an existing macro, or you can define a macro on the spot by clicking the Define Macro button in the InfoBox.

Manipulating Worksheet Records

Because a worksheet can display large amounts of data, it can sometimes be a handy view for editing database information. Using a worksheet, you can do the following:

- Edit existing data
- Add and delete records
- Select subsets of records for display in a worksheet
- Arrange the order in which the records are displayed
- Copy information from the worksheet to the Clipboard

Editing Data. To edit an individual data value in a worksheet, follow these steps:

1. Double-click the cell.
2. When the text cursor appears, make any editing changes you want.
3. To store your edits to the database, either press Enter or click another worksheet cell. To restore the original cell value, press Esc.

Adding and Deleting Records. Because a worksheet offers a handy view of your data, you may prefer to use it as a vehicle for adding and deleting records. Of course, when you add new records, you can insert values only for those fields displayed in the worksheet. This isn't a serious restriction because you can easily add new fields to the worksheet—even on a temporary basis.

Adding Records. To add one or more new records, follow these steps:

1. Click the New Record button on the action bar or press Ctrl+N. Approach inserts a blank line at the bottom of the worksheet and moves the text cursor to the left-most cell there.
2. Enter the data values for the new record. To move from one cell to the next, press Tab or use the mouse.

If you press Tab when the cursor is positioned in the last cell of the new record, Approach automatically creates another blank line and tabs to its left-most cell, where you can begin adding another record.

Deleting Records. To delete one or more records, follow these steps:

1. Select the record you want to delete by clicking next to it in the row gutter. To select multiple adjacent records, drag the pointer down or up after the first record is highlighted (see fig. 14.19).

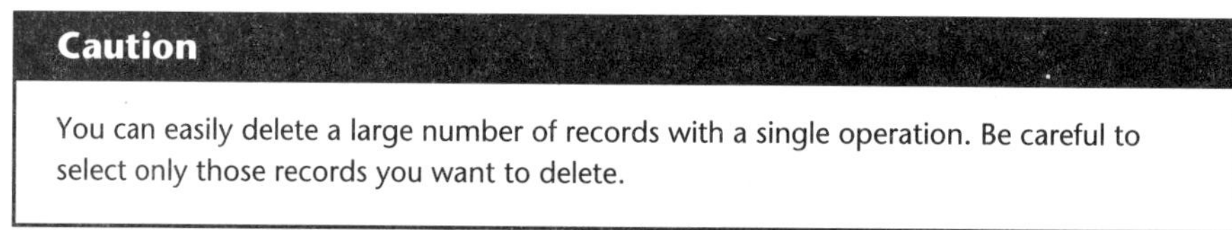

Caution

You can easily delete a large number of records with a single operation. Be careful to select only those records you want to delete.

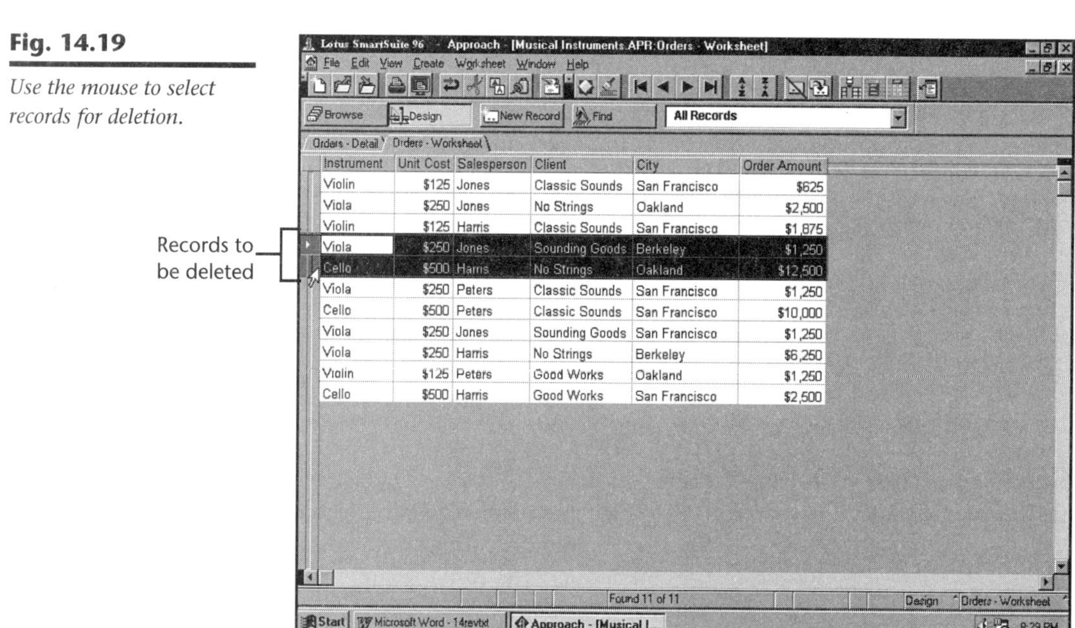

Fig. 14.19

Use the mouse to select records for deletion.

2. To delete the selected records, do one of the following:
    - Click the Delete Current Record icon.
    - Open the Edit menu and choose Cut or Clear.
    - Press Ctrl+Delete or the Delete key.
    - Open the Worksheet menu and choose Delete Selected Records.

After asking you for verification, Approach deletes the records you selected.

> **Note**
>
> You can't delete selected groups of cells in a worksheet. You can delete only entire records. You can, however, erase the contents of individual cells.

Finding and Sorting Records. By using standard Approach commands, you can sort the order in which the records appear in a worksheet. You can also use Find commands to select subsets of records for display. Approach also lets you name and save frequently performed finds and sorts. These can be selected from the action bar.

To sort the records displayed in a worksheet, open the Worksheet menu and choose Sort. The steps for performing these finds and sorts are described elsewhere in this book and aren't repeated here. (Sorting records is described in Chapter 5, "Working with Your Data"; Chapter 6, "Finding Records," describes how to perform finds.)

To display a subset of the records in the database, follow these steps:

1. Open the Worksheet menu and choose Find, and then choose Find again; or click the Find button on the action bar. Then enter the correct find criteria in the blanks (see fig. 14.20).
2. Specify the records you want to display by entering the search criteria in the appropriate column.
3. For more complex searches, click the Find Assistant button in the action bar. As shown in figure 14.21, Approach's Find/Sort Assistant guides you through constructing a search that might include the following:
    - Duplicate records
    - Finds based on a formula or calculation
    - SQL queries
    - Highest, lowest, or unique values

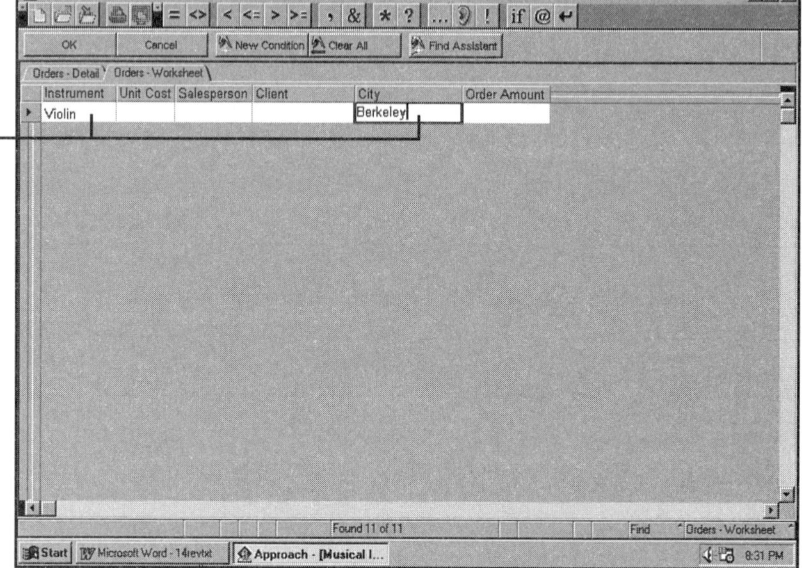

Fig. 14.20

Enter the search criteria for selecting a subset of records.

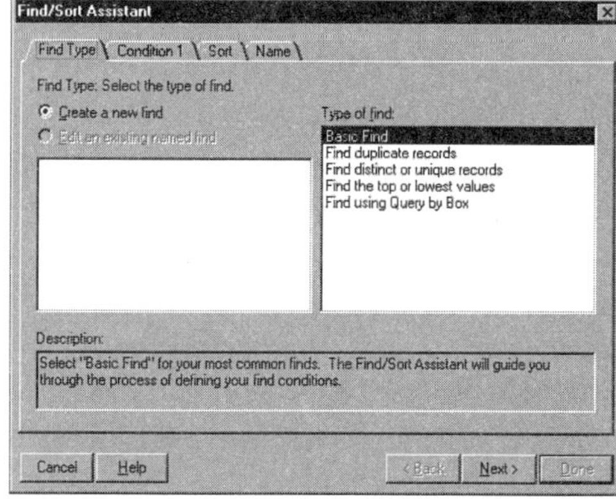

Fig. 14.21

The Find/Sort Assistant guides you through complex searches.

4. When you've finished entering your search criteria, click OK to begin the search.

Approach finds and displays only those records matching your search criteria.

Copying Data to the Clipboard. You can copy part or all of a worksheet to the Clipboard. From there, you can then paste, link, or embed the information into a document in another application, as follows:

- As tab-delimited values, with a hard return inserted at each end of record. This format would be useful, for example, for pasting into an Ami Pro document or a Lotus 1-2-3 spreadsheet.

- As a graphic in Windows Metafile (.WMF) format. For instance, you can paste a group of cells into a frame within an Ami Pro document where it can then be manipulated as an ordinary graphic.
- As an embedded or linked OLE object.

Copy part or all of a worksheet, as follows:

1. Select the cell or cells you want to copy. To select the entire worksheet, click the upper left corner of the worksheet at the intersection of the row and column gutters.
2. Open the Edit menu and choose Copy or press Ctrl+C. Approach copies the selected information to the Clipboard.

Using Crosstabs

A *crosstab*, which is short for *cross-tabulation worksheet*, is a special type of worksheet that summarizes many rows of information from a database. A crosstab can display summaries based on one, two, or several fields, and the crosstab calculations can be sums, numbers, averages, or other statistical measures.

Figure 14.22 shows a simple type of crosstab for the Orders database described earlier in this chapter. This crosstab summarizes the sales information from the database, categorized by the different values found in the INSTRUMENT field. The left-most column lists the different instruments sold (cello, viola, and violin), and the numbers in the second column are the total number of each type sold. The top row lists the name of the summary field, NUMBER OF ITEMS, which is used in calculating these totals.

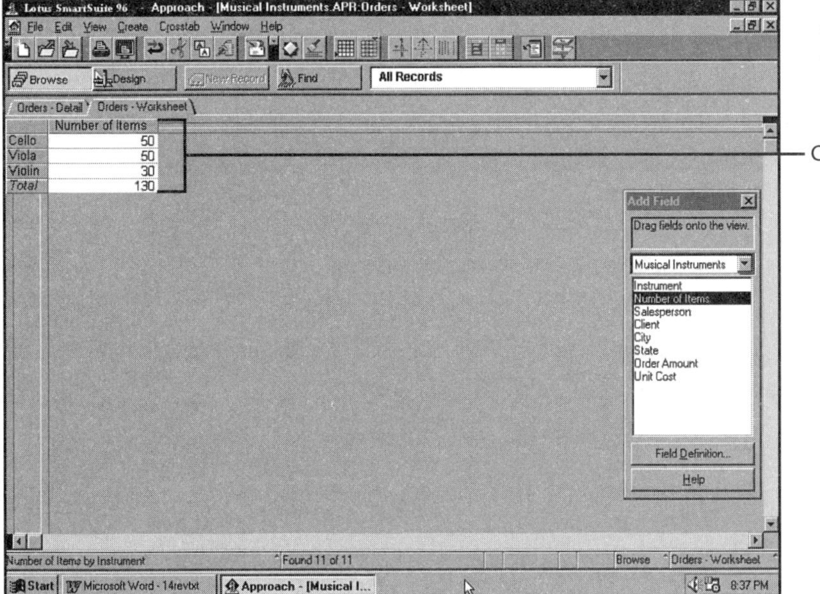

Fig. 14.22

A crosstab view summarizes database information over a single field.

A crosstab view is an extremely flexible tool for analyzing database information. For instance, if you're not quite satisfied with the type of summary information displayed by a crosstab, you can easily modify it to display other summary information by adding and deleting fields.

Unlike a worksheet, a crosstab displays summary information about a database rather than show individual database values. Crosstabs are useful because they can condense a great deal of information into a small amount of space. For example, if a musical instrument dealer is doing a yearly budget, he may want to know the total yearly sales of each instrument type, but he won't care about the details of each sale, such as who bought which instruments.

A crosstab can summarize information by number, average, or other statistical measures. You can create a crosstab to display summary information based on the values in one or more fields. Approach's intuitive interface makes it easy to create these different types of crosstabs. Moreover, you can change a crosstab as you work with it so that you can quickly and easily see a variety of different perspectives on a database.

Looking at Some Crosstab Examples

The data from the Orders database illustrates some of the different types of crosstabs you can create. In this particular database, each record represents an order placed by a customer for a certain number of instruments of a particular type.

Figure 14.23 shows a common type of crosstab, based on the values in the following three fields:

- *INSTRUMENT.* The type of instrument sold in any particular order.
- *NUMBER OF ITEMS.* The number of instruments sold in each order.
- *CITY.* The city in which a customer does business.

This crosstab shows the total number of instruments sold, categorized by instrument type and by city. The types of instruments are shown in the left-most column and the city names are listed in the top row. The NUMBER OF ITEMS field furnishes the numeric data for the body of the crosstab. A glance at this data indicates that 25 cellos have been sold to customers in Oakland and 10 violas were sold to customers in San Francisco.

Notice that the second row of the field labels shows the name of the field used in performing the summary calculations—NUMBER OF ITEMS, in this example. This is called the *summary calculations label.*

Figure 14.22 shows a more condensed type of crosstab, which summarizes total instrument sales broken down only by instrument type. Again, the NUMBER OF ITEMS field furnishes the numeric data for the summary values in the body of the crosstab.

You can create a crosstab that summarizes information based on several fields. For instance, the crosstab in figure 14.24 shows summary information on instrument sales broken down by instrument, city, and also by salesperson. This crosstab shows that 10 violins were sold in Oakland by a salesperson named Peters.

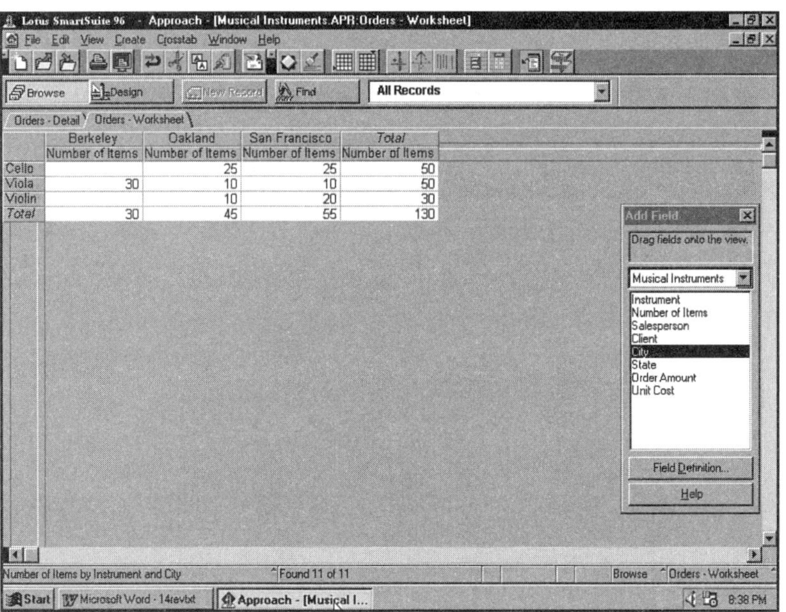

Fig. 14.23

This crosstab summarizes instrument sales by instrument type and city.

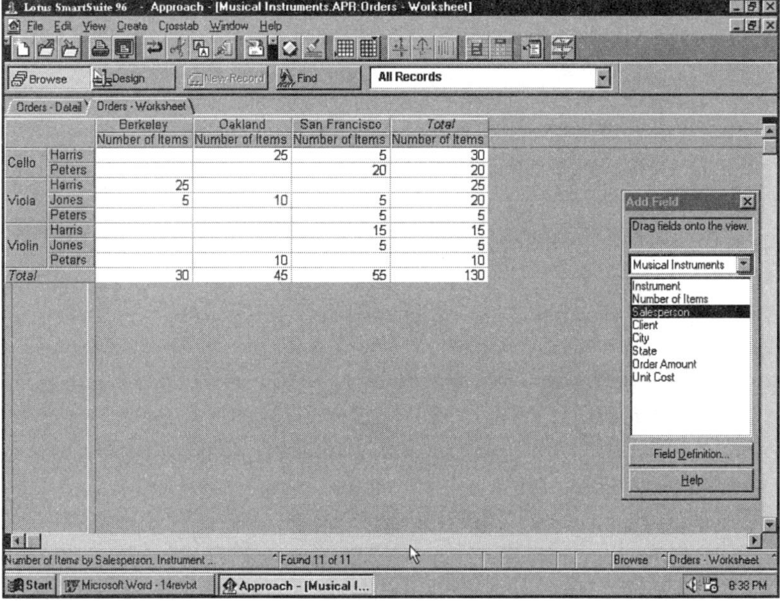

Fig. 14.24

This crosstab summarizes instrument sales by instrument type, city, and salesperson.

Creating a Crosstab

The same basic steps are used for creating all types of crosstabs. You choose the fields from which the summary information is to be drawn, and you select the type of crosstab calculation you want. Approach automatically assigns a name such as Crosstab 1 to the new crosstab, but you can change the name later to something more specific.

To create a new crosstab, follow these steps:

1. Open the Create menu and choose Crosstab. Approach displays the Crosstab Assistant dialog box, as shown in figure 14.25.

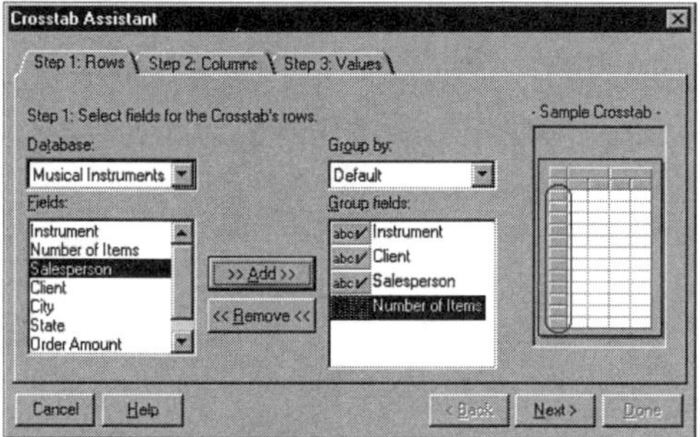

Fig. 14.25

Use the Crosstab Assistant to select the fields for a new crosstab.

> **Note**
>
> At each step in using the Crosstab Assistant, the diagram at the right side of the dialog box illustrates which items you're now selecting.

2. Make sure that the Step 1: Rows tab is selected.
3. Select the field (or fields) you want to use for the rows of the crosstab. For the crosstab shown in figure 14.22, for example, the INSTRUMENT field was selected.
4. Move the field name into the Group Fields list box, either by clicking the Add button or by double-clicking the name in the Fields list. If you want to remove a field you've selected, highlight it in the Group Fields list box and either double-click it or click the Remove button.
5. The Crosstab Assistant also lets you make your crosstab easier to read by grouping related items under the same heading. For example, with a numeric field, you can group numbers from 1-10, 11-20, 21-30 and so on. You can group character fields by the first one to five letters or group dates by month, quarter, year, and so on. Groupings are especially useful if your crosstab stacks several fields in the same row.

   To group a field's data, click the button beside the field in the Group Fields list box. Select the best grouping from the popup list.

6. Click either the Step 2: Columns tab at the top or the Next button to select columns for your crosstab.
7. Choose the field (or fields) for the columns of the crosstab. For example, for the crosstab in figure 14.23, the CITY field was chosen.
8. Click either the Step 3: Values tab at the top or the Next button.
9. Select the field to be used as the basis of the crosstab summary calculations.
10. From the drop-down list at the top, select the type of summary calculation you want performed. This calculation is applied to the field you selected in step 7. For the crosstab in figure 14.22, for instance, the Sum function was chosen.
11. Click the Done button. Approach creates and displays the new crosstab.

Performing Standard Operations with Crosstabs

Most of the operations available with worksheets are also available with crosstabs, including the following:

- Customizing the background and border colors of all the cells in a column
- Adjusting the font, alignment, and color of the text in the cells of a column
- Adjusting the width of individual columns
- Customizing the appearance of individual row and column labels
- Creating multiple panes for viewing of up to four different parts of a crosstab
- Changing the name of the crosstab
- Assigning macros to the crosstab
- Setting parameters for printing a crosstab

Because of their nature, crosstabs don't lend themselves to some operations that are available with worksheets. These include the following:

- You may not be able to edit the row or column labels if they represent actual data values in the database.
- You can't edit the values in the body of a crosstab, because they're the results of summary calculations.
- You can't change the order of data appearing in rows or columns. Approach automatically sorts these items alphabetically.

You can perform a variety of operations on crosstabs that aren't available to worksheets or any other type of view. These are described in the following sections.

Special Crosstab Operations

Because of the unique qualities of crosstabs, Approach offers several crosstab operations that give you a great deal of flexibility. For example, you can change the height of individual rows, and you can customize groups of cells on a row-by-row basis. You can also edit the label that defines the type of information that's summarized in a crosstab.

You can add and delete fields in a crosstab; however, these operations have entirely different meanings compared to the equivalent operations with worksheets.

Adjusting Row Height and Appearance. As with worksheets, you must first select the group of crosstab cells you want to customize. You can use nearly all the operations listed in table 14.1 for selecting various parts of a crosstab. However, a few differences are listed in the following table.

To Select	Operation
The entire crosstab, including labels	Click the upper left corner of the crosstab at the intersection of the row and column gutters.
All the row and column labels (both of the top two rows of column labels)	Click twice in the upper left corner of the crosstab.

You can adjust the height of individual rows, as follows:

1. Click the row gutter on the bottom border of the row until the pointer changes to a double arrow, as shown in figure 14.26.
2. Drag the pointer up or down to resize the row.

Fig. 14.26

You can adjust the height of individual rows using the same field of a crosstab.

Click and drag to adjust row height

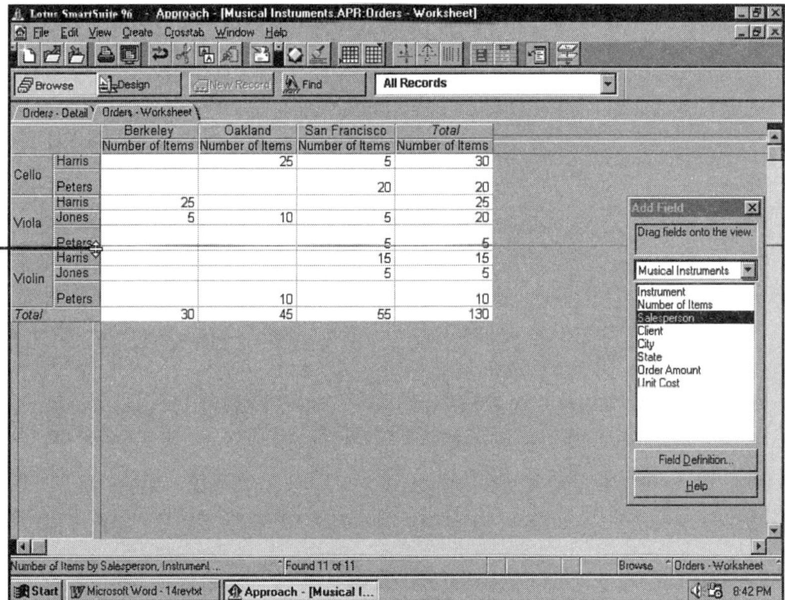

Adding and Deleting Fields. You can easily change the basic meaning of a crosstab by adding and deleting fields. When you add a new field, Approach recalculates the entire crosstab, calculating new summary information based on the values in the new field as well as by those of the original fields.

Adding a New Field. You can drag a field name either to the left edge of the crosstab or to the top, depending on how you want the new crosstab to appear. As you position the name, a black placement bar appears, indicating where the new field values will appear.

The crosstab shown in figure 14.27 summarizes sales information by salesperson and city. In figure 14.28, the INSTRUMENT field name is positioned to the right of the SALESPERSON field values. When the INSTRUMENT field is added to the crosstab, Approach calculates new summary information based on the fields SALESPERSON, CITY, and INSTRUMENT, as shown in figure 14.29.

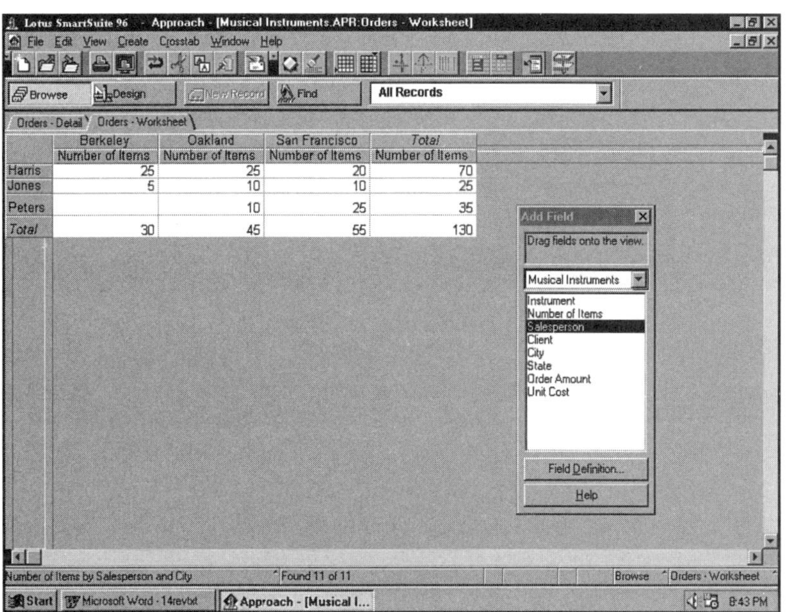

Fig. 14.27

A crosstab based on values in the SALESPERSON and CITY fields gives geographic sales concentrations at a glance.

Fig. 14.28

To insert a new field into a crosstab, drag it from the Add Field dialog box to the column or row gutter.

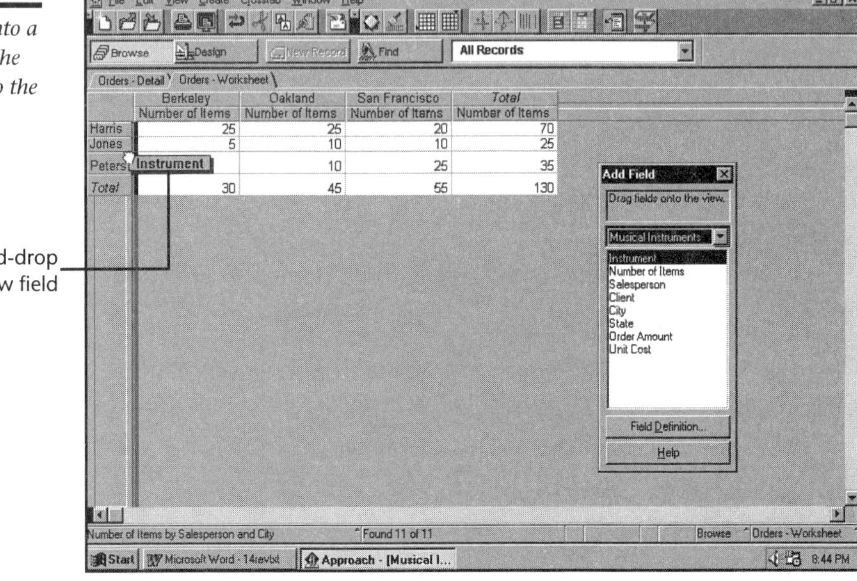

Fig. 14.29

The new crosstab, based on values in the fields Salesperson, City, and Instrument, makes it easy to discover where certain instruments—and salesmen—work best.

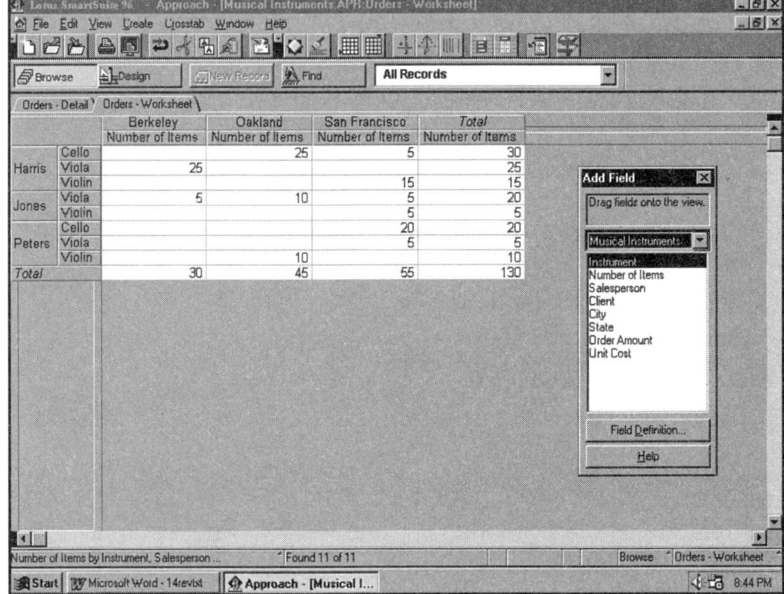

To add a new field to a crosstab, follow these steps:

1. Display the Add Field dialog box. To accomplish this, either click the Add Field icon or open the Crosstab menu and choose Add Field.
2. To add a new field, drag its name from the Add Field dialog box onto the crosstab.

Note that when you add a new field to a crosstab, the resulting summary information is exactly the same regardless of where you place the new field. However, the exact placement order of this information depends on where you place the new field name.

Deleting a Field. Deleting a field from a crosstab has exactly the opposite effect from adding a field. Approach automatically recalculates the summary information based on the remaining fields.

To delete a field from a crosstab, follow these steps:

1. Click anywhere on the row or column of values for that field.
2. When the pointer changes to the shape of a hand, click again in the same place, and drag the field name up and off the crosstab.

Approach displays the new crosstab, basing the new calculations on the remaining fields.

Adding and Deleting Summary Rows and Columns. Each time you create a new crosstab, Approach automatically inserts summary columns and rows. For example, in the crosstab shown in figure 14.23, the far right column lists the total number of each type of instrument sold. If you prefer not to have these totals displayed, you can delete the row, the column, or both.

To delete the row or column of totals, click the row or column label and release the mouse button. When the pointer changes to a hand, drag the row or column away from the crosstab.

If you later change your mind, you can redisplay either or both the row and column totals by opening the Crosstab menu and choosing Summarize Rows or Summarize Columns. The corresponding totals row or column is added to the crosstab.

From Here...

Worksheets and crosstabs are powerful tools you can use when working with databases. Worksheets allow you to view and edit information in columnar format, whereas crosstabs offer a convenient mechanism for viewing summary information from all or part of a database file.

You can enhance the usefulness of worksheets and crosstabs by using other Approach features, such as charting, finding, and sorting groups of records. For more information, refer to the following chapters in this book:

- Chapter 5, "Working with Your Data," contains information about sorting groups of records.
- Chapter 6, "Finding Records," describes how to find selected groups of records.
- Chapter 15, "Creating Charts," tells you how to create graphical charts that let you visually analyze your data.

CHAPTER 15

Creating Charts

By using the charting feature of Approach, you can create a wide variety of charts to enhance your tables. Each chart you create is stored as a separate view, and you can easily retrieve any particular one by selecting its name.

In this chapter, you learn how to

- Distinguish between different types of charts
- Create a new chart
- Modify existing charts
- Customize a chart with legends, titles, and axes information
- Drill down to a chart's underlying data
- Enhance charts with other text and graphics objects

The charts shown in this chapter are based on sales figures from an Orders database for a musical instrument dealer. In this database, each record represents a single order placed by a customer. Each order is for a number of instruments of a single type (such as violins).

Table 15.1 shows the data used for generating these charts. The fields in this table have the following meaning:

Field	Contents
INSTRUMENT	Type of instrument sold
NUMBER OF ITEMS	Number of instruments sold
SALESPERSON	Name of salesperson making sale
CLIENT	Name of person or company buying instruments

Table 15.1 Sample Data

Instrument	Number of Items	Salesperson	Client
Violin	5	Jones	Classic Sounds
Viola	5	Jones	No Strings
Violin	15	Harris	Classic Sounds
Violin	5	Jones	Sounding Goods
Cello	5	Harris	No Strings
Viola	8	Peters	Classic Sounds San Francisco
Cello	3	Peters	Classic Sounds Oakland
Viola	5	Jones	Sounding Goods Berkeley
Viola	5	Harris	No Strings San Francisco
Violin	5	Peters	Good Works Oakland
Cello	2	Harris	Good Works San Francisco

Using Charts

When creating a new chart, you can choose from a wide variety of types, including bar charts, pie charts, and many others. For each chart type, Approach offers a wide range of features that you can customize, such as three-dimensional effects, titles, legends, and many others. This section shows samples of the more commonly used types of charts you can create with Approach. These samples are representative only because so many options are available for each chart type.

Using Bar Charts

Bar charts are one of the most popular formats for displaying different types of information. Typically, the x-axis of a bar chart displays the different values stored in a field, while the values on the y-axis represent totals for those values.

For example, figure 15.1 illustrates a bar chart showing a breakdown of instrument sales. Here, the x-axis lists the different types of instruments, while the y-axis shows total number of each type sold. This bar chart offers a good visual representation of the relative sales numbers.

You can enhance the appearance of bar charts by including special effects, such as depth and grid lines. When these modifications are applied to the bar chart in figure 15.1, the result is shown in figure 15.2. These enhancements—as well as many others—are available with most of the chart types in Approach.

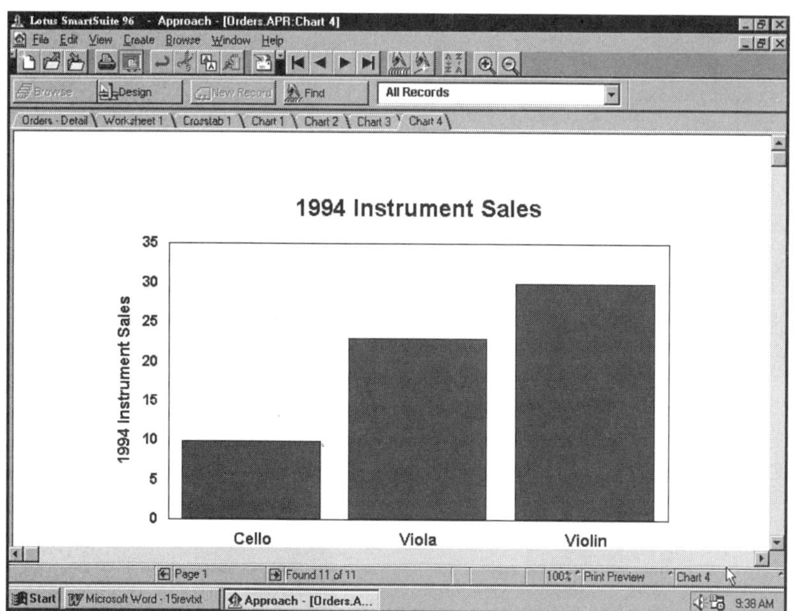

Fig. 15.1

A two-dimensional bar chart displays numbers for each field of data and is a good way to compare relative amounts.

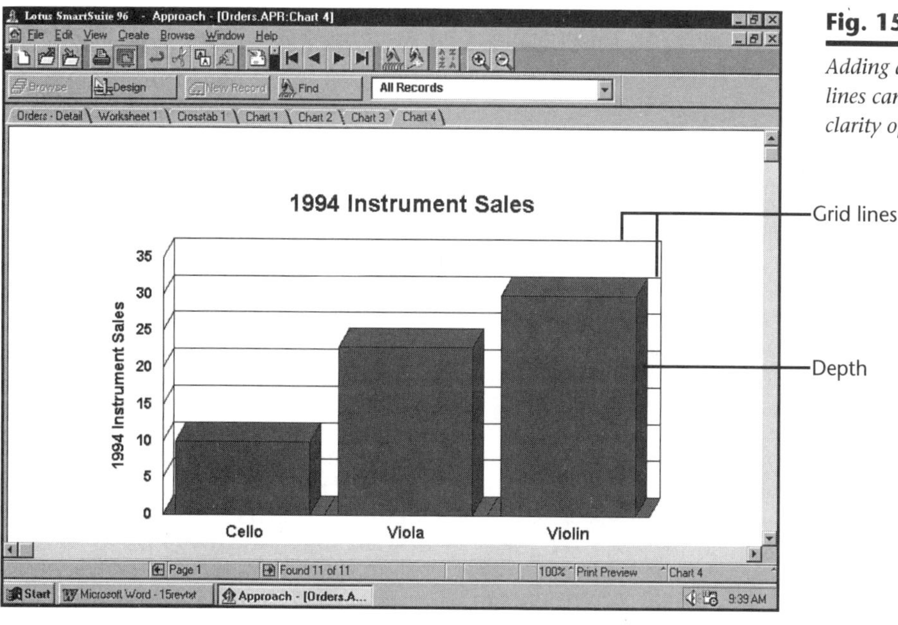

Fig. 15.2

Adding depth and grid lines can improve the clarity of a chart.

A bar chart is also a convenient tool for displaying values from more than one series of data. (A *series* is a subset of data within a database.) Using the data in table 15.1 as an example, you can break down the total instrument sales by individual salesperson, so that the sales for each salesperson is a separate series. The result is the chart shown in figure 15.3.

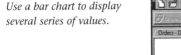

Fig. 15.3

Use a bar chart to display several series of values.

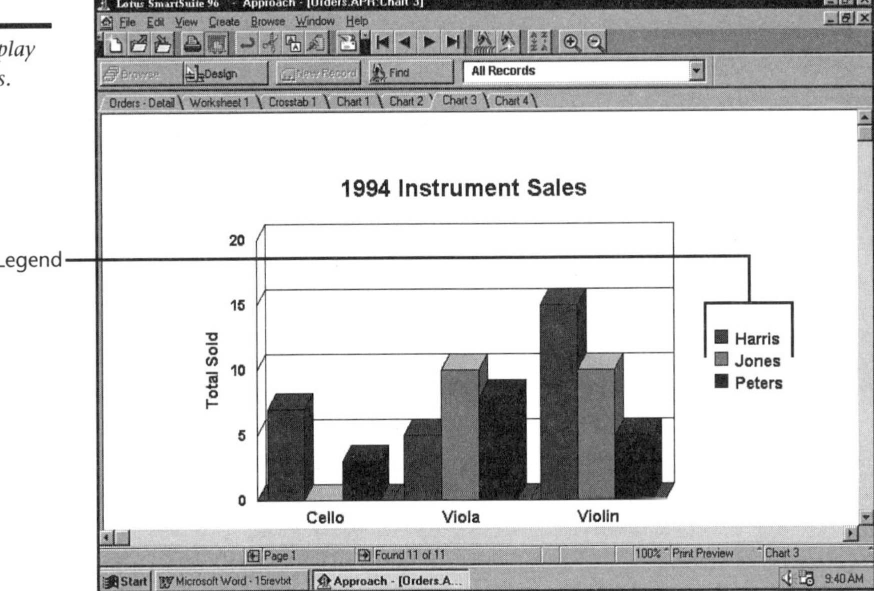

Note that figure 15.3 contains a legend that serves to identify the different series included in the chart. You can optionally include a legend with most types of charts, and—like other chart features—you can customize the appearance of the legend.

Another variation on the bar chart is the *three-dimensional perspective* variety, such as the one shown in figure 15.4. Notice how this chart differs from the one shown in figure 15.3, although both are drawn in three dimensions. Be careful, however, because the extensive use of 3-D bars can make your chart difficult to interpret.

Figure 15.5 shows a type of bar chart in which the bars are drawn horizontally instead of vertically. There is no particular advantage in using a horizontal bar chart as opposed to a vertical one. The type you use is a matter of personal preference, but should be chosen to display your data to the best advantage.

Figure 15.6 shows still another type of bar chart: the *stacked bar chart.* Here, the values for different series are placed directly on top of each other. This type of chart allows you to directly see various totals.

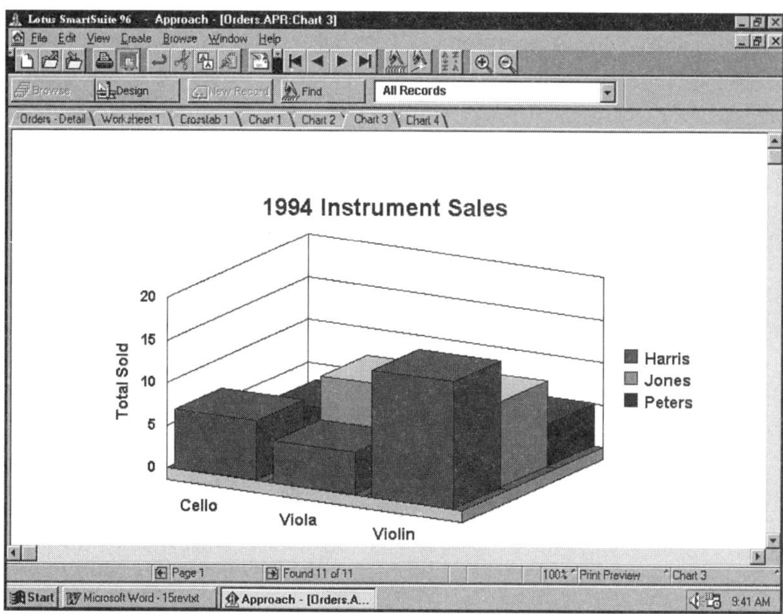

Fig. 15.4

A three-dimensional chart gives a new perspective to data.

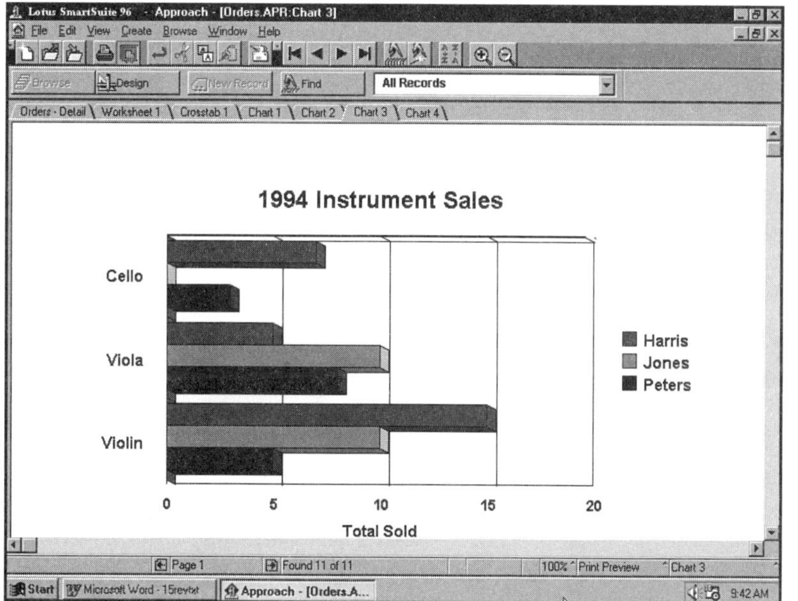

Fig. 15.5

Information can be displayed horizontally instead of vertically.

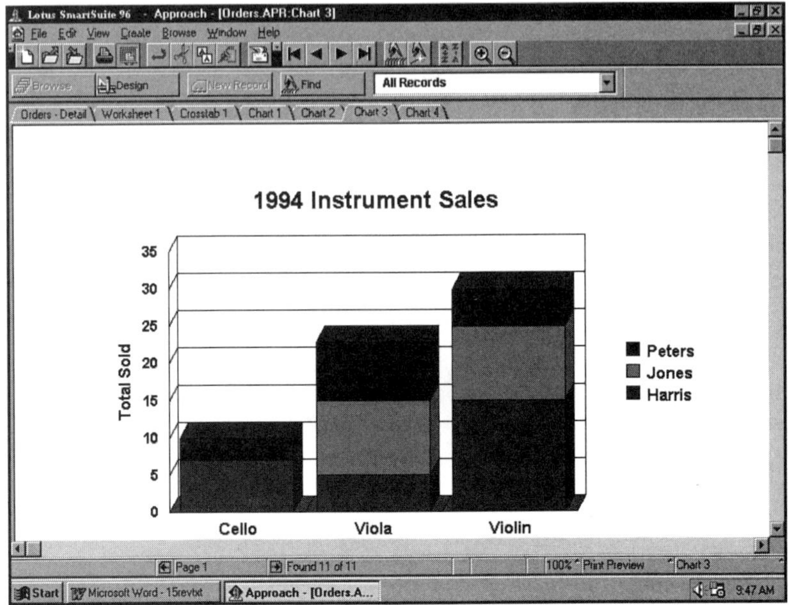

Fig. 15.6

A stacked bar chart offers a total picture of the amount, but breaks it down further according to a second data series.

Using Pie Charts

Pie charts are extremely popular, possibly because they remind us of food. They also are a good way of representing relative proportions in a set of numbers, as shown in figure 15.7. An *exploded pie chart,* like the one in figure 15.8, adds a particularly dramatic touch and helps the viewer distinguish important information. To "explode" a pie chart, simply click the appropriate slice and drag it away from the pie.

A pie chart can display the information from only one series of data. For example, a pie chart can illustrate the total number of each type of instrument sold, but it can't display the total number of each type of instrument sold by each salesperson.

The legend shown in figures 15.7 and 15.8 is optional. You can control its placement and appearance as you can with legends for other types of charts.

Using Line and Scatter Charts

Although not quite as striking as three-dimensional bar or pie charts, *line charts* (also called x-y charts) and *scatter charts* are alternative ways of displaying relative values. Figure 15.9 shows an example of a line chart. A scatter chart is simply a line chart without the solid lines connecting the individual points.

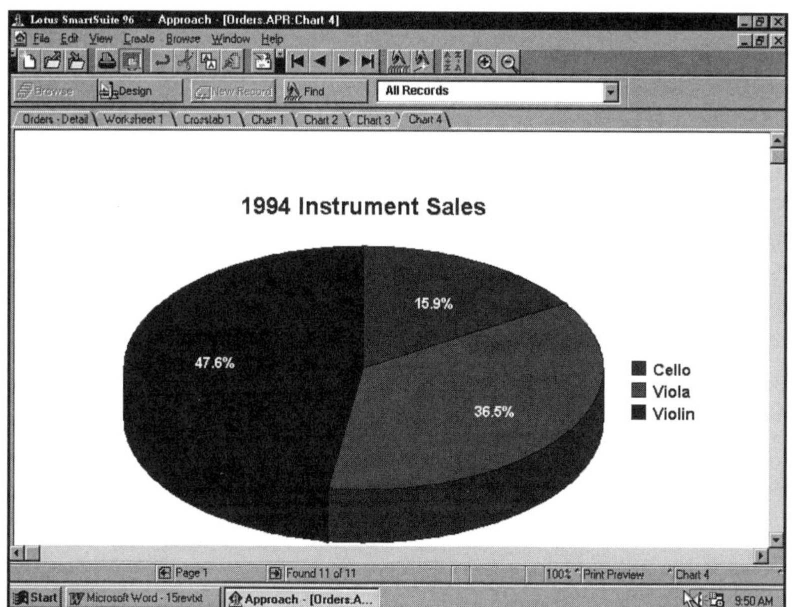

Fig. 15.7

A pie chart shows "slices" of your data and is an excellent way to compare a single data series.

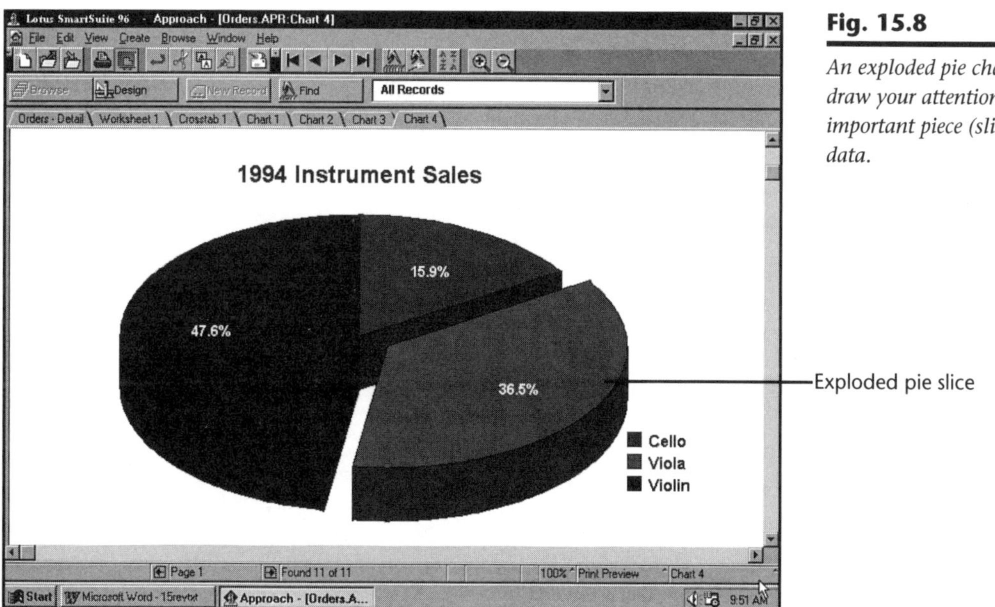

Fig. 15.8

An exploded pie chart can draw your attention to an important piece (slice) of data.

Fig. 15.9

A line chart tracks data series over several intervals.

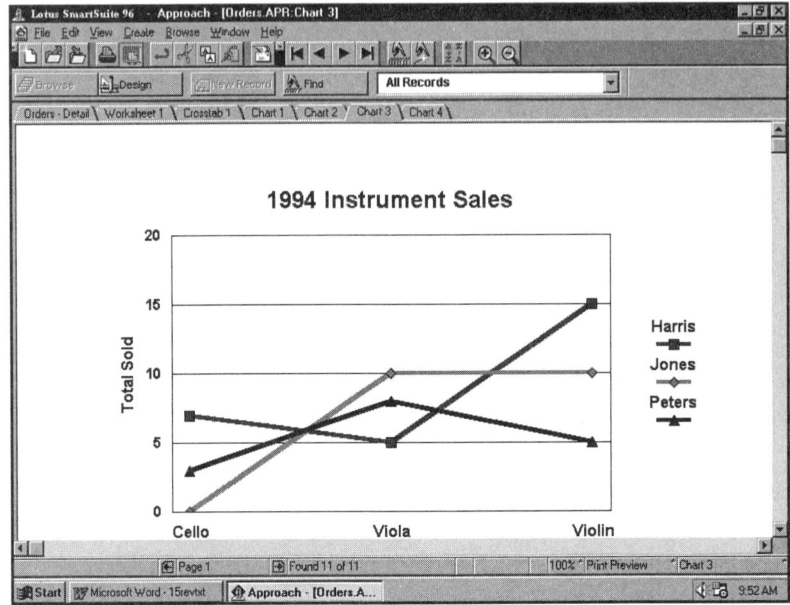

Using Area Charts

An *area chart,* such as the one shown in figure 15.10, is effective in portraying a change of values with respect to time or another variable. The advantage of using an area chart is that you can use it to show cumulative totals. For example, the vertical heights on the chart in figure 15.10 show total sales for each instrument type.

Fig. 15.10

An area chart stacks items for a cumulative total.

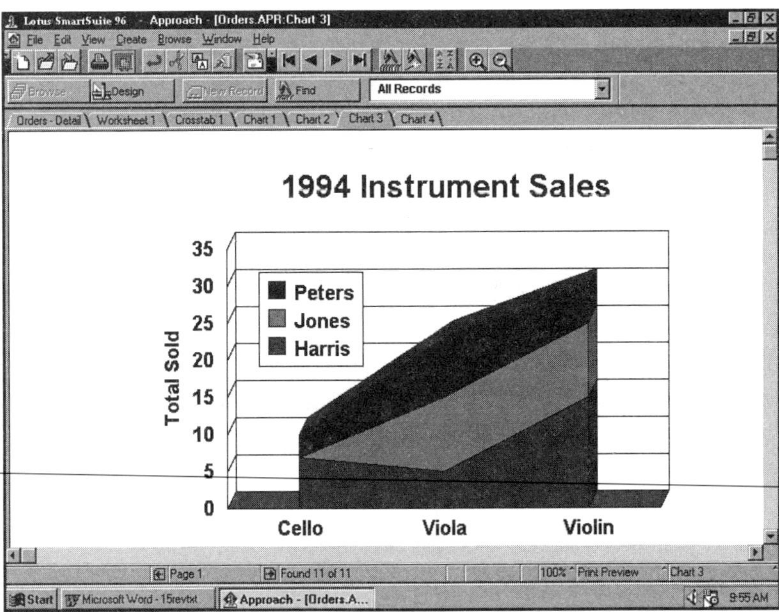

Using Other Chart Types

Approach supports four other types of chart: the *Hi/Lo/Close/Open* (HLCO), *radar, mixed,* and *number grid* charts. Although you'll rarely need them, you should familiarize yourself with their application.

- *HLCO charts* are useful for tracking numbers that fluctuate over a given period of time. Stock market reports are a common type of HLCO chart.
- *Radar charts* compare data series with a great many variables, letting you see where data overlaps.
- *Mixed charts* are standard chart types with an additional data series plotted on the same chart, using a different chart type. In the music store example, you could chart each salesperson's total sales using a bar graph, and then add a line graph showing average sales per order for each salesman (see fig. 15.11). You can combine line, bar, and area chart types only.

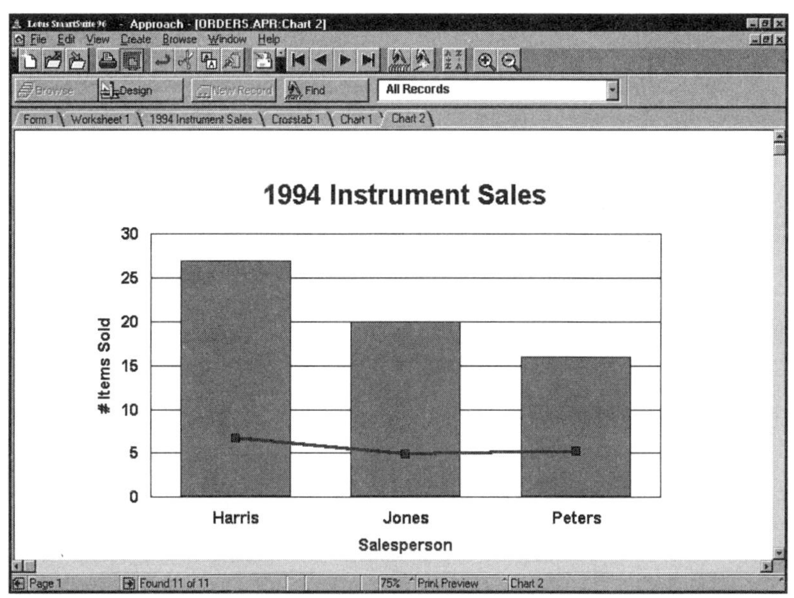

Fig. 15.11

A mixed chart type makes it easy to compare different types of data, such as total sales versus average sales per order.

- *Number grid charts* are exactly what they sound like: a grid of numbers, much like you'd see in an Approach crosstab or worksheet, but with a more professional appearance.

Creating a New Chart

You can create a chart in two basic ways. The standard method is to use the Chart Assistant, which guides you through the steps for selecting the various chart elements. Alternatively, you can have Approach automatically create a chart directly from a crosstab view.

> **Note**
>
> You can't view a chart in Browse mode. Switch to Print Preview to see the finished chart after making your changes in Design mode.

The first step in creating a new chart is to select the records you want to include by performing a standard find. If you skip this step, Approach will automatically use all records in the current database.

After choosing the records to be charted, you can set up the basic format for the new chart. This includes the type of chart, the style and layout, and the fields to be plotted. Approach will then display the chart on-screen. If you want, you can then customize the chart by using the wide variety of tools at your disposal.

Selecting the Data You Want to Chart

To chart a subset of records from a database, you must specify them as follows:

1. Switch to any convenient form, worksheet, or report for the table you want to chart.
2. By using a Find command, enter a query to specify the records you want to use.
3. Create the chart, as described in the following sections.

> **Note**
>
> For more information on performing a find operation, refer to Chapter 6, "Finding Records."

Choosing the Chart Options

After you select the records to be plotted, you can create the chart. Choose the type of chart you want, the fields to be displayed on the x- and y-axes, and—if you plan to chart more than one series—the field to be used for isolating the different series. You can also override the default name supplied by Approach for the chart and select your own.

> **Note**
>
> A *series* is a subset of data for a particular field value. If you create a chart showing company sales by salesperson, for example, there will be a separate series of data for each salesperson.

> **Note**
>
> When you create a new chart, you're limited to bar, line, area, and pie chart types. Later, when the chart is on-screen, you can switch to one of the many other types available.

Follow these steps to create a new chart:

1. Open the Create menu and choose Chart. Approach displays the Chart Assistant dialog box (see fig. 15.12).

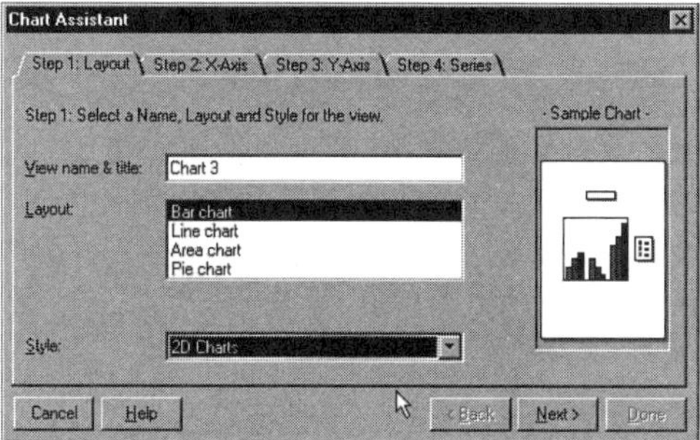

Fig. 15.12

Choose the basic layout features for the chart.

2. Make sure that the left tab at the top of the Assistant is selected (the one labeled Step 1: Layout). Then fill in the options as shown in figure 15.12. At each step, the Sample Chart display on the right indicates which part of the chart you're now choosing.
3. Click the tab at the top labeled Step 2: X-Axis or click the Next button.

> **Note**
>
> If you select pie as the type of chart, the Step 2: X-Axis tab at the top changes to Pie Fields. Also, if you're creating a pie chart, skip to step 8 after you complete step 3.

4. When the next display appears, select the field whose values you want on the x-axis (see fig. 15.13).

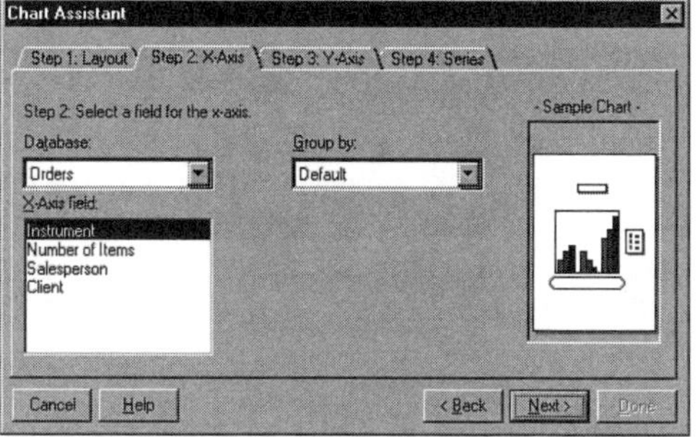

Fig. 15.13

Choose the field whose values will be displayed on the x-axis of the new chart.

5. Click the Next button or the tab at the top labeled Step 3: Y-Axis. The screen then switches to the display shown in figure 15.14.

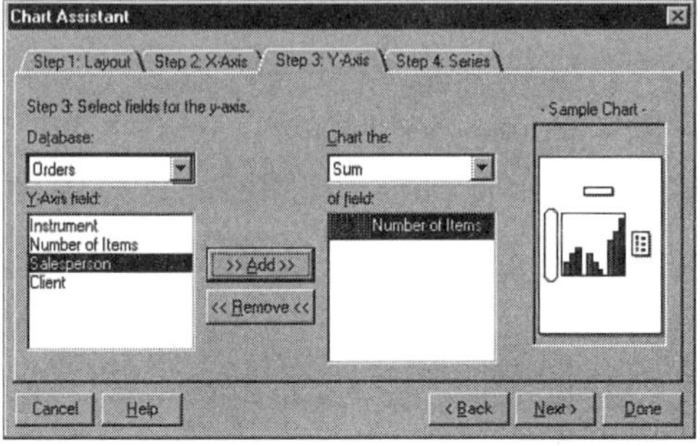

Fig. 15.14

Choose the field whose values will appear on the y-axis of the new chart.

6. Select the field whose values you want on the y-axis.
7. Choose the type of calculation you want performed on the field you selected in step 6 (the most common selection is Sum).
8. Click the top tab labeled Step 4: Series or click the Next button, and you'll see the screen shown in figure 15.15. (If you plan to display only one series of values on the new chart, skip this step.)

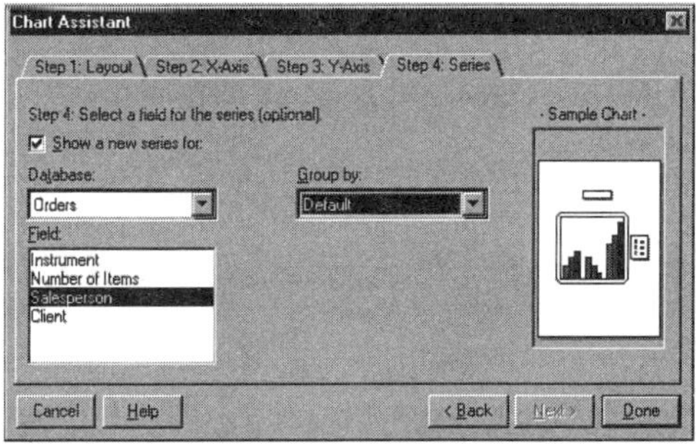

Fig. 15.15

Select the field that will add a second series of data to the chart to break it down into additional categories.

9. Choose the field whose values are to determine the different series in the chart. For example, if you select the Salesperson field, each individual name in this field will be the basis of a different series.

> **Tip**
>
> If you have many different items to graph, you sometimes can save space by grouping them into related categories. For example, rather than display the test scores of each student in a class, you could group the students' names alphabetically. To do this, choose the optional Group By drop-down list on the panel. You can group items by the first one through five characters in the field.

10. Click the Done button. Approach displays the new chart on your screen.

Creating an Instant Chart

If you're working with a crosstab view, you can bypass the steps described earlier for creating a new chart and let Approach automatically use the crosstab layout to create a vertical bar chart for you. This type of chart is called an instant chart because Approach automatically makes all the choices necessary to create the chart. If necessary, you can modify the chart by using the procedures described throughout the second half of this chapter.

> **Note**
>
> For more information on crosstabs, see Chapter 14, "Using Worksheets and Crosstabs."

Suppose that you're working with a simple crosstab based on the values of two fields, such as the one shown in figure 15.16. This crosstab lists the sum of the field NUMBER OF ITEMS over all records for the various types of instruments. If you create an instant chart from this crosstab, it will be similar to the one shown in figure 15.17.

	Number of Items
Cello	10
Viola	23
Violin	30
Total	63

Fig. 15.16

The numbers displayed in a simple crosstab may not give the viewer an immediate picture of the data.

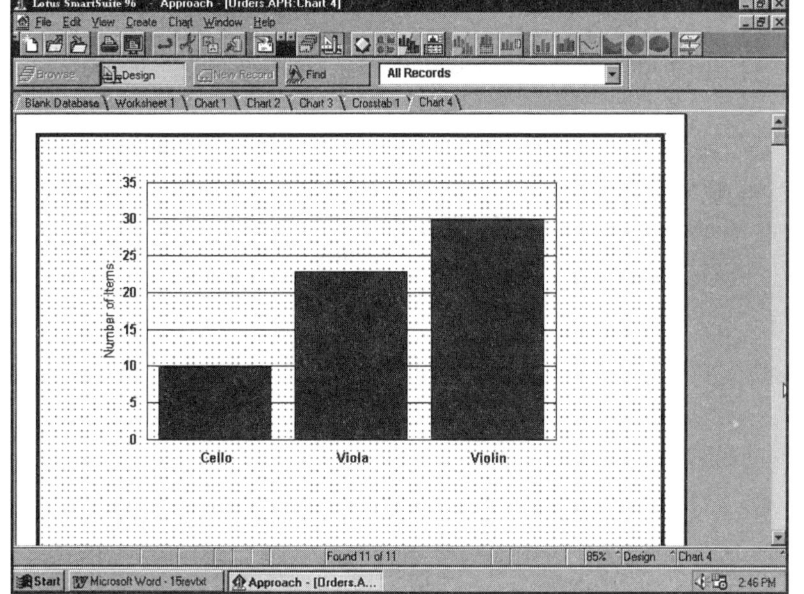

Fig. 15.17

You can have Approach automatically create an instant chart from the simple crosstab in figure 15.16, providing more effective interpretation for the viewer.

Similarly, a chart created from a crosstab based on three fields will be a bar chart showing several series of data. The field values in the first column of the crosstab will be displayed on the x-axis of the chart, while the field values displayed in the first row of the crosstab will furnish the values for the different series.

To create an instant chart from a crosstab, first select that crosstab as the current view; then either click the Chart Crosstab icon, or open the Crosstab menu and choose Chart Crosstab. Approach generates and displays the chart.

Modifying an Existing Chart

Because you can modify just about any part of any chart, you have enormous control over its appearance. The following are some of the types of changes you can make:

- *Chart data.* You can change the fields whose values are displayed in a chart.
- *Chart type.* With a simple mouse click, you can change a chart from one type to another. For instance, you can easily switch from a bar chart to a pie, area, or other type of chart.
- *Chart layout.* The layout of a chart refers to whether a grid and/or legend are displayed with a chart.
- *Chart elements.* Each chart contains a variety of different bits and pieces, such as a title, legend, labels, and many other items. You can modify the appearance of these elements and, in many cases, you can also control their position.

Note

You can view a chart in Print Preview or Design mode. To make any changes to a chart, however, you must be in Design mode, with the chart you want to modify selected. Furthermore, you must make sure that the option Show Data on the View menu is selected.

Changing the Data in a Chart

When you create a chart, you select the fields whose values are to be displayed. If necessary, you can modify the chart later by selecting different fields. You can even change a chart that displays a single data series, so that it displays multiple series.

To select a different set of data to be displayed by the chart that's now displayed, follow these steps:

1. Open the Chart menu and choose Chart Data Source. The Chart Data Source Assistant dialog box appears (see fig. 15.18).

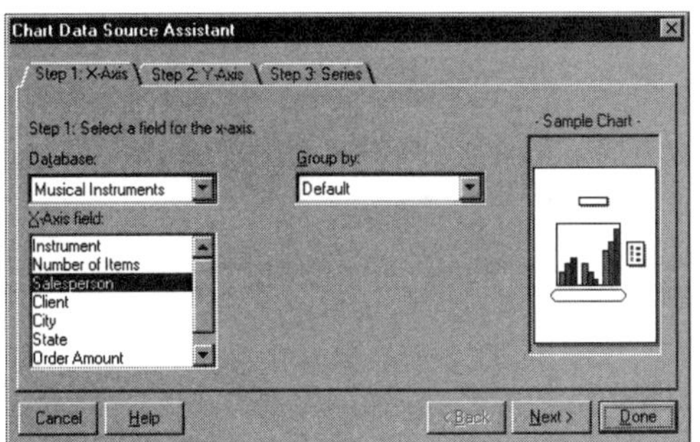

Fig. 15.18

Use the Chart Data Source Assistant dialog box to select a different data set for a chart.

> **Note**
>
> Using the Chart Data Source Assistant dialog box is nearly identical to using the Chart Assistant. However, the labels of the top tabs are arranged somewhat differently.

2. Choose the new fields for the x-axis and y-axis.
3. To display multiple series, click the Step 3: Series tab. Then choose the field whose values will define the different series.
4. After making your selections, click the Done button. Approach will then recalculate and display the modified chart.

Using the Chart InfoBox

To make most changes to a chart, you use its InfoBox. As with other parts of Approach, the InfoBox contents depend on the objects selected. Once the InfoBox is displayed, however, you can use its drop-down objects list to select the part of your chart you want to modify. You also can leave the InfoBox on-screen while you select different parts of a chart for customizing, and then immediately switch back to the InfoBox to make your changes.

You can display the InfoBox for a chart by using any of the following methods:

- Click the InfoBox icon.
- Open the Chart menu and choose Chart Properties.
- Press Ctrl+E.
- Double-click anywhere on the chart.

The contents of the InfoBox change, depending on which part of the chart you've selected. However, its basic appearance remains the same, like that shown in figure 15.19.

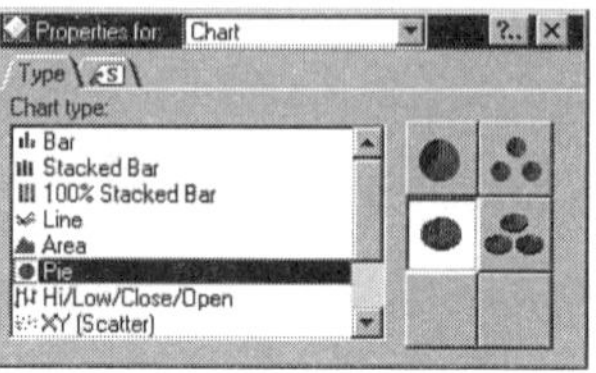

Fig. 15.19

Customize a chart by using its InfoBox in Design mode.

To select which part of a chart you want to modify, pull down the list box at the top, as shown in figure 15.20, and then make your selection. You can also directly click the chart item you want to modify, in which case the InfoBox will automatically display the appropriate options for you to modify.

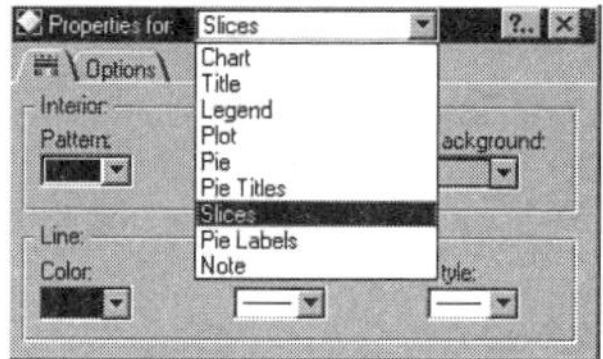

Fig. 15.20

Select a chart element by selecting its name from the InfoBox drop-down list.

As in other sections of Approach, different tabs on the InfoBox control the format, colors, styles, and other aspects of the chart. You can choose to hide certain slices of a pie chart, for example, or change colors and patterns of chart elements. The tabs will change according to the chart object you've selected, displaying only the appropriate controls.

> **Note**
>
> When working with the InfoBox, the summary panel InfoBox may sometimes appear, often caused by clicking outside the chart area. Clicking somewhere on the chart will return you to chart properties.

Using the Chart SmartIcon Bar

When you create a new chart or move to a chart page, Approach automatically displays a special Chart SmartIcon bar. Clicking these icons opens the InfoBox to the most commonly performed chart modification tasks.

Modifying Text. By changing the type face, size, attributes, alignment, and numeric formatting, you can change the appearance of any text element on a chart. To make these adjustments to a text element, select that element and then use the top four buttons on the upper left part of the InfoBox.

Note

When the InfoBox for a chart is displayed, you can select an entire text element by clicking it once; its four handles will then appear. In some cases, you can select just part of a text element by double-clicking it and then highlighting the text you want to customize.

Caution

Don't try to delete a text element by using the Delete or Backspace key—or by opening the Edit menu and choosing Cut. If you do, the entire chart will disappear. Here's why: If you look closely, any chart you're working with is always selected. You can see this by noticing that its four selection handles are visible. When you press the Delete or Backspace key, anything that's selected is deleted—in this case, the entire chart.

To change the font and attribute of the text you've selected, click the InfoBox fonts tab. The fonts page lets you change fonts, colors, and related text attributes (see fig. 15.21).

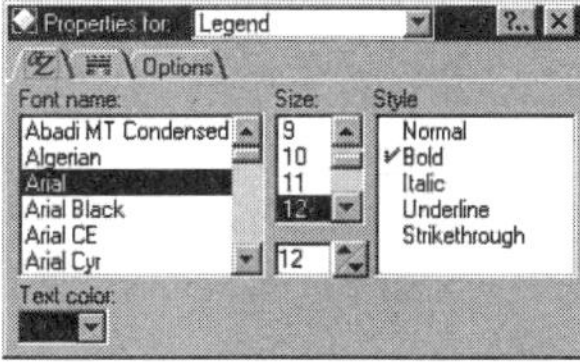

Fig. 15.21

You can customize text fonts and attributes.

To customize the format for numeric information, click the number tab and then make your selections from the displayed options (see fig. 15.22). Approach will let you select only those number formats that are appropriate. For example, if you've selected slice labels in a pie chart, which are expressed as a percentage, you can't change to a currency format.

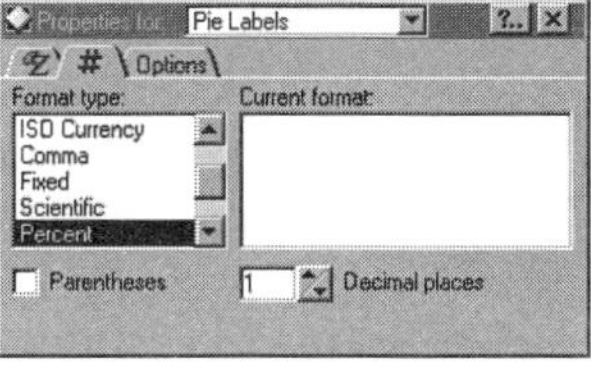

Fig. 15.22

Data type permitting, use the InfoBox to change text numeric formats.

To customize the display and placement of text, click the Options tab in the InfoBox. You then can choose which labels or titles to display and where to display them. Where appropriate, Approach lets you place text inside or outside of the chart area (see fig. 15.23).

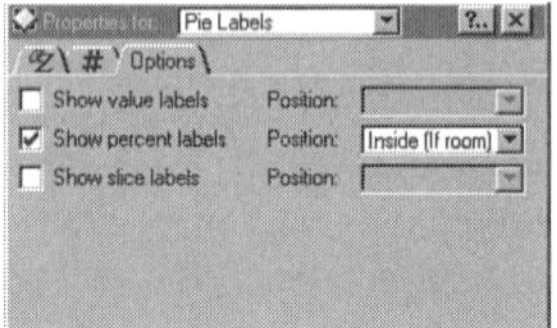

Fig. 15.23

You can change the content and placement of titles and labels using InfoBox tabs.

Modifying Lines, Patterns, and Colors. Many components of a chart contain straight lines and closed and filled areas. Use the colors page on the InfoBox to modify these attributes, as follows:

- To customize the color of a line or filled area you've selected, click the down arrow beside the color box and choose from the color grid that appears (see fig. 15.24).

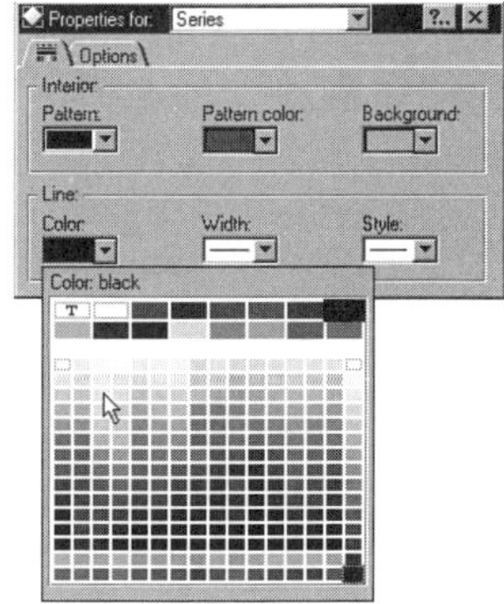

Fig. 15.24

Use these options to customize the color and patterns of lines and filled areas.

- To customize a line, click the down arrows for width and style (see fig. 15.25), and then make your changes.

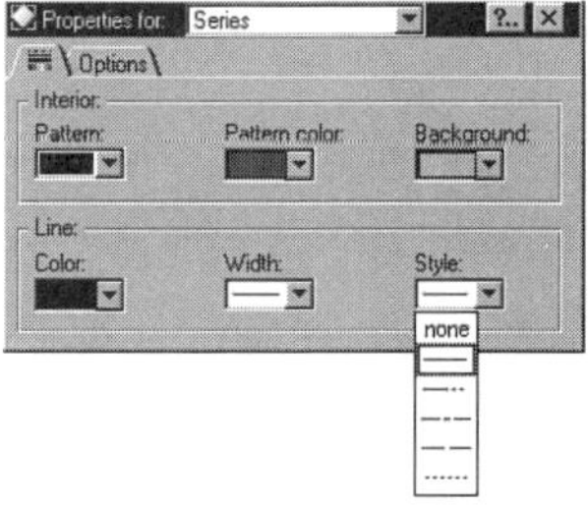

Fig. 15.25

Use these options to customize the style and width of a line.

Modifying the Chart Type

When you create a new chart, you must choose one of the four basic types: line, bar, area, or pie. However, you can later change the chart type—choosing from a much wider variety—and change the inclusion or placement of chart elements. To make your changes, follow these steps:

1. Make sure that the chart is on-screen. If necessary, double-click the chart to bring up the InfoBox.
2. Pull down the list box at the top of the InfoBox and choose Chart from the list (see fig. 15.26).

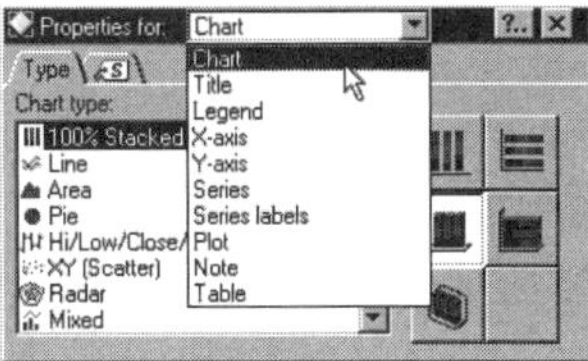

Fig. 15.26

Change the chart type using this drop-down list.

3. The chart pages will appear. Choose the new type of chart from the list box on the left.
4. You can choose to add two- or three-dimensional aspects as well as depth to your chart by using the buttons to the right. Your chart will change to reflect your selections (see fig. 15.27).

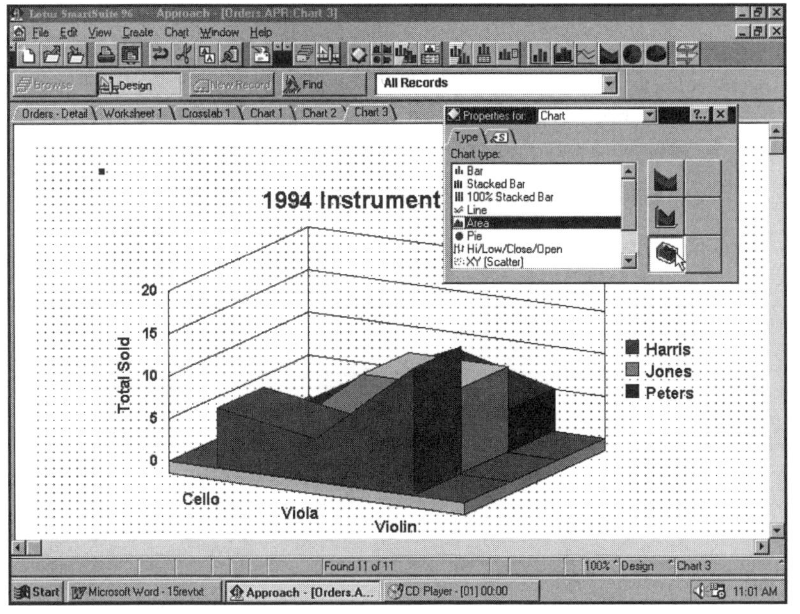

Fig. 15.27

Add depth to your chart by using these InfoBox buttons.

Drilling Down to Chart Data

You can check the underlying data in your chart by making sure that you're in Design mode, and then clicking on an element (say, a slice in a pie chart or a bar segment in a bar chart). Click the Drill Down to Data SmartIcon, or open the Chart menu and choose Drill Down to Data; Approach will build a new worksheet page listing only the data that produced that data element (see fig. 15.28).

Fig. 15.28

You can view single data elements of a chart by using the Drill Down to Data button.

Instrument	Salesperson	Number of Items
Violin	Jones	5
Viola	Jones	5
Violin	Jones	5
Viola	Jones	5

Drilling down is an easy way to analyze chart numbers without having to build a separate worksheet or report for each data element.

Customizing the Chart Elements

Each type of chart has its own set of elements, and you can customize most of them. This section describes how to customize the elements that are common to most chart types. Figure 15.29 shows the standard elements of a chart. (You probably will never use them all in a single chart; they're included here for illustration purposes only.)

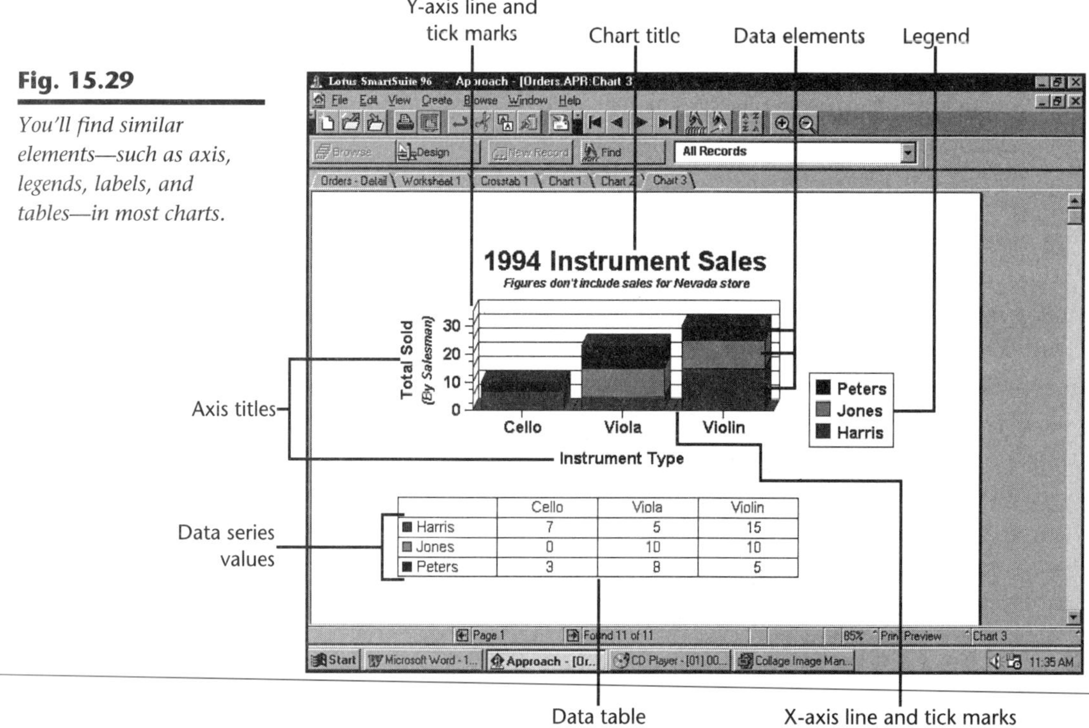

Fig. 15.29

You'll find similar elements—such as axis, legends, labels, and tables—in most charts.

The common chart elements are as follows:

- The *chart title* is a heading for the chart.
- The *legend* identifies individual data elements when a chart contains more than one series.
- *X-axis and y-axis components* (including titles, lines, tick marks, and value labels) identify and quantify the information being charted.
- The *note* adds an explanation to the chart; it can be added in several preset positions, or later selected and moved into the desired position.
- The *data table* shows actual values for a chart's data elements and is especially useful when more than one series is used. It takes the place of a legend (series value labels are given in the row labels on the left). The data table normally puts values listed on the x-axis as column headings. Actual data (x-axis values) appears as the body of the table.

To customize these elements, you must first display the InfoBox, using any of the methods described earlier. Then, to select the part you want to change, you can do either of the following:

- Click the top drop-down list box (refer back to fig. 15.20) and select the element containing the part you want to customize.
- Click directly on the part of the chart you want to customize.

When you select the element you want—using either of the preceding methods—the entire right section of the InfoBox changes, displaying options specific to that element. In some cases this could include a list, from which you select the particular part of the element you want to customize.

For some elements, several tabs may become visible at the bottom of the InfoBox, offering other options.

Tip

You can click the Show (element) check boxes to display or hide many of the chart elements. To delete a particular element from the chart, click it and then deselect the Show (element) check box.

Adding a Chart Title. When Approach creates a new chart, it won't automatically affix a title at the top. You can add one by selecting Title from the InfoBox drop-down list. You can customize your title in the following ways using the font, color, and Options pages:

- Create and edit up to three lines of title text (see fig. 15.30).
- Customize the background and frame of the title box.
- Change the font, style, color, and position of the title text.

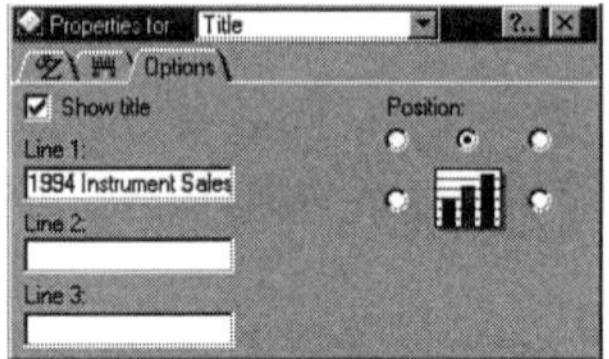

Fig. 15.30

You can customize a chart's title.

Tip

You can double-click the title text and edit it in place.

Adding a Legend. If a chart contains a legend, you can customize it in the following ways:

- Change its position with respect to the chart
- Edit any part of the legend text
- Change the font, style, and color of the legend text
- Customize the frame surrounding the legend

To customize a legend, first select it so that the InfoBox appears, as shown in figure 15.31. (Alternatively, you can select Legend from the drop-down list box at the top of the InfoBox.) You can then use the various InfoBox options to make your changes.

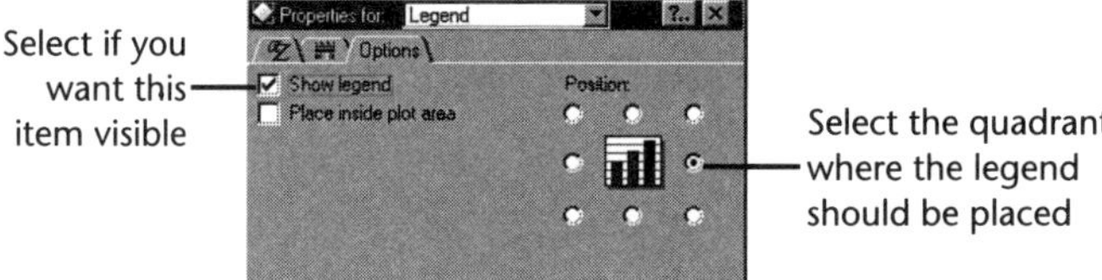

Fig. 15.31

Use these options to customize a chart legend.

Inserting a Note. You can insert a one- to three-line note at the bottom left, right, or center of a chart. You can customize this note and move it to another position later, using the same types of options available for the chart title and legend.

To create a note, follow these steps:

1. Pull down the list box at the top of the InfoBox, and then select the Note option.
2. Make sure that the Show Note box is checked.
3. Enter the desired text into the boxes marked Line 1, Line 2, and Line 3. A new line appears below the chart, and the InfoBox takes on the appearance shown in figure 15.32.
4. To reposition the note, click it once and then drag it to where you want it.

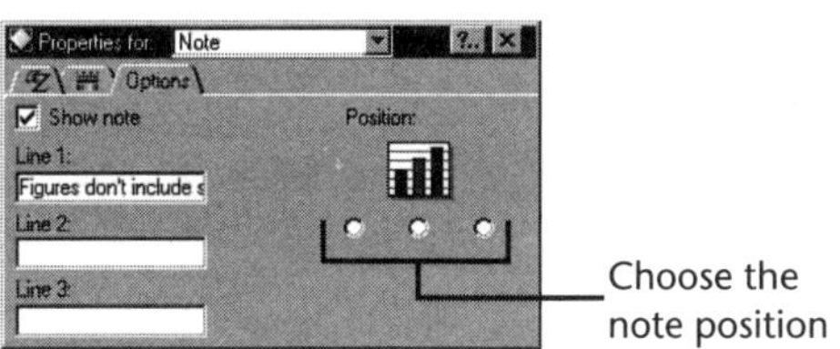

Fig. 15.32

You can create and customize a note for a chart.

Customizing the X- and Y-Axes. With the exception of pie charts, all other chart types use x- and y-axes. Each axis includes the following parts, which you can individually customize:

- Title and subtitle
- Axis line
- Tick marks
- Labels for data values on the axis
- Range and scale for the axis data values
- Major grid lines

Tip

You can hide all the components of the axis by deselecting the Show (element) option in the InfoBox.

To customize the components of either the x-axis or y-axis, select it from the drop-down list at the top of the InfoBox. Alternatively, you can click any part of the axis you want to modify. The InfoBox will then take on the appearance shown in figure 15.33.

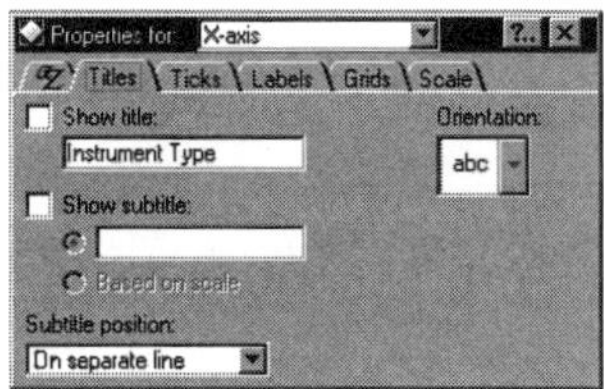

Fig. 15.33

Use these options to customize either axis of a chart.

Adding a Title and Subtitles. Approach sets the title for each axis to the name of the field whose values are shown on that axis. You can edit this title by double-clicking it and then making your changes.

You can also add a subtitle to each axis, as follows:

1. Select the x-axis or y-axis from the InfoBox drop-down list. Then click the Titles tab (see fig. 15.34).

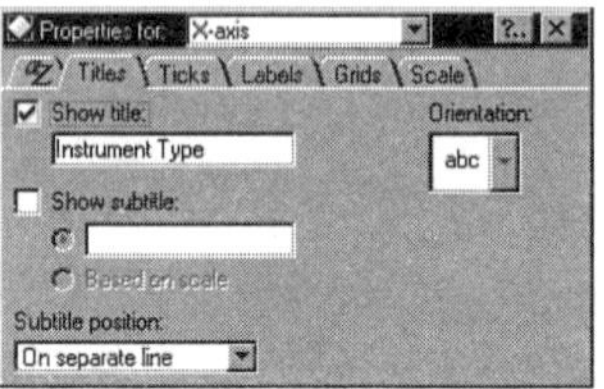

Fig. 15.34

You can add titles and subtitles to chart axes.

2. Click the Show Title check box and enter the desired text. On the y-axis, you can choose to display text horizontally, vertically facing left, or vertically facing right.
3. If you want to add a subtitle, click the Show Subtitle check box and enter your text. You can choose to display it on the same line as the title or on a new line. If you choose to display it on the same line as the title, you can change the font to distinguish it.

> **Note**
>
> You can choose to display a subtitle—when the scale of the chart permits it—by clicking the Based on Scale radio button.

Customizing a Chart Axis. You can change the following components of an axis by using its InfoBox:

- Color, pattern, and style of lines and text
- Tick marks
- Range and scaling of data values
- Grid lines

Approach automatically selects the best scale for viewing chart data. You can alter that scale and data range manually by following these steps:

1. Pull down the list box at the top of the InfoBox, and select either X-axis or Y-axis.
2. Select the tab marked Scale (see fig. 15.35).

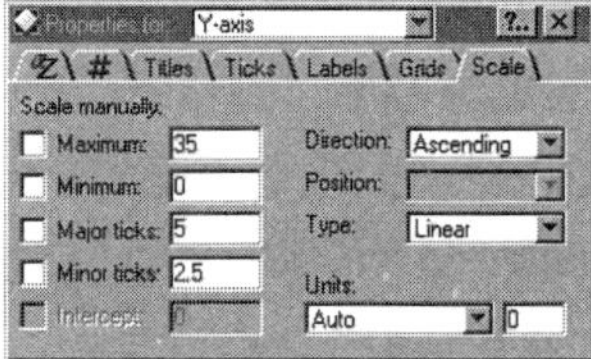

Fig. 15.35

The scale and placement of grid lines and tick marks help you compare values.

3. The current minimum and maximum tick mark values will be shown. Edit them as necessary. Your chart will resize to fit your new values.

Note

The scale options apply to an axis only if it displays numeric values.

Adding Grid Lines and Tick Marks. Grid lines and tick marks can help you read and interpret various types of charts, and you can optionally display grid lines for most chart types—pies being the notable exception.

When you display horizontal or vertical grid lines on a chart, they appear at the positions of the major tick marks on the corresponding axis. You can display these grid lines even if you hide these tick marks.

To display and customize either the vertical or horizontal grid lines for a chart, follow these steps:

1. Pull down the list box at the top of the InfoBox.
2. Select either the x- or y-axis.
3. Select the Grids tab (see fig. 15.36).

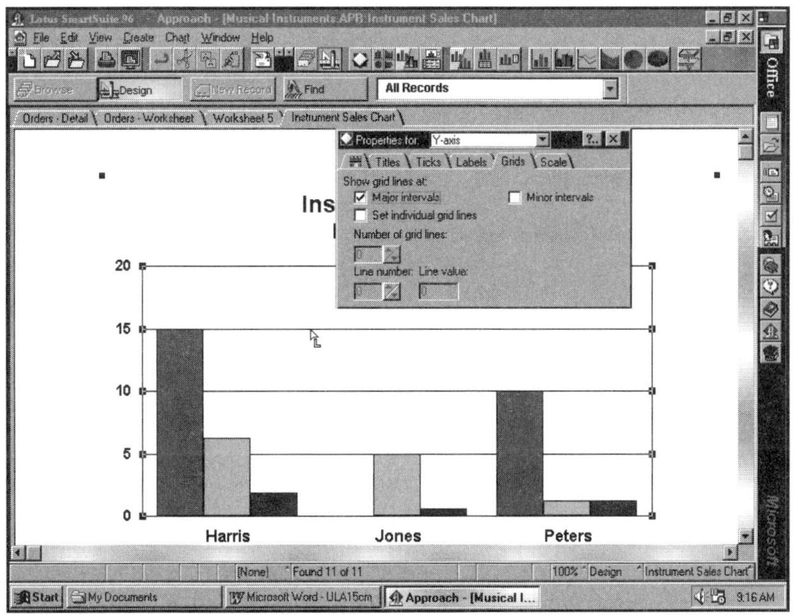

Fig. 15.36

The Grid page controls how x- or y-axis gridlines are displayed.

4. Click the Show Grid Lines At check box to display Major Intervals and Minor Intervals, as desired. You can let Approach set grid-line intervals automatically at preselected intervals, or you can set each grid mark by hand. The options displayed will depend on the axis chosen.

To display and customize the vertical and horizontal tick marks on a chart axis, follow these steps:

1. Pull down the list box at the top of the InfoBox.
2. Select either the x- or y-axis.
3. Select the Ticks tab and make sure that the Show Axis Line box is checked (see fig. 15.37).

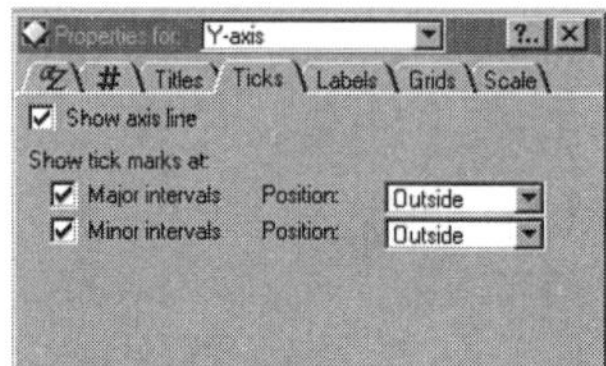

Fig. 15.37

The Ticks page in the InfoBox controls intervals on the x- and y-axes.

4. Click the boxes to select Show Tick Marks At Major Intervals and Minor Intervals. You can choose to extend the tick marks outside the chart (pointing toward value labels) or to keep them inside.

Deleting a Chart

You can easily delete a chart that's no longer of use to you. To accomplish this, use virtually the same steps you would for deleting any other type of view.

To delete a chart, follow these steps:

1. Display the chart you want to delete. The easiest way to accomplish this is to click the tab for that chart in the upper part of the Approach window.
2. Pull down the Edit menu and choose Delete Chart.
3. When Approach asks you to verify your deletion, choose Yes.

Enhancing a Chart with Text and Graphics

You can add dramatic impact to your chart by inserting additional text and graphics elements. For instance, you could add special text labels (in addition to those available as standard chart features), or you could insert a company logo. Figure 15.38 shows a chart containing both of these types of elements.

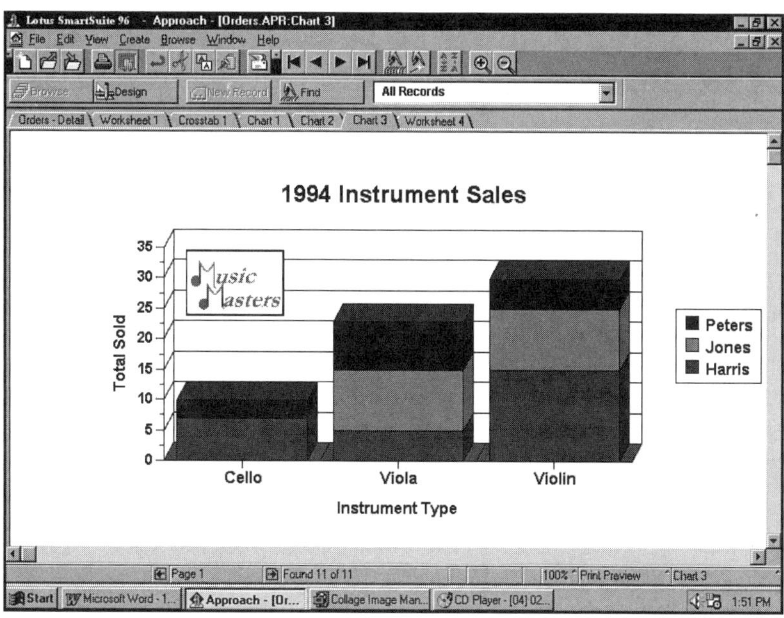

Fig. 15.38

You can add text and graphics elements to give your chart a more professional appearance.

You can add the following types of objects to a chart:

- Text objects
- Circles and ellipses
- Squares and rectangles
- Graphics images from other files
- Macro buttons

To add any of these elements, use the same techniques you would use for adding them to other types of Approach views. Suppose that you want to add a special logo to a chart, such as the Music Masters logo shown in figure 15.38. To insert this title as a text object, follow these steps:

1. Make sure that you're in Design mode; then open the Edit menu and choose Picture and then Import.
2. Select the picture file you want to import and click OK.
3. Your picture will appear on the chart page. You can resize or move it.

Adjusting Chart Parameters

When adding elements to a chart, you may need to resize and adjust the chart and some of its elements to make everything fit. In addition to customizing the various bits and pieces that make up a chart, you can also adjust several parameters that affect the overall chart. These parameters include the following:

- Chart name
- Position of the chart on the page
- Background color
- Macros associated with the chart
- Printing the chart

Resizing the Chart

To resize the chart, click it once, and then click one of the handles that appear. Drag the handle to enlarge or shrink the chart.

You may need to reduce the viewing size of the chart (to 85 percent or less) so that you can see and manipulate handles easily.

Changing the Chart Name

When you create a new chart, Approach automatically assigns it a name: Chart 1, Chart 2, and so on. You can change it to a more descriptive name. To accomplish this, double-click the chart name on the tab at the top of the chart window, and then type the new name.

> **Note**
>
> You must be in Design mode to change a chart's name.

Adjusting the Chart Position

Each chart occupies an entire page on-screen—or when printed—and you can reposition the chart anywhere on that page. To accomplish this, follow these steps:

1. Click the Zoom button on the status bar or choose Zoom Out from the View menu to reduce the size of the page until the entire page appears on-screen.
2. Click and hold the mouse button down anywhere within the chart handles.
3. Holding the mouse button down, reposition the chart where you want it on the page.

Changing the Background Color

You can adjust the color of the page that serves as a background for a chart. To accomplish this, follow these steps:

1. Click anywhere on the chart, so that the four chart handles appear.
2. Double-click anywhere outside the chart handles. You'll then see the summary panel InfoBox. Click the colors tab.

> **Note**
>
> Each chart appears in its own separate summary panel, which, when printed, appears on its own page.

3. Pull down the Fill Color list box.
4. Click the color you want as the chart background.

> **Caution**
>
> Be sure not to double-click the control box for either the chart or the Approach window. If you do, Windows will attempt to exit either from the chart or from Approach itself.

5. To remove this InfoBox from the screen, double-click its control box in the upper left corner.

Associating Macros with a Chart

You can associate a pair of macros with each chart: one to execute when you display the chart and the other when you exit from the chart. To make your selections for the current chart, follow these steps:

1. Double-click anywhere outside the chart area defined by its four handles. The InfoBox will appear with the chart name in the Properties For box at the top.
2. Select the Macros tab (see fig. 15.39).

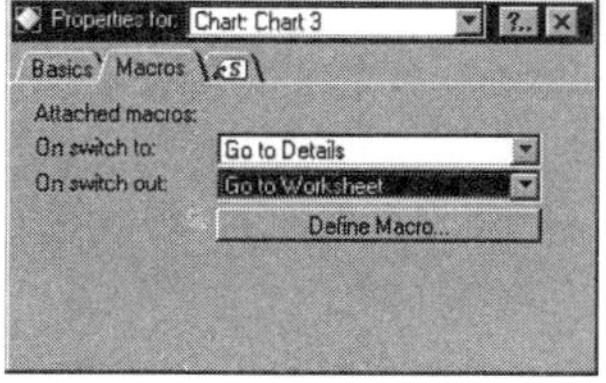

Fig. 15.39

You can choose to activate macros when entering and exiting a chart.

3. Click the drop-down list and select the macros to execute when opening and when exiting the chart.

This assumes that you've already created the macros you plan to use with the current chart. You also can create one or both macros from within the InfoBox. For each macro you want to create, click the Define Macro button, and then follow the usual procedure for creating macros. (For more information on creating macros, see Chapter 13, "Automating Your Work.")

Printing a Chart

Printing a chart is usually quite straightforward, involving only three steps:

1. Open the File menu and choose Print.
2. Select the print options you want.
3. Click OK to start printing.

If you have a color printer, the colors will probably be pretty close to those on-screen, although you can experiment a bit with Approach's wide range of colors to get just the output you want.

If you're using a black-and-white printer, each chart will be printed in various shades of gray. Depending on the type of printer, you'll be pleasantly or unpleasantly surprised with the output. However, by experimenting with the various colors offered by Approach, you should be able to select tones that produce pleasing printouts.

Here are a few pointers for printing charts:

- For black-and-white printers, consider restricting the colors for the various chart elements to different shades of gray. This will simplify your experimentation to find suitable print colors, although it will somewhat deaden the images on your color monitor.
- To minimize the print time while generating experimental printouts—which can be considerable for most types of charts—use the lowest possible resolution available for your printer. For example, for HP LaserJet printers, you can use the Print Quality option on the Print dialog box to select 75 or 150 dpi (dots per inch). Then, when you've established the color scheme you want for your printouts, switch back to the printer's highest resolution.
- Some charts may look better when printed in landscape orientation. To switch to landscape, open the File menu, choose Print Setup, and then choose the Landscape option.

From Here...

This chapter has focused on using charts, which is one of Approach's most sophisticated methods for displaying stored information. By using the tools described in the chapter, you can create a wide variety of different chart types. You can also customize your charts in many different ways.

To learn about other important areas relevant to database management, refer to the following chapters in this book:

- Chapter 14, "Using Worksheets and Crosstabs," describes how to create crosstabs, which simplify creating charts.
- Chapter 16, "Exploring Advanced Database Relationships," explains the basics of using databases that consist of multiple tables. By using the information in this chapter, you'll be able to create a single chart containing information from several related tables.

CHAPTER 16

Exploring Advanced Database Relationships

Up to this point we've used Approach for one-to-one, many-to-one, and one-to-many relationships. In this chapter, you'll look at the remaining relational database case: a many-to-many relationship. For example, one purchase order can apply to many parts in your inventory database, and one part may be on order by many purchase orders. What's not obvious is the need for an intermediate database to resolve this many-to-many relationship!

In this chapter, you learn how to

- Recognize a many-to-many relationship
- Resolve many-to-many database dilemmas
- Use Approach to create a many-to-many relationship
- Join many-to-many relational databases
- Design forms for many-to-many relationships

Describing a Many-to-Many Relationship

Relational databases work well as long as the records in the joined databases are related by either a one-to-one, many-to-one, or a one-to-many relationship (see Chapter 8, "Understanding Relational Databases"). With these types of relationships, one or more fields stored in the related databases provide the linking information. However, relational technology can't handle databases related in a many-to-many relationship, which occurs when one record in Database A is related to many records in Database B and one record in Database B is related to many records in Database A.

A common many-to-many relationship occurs between purchase orders and parts. One purchase order can include many part numbers and any part number can appear in multiple purchase orders (see fig. 16.1). With such relationships, you can't join the databases with one set of linking fields.

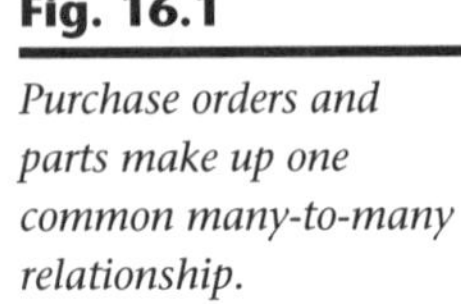

Fig. 16.1

Purchase orders and parts make up one common many-to-many relationship.

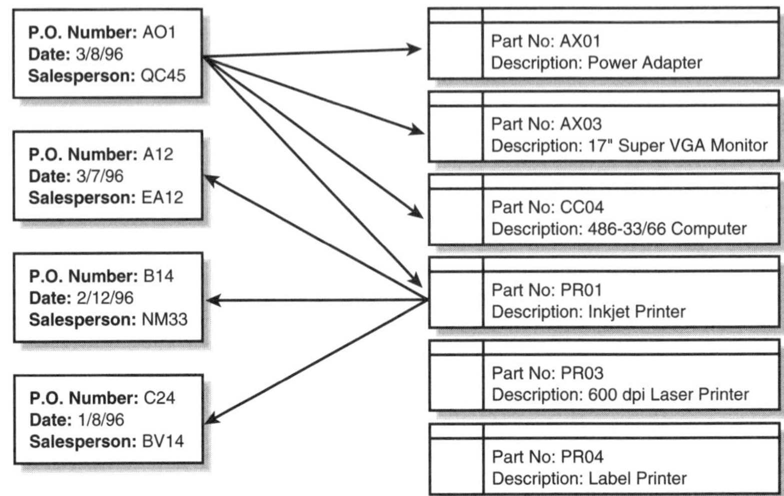

Resolving a Many-to-Many Relationship

To properly maintain a many-to-many relationship, you must add another database to your application. This intermediate database connects each of the original many-to-many databases in a one-to-many relationship. Thus, the intermediate database must contain at least two fields: a field to join relationally to the first database, and a field to join relationally to the second database. In database jargon, you're *resolving a many-to-many relationship*. Each main database contains one or more fields, sometimes called *key fields*, which uniquely identify a record in the main database. You must then link the intermediate database to the key field(s) in each main database. The intermediate database can also contain information specific to the relationship between the two main databases, such as the quantity on order in the purchase order example. Figure 16.2 shows how the intermediate database connects two many-to-many databases.

By using the Purchase Orders/Parts model, for example, you can add a new intermediate database called Line Items. The Line Items database relates the Purchase Order database to the Parts database as follows:

- *Purchase Order-to-Line Items relationship:*

  Each purchase order record can link to multiple line item records using a PO NUMBER field.

  Each line item record can link to only a single purchase order record.

- *Parts-to-Line Items relationship:*

  A part record can be linked to multiple line items using a PART NUMBER field.

  Each line item record can link to a single part record.

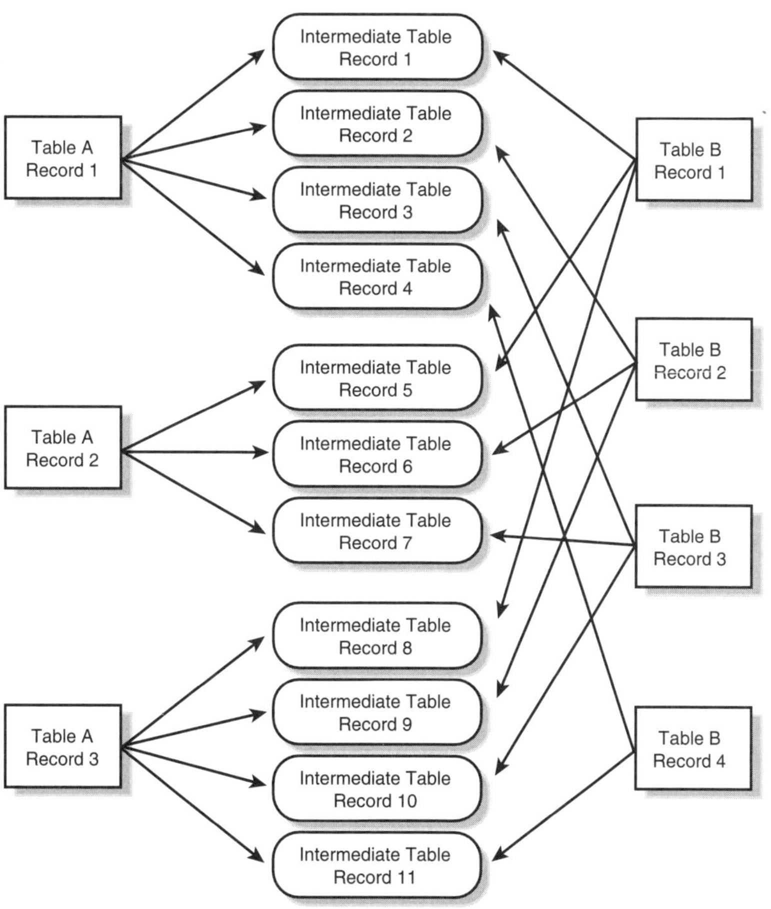

Fig. 16.2

An intermediate database resolves a many-to-many relationship into two one-to-many relationships.

The Line Items database shows one record for each occurrence of a particular part number on a particular purchase order. The key field in the Purchase Order database (for example, PO NUMBER) relationally links the Line Items database to the Purchase Order database. The key field in the Parts database (for example, Part Number) relationally links the Line Items database to the Parts database. Figure 16.3 shows how this example might look.

Note

A Line Items database record can also contain other information, such as the quantity and price of each part ordered on the purchase order or a description of the alterations to the part that have been requested. Including such information in the Line Items database makes sense because it refers to a particular part number on a particular purchase order.

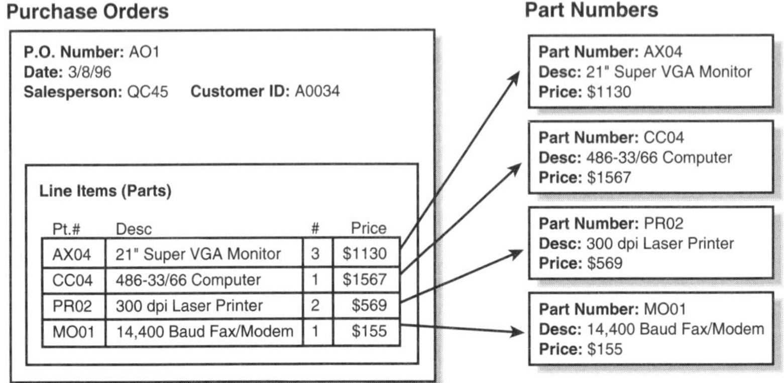

Fig. 16.3

The Purchase Orders and Parts databases can be related through the PO Line Items database.

Using Approach to Set Up a Many-to-Many Relationship

Once you understand that the problem you're dealing with is a many-to-many relationship, you can create the proper databases in Approach for this relationship.

To set up an application that links two databases in a many-to-many relationship through an intermediate one-to-many database, you must perform three steps:

1. Create three databases.
2. Relationally link the databases.
3. Build the forms.

Creating the Databases

You begin setting up your many-to-many environment by creating three databases. First, build the two main databases that have the many-to-many relationship (the Purchase Order and Parts databases). Then, build the intermediate database to connect them (the Line Items database), as shown earlier in figure 16.3.

If Owl Publishing decides to sell books and reading accessories, for example, the company needs three databases to keep track of its business:

- A Purchase Orders database to store purchase order information
- A Parts database to store part information (such as books and bookmarks)
- A Line Items database to relate the Purchase Orders database to the Parts database

Building the Purchase Orders Database. To build the Purchase Orders database, follow these steps:

1. Display the New dialog box by opening the File menu and choosing New Database, or clicking the New Database icon on the SmartIcon bar.

2. Make sure that Blank Database is selected, and then click OK.
3. Type **Purchase Orders** in the File Name text box; then click the Create button. The Creating New Database: Purchase Orders dialog box appears.
4. Use the field definitions in the following table for the Purchase Orders database. Type the name of the field in the Field Name column and choose the field type from the Data Type drop-down list. Default field sizes will appear as you create each field; it's not necessary to change them.

Field Name	Data Type	Size
PO_NUMBER	Text	10
SALES_ID	Text	10
DATE	Date	Fixed
CUSTOMER_ID	Text	10

5. The default form, Blank Database, appears automatically. Switch to Design mode by clicking the Design button on the action bar (see fig. 16.4).

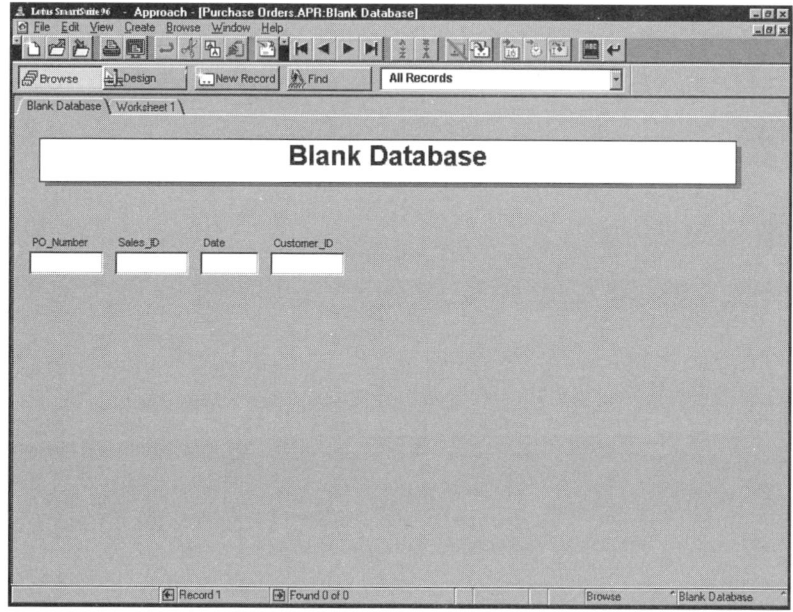

Fig. 16.4

The Purchase Order form is the first form you need in creating a many-to-many relationship.

6. Double-click the tab labeled Blank Database at the top of the form to edit it; then type **Purchase Order** as the form's new tab label.
7. The form title (the white box at the top of the form containing the words Blank Database in large letters) should also change. Select the title and then double-click anywhere in the white text area to select the text for editing and replace *Blank Database* with **Purchase Order**.

8. Open the File menu and choose Save Approach File. The Save Approach File dialog box appears.
9. Click Save to save the Approach file.

Building the Parts Database. Now you need to create a Parts database to store information about Owl's books and accessories. Follow these steps:

1. Open the File menu and choose New Database, or click the New Database SmartIcon. The New dialog box appears.
2. Select Blank Database and click OK.
3. Type `Parts` in the File Name text box and click Create to open the Creating New Database dialog box.
4. Use the field definitions in the following table for the Parts database. Type the name of the field in the Field Name column, select the field type from the Data Type drop-down list, and enter the size in the Size column (if necessary).

Field Name	Data Type	Size
PART NUMBER	Text	10
SHIPPING WEIGHT	Numeric	4
IN STOCK	Numeric	4
DESCRIPTION	Text	50
PRICE	Numeric	10.2

5. Click OK in the Creating New Database dialog box to create the database and view the default form (see fig. 16.5).

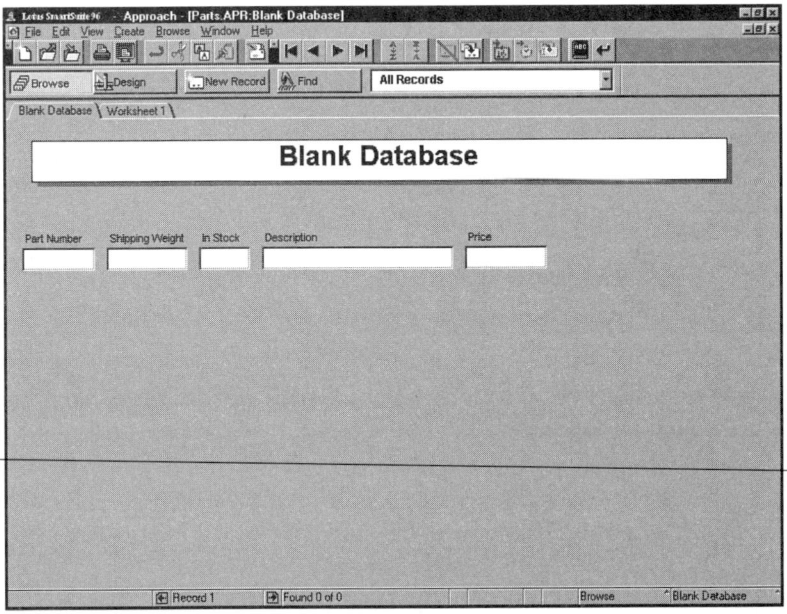

Fig. 16.5

The Part Data Entry form is the second form you need to create a many-to-many relational database.

6. Click Design on the action bar, and then double-click the tab labeled Blank Database to enter edit mode. Type **`Part Data Entry`** to change the tab label.
7. Double-click the form title and then change the default title by typing **`Part Data Entry`**.
8. Click the Browse button on the action bar, and then click the tab marked Worksheet 1 to enter the default forms worksheet. Now enter the following records into the Parts database:

PART NUMBER	SHIPPING WEIGHT	IN STOCK	DESCRIPTION	PRICE
AX01	2	15	Book—Library Management	12.95
AX02	3	12	Book—Books in Print	39.95
AX03	2	7	Book—Famous Authors	29.95
AX04	102	2	Book—Encyclopedia of Owls	1129.95
CC01	45	23	Mahogany Bookcase	888.00
CC02	40	13	Mahogany Lectern	906.00
CC03	46	12	Brass World Globe	1250.00
CC04	87	10	Ivory Inlaid Teak Globe	1567.00
MO01	3	300	Magnifying Glass	24.95
MO02	3	90	Hands-Free Book Holder	129.95
PR01	1	40	Cat Bookmark	3.99
PR02	1	40	Horse Bookmark	5.99
PR03	1	40	Brass Angel Bookmark	15.99
PR04	1	4	Gold Star Bookmark	24.99

9. Open the File menu and choose Save Approach File. The Save Approach File dialog box appears.
10. Keep the default name for the Approach file. Click Save to save it.
11. Close the Parts Approach file by choosing Close from the File menu.

Building the Line Items Database. Finally, you need to create a PO Line Items database, which you'll use to relate the purchase orders in the Purchase Orders database to the parts in the Parts database. Follow these steps:

1. To display the New dialog box, open the File menu and choose New Database, or click the New Database icon on the SmartIcon bar.
2. Make sure that Blank Database is selected; then click OK.
3. Type **`PO Line Items`** in the File Name text box, and then click the Create button. The Creating New Database: PO Line Items dialog box appears.

4. Use the field definitions in the following table for the PO Line Items database. Type the name of the field in the Field Name column and choose the field type from the Data Type drop-down list, changing the default size if necessary.

Field Name	Data Type	Size
PO NUMBER	Text	10
PART NUMBER	Text	10
COLOR	Text	10
QUANTITY	Numeric	4

5. Click OK in the Creating New Database dialog box to create the database and view the default form (see fig. 16.6).

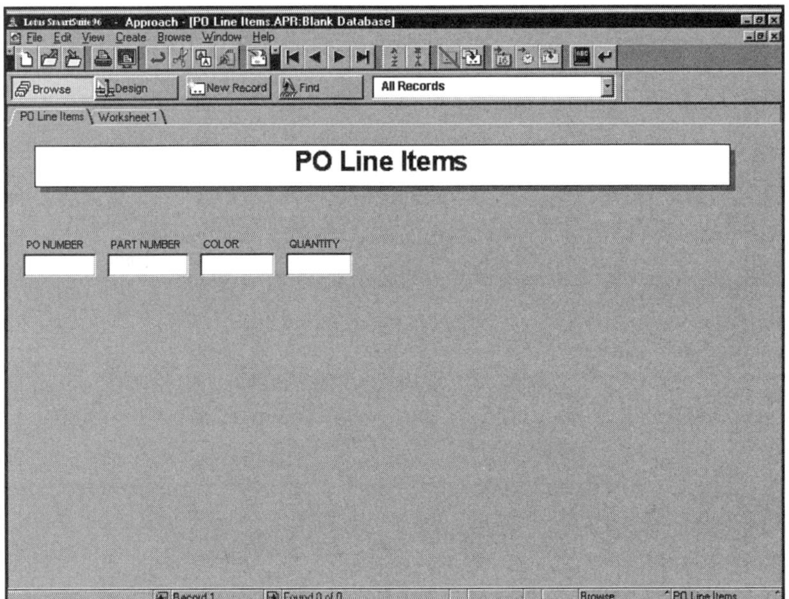

Fig. 16.6

The PO Line Items database ties the Purchase Orders database to the Parts database.

6. Switch to Design mode and double-click the Blank Database tab to select the tab text. Now type **`PO Line Items`**.
7. Double-click the form title to get into text editing mode. Change the default text (*Blank Database*) by highlighting it and typing **`PO Line Items`**.
8. Open the File menu and choose Save Approach File. The Save Approach File dialog box appears.
9. Keep the default name for the Approach file. Click Save to save the file.
10. Close the PO Line Items Approach file by choosing Close from the File menu.

Joining the Databases

Joining databases establishes the relational links between them. A *join* links a field in a specific Approach file to its identical counterpart in another Approach file. For these steps, all the joins are done in the Purchase Orders Approach file. Join the databases in the following order:

1. Join the first many database to the intermediate database (that is, join the Purchase Orders database to the PO Line Items database). You'll set the join options so that:
   - If no matching record exists in the intermediate database, Approach creates a record automatically.
   - If you delete a record in the main (Purchase Orders) database, Approach deletes all matching records in the intermediate (PO Line Items) database.
2. Join the intermediate database to the second many database (that is, join the PO Line Items database to the Parts database).

In the Owl Publishing example, follow these steps to join the Purchase Orders, PO Line Items, and Parts databases together:

1. If the Purchase Orders Approach file isn't open, open it by choosing Open from the File menu.
2. Open the Create menu and choose Join. The Join dialog box appears.
3. Click Open. The Open dialog box appears.
4. Select PO Line Items.dbf from the database file list and then click Open. The PO Line Items database appears in the Join dialog box.
5. Select the PO_NUMBER field in the Purchase orders database box.
6. Select the PO NUMBER field in the PO Line Items database box.
7. Click Join. A line appears between the Purchase Orders and PO Line Items database boxes.
8. Click the Options button to open the Relational Options dialog box.
9. Select both Insert check boxes and the first Delete check box (see fig. 16.7). Make sure that the last Delete check box is not selected. Click OK to close the Relational Options dialog box.

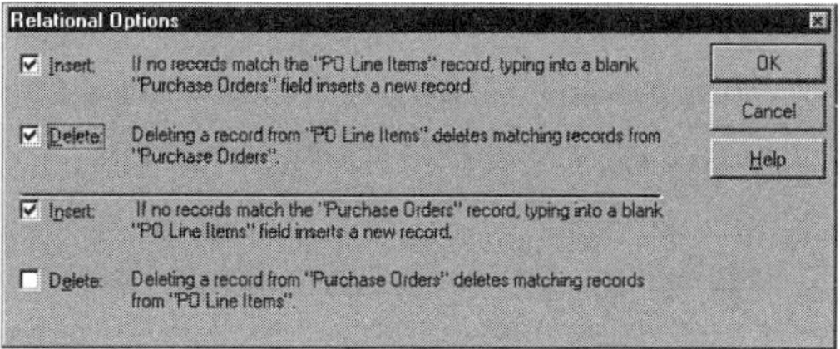

Fig. 16.7

Set your options for the relationship between Purchase Orders and PO Line Items.

10. Click Open in the Join dialog box. The Open dialog box appears.
11. Select Parts.dbf from the database files and click Open to close the Open dialog box. The Parts database appears in the Join dialog box.
12. Select the PART NUMBER field in the PO Line Items database box.
13. Select the PART NUMBER field in the Parts database box.
14. Click Join. A line appears between the PO Line Items and Parts database boxes. The Join dialog box should now look like figure 16.8.

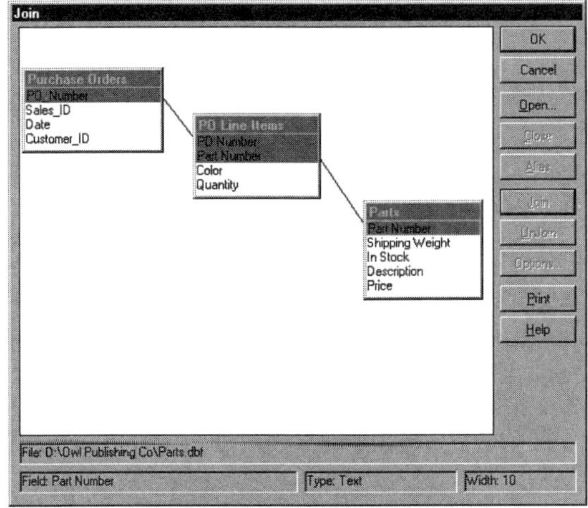

Fig. 16.8

Link Purchase Orders to Parts through the PO Line Items database.

15. Click OK to create the joins.
16. Save the Approach file by opening the File menu and choosing Save Approach File.

Designing the Forms

Although you can enter the records into each database in the Approach file on separate forms, creating a single form for most of the information is usually best. Building this type of form by using repeating panels is straightforward.

Ordinarily, you have greater interest in one of the two main databases (Purchase Orders and Parts). In the Purchase Order application, for example, you use the purchase order form (the main database is Purchase Orders) most often. But you can create a Part Data Entry form (the main database is Parts) within the same Approach file to add new part numbers.

To create a form that displays information from one of the main databases as well as the intermediate database, add a repeating panel from the intermediate database (PO Line Items) to the form based on a main database (Purchase Orders). (See Chapter 9, "Designing Advanced Forms," for more information about repeating panels.)

> **Note**
>
> Because of the relational link, information stored in the other main database (Parts) can be displayed in the repeating panel based on the intermediate database (PO Line Items). You can display a part's price (the PRICE field in the Parts database) in the repeating panel on the Purchase Order form, for example.

Adding Forms and a Repeating Panel. Owl Publishing wants to create a Purchase Order form. From this form, the company can set up new Purchase Orders and add line items, each referencing an individual part number to the purchase order. First, add two forms to the Purchase Orders application to display records from the PO Line Items and Parts databases respectively. Then complete the Purchase Order form that you started earlier. To accomplish this task, follow these steps:

1. If the Purchase Orders Approach file isn't open, open it.
2. Switch to Design mode by clicking the Design button on the action bar.
3. Open the Create menu and choose Form. In the Form Assistant, type **`Line Items`** in the View Name & Title text box. Select Standard from the SmartMaster Layout list and leave the Style list set to Default.
4. Click the Next button. Select the PO Line Items database and Add all the fields in the PO Line Items database to the Fields to Place on View list. Click Done to create the Line Items form.
5. Open the Create menu and choose Form. In the Form Assistant, type **`Parts`** in the View Name & Title text box. Select Standard from the SmartMaster Layout list and leave the Style list set to Default.
6. Click the Next button. Select the Parts database and Add all the fields in the Parts database to the Fields to Place on View list. Click Done to create the Parts form.
7. Switch to the Purchase Order form. Open the Create menu and choose Repeating Panel. The Add Repeating Panel dialog box opens.
8. Select the PO Line Items database from the Database drop-down list. This will be the main database for the repeating panel.
9. Select Part Number, Color, and Quantity from the Fields list box.
10. Choose Add or double-click each field to move the selected fields to the Fields to Place in Panel list.
11. Click OK. A repeating panel appears on the Purchase Order form.
12. Use the Text tool on the tools palette (press Ctrl+L if the palette isn't visible) to change the headings above the repeating panel that Approach created from the field names in your database, if necessary (see fig. 16.9).

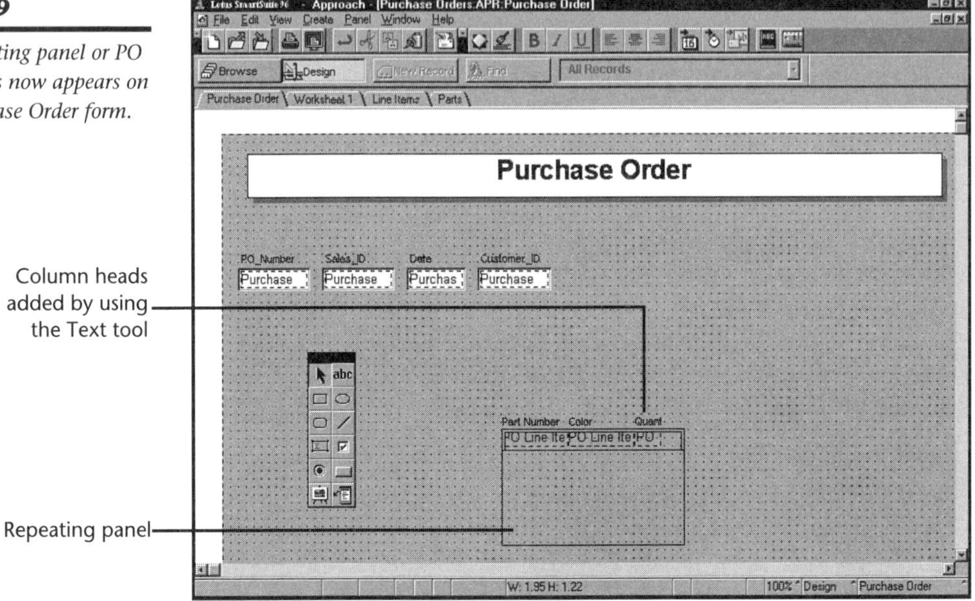

Fig. 16.9

The repeating panel or PO Line Items now appears on the Purchase Order form.

To ensure that you enter only valid part numbers in the repeating panel, follow these steps:

1. Switch to Design mode, if necessary. Select the PART NUMBER field in the repeating panel on the Purchase Order form.
2. Open the Create menu and choose Field Definition. The Field Definition dialog box appears.
3. Click the Options button to expand the Field Definition dialog box and display the Default Value and Validation tabs. Select the Validation tab to display the Validation page.
4. Select the In Field check box.
5. Select the Parts database from the drop-down list.
6. Select the PART NUMBER field from the list box.
7. Click OK to close the Field Definition dialog box.

To make room for more fields in the repeating panel, click outside a field in the first line of the repeating panel. A gray border appears around this line. Resize the border to the right to make the repeating panel larger. (Resizing this border is done in the same way as resizing a field.)

To add the PRICE field from the Parts database to the repeating panel, follow these steps:

1. Click the Draw Field tool on the tools palette. (If the tools palette isn't visible, open it by choosing Show Tools Palette from the View menu or by pressing Ctrl+L.)

2. Drag a rectangle inside the empty portion of the first line of the repeating panel. If it's not already visible, the field InfoBox appears.
3. Select the Parts database from the drop-down list of databases.
4. Select the PRICE field from the Field list box.
5. Make sure that no Borders options are selected in the colors page.
6. Click the first (text) tab in the field InfoBox and then click the Label radio button. Make sure that No Label is selected in the Label Position drop-down box.
7. Drag the sizing handles for the PRICE field so that they're entirely contained within the first line of the repeating panel.
8. Use the Text tool on the tools palette to modify the heading for the PRICE field, if necessary.
9. Select the PRICE field in the repeating panel.
10. Switch to the format (#) page in the InfoBox. Select Currency from the Format Type drop-down list.
11. Select United States from the Current Format drop-down list.
12. Click the up arrow by the Decimal Places spin box to 2.
13. Switch to Browse mode and view the Purchase Order form. The PRICE field now appears in the repeating panel (see fig. 16.10).

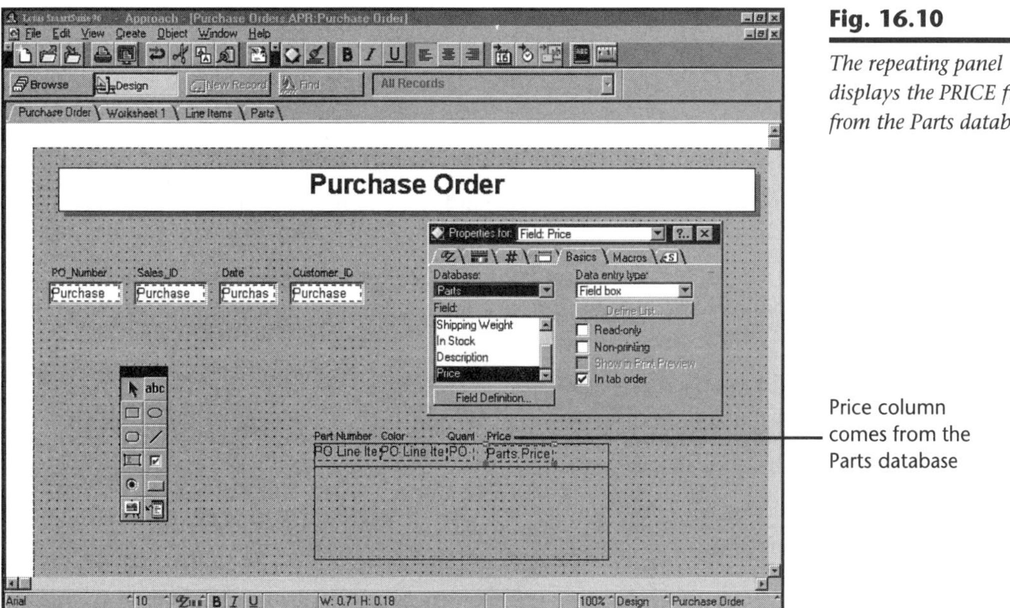

Fig. 16.10

The repeating panel displays the PRICE field from the Parts database.

Extending the Total for Each PO Line Item. Continuing the Owl Publishing example, suppose that you want to calculate the total for each line in the repeating panel on the Purchase Order form. To do this, follow these steps:

1. Switch to Design mode.
2. If the repeating panel isn't large enough for another field, enlarge the panel by clicking the first line and then dragging the right border.
3. Click the Draw Field tool on the tools palette.
4. Drag a rectangle inside the top line of the repeating panel. If it isn't already visible, the field InfoBox appears.
5. Click the Field Definition button. The Field Definition dialog box appears.
6. Scroll down to an empty line and type **`LineTotal`** in the Field Name column. Select Calculated as the data type. The Field Definition dialog box expands to display the Define Formula page.
7. Type **`"Parts".Price * "PO Line Items".Quantity`** in the Formula text box. You can also select the databases and click the field in the Fields list box.
8. Click OK to close the Field Definition dialog box.
9. On the Colors page of the InfoBox, make sure that no Borders options are checked. On the Fonts page, click the Label radio button and make sure that No Label is selected in the Label Position drop-down box.
10. Drag the sizing handles for the LineTotal field so that the field is completely within the top line of the repeating panel.
11. Use the Text tool on the tools palette to modify the heading for the LineTotal field, if desired.
12. Select the LineTotal field in the repeating panel.
13. Switch to the format (#) page in the InfoBox. Select Currency from the Format Type list.
14. Select United States from the Current Format drop-down list.
15. Click the up arrow next to the Decimal Places spin box twice to move from 0 to 2, if necessary.
16. Switch to Browse mode to view the Purchase Order form. The LineTotal field is now available in the repeating panel. Enter a few sample line items as shown in figure 16.11 to make sure that your form is working correctly.

Adding a Total for the Purchase Order. Owl Publishing also needs a field that totals the amount of each purchase order. To add such a field, follow these steps:

1. Switch to Design mode.
2. Click the Draw Field tool on the tools palette.
3. Drag a rectangle near the repeating panel. If it isn't already visible, the field InfoBox appears.
4. Click the Field Definition button. The Field Definition dialog box appears.
5. Scroll down to an empty line in the Field Definition dialog box. Type **`Order Total`** in the Field Name column and select Calculated as the data type. The Field Definition dialog box expands to display the Define Formula page.

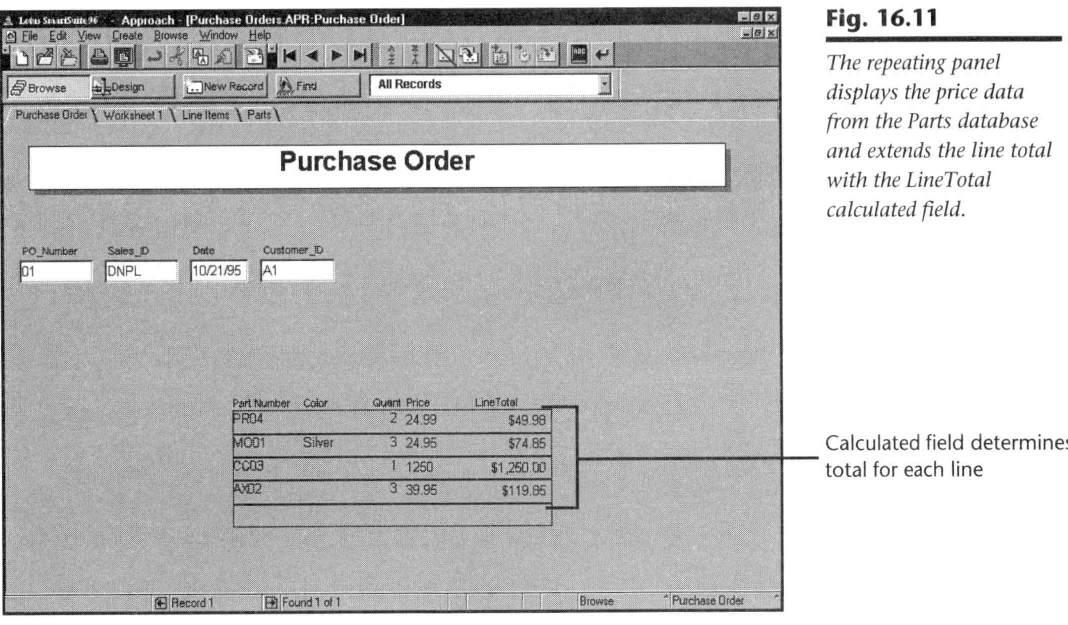

Fig. 16.11

The repeating panel displays the price data from the Parts database and extends the line total with the LineTotal calculated field.

6. Type **`Ssum(LineTotal)`** in the Formula text box or select it from the Fields and Functions scroll boxes.
7. Click the Define Summary tab to switch to the Define Summary page. Choose Summary Of All Records In PO Line Items from the Summarize On drop-down list.
8. Click OK to close the Field Definition dialog box.
9. The Order Total field should still be selected. Switch to the format (#) panel. Select Currency from the Format Type drop-down list. Choose United States in the Current Format drop-down list and click the up arrow next to the Decimal Places spin box twice to move from 0 to 2.
10. Switch to Browse mode to view the Purchase Order form. The Order Total field displays the total amount of the purchase order (see fig. 16.12).

Enhancing the Usability of the Purchase Order Form. The Owl Publishing employees assigned to fill out the Purchase Order form are having trouble with the Part Number field in the repeating panel. If they don't know the part number, the drop-down list of part numbers (supplied by Approach due to the validation rules you set up) are no help. Changing the drop-down list to display the part descriptions corrects the problem. To modify the list, follow these steps:

1. Switch to Design mode. Move to the Purchase Order form, if necessary.
2. Double-click the Part Number field in the repeating panel. If it wasn't already visible, the InfoBox for the PO Line Items Part Number field appears. Notice that the field has the Data Entry Type drop-down list on the Basics page.

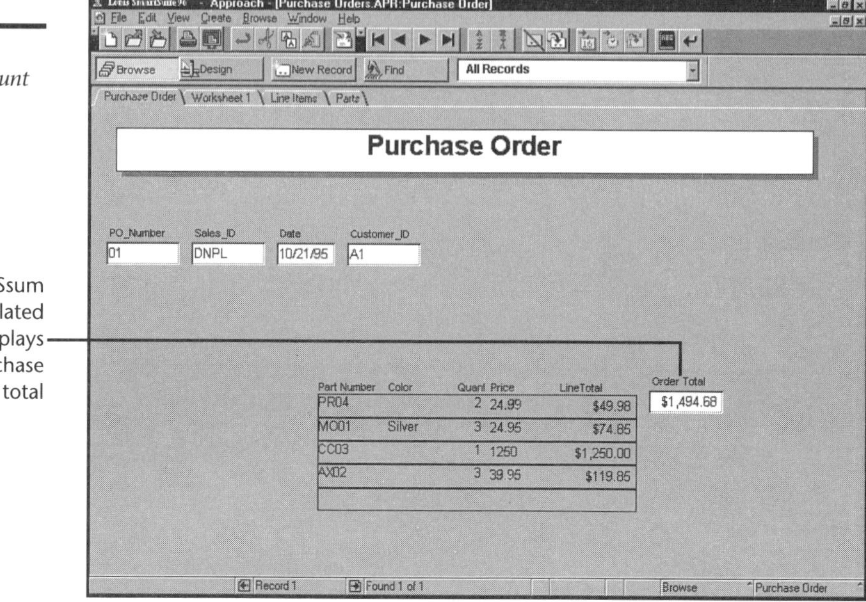

Fig. 16.12

The Order Total field displays the total amount of the purchase order.

An Ssum calculated field displays each purchase order's total

3. Click the Define List button to open the Drop-Down List dialog box.
4. Choose the Create List Automatically from Field Data radio button.
5. Select the Parts database from the drop-down list of databases. Choose Part Number from the Field to Create List From list.
6. Check the Show Description Field check box.
7. Select the Description field from the Parts database.
8. Click OK to close the Drop-Down List dialog box.
9. Switch to Browse mode and choose the Part Number field in the repeating panel. A list of part descriptions appears. When you select a description, its part number is entered into the PO Line Items Part Number field in the repeating panel (see figs. 16.13 and 16.14).

Adding Inventory Functions. The Owl Publishing employees want to transfer directly from any line item in the repeating panel to the Parts record for that line. They then can make inventory adjustments and so forth. To do so, follow these steps:

1. Switch to Design mode.
2. Open the Edit menu and choose Macros to open the Macros dialog box. Choose New. The Define Macro dialog box opens. (Chapter 13, "Automating Your Work," provides more details on creating Approach macros.)
3. Type `Go To Part Number` in the Macro Name text box.
4. On the first line in the Options section, select the View command from the Command column's drop-down list.

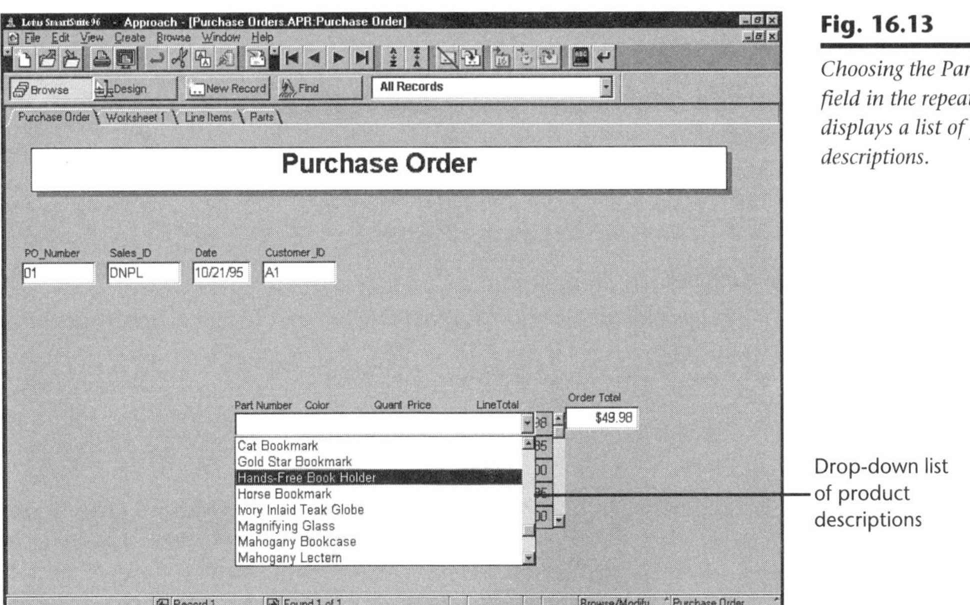

Fig. 16.13

Choosing the Part Number field in the repeating panel displays a list of product descriptions.

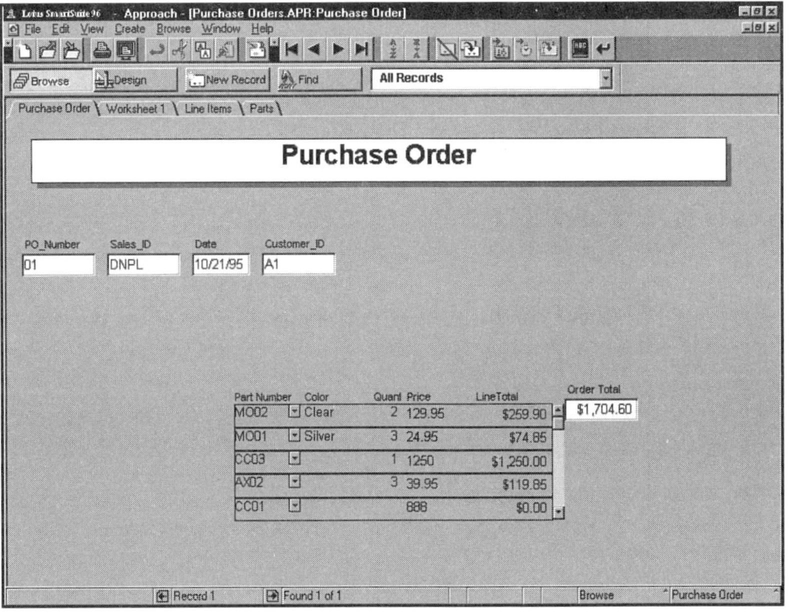

Fig. 16.14

Select a description to place the associated part number into the Part Number field.

5. Choose Parts from the list of available forms and reports in the Switch, Show, or Hide Views section near the bottom of the dialog box.
6. Click the Command column on the second line of the Options section. Choose Records from the drop-down list.

7. Choose Current Record in the Go To, Hide, Duplicate, or Create a Record section.
8. Click OK to close the Define Macro dialog box. Choose Done to close the Macros dialog box.
9. Click the Button tool on the tools palette.
10. Drag a rectangle in an empty section of the repeating panel's top line. (Resize the top line, if there are no empty sections.) If it wasn't already visible, the Button InfoBox appears.
11. On the Macros page of the Button InfoBox, select Go to Part Number from the On Clicked drop-down list.
12. Switch to the Basics page. Type **Part #** in the Button text box.
13. Switch to Browse mode and click a button on a line in the repeating panel. Approach switches to the Parts record for that line (see figs. 16.15 and 16.16).

Adding Order Information to the Parts Form. Owl Publishing wants to determine which Purchase Orders include a certain part number. The company can then determine who's affected when a part is unavailable. To do so, follow these steps:

1. Switch to Design mode.
2. Select the Parts form from the tabs or from the status line at the bottom left of the screen.
3. Open the Create menu and choose Repeating Panel. The Add Repeating Panel dialog box appears.
4. Select PO Line Items from the Database drop-down list.
5. Select PO Number, Color, and Quantity from the Fields list.
6. Choose Add to move the chosen fields from the Fields list to the Fields to Place in Panel list, or double-click each field.
7. Click OK.
8. Use the Text tool on the tools palette to modify the headings for the repeating panel, if desired (see fig. 16.17).

Tip

Change the information in the repeating panel only on the Purchase Order form. To keep users from changing the information in the repeating panel on the Parts form, open the InfoBox, click each field in the panel, and then check the Read-Only check box in the Basics page.

Adding a Customer Database. The Purchase Orders database contains a CUSTOMER_ID field to identify the customer of the purchase order. You can create a Customer database with name and address information for all your customers. The Customer database also contains a CUST ID field to join it to the Purchase Orders database (see fig. 16.18).

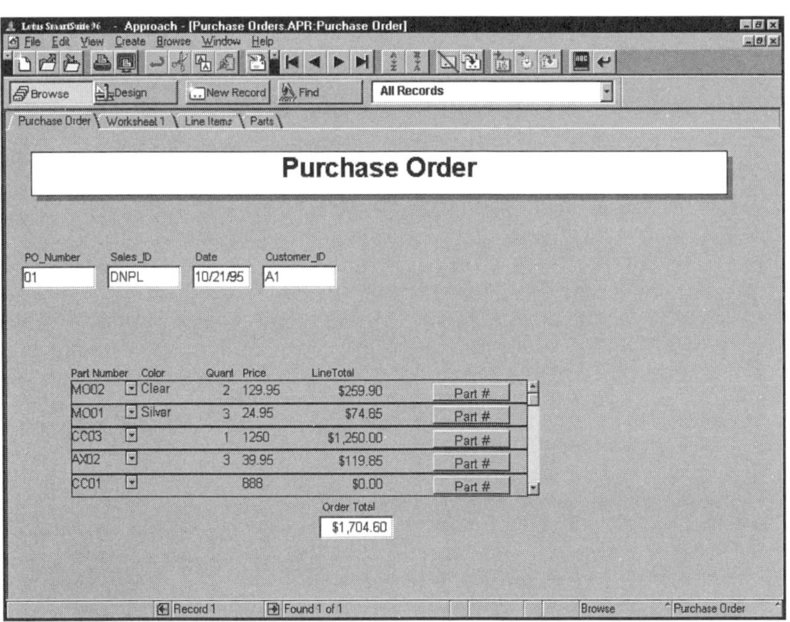

Fig. 16.15

If you click a button for a record in the repeating panel…

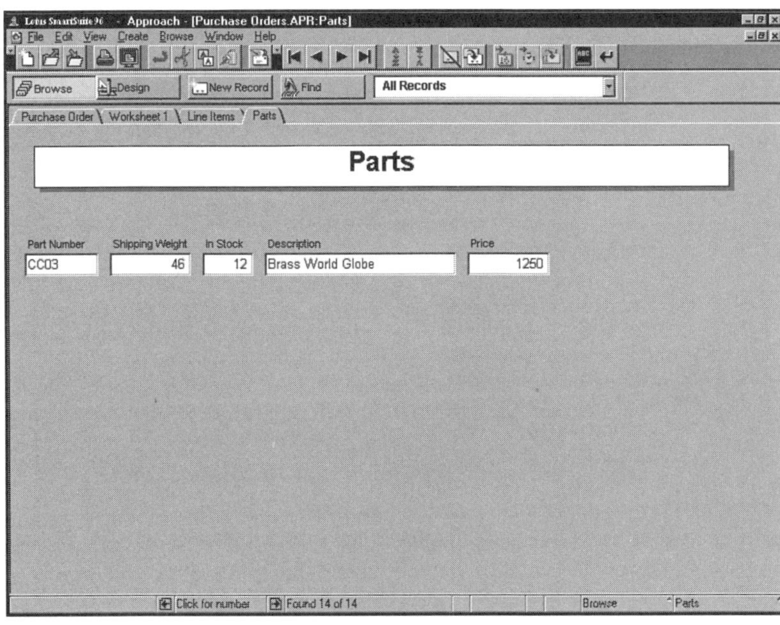

Fig. 16.16

…you're transferred to that database record, as shown on the Parts form.

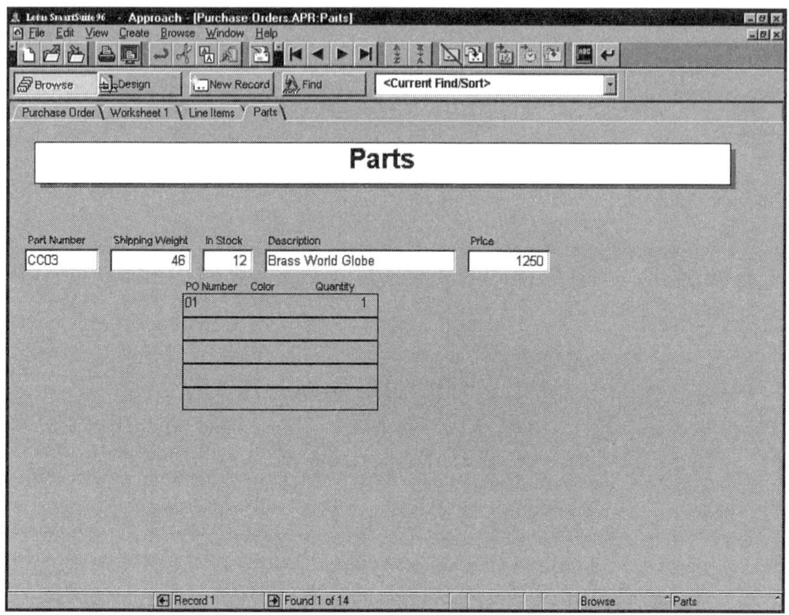

Fig. 16.17

A repeating panel on the Parts form shows which Purchase Orders contain a particular part.

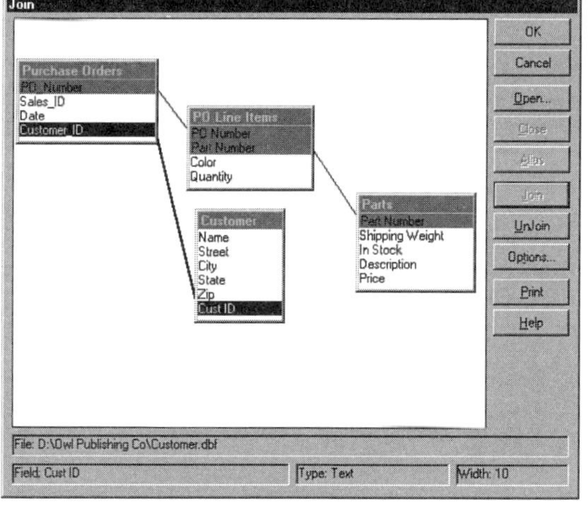

Fig. 16.18

The Join dialog box links Purchase Orders to Customer.

If you place the name and address fields from the Customer database on the Purchase Order form, the customer information is displayed when you fill in the Purchase Orders CUSTOMER_ID field on the Purchase Order form (see fig. 16.19).

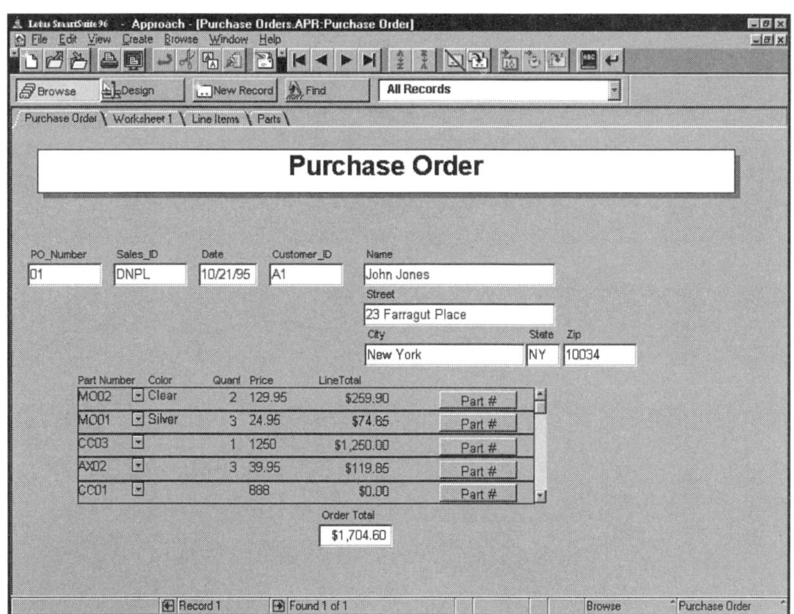

Fig. 16.19

The Purchase Order form can display customer information from the Customer database.

From Here...

This chapter has given you a brief introduction into some of the more powerful uses of Approach. After you work with databases for a short time, you'll see how most problems can be broken down into one-to-many or many-to-many cases. Once these cases are defined, you can use the techniques learned in this chapter and throughout this book to create useful forms and reports using Lotus Approach.

For more information, refer to the following chapters:

- Chapter 8, "Understanding Relational Databases," discusses how relational databases are formed and used.
- Chapter 9, "Designing Advanced Forms," shows you how to create forms that display information from several databases.
- Chapter 12, "Creating Advanced Reports," tells you how to develop reports that take full advantage of relational databases.

CHAPTER 17

Customizing Approach

Approach offers you several different ways to change the functions available to users of your application as well as the look and feel of your application. This is helpful not only for setting personal preferences, but also when developing database applications for others to use.

Customization is more than changing how the screen looks. It can also affect how the data is displayed and how you work in designing a database.

In this chapter, you learn how to

- Customize the SmartIcon toolbar and the action bar
- Define custom menus
- Create custom SmartMasters
- Change display defaults
- Set up Approach's phone dialer to work with your modem
- Establish preferences for specific database types

Customizing the SmartIcon Bar

Approach lets you customize the appearance of the SmartIcon bar. You can add icons to or remove icons from any set on the current SmartIcon bar to better suit your needs. You can also change the position of the SmartIcon sets individually on-screen and change the size of the displayed icons. You can choose to display help balloons automatically or by right-clicking.

You can use your new design to replace an existing SmartIcon set or to create a new SmartIcon set. If you customize a SmartIcon set associated with a mode (for example, the Browse SmartIcon set), Approach displays the customized version of the SmartIcon set in the toolbar area or wherever you want it when you switch to that mode. You also can create SmartIcon sets that display only when the action bar is disabled.

Approach keeps separate SmartIcon set files for different combinations of modes (Browse, Design, Find, or Preview) and view types (Form, Report, Mailing Label, Form Letter, Worksheet, or Crosstab). From the File menu choose User Setup, and then choose SmartIcons Setup to view the SmartIcons Setup dialog box (see fig. 17.1).

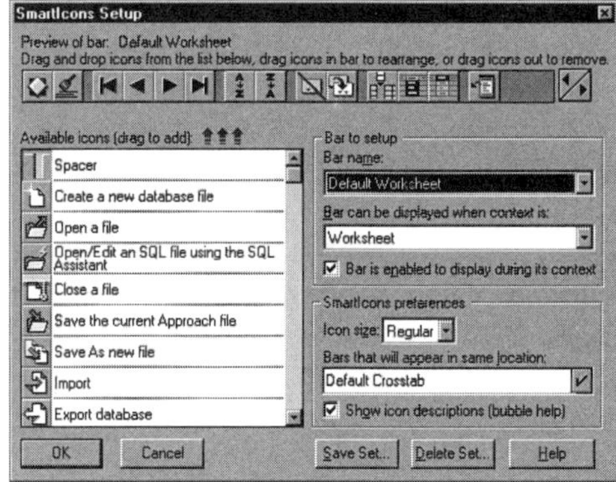

Fig. 17.1

The SmartIcons Setup dialog box shows the default set for a worksheet.

Approach displays the currently selected SmartIcon set at the top of the SmartIcons Setup dialog box. The Bar Name drop-down list shows the name of the bar now on display. The default is the set name of the currently open SmartIcon set. If you want to modify a different SmartIcon set, select the set name you want to use from this list.

You can choose when to display the currently selected SmartIcon set by using the Bar Can Be Displayed When the Context Is list box, below the Bar Name setting. Approach lets you choose whether to display a SmartIcon set always, as shown here, or only during certain modes and conditions.

Tip

Approach has several different default SmartIcon sets, each specific to a certain mode or type of view.

The list box on the left side of the SmartIcons Setup dialog box displays all the SmartIcons that you can place in the currently selected SmartIcon set. The following sections explain how to use these list boxes and customize the SmartIcon settings.

Adding Icons to a SmartIcon Set

To add an icon to the current set in the SmartIcon bar, click the icon you want to add from the list of available icons on the left side of the SmartIcons Setup dialog box.

Drag the icon onto the bar at the top of the dialog box; then release the mouse button. Approach inserts the new icon into the set.

Note

You can modify a SmartIcon set only by using the mouse. The keyboard can't be used.

If you drop the new icon on top of an existing icon, the existing icon (and all icons to the right of it) move over to make room for the new icon. To add an icon to the end of the set, use the left/right arrow buttons to the right of the bar to scroll through the icons until you reach the end. Then drop the new icon into the empty space.

Tip

To make your SmartIcon set easier to use, group the icons for related operations together. Drag the Spacer icon (at the top of the icon list) to the right of your group to separate it from the next group of icons on the bar.

Removing Icons

To remove an icon from a SmartIcon set, use the mouse to select the icon you want to remove from the set of icons at the top of the SmartIcons Setup dialog box. Drag the icon anywhere outside the set and release the mouse button. The SmartIcon disappears from the set.

Using Icon Descriptions (Bubble Help)

The SmartIcons Setup dialog box has a check box for Show Icon Descriptions. When it's turned on, this setting provides a help bubble when the mouse pointer lingers over a SmartIcon (see fig. 17.2). This check box controls bubble help for all SmartIcon bars, not just the one now in use. When the check box is deselected, the help balloons are still available by right-clicking a SmartIcon.

Tip

You don't need to save the current SmartIcon set to save changes to the help balloons. The changes are saved when you click OK in the SmartIcons Setup dialog box.

Fig. 17.2

Help balloons provide descriptions for the SmartIcons.

Saving Changes to a SmartIcon Set

The changes you make to a SmartIcon set normally last only through the current Approach session. To make the changes permanent, you must save them by clicking the Save Set button in the SmartIcons Setup dialog box. After you're given an opportunity to change the set name, a message box will appear asking whether you want to overwrite the current SmartIcon set. Click Yes, and your new set will replace the old one.

If you want to save your changes as a new set of SmartIcons, follow these steps:

1. Click the Save Set button. When the Save As SmartIcons File dialog box appears, type the name of the new set in the box provided.
2. Click OK to save the SmartIcon set in the default directory. Otherwise, click Browse. The Save As dialog box appears (see fig. 17.3), and you can save the set in any folder you want.

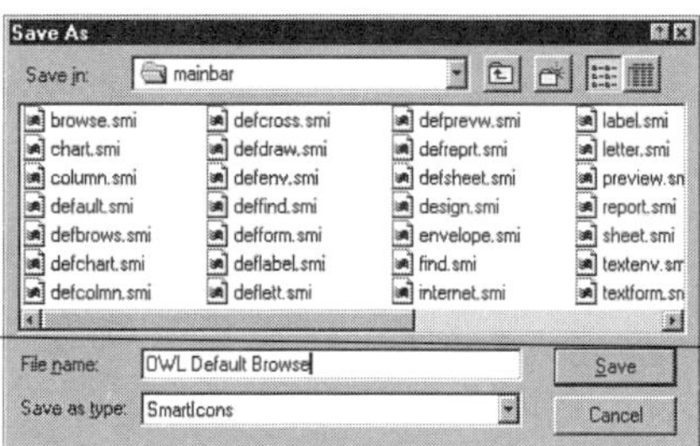

Fig. 17.3

When finished, you can save your custom set of SmartIcons.

3. Type the name of the new SmartIcon set in the File Name text box. Check the Save As Type drop-down list box to make sure that SmartIcons is selected; then click Save.

Renaming a SmartIcon Set

Approach lets you replace the name of the SmartIcon set with a different name. Follow these steps:

1. Open the SmartIcons Setup dialog box by opening the File menu and choosing User Setup and then SmartIcons Setup.
2. Open the file by selecting its set name from the Bar Name drop-down list in the SmartIcons setup dialog box.
3. Choose Save Set. The Save as SmartIcons File dialog box appears.
4. Change the name in the SmartIcons Bar Name text box.
5. Click OK. Approach displays a dialog box warning you that the file name exists.
6. Click Yes to save the changes.

Deleting a SmartIcon Set

Approach allows you to delete a SmartIcon file. Follow these steps:

1. Open the SmartIcons Setup dialog box by opening the File menu and choosing User Setup and then SmartIcons Setup.
2. Choose Delete Set in the SmartIcons Setup dialog box. The Delete Sets dialog box opens.
3. Scroll through the list and select the set name for the SmartIcon set you want to delete.
4. Click OK to delete the set.
5. Approach asks you to confirm the deletion. Click Yes to delete the set.

Changing the Icon Size

Approach can display icons on the SmartIcon bar in two sizes: regular and large. As you may expect, the large icons take up more room, so fewer of them can fit on the SmartIcon bar. The graphics are somewhat more detailed and easier to recognize, however. In the Icon Size drop-down box, choose the size you want and then click OK.

Changing the Position of any SmartIcon Set

You can put a set of SmartIcons at the top of the screen (the default position), at the bottom, or against the left or right sides. You can also place the SmartIcon set in its own window anywhere in the workspace.

To reposition a SmartIcon set, move the mouse pointer to the left end of the set. As you approach the dark area, the arrow will change to an open hand. Now click and hold down the mouse button. The hand will change into a closed fist, indicating that you can drag the set to the desired position.

The set will change shape according to position. At the top and bottom of the screen, it will become a long horizontal bar. To the left and right, it will change to a vertical bar, and in the center it will become a smaller floating toolbar, which you can resize to any rectangular shape as desired (see fig. 17.4).

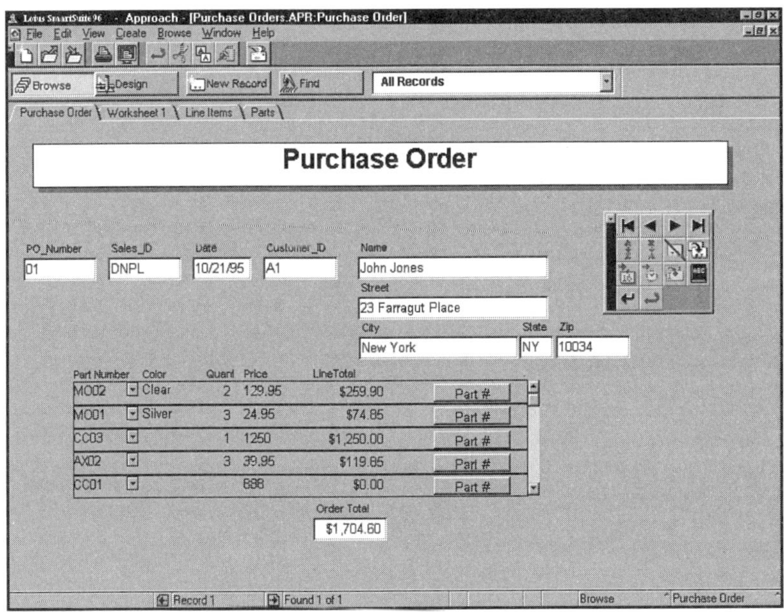

Fig. 17.4

Select where the SmartIcon set is placed by dragging and dropping it anywhere on-screen.

When you place a SmartIcon set in a floating window by repositioning it in the workspace, you have much more flexibility in determining its position and size. You can also display a larger number of icons than you can in a standard SmartIcon bar area.

To reposition this window, move the mouse pointer anywhere in the window, hold down the mouse button, and drag the window to its new location. To resize the window, drag the window borders until you establish the new size. You can't stretch the window to a size larger than necessary to display the current set of SmartIcons, but you can shrink the window so that some icons aren't displayed.

To hide a floating SmartIcon window, click the control box in the upper left corner and select the option desired. Hiding the SmartIcon window in one mode leaves it visible in other modes.

To redisplay a hidden SmartIcon window, open the View menu and choose Show SmartIcons to turn them all off, and then choose this option again to show the hidden one.

Repositioning the Action Bar

Just as you can reposition the SmartIcon bars, Approach lets you reposition or hide the action bar. You can move the action bar to the bottom, left, right, or top of the workspace, or it can float in its own window within the workspace. There are two ways to do this:

- Right-click while positioned anywhere on the bar between the buttons. Choose the new position for the action bar from the docking menu that appears (see fig. 17.5).

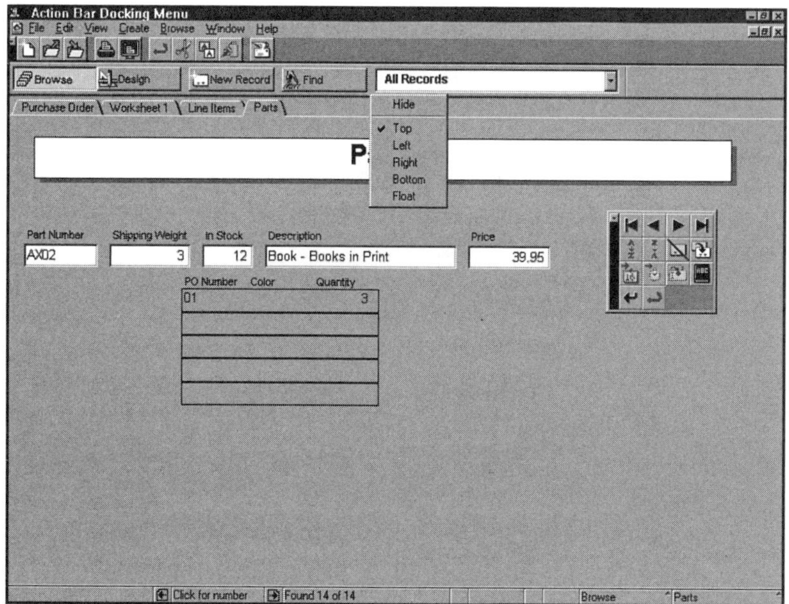

Fig. 17.5

Choose where to place the action bar by clicking and dragging or by right-clicking to use the docking menu.

- Move the mouse anywhere on the action bar between the buttons. Click the left mouse button and drag the outline of the bar to the desired position and release.

If the action bar has been hidden, you can redisplay it by opening the View menu and choosing Show Action Bar.

Customizing Menus

Attaching custom menu(s) to a view or set of views restricts the application's user to access only a certain set of menu selections. Each view can have its own custom menu. A custom menu can be used for each view in an Approach file, or a combination of menus can be used in an Approach file.

Custom menus are especially useful when creating a database application where the users won't be familiar with Approach. You can control a user's actions by restricting which menu items are available on different views. Also, you can change the wording of the menu names and commands to make them more meaningful to your user set.

Caution

If a menu item isn't available in the current custom menu, the SmartIcon that performs the same task, if present, won't work.

Custom menus are available for Browse mode only. Menu selections that aren't applicable in a certain mode, such as the Actual Size menu item in Browse mode, will be dimmed.

Defining and Editing Custom Menus

You can define or modify custom menus in Design mode only. From the Create menu choose Custom Menu to display the Customize Menus dialog box (see fig. 17.6).

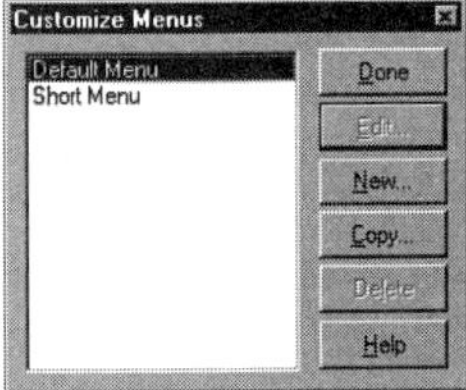

Fig. 17.6

You can design several custom menus.

The Customize Menus dialog box lists all the currently defined menus. It has a series of buttons for creating and maintaining custom menus:

- Done closes the dialog box and saves any changes you have made to the menus.
- Edit allows you to change the currently selected set. The Default Menu and Short Menu can't be edited.
- New starts a new custom menu.
- Copy copies the currently selected menu.
- Delete removes the selected custom menu. The Default Menu and Short Menu can't be deleted.

Select the Default Menu and choose Copy to open the Define Custom Menu Bar dialog box (see fig. 17.7). Use this dialog box to define or modify custom menus. The Define Custom Menu Bar dialog box has three numbered sections.

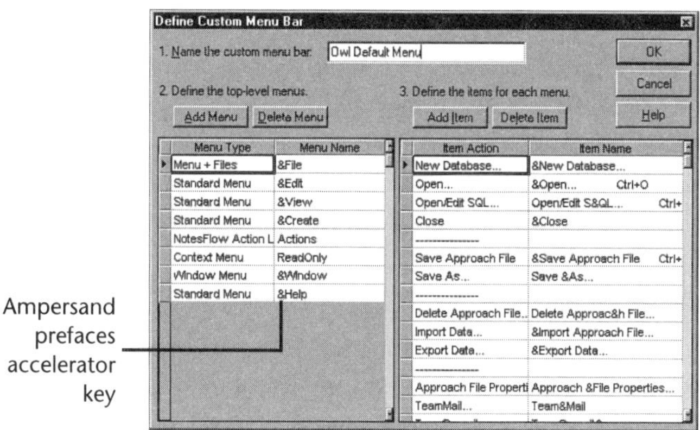

Fig. 17.7

Define menu selections in the Define Custom Menu Bar dialog box.

Naming the Custom Menu. The first numbered section, at the top of the Define Custom Menu Bar dialog box, names the menu. When you create a new menu, Approach will give the menu a default name. You can keep this name or give the menu a new, unique name by typing the name in the text box.

Selecting the Top-Level Menu Items. The second section of the dialog box, the listings on the left, shows the top-level menu item(s).

The Menu Type is listed in the left column. A new type can be selected by clicking the menu type box and then choosing the desired type from a drop-down list or by typing the first letter of the menu type. The text for the Menu Type can't be edited.

There are seven types of top-level menus:

- Standard Menu displays the menu items defined in the box on the right side of the dialog box.
- Menu + Files displays the menu items defined in the box on the right side of the dialog box and, at the bottom of the menu, lists the five most recently opened Approach files.
- Window Menu displays the menu items defined in the box on the right side of the dialog box and a list of the currently open Approach files.
- Context Menu varies by the view type and current mode. The Context menu can't be modified.

> **Tip**
>
> The Context menus can't be changed, but you can include on other menus items that appear on the context-sensitive menus.

- Macro List Menu contains all macros defined to display in a menu. It can't include any other types of menu items.

- View List Menu contains only those views defined to display in Browse mode. It can't include any other types of menu items.
- NotesFlow Action List Menu contains menu items used to trigger Notes commands and macros from within Approach applications.

> **Note**
>
> The Macro List and View List menu types don't display any menu items. If you need a menu that combines macros, views, and standard menu items, use one of the menu types that can include items. Defined views and macros show up in the Item Action list for inclusion on other menus.

The Menu Name—what's actually displayed in the menu bar—is the second column of items in this section. The name can be modified for all menu types except the Context menu. The menu name can have an accelerator, which allows it to be accessed with an Alt+key combination. To define an accelerator, put an ampersand (&) before the letter that will be underlined. For example, &File displays as File and can be accessed by selecting Alt+F.

Menus are added or removed by clicking the Add Menu and Delete Menu buttons. The current menu, either for editing or deleting, is the one with the triangle selection pointer in the box to the left. When a top-level menu is removed, so are all of its related items.

Defining Menu Commands. The third section of the Define Custom Menu Bar dialog box is where you define the individual menu items for each top-level menu. The items displayed in this section are for the currently selected menu item (see fig. 17.8). For the menu types that can't be edited or can't have commands added—Context, Macro List, View List, and NotesFlow Action List—this area will be empty, and the Add Item and Delete Item buttons will be dimmed.

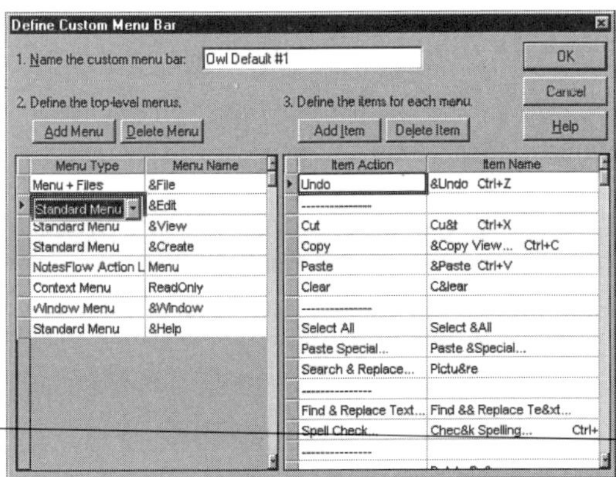

Fig. 17.8

The menu items on the right are for the Default Menu while in Browse mode.

Menu items are added in the same way as the menu names. Use the Add Item button to add a new line. The items are selected from a drop-down list. This list also includes all currently defined macros and views. After an Item Action is selected, the corresponding Item Name section is filled in with the default name. Item actions can't be edited, but item names can. Again, an accelerator can be added with the use of the ampersand, such as &Paste for Paste. You can delete the current item by clicking the Delete Item button.

Tip

The spacer, a dashed line that separates sections within a menu, is included as a menu item. Use it to group similar menu choices together.

Caution

It's possible to add more menu items than can be displayed in the current resolution. In this case, the menus won't scroll to reveal the items that are defined but not displayed. If you're developing menus for others, check the menus in VGA resolution (standard 640×480) to guarantee that all items will be accessible.

Creating a Custom Menu from an Existing Menu. If you'd like a custom menu that's similar to the existing menu, the easiest way to create the new menu is to modify an existing menu bar. For example, you might want a menu similar to the Approach default menu. To define a custom menu bar based on an existing menu, follow these steps:

Note

These steps are presented sequentially, but editing doesn't have to follow this exact order.

1. In Design mode, click Create on the menu bar and choose Custom Menu.
2. Select the menu you want to duplicate and click the Copy button.
3. The Define Custom Menu Bar dialog box opens. Change the menu name, if you want.
4. To remove any existing top-level menus that won't be needed, select the Menu Type box and click the Delete Menu button.
5. Add any new top-level menus by clicking the Add Menu button. Choose the menu type from the drop-down list if it's different from the Standard Menu default.
6. Edit any menu names if you want to rename any top-level menus.

7. Select the top-level menu for which you'd like to edit the items. The selected menu will have a triangle to the left of its menu type.
8. Remove any unwanted menu items from the current menu by selecting the item and clicking the De<u>l</u>ete Item button. The selected item will have a triangle to the left of its item action.
9. Add any new items by clicking the Add <u>I</u>tem button, and then choose the desired item action from the drop-down list.
10. Edit the item name, if you want to rename an item.
11. Reorder any menu items by dragging and dropping in the Menu Items list (see fig. 17.9). Select an item by clicking the selection triangle to the right of the item name; the pointer will change to a hand. Drag the item up or down in the list. The hand pointer is attached to a box, which represents the item, and a dark line appears to show where the item would be inserted when dropped. To drop an item into a new position, release the mouse button.
12. Reorder any top-level menus using the same drag-and-drop method. Select the menu, and then move it up or down in the list and drop it into its new position.

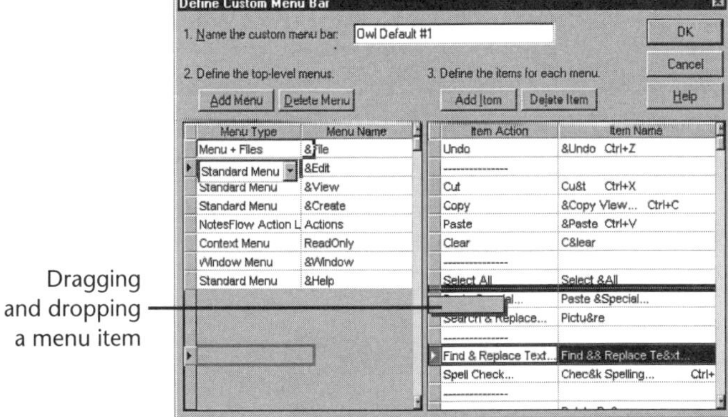

Fig. 17.9

Use drag-and-drop to change the order of items in a menu.

Creating a New Custom Menu. You also can create a custom menu from the ground up rather than use an existing menu as a guide. This is often easier for short menus or menus that won't follow the standard Approach default menu structure. To create a new menu, follow these steps:

> **Note**
>
> These steps are presented sequentially, but editing doesn't have to follow this exact order.

1. In Design mode, open the Create menu and choose Custom Menu.
2. Click the New button.
3. The Define Custom Menu Bar dialog box appears. Change the menu name, if you want.
4. Add any new top-level menus by clicking the Add Menu button. Choose the menu type from the drop-down list if it's different from the default Standard Menu.
5. Edit any menu names if you want to rename any top-level menus.
6. Select the top-level menu for which you'd like to edit the items. The selected menu will have a triangle to the left of its menu type.
7. Add any new items by choosing the Add Item button, and then by choosing the desired Item Action from the drop-down list.
8. Edit the Item Name, if you want to rename an item.
9. Reorder any menu items by dragging and dropping in the Menu Items list. Select an item by clicking the selection triangle to the right of the item name; the mouse pointer changes to a hand shape. Drag the item up or down in the list. The hand pointer is attached to a box, which represents the item, and a dark line appears to show where the item would be inserted when dropped. To drop an item into a new position, release the mouse button.
10. Reorder any top-level menus by the same drag-and-drop method. Select the menu, and then move it up or down in the list and drop it into its new position.
11. If you need to remove any top-level menus, select the menu and click the Delete Menu button. If you need to remove any menu items, select the menu item and click the Delete Item button.

Editing an Existing Custom Menu. Editing an existing custom menu is very similar to creating a new menu by copying an existing menu. Follow these steps:

1. Switch to Design mode.
2. Open the Create menu and choose Custom Menu.
3. Click the custom menu you want to edit.
4. Click the Edit button.

From this point, you can continue from step 3 earlier in the section "Creating a Custom Menu from an Existing Menu."

Duplicating a Custom Menu

To make a duplicate of a defined custom menu, follow these steps:

1. Switch to Design mode.
2. Open the Create menu and choose Custom Menu.

3. Click the custom menu that you want to duplicate.
4. Click the Copy button.
5. If you want to edit the new menu, select it and click the Edit button. Or click Done to close the Customize Menus dialog box.

Attaching a Custom Menu to a View

A custom menu is attached to a view through the InfoBox. The menu is attached in Design mode, but it's used only in Browse mode.

Because menus are attached to views, you must attach a custom menu to each view individually. If you duplicate a view with a custom menu, however, the custom menu will be attached to the duplicate.

> **Note**
>
> Custom menus aren't used in Design mode, so the menu bar won't change immediately after attaching a custom menu in Design mode. To view a custom menu bar, attach the menu and switch to Browse mode.

To attach a custom menu to a view, follow these steps:

1. Switch to Design mode and move to the view to which you want to attach the custom menu.
2. Define the custom menu, if it's not already defined.
3. Open the InfoBox for the view and switch to the Basics page (see fig. 17.10).

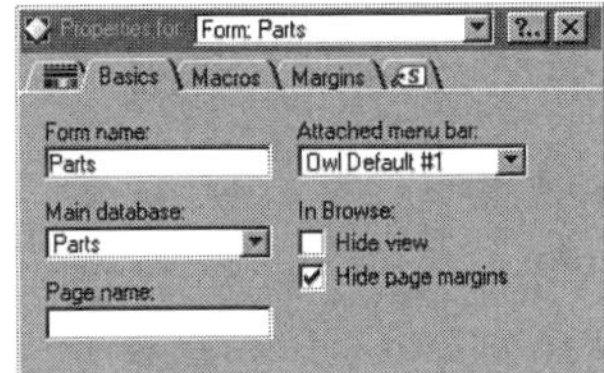

Fig. 17.10

The InfoBox for a view lists the attached custom menu name.

4. From the Attached Menu Bar drop-down list, choose the menu bar that you want attached to the current view.
5. Switch from Design mode to Browse mode to view the Custom Menu bar (see fig. 17.11). Remember, if a menu item isn't present in the view's current menu, the corresponding SmartIcon won't work either.

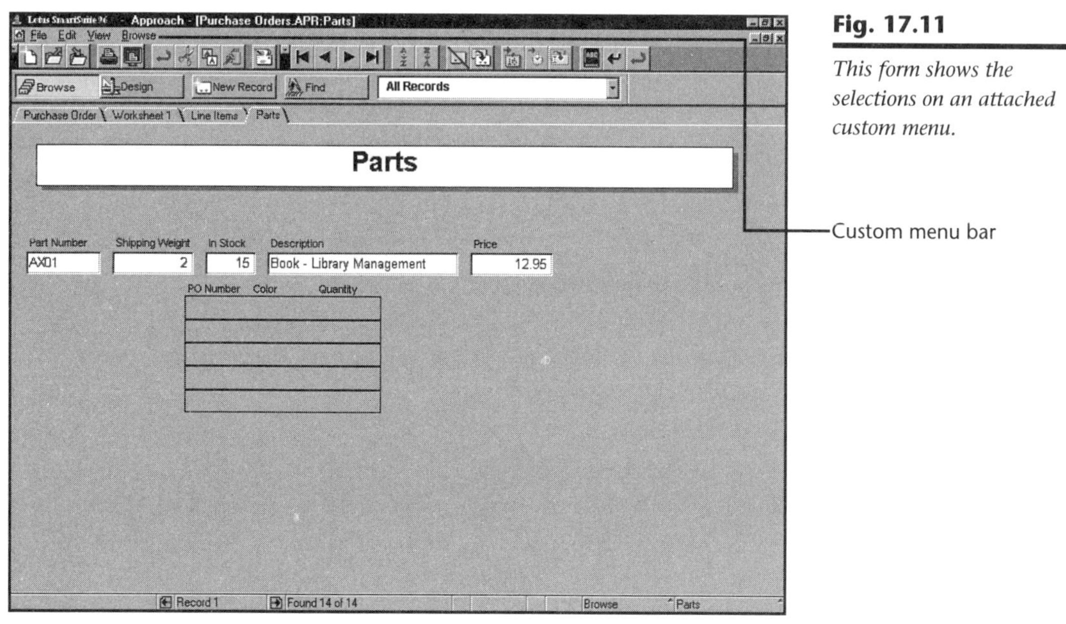

Fig. 17.11

This form shows the selections on an attached custom menu.

Removing a Custom Menu from a View

Custom menus are attached to a view through the InfoBox. The menus can be attached or modified only in Design mode.

To remove a custom menu from a view, follow these steps:

1. Switch to Design mode and move to the view from which you want to remove the custom menu.
2. Open the InfoBox for the view and go to the Basics page.
3. From the Attached Menu Bar list, choose the Default Menu to return to the Approach default for this view.

Deleting a Custom Menu

Custom menus can be deleted only in Design mode. To delete a custom menu, follow these steps:

1. In Design mode, open the Create menu and choose Custom Menu.
2. Select the custom menu that you want deleted by clicking it.
3. Click the Delete button.
4. When you're asked to confirm that you want to permanently delete the menu, choose Yes. If you choose No, you cancel the delete. With either choice, you return to the Customize Menus dialog box.
5. Perform any other modifications or click Done to close the dialog box.

If you delete a menu that's now being used, any view that it was attached to will revert to the default menu.

Creating Custom SmartMasters

It's easy to turn a frequently used Approach application you've developed into a SmartMaster template others can use. To build your own template, follow these steps:

1. Open the Approach file for the application you want to use as a SmartMaster. Then open the File menu and choose Save As.
2. Choose the SmartMaster file format (.MPR) in the Save As Type drop-down list box and click Save (see fig. 17.12).

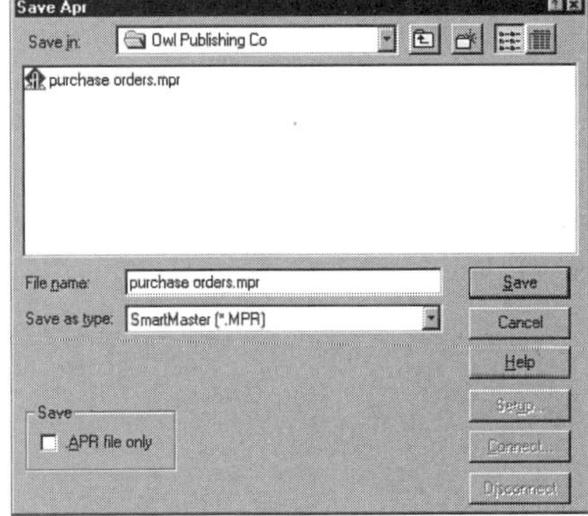

Fig. 17.12

Create your own SmartMaster templates from existing database application files.

3. Approach will save the standard Approach file as an .MPR type of file, and then display another Save As dialog box.
4. Change the name and/or file location for the database file. Then choose whether you want to save an exact copy (with current data), a blank copy (with all fields and properties but no data) or the original file itself. Click Save to save your database file.

If you have joined databases in this application, you must repeat the last two steps for each database.

Tip

If you want your new custom SmartMaster to appear in the opening Welcome box and New Database window, save it to the Approach SmartMaster directory.

Setting the Display Defaults

Approach allows each user to customize his or her own desktop working environment. This includes what the working window will look like, which tools will be available in Design mode, and the settings chosen for default views. These display defaults are set on the Display page of the Approach Preferences dialog box (see fig. 17.13). This dialog box can be opened in any mode except Find. To open the dialog box, open the File menu and choose User Setup and then Approach Preferences.

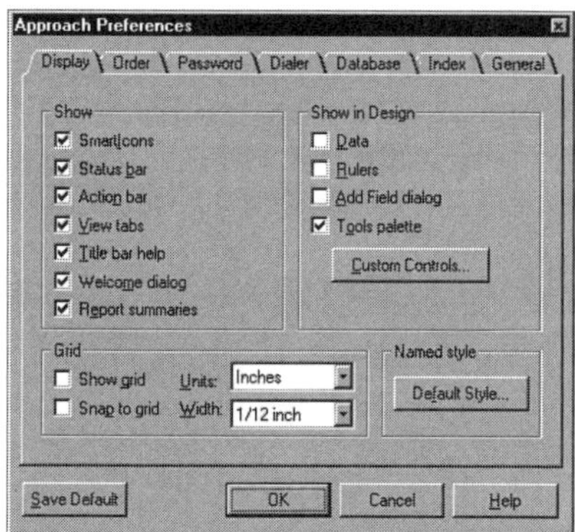

Fig. 17.13

Use the settings on the Display page to adjust your desktop working environment.

> **Note**
>
> The Display page sets permanent defaults for an Approach file. This varies from setting the options with menu commands or SmartIcons, which are set just for the current session.

General Screen-Item Defaults

The Show section of the Display page affects items in the Approach main window (see fig. 17.14).

Each item is either turned on or off. These settings can be just for the current Approach file. Or, if you adjust a setting and click the Save Default button, this setting will also become the default for new Approach files.

These items are controlled in the Show section:

- *SmartIcons.* This turns the SmartIcons on or off for the Approach file for all modes. Any other open Approach files still have the use of SmartIcons. By contrast, opening the View menu and choosing Show SmartIcons turns the SmartIcons on or off for all currently open Approach files.
- *Status Bar.* This selection turns the status bar on or off for all currently open Approach files, the same as opening the View menu and choosing Show Status Bar.

- *Action Bar*. This selection turns the action bar on or off for all currently open Approach files, the same as opening the View menu and choosing Show Action Bar.
- *View Tabs*. An Approach file's view tabs either are displayed or not, depending on this setting. To turn tabs off for individual views, use the In Browse Hide View check box in the view's InfoBox.
- *Title Bar Help*. This displays a help message for the selected menu item, but is different from the help balloons that are available for SmartIcons. The help message is displayed in the title area of the Approach window's title bar.
- *Welcome Dialog*. When enabled, the Welcome dialog box appears whenever you start Approach or close all Approach files in an Approach session. The Welcome dialog box allows you to quickly open your most recently opened files, create a new file from a SmartMaster template, and have access to the standard File Open and New Database dialog boxes.
- *Report Summaries*. Checking this box makes sure that you'll see the summaries of a report by restricting display options to Print Preview or Design mode. You must make sure, however, that you also have Show Data checked on the View menu if you are in Design mode.

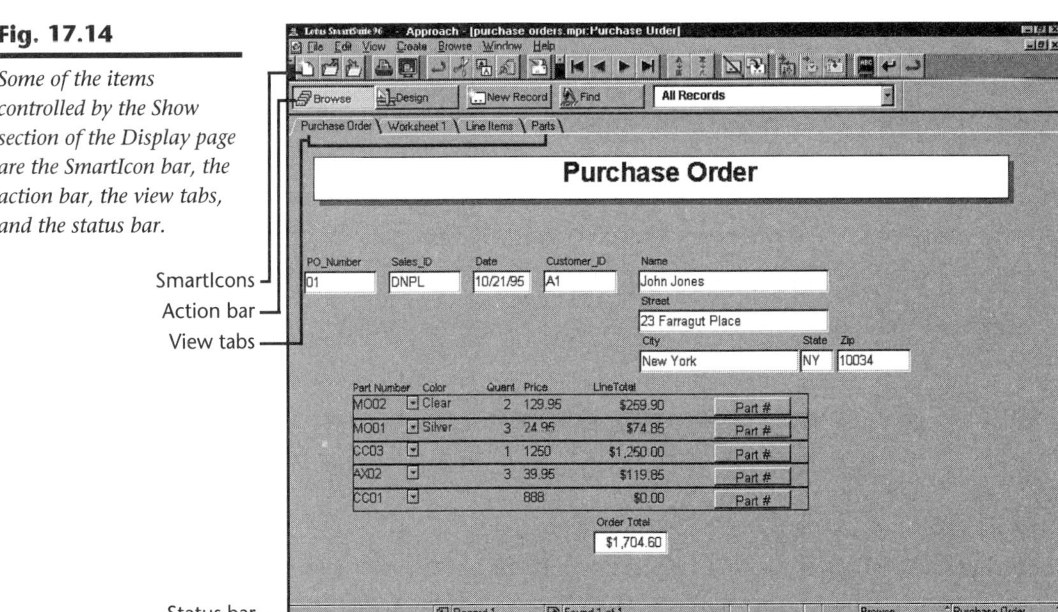

Fig. 17.14

Some of the items controlled by the Show section of the Display page are the SmartIcon bar, the action bar, the view tabs, and the status bar.

Design Screen Items

The items in the Show in Design area of the Display page adjust the various tools available to most views in Design mode (see fig. 17.15).

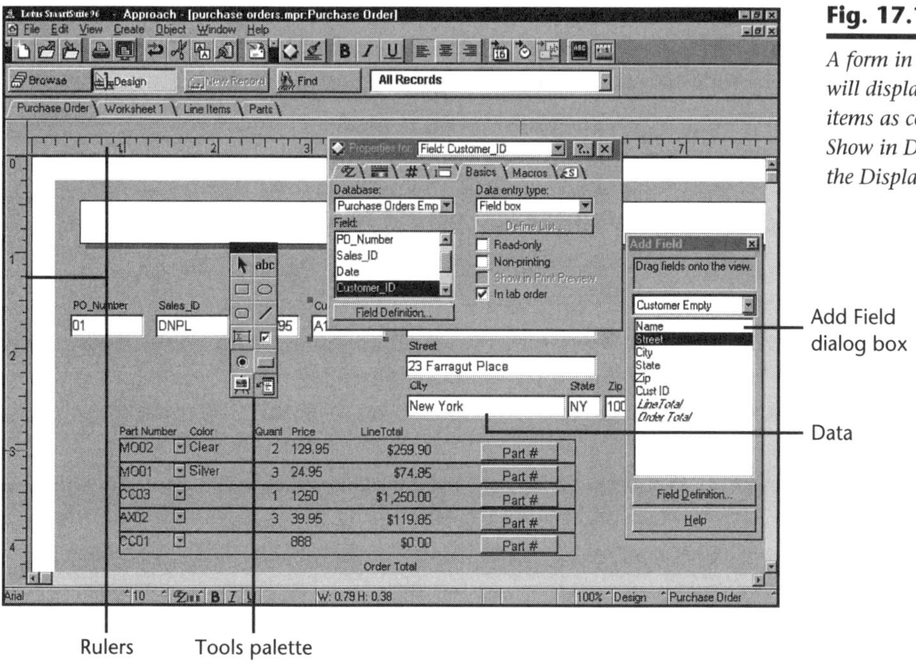

Fig. 17.15

A form in Design mode will display only screen items as controlled by the Show in Design section of the Display page.

> **Note**
>
> Worksheets and crosstabs are slightly different from other view types in the tools available. Because they don't allow added objects or free-form design, the tools palette and rulers aren't available on either view type. Also, worksheets and crosstabs are the only view types that can have the Add Field dialog box and InfoBox active in Browse mode.

Each item is either turned on or off. These settings can be just for the current Approach file. If you adjust a setting and click the Save Default button, this setting will also become the default for new Approach files.

The Show in Design section controls the following items:

- *Data*. When this item is selected, data will be showing when you're in Design mode. The setting is saved in the file, but it can be changed temporarily by opening the View menu and choosing Show Data.
- *Rulers*. This controls whether rulers will be on by default in Design mode. You can temporarily change this setting by opening the View menu and choosing Show Rulers (or pressing Ctrl+J).
- *Add Field Dialog*. The Add Field dialog box is a quick way to add new fields to a view, or to display the Field Definition dialog box to define new fields. You can temporarily close the Add Field dialog box by clicking the Close box in the upper right corner, or by using the context menu's current Add Field section.

- *Show Tools Palette.* The tools palette is a floating set of buttons for drawing shapes and lines, creating text blocks, and adding fields to a view. You can temporarily remove it from your screen by opening the View menu and choosing Show Tools Palette (or pressing Ctrl+L).

  You also can add OLE custom controls to your tools palette by clicking the Custom Controls button and selecting from the displayed list in the Custom Controls dialog box. In Design mode, you can add these control objects to the background of a form, report, mailing label, or form letter. A custom control may be as simple as a tool to draw a pentagon on the view or a program that retrieves and updates stock prices, for example. Custom controls aren't part of Approach, but may be written in LotusScript or purchased from third-party vendors. They must be installed and registered before they can be selected from the Custom Controls dialog box.

Note

The overall concept of OLE, or object linking and embedding, is discussed in more detail in Chapter 19, "Using Approach with the Lotus SmartSuite." Other uses of OLE by Approach are described in Chapter 9, "Designing Advanced Forms," and Chapter 18, "Importing and Exporting Files."

Grid Defaults

The *grid* is a series of points at a certain interval (see fig. 17.16). It's available when you're in Design mode for all views except worksheets and crosstabs. You can use the grid as a general guide or, with the Snap to Grid setting, items can be easily aligned to various grid points. The grid interval can be set by the user in inches or centimeters.

These grid settings are available:

- *Show Grid.* When this check box is selected, the grid will be displayed when you're in Design mode. The grid is displayed as a series of dots. You can temporarily override this setting by opening the View menu and choosing Show Grid.
- *Snap to Grid.* "Snap to" refers to how objects behave when being moved across the grid. The objects are attracted to grid points and seem to "snap" to a point when moved close to one. The grid doesn't have to be showing for objects to snap to the grid. You can temporarily override this feature by opening the View menu and choosing Snap to Grid (or pressing Ctrl+Y).
- *Units.* This setting is chosen from a drop-down list, and is in inches or centimeters.
- *Width.* The widths available are also chosen from a list and depend on which units of measurement are used. The grid settings for inches are from 1/16 to 1/2 of an inch. The grid settings for centimeters are from 0.1 to 1 centimeter.

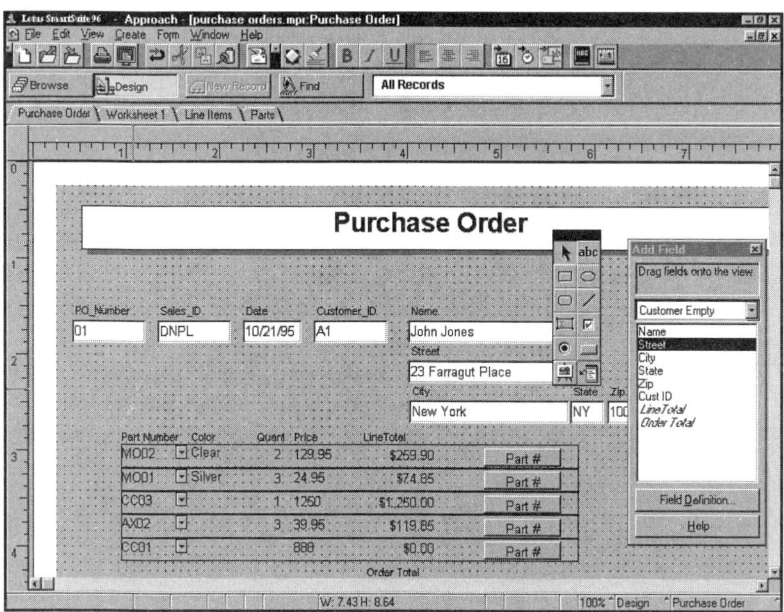

Fig. 17.16

Use the grid to align design objects.

Default Style

The Default Style button in the Named Style section of the Approach Preferences dialog box's Display page allows you to set what will be used by the Assistants as the default for any view. By using the Define Style dialog box, you can set the following attributes:

- Font
- Lines and Colors
- Label
- Picture
- Background

Working with this section is the same as when creating a named style. (For more information on named styles, see Chapter 3, "Building Data Input Forms.")

The default style is saved with the Approach file. If you click the Save Default button, this default style gets used for all new Approach files. If no Approach file is open, click Save to make your choices the new default style.

Setting the Phone Dialer Options

The Dialer page in the Approach Preferences dialog box sets default options for the autodialer (see fig. 17.17). These defaults are for the current Approach file or, if you click the Save Default button, are available to all Approach files. (To open the dialog box, open the File menu and choose User Setup, and then Approach Preferences.)

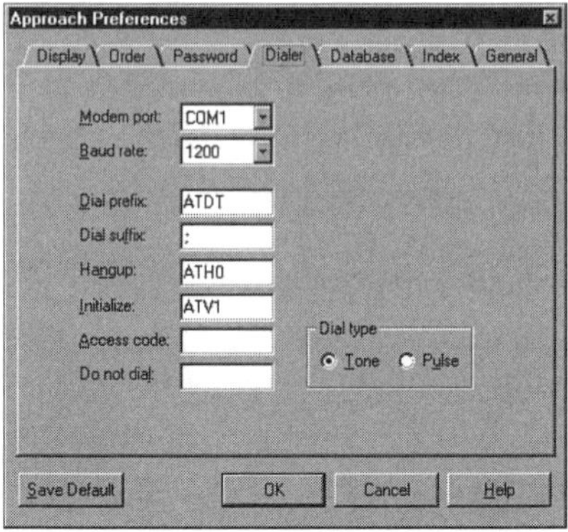

Fig. 17.17

Configure your modem to dial for you from the Dialer page.

Tip

You can dial a phone number by selecting a field that contains a number and choosing Dial from the Browse or Worksheet menu. Dialing is also available as a macro command.

These are the settings on the Dialer page:

- *Modem Port.* Use this drop-down list to select the communications port used by your modem.
- *Baud Rate.* Select the highest baud rate, from 110 baud to 19.2 kilobaud, that your modem can use.
- *Dial Prefix.* This is the command sent to the modem before the number is dialed. Unless you know you need a different prefix, leave this setting at the default (ATDT). This sends a command to your modem telling it to dial using tones rather than pulse.
- *Dial Suffix.* This command is sent after the number is dialed.
- *Hangup.* This command tells the modem to hang up the phone.
- *Initialize.* If your modem uses a certain initialization string, it needs to be typed into this box. Consult your modem manual for the proper string.
- *Access Code.* The access code is used if you need to dial a number, such as a 9, to get to an outside line. Place a comma after the code to pause while you're connecting to the outside line. If the pause time isn't long enough, add another comma to add another 2 seconds to the pause time.
- *Do Not Dial.* Use this for the local area code or any other numbers or characters that might be in the field you're dialing from that you don't want the phone to dial.
- *Dial Type.* This is Tone or Pulse, depending on what your phone lines can use. Most telephones use Tone. If you click Pulse, Approach automatically changes the Dial Prefix to ATDP, which sets the modem to use pulse dialing rather than tone.

Setting General Working Preferences

The General page in the Approach Preferences dialog box contains items that customize how you'd like Approach to act in various situations (see fig. 17.18). If you click the Save Default button, the settings are saved as defaults. Otherwise, they're just set for the current Approach file. (To open this dialog box, open the File menu and choose User Settings and then Approach Preferences.)

Fig. 17.18

Adjust your working preferences on the General page.

Table 17.1 shows the General page's settings, according to section.

Table 17.1 General Settings of the Approach Preferences Dialog Box

Setting	Description
Show Settings	
Calculated Fields in the Join Dialog	Calculated fields will appear in italics at the bottom of the field list, after the database fields. A field list shows database fields and the calculated fields that refer to fields in the listed database (and only the listed database), and it doesn't include summary fields.
Add Field Dialog After Creating New Fields	If this setting is on, any time you use the Field Definition dialog box and define a new field or fields, you'll automatically be given the option to add the new fields from the Add Field dialog box to the current view. Then, if you close the Add Field dialog box, it brings up a dialog box with the option to change to Browse mode or remain in Design mode.
Cancel Macro Dialog When Running Macros	The Cancel Macro dialog box is a visual clue that a macro is running. It also has a Cancel button. Whether or not this button is displayed, you usually can cancel macros by pressing Esc. This is a very helpful setting when testing new macros that may not do what you intended.

(continues)

Table 17.1 Continued

Setting	Description
Navigation Settings	
Use Enter Key to Move Between Fields	This user preference lets you press Enter to move between fields when entering data. Note that you must use Ctrl+Enter to put a new line into a text or memo field when this option is selected.
Expand Drop-Down Lists Automatically	Select this setting if you want a field's drop-down list to appear as soon as your cursor enters the field.
Data Settings	
Download Data Before Print Preview	Downloading data is most useful when working in a shared-file environment or with SQL or ODBC data. The current set of data is downloaded to your local computer's hard drive. This means that you don't have to worry about updates from other users or server access time while working with the downloaded set.
Lock Records Using Optimistic Record Locking	This setting is for applications with users working in a multiuser networked environment, and should be set to the same value for all users of the same applications. Optimistic record locking allows multiple users to update the same record. If two users are viewing a record and both users try to save their changes, the second one attempting the save will get a warning that the record has been modified since they received the data. If this setting is off, the first person to use a record can change fields; all other users can view the record but can't change it.

Setting Database Preferences

Database preferences vary by database type. To set the preferences for a certain database type, a database of that type needs to be accessed in the current Approach file. For example, to set the preferences for a Paradox database, you'll need to open a Paradox database. This is the same for the SQL or ODBC tables.

To open the Approach Preferences dialog box, open the File menu and choose User Setup and then Approach Preferences.

Setting Case Sensitivity on Paradox 4.0 Files

Normally, Paradox 4.0 file searches aren't case-sensitive. If you open a Paradox 4.0 file and use the Database page of the Approach Preferences dialog box, however, you'll be able to activate case sensitivity (see fig. 17.19). Notice, however, that this doesn't apply to earlier versions of Paradox.

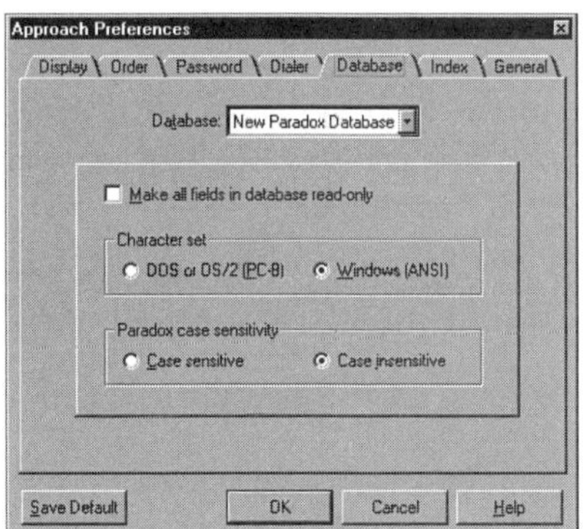

Fig. 17.19

Paradox's case-sensitivity settings are on the Database page when a Paradox file is available.

Note

Paradox 3.5 files are always case-sensitive.

After you click OK to close the Approach Preferences dialog box, a warning box informs you to close and reopen the file for the new case-sensitivity setting to take effect.

Including Lotus Notes, Microsoft Access, SQL, and ODBC Databases

Different options are displayed in the Database page of the Approach Preferences dialog box for these types of databases. Changing an option here will affect every database of its type that you use in Approach. You can choose

- Read-only access for Lotus Notes, Access, SQL, and ODBC files
- Display of SQL tables in file name lists

Caching SQL Tables

The Database page on the Approach Preferences dialog box also has a setting that allows the user to cache SQL table (database) names in an Approach session. When the names are cached, they're copied to the user's computer, and a list of names doesn't need to be generated from the network server every time a dialog box—such as Open or New, which contain a list of the table names—is opened.

Caution

When table names are cached, they don't get updated as you and other users insert or delete tables. The table names at the beginning of the next Approach session will reflect any changes.

From Here...

In this chapter, you learned how you can use the customization options in Approach to develop and enhance your database applications. To learn more about automating your application through macros, read this chapter:

- Chapter 13, "Automating Your Work," shows how Approach macros can be used for most tasks, including navigating through different views, finding records, and printing reports.

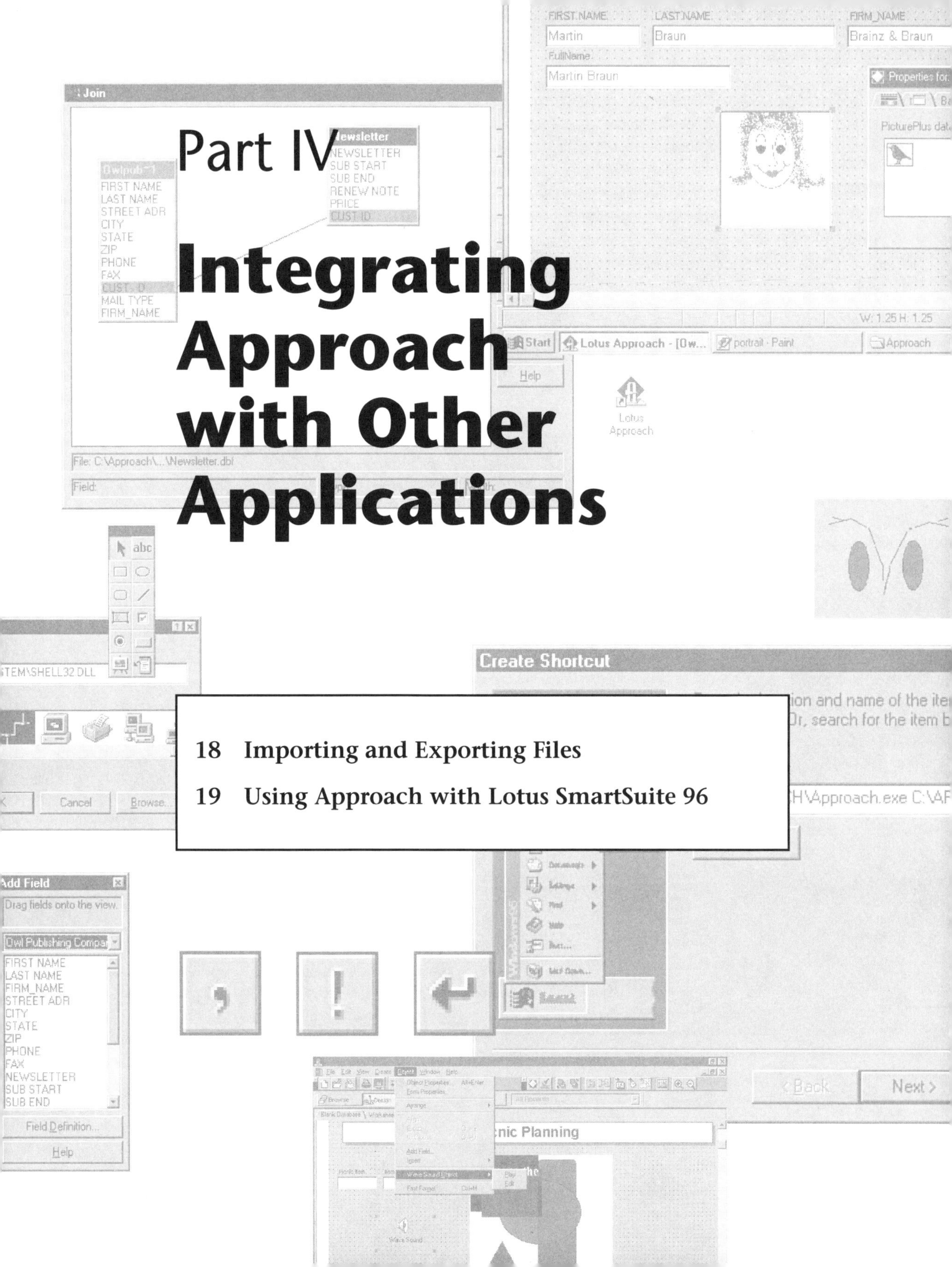

Part IV

Integrating Approach with Other Applications

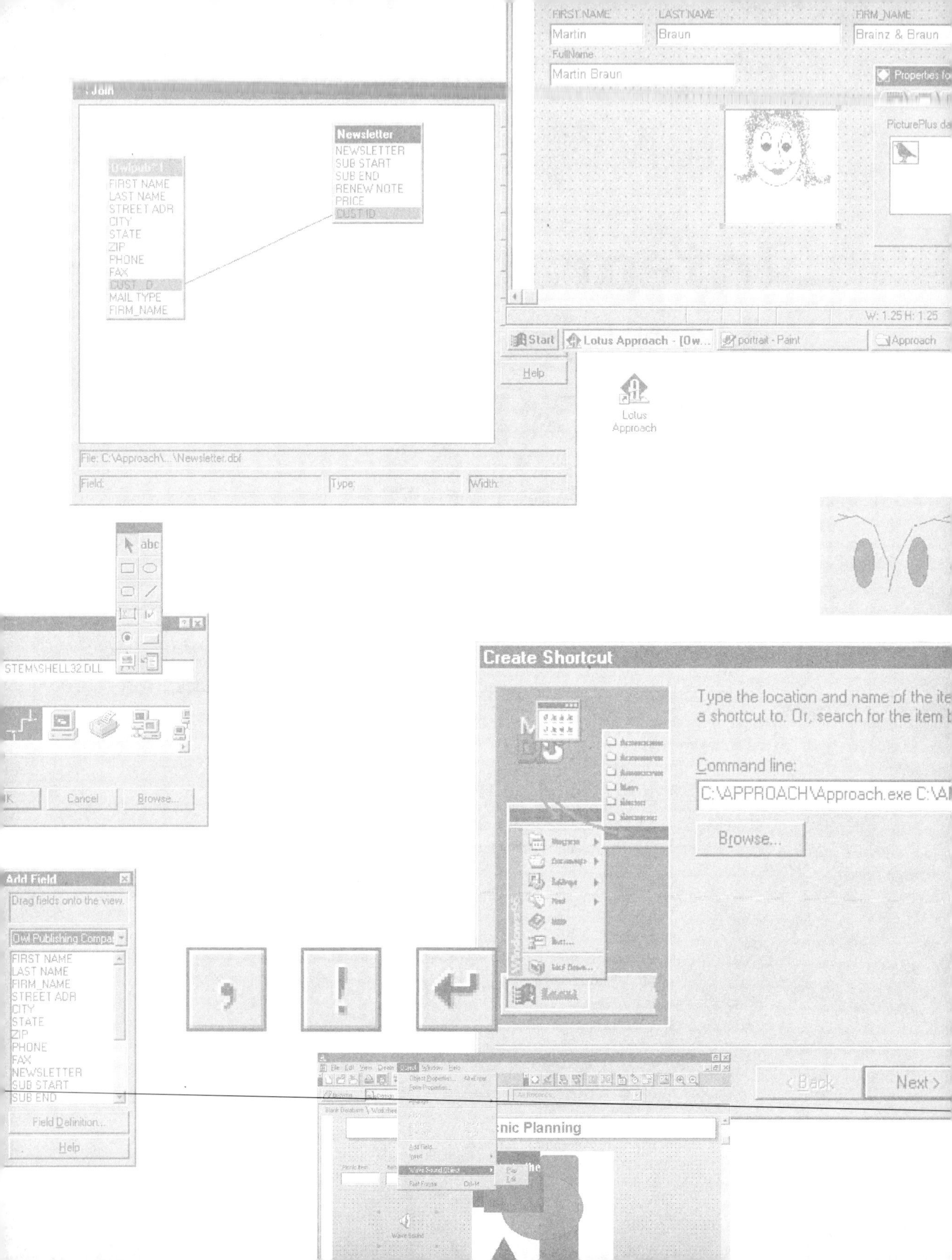

Join
Newsletter
NEWSLETTER
SUB START
SUB END
RENEW NOTE
PRICE
CUST ID
FIRST NAME
LAST NAME
STREET ADR
CITY
STATE
ZIP
PHONE
FAX
CUST_ID
MAIL TYPE
FIRM_NAME
File: C:\Approach\...\Newsletter.dbf
Field:
Type:
Width:
Help
FIRST NAME
LAST NAME
FIRM_NAME
Martin
Braun
Brainz & Braun
FullName
Martin Braun
PicturePlus
W: 1.25 H: 1.25
Start
Lotus Approach - [Ow...
portrait - Paint
Approach
Lotus Approach
STEM\SHELL32.DLL
Cancel
Browse...
Create Shortcut
Type the location and name of the ite
a shortcut to. Or, search for the item b
Command line:
C:\APPROACH\Approach.exe C:\A
Browse...
< Back
Next >
Add Field
Drag fields onto the view.
Owl Publishing Compa
FIRST NAME
LAST NAME
FIRM_NAME
STREET ADR
CITY
STATE
ZIP
PHONE
FAX
NEWSLETTER
SUB START
SUB END
Field Definition...
Help
nic Planning

CHAPTER 18

Importing and Exporting Files

For those of you who have your data already on your computer, Approach offers many options to get your data into an Approach application—even if it's not in a database format that Approach can "open" directly. For example, you may have a name and address list in a text file and want to use the new Contacts SmartMaster that comes with Approach to get up and running quickly. Or you may own another database program and want to use its databases in Approach. *Importing* is the process of bringing outside data files into Approach databases.

Another common situation that occurs is the need to give your database to someone who wants to use it in a text-file or spreadsheet format. *Exporting* is the process of taking your Approach databases and creating files that you can use with other software, such as word processors, spreadsheet programs, and other database managers.

By using Approach, you can import and export database information in a variety of different data formats. With this flexibility, you can sort, store, and update information selectively. Importing and exporting also allows you to move information into and out of non-database formats to exchange data with applications that use a proprietary format.

Similar to sharing data, you can also share views that are already created by importing an Approach file. Approach views can also be inserted into other applications, such as a word-processor document, by using Approach as an OLE server.

In this chapter, you learn how to

- Import data into Approach from another database, from a text file, and from a spreadsheet
- Export data from Approach to other databases, to a text file, and to a spreadsheet
- Import other data from other Approach files
- Create Approach OLE Server objects for use in other applications

Importing Data

Importing information into Approach allows you to use Approach's powerful database tools and SmartMasters to view and modify the data.

Approach lets you specify the fields from which information is imported and the fields in the open database into which that information is placed. You can use the Import feature to add records to the end of a database, update existing records, or a combination of both.

Using the Import Setup Dialog Box

The Import Setup dialog box is used to map fields in the selected Approach database that will receive data from the imported data fields. It also lets you browse through the records being imported so that you don't have to guess which field might have the data that goes into a particular database field. This is especially helpful for data coming from a spreadsheet or text file that doesn't have predefined field names. The Import Setup dialog box also shows the number of records contained in the file being imported (see fig. 18.1).

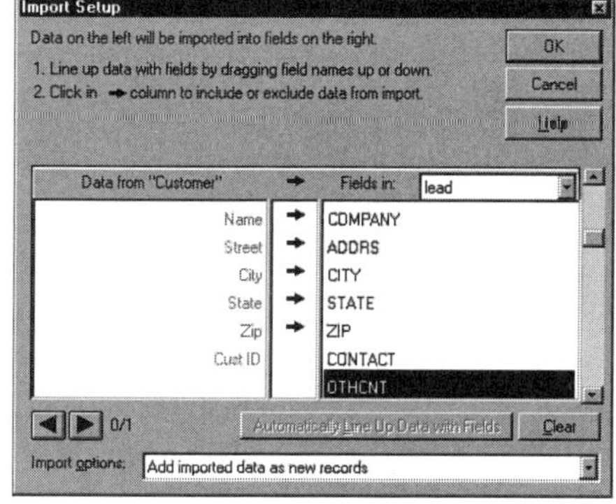

Fig. 18.1

The Import Setup dialog box maps imported data to existing data.

The fields in the file being imported are listed on the left side of the Import Setup dialog box. The destination Approach database name and its fields are listed on the right. The destination field names can be moved up or down to match the proper importing field. To map the importing and destination field names together, you need to position them across from each other and insert an arrow in the middle column to connect them.

The previous and next buttons in the lower left corner of the dialog box (represented by a left-facing triangle and right-facing triangle) are used to browse the data in the importing file. The first record, 0, generally contains field names. Subsequent records contain actual data. This comes in handy if you can't identify fields by name and need to see actual data to map them.

The Import Setup dialog box is also used to set the add or update options for the data from the importing file. The Import Options drop-down list contains the options available to you based on the type of file you are importing. The imported data can complete the following tasks:

- *Add Imported Data as New Records.* Append new records to the end of the destination database as new records.
- *Use Imported Data to Update Existing Records.* Update only existing records in the selected Approach database that match specified criteria. Only those records in the database's current found set will be updated.
- *Use Imported Data to Update & Add to Existing Records.* Update existing records that match specified criteria and append as new any records that don't match. Once again, only those records in the database's current found set will be updated.

When using an import option that updates records—often called *merging files*—the Import Setup dialog box changes to allow you to set criteria for matches (notice in fig. 18.2 that an additional column for checking has been added to the right side). This file-matching criteria should be something unique, such as customer name, an employee number, or a combination of name and telephone number. The fields that are marked as matching criteria are automatically mapped to each other if you haven't already done so.

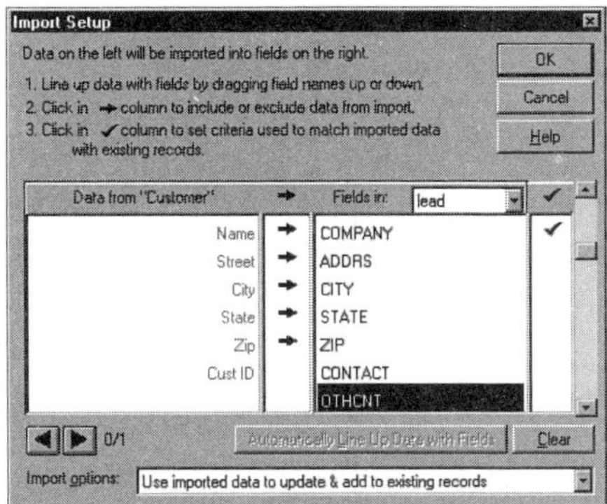

Fig. 18.2

This import updates records that exactly match the Name field to the Company field.

Note

You can't use the update options with spreadsheet, text, or delimited text files. To update using these file types, first import the data into a new database and save it as a regular database (.DBF) file. Use this file to update your database.

To import data, updating only those records that match an exact criteria, follow these steps:

1. In Approach, open the database into which you want to import data; this database is now known as the current Approach database.
2. Switch to Browse mode.
3. Open the File menu and choose Import Data. The Import Data dialog box appears (see fig. 18.3).

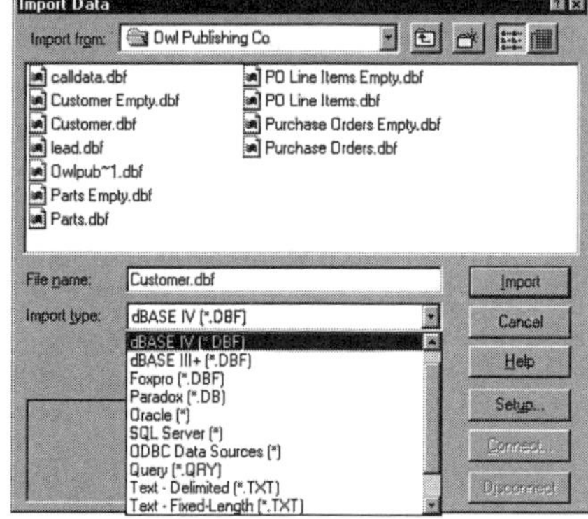

Fig. 18.3

You use the Import Data dialog box to select the file or database from which you're importing.

4. Select the type of file you're importing from in the Import Type drop-down list. If you're importing from a text or spreadsheet file, another dialog box may appear for information specific to that type. Refer to the later section specific to importing that file type for more details.
5. Use the Import From drop-down list at the top of the dialog box to select the drive and folder that contain the file you want to import.
6. Select the file you want to import from—the importing database—in the file list box. Its name will appear in the File Name text box below the list box.
7. Click Import. The Import Setup dialog box appears.

> **Note**
>
> If a field in the importing file and a field in the current Approach database have the same name, Approach maps them automatically. These mapped fields have arrows between them when the Import Setup dialog box appears.

8. If the current Approach file contains multiple joined databases, select the destination database from the drop-down list of databases.

Caution

If your Approach file contains joined databases, you can import information into only one database at a time. Changing which database you're importing into erases any mappings you've established.

9. Set the Import Options to use imported data to match existing records. The dialog box changes to allow you to set a matching criteria.
10. Move the destination database field names up or down, if necessary, to line them up with the proper fields from the import file. To move a database field, click the field so it's selected. The cursor changes to include up and down arrows to show that the field can be moved. Drag the field to the new position and release. The field you dragged switches places with another field (see fig. 18.4).

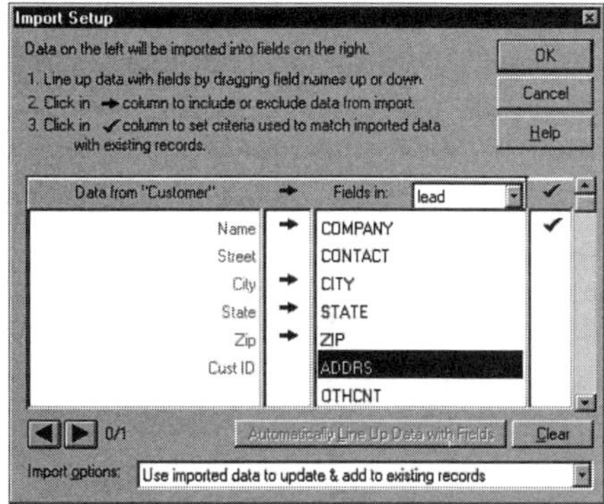

Fig. 18.4

Drag the destination database field names up or down to align with importing fields.

Note

Calculated and variable fields aren't displayed in the Import Setup dialog box because they're a part of the Approach file, not stored in a database.

11. After a pair of importing and database field names are lined up properly, click the check column between them for an arrow to show that the two are mapped to each other.

Note

Only the database fields in Import Setup that have an arrow from an importing field will receive data. If the Import Setup dialog box shows more fields in the importing file or Approach database, use the scroll bar to scroll through the fields and check that all fields that should be receiving data are properly set.

> **Note**
>
> The two mapped fields should have the same field type. If they don't, Approach doesn't import the value from the importing field into the database, with one exception: You can import any field type into a text-type field. It's also important that the Approach database field is the same length or longer than the importing field. If it's shorter than the importing field, the incoming data will be truncated to the length of the database field.

12. Repeat steps 10 and 11 for every field you want to map. Be sure to scroll the lists if the importing or approach database field lists contain more fields than are shown in the dialog box.

> **Note**
>
> If you need to unmap a pair of fields, click the arrow to turn it off. To clear all set mappings, click the Clear button in the Import Setup dialog box. To redo all automatic mappings (based on name), first make sure that no field names are mapped; then click the Automatically Line Up Data with Fields button.

13. Click OK in the Import Setup dialog box.

Approach imports the fields from the selected database or file, merging matching records into the selected Approach database. Because you're not adding any records that don't match, the record counter should remain the same.

Importing Data from a Specific File Type

Since Approach can import from a wide range of file types, some additional information may be necessary when importing from specific file types.

> **Tip**
>
> If you're going to create a new Approach database from an existing dBASE, Paradox, or FoxPro file, open the file directly. Use the Import Setup dialog box to update or consolidate information.

Importing Data from Another Database

Approach can easily import information in dBASE-, Paradox-, and FoxPro-format databases. You can import information stored in any of these formats into an open database in Approach. This capability is very useful if you have similar information stored in several different databases. For example, you may have multiple databases with customer information. Approach lets you consolidate data in these databases into a single Approach database. You can do this even if the imported databases are of different database formats.

Importing Data from a Text File

You can import information from a delimited or fixed-length text file. Because many current software packages can export data to a text file, you may find this useful.

> **Note**
>
> If you're starting a new database from a text file, you don't need to create a database and then import the data. Open the File menu and choose Open. You can select the text-file type in the Open dialog box. Approach will open the file and convert it to a database for you.

Importing Data from a Delimited Text File. A delimited text file has a special format that allows Approach to find field data to import. Each text line (ending with a carriage return/line feed combination) is treated as a single record to import. Within the line, special characters called *delimiters* separate the text into fields. Commas and tab characters are often used as delimiters, although you can use almost any character as a delimiter. In the following example, the text-file database has one record per line, and fields are comma-delimited:

```
"George","Smith","45 A Street","Carmichael","CA","90569"
"Joseph","Jordan","1290 Fortune Street","Lansing","MI","59067"
"Fred","Grossman","67709 Chadworth Ave","New York","NY","10089"
"John",,"39023 Palm Drive","Palm Springs","CA","96890"
```

In a delimited text file, fields that contain carriage-return characters or the delimiter character can be imported if the entire field is enclosed in double quotation marks. Fields enclosed in double quotation marks should begin immediately after the delimiter, or the quotation marks will be interpreted as a character in the field.

Fields that aren't enclosed in double quotation marks should import correctly even without the quotation marks, as long as the delimiter character or a carriage return isn't contained in the field.

> **Note**
>
> The text file should have the same number of fields on every line. If information in one of the fields is missing, you must indicate the presence of the missing field with a delimiter. In the preceding example, because the second field (last name) is missing from the last text line, an extra comma has been inserted, indicating the end of the missing field.

When you choose delimited text as the file type in the Import Data dialog box, the Text File Options dialog box opens (see fig. 18.5). Set the file options as necessary in the Text File Options dialog box:

- Use the Separate Fields With section of the dialog box to set the delimiter. If the delimiter isn't listed, type it in the text box next to Other.

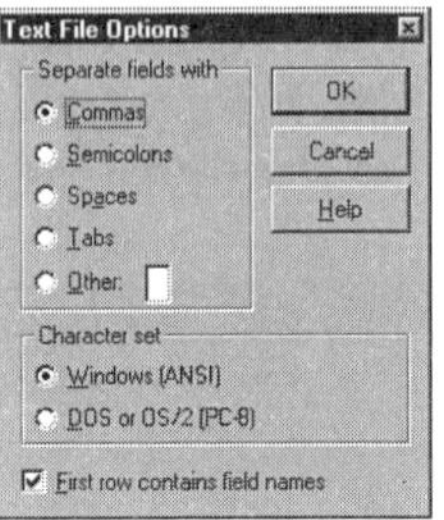

Fig. 18.5

The Text File Options dialog box contains settings specific to delimited text files.

- Select the proper character set (Windows or DOS) for the file. This is especially important if the file you're importing from has international characters.

  The character set determines how you enter special characters that aren't on the keyboard. For example, if you're using the DOS set and want to type the symbol for yen (¥), press Alt and type 157 on the numeric keypad. With the Windows set, press Alt and type 165 on the numeric keypad.
- Select the check box if the first row contains field names. You don't want to import the field names as field data.

Click OK to proceed to the Import Setup dialog box. Refer to "Using the Import Setup Dialog Box" earlier in this chapter for details.

Importing Data from a Fixed-Width Text File. In a fixed length text file, each record has a certain number of character spaces reserved for each field. Using this information, you know where each field starts and ends. Because you already know the position of each field, there are no delimiters. The preceding delimited file data might be stored in a fixed-width file, as follows:

```
George  Smith        45 A Street       Carmichael    CA90569
Joseph  Jordan     1290 Fortune Street Lansing       MI59067
Fred    Grossman  67709 Chadworth Ave  New York      NY10089
John              39023 Palm Drive     Palm Springs  CA96890
```

For this file, the first field is 8 characters wide, the second is 10 characters, and so on. It's important to know where each field begins and ends in a fixed-width text database. If this information isn't correct, odds are that the data imported won't be, either.

Fixed-length text files have their own Fixed Length Text File Setup dialog box so you can describe where each field begins or ends. In figure 18.6, the information for several fields has been entered. Approach has used the starting point and width to fill in the starting point for the second field. All fields to be imported need to be defined in this dialog box.

For each fixed-length record field, you can perform several tasks:

- Select the proper character set (Windows or DOS) for the file. This is especially important if the file you're importing from has international characters.
- Type a field name, data type, starting position, and width.

- Select the check box if the first row contains field names. You don't want to import the field names as field data.

Tip

If the first row of your fixed-width text file contains the field names and is correctly spaced, Approach will automatically measure and set up the import. Just click the First Row Contains Field Names check box.

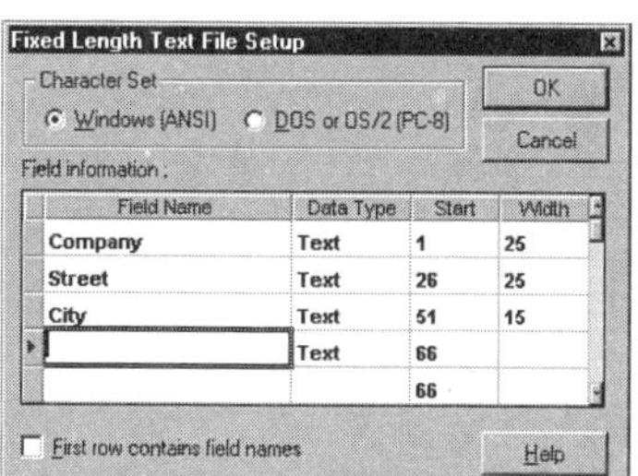

Fig. 18.6

Use the Fixed Length Text File Setup dialog box to describe field width and placement.

After all the fields are defined, click OK to proceed to the Import Setup dialog box. Refer to "Using the Import Setup Dialog Box" earlier in this chapter for details.

Importing Data from a Spreadsheet. Because spreadsheets such as Lotus 1-2-3 for Windows or Microsoft Excel have rudimentary database capabilities, a significant amount of data that should be stored in databases is instead stored in spreadsheets. Also, spreadsheets display data in a format that many people are comfortable with—a table. In the table, each column in the spreadsheet is treated as a field, and each row is a record. Spreadsheets have limited database capabilities, however. You may want to import data from a spreadsheet into Approach to make use of Approach's extensive database capabilities.

Tip

If you're starting a new database from a spreadsheet file, you don't need to create a database and then import the data. Open the File menu and choose Open. Within the Open dialog box you can select the spreadsheet file type. Approach will open the file and convert it to a database for you. Use the Approach worksheet created for you to see your data in table format.

A spreadsheet file must follow a special format before you can import its contents into an open database. Each row must be one record, and each column must be a field.

If your spreadsheet is divided into "ranges," after you choose the spreadsheet file in the Import Data dialog box, a second dialog box opens (see fig. 18.7). This dialog box contains a list of all the named ranges that contain data. In the Select Range dialog box, you can also tell Approach to skip the first row that contains field names, if necessary.

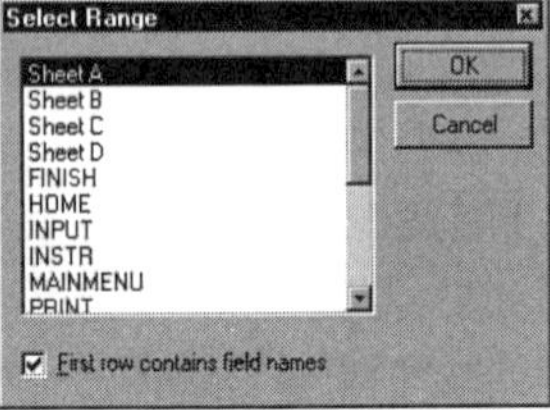

Fig. 18.7

Use the Select Range dialog box to choose the sheet or named range you want to import.

> **Note**
>
> You don't need to delete blank rows in a spreadsheet before you import data from that spreadsheet—Approach doesn't import the blank rows.

After selecting the range for import, click OK to proceed with the Import Setup dialog box. Refer to "Using the Import Setup Dialog Box" earlier in this chapter for details.

> **Note**
>
> In Excel, a column can hold a date and a time (such as 2/24/93 9:46pm). If a column in the Excel file is formatted in this manner, Approach lists that column twice in the Fields to Map list box—once as a date field, and once as a time field (for example, for column A, A DATE and A TIME).

Exporting Data

Approach lets you export information to the following types of files:

- Other database formats
- Text files
- Spreadsheets

By exporting data into other files, you can work with your data outside Approach. For example, you can work with text-file data in a word processor, or use the sophisticated mathematical functions of a spreadsheet in an exported spreadsheet-format file.

Exporting data also allows you to change the order in which the records are stored, choose a subset of your data, or both.

> **Note**
>
> Non-summary calculated fields and variable fields can be exported. They become standard database fields and contain their value at the time of export for each record.

Choosing Records to Export

You may find it useful to perform a find on your Approach database before exporting records. If you perform a find, Approach exports only those records from the current found set. To perform a find before exporting, follow these steps:

1. Switch to Browse mode.
2. Select the view you want to use to create the find by selecting its tab or by selecting the view name from the status bar.
3. Click the Find button on the action bar.
4. Type the find criteria on the form.
5. Press Enter or click OK on the action bar to execute the find and create the found set.

Ordering Exported Records

Approach exports records from the currently open database in their current sort order. Thus, when exporting records, you may find it helpful to sort the records in the current found set before performing the export. The records appear in the destination file in the order in which they're sorted.

Tip

If you want to perform a find and a sort for the exported data, do the find first and then the sort. This limits the number of records sorted to the found set and is the more efficient way to handle this situation.

Note

If you've used the Order tab in the Approach Preferences dialog box to set a default sort order on your database, the records are exported in that order. (To access the Approach Preferences dialog box, from the File menu choose User Setup and then Approach Preferences.)

To perform a sort before exporting records, follow these steps:

1. Switch to Browse mode.
2. Open the Browse menu and choose Sort and then Define. You can also press Ctrl+T or, if it's present, click the Define Sort SmartIcon. The Sort dialog box appears.
3. Select the database you want to sort from the drop-down list under the Database option.
4. In the Fields list box, select the field you want to sort.

> **Note**
>
> You can sort on a summary field, but you can't export a summary field.

5. Click Add or double-click the selected field to move the field to the Fields to Sort On list box. Adjust the sort direction (Ascending or Descending), if needed.
6. Repeat steps 4 and 5 as needed to add more fields to the sort. You can select fields from multiple databases if the current Approach file contains joined databases.
7. Click OK in the Sort dialog box to perform the sort.

Using the Export Data Dialog Box

Approach lets you export information from the currently open Approach database or databases to a new file. This process is useful if you want to create a new file that has the following:

- Records stored in a specific order. Exporting records is the only way to reorder your records physically, although opening the File menu and choosing User Setup and then Approach Preferences allows you to set a permanent display order on the database.
- Only a subset of the records in the currently open database.

> **Note**
>
> See the earlier sections "Choosing Records to Export" and "Ordering Exported Records" for more information about using the Export Data dialog box.

To export information from an open Approach database to a new file, follow these steps:

1. Open the database from which you want to export information.
2. Switch to Browse mode.
3. If desired, perform a sort or find on the records in the open database. If you want to perform a sort and a find, do the find first.
4. Open the File menu and choose Export Data. The Export Data dialog box appears (see fig. 18.8).
5. Select the export database file type from the Export Type drop-down list.
6. Use the Export To drop-down list and the folders list to select the drive and folder in which you want to store the exported file.
7. Type the name of the export file in the File Name text box.

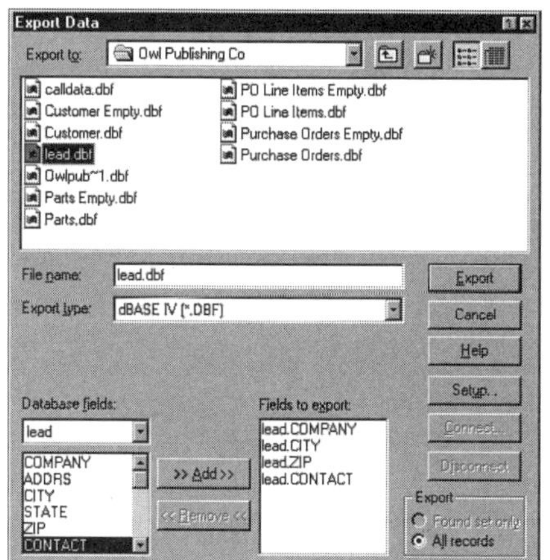

Fig. 18.8

Set file export options in the Export Data dialog box.

8. Select a set of fields to export. If the current Approach file contains multiple joined databases, select one database from which you want to export fields. The fields in the selected database appear in the Database Fields list box beneath the selected database name.
9. Select a field in the Database Fields list box. The order in which you select fields determines their order in the new database.
10. Click Add or double-click the selected field to move the field to the Fields to Export list box.

Note

To remove a field from the Fields to Export list box, select the field and click Remove, or double-click the field.

11. Repeat steps 8 through 10 for all databases and fields you want to export.

Tip

You can export fields from more than one database using the Database Fields drop-down box. Your current main database, which is determined by the view from which the export is initiated, controls the number of records created and exported. If a related database has more than one record per main database record, multiple records containing the main database fields and fields from each related record will be created and exported.

12. Select one of the following options from the Export section of the Export Data dialog box:

Button	Description
All Records	Exports all records in the currently open database. Records are exported in their true order in the database, even if a default sort order has been set.
Found Set Only	Available only if you perform a find or a sort before starting the export. If you select this option, records are exported in their current or default sort order, and only records in the found set are exported.

Note

If you've sorted *all* the records, you must select the Found Set Only radio button, or the destination file won't have sorted records.

13. Click Export in the Export Data dialog box.

Approach creates a new file or database with the selected fields and exports the selected records.

Exporting Data to Another Database. Choose the database type you'll be exporting to in the Export Type list box in the Export Data dialog box. The database type that you export to doesn't have to be the same type that you're exporting from. For example, you can export to create a Paradox database from a dBASE database.

Note

If the export database is a Paradox database, the Choose Key Field dialog box appears. Choose one or more of the fields from the list of fields to be the key field. You can also choose Add Key Field to have Approach create a serial key field.

Exporting Data to a Text File. Approach allows you to export information from the currently open Approach database to a text file. This capability is handy if you want to use the information in a word processor or another application that can't read database-format files. As with importing, the exported text file can be delimited or fixed-length.

Exporting Data to a Delimited Text File. To export the currently open database to a delimited text file, follow these steps:

1. Open the database from which you want to export information.
2. Switch to Browse mode.
3. If you want, perform a sort or find on the records in the open database.

4. Open the File menu and choose Export Data. The Export Data dialog box appears.
5. Select the delimited text file type from the Export Type drop-down list.
6. Use the Export To drop-down box to select the drive and folder where you want to store the exported text file.
7. Choose the fields to export. This is covered in more detail earlier in the section "Using the Export Data Dialog Box."
8. Select All Records or Found Set Only from the Export section of the Export Data dialog box.
9. Click Export in the Export Data dialog box. The Text File Options dialog box appears (refer back to fig. 18.5).
10. Choose a delimiter. If you choose Other, type the delimiter character into the text box to the right of the option.
11. Choose one of the following Character Set options to select the character set for the text file:
    - Choose the Windows (ANSI) option if you're exporting to a Windows text file.
    - Choose the DOS or OS/2 (PC-8) option if you're exporting to a DOS or OS/2 application.
12. Choose whether the first row of the exported file will contain field names.
13. Click OK in the Text File Options dialog box.

Approach creates the new, delimited text file with the selected fields and exports the current found set of selected records to that file. Each record in the database appears as one line in the text file. Each field in the database becomes a portion of a line, separated from the next field by the delimiter character.

> **Note**
>
> Fields will be exported with double quotation marks at the beginning and end of each field. Carriage returns and delimiters within a field will remain intact.

Exporting Data to a Fixed-Length File. In a fixed-length text file, each field has a specific starting and ending point. For example, a FIRST NAME field might be defined as 10 characters. In the text file, it would start at position 1 and end at position 10. The next field would start in the position that immediately follows (position 11).

To export data to a fixed-length text file, set up the Export Data dialog box as described earlier in the section "Using the Export Data Dialog Box." For this example, however, select fixed-length text in the Export Type drop-down list.

Click Export in the Export Data dialog box to bring up the Fixed Length Text File Setup dialog box. In this dialog box, you can do the following:

- Set the character set (Windows or DOS).
- Adjust the field widths, if necessary.
- Choose whether the first row contains field names in the exported file.

Exporting Data to a Spreadsheet. Approach lets you export data to a spreadsheet. After you store data in a spreadsheet, you can use the spreadsheet software's powerful mathematical functions to manipulate the data. Excel (.XLS) and Lotus 1-2-3 (.WK1) are spreadsheet types supported for export.

To export data to a spreadsheet, choose the desired type in the Export Type drop-down list in the Export Data dialog box, set export options as desired, and click Export.

Importing an Approach File

An Approach file (.APR) contains information about all the views, forms, reports, form letters, mailing labels, worksheets, crosstabs, charts, macros, database field objects, calculated fields, and variable fields defined within it.

You can import an Approach file into the currently open Approach file. This allows you to use the views, macros, field objects, and calculated and variable fields in the imported Approach file in the currently open Approach file. Database contents won't be imported.

When you import an Approach file, you map database fields available to the currently open Approach file to field objects (in views, macros, and so on) in the imported Approach file. If no field in the current databases is mapped to a field object in the imported Approach file, that field object won't display anything wherever it appears. Any macros or calculations that refer to that unmapped field object won't run or evaluate.

Note

Importing an Approach file, as opposed to importing a database, doesn't affect the data stored in the database in any way.

To import an Approach file, follow these steps:

1. Open the Approach application into which you want to import another Approach file. This open file is the destination Approach file.
2. Switch to Design mode.
3. Open the File menu and choose Import Approach File. The Import Approach File dialog box appears (see fig. 18.9).
4. Use the Import From drop-down list and the folders list box to select the drive and folder that contain the Approach file you want to import. Click the folder to open it and display the files within it.

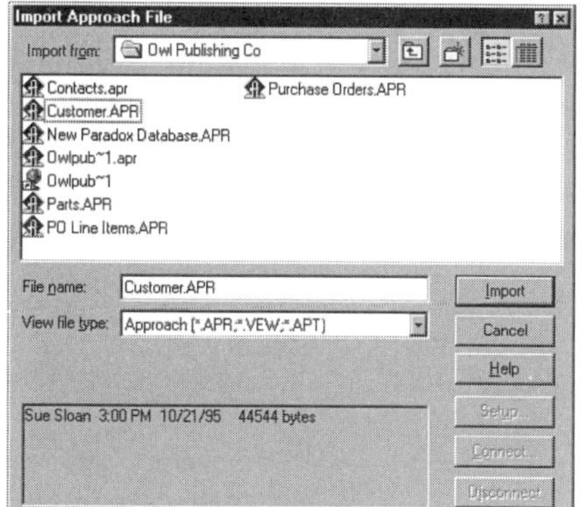

Fig. 18.9

Choose an Approach file to import from the Import Approach File dialog box.

5. Select the Approach file you want to import by clicking its name or by typing it in the File Name text box.
6. Click Import. The Import Approach File Setup dialog box appears (see fig. 18.10).

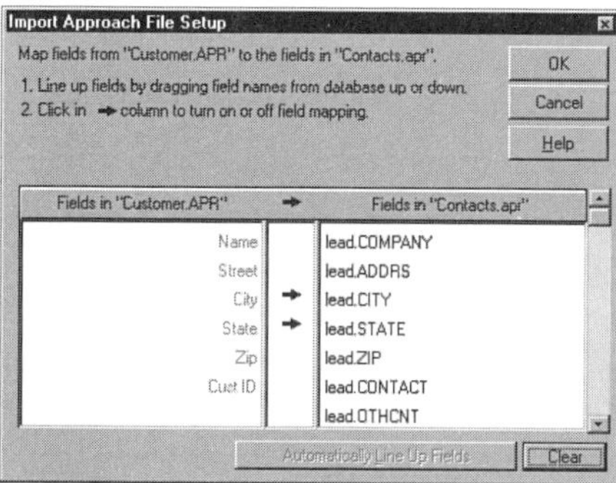

Fig. 18.10

Use the Import Approach File Setup dialog box to map current database fields to those field objects in the imported Approach file.

You use the Import Approach File Setup dialog box to map the field object names in the importing Approach file to the fields in databases available to the open Approach file. To map fields, follow these steps:

1. Any fields that match by name will be mapped automatically. To unmap those fields, click the arrow between them.

> **Note**
>
> If the current open Approach file contains multiple joined databases, all fields are listed by *DATABASENAME:FIELDNAME*. This is different from importing data because the Approach file needs to know which field to display for each field object referenced in the importing Approach file. Also, because you're not importing data, all field objects, including calculated and variable fields, show up in the current open Approach file when the import is completed.

2. Move any field in the current open Approach file, if necessary, so it's directly across from the field object to which it will be mapped. To move a field, click the field so that it's selected. The cursor changes to show that the field can be moved. Drag the field to the new position and release the mouse button. The field you dragged switches places with the field whose position it now occupies.
3. To map the two selected fields, click the arrow column between the two fields so that an arrow appears between them.
4. Repeat steps 1 through 3 for every field you want to map. For a pair of fields to be mapped, they must have an arrow between them.

> **Note**
>
> To clear all field mappings, click the Clear button. To redo all automatic mappings—those based on matching names—click the Automatically Line Up Fields button. (This button is inactive if any fields on the list are already mapped.)

5. Click OK in the Import Approach File Setup dialog box. Approach imports the source Approach file into the current open Approach file. All the views, macros, field objects, and calculated and variable fields in the source Approach file are available for use.

> **Note**
>
> Any fields that aren't mapped when the Approach file is imported appear as `NO FIELD REFERENCE` in Design mode with Show Data mode turned off. With Show Data mode turned on, the unmapped fields are blank. Use the InfoBox to assign database fields to these unmapped fields if you want to use them, or delete them from the views.

Creating Approach Objects for Other Applications

Approach is an object linking and embedding (OLE) server. This means that Approach lets you create objects that can be linked or embedded into another Windows application (called a *container application*). Your OLE object can then be activated—within, for example, a document in AmiPro or Word for Windows—giving you access to an Approach view or application without completely switching to Approach from your current environment.

When you're in a container application, like AmiPro, you can use an Approach OLE object in one of two ways:

- An OLE linked object gives other applications access to a copy of an Approach view or application, but the original object stays in its original source files (an

Approach file with/without databases). When the Approach object is activated in the other application, the linked object is updated to reflect any changes to the original object. In this way, changes you make to the original Approach application are available to the users of the linked object, and the databases are updated in the original source files.

- An OLE embedded object is a copy of the entire object (the Approach file with/without data) embedded in another application. The changes made in that application, to the Approach file or the data, are limited to the application and not reflected in the original source files.

A linked or embedded Approach object can have access to data. It might be helpful to link a commonly used crosstab into a word-processing document, for example, so that the crosstab can be activated and printed whenever the document is used. The document would display the current data and format of the original object in Approach.

The default OLE object created in Approach, such as a form object, is an object with a link to its original database. For it to use that data, the database has to be present.

> **Note**
>
> Approach must be installed on your computer or your network server computer to activate an Approach object.

If the database is no longer present, or if the object is activated on a machine that doesn't have access to the database, the Approach file displays a message that the database can't be found and asks whether you want to open a different one. At this point, you can choose to open the object with a different database or cancel.

An option with an Approach object is to include data within the object. With this option, the person who'll be using the object doesn't need the original database present to view or use the data. Of course, at this point there's no longer a link back to the original data source, so any changes made to this copy won't be reflected in the original.

An Approach object with data is stored as an Approach Transfer file (.APT), which is limited to using existing views and data. To get a fully modifiable copy of the view(s) and data, you can open the File menu and choose Save As to create a fully functional Approach file (.APR) with databases.

Creating an Approach OLE Object in Approach

An Approach object created within Approach has two options for including views—the current view and all views in the Approach file. For either option, there are also five options for including data:

- All databases
- Found set

- Current record
- Blank databases
- No databases

To create an Approach object within Approach, follow these steps:

1. Switch to Browse mode and use the tabs to move to the view you want to use.
2. Open the Edit menu and choose Copy View to open the Copy View to Clipboard dialog box (see fig. 18.11). Choose either to copy the current view only or to copy all views to be embedded in your object, and which data will be included. Then click OK.

> **Note**
>
> Copy View is available only if nothing else (no field or button) is selected in the view. If you see the regular Copy command, press Esc to deselect whatever was selected.

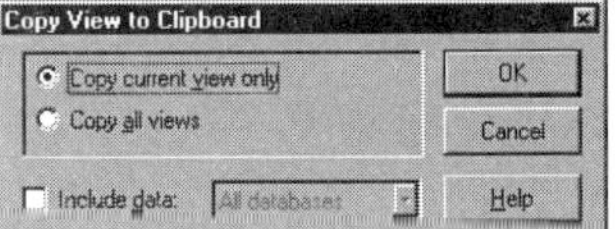

Fig. 18.11

Use the Copy View to Clipboard dialog box in Approach to create OLE objects.

3. Switch to the application where you want to link or embed the Approach object.
4. In the application where you want to paste the object, open the Edit menu and choose Paste Special. The Paste Special dialog box appears, listing the options for pasting in the Approach object (see fig. 18.12).

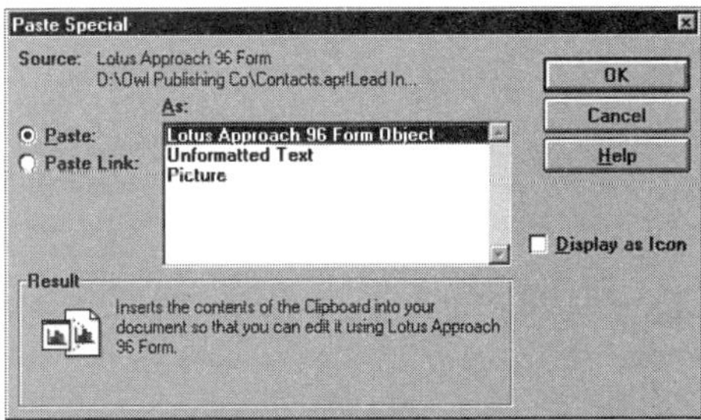

Fig. 18.12

Use the Paste Special dialog box to add an Approach object to a client (container) application.

5. Select the desired option and select Paste or Paste Link. Then Click OK. The object is inserted into the container application (see fig. 18.13).

To activate the Approach object, double-click anywhere within the object. You can also select the object, open the Edit menu, and choose Edit Approach Object.

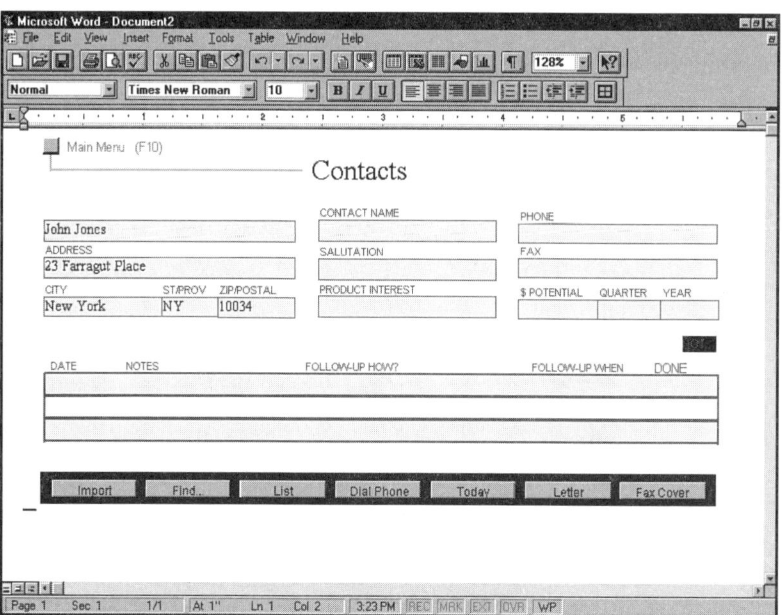

Fig. 18.13

An Approach form object is embedded into a Word for Windows document.

Creating an Approach OLE Object in Another Application

To create an Approach OLE object within a container application, follow these steps:

1. Start by opening the application. From the Insert menu, choose Object. The Object dialog box appears, listing all OLE server applications now installed on your machine (see fig. 18.14).

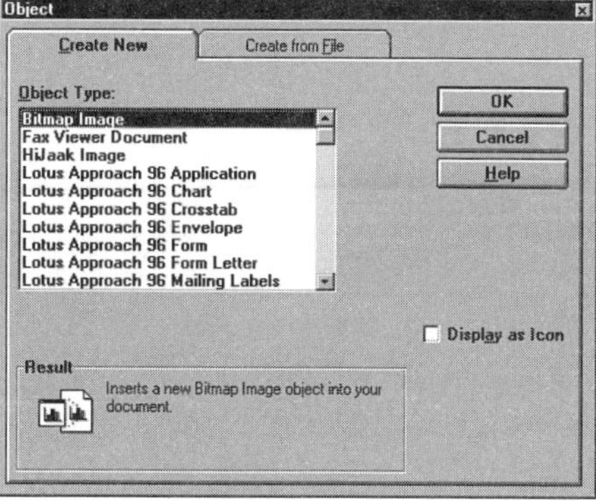

Fig. 18.14

The Object dialog box lists possible object types.

> **Note**
>
> The list of objects that can be created will vary depending on the software installed on your machine. Don't be surprised if your list or your dialog box looks different from the figure.

2. Select the Approach object of your choice, such as an Approach form object. Click OK. This brings up the standard Approach Open dialog box (see fig. 18.15).

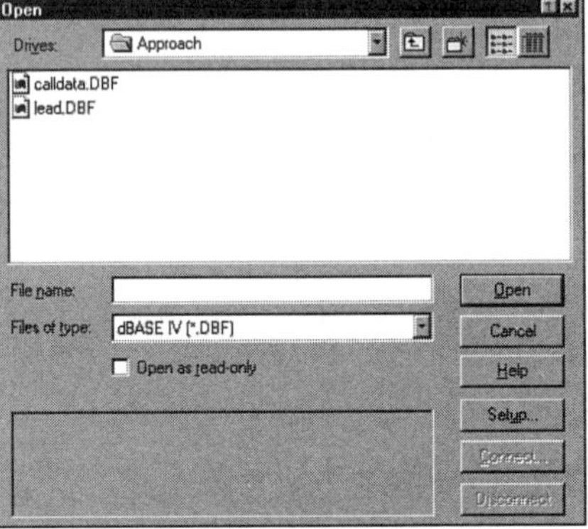

Fig. 18.15

Creating an Approach object starts by opening the database file.

3. Select the file type you're using for the object from the Files of Type drop-down list.
4. Use the Drives drop-down list and the folders list box to select the drive and folder that contain the database you want to use.
5. Select the file you want to use and click Open.
6. The Approach Assistant that's used to create the type of object selected appears. Because the object in this example is an Approach form object, the Approach Form Assistant dialog box opens (see fig. 18.16).

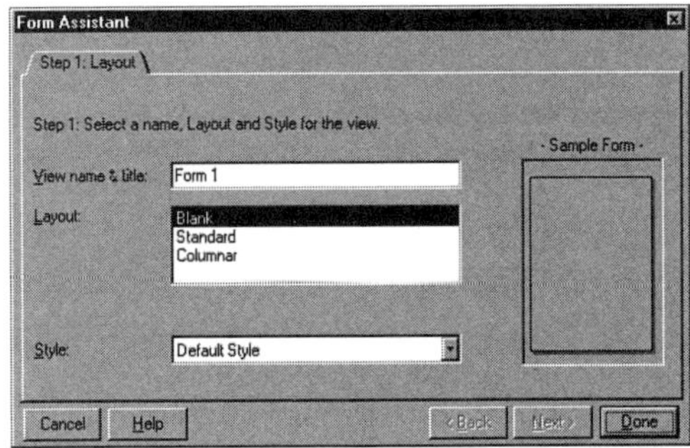

Fig. 18.16

Use the Approach Form Assistant dialog box to create an Approach Form Object.

7. Use the Form Assistant to create the form or object you've selected.

To activate the Approach object, double-click it. You can also select the object, open the Edit menu, and choose Edit Approach Object.

From Here...

As you've learned, much of Approach's versatility lies in its capability to interchange data between different formats. This capability is fully highlighted when doing imports and exports.

By importing Approach files, you can use stored views, macros, and calculated and variable fields from within a different Approach file. You don't need to re-create all the work it took to create the original.

With Approach's OLE capabilities, you can have Approach access your data from within any application that can serve as an OLE client (container application).

To learn more about using Approach with other applications in the Lotus SmartSuite, refer to the following chapter:

- Chapter 19, "Using Approach with Lotus SmartSuite 96," describes how you can use Approach as an OLE client or server for the other applications in the SmartSuite. It can also be used to display, enter, or report on Lotus 1-2-3 spreadsheet data.

CHAPTER 19

Using Approach with Lotus SmartSuite 96

The Windows 95 environment and Lotus SmartSuite 96 integration of applications make it easy to use many different types of applications together. The built-in Windows features of the Clipboard and object linking and embedding (OLE) can instantly share text, graphs, charts, pictures, and database information between applications.

In this chapter, you learn how to

- Use the Lotus SmartCenter to organize and launch your applications, and to access your Lotus Organizer address book and calendar
- Use the Windows Clipboard to copy or cut data from one Lotus application to another
- Use OLE to link information from Lotus 1-2-3 or Word Pro to Approach
- Use the drag-and-drop features of OLE 2 with Approach
- Update OLE-linked information
- Embed a Freelance picture into Approach or embed an Approach database into Word Pro
- Create an Approach report or dynamic crosstab directly from Lotus 1-2-3 data
- Open a named Lotus 1-2-3 range from Approach
- Use a cross-application SmartMaster to quickly implement a common business application

Using the Lotus SmartCenter

The SmartCenter is a set of "drawers" that appears on your desktop after installation of the SmartSuite. Although it can be moved, it's initially placed opposite the Windows 95 taskbar. A drawer can be opened and closed by clicking the drawer front. If you open the SmartSuite drawer, you'll find another level of organization, called *folders*, which can be opened by clicking a folder title. By using the SmartCenter, you can easily find and launch your SmartSuite applications and files, regardless of which window is now active. Although other drawers and folders can be added at any time, the default set is as follows (see fig. 19.1):

- *SmartSuite drawer.* Contains folders with shortcuts to your Lotus applications and SmartMasters. You can launch Approach 96 directly by clicking this drawer and then clicking the Lotus Approach icon in the Lotus Programs folder. You can add non-Lotus application shortcuts to existing or new folders at any time.

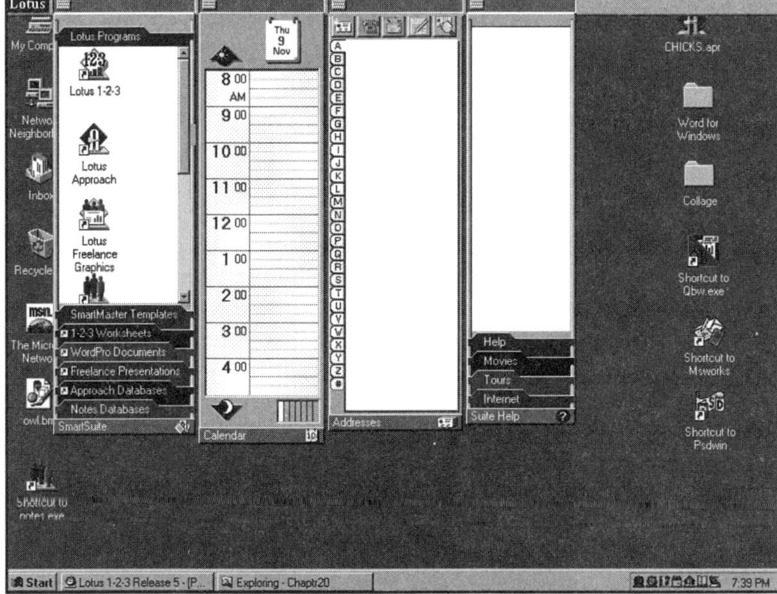

Fig. 19.1

You can easily launch Approach from the Lotus SmartCenter's SmartSuite drawer. The drawer will automatically close so that it doesn't overlay your Approach window.

- *Calendar drawer.* Displays your Organizer calendar, defaulting to today's entries.
- *Addresses drawer.* Lists names of people from your Organizer, Notes, or cc:Mail address book. You can exchange an Approach dBASE-type file with Organizer by using the import and export methods discussed in Chapter 18, "Importing and Exporting Files."
- *SuiteHelp drawer.* Contains a variety of online help in folders. In addition to regular help text, there are ScreenCam movies, tours of the products, and access to the IBM and Lotus home pages on the Internet.

Note

If you installed the SmartSuite from CD-ROM, the printed manuals you bought are brief introductions only. To access the full product documentation, you must install the DocOnline feature, which adds a folder to the SuiteHelp drawer and installs the Acrobat Reader 2.1 to let you view and print the manuals from the CD-ROM.

Adding an Approach Application to the SmartCenter

You can add your own drawer to the Lotus SmartCenter. Lotus provides an Add Assistant to guide you through the steps for creating a new drawer. Follow these steps:

1. Click the cabinet menu button (the Lotus button at the left end of the SmartCenter).
2. Choose Add Drawer from the menu. The Add Drawer dialog box appears, showing the Step 1: Type page.
3. Select a drawer type from the Pick the Drawer Type list box; choose File Type for this drawer.
4. Click Next or the Step 2: Basics tab to go to the next page.
5. Type a name in the Drawer Label text box and select a drawer handle from those available from the Drawer Handle drop-down list.
6. Click Done. Your new drawer appears at the right side of the existing drawers in the SmartCenter.
7. Drag and drop the drawer anywhere you want it in the SmartCenter.

Adding a Folder to the SmartCenter

You can also add folders to the SmartSuite and SuiteHelp drawers, or to a file type drawer you've created yourself. Follow these steps:

1. Click the file drawer you just added to the SmartCenter to open it.
2. Right-click the gray area at the top of the open file drawer to display a menu of options for the drawer.
3. Choose Add Folder from the menu that appears.
4. From the Browse for Folder dialog box, click a folder, such as Owl Publishing's folder, to add as a new divider.

> **Tip**
>
> You can also drag a folder from your desktop and drop it into an open folder drawer.

5. Click OK. The contents of the selected folder appear as icons in your new SmartCenter folder. These are now available for you to use as shortcuts to the files and applications that folder contains (see fig. 19.2).
6. Click the front of the file drawer to close it.

Fig. 19.2

Owl Publishing has its own drawer in the Lotus SmartCenter.

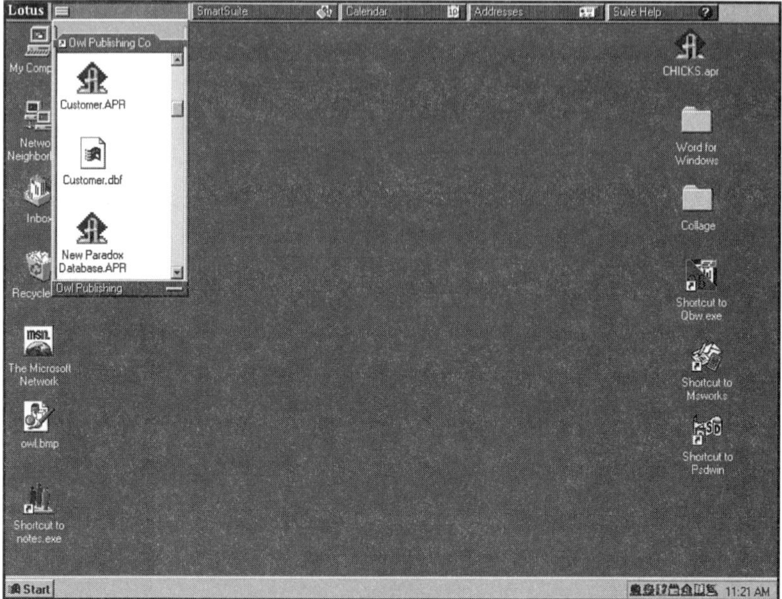

Sharing Data with Approach

The entire Lotus SmartSuite 96 and nearly all Windows 95 applications allow you to take advantage of certain data-sharing techniques. For example, if you want to send a company letter, you can create your logo in Freelance, include a performance chart from Lotus 1-2-3 that's based on a database you created in Approach, and type your letter in Word Pro. All the pieces of your letter could be created in their respective applications and linked together for a complete printout. By integrating with Word Pro, 1-2-3, and Freelance, Approach lets you easily take advantage of the Windows Clipboard and OLE.

By using the Clipboard, you can directly cut text and images from any application and paste them into an Approach view. For example, you can create your company logo by using Freelance 96 and paste it directly onto your Approach company invoice form. You can also take any Approach view and copy it into another application. For example, you could include a form you created in Approach for a survey in the letter you create in Word Pro.

OLE is an advanced tool that lets you share objects between applications and modify the information that an object represents using the original program. There are two methods for sharing objects using OLE:

- *Embedding* your company logo into an Approach invoice form allows you to store the logo object directly in the actual Approach form. You can then access the program it was created in directly from the embedded logo object, make changes to it, and have those changes saved in the Approach form.

- *Linking* your company logo into an Approach form is similar to embedding, except the object isn't stored in the actual Approach form. You can display linked objects on your form as an icon, or you can see the contents of the object—the company logo, in this example. You would use linking for objects that belong to another application, such as a company spreadsheet that's updated by another department. That way, you would always have current information displayed in your Approach form.

OLE 2 adds drag-and-drop capability between applications that support it. For example, you can drag a 1-2-3 range and drop it into an Approach view.

Note

Both applications must support OLE drag-and-drop for this to work. Consult your application's documentation to see if this is supported and how the resulting object is handled in that application.

With 1-2-3, Approach is more closely integrated because the two applications are natural partners in managing and analyzing data arranged in tables. Installing Approach 96 adds additional menu commands to 1-2-3 that let you directly access some of Approach's powerful database features. From 1-2-3 you can directly create Approach forms, reports, crosstabs, and mailing labels. Don't forget that Approach also lets you access tabled 1-2-3 information as a database type if you need to use the entire set of data in the 1-2-3 file.

Using the Clipboard

The Windows Clipboard is the broadest and easiest way to share information between two separate applications. All Windows programs support the Clipboard for inter-application data copying. By using the Edit menu's Copy and Cut commands, you can place data from virtually any application into the Clipboard. The Clipboard can hold text, graphics, tables, charts, and bitmaps. The only limitation to what the Clipboard can hold is your PC's available memory.

After you copy your data into the Clipboard, you can view, save, or use the information in another Windows application. To view or save the data in the Clipboard, open the Clipboard Viewer (from the Windows Start menu, choose Programs, Accessories, and then Clipboard Viewer). To put the data into a different application, simply switch to that application and choose Paste from the Edit menu. The data stored in the Clipboard is pasted onto your screen as a part of your current view in Approach.

The data pasted into your application is a *duplicate* of the data you copied to the Clipboard. There are no links between the original and duplicate. Changes made to the data copied from the source application aren't reflected in the original application.

Copying and Pasting Information from Freelance to Approach

It's easy to use the Clipboard to copy desired information. To copy a logo from Freelance into an Approach application, follow these steps:

1. Open the Freelance file that contains the logo you want to copy.
2. Select the logo using the Freelance Pointer tool.
3. From Freelance, open the Edit menu and choose Copy (or press Ctrl+C) to copy the logo to the Windows Clipboard (see fig. 19.3).

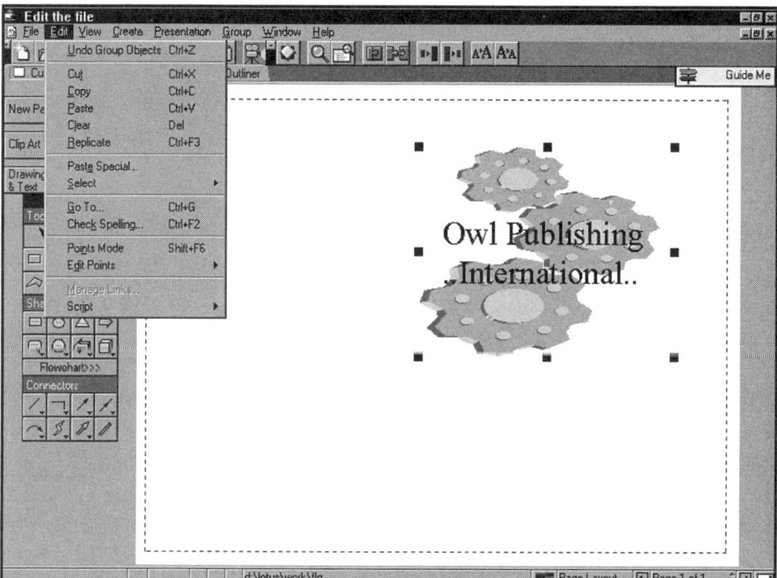

Fig. 19.3

After selecting the logo, copy it to the Windows Clipboard.

4. Open the Approach file that you want to paste the logo into and make sure that you're in Design mode on the view where you want to put the logo.
5. Open the Edit menu and choose Paste (or press Ctrl+V) to paste the logo from the Windows Clipboard (see fig. 19.4).
6. Use your mouse to resize and move the logo on your Approach form.

Copying and Pasting Information from Approach to 1-2-3

You can also use the Windows Clipboard to paste Approach information into other SmartSuite applications. For example, when you paste an Approach form into Word Pro, you get an image of the form framed by a Word Pro image box.

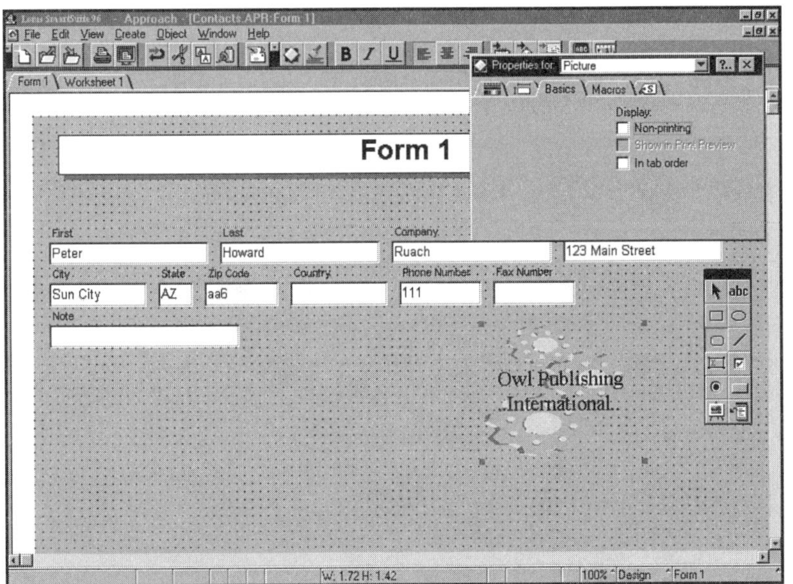

Fig. 19.4

Paste the logo onto your Approach form and resize it to fit the space on the form.

Pasting an Approach view into Lotus 1-2-3 can offer extra benefits. Since Approach's worksheets and 1-2-3's spreadsheets are in column format, you can paste Approach database information directly into 1-2-3 rows and columns. This way, you easily can analyze your data and make complex graphs and charts by using 1-2-3's full power. Although you can copy other Approach views (forms, reports, mailing labels, charts, crosstabs, and form letters) into 1-2-3, the worksheet is the most useful.

To copy an Approach worksheet into a 1-2-3 spreadsheet, follow these steps:

1. Open the Approach application and access the worksheet you want to copy from.
2. Open Approach's Edit menu and choose Select All to highlight the entire view.
3. Open Approach's Edit menu and choose Copy, or press Ctrl+C (see fig. 19.5).

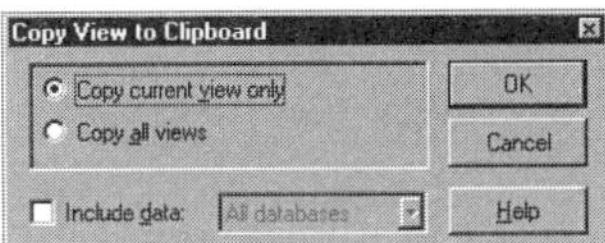

Fig. 19.5

After choosing Copy, you can copy only the current view or all the views in the application to the Windows Clipboard.

The worksheet is copied to the Windows Clipboard. You can see the current data in the Windows Clipboard by using the Windows Clipboard Viewer (see fig. 19.6).

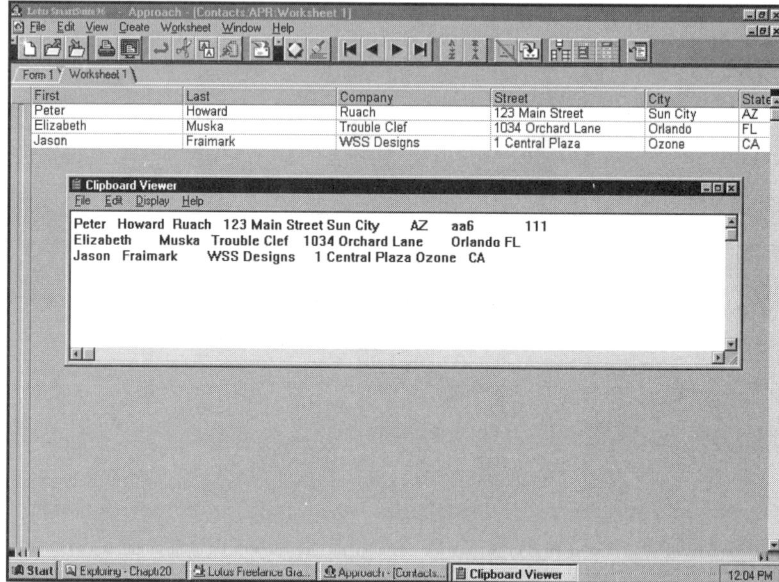

Fig. 19.6

This is how your worksheet will look in the Windows Clipboard Viewer.

4. Open the 1-2-3 spreadsheet into which you want to paste the view.
5. In 1-2-3, open the Edit menu and choose Paste to paste the Approach view from the Windows Clipboard into the 1-2-3 row-and-column format (see fig. 19.7).

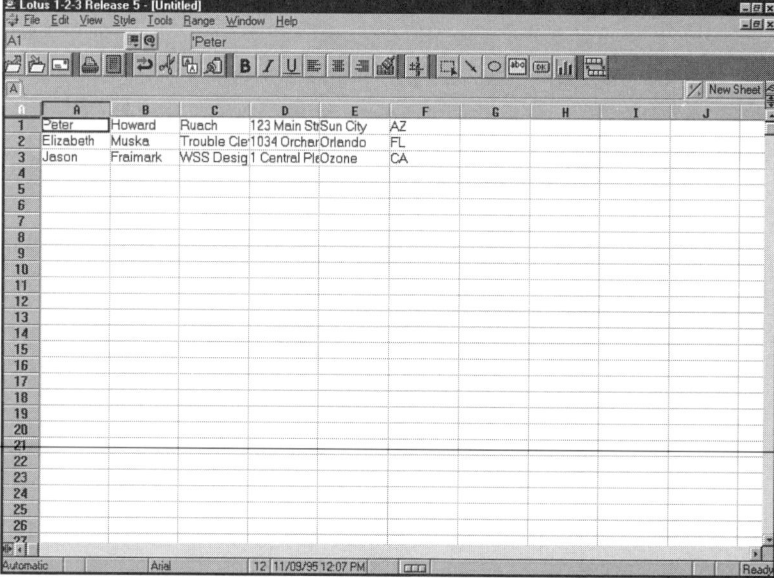

Fig. 19.7

Paste the Approach worksheet data directly into 1-2-3 as rows and columns.

Using Object Linking and Embedding (OLE)

Although the Clipboard allows wide flexibility of data sharing by copying the data from one Windows application to another, OLE takes sharing to another level. By using OLE, you can share the same copy of the data between applications, and maintain the data for all the applications at one time using the original Windows program where the data was created.

Linking and embedding are similar concepts, but there's an important difference between the two. Linking creates an image of your data (or an icon representing it) in an application other than the one it was created with. Embedding your data actually stores the original data in another application's file.

For example, you can link the logo you created in Freelance to an Approach form. To change the logo in the future, you can simply change the Freelance file rather than repaste an updated logo into Approach. In this example, you can see and print the logo in Approach, and an actual link is placed in your Approach file connecting the logo object to the Freelance file containing the logo. This link is regularly updated and the changes made to the Freelance file are immediately visible in your Approach form. To access Freelance directly from Approach, go into Design mode and double-click the logo object.

> **Note**
>
> For links to keep working, linked files must be kept in their original locations. These linked files can be numerous and difficult to track. Also, information is automatically updated in the linked files without your control.

Linked objects are primarily useful if you have data that's common to many applications and might change in the future. Such changes would automatically change the linked applications to provide the most current data. It's also beneficial to link your applications together if you have many programs that use the same data. This saves you time and maintains continuity in your files. If your logo is used in Approach, Word Pro, Freelance, and 1-2-3 for various reports and letters, for example, it is easier to change the logo in one file and have those changes reflected in all your applications.

Embedding also allows you to share information between Windows applications. When you share Windows data using embedding, the information is directly inserted into the indicated program file. Whereas linking stores a connection to a file, embedding stores a copy of the actual data file (logo in this case) in the Approach file for the form you embedded it into. No link is established to the original data file. Any changes made to the original data file aren't reflected in the embedded data.

However, you can still change the embedded logo data. Because all the information necessary is stored in the Approach file, you can automatically open Freelance from

Approach. The embedded information appears in Freelance in a window where changes can be made. These changes are saved directly into the Approach file and don't change the original logo file.

Embedding is particularly useful when you need to move your Approach files from one machine to another. Embedding data into Approach gives you the flexibility to decide when information is updated (linked data will update automatically). Also, you use only one Approach file to store information from multiple applications, which allows you to move the file to different computers. One drawback to embedding is the increased size of the Approach file containing the embedded data.

Linking Data with Approach

Linking data between Lotus SmartSuite applications is an important part of application design and development in Approach. You can, in effect, use the "right tool for the right job," thus improving your productivity and possibly that of those who use your applications.

Linking 1-2-3 Information into Approach

If a set of numbers is normally or more easily maintained in 1-2-3, and you need to keep your copy of that data in your Approach application current, you need to link the data. To create a link in Approach from 1-2-3 data, follow these steps:

1. Open the 1-2-3 file you want to link to Approach.
2. Highlight the 1-2-3 cells you want to link to in your Approach application (see fig. 19.8).

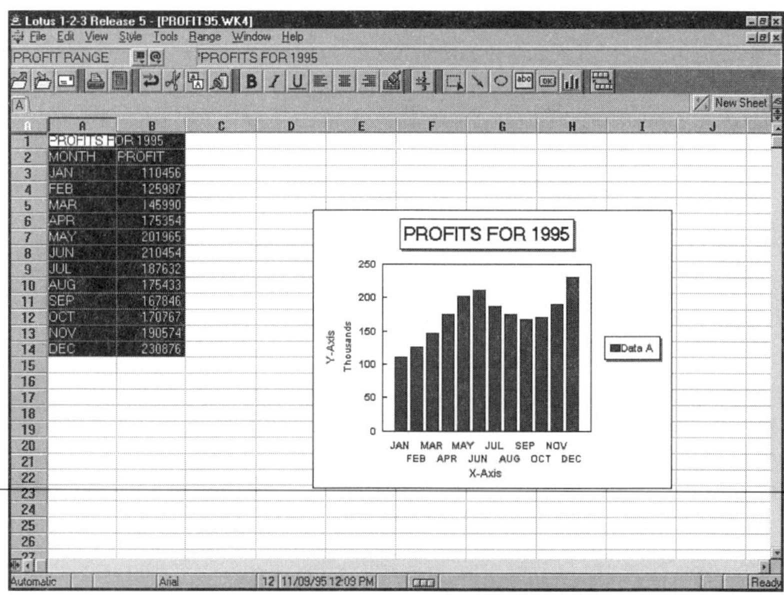

Fig. 19.8

Select the 1-2-3 cells that you want to link to Approach.

3. Open the Edit menu and choose Copy to copy the 1-2-3 information to the Windows Clipboard.
4. Open your Approach application and switch to Design mode on a form where you want the 1-2-3 data to appear.

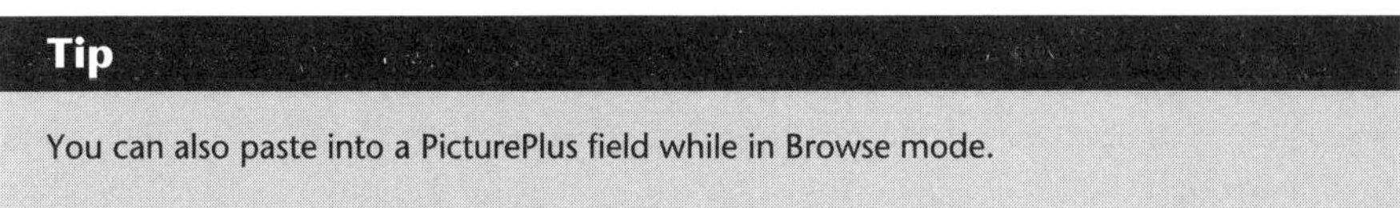
Tip

You can also paste into a PicturePlus field while in Browse mode.

5. Open Approach's Edit menu and choose Paste Special to open the Paste Special dialog box.
6. Select Paste Link to create a link to the original 1-2-3 document and then click OK (see fig. 19.9).
7. Your linked data should now appear in your Approach form (see fig. 19.10).

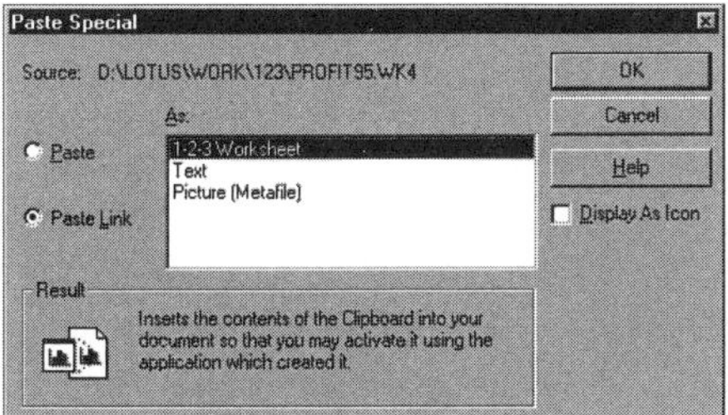

Fig. 19.9

Select Paste Link to create a link between the 1-2-3 file and Approach.

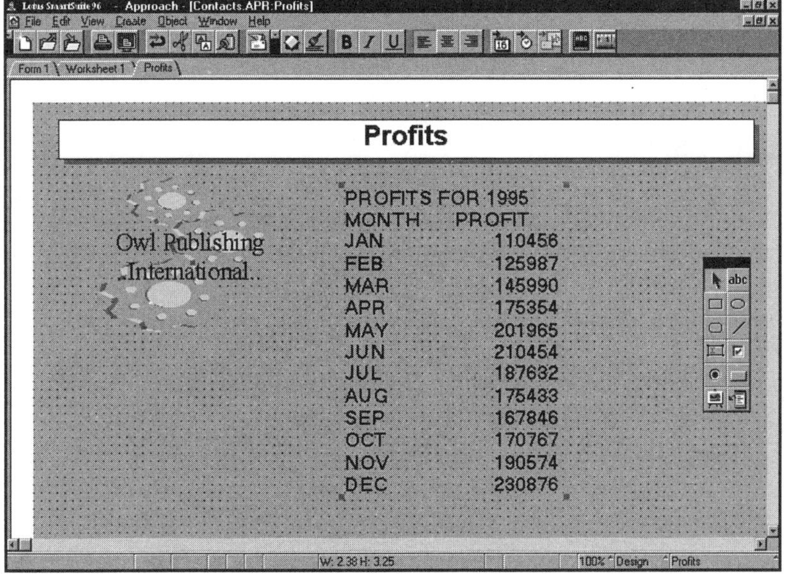

Fig. 19.10

You can reposition and resize the linked data as needed in your Approach view.

> **Note**
>
> In Approach, the mouse pointer changes into a hand shape when it's positioned over linked or embedded information.

Updating Linked Information

You can easily update your linked 1-2-3 information from Approach. Through Approach you can start 1-2-3, modify your information, and have those changes reflected in your Approach form.

To update your linked 1-2-3 information from Approach, follow these steps:

1. Open your Approach application with 1-2-3 data linked to it. (Make sure that you're in Design mode or accessing a PicturePlus field in Browse mode.)
2. Double-click the 1-2-3 linked data object to launch 1-2-3 with your linked file.
3. Make the appropriate changes in 1-2-3.
4. Save the changes, exit 1-2-3, and notice the updated information in Approach.

Linking Approach Data to Word Pro

Not only can you link SmartSuite files to Approach, but you can link your Approach databases to other Lotus applications. For example, you can link an Approach worksheet to a Word Pro document so that the data will appear in the document. By linking the information to Word Pro, if you add, modify, or delete database records, your Word Pro document will reflect the most current Approach information.

To create an Approach link in Word Pro, follow these steps:

1. Open your Approach application and select the worksheet you want to link to Word Pro.
2. In Approach, open the Edit menu and choose Select All to highlight the entire view.
3. Open the Edit menu and choose Copy to copy the current worksheet into the Windows Clipboard.
4. Open the Word Pro document into which you want to link the Approach data.
5. Open Word Pro's Edit menu, choose Paste Special, and then select Paste Link to paste the Approach link into Word Pro. The information automatically appears in a Word Pro frame.
6. Size the frame to use in your Word Pro document (see fig. 19.11).

Linking by Using OLE 2 Drag-and-Drop

Approach 96, as well as 1-2-3 and Word Pro, supports the OLE 2 drag-and-drop method for linking objects with other applications. By using the 1-2-3 data selected earlier in figure 19.8, you can drag the range highlighted into your Approach application by following these steps:

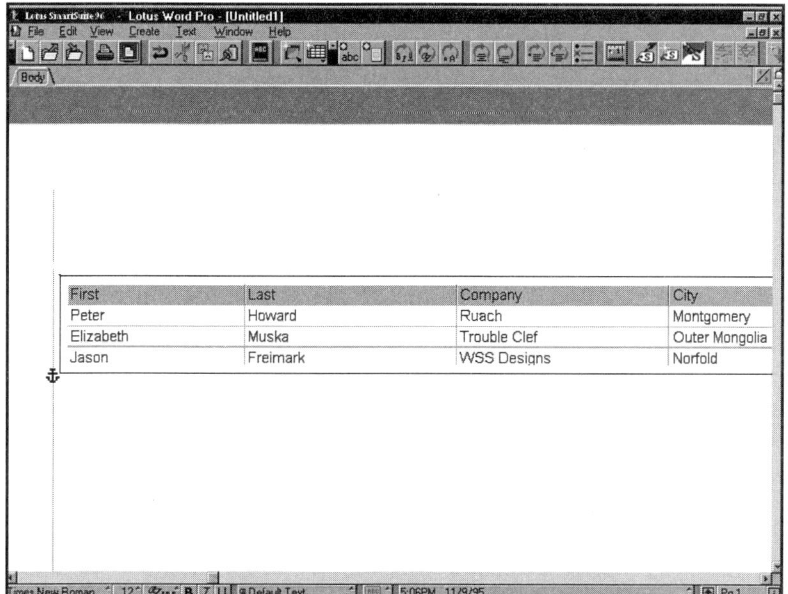

Fig. 19.11

The OLE-linked Approach object appears in a frame in your Word Pro document and will stay current with your Approach database.

1. Open your Approach application, and select the view in which you want to place the linked 1-2-3 data. Make sure that you're in Design mode; then minimize the application to the Windows 95 taskbar.
2. Open the 1-2-3 application that contains the data range desired. Highlight the range.
3. Drag the range from 1-2-3 to the Approach button on the Windows 95 taskbar.

   To do this, move the mouse pointer over the edge of the object to be dragged. When the mouse pointer changes into a hand shape, start the drag-and-drop operation by holding down the left mouse button and moving the mouse pointer, dragging the object with you. Don't release the button until you're ready to drop the object in your Approach view.
4. The Approach application window appears. Position your mouse pointer where you want the data and drop it by releasing the mouse button.

If you do the drag-and-drop from 1-2-3 and don't have an Approach application file in Design mode, Approach creates a new application including the Blank Database form and Worksheet 1 for your 1-2-3 data range.

Updating Approach Links

After you create a link between Approach and an object created by another application, that connection is saved with the Approach file. The default settings for creating a link ensure that updates to the linked data automatically occur in your Approach application.

Sometimes you need to change the link options, however. If your linked Freelance file is moved to a new disk location and you want Approach to keep the link active to the new location, you'll want to change the link source file. Sometimes you won't want Approach to automatically update linked files, or even break the link between the applications entirely.

You can easily accomplish these tasks through Approach by using the Links dialog box. From this dialog box, you can change the default link update status, change the link source file, or completely break the link.

To make these changes, open your Approach file with the linked object in it and make sure that you're in Design mode. Open the Edit menu and choose Manage Links to bring up the Links dialog box (see fig. 19.12). Select the link to be modified from those displayed in the As list box.

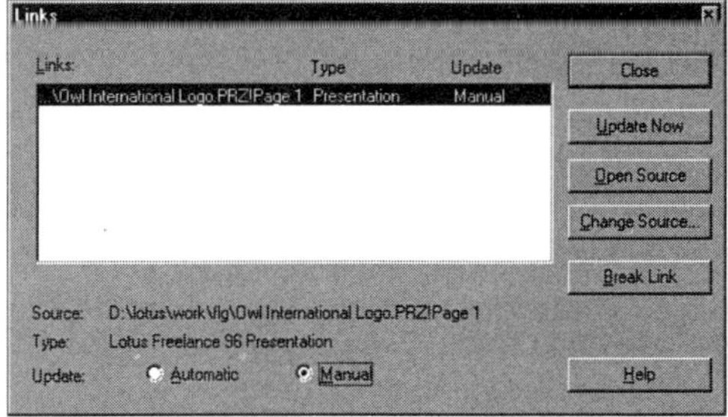

Fig. 19.12

Click the Manual radio button to disable the automatic link for updates for the selected link.

> **Note**
>
> If the linked object you want to change is in a PicturePlus field in your database, you must be in Browse mode to update it. Display the record that contains the object on a form and select the PicturePlus field to identify which object you want to modify. Then proceed as described here for other types of linked objects.

Sometimes you don't want Approach to automatically update from your linked document. If you're making multiple modifications to your company logo and using Approach at the same time, you may want to disable the automatic link update command until all your changes are finished. This helps ease the load on your computer's memory because Approach won't constantly update the files linked to it. To disable the automatic link update command, first select the link you want to modify in the

Links dialog box. Click the Manual radio button to have Approach update your linked documents at your manual command. Of course, the link is still maintained, and you can switch it back to automatic update any time in the future.

After switching the link update mode from Automatic to Manual, you must manually refresh Approach to reflect updated linked information. If you click the Update Now button in the Links dialog box, Approach updates your selected link.

If you want to change a linked document, you can click the Open Source button in the Links dialog box. This command opens the original application where this object was created using the linked data. You can also double-click the linked object directly from Approach when in Design mode to launch the original application.

Sometimes you may need to update the actual link between Approach and the data file. If you reorganize your hard drive or place a file on a server, you need to tell Approach of the new location. To do so, click the Change Source button in the Links dialog box. Approach then allows you to scan through your hard drive and select a different file to link to.

Note

If you change an Approach link to an incorrect file, you lose the ability to update that information automatically. Change the link source again to the correct file to regain object linking update capabilities.

Finally, sometimes you may want to break your link between Approach and the other application permanently. By breaking the link, you still retain the data image in your Approach file. Any changes made to the linked file won't update your Approach file. To break your link, click the Break Link button in Approach's Links dialog box.

Tip

To make your linked changes permanent, you must save your Approach file. That way, if you accidentally update or break a link or change the source to the wrong file, you can revert to your last saved version.

Embedding Data into Approach

Object embedding allows you to store another application's data directly in an Approach file. By embedding the data, you can move your Approach files to different machines without worrying about links to other files. You also can still make changes to the data using the original application, as long as that application is installed on the new machine.

Embedding a Freelance Object into Approach

Because of Freelance's built-in drawing and presentation development capabilities, you may want to use it to create an image or an entire presentation of images and embed that object in your Approach application. To embed a Freelance object into Approach, follow these steps:

1. Create your Freelance logo, image, or presentation.
2. Open Freelance's View menu and choose Page Sorter to view all your Freelance slides in the current presentation.

> **Note**
>
> You must be in Page Sorter mode to embed a Freelance presentation into Approach. If you select a single page's symbol and try to copy it into the Windows Clipboard, Approach doesn't recognize it as a specific Freelance file, and the image pasted isn't an embedded file.

3. Open the Edit menu and choose Copy (or press Ctrl+C) to copy the presentation into the Clipboard.
4. Open the Approach file into which you want to place the embedded presentation, and enter Design mode on the desired view.
5. Open the Edit menu and choose Paste Special to open the Paste Special dialog box (see fig. 19.13).
6. Make sure that the Paste radio button is selected and then click OK. The Freelance presentation is embedded into Approach.

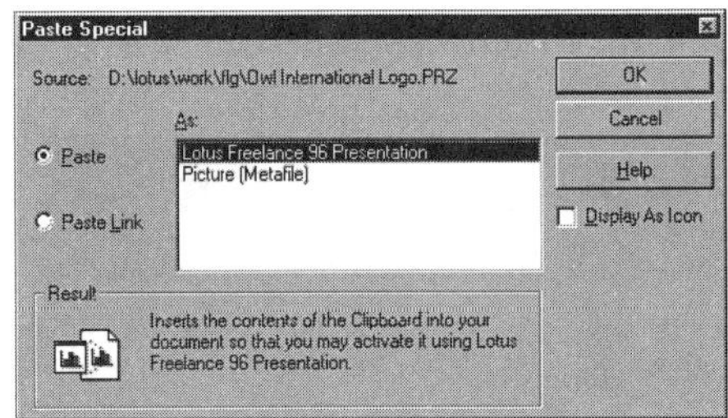

Fig. 19.13

Choose Paste to embed the Freelance presentation into Approach.

Embedding an Approach View into Word Pro

You can also embed an Approach view into other SmartSuite applications. This saves you the time involved in retyping a worksheet or form in Word Pro. In this case, you aren't expecting the document to be kept current with the data; otherwise, you would have used a link and sent the document on disk or via e-mail.

To embed an Approach view into a Word Pro document, follow these steps:

1. Open the Approach file that you want to embed and access a worksheet view.
2. Open Approach's Edit menu and choose Select All to highlight the entire view.
3. Open the Edit menu and choose Copy (or press Ctrl+C).

> **Note**
>
> If you were copying a view other than a worksheet, you would choose Copy View from the Edit menu.

4. The Copy View to Clipboard dialog box appears. Select Copy This View Only to copy your current view into the Clipboard.
5. Open a Word Pro document and choose Paste Special from the Edit menu.
6. Choose the Paste radio button and then select Lotus Approach 96 Worksheet Object type from the As list box to embed the Approach view into Word Pro (see fig. 19.14).

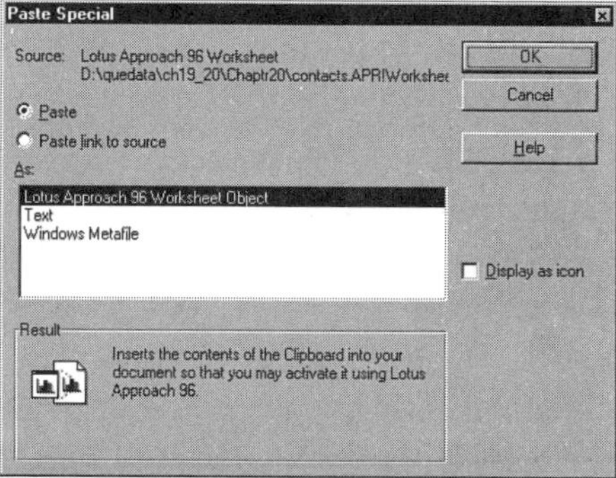

Fig. 19.14

Choose Lotus Approach 96 Worksheet Object to embed an Approach worksheet view into Word Pro.

> **Tip**
>
> Word Pro automatically creates a frame when the file is embedded into it. You can use the mouse to resize this frame to make it easier to use in your document.

7. Double-click the object to open Approach with the embedded data in it (see fig. 19.15).

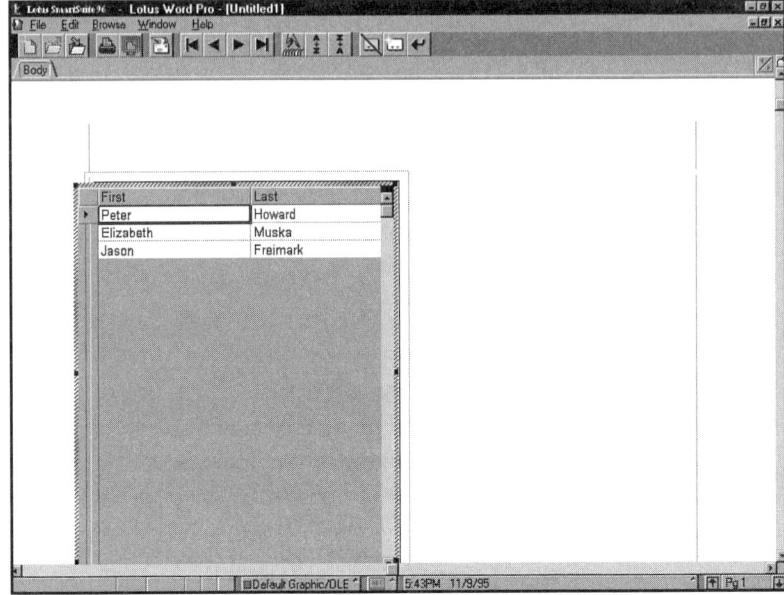

Fig. 19.15

Notice that the items on the menu bar and the SmartIcons are from Approach, even if the title bar still states that you're in Word Pro when you access an embedded Approach object in Word Pro.

Advanced Integration with Lotus 1-2-3

Besides using the Windows Clipboard and OLE features, Approach also provides additional built-in functionality for Lotus 1-2-3 users.

During installation, if Approach detects 1-2-3 on your system, extra menu commands are added to 1-2-3. This happens automatically when installing SmartSuite 96 too. These new commands allow you to use Approach's Form Assistant, Report Assistant, Crosstab Assistant, and Mailing List Assistant features in 1-2-3. To access these commands, open 1-2-3's Tools menu and choose Database.

Select the 1-2-3 information you want to use with your mouse, and run one of these new commands. Approach is automatically started, and you can create new forms, reports, crosstabs, and mailing lists with 1-2-3 data. When you finish using Approach, the new object is automatically embedded into your 1-2-3 spreadsheet.

You can also open named 1-2-3 ranges directly from Approach. By using these named ranges, you can load data into your spreadsheet directly from Approach.

Creating a Report Directly from 1-2-3 Data

Use one of the new 1-2-3 commands installed with Approach to create a report directly from your spreadsheet data. Select the columns you want to use to create a report, and then open Approach's Report Assistant from 1-2-3. Add the fields you want, and let Approach create a complete report for you!

To create a sample report from 1-2-3 information, follow these steps:

1. Create your 1-2-3 spreadsheet. Ensure that each column is named. Approach uses the column name as a field name.
2. Select the cells from which you want to create your report, including the titles.

> **Note**
>
> Your columns must have text labels in them. Approach uses these labels as field names that you can place on your report. Without column labels, 1-2-3 won't start Report Assistant.

3. In 1-2-3, open the Tools menu and choose Database and then Report to start Approach and access the Report Assistant dialog box (see fig. 19.16).

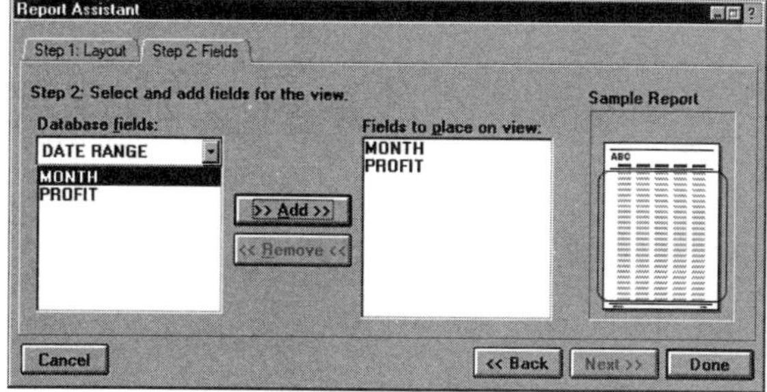

Fig. 19.16

Choose the 1-2-3 columns from the range you want to place in your Approach report.

4. Select the report type you want to use, add the desired fields to your report form, and click the Done button. Approach automatically creates the report for you (see fig. 19.17).
5. Once you exit Approach, an embedded file icon appears in 1-2-3. You can double-click this icon to access your newly created report.

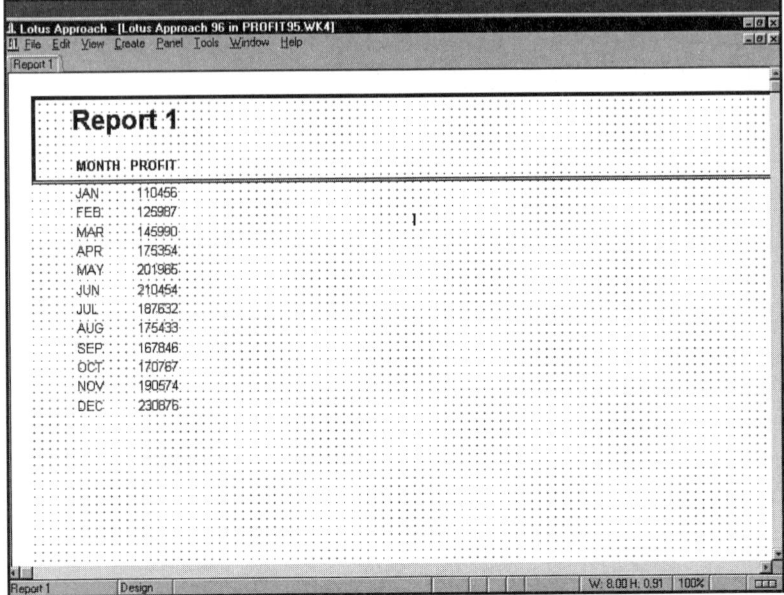

Fig. 19.17

Your newly created report appears in Approach.

Opening a Named 1-2-3 Range from Approach

Approach also lets you open a named 1-2-3 range. You can easily set up a named range in your 1-2-3 spreadsheet to open under Approach by selecting the cells that you want in the named 1-2-3 range, using 1-2-3 to name the range, and then opening the range from Approach.

To create and open a named 1-2-3 range from Approach, follow these steps:

1. Open your 1-2-3 spreadsheet.
2. Select the cells you want included in the named range.

> **Note**
>
> You must have text column headers for your highlighted cells so that 1-2-3 can correctly save the named range.

3. From 1-2-3, open the Range menu and choose Name. Enter an appropriate name for your data range in the Name text box and click OK.
4. Start Approach and open the File menu and choose Open (or press Ctrl+O).
5. Scroll through the Files of Type drop-down list in the Open dialog box and select 1-2-3 Ranges (*).
6. Your 1-2-3 spreadsheet file automatically appears in the Drives text box, and you can see the list of named ranges in that file in the middle of the Open dialog box. Select the named range and click OK (see fig. 19.18).

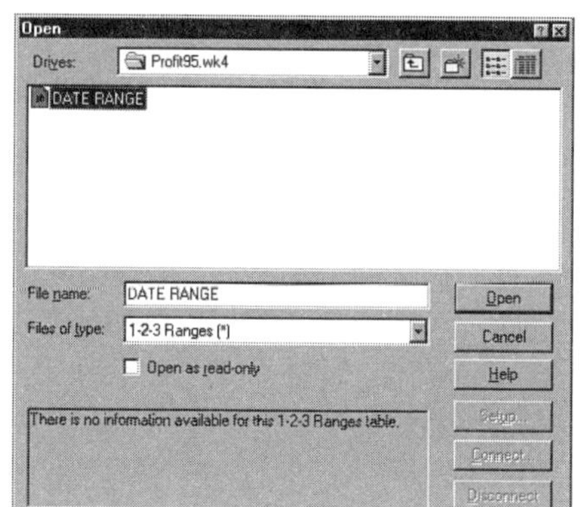

Fig. 19.18

Select 1-2-3 Ranges (*) and then highlight the named range that you want Approach to open.

Using Cross-Application SmartMasters

The SmartSuite drawer in the SmartCenter contains cross-application SmartMasters. Each SmartMaster provides a template for a common business application using two or more SmartSuite programs with shared data objects like those discussed in this chapter.

To use a SmartMaster, just open the SmartMaster Templates folder in the SmartSuite drawer and click the one that appears to match your needs most closely. You can then tailor the application using the skills you've developed in this book.

From Here...

In this chapter, you learned how to use the integrated features of the Lotus SmartSuite with Approach 96. By using the Windows Clipboard, you can copy data back and forth between multiple applications. Object linking and embedding gives you the advanced flexibility to share and update information. You can update and link graphics, text, and spreadsheets into Approach files, and modify them with their original application.

You also learned how to use some of the features more closely integrated between 1-2-3 and Approach. Approach can directly access 1-2-3 data and create powerful reports, forms, and mailing lists with a few mouse clicks. To learn more about using Approach with OLE, refer to the following chapters:

- Chapter 9, "Designing Advanced Forms," describes embedding OLE objects in forms and reports.
- Chapter 17, "Customizing Approach," discusses adding custom controls to your applications using OLE.
- Chapter 18, "Importing and Exporting Files," also describes OLE and explains more about how OLE works.

Index

Symbols

A

B

C

D

E

F

G

H

L

M

N

O

P

Q

R

S

T

U

V

W

X

Y

Z

Complete and Return this Card for a *FREE* Computer Book Catalog

Thank you for purchasing this book! You have purchased a superior computer book written expressly for your needs. To continue to provide the kind of up-to-date, pertinent coverage you've come to expect from us, we need to hear from you. Please take a minute to complete and return this self-addressed, postage-paid form. In return, we'll send you a free catalog of all our computer books on topics ranging from word processing to programming and the internet.

Mr. ☐ Mrs. ☐ Ms. ☐ Dr. ☐

Name (first) ☐ (M.I.) ☐ (last) ☐

Address ☐

City ☐ State ☐ Zip ☐

Phone ☐ Fax ☐

Company Name ☐

E-mail address ☐

1. Please check at least (3) influencing factors for purchasing this book.

- Front or back cover information on book ☐
- Special approach to the content ☐
- Completeness of content ☐
- Author's reputation ☐
- Publisher's reputation ☐
- Book cover design or layout ☐
- Index or table of contents of book ☐
- Price of book ☐
- Special effects, graphics, illustrations ☐
- Other (Please specify): ______ ☐

2. How did you first learn about this book?

- Saw in Macmillan Computer Publishing catalog ☐
- Recommended by store personnel ☐
- Saw the book on bookshelf at store ☐
- Recommended by a friend ☐
- Received advertisement in the mail ☐
- Saw an advertisement in: ______ ☐
- Read book review in: ______ ☐
- Other (Please specify): ______ ☐

3. How many computer books have you purchased in the last six months?

- This book only ☐
- 3 to 5 books ☐
- 2 books ☐
- More than 5 ☐

4. Where did you purchase this book?

- Bookstore ☐
- Computer Store ☐
- Consumer Electronics Store ☐
- Department Store ☐
- Office Club ☐
- Warehouse Club ☐
- Mail Order ☐
- Direct from Publisher ☐
- Internet site ☐
- Other (Please specify): ______ ☐

5. How long have you been using a computer?

- ☐ Less than 6 months
- ☐ 6 months to a year
- ☐ 1 to 3 years
- ☐ More than 3 years

6. What is your level of experience with personal computers and with the subject of this book?

	With PCs	With subject of book
New	☐	☐
Casual	☐	☐
Accomplished	☐	☐
Expert	☐	☐

Source Code ISBN: 0-7897-0208-8

7. Which of the following best describes your job title?

Administrative Assistant ☐
Coordinator ☐
Manager/Supervisor ☐
Director ☐
Vice President ☐
President/CEO/COO ☐
Lawyer/Doctor/Medical Professional ☐
Teacher/Educator/Trainer ☐
Engineer/Technician ☐
Consultant ☐
Not employed/Student/Retired ☐
Other (Please specify): ______________ ☐

8. Which of the following best describes the area of the company your job title falls under?

Accounting ☐
Engineering ☐
Manufacturing ☐
Operations ☐
Marketing ☐
Sales ☐
Other (Please specify): ______________ ☐

9. What is your age?

Under 20 ☐
21-29 ☐
30-39 ☐
40-49 ☐
50-59 ☐
60-over ☐

10. Are you:

Male ☐
Female ☐

11. Which computer publications do you read regularly? (Please list)

____

Comments: ______________________________

Fold here and scotch-tape to mail.

NO POSTAGE NECESSARY IF MAILED IN THE UNITED STATES

BUSINESS REPLY MAIL
FIRST-CLASS MAIL PERMIT NO. 9918 INDIANAPOLIS IN

POSTAGE WILL BE PAID BY THE ADDRESSEE

ATTN MARKETING
MACMILLAN COMPUTER PUBLISHING
MACMILLAN PUBLISHING USA
201 W 103RD ST
INDIANAPOLIS IN 46290-9042